59 *American Literary Critics and Scholars, 1800-1850*, edited by John W. Rathbun and Monica M. Grecu (1987)

60 *Canadian Writers Since 1960*, Second Series, edited by W. H. New (1987)

61 *American Writers for Children Since 1960: Poets, Illustrators, and Nonfiction Authors*, edited by Glenn E. Estes (1987)

62 *Elizabethan Dramatists*, edited by Fredson Bowers (1987)

63 *Modern American Critics, 1920-1955*, edited by Gregory S. Jay (1988)

64 *American Literary Critics and Scholars, 1850-1880*, edited by John W. Rathbun and Monica M. Grecu (1988)

65 *French Novelists, 1900-1930*, edited by Catharine Savage Brosman (1988)

66 *German Fiction Writers, 1885-1913*, 2 parts, edited by James Hardin (1988)

67 *Modern American Critics Since 1955*, edited by Gregory S. Jay (1988)

68 *Canadian Writers, 1920-1959*, First Series, edited by W. H. New (1988)

69 *Contemporary German Fiction Writers*, First Series, edited by Wolfgang D. Elfe and James Hardin (1988)

70 *British Mystery Writers, 1860-1919*, edited by Bernard Benstock and Thomas F. Staley (1988)

71 *American Literary Critics and Scholars, 1880-1900*, edited by John W. Rathbun and Monica M. Grecu (1988)

72 *French Novelists, 1930-1960*, edited by Catharine Savage Brosman (1988)

73 *American Magazine Journalists, 1741-1850*, edited by Sam G. Riley (1988)

74 *American Short-Story Writers Before 1880*, edited by Bobby Ellen Kimbel, with the assistance of William E. Grant (1988)

75 *Contemporary German Fiction Writers*, Second Series, edited by Wolfgang D. Elfe and James Hardin (1988)

76 *Afro-American Writers, 1940-1955*, edited by Trudier Harris (1988)

77 *British Mystery Writers, 1920-1939*, edited by Bernard Benstock and Thomas F. Staley (1988)

78 *American Short-Story Writers, 1880-1910*, edited by Bobby Ellen Kimbel, with the assistance of William E. Grant (1988)

79 *American Magazine Journalists, 1850-1900*, edited by Sam G. Riley (1988)

80 *Restoration and Eighteenth-Century Dramatists*, First Series, edited by Paula R. Backscheider (1989)

81 *Austrian Fiction Writers, 1875-1913*, edited by James Hardin and Donald G. Daviau (1989)

82 *Chicano Writers*, First Series, edited by Francisco A. Lomelí and Carl R. Shirley (1989)

83 *French Novelists Since 1960*, edited by Catharine Savage Brosman (1989)

84 *Restoration and Eighteenth-Century Dramatists*, Second Series, edited by Paula R. Backscheider (1989)

85 *Austrian Fiction Writers After 1914*, edited by James Hardin and Donald G. Daviau (1989)

86 *American Short-Story Writers, 1910-1945*, First Series, edited by Bobby Ellen Kimbel (1989)

87 *British Mystery and Thriller Writers Since 1940*, First Series, edited by Bernard Benstock and Thomas F. Staley (1989)

88 *Canadian Writers, 1920-1959*, Second Series, edited by W. H. New (1989)

89 *Restoration and Eighteenth-Century Dramatists*, Third Series, edited by Paula R. Backscheider (1989)

90 *German Writers in the Age of Goethe, 1789-1832*, edited by James Hardin and Christoph E. Schweitzer (1989)

91 *American Magazine Journalists, 1900-1960*, First Series, edited by Sam G. Riley (1990)

92 *Canadian Writers, 1890-1920*, edited by W. H. New (1990)

93 *British Romantic Poets, 1789-1832*, First Series, edited by John R. Greenfield (1990)

94 *German Writers in the Age of Goethe: Sturm und Drang to Classicism*, edited by James Hardin and Christoph E. Schweitzer (1990)

95 *Eighteenth-Century British Poets*, First Series, edited by John Sitter (1990)

96 *British Romantic Poets, 1789-1832*, Second Series, edited by John R. Greenfield (1990)

97 *German Writers from the Enlightenment to Sturm und Drang, 1720-1764*, edited by James Hardin and Christoph E. Schweitzer (1990)

98 *Modern British Essayists*, First Series, edited by Robert Beum (1990)

99 *Canadian Writers Before 1890*, edited by W. H. New (1990)

100 *Modern British Essayists*, Second Series, edited by Robert Beum (1990)

101 *British Prose Writers, 1660-1800*, First Series, edited by Donald T. Siebert (1991)

102 *American Short-Story Writers, 1910-1945*, Second Series, edited by Bobby Ellen Kimbel (1991

103 *American Literary Biographers*, First Series, edited by Steven Serafin (1991)

104 *British Prose Writers, 1660-1800*, Second Series, edited by Donald T. Siebert (1991)

105 *American Poets Since World War II*, Second Series, edited by R. S. Gwynn (1991)

106 *British Literary Publishing Houses, 1820-1880*, edited by Patricia J. Anderson and Jonathan Rose (1991)

107 *British Romantic Prose Writers, 1789-1832*, First Series, edited by John R. Greenfield (1991)

108 *Twentieth-Century Spanish Poets*, First Series, edited by Michael L. Perna (1991)

109 *Eighteenth-Century British Poets*, Second Series, edited by John Sitter (1991)

110 *British Romantic Prose Writers, 1789-1832*, Second Series, edited by John R. Greenfield (1991)

111 *American Literary Biographers*, Second Series, edited by Steven Serafin (1991)

112 *British Literary Publishing Houses, 1881-1965*, edited by Jonathan Rose and Patricia J. Anderson (1991)

113 *Modern Latin-American Fiction Writers*, First Series, edited by William Luis (1992)

114 *Twentieth-Century Italian Poets*, First Series, edited by Giovanna Wedel De Stasio, Glauco Cambon, and Antonio Illiano (1992)

115 *Medieval Philosophers*, edited by Jeremiah Hackett (1992)

116 *British Romantic Novelists, 1789-1832*, edited by Bradford K. Mudge (1992)

117 *Twentieth-Century Caribbean and Black African Writers*, First Series, edited by Bernth Lindfors and Reinhard Sander (1992)

118 *Twentieth-Century German Dramatists, 1889-1918*, edited by Wolfgang D. Elfe and James Hardin (1992)

119 *Nineteenth-Century French Fiction Writers: Romanticism and Realism, 1800-*

(Continued on back endsheets)

American Newspaper Publishers, 1950–1990

Dictionary of Literary Biography® • Volume One Hundred Twenty-Seven

American Newspaper Publishers, 1950–1990

8962

Edited by
Perry J. Ashley
University of South Carolina

A Bruccoli Clark Layman Book
Gale Research Inc.
Detroit, London

Printed in the United States of America

Published simultaneously in the United Kingdom
by Gale Research International Limited
(An affiliated company of Gale Research Inc.)

The paper used in this publication meets the minimum requirements
of American National Standard for Information Sciences—Permanence
Paper for Printed Library Materials, ANSI Z39.48-1984. ∞ ™

Library of Congress Catalog Card Number 92–42531
ISBN 0–8103–5386–5

10 9 8 7 6 5 4 3 2 1

I(T)P™

The trademark **ITP** is used under license.

To

Rachel and Anna

Enough light to brighten

a grandfather's life

Contents

Plan of the Series

. . . Almost the most prodigious asset of a country, and perhaps its most precious possession, is its native literary product – when that product is fine and noble and enduring.

Mark Twain*

The advisory board, the editors, and the publisher of the *Dictionary of Literary Biography* are joined in endorsing Mark Twain's declaration. The literature of a nation provides an inexhaustible resource of permanent worth. We intend to make literature and its creators better understood and more accessible to students and the reading public, while satisfying the standards of teachers and scholars.

To meet these requirements, *literary biography* has been construed in terms of the author's achievement. The most important thing about a writer is his writing. Accordingly, the entries in *DLB* are career biographies, tracing the development of the author's canon and the evolution of his reputation.

The purpose of *DLB* is not only to provide reliable information in a convenient format but also to place the figures in the larger perspective of literary history and to offer appraisals of their accomplishments by qualified scholars.

The publication plan for *DLB* resulted from two years of preparation. The project was proposed to Bruccoli Clark by Frederick C. Ruffner, president of the Gale Research Company, in November 1975. After specimen entries were prepared and typeset, an advisory board was formed to refine the entry format and develop the series rationale. In meetings held during 1976, the publisher, series editors, and advisory board approved the scheme for a comprehensive biographical dictionary of persons who contributed to North American literature. Editorial work on the first volume began in January 1977, and it was published in 1978. In order to make *DLB* more than a reference tool and to compile volumes that individually have claim to status

as literary history, it was decided to organize volumes by topic, period, or genre. Each of these free-standing volumes provides a biographical-bibliographical guide and overview for a particular area of literature. We are convinced that this organization – as opposed to a single alphabet method – constitutes a valuable innovation in the presentation of reference material. The volume plan necessarily requires many decisions for the placement and treatment of authors who might properly be included in two or three volumes. In some instances a major figure will be included in separate volumes, but with different entries emphasizing the aspect of his career appropriate to each volume. Ernest Hemingway, for example, is represented in *American Writers in Paris, 1920–1939* by an entry focusing on his expatriate apprenticeship; he is also in *American Novelists, 1910–1945* with an entry surveying his entire career. Each volume includes a cumulative index of the subject authors and articles. Comprehensive indexes to the entire series are planned.

With volume ten in 1982 it was decided to enlarge the scope of *DLB*. By the end of 1986 twenty-one volumes treating British literature had been published, and volumes for Commonwealth and Modern European literature were in progress. The series has been further augmented by the *DLB Yearbooks* (since 1981) which update published entries and add new entries to keep the *DLB* current with contemporary activity. There have also been *DLB Documentary Series* volumes which provide biographical and critical source materials for figures whose work is judged to have particular interest for students. One of these companion volumes is entirely devoted to Tennessee Williams.

We define literature as the *intellectual commerce of a nation:* not merely as belles lettres but as that ample and complex process by which ideas are generated, shaped, and transmitted. *DLB* entries are not limited to "creative writers" but extend to other figures who in their time and in their way influenced the mind of a people. Thus the series encompasses historians, journalists, publishers, and screenwriters. By this means readers of *DLB* may be aided to perceive literature not as cult scripture in

---

the keeping of intellectual high priests but firmly positioned at the center of a nation's life.

DLB includes the major writers appropriate to each volume and those standing in the ranks immediately behind them. Scholarly and critical counsel has been sought in deciding which minor figures to include and how full their entries should be. Wherever possible, useful references are made to figures who do not warrant separate entries.

Each *DLB* volume has a volume editor responsible for planning the volume, selecting the figures for inclusion, and assigning the entries. Volume editors are also responsible for preparing, where appropriate, appendices surveying the major periodicals and literary and intellectual movements for their volumes, as well as lists of further readings. Work on the series as a whole is coordinated at the Bruccoli Clark Layman editorial center in Columbia, South Carolina, where the editorial staff is responsible for accuracy of the published volumes.

One feature that distinguishes *DLB* is the illustration policy – its concern with the iconography of literature. Just as an author is influenced by his surroundings, so is the reader's understanding of the author enhanced by a knowledge of his environment. Therefore *DLB* volumes include not only drawings, paintings, and photographs of authors, often depicting them at various stages in their careers, but also illustrations of their families and places where they lived. Title pages are regularly reproduced in facsimile along with dust jackets for modern authors. The dust jackets are a special feature of *DLB* because they often document better than anything else the way in which an author's work was perceived in its own time. Specimens of the writers' manuscripts are included when feasible.

Samuel Johnson rightly decreed that "The chief glory of every people arises from its authors." The purpose of the *Dictionary of Literary Biography* is to compile literary history in the surest way available to us – by accurate and comprehensive treatment of the lives and work of those who contributed to it.

The *DLB* Advisory Board

Introduction

Never in the history of mankind have the channels of communication expanded as rapidly as during the last half of the twentieth century. Five hundred years intervened between the 1440s, when Johannes Gutenberg began the printing revolution, and the 1940s, when printed materials – newspapers, magazines, and books – reached their zenith as the primary means for the mass dissemination of information, mostly to national audiences. In the fifty years since World War II began and the discovery that radar could be used to "bounce" pictures around the world, more than three hundred satellite-delivered world systems have developed, serving hundreds of millions of households, thereby inaugurating the age of electronic communication and making possible what Canadian educator Marshall McLuhan called the "global village." In 1990 it was estimated that in developing countries there are more homes with television sets than with toilets.

Because of their persuasive influence on the political, social, and cultural systems of the world, television networks are being called the "Third Superpower," making it increasingly more difficult for totalitarian countries, such as Communist China, to control the infusion of "undesirable" cultural and political ideas. For instance, Ted Turner's Cable News Network is now available in about 150 countries. As a consequence, cultural diffusion among different peoples, which previously took many generations to transpire, can now be accomplished in a few years – or even months.

This volume does not, however, struggle with the worldwide implications of media development, except for those changes that have had an impact on American newspaper journalism. This volume – as previous *Dictionary of Literary Biography* volumes on American newspaper journalists do – concentrates on American newspaper developments and the role these newspapers continue to play in the nation's communication spectrum. This volume deals with those individuals who have published major newspapers with regional and national reputations and have put together newspaper chains, multimedia corporations, and media conglomerates. Even though many of the individuals included in this volume have been widely recognized as writers and ed-

itors, this volume emphasizes their roles as publishers and business managers.

At the end of the twentieth century, newspapers continue to be so commonplace in the everyday lives of the American people that social observers, particularly historians, tend to overlook them as a vital institution providing an indispensable service – the delivery of in-depth information and opinion. For two centuries before the 1890s and the discovery of the "mass market" of readers by national magazines, this function was served almost solely by newspapers for the average American. In observing the phenomenal nineteenth-century growth of American cities and the impact it had on newspapers, sociologist Robert E. Park noted in 1925 that "if public opinion is to continue to govern in the future as it has in the past, if we propose to maintain a democracy as Jefferson conceived it, the newspaper must continue to tell us about ourselves. We must somehow learn to know our community and its affairs in the same intimate way in which we knew them in the country village." He suggested that newspapers should continue "to be the printed diary of the home community," as local news "is the very stuff that democracy is made of."

If Park had been observing the function of the American media during the 1992 presidential election, he might have further noted that newspapers provide not only "the printed diary of the home community" but of the national and world communities as well. And the financial independence achieved by the American media during the twentieth century has led to the editorial independence that permitted and encouraged a raging national debate about the patriotism and personal integrity of the candidates, the national debt, and the gridlock in national politics between Republican President George Bush and a Democrat-controlled Congress – all without fear of retribution from the winning candidates after the election.

In 1990 American journalism celebrated its tricentennial – three hundred years of newspaper publishing in this country. Therefore, it seems fitting that this volume – with the four previous *DLB* volumes on American journalists – completes the story of the leaders in American newspaper journalism during those three centuries. It also seems fitting to present the readers of this volume with not only the last forty years in this history, but also an overview of the entire history of U.S. newspaper publishing.

The three centuries of newspaper publishing in this country can be divided almost equally into one-century segments – eighteenth century: the colonial beginnings, the struggle for press freedom, and the service newspapers provided as the conduit through which the debates over separation from England and the adoption of the Constitution could flow; nineteenth century: the development of modern journalism, with an orientation to and support from the reading public and independence from partisan politics; and twentieth century: financial independence from partisan pressures, growth in numbers and readership of newspapers, competition for the delivery of news and information, and consolidation in the ranks of newspapers.

For the first 150 years of U.S. newspaper publishing – until the midpoint of the nineteenth century – newspapers in this country were basically controlled by politicians and political parties. Consequently, as long as most newspaper publishers were forced to rely on political patronage for financial stability – be they appointed as local postmaster, awarded the governmental printing contract, or designated as the official paper for government advertising – they were not free to exercise political independence on the editorial page. The press was so closely aligned with party functions that most editors became part of the party system. True, there were national debates on public issues during the late eighteenth and early nineteenth century. However, these were directed by the political parties and were not centered on the needs and interests of the American people as determined by an independent press.

In 1690 the first American newspaper – Benjamin Harris's *Publick Occurrences* – was banned after one issue, because Harris had not submitted to the colonial licensing laws. The years between that event and the American Revolution represented constant struggles by newspaper publishers to exercise their right as "free born British citizens" to print without prior restraint the social, political, and economic debates of the day. Borrowing from the Age of Enlightenment, writers such as "Father of Candor" argued that ideas and opinions that do not lead to destruction of life or property should be of no concern to the civil authority and that only those expressions that lead to civil disorder should be tried in the courts. Lawyers argued, as Andrew Hamilton did in 1735 in the case of John Peter Zenger, that printer/editors had the right to express

their opinions and to defend them on the basis of their truth and that a jury selected from the community should determine guilt or innocence.

As these debates continued, colonial printers were laying the foundation for American journalism: John Campbell, with the consent and approval of the royal governor, began the *Boston News-Letter* as the first continuous newspaper in the American colonies; James Franklin defied the licensing system by publishing the *New-England Courant* as a lively, controversial newspaper that challenged the political establishment; Andrew Bradford founded the *American Mercury* as the first newspaper outside of Boston; and William Park started the first newspapers in both Maryland and Virginia. At the same time, such entrepreneurs as Benjamin Franklin and James Parker established, through various partnerships and copublishing arrangements, rudimentary newspaper "chains."

After the Stamp Act of 1765 and as the Revolutionary War approached, newspaper editors discovered that it was a time when one had to choose sides. As journalism historian Frank Luther Mott observed, there seemed to be no middle ground for newspaper publishers. They were told, "You can not carry water on both shoulders"; "You are either for us or against us"; and "Liberty of the press belongs only to those who speak for liberty."

There are also many examples of growing public support for the colonial press during and after the 1765 Stamp Act crisis. John Holt, owner of the *Weekly Gazette and Post-Boy* in New York, found a warning letter thrown through the door of his printing shop: "We are encouraged to hope you will not be deterred from continuing your useful Paper by groundless Fear of the detestable Stamp-Act. However, should you at this critical Time shut up the Press and basely desert us, depend on it, your House, Person and Effects, will be in imminent Danger; We shall therefore expect your Paper on Thursday as usual." Thereafter, Holt's newspaper came out on Thursday "as usual."

Printers also found that the popularly elected colonial assemblies and grand juries were willing to protect the rights of citizens, including printers and publishers. Therefore, newspaper publishers began to align themselves with the opposing factions in the debate that eventually led to separation from British authority. Patriot editors such as William Bradford III, Benjamin Edes, John Holt, and Isaiah Thomas risked imprisonment and confiscation of property for their support of independence. Their printing of the fiery writings of such patriots as Samuel Adams and Thomas Paine led British authorities to dub their printing plants "sedition factories." On the other side, Loyalist editors such as James Rivington faced the threat of mob violence for their opposition to breaking away from the mother country. There were some editors, such as William Goddard, who courageously resisted pressures from both sides and allowed both points of view a forum for expression in their newspapers.

In spite of the gains in press freedom and the public and private support for the concept, printers were still intimidated by government authorities. In 1773, only two years before the battles of Lexington and Concord, Thomas Powell, a partner on the *South Carolina Gazette,* was charged with contempt of parliamentary privilege by the South Carolina governor's council for running a story about the meeting of the assembly without having been given prior permission to include the article in his newspaper. And, even though newspaper publishers had generally won the right to publish without prior restraint and to have truth accepted in cases of seditious libel, there was no legal guarantee of these rights.

The Revolutionary War proved that newspapers could play an essential role in a time of dramatic social change. As he researched the causes leading to the Revolution, historian Arthur Schlesinger, Sr., concluded that the newspapers were so deeply involved in the patriot cause that the war could not have succeeded without an "alert and dedicated press." He notes that when the Continental Congress decided on 4 July 1776 that independence was the course that the colonies should take, it was readily apparent that the press had played a major role in molding public sentiment for the move. Mott said that during this turbulent period newspaper reading became a regular habit of the American people, and, because of the extra demand for information, some newspapers broke journalistic tradition by publishing more than once a week, thus paving the way for the daily press. There is little doubt that the conflict established the opinion-making function of the press. Most of all, freedom of the press took firm root, leading to the greatest American tradition: freedom of utterance.

In the post-Revolutionary years — when the attention of the nation was turned to debates over the adoption of the Constitution, alliance with France, the relative strength of the new states compared to the national government, and political-party control over the central government — the press once again was divided, as editors chose sides with political parties and, in return, received financial support and political patronage from the dominant parties.

These issues were battled out, sometimes with vitriolic and scurrilous invective, by such Federalist editors as William Cobbett, John Fenno, Benjamin Russell, and Noah Webster, and by such Republican (Democratic) editors as Benjamin Franklin Bache, William Duane, Philip Freneau, and Samuel Harrison Smith.

By the last decade of the eighteenth century, the tradition of a free and outspoken American press was established; the immediate problem was to secure legal guarantees of these rights. Even though each newspaper's circulation seldom exceeded five hundred copies a week during this period, they were considered so crucial to America's emerging democracy that nine of the first thirteen states independently guaranteed freedom of the press before Congress passed the First Amendment in 1789. However, in spite of the First Amendment guarantee of freedom of the press, there were still attempts to use government power to silence editorial opponents, mainly through libel suits and the short-lived Alien and Sedition Acts of 1798. The remaining right basic to a free press — truth as a defense in libel cases — began to be worked into state laws by the first decade of the nineteenth century. In 1814 the Supreme Court validated this claim.

By the end of the eighteenth century, the population of the United States reached 5.3 million, citizens moved inland away from the coastal cities, three new states were brought into the Union, and westward expansion was well under way. Consequently, distance was beginning to be a major factor in the circulation of news throughout the country. As a result newspapers began to replace town meetings, taverns, churches, and post offices as the primary forum by which Americans debated major national issues.

As the nineteenth century opened, all of the new states and most of the older ones began to incorporate universal white-male suffrage into their constitutions, and a new age of egalitarianism was inaugurated. By the second decade of the nineteenth century, the focus and strength of the nation were turned to westward expansion, economic growth and development, political equality, and a free-enterprise democracy.

Historian Michael Schudson observed that by the midpoint of the nineteenth century, America was transformed from a "liberal mercantilist republic, still cradled in aristocratic values, family and deference, to an egalitarian market democracy, where money had new power, the individual new standing, and the pursuit of self-interest new honor." Such a transformation demanded public education and the means by which newly franchised voters could be informed, participating citizens. The emphasis within the press once again shifted to reflect these needs. Newspapers either changed their content to meet the demands of their readers or were forced to yield to the new penny press.

The penny press – a press for the masses – began in 1833 with Benjamin Day's *New York Sun* and grew in response to the need for political, economic, and social information. The editors soon found that if they were to gain the patronage and support of their working-class readers, their newspapers had to support the "causes" of those readers. Therefore, newspaper publishers, such as Horace Greeley with the *New York Tribune,* began to use their publications to explore such broad public issues as public education, westward expansion, limited forms of socialism, the labor movement, woman's rights, prohibition, experimental farming, and the abolition of slavery.

James Gordon Bennett's *New York Herald* set the pace for changes in news content and writing style in order to meet the needs of a barely literate readership. The style was greatly simplified and couched in the language of the readers; local news was emphasized; reporters were sent to police courts to cover the drama of life from the tenements; and sensationalism was introduced to provide spice for those readers who felt there was little in their own lives. But, most of all, the penny press introduced the "London Plan," by which newspapers were sold on the street by the single copy. Instead of having to pay six dollars to ten dollars a year – several weeks' wages – in advance for a newspaper subscription, the average working-class American found he could buy a copy of his favorite newspaper for one or two pennies on his way home from work each day.

As a result the press for the masses grew to unprecedented levels in only a few years. The number of daily newspapers increased from 42 in 1820 to 574 by 1870, while the number of weeklies rose from 512 to 5,091 in the same half century. While the population increased about 400 percent, the circulation of the daily press bounded forward at the astronomical rate of 7,700 percent, from about 33,000 in 1820 to 2,601,000 in 1870.

Mechanical innovations were also essential to the rise of the mass-circulated, "populist" press. The introduction of the steam-powered cylinder press during the first decades of the century increased daily production rates to almost ten thousand "perfected" newspapers per hour by 1870. The telegraph, introduced in 1844, expanded the potential of daily newspapers by providing instantaneous news, especially to the growing inland daily press. By 1870 there were more than one hundred thousand miles of telegraph lines bringing fresh intelligence on a continual basis. Distribution of newspapers was further enhanced by the advent of the railroad in the 1830s; by 1870 more than fifty-two thousand miles of rails carried news across the nation.

In addition to the mass-circulation penny press, smaller papers sprang up in the first half of the nineteenth century to promote various social and economic views. These special-interest newspapers represented such groups as farmers, religious denominations, laborers, blacks, populists, immigrants, suffragists, and abolitionists. These periodicals searched for means by which their constituents could be brought into the mainstream of American society; opposed the dominant political and economic structure; emphasized the importance and prominence of their leaders; and hoped to educate the rest of society to the particular plights of their groups. The ranks of this press grew so widespread by the end of the century that an estimated 50 percent of the American population was represented by these specialized periodicals.

The petty feuds of the party journalists were swallowed up in the vastly greater conflict that began the American Civil War in April 1861. J. Cutler Andrews, a historian specializing in newspaper reporting during the Civil War, has identified at least six hundred correspondents, photographers, and illustrators – approximately four hundred for the Northern press and another two hundred for the Southern press – who covered all fronts for an anxious American audience. Special national publications such as *Frank Leslie's Illustrated Newspaper* brought the look of war to its readers with woodcuts based on sketches by its artists in the field. Mathew Brady introduced the concept of photojournalism, and Thomas Nast became the father of editorial cartooning.

With extensive use of the telegraph, it was possible for morning newspapers to report battles from the day before, leading to the first major concern by military leaders about the control of vital wartime information. As a result both the Union and the Confederate governments placed restrictions on the movements of correspondents and introduced censorship as a means of protecting troop movements and casualty information. Newspaper publishers found, however, that they needed to withhold military news until it was no longer damaging to "the cause" – thus setting the standard of voluntary cooperation by American media with the military during future wartime crises.

During the last three decades of the nineteenth century, the American newspaper was going through the final stages of its evolution from a vehicle of opinion into a medium that emphasized news, human interest, and entertainment and introduced advertising as a major source of income. With added revenues from sales of newspapers and advertising, newspaper publishers began exercising independence from domination by political parties. As Whitelaw Reid of the *New York Tribune* saw it, this independence gave newspaper editors the opportunity to sever their party affiliations; more important, in his view, was the new freedom to criticize political parties from within. Mott says that "a chief reason for this change was the shift in emphasis from editorial comments and preoccupation with affairs of government to wider fields of news and to more-intimate human interests. This change in the news concept took newspapers away from the politicians and put them in the hands of reporters." This new approach should not be interpreted to mean that journalists were no longer interested in politics. Horace Greeley, the best-known editor of his time, ran for the presidency on the Democratic ticket in 1872. Other editors still endorsed party leaders in national, state, and local elections. Editors and publishers, such as Murat Halstead, Whitelaw Reid, Carl Schurz, and Henry Watterson, were frequently named as delegates to state and national conventions and usually served on critical committees, such as platform and rules.

This was, however, the age of "New Journalism," with Joseph Pulitzer setting the pace. In his prospectus for the *New York World* the day after he purchased the paper in 1883, Pulitzer noted that there was room in New York City for a newspaper "that is not only cheap but bright, not only bright but large, not only large but truly democratic – dedicated to the cause of the people rather than that of purse potentates – devoted more to the news of the New than the Old World that will expose all fraud and sham, fight all public evils and abuses – that will serve and battle for the people with earnest sincerity."

Historians Edwin and Michael Emery have characterized the daily newspapers of this period as "low-priced, aggressive, and easily read" and noted that they appealed "to the mass audience through improved writing, better makeup, use of headlines and illustrations and a popularization of their contents." The average reader in the late nineteenth century bought newspapers for local news, human interest, romance, tragedy, conflict, entertainment, and, perhaps, editorial opinions. In the attempt to catch the attention of the average citizen and barely literate immigrant, some metropolitan newspapers drifted back into sensationalism, which led by the late 1890s to the era of "Yellow Journalism." It was an age in which news was "marketed," and those newspapers that were successful in meeting the needs of the public survived.

In these same three decades the United States was rapidly moving from an agrarian to an industrial society, a movement that brought with it demands for social, political, and economic reforms. The rapid growth of the cities was far outstripping the capacity of local governments to provide critical services; someone was needed to champion the causes of urban, working-class Americans. Newspaper publishers and editors did this work through their famous editorial campaigns and crusades aimed at making life better for all. The *New York Tribune* promoted a fresh-air fund; the *New York World* campaigned for funds to build a pedestal for the Statute of Liberty; the *Kansas City Star* promoted community improvements and helped run gamblers and prostitutes out of the city; and the *Chicago Daily News* advocated a fresh-air sanatorium. Wide-scale moves were also undertaken to dislodge the political-party "machines" through revisions of election procedures. In 1870 *Harper's Weekly* and the *New York Times* teamed up with reform Democrat Samuel J. Tilden to investigate fraud, graft, and corruption in New York City politics by the Tammany Hall organization, which eventually led to the trial and conviction of William "Boss" Tweed for extorting millions of dollars from the public treasury.

It was also a time when newspapers engaged in extensive stunts and promotions in an effort to gain even more widespread readership. Jules Verne had just written the novel *Around the World in Eighty Days* (1873). Could it be done? The *New York World* sent "Nellie Bly" (Elizabeth Cochrane) and two male companions on a similar trip. She returned to much fanfare in New York seventy-two days, six hours, eleven minutes, and fourteen seconds later. The *New York Herald* learned that an American missionary had been "lost" in Africa for several years. As a promotion the newspaper outfitted an expedition and sent the adventurer Henry Stanley up the Nile River to a well-publicized meeting featuring the famous greeting, "Dr. Livingstone, I presume."

Between the Civil War and World War I, more than 25 million immigrants came to the "land of promise." They needed some means to help overcome what historian Oscar Handlin calls "the shock of alienation" in their efforts to separate from an old culture and become assimilated into a new one. For instance, the census of 1900 shows that one out of seven persons living in the United States was foreign-born and that one-third of the population was either foreign-born or first-generation American. As the populations of individual communities swelled with the influx of new immigrants, mutual aid societies were formed to help provide for such needs as housing, food, and work. The mutual-aid societies began to publish newspapers in the immigrants' native languages, reporting activities within the community that were ignored by the English-language press while keeping the immigrants informed about world affairs. The influx of immigrants led to an increase in foreign-language newspapers, from 315 in 1880 to 1,323 in 1917.

Growth in the number of newspapers published and aggregate circulation was astounding during the last thirty years of the nineteenth century. While the population of the country was doubling to almost 76 million by 1900, the total number of daily newspapers was increasing fourfold, and their total circulation was increasing sixfold. Using census data and the few newspaper directories that were available for the period, Alfred McClung Lee estimated that there were 574 daily newspapers with a total circulation of 2.6 million published in 1870, and that by 1899 the number of daily papers had grown to 2,226, with a total circulation of 15 million. At the same time the nondaily press — the weekly, biweekly, and triweekly newspapers — increased from 4,500 newspapers in 1870 to about 16,000 by the turn of the century. Mechanical developments — stereotyping, the typecasting machine, the web-perfecting press, photoengraving, and color printing — made possible the great circulation wars in cities such as New York.

The nineteenth century was also a period of almost blind faith in what was printed in newspapers. This was exemplified in 1897 when Virginia O'Hanlon wrote to the *New York Sun:* "Dear Editor: I am eight years old. Some of my little friends say there is no Santa Claus. Papa says 'if you see it in The Sun it's so.' Please tell me the truth, is there a Santa Claus?" Editor Francis P. Church wrote the classic response:

> Virginia, your little friends are wrong. They have been affected by the skepticism of a skeptical age. They do not believe except they see....
>
> Yes, Virginia, There is a Santa Claus. He exists as certainly as love and generosity and devotion exist, and you know they abound and give to our life its highest beauty and joy. Alas! how dreary would be

the world if there were no Virginias. There would be no childish faith then, no poetry, no romance, to make tolerable this existence....

> No Santa Claus! Thank God! he lives and he lives forever. A thousand years from now, Virginia, nay, ten times ten thousand years from now, he will continue to make glad the hearts of childhood.

The first half of the twentieth century was a transitional period from the highly personalized journalism of the nineteenth century to the corporate journalism of today — a time in which the existence of one newspaper publishing firm in each city was becoming the rule rather than the exception and in which the surviving newspapers were increasingly being run as business enterprises by professional managers rather than as vehicles for the expression of individual editors' beliefs. The years between 1900 and World War II have been romanticized as the era of the wisecracking, hard-drinking reporter who outdid the police in solving crimes while seeking out scandals that would become the next day's titillating headlines. This stereotype — immortalized by Ben Hecht and Charles MacArthur in their 1928 play, *The Front Page,* and in countless films and television programs — has a basis in fact. The flamboyant personalities in the raucous world of vaudeville-style journalism depicted in *The Front Page* were patterned after real-life reporters and editors whom the playwrights had known during their own newspaper days in Chicago. Some journalists actually did succeed in solving crimes and tracking down malefactors where the police had failed.

At the same time, however, most newspapers were establishing reputations for solid, factual reporting of the news. In New York, Adolph Ochs was making the *Times* "the newspaper of record" that published "all the news that's fit to print." The *Christian Science Monitor,* founded by Mary Baker Eddy in 1908 to "injure no man, but bless all mankind," was becoming a truly national newspaper that increased its daily circulation to almost 150,000 without emphasizing crime, sex, or violence.

Editorial campaigns and crusades intensified during the early years of the twentieth century in both the responsible and the sensational press. Newspapers in many cities attacked political-party machines while fighting fraud and corruption in local, state, and national government. They argued for reform in the penal system; advocated the initiative, referendum, and recall; proposed the popular election of U.S. senators; campaigned for the regulation of railroad and utility rates; and continued to support the labor movement. When World War I engulfed Europe, most of these newspapers reflected the isolationist sentiments of many of their readers; but after the United States entered the conflict, they gave vigorous support to the war effort.

However, the most important changes in newspaper journalism were the expanded coverage of government, the beginning of interpretative reporting, and the introduction of syndicated columnists. Signed columns had appeared as early as the 1890s but tended to focus on humor, literature, or local-color reporting. Columns primarily devoted to appraising political and economic affairs did not appear until the 1920s, with the work of David Lawrence, Mark Sullivan, and Frank Kent. By the late 1930s columnists such as Heywood Broun, Walter Lippmann, and Raymond Clapper were being syndicated in hundreds of newspapers. In 1937 the *New Republic* observed that much of the influence once "attached to the editorial page has passed to the columnists." Even though the political pundits were the most prominent, other writers and columnists were widely read and enjoyed. Red Smith and Grantland Rice expounded on the great and near great in sports; Ring Lardner offered humor and social commentary; Walter Winchell created the show-business gossip column; and Marie Manning (Beatrice Fairfax) and Elizabeth Gilmer (Dorothy Dix) set the pattern for advice columnists to follow.

The coverage of World War II was probably American journalism's greatest achievement during these years. The *New York Times,* the *New York Herald Tribune,* the *Christian Science Monitor,* the *Chicago Tribune,* the *Chicago Daily News,* and the Scripps-Howard Newspaper Alliance are usually cited for their extensive coverage through the excellent work of correspondents such as Webb Miller, Edgar Ansel Mowrer, Paul Scott Mowrer, Anne O'Hare McCormick, and the GIs' friend, Ernie Pyle.

The increasing power and influence of the press during the early part of the century provoked a reaction in the form of the first major examination and criticism of American journalism. Newspaper publishers, many of whom had become men of great wealth, found themselves under attack from two directions: they were distrusted by the wealthy for supporting reforms that were contrary to the interests of their own class; and they were suspected by progressive reformers of hypocritically seeking to curry favor with the working class only to sell more papers and thereby acquire even more wealth for themselves. E. W. Scripps summarized the attitude of some of these publishers when he said, shortly before his death: "The loneliness of my life is great. I am hated by the rich for being a renegade, and I am hated by the poor for being rich. I am not wise enough or learned enough to be an acceptable member of the highbrow club. I have learned too many things to make me a comfortable companion of the man in the field, or the street and in the shop."

In order to try to overcome their feeling of isolation, some publishers began to share their riches with their communities and their profession. William Randolph Hearst gave $1 million to the University of California for a woman's gymnasium in honor of his mother, bought and gave to the state of Illinois the Abraham Lincoln homestead, and donated the Greek Theater to the city of Berkeley, California. *San Francisco Chronicle* publisher M. H. De Young left his outstanding art collection to the city of San Francisco, where it is housed in a museum bearing his name. Lucius Nieman's widow gave *Milwaukee Journal* stock to Harvard University in order to establish a continuing-education program for working journalists, and Scripps provided funds for the Foundation for Research in Population Problems at Miami (Ohio) University and the Scripps Institute of Oceanography at the University of California.

The number of U.S. daily newspapers grew until a peak of about 2,600 was reached around 1915, then declined to 1,772 in 1950, leaving less than 10 percent of American cities with competing newspaper organizations. However, the circulation of those newspapers that remained showed a rapid growth: while the population of the United States doubled between 1900 and 1950, the aggregate circulation of all daily newspapers increased 260 percent, from 15 million to about 54 million. More Americans than ever were reading newspapers, but there were fewer newspapers for them to read. Only those newspapers that best served the needs of the readers would survive.

The reduction in the number of newspapers was partly due to mergers and consolidations, which accelerated during this period. Mott suggests that the lack of reader interest in newspapers representing different political viewpoints – as well as mounting production costs – led to the combining of morning and evening papers under common ownership in many cities. Many newspapers escaped mergers only to become parts of chains – or "groups," as chain owners preferred to call such arrangements. These multiple ownerships increased strikingly. In 1900 ten chains published 32 newspapers, representing less than 15 percent of total daily circulation. By 1954 ninety-five chains controlled 485 dailies, representing about 45 percent of total circulation.

During the first half of the century, for the first time, two other media competed with newspapers for the attention, time, and advertising dollars of the American public – popular magazines and radio. Mass-circulation magazines, which had originated during the 1890s, reached a total circulation of about 400 million by 1950, thereby bringing information, opinions, and entertainment into millions of new American homes. By 1960 census data showed that 81 percent of American homes received one or more magazines on a regular basis. Radio – which went commercial in 1920, when KDKA in Pittsburgh, Pennsylvania, broadcast its regularly scheduled programs – had almost three thousand stations on the air by 1950 and was heard in 96 percent of American homes.

By 1900 popular magazines were beginning to enter the average America home and, therefore, were competing with newspapers for the attention and leisure time of American readers. However, in the first half of the century the average workweek declined from sixty to forty hours; the average education increased from a third- to a ninth-grade level; disposable household income escalated rapidly; and new American businesses searched for a national advertising medium. As a result magazine reading began to absorb some of the extra leisure hours available to American workers and did not take away from the time they spent with their newspapers. Instead, magazines began to provide for what appeared to be an insatiable demand for additional news, opinions, and entertainment.

Even though radio did not become a commercial medium until 1920, World War I was a harbinger of the international implications of electronic communication, especially broadcasting. When World War I broke out in Europe in 1914, the British used the transatlantic cable to propagandize Americans. When it came time to demand surrender from the Germans and for President Woodrow Wilson to project his Fourteen Points plan for ending the war, those messages were first broadcast to Germany by radio.

However, radio was not in the news business; it was basically an entertainment medium. By the 1930s radio had spread to most American homes, offering such entertainment programs as *Lum and Abner* and *Amos 'n' Andy* and such performers as Jack Benny and Edgar Bergen. Radio had covered national election returns since 1916, President Franklin D. Roosevelt's "Fireside Chats" during the depths of the Depression, and the major sports events of the time. It did not, however, pose an immediate threat for the newspaper audience until World War II. Early radio com-

mentators scrambled to Europe in 1936 to broadcast live from the opposing lines of the Spanish civil war and in 1939 to report from London rooftops about the great destruction and anxiety caused by the German air raids on the city. Before World War II less than 5 percent of radio time was devoted to news presentations, but this figure increased to as much as 30 percent for some stations during the war years.

Television, still in an experimental state during most of this period, began broadcasting in 1939 when Roosevelt cut the ribbon to open the New York World's Fair, becoming the first American president to appear on television. The medium advanced from 9 stations and eight thousand home receivers in 1945 to 97 stations and 6 million receivers in 1950; even so, in 1950 only 13 percent of American homes had television sets. Two years later the Federal Communications Commission lifted the freeze on new stations, and television boomed during the 1950s, as radio had in the 1920s, reaching 156 stations and 55 million sets by 1960.

Several factors dominated American journalism during the last half of the twentieth century: competition for the delivery of news, information, and entertainment; further consolidation in the ranks of newspapers; the development of cross-media ownership and media conglomerates; the introduction of television, and eventually cable television, into most American homes; the expansion of radio into FM broadcasting; the intrusion of computers in newspaper newsrooms; and the transmission of information and programming via satellite, creating the first "global" communications systems.

In the half century since televison was introduced, it has become the most pervasive medium in all American homes. By 1990 the Nielsen research organization reported that the average American spent four hours each day watching television and about three hours listening to radio. The average American spent only forty-six minutes each day reading newspapers. Television could inform and entertain the American public with less effort on the part of the consumer and add two new dimensions, motion and sound. However, by 1990 broadcast audiences were fragmented among the various radio and television stations. While local television stations were struggling to reach 20 percent of the households in their viewing audiences and radio stations were having difficulty reaching as little as 10 percent, local newspapers were still entering about three-fourths of American homes.

The potential impact of television was dramatically demonstrated in the 1950s when Edward R. Murrow exposed Senator Joseph McCarthy's attacks on alleged Communists as a "Red hunt." In the late 1960s the Vietnam War was made a "living room war" when television commentators, such as Walter Cronkite, helped convince the American people that the country was hopelessly mired in a jungle quagmire. During Operation Desert Storm in 1991 the governments of the United States, Iraq, and the rest of the world watched as CNN correspondent Peter Arnett broadcast live from Baghdad, reporting the activities of the war as they occurred.

The competition from television for Americans' leisure time, rapidly rising costs of production, distribution problems to suburban areas, and shrinking advertising dollars were largely responsible for the decline in the number of daily newspapers, mostly afternoon editions, and the death of such magazines as *Look, Life, Collier's,* and the *Saturday Evening Post.* In 1950 there were 1,772 daily newspapers with a total circulation of 54 million, but the number declined to 1,611 by 1990, although total daily circulation stabilized at about 62 million in the mid 1980s. Four newspapers – the *Wall Street Journal, USA TODAY,* the *New York Times,* and the *Los Angeles Times* – each exceeded 1 million in average daily circulation. However, the average daily newspaper still had a circulation of less than thirty thousand and was published in a medium- to small-sized city – often too small to support a local television station – and was the only source of comprehensive information for its community.

In spite of the overall concern that newspapers were being swallowed up by the media giants and that absentee ownership would inhibit editorial initiatives, many courageous editorial stands were taken by the press from 1950 to 1990. The most noteworthy was the publication of the Pentagon Papers in 1971 by the *New York Times,* showing that the government had been less than honest with the American people about the Vietnam War. In 1972 extensive investigative reporting by the *Washington Post* after the break-in at the Democratic Headquarters in the Watergate Building led to the resignation of President Richard Nixon.

Newspaper crusades, however, were not limited to Washington and New York. Hodding Carter, Jr., won a Pulitzer Prize in 1946 for courageous editorials on racial, religious, and economic intolerance in Mississippi; John Heiskell's *Arkansas Gazette* opposed Gov. Orval Faubus's move to block Little Rock school integration; Barry Bingham, Sr., used the *Louisville Courier-Journal* to campaign against abusive strip-mining practices in Kentucky; and Howard Rock's *Tundra Times* crusaded against the Atomic Energy Commission's plan to detonate six atomic bombs at Cape Thompson in order to create a harbor to facilitate the transportation of Alaska's mineral resources.

By the 1990s independent newspapers, once controlled by family interests, were being bought by newspaper groups that employed professional managers and were thus taking on the trappings of corporate business. For instance, the Bowles family, after many generations of newspaper interests, sold its Springfield, Massachusetts, newspapers to S. I. Newhouse in the 1960s; the Cowles family, for decades the dominant newspaper family in Iowa, sold the *Des Moines Register* to the Gannett Company for $160 million in 1985; and Bingham, once the patriarch of Kentucky journalism, sold the *Louisville Courier-Journal* and *Louisville Times* to Gannett in 1986. In these cases ownership of the newspapers passed to stockholders, for whom the major concern was no longer the general welfare of the communities but the "bottom line" – annual profits and return on investment. However, editorial independence of the local newspaper appears to be more extensive than in the past when publishers such as Hearst and Scripps – who had their own political ambitions and agendas – dictated editorial policies, including political endorsements. As long as newspaper properties are profitable, there seems to be little interference with local editorial decisions from the stockholders and corporate offices. However, when the national recession of the late 1980s hit the newspaper business, many local editors learned that declining profits for their newspapers led to reduced newsroom budgets and fewer staff members to give what they considered adequate coverage to community activities – what some local editors label "budgetary tyranny."

Of the 1,611 daily newspapers published in 1990, 133 groups owned 75 percent and controlled 81 percent of the total daily circulation. Even though some groups – such as Thomson Newspapers, with 124, and Gannett, with 81 – had large numbers of newspapers, they did not control a large percentage of the total circulation and certainly did not possess concentrated circulation in one geographic area. Many groups' newspaper holdings had modest circulations and were concentrated in smaller cities. For instance, the Donrey Media Group was the third largest group, with 56 newspapers, but the average daily circulation of those newspapers was only 13,800. Two-thirds of the newspaper groups had 5 or fewer daily newspapers in their organizations.

Only thirty-seven American cities still have competing newspaper companies. New York had nine metropolitan daily newspapers in the late 1940s but only three citywide dailies after 1967. Several of the old, traditional rival newspapers – the *World-Telegram and Sun,* the *Journal-American,* and the *Herald Tribune* – were merged into the *World Journal Tribune* in 1966 in an effort to salvage some of their heritage of strong newspaper leadership. However, this publication failed in 1967 because of continuing disputes with labor unions over production automation, ending the legacy of many bitter rivalries in New York City between competing newspaper publishers – James Gordon Bennett and Horace Greeley, Joseph Pulitzer and William Randolph Hearst, and Charles Dana and Whitelaw Reid.

In 1990 some of the largest metropolitan markets – including Boston, Chicago, Los Angeles, Houston, Dallas, Denver, and Washington – had as many as twenty television stations and scores of radio stations but no more than two competing citywide newspapers. Many other large cities – such as Detroit, Seattle, San Francisco, Saint Louis, Philadelphia, Miami, and Cleveland – that once supported competing daily newspapers now have either a joint-operating agreement between two companies or only one newspaper company that publishes both morning and evening editions.

Traditional newspaper publishing companies have expanded into cross-media ownership. By 1990 the New York Times Company – which in 1950 was devoted almost exclusively to publishing the *Times* – published twenty-five daily and nine nondaily newspapers; was part owner of the *International Herald Tribune* published in Paris; owned five television and two radio stations; and had equity interests and partnerships in four paper companies. The Gannett Company, begun in the 1920s by Frank E. Gannett as a small upstate New York group, had grown to include eighty-one daily and seventy-six nondaily newspapers; ten television and fifteen radio stations; *USA TODAY, USA Weekend,* and *USA Baseball Weekly;* and the largest outdoor-advertising company in North America. At the same time the Hearst Corporation controlled only twelve daily newspapers but had diversified with ownership of six television and seven radio stations; thirteen monthly consumer magazines; twenty business publications; two book companies; a partnership in two cable-television companies; and the King Features Syndicate.

An example of a lesser-known cross-media corporation is Multimedia in Greenville, South Car-olina, begun by Roger Peace in 1968. By 1990 it included thirteen daily newspapers (three morning-and-evening combinations) published in ten cities in nine states; forty-nine nondaily newspapers; four television and eight radio stations; and more than one hundred cable-television franchises in Illinois, Kansas, North Carolina, and Oklahoma. Multimedia Entertainment produces and syndicates television programs featuring Phil Donahue, Sally Jessy Raphael, and Rush Limbaugh.

The major concern about the development of media conglomerates and too much control of the American media by one organization accelerated in the 1980s. Cross-media ownership is probably best exemplified by Capital Cities/ABC, the parent corporation of the American Broadcasting Company. Capital Cities/ABC publishes eight daily and seventy-seven weekly newspapers and thirty-nine shopping guides. It also owns and operates ABC Television, providing programming to 222 affiliated stations; six radio networks with 3,245 affiliated stations; eight television and twenty-one radio stations; and a majority interest in the Arts & Entertainment and Lifetime cable services. Foreign ownership in the U.S. media, always a cause for alarm, began to develop by the 1990s. Thomson Newspapers, with Lord Roy Thomson of Australia as principal owner, became the largest newspaper group in the United States. Rupert Murdoch's News Corporation published only three daily newspapers but also owned seven television stations, fourteen business publications, 20th Century-Fox films, and the Fox Broadcasting Company.

A few wealthy individuals entered the newspaper business as a benevolent service to their communities. Dorothy Schiff, a wealthy New York socialite, bought the ailing *Evening Post* in 1939. Marshall Field III – whose family had amassed a fortune from department stores, banking, railroads, and real estate – began the *Chicago Sun* in 1941 as morning competition for the ultraconservative *Chicago Tribune.* He also invested $5 million in *PM,* an adless newspaper in New York City. John Hay Whitney, a New York financier and ambassador to the Court of Saint James, was encouraged to invest in the *New York Herald Tribune* in an effort to keep the newspaper afloat.

In other cases wealthy newspaper publishers have shared their fortunes through benevolent activities, such as support for community social and cultural activities, building programs, innovative educational activities, and scholarships. The Cowles Foundation established the Willkie House, a black community center in Des Moines, in honor of presidential candidate Wendell Willkie. George Barry Bingham, Sr., contributed 5 percent of the Courier-Journal Company's pretax earnings to local charities and supported the development of the Kentucky Center for the Arts Endowment Fund. The Peace family heirs made major contributions to the Peace Center for the Performing Arts and the Roger C. Peace Rehabilitation Hospital, both in Greenville, South Carolina. The Gannett Company set up a foundation, valued at $700 million in 1992, to support the Freedom Forum, "devoted to promoting free press, free speech and free spirit of all people." The Samuel I. Newhouse Foundation was a major benefactor of the Newhouse Center for Law and Justice at Rutgers University, the Mitzi E. Newhouse Theater at Lincoln Center in New York City, and the S. I. Newhouse School of Public Communications at Syracuse University. Bernard Kilgore began the Dow Jones Newspaper Fund to provide internships on American newspapers to encourage college students to enter journalism.

Even though the newspaper industry was slow in responding, the electronic revolution that began with World War II had a major impact on newspaper production by the end of the century. By the 1960s newspapers were beginning to be printed by the photographic, offset process instead of "hot metal" – introduced a century earlier by Mergenthaler's "Lin-O-Type" machine. In the 1970s the first computers were introduced in newsrooms, leading to the complete pagination of copy, headlines, and illustrations by copy editors, thereby bypassing the more traditional functions of typesetters, compositors, and stereotypers. By the 1980s, with the use of satellite technology, some major newspapers, such as the *Wall Street Journal* and *USA TODAY,* were able to relay full-page formats to remote printing plants throughout the country for simultaneous production and delivery of their publications. In an attempt to be more competitive with the broadcast media, some newspapers experimented with – rather unsuccessfully – electronic, in-home delivery of news. These innovations in production caused major stress between newspapers and the traditional printers' unions, particularly in heavily unionized metropolitan centers such as New York City.

The decline in the number of newspapers and the high cost of entering the newspaper-publishing field have caused concern about the reduced number of media "voices" remaining for the American people to exchange ideas, information, and opinions. However, in the early 1990s there are more media outlets available than at any other time in the history of this country. There are 1,611 daily and approximately 7,500 nondaily newspapers. There are almost 1,500 television and 11,000 radio stations; 11,300 cable-television systems with an average of 30 channels each; at least 12,000 magazines (with some estimates as high as 50,000 for periodicals in magazine format); and more than 50,000 new books published each year. This is a total of more than 90,000 "channels" – up from less than 20,000 in 1950 – by which the American people can communicate with each other. Americans now have more information available to them than ever before – and probably feel overwhelmed by the deluge.

Beginning with the rise of television in the 1950s, media critics have suggested that the print media would soon cease to exist. Through an extensive marketing campaign the broadcast industry has convinced most observers that television is the primary, if not the only, source of news for the American people. In spite of the fact that practically all American homes have radios and televisions and cable television is in about two-thirds of those homes, these broadcast media are not serving their communities with the news and information necessary to everyday life. Consequently, newspapers continue to be the only daily medium to give comprehensive, in-depth accounts of the news, social and political commentary, investigative reporting, and news analysis.

In general, broadcasters provide little coverage of – and most cable systems ignore – local news. Even in cities large enough to have competition from radio, television, and cable systems, media research shows that the local newspaper remains the only medium to concentrate on local news. Only the local newspaper, daily or weekly, continues to give comprehensive coverage of matters of local interest, such as local government, public schools, and election results; community fund drives, recognition of community volunteers, and "mutual aid" and benevolent activities; letters to the editor, editorials, and advice columns; fiftieth wedding anniversaries, debutante balls, reunions, and homecomings; book, music, and theater reviews; local attractions, travel opportunities, and leisure-time pursuits; Eagle Scout awards, high school sports, and scholastic honors; public-meeting notices, public hearings, and bid openings; birth, marriage, and death announcements; and display and classified advertisements, local sales promotions, and coupons.

Historians traditionally have used the files of local newspapers not only as a source of vital statistics but also as a record of life in various communities: how residents lived; what they paid for homes, automobiles, dresses, suits, and food; how they entertained themselves; and whom they chose to govern their communities. It is inconceivable that this documentation will be abandoned without being replaced by some other form of permanent record that is as good or better.

It has been said that the average American can expect his name to be in a newspaper at least three times – at birth, marriage, and death. If this is the case, and, as Robert E. Park suggests, "local news is the very stuff that democracy is made of," and if no other medium provides comprehensive local news coverage, then it follows that the local newspaper must continue "to be the printed diary of the home community."

– Perry J. Ashley

Acknowledgments

This book was produced by Bruccoli Clark Layman, Inc. Karen L. Rood is senior editor for the *Dictionary of Literary Biography* series. David Marshall James was the in-house editor.

Production coordinator is James W. Hipp. Photography editors are Edward Scott and Timothy C. Lundy. Layout and graphics supervisor is Penney L. Haughton. Copyediting supervisor is Bill Adams. Typesetting supervisor is Kathleen M. Flanagan. Samuel Bruce is editorial associate. Systems manager is George F. Dodge. The production staff includes Rowena Betts, Steve Borsanyi, Barbara Brannon, Teresa Chaney, Patricia Coate, Rebecca Crawford, Margaret McGinty Cureton, Denise Edwards, Sarah A. Estes, Joyce Fowler, Robert Fowler, Brenda A. Gillie, Bonita Graham, Jolyon M. Helterman, Ellen McCracken, Kathy Lawler Merlette, John Myrick, Pamela D. Norton, Thomas J. Pickett, Patricia Salisbury, Maxine K. Smalls, Deborah P. Stokes, and Wilma Weant.

Walter W. Ross and Suzanne Burry did library research. They were assisted by the following librarians at the Thomas Cooper Library of the University of South Carolina: Linda Holderfield and the interlibrary-loan staff; reference librarians Gwen Baxter, Daniel Boice, Faye Chadwell, Cathy Eckman, Rhonda Felder, Gary Geer, Qun "Gerry" Jiao, Jackie Kinder, Laurie Preston, Jean Rhyne, Carol Tobin, Carolyn Tyler, Virginia Weathers, Elizabeth Whiznant, and Connie Widney; circulation-department head Thomas Marcil; and acquisitions-searching supervisor David Haggard.

American Newspaper Publishers, 1950–1990

Dictionary of Literary Biography

Frank Bartholomew
(5 October 1898 – 26 March 1985)

Alfred Lawrence Lorenz
Loyola University in New Orleans

MAJOR POSITIONS HELD: Pacific Coast Division manager (1925–1955), vice-president (1938–1954), first vice-president (1954–1955), president (1955–1958), United Press; president (1958–1962), chairman of the board (1962–1972), United Press International.

BOOK: *Bart: Memoirs of Frank H. Bartholomew* (Sonoma, Cal.: Vine Brook Press, 1983).

SELECTED PERIODICAL PUBLICATION – UNCOLLECTED: "Putting the 'I' into U.P.I.," *Editor & Publisher,* 115 (25 September 1982): 25–26, 32, 50, 52, 56.

Frank Harmon Bartholomew enjoyed a half-century career with United Press, rising from reporter to chairman of the board. As a reporter, he helped to create the news service's history. As president, he crafted its merger with International News Service in 1958. As chairman, he presided over the beginning of its decline into bankruptcy and near death.

Bartholomew was born in San Francisco on 5 October 1898 to John and Kate Schuck Bartholomew. He grew up in Portland, Oregon, where he moved with his mother when his parents separated, and attended Oregon Agricultural College (later Oregon State University) there. He began his career in journalism at age fifteen by producing a one-page newspaper, the *Portland Recorder*. He promised weekly editions at fifteen cents a

month, but he published only the edition of 2 February 1914. After graduation from high school, he became a reporter for a short while for the *Portland Oregonian*. Later, he worked for brief periods as a reporter for the *Albany* (Oregon) *Evening Democrat*, managing editor of the *Oregon City Courier*, sports editor of the *Vancouver* (British Columbia) *Sun*, and reporter for the *Portland Evening Telegram*. He entered Oregon Agricultural College during World War I and enlisted in the Student Army Training Corps, establishing a company newspaper as a money-making venture. In 1918 he served as a first lieutenant in the U.S. Army. When the war ended, he returned to the *Evening Telegram*. He took a leave of absence to go to Hollywood to write captions for short films that preceded feature movies of the silent era, but he returned to journalism within a few weeks.

Bartholomew began his United Press career in 1921 as a reporter and manager for the Portland bureau. To his fellow Unipressers, he was always Bart. He towered over most other men, and as he grew older, he became increasingly bald. He was a soft-spoken man with a quick smile, informal and at ease in his dealings with others, but fast-moving and efficient at whatever he did.

In 1922 Bartholomew was sent to Los Angeles to take over the bureau there and cover the movie industry. That was also the year of his marriage to Antonia Luise Patzelt and of still another move, to Kansas City, where he worked as a salesman in United Press's Southwest Division. In 1925 he was appointed manager of the Pacific Coast Division in

Frank Bartholomew at the border between East and West Berlin, 1959 (from Bart: Memoirs of Frank H. Bartholomew, *1983)*

San Francisco, his work base for the next thirty years and his home for the rest of his life. Beginning in 1943 he lived in nearby Sonoma, at the Buena Vista Vineyards, a five-hundred-acre winery that he bought at a state auction for $17,600. There, he produced his own wine and found diversion from his work. UP was never far from his thoughts, however. He tacked to his library wall a plaque with words Stephen Vincent Benét wrote about the company in *Fortune* in 1933: "Unipressers are bound in an unusual *esprit de corps,* hard to define but nonetheless real. No doubt it has something to do with the UP's fearless independence."

Although he was beginning to show himself to be a capable businessman, Bartholomew was always a working journalist. He was on vacation with his wife near Santa Barbara in July 1925 when the city was shaken by one of the worst earthquakes in its history. Bartholomew gathered what information he could, but he had no way to get it on the UP wire. Power lines were down, and telephone communications were out. A UP telegrapher who arrived from Los Angeles, Tom Kelly, found a telegraph line and powered it by running a cable from Bartholomew's car. Throughout the day and well into the next morning, Bartholomew wrote and Kelly clicked his story out in dots and dashes to UP clients across the country. Backed up later by other reporters from Los Angeles, the two stayed on the scene throughout the week, and for several days theirs was the only news the rest of the country had of the earthquake and its aftershocks.

Bartholomew's skills as a salesman helped United Press to become firmly entrenched in newspapers in the states that made up his Pacific Coast Division. All but one of the dailies in Nevada became subscribers. In California, UP had twice as many clients as the other news services combined. In 1930 he was put in charge of serving UP clients in Mexico, Central America, and Australia. In 1938 he was made a vice-president of the company.

After the Japanese bombed Pearl Harbor in December 1941, Bartholomew shipped out from San Francisco to Hawaii in a navy convoy, then flew to New Caledonia in the bay of a cargo plane loaded with incendiary hand grenades. He covered the war in New Guinea and, later, the campaign in the Aleutians and the battles for Okinawa and the Philippines. He kept tabs on the Pacific contingent

J. D. Gortatowsky, a Hearst Corporation executive, and Bartholomew during negotiations for the 1958 merger of Hearst's International News Service with United Press to form United Press International (from Bart: Memoirs of Frank H. Bartholomew, 1983)

of UP war correspondents and filed stories from the island battlefields himself.

Bartholomew entered Tokyo ahead of the U.S. Army in August 1945 to reopen the United Press bureau, then led the UP staff in covering the Japanese surrender aboard the battleship *Missouri*. A few days later he attempted an interview with Prime Minister General Hideki Tojo, but while he was making the arrangements at Tojo's home in suburban Tokyo, a U.S. officer appeared with orders to arrest Tojo. The Japanese leader withdrew to the interior of his house and shot himself with a U.S. Air Force pistol. Through an interpreter Bartholomew recorded, and later reported, what Tojo thought were his last words, though the Japanese leader recovered to stand trial and be hanged for war crimes.

Bartholomew also covered the dawn of the atomic age. While in Japan he visited Hiroshima. He reported on the postwar atom bomb tests at Bikini Atoll and the early nuclear tests in the Nevada desert.

In 1949 he was shuttling between Japan and China when the Communist forces of Mao Tse-tung wrested control of China from Chiang Kai-shek. He was in Shanghai when Mao's troops advanced on the city and found himself working as executive to pay off the Chinese staff of the United Press bureau in silver coins and as reporter covering the story. He escaped on a flight that lifted off one end of the runway while Communist troops were overrunning the far end.

When the Korean War broke out, he put on his correspondent's uniform once more. He was in Kaesong, North Korea, in 1951 during negotiations preliminary to truce talks, and in reading some of the planning documents he learned that news personnel from United Nations countries were to be barred from the meetings. Bartholomew protested to the UN commander, Gen. Matthew B. Ridgeway, with the result that the meetings at Kaesong and the peace talks at Panmunjom were opened. In 1954 and 1955 Bartholomew covered the Vietnamese struggle against the French.

His battlefield work won Bartholomew a wall of awards, including the Omar N. Bradley Award of the Veterans of Foreign Wars, the combat reporting award of the American Gold Star Mothers, and the Texas Journalistic Conference Medal for "12 years of hazardous and brilliant reporting of the wars of the Pacific." He also won a reputation as a strong administrator who could delegate authority and develop talent, and one who could operate on a tight budget—always a cardinal virtue at United Press. He excelled at planning and at bringing his plans to fruition. He knew how to sell the service and how to handle the clients to whom he had sold it. As a result, although he had never worked in New York, he was well respected in the company's *Daily News* Building headquarters. In 1954 he was named first vice-president, and on 6 April 1955, when Hugh Baillie, who had been president of the company for twenty years, moved up to chairman of the board, Bartholomew was made president of United Press.

The company that Bartholomew took over had a spurt of growth in the decade after World War II. In the early 1950s the company pioneered the use of the Teletypesetter, a revolutionary device that allowed stories to go from wire service to newspaper already hyphenated and capitalized where necessary, and column-justified. It also produced a paper tape that could be fed into typesetting machines. In 1952 UP acquired Acme Newspictures, and the following year it put into service the Unifax, the first fully automatic facsimile receiver producing sharp and affordable photographs.

E. W. Scripps had established the United Press as a collective news operation for his newspapers in 1907 as a means of holding down costs of covering the news around the world, and largely in reaction to the restrictive membership policies of the Associated Press. William Randolph Hearst set up the International News Service for his newspapers in 1910, also for reasons of economy. Bartholomew's major achievement as president was the engineering of a merger between the two. His reason was simple: "Costs of covering the world newsfront have risen steadily with the rapidly improving means of transmitting both news and pictures and electronic processes."

After lengthy secret and delicate negotiations, an agreement was signed in New York's Drake Hotel on 16 May 1958 and toasted with four bottles of Buena Sonoma Valley champagne from Bartholomew's own winery. A week later a report went out on the new company's wires announcing

Bartholomew received this award, named after the second general manager of the United Press, at the American Newspaper Publishers Association annual meeting in 1978 (from Bart: Memoirs of Frank H. Bartholomew, *1983).*

"the news service which will embrace the largest number of newspaper and radio clients ever served simultaneously by an independently operated news and picture agency." Bartholomew was made president of the new company, United Press International.

UPI flourished during Bartholomew's presidency. When he took office, UP served 4,654 clients and had 160 bureaus. He reported in 1960 that the fledgling UPI counted 10,000 employees operating out of 234 bureaus in 57 countries. It served 1,656 newspapers and 1,996 radio and television stations in the United States, and 1,393 newspapers and 321 radio and television stations overseas. By the time he stepped down in 1972, the client list had grown to 6,512, and the number of bureaus to 261. It also had begun preparations to enter the age of computers and satellites. Bartholomew's prime responsibility was to see to it not only that the business was profitable, but that the service adhered to his guidelines: "truly objective reporting, readable fast and complete. We are in effect photographers of the world scene, and usually no retouching is necessary. We want to tell what happened, not necessarily our opinion of what it means; we can safely leave that to the editorial pages and to the news analysts."

Bartholomew was president of United Press International until 1962, when he became chairman of the board. He retired a decade later to a home in Glenbrook, Nevada, where he worked on his memoirs with the aid of George McCadden, a former Unipresser. Bartholomew died of cancer there on 26 March 1985.

The years following Bartholomew's retirement and death saw a rapid deterioration of United Press International. The company had begun losing money in 1962. Costs of news gathering were increasing ever more rapidly. The economics of the news industry were changing in response to changing demographics of American cities, declining reading habits, and increased television viewing. Many evening newspapers—the core group of UPI clients—died out or converted to morning publication. The AP, which had long had a restrictive membership policy, had turned to its advantage a 1945 Supreme Court ruling outlawing the policy by signing up large numbers of UP, then UPI, clients.

Bartholomew's wire service had to cut rates to keep up with the competition. Newspapers had the advantage of being able to afford two wire services, but UPI suffered a loss of income, and that resulted in a reduction in services. UPI cut where it thought it could most easily do so—in Europe—but that lessened its reporting strength there and made it less attractive as a news service. In addition, prestige newspapers such as the *New York Times, Washington Post,* and *Los Angeles Times* began selling supplemental news reports, creating more competition for the company. All the while, UPI had to fight an old prejudice of many editors that it was not quite the equal of the AP. When newspapers started to cut costs as their own costs increased and revenues declined, they found UPI expendable.

In 1982 UPI published a colorful booklet touting seventy-five years of its journalistic achievements. On the inside cover was a photo of Scripps

and his statement, "I regard my life's greatest service to the people of this country to be the creation of the UP." But even as the booklet was being printed and distributed, the E. W. Scripps Company was looking for a buyer. UPI was suffering annual operating losses of nearly $2 million, and the losses were mounting. Later in the anniversary year, the Media News Corporation of Douglas Ruhe and William Geissler bought the company. They were incapable of damming the flood, however, and in 1985, while Bartholomew was suffering his final illness, their United Press International was tumbling into bankruptcy. On 28 April 1985, one month after his death, UPI filed for Chapter 11 protection. The owners claimed $40 million in debts, with assets of $24 million.

Mario Vazquez Raña, an owner of chains of appliance stores and newspapers in Mexico, bought the company in 1986 for $41 million, but his efforts to reverse its losses were inadequate. In 1987 it was reportedly losing $1 million each month. Vasquez Raña sold UPI in 1988 for $55 million to the WNW (World News Wire) Group, owned by Earl Brian, who put the wire service under a subsidiary, Infotechnology. Still, it hemorrhaged, losing a reported $16 million during the first year of Brian's ownership.

By 1991 UPI was back in bankruptcy court, once again seeking protection from its creditors. Its liabilities had grown to $65 million, and its assets had shrunk to $22 million. It counted only 2,000 clients (an exaggeration by some estimates), and it was losing $150,000 to $200,000 each month. The court subsequently sold UPI at auction to Middle East Broadcasting Center Ltd., an Arabic television network based in London, for $3.95 million. The agreement to purchase was made on 28 June 1992, thirty years after Bartholomew had stepped down as president.

References:

Gregory Gordon and Ronald E. Cohen, *Down to the Wire: UPI's Fight for Survival* (New York: McGraw-Hill, 1990);

Joe Alex Morris, *Deadline Every Minute: The Story of the United Press* (Garden City, N.Y.: Doubleday, 1957).

George Barry Bingham

(10 February 1906 – 15 August 1988)

Michael D. Murray
University of Missouri–St. Louis

MAJOR POSITIONS HELD: Assistant to the publisher, *Louisville Courier-Journal* (1933–1937); publisher (1937–1941), president and editor (1945–1961), editor and publisher (1961–1971), *Louisville Courier-Journal* and *Louisville Times*; chairman of the board, Louisville Courier-Journal and Louisville Times Company (1971–1986).

George Barry Bingham built an influential and highly respected communications empire in Louisville, Kentucky, then dismantled it shortly before his death. Owner of the *Louisville Courier-Journal,* the *Louisville Times,* a major printing company (Standard Gravure), WHAS-TV, and two radio stations, Bingham was at the forefront of liberal causes, a strong advocate of civil rights, education, and the Democratic party. Seventy percent of the households in Louisville subscribed to Bingham's nationally recognized newspapers during his tenure as editor (1945–1971). Also during that period his newspapers won eight Pulitzer Prizes, and the *Courier-Journal* was twice listed among the top ten newspapers in the United States by *Time* magazine. Bingham's reputation for fairness, evenhandedness, and forthrightness stood in stark contrast to internal family dissension, which became a matter of public interest. Toward the end of his life, concerns over management became widely known and eventually influenced the sale of the media properties.

Barry Bingham was the son of Robert Worth Bingham and Eleanor Everett Miller Bingham. Robert's family operated a military academy in North Carolina, the Bingham School, for three generations before Barry's father decided to relocate to Louisville and pursue the legal profession. In Kentucky he met and married his first wife, Barry's mother, who had three children: Robert Worth Bingham, Jr., Henrietta Worth Bingham, and Barry, the youngest, who occupied much of the energy and affection of his mother because of his frequent illnesses as a child. In a 1913 automobile accident Eleanor shielded Barry from injury but in-

Barry and George Barry Bingham in the pressroom of the Louisville Courier-Journal *(by permission of the* Louisville Courier-Journal*)*

curred a fractured skull. Barry was unconscious and then awoke to find his mother on the verge of death. His father, who had traveled to Cincinnati to fulfill duties as a judge, returned immediately to Louisville in time to be with his wife at her passing six hours later. The judge was reportedly distraught but escaped depression by throwing himself into his

Bingham's parents, Eleanor Miller and Robert Worth Bingham. Robert purchased the Louisville Courier-Journal *and* Louisville Times *in 1916 (from Sallie Bingham,* Passion and Prejudice: A Family Memoir, *1989).*

work, occasionally taking his family on short vacations.

On a summer trip to Asheville, North Carolina, Robert, Sr., became reacquainted with Mary Lily Kenan Flagler, a widow whom he had known as a young man. Flagler's deceased husband, Henry, had been a partner with John D. Rockefeller in Standard Oil and had left an estate of close to $100 million to his widow. In 1916 Robert, Sr., married the Standard Oil heiress, regarded as the wealthiest woman in the United States, which created suspicion among members of her family of his fortune hunting. They were unaware of her financial commitments to her new husband, which included both securities to provide him with a sizable income and payment of debts the judge had incurred in his financial dealings. This skepticism grew considerably after her death, with part of the inheritance creating the financial basis for the Bingham family publishing empire. Allegations regarding Robert's involvement in the death of his second wife on 27 July 1917 later became the sub-

ject of considerable research, accounts hotly contested by his son Barry. She apparently died of heart failure resulting from heavy doses of morphine, prescribed by a physician for her edema of the brain.

Robert, Sr., had major political ambitions and was regarded as an internationalist in his thinking. He served as municipal judge and mayor of Louisville, joined in founding a club to take over operations of Churchill Downs (home of the Kentucky Derby), pushed for economic development, and encouraged political recognition and public office for blacks. He bought the morning *Courier-Journal* and afternoon *Louisville Times* in 1916 and is credited with being one of the first publishers to divorce strict party affiliation from automatic candidate endorsement by his newspapers. He worked for social justice and supported improvement in education, especially for blacks in Louisville and rural slum-dwellers throughout Kentucky. He also insisted on global coverage for his papers, which was unusual in that region at that time. In spite of these innova-

Bingham and his wife, Mary, with George Norton during the 1930s (from Sallie Bingham,
Passion and Prejudice: A Family Memoir, *1989)*

tions for what were then small southern dailies, he was not regarded as a great newspaperman, but one who set the stage for his son.

Barry grew up in Louisville and attended the Richmond School. He studied briefly at the Bingham School in North Carolina, but most of his secondary education came at the Middlesex School in Concord, Massachusetts. He entered Harvard University in 1924. He was graduated magna cum laude four years later with a B.A. degree in English and began contributing on a free-lance basis to the Louisville newspapers, working at WHAS-AM radio, and writing an extended novel. He eventually learned the newspaper trade as a police reporter for the *Times*. In 1931 he married Mary Clifford Caperton, whom he had met while performing in theatrical productions at Harvard. A native of Richmond, Virginia, she had worked as a correspondent for the *Christian Science Monitor* while still a student at Radcliffe.

Franklin D. Roosevelt was regarded as a national hero in the Bingham household, and from 1933 until his death in 1937, Robert, Sr., served as Roosevelt's ambassador to Great Britain. He was well liked by the British and received honorary de-

grees from Oxford, Cambridge, and the University of London. Meanwhile, Barry advanced to the Washington bureau of the *Courier-Journal* and became company secretary, then associate publisher, and, just before his father's death, copublisher. Robert, Sr., believed the newspapers needed to be controlled by a single person, and he made Barry sole inheritor of family stock.

In order to help the newspapers gain nationwide acclaim, Bingham recruited Mark Foster Ethridge, who had served as assistant general manager of the *Washington Post* and president and publisher of the *Richmond Times-Dispatch*. This ambitious new general manager proceeded to help build the reputation of the Louisville publications toward independent, progressive, liberal policy and opinion. Ethridge hired Jim Pope from the *Atlanta Journal* to be his managing editor and boasted seven Nieman Fellows from Harvard on his staff. He enhanced the appearance of the newspapers – introducing a new, easy-to-read typeface and Sunday magazine printed in color – and foreign coverage increased even more.

When Bingham departed the enterprise for military service in 1941, Ethridge was left to run the newspaper, while Mary became vice-president and director of the Courier-Journal and Times Company and WHAS radio and a member of the editorial board. During this period Bingham served as a public relations officer in the U.S. Naval Reserves, with duty in the European theater and with the Pacific fleet. He received the Bronze and Silver Stars and witnessed the Japanese surrender aboard the USS *Missouri*. He was discharged with the rank of commander in 1945 and returned to begin a major construction project on a new facility to house his properties. Completed three years later, it was built, as some political partisans were apt to point out, four blocks south of the Mason-Dixon Line. One of Bingham's ancestors was a Confederate colonel who fought at Appomattox; a worn rebel flag was passed down and once displayed in the newspaper office. For many years, dating back to the early editorship of the legendary Col. "Marse Henry" Watterson, who wrote the editorial "To Hell with the Hohenzollerns and Hapsburgs," the *Courier-Journal* had gained a reputation as the strongest journalistic voice in the South. Although the direction changed under Bingham ownership, becoming in time new liberal Democratic and "New Deal," the newspaper retained its status as a leading southern paper, on the cutting edge of liberal causes.

Over the years editorial stands against the poll tax, government corruption, and Kentucky strip mining added to the reputation of the Bingham publications and their statewide influence and readership. In 1949 President Harry Truman made Bingham chief of the Marshall Plan in France, and in that position Bingham worked directly with Averell Harriman and Dean Acheson, distributing foreign aid and helping to rebuild the French economy. At the same time Bingham continued to keep his hand in affairs in Louisville, taking a strong interest in local government and community projects, while Ethridge continued to build circulation statewide. Bingham and his wife institutionalized involvement by the paper in community affairs to some extent by insisting, for example, on contributing 5 percent of his company's pretax earnings to local charities. He lived at Melcombe, the family estate, just fifteen minutes away from his office at the *Courier-Journal,* and supported community causes such as developing the Kentucky Center for the Arts Endowment Fund, which he chaired. Bingham also exerted considerable influence in Democratic politics, usually behind the scenes, although in 1956 he made a formal, public commitment, devoting himself full-time to the candidacy of Adlai E. Stevenson, serving as cochairman of his Presidential Committee.

Regarded as a remote, reserved character to many, including his employees, Bingham was highly respected as something of a patrician figure, always on the side of liberalism and equality in what was often regarded as an archconservative community. An Episcopalian and member of several elite private clubs, his keeping an ironclad-monopoly newspaper open for both public scrutiny and criticism stood as something of a paradox that newspaper people themselves regarded with a degree of awe and appreciation. Bingham was credited in a 1950 issue of *The Reporter* for playing a major role in Louisville's graft-free status among big cities of that era and helping to improve literacy and primary and secondary education. He and Mary were also applauded for excellence in editorial attention to important issues and for creating a moral climate in which equality in education could prosper. Their attentiveness to the arts helped to create summer opera, a first-class symphony orchestra, and a playwriting competition of national repute.

By 1952 the *Courier-Journal* was ranked by *Time* magazine in the top four newspapers in the country behind the *New York Times, St. Louis Post-Dispatch,* and *Christian Science Monitor.* Controversial issues, such as unionization, integration, and busing – hotly debated throughout the country and especially in the southern states – were covered comprehensively by all Bingham enterprises, print and broadcast. The cross-ownership issue, regarding the propriety of the same company operating both newspaper and broadcast outlets dominant within the same media market, also received significant coverage.

Self-criticism or lack of it, long an issue in overall newspaper criticism by outsiders, was addressed by the *Courier-Journal* with the establishment of the nation's first newspaper ombudsman. Such innovations were encouraged, and indeed enhanced, by Bingham's personal campaigns to improve the performance of his various properties, satisfying both liberal political agendas and more popular community interests, including his newspapers' sports emphasis, with special attention to horse racing, professional boxing, and, more recently, both Kentucky and Indiana college basketball.

In spite of his enormous success in the field of mass communication, Bingham faced personal tragedies and challenges. In 1964 his son Jonathan was killed in an electrical accident. Another son, Worth, who had worked in management at both the *Courier-Journal* and *Times,* died in an accident two years later. His third son, Barry, Jr., who had experience at both the CBS and NBC television networks in New York, was stricken with Hodgkin's disease after taking over as president of the Courier-Journal and Times Company in 1971. Bingham's namesake was treated and recovered from the illness but was challenged a decade later by his sister Sallie, a writer, over his ability to manage the company effectively.

Barry, Jr., sat on the board of the family business with his wife, his mother, his sister Eleanor Bingham Miller, Sallie, and his sister-in-law, Joan. Since Sallie had become book-review editor of the *Courier-Journal,* she was in a position to question Barry, Jr.'s corporate decision making from an insider's perspective. She wrote a family memoir, *Passion and Prejudice* (1989), in which she offered a personal view of family matters. Barry, Jr., had asked the female family members to resign from the board in 1984, and Sallie charged that sexism was involved in her brother's request, since the father and son would remain as the only family members on the board. Sallie negotiated to sell her shares of stock in the company.

Eventually Barry, Sr., declared the company's properties to be for sale to "divergent interests." In making the announcement on 9 January 1986, Bingham cited an unpredictable future market in print and electronic communication, material and equipment costs, and tax policies not favoring family-held corporations. His son strongly and publicly objected to the sale, which was announced on 18 May 1986. The Gannett Company, whose daily newspapers had a combined circulation at that time of more than six million, acquired the Louisville papers for more than $300 million.

Gannett chairman Allen Neuharth said the acquisition was like winning the Triple Crown in racing, because within a sixteen-month period his company had successfully bid for two other highly regarded daily newspapers, the *Des Moines Register* and the *Detroit News.* At the time of the sale, Barry, Sr., said: "It is not easy for me to see the *Louisville Courier-Journal* and *Louisville Times* pass from my family to other hands. Change is an inevitable rule of life, however." He added that management by more than one individual made decision making difficult. National newspaper accounts prior to the sale had pointed to drawbacks for potential buyers at the time, including a flat economy and expensive statewide circulation that the *New York Times* maintained had been kept by the Binghams more for tradition than profit.

The sale of the properties and family bickering created an intense national spotlight. CBS-TV's

Dust jacket for the 1989 book in which Bingham's daughter expresses her displeasure with family management of the Louisville newspapers

popular *60 Minutes* program profiled the family and its turbulent internal problems, for example, while Sallie appeared on television talk shows, discussing her position in the family controversy and her book. Barry, Sr., had fought to stop publication of another book, *The Binghams of Louisville: The Dark History Behind One of America's Great Fortunes* (1987), which alleged that his father had contributed to the death of his second wife. Bingham provided the planned publisher of that book, Macmillan, with a detailed memorandum of alleged misstatement of fact. A revised version was put out by Crown in 1987 with changes it reported as insignificant. Two other books, *House of Dreams: The Bingham Family of Louisville* (1988) and *The Patriarch: The Rise and Fall of the Bingham Dynasty* (1991), address the family history in less controversial accounts.

Ironically, Barry, Jr., who offered his resignation on the sale of the properties, was asked to stay on as editor and publisher until other family properties were sold. He had announced reaching a full understanding of responsibilities with his father during the period the companies were for sale, something he said he regarded as a "healing" arrangement. At the time he decided to sell, Barry, Sr., said: "My family group has expanded beyond my three surviving children to include nine grandchildren. . . . Divergent interests are bound to develop among so many individuals, as they have done in our children's generation. As a senior member of my family, I must try to foresee as clearly as I can the future needs and desires of all." When the sale of the *Courier-Journal* and *Times* was completed, he added: "There were no winners." Barry, Sr., died of a brain tumor on 15 August 1988 at his home in Glenview, Kentucky.

References:

Sallie Bingham, *Passion and Prejudice: A Family Memoir* (New York: Knopf, 1989);

Marie Brenner, *House of Dreams: The Bingham Family of Louisville* (New York: Random House, 1988);

Nancy Rivera Brooks, "Gannett Acquires Louisville Papers," *Los Angeles Times,* 20 May 1986, IV: 1;

David Leon Chandler, *The Binghams of Louisville: The Dark History Behind One of America's Great Fortunes* (New York: Crown, 1987);

Geraldine Fabrikant, "Courier-Journal Chief to Stay in Job," *New York Times,* 21 January 1986, p. D6;

Alex S. Jones, "Sale of Bingham Papers Nears," *New York Times,* 16 May 1986, p. D3;

James Kelly, "Slugging It Out in Louisville," *Time,* 127 (20 January 1986): 76;

Andrew Radolf, "Family Feud," *Editor & Publisher,* 119 (18 January 1986): 10–11, 37;

Eleanor Randolph, "Gannett Bid Nets Louisville Newspapers," *Washington Post,* 20 May 1986, p. E1;

J. Y. Smith, "Barry Bingham Sr. Dies at 82; Built Communications Empire," *Washington Post,* 16 August 1988, p. B7;

Susan E. Tifft and Alex S. Jones, *The Patriarch: The Rise and Fall of the Bingham Dynasty* (New York: Summit, 1991);

Joe Ward, "Barry Bingham Sr., Former Publisher of *Courier-Journal,* Dies at Age 82," *Louisville Courier-Journal,* 16 August 1988, p. A1;

Llewellyn White, "Papers of Paradox: The *Louisville Courier-Journal* and *Times* Confound Critics of Press Monopolies," *Reporter,* 2 (31 January 1950): 22–26.

Papers:

Most of Bingham's papers are at the Schlesinger Library, Radcliffe College; others are at the Houghton Library, Harvard University.

Erwin Dain Canham

(13 February 1904 – 3 January 1982)

June N. Adamson
University of Tennessee

MAJOR POSITIONS HELD: Managing editor (1942–1945), editor (1945–1964), editor in chief (1964–1974), editor emeritus (1974–1982), *Christian Science Monitor*; U.S. delegate to United Nations (1949); president, U.S. Chamber of Commerce (1959).

BOOKS: *Awakening: The World at Mid-Century* (New York: Longmans, Green, 1951);
New Frontiers for Freedom (New York: Longmans, Green, 1954);
Commitment to Freedom: The Story of the Christian Science Monitor (Boston: Houghton Mifflin, 1958);
A Christian Scientist's Life, published with DeWitt John, *The Christian Science Way of Life* (Englewood Cliffs, N.J.: Prentice-Hall, 1962);
The Ethics of United States Foreign Relations (Columbia: University of Missouri Press, 1966).

SELECTED PERIODICAL PUBLICATIONS –
UNCOLLECTED: "Two-Hour Coexistence with Mr. K.," *Saturday Review,* 42 (28 February 1959): 31;
"Effective Modern Education as the Layman Sees It," *National Education Association Journal,* 48 (March 1959): 12–18;
"The Value of Self Criticism for Business and Labor," *Vital Speeches,* 26 (15 December 1959): 147–150;
"A Look at National Goals," *PTA Magazine,* 56 (September 1961): 24–26;
"Why the Monitor Changed," *Saturday Review,* 48 (10 April 1965): 78–79;
"Public Looks at Labor," *DUNS Reviews,* 89 (January 1967): 81.

Erwin Dain Canham was editor of the *Christian Science Monitor* for nearly three decades; before that he served the newspaper as bureau chief in Geneva, Switzerland, and Washington, D.C. He perpetuated and enlarged founder Mary Baker Eddy's goal of giving readers the tools with which to work

Erwin Dain Canham (courtesy of Christian Science Center Archives)

out their salvation. Indeed Canham helped make the *Christian Science Monitor* a nationally and internationally respected newspaper for significant regional articles, arts features, and Washington and foreign correspondence. Intertwined with these accomplishments was his strong sense of ethics. He was widely known and respected in the United States for ethical views on many topical subjects, which he gave in commentaries on weekly network radio and television programs. He also presented them in his speeches and his long-running *Monitor* column, "Let's Think." Prisoners holding hostages called for Canham to help negotiate their grievances. Presidents called on him to serve on investigating committees. He was decorated by the

The American delegation at the UN General Assembly, 1949. Canham is third from left in the back row; in the front row are Eleanor Roosevelt, Philip C. Jessup, John Foster Dulles, Warren R. Austin, and Dean Acheson.

British Empire, France, Greece, Germany, and Austria and earned many other honors around the world.

In his leadership position with the *Monitor,* he strengthened coverage of foreign news and trained staff specialists in many areas. At the time of Canham's death, Saville R. Davis, former managing editor of the paper, said, "The paper had expert editors before him, and they were competent professionals, but a more intense journalistic competence was developed under Canham." He was widely respected for his knowledge of international affairs and for his familiarity with political and business leaders around the world.

Canham was born on 13 February 1904 in Auburn, Maine, the son of Vincent Walter Canham and Elizabeth Gowell Canham, whom he joined in becoming a Christian Scientist, a devotion that pervaded his life. He taught generations of students in the Christian Science Sunday School and made many other contributions to the faith, including service as president of the church.

His interest in journalism began early, because his father was agricultural editor of the *Lewiston* (Maine) *Sun and Journal.* Erwin was eight years old when he stood on a chair in front of an old-fashioned telephone to take down items for publication. At fourteen he became a general-assignment reporter for the paper during the World War I manpower shortage.

He worked as a correspondent for eight different newspapers while attending Bates College in Lewiston. Following his graduation in 1925, he began his long career with the *Monitor* by spending a year as a general-assignment reporter before leaving Boston to attend Oxford University as a Rhodes Scholar. However, he did not desert the paper; while he was studying in England, he also covered the League of Nations for the *Monitor.* He earned B.A. and M.A. degrees from Oxford in 1929. When he rejoined the newspaper full-time, he began his swift rise through the ranks of its journalists, becoming managing editor (1942), editor (1945), and then editor in chief (1964).

Canham in conference in his Christian Science Monitor *office. Behind him is a portrait of Christian Science founder Mary Baker Eddy (courtesy of Christian Science Center Archives).*

Canham later discussed his academic weaknesses during his high-school years in *A Christian Scientist's Life* (1962): "Perhaps my grammar school training had not been good enough, perhaps I had not learned to study, perhaps I had not come of intellectual age." However, his intellect was sparked when he collaborated with a fellow student on the senior-class play, "The Middle Path," devoted to the bitter labor struggles of 1920–1921. Canham recalled that once he was in college, "the spiritual and intellectual ferment that had been happily boiling up in me began to take hold." During his senior year he went on a debating tour of Great Britain, and while in Edinburgh he was offered the job with the *Monitor*. In Edinburgh he debated on a subject for which neither he nor his colleagues were prepared – prohibition – and they won the pro argument, at least in part because of citations of "the rather squalid crowds pouring in and out of the public houses on an Edinburgh Saturday

night." He later commented on H. L. Mencken's reaction to prohibition:

Perhaps nobody has written more vitriolic attacks on prohibition and abstinence than the late Henry L. Mencken, and there aren't many people with whom I would disagree more on moral issues. But Mr. Mencken and I, while on newspaper trips, were on the best of terms. More than once he saw to it that I got my ginger ale or tomato juice, despite his panegyrics on beer. He had also written many ungracious and untrue things about Christian Science. I did not mawkishly ignore these elements in Mr. Mencken's character, but I always tried to see the true man of God's creation beneath his shell of cynicism and atheism. I admired his immense journalistic virtuosity and was vastly entertained by his presence.

A Christian Scientist's Life presents similar observations about many well-known persons on the national and international scenes. He also wrote of seeing the true face of Germany both before and

THE CHRISTIAN SCIENCE MONITOR

BOSTON, TUESDAY, JANUARY 14, 1969 — *An International Daily Newspaper* — K — VOL. 61, NO. 41 THREE SECTIONS — MIDWESTERN EDITION • 10c

FOCUS on Britain

What's ahead . . .

There is every reason to believe that Britain's rising tide of nationalism will carve out even higher bench marks in 1969.

The year will almost certainly see a start made on restructuring the government and constitution of the United Kingdom of Great Britain and Northern Ireland.

Welsh and Scottish nationalists have notched up considerable successes at the polls. The Plaid Cymru in Wales has widened its hold on the popular vote by 30 percent in two years. A bill now is being prepared for Scottish independence.

Even nationalists in the county of Cornwall—the supporters of "Mebyon Kernow"—are laying plans to put up their own election candidates.

The civil-rights troubles of Northern Ireland, which already has its own Parliament and government as well as representation at Westminster, raise further doubts about the viability of the present UK system.

Liberal and Conservative Parties have taken due note. Both now have reform programs aimed at satisfying nationalist demands while retaining the UK's overall integrity.

Polls show that most nationalist support comes from dissatisfied Labourites. Hence the Labour government feels it must make a move before the next election.

⊕

Britain has had a bill of rights since 1689. Is it time for a new one?

A working group of the organization which ran Human Rights Year (1968) thinks it is.

It proposes that a human-rights commission be set up to handle all complaints from citizens.

This step, the group suggests, should be followed by a new bill which would gather together all rights statutes into a single legal document.

Britain's original declaration and bill of rights include some of what are generally accepted today as basic human rights, but not all of them. And the bill itself is not covered by constitutional guarantee.

Other rights have now been put into law. But, without the protection of the constitution, these also could be changed by parliamentary vote.

Furthermore, the 1689 bill was mainly concerned with protecting Parliament from the sovereign. A new bill would protect the people from the government machine.

Trends . . .

It's been feared that those flareups between Protestant and minority Roman Catholics might make industries shy away from Northern Ireland.

Now that feeling is changing. If the dissension has any adverse effect on the government's program to attract new industries, this, it is believed, will be only temporary.

Why? Nothing succeeds like success. And statistics just released show that output of Ulster firms continues steadily upward.

Estimated gross output of companies employing 25 or more persons rose from £880 million ($2.1 billion) in 1966 to £923 million in 1967—a 5 percent jump.

And this was achieved with a smaller labor force earning wages that grew from £682 to £730 in that 12-month period.

How and why . . .

One of society's contradictions is that lawbreakers usually know far more about the law than law-abiding citizens, who rarely if ever see the inside of a court.

Britain's Haldane Society, an association of lawyers, would like to change that. They feel that if a child can be helped to understand the laws that govern his society, then perhaps he will have respect for them.

So the association is proposing that a basic legal education be taught to all children in British secondary schools. The emphasis would be on the nature of law and how it works rather than on its specific content.

The lawyers further suggest that law courses should be made available to adults who don't necessarily have academic qualifications but who want to learn about their country's legal system in their spare time.

Every citizen, says the society, should know about the effect of law on his everyday life.

⊕

For rent: Instant church.

A prefabricated, collapsible, movable building, it's been designed in Britain to serve new housing developments.

With this kind of church building available at a nominal rent, it is hoped that people in housing developments will in time raise enough funds to build their own permanent church.

Then the prefab can be dismantled and transported to some new location in need of a church or community center.

The first of these buildings is expected to serve a new housing area in Sussex.

The idea is quickly spreading. Church authorities across the country are eagerly mulling over its possible uses in their communities.

Where to look

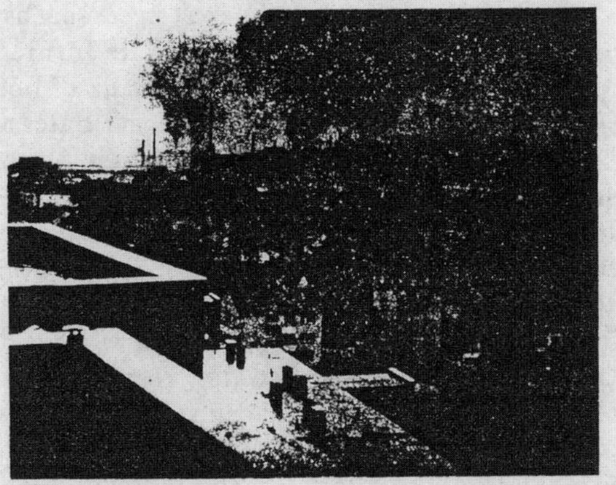

Bundesbildstelle

Joint-operation clouds blur German industrial scene

'Mitbestimmung'

West German industrial future tugged three ways by government, management, unions

By Harry B. Ellis
Staff correspondent of The Christian Science Monitor

Bonn

An elusive concept called "Mitbestimmung" is being tossed about like a political hot potato among political parties and trade unions in West Germany.

"Mitbestimmung" means industrial codetermination, or the sharing of management responsibilities within a firm by employers and workers.

The practice was established in 1951 in the West German coal, iron, and steel industries and the following year was extended in attenuated form to the rest of German industry.

The Federation of German Trade Unions now demands that the coal, iron, and steel model be applied to the 400 largest industrial firms in West Germany.

Management vigorously objects. The political parties, facing a national election this September, are hoping to postpone the issue until a new Parliament is elected.

The Social Democratic Party (SPD), led by Foreign Minister Willy Brandt, gingerly sides with the trade unions—the strongest element of Social Democratic support.

Worker apathy found

Chancellor Kurt Georg Kiesinger's Christian Democratic Union (CDU) is split on the issue, though its sister party — the Christian Social Union (CSU) of Bavaria — comes down squarely on the employers' side.

The concept is elusive, because no one quite knows what the trade-union federation is aiming at or how the system would work.

A public-opinion survey carried out by the Institute for Applied Social Science found that 71 percent of West Germans in principle wanted workers to participate in management decisions.

But workers themselves — as distinct from their trade-union officials — seem apathetic on the question. Many workers queried did not know who, if any, of their representatives sat on boards of directors.

The issue, in other words, currently is being pushed, not by workers en masse, but by their trade-union officials, grouped within the trade-union federation.

Under the 1951 law, each coal and steel company has an 11-man board of directors. Five members represent management, five labor, and the chairman is neutral.

The system has worked generally smoothly. Indeed, it was faster for coal companies

★ Please turn to Page 4

Arab bloc hopeful of U.S. shift

By John K. Cooley
Staff correspondent of The Christian Science Monitor

Amman, Jordan

The Arab world hopes against hope that the anticipated resumption of United States-United Arab Republic diplomatic relations will be a good omen for peace.

The prospect pleases many members of King Hussein's government here. The King, now visiting London, unlike five other Arab rulers, never followed President Nasser's example by breaking with Washington during the June, 1967, Arab-Israeli war.

"Next week [with the inauguration of Richard M. Nixon] just might mean the beginning of many good things," said one Jordanian official. "We hope for a great deal from the new Nixon administration."

This hope has stirred faintly since the Mideast tour last month of William W. Scranton, President-Elect Nixon's special peace emissary.

At the Allenby Bridge between East Jordan and the Israeli-occupied West Bank, where Mr. Scranton spoke his now-famous phrase about the need for a "more even-handed" United States Middle East policy, there was some skepticism.

While two correspondents and a group of

★ Please turn to Page 6

Inside today

Midwinter vacation? Here's a wide selection

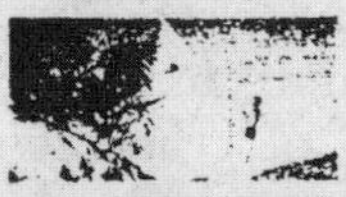

Surfing in Hawaii, snowmobile tours to Yellowstone, mountaineering by burro in Jamaica, Motorailroad travel in Britain, chalet renting in the Swiss Alps, air and sea cruising almost anywhere—these are among the travel delights covered in today's Midwinter Vacation Issue.

Second section

U.S. hopes for answers in Soviet Venus probe

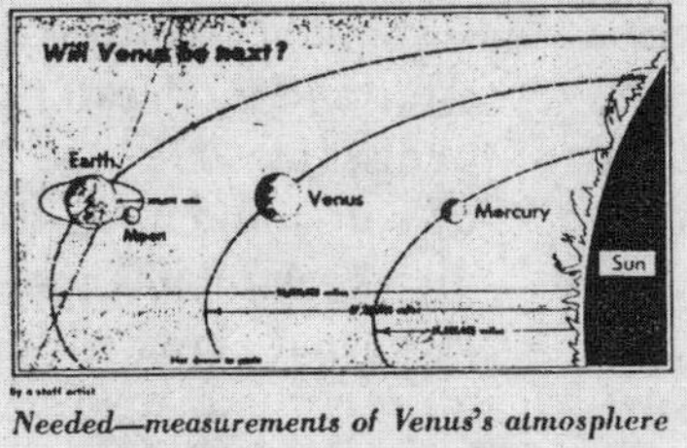

By a staff artist

Needed—measurements of Venus's atmosphere

By Robert C. Cowen
Natural science editor of The Christian Science Monitor

Pasadena, Calif.

American planetary scientists are cheering on the two new Soviet Venus probes with hopes that, this time, the automatic machinery will do its job.

"The thing to hope that the Russians will do is make a really good set of measurements of lower atmosphere composition," explains Dr. Lewis D. Kaplan, planetary atmospheres scientist at the Jet Propulsion Laboratory (JPL) here.

"This was done badly last time," he says. "What we all would like are measurements of things like water vapor or methane in the lower atmosphere and really good measurements of surface temperatures and pressure."

On Oct. 18, 1967, the Soviet Venera 4 reportedly soft landed on Venus. The American Mariner 5 craft, built and commanded by JPL, flew within 6,400 miles of the planet the next day.

The Soviets reported a surface pressure of 12 to 22 times the sea-level pressure at earth. They reported a surface temperature of 536 degrees F. in an atmosphere largely made of carbon dioxide.

Findings conflict

The pressure and temperature data didn't jibe with findings from Mariner 5 and ground-based radar and radio observations. If the Soviets were right, the radius of Venus would be some 20 to 35 kilometers larger than the American findings indicated.

On the other hand, everything matched nicely if scientists assumed that the Soviet data actually referred to a level high in the Venus atmosphere rather than the surface.

Last fall, it turned out that the Soviet probe very likely had failed at high altitude. Its final data appear to have come from a level perhaps 20 miles high rather than from the surface.

This suggests that surface conditions are even more severe than those first reported by the Soviets. An average surface pressure of perhaps 100 atmospheres and average surface temperature close to 800 degrees F. are indicated. The 800 degree temperature would agree with radio measurements made from the ground.

Two probes on way

Now the Soviets have set out to try to get unambiguous data all the way to Venus's surface. The probe Venera 5, launched Jan. 5, is to land on Venus's sunny side sometime next May. Venera 6, launched Friday, reportedly is aimed for the dark side.

"This time," Dr. Kaplan observed, "I think the Russians know what the Venus atmosphere is like and will not underdesign their equipment, as was the case before.

"There may be interesting kinds of clouds lower down in the Venus atmosphere. It's hot enough so that things like mercury and some of its compounds should volatilize. There may be clouds of that there.

"I hope the Russians will take particle samples and analyze them as the probe drops down. They could use a mass spectrometer [an instrument for determining the masses of different particles]. Certainly, we would know how to do this if we had a spacecraft with the weight of the Russian ones."

Its disk shrouded by a perpetual cloud

★ Please turn to Page 3

It's all technology's fault—or is it?

By Florence Mouckley
Staff correspondent of The Christian Science Monitor

London

Technology and the layman are still not speaking to each other.

There was an opportunity for them to kiss and make up at London's current Inventions and New Products Exhibition but the chance was muffed.

It's all technology's fault.

It can't seem to explain itself except in its own complicated terms.

Mental feedback: 'Nil'

True, the LINPEX '69 show—the London International Inventions and New Products Exhibition—is aimed at the engineer, the chemist, the technology expert, and the like. But even more so is it programmed at the nontechnical businessman and ordinary person with some ready money to invest.

There may be a new invention with potential lurking among those on display at LINPEX '69. But the chances are the scientifically unsophisticated investor will pass it right by.

Certainly, if industry, science, and applied technology were "sending," this particular laywoman was not "receiving."

As I read and reread, word by agonizing word, the description of a new computer, the mental feedback I kept getting was, "How's that again?"

The only input I processed was that the maker of this new computer was anti the new decimal system that is coming in in Britain.

The description reads in part:

". . . the . . . computer [is] printed on flexible cheap plastic for shifting the rotor with the left thumb while the stator is held firm and the right hand is free to use the magnifier pencil for extra precision. The existing rigid devices are as unsuited for rapid computing as is the denary (decimal) notation. In scale-16 the L (the symbol re-

★ Please turn to Page 6

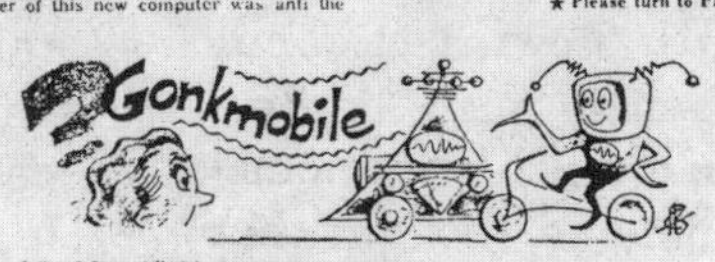

By Henry C. Benson, staff artist

Gonks from outer space . . .

2nd Cl Post Pd at Boston, Mass., and add'l offices

January 14, 1969

Front page of the Christian Science Monitor, *14 January 1969*

after 1932, notably in Geneva and Lausanne, "when Nazi stooges came to attack and ruin the fine journalists who had for years represented the upstanding newspapers of Germany in which for a century liberalism had been fighting a losing battle with militarism and hate."

Canham cited two events that were especially meaningful to him during his years as editor of the *Monitor*. The first was an address that he delivered at Yale University in 1950, "The Authentic Revolution," which remained in reprint demand for many years. He presented a revision of this address as the Fourth of July oration at Faneuil Hall in Boston in 1962. The second event he often cited was his part in helping to quell the riot in the Massachusetts State Prison at Charleston in 1955. He wrote of the experience in the *Monitor*: "To have the privilege of restoring hope to 4 desperate men threatening the lives of 11 others, and perhaps more, is the deeply humbling experience 7 Boston citizens had during the last 24 hours." Actually, he was the first person to be invited to enter — alone.

As a Christian Scientist, Canham followed Eddy's philosophy, "to injure no man, but to bless all mankind." In practice this meant little emphasis on news of crime, violence, and disasters and greater attention to topics of long-term importance. To criticism that the *Monitor* gave little attention to medical news because of the church's emphasis on spiritual healing, Canham responded that much of medical news was of transient significance.

The *New York Times* reported in January 1982 that by the mid 1960s Canham's view was that radio and television had forced newspapers to go beyond "the mere reporting of the event" and that editors should "press the task of reporting more deeply and widely." However, he stressed that reporters must avoid coloring their articles with opinion. The *Times* called Canham's career "an unusual combination of two deep interests: religious concern and a nose for news." The *New York Herald Tribune* described him in 1961 as "anything but humorless, [with a] slightly pursed countenance and a conversational manner that plainly abhors superfluous small talk. . . . Some who know him well say he is a devastating mimic." One little-known fact about Canham is that he was nicknamed "Spike" by Roscoe Drummond, a well-known journalist and sometime *Monitor* colleague. Drummond thought that Canham's air of dignity and scholarship needed that kind of counterbalance.

Unlike many newspaper editors who declined involvement with any organizations or businesses, Canham had no such hesitation; in fact, he saw this work as part of his mission. He served as a delegate to the United Nations Geneva conference on freedom of information in 1949, and later as chairman of the U.S. advisory commission on information for the U.S. Information Agency. He saw no conflict of interest in serving as a director of the John Hancock Mutual Life Insurance Company and the Federal Reserve Bank of Boston and as a trustee of Wellesley College, Bates College, the Boston Public Library, and the Boston Museum of Fine Arts.

He came under severe criticism when he accepted the presidency of the U.S. Chamber of Commerce in 1959. Some editors "thought they had caught him with his hand in the jam," *New York Herald Tribune* writer Edgar A. Comee reported. "They tartly recalled the frequent Canham strictures against the growing subversion of journalistic objectivity by, among others, the public relations finger men of big business. . . . It was a thought that also occurred to many on the *Monitor*'s own staff." Comee speculated that Canham's motives were to help liberalize the U.S. Chamber's approach to a changing world and to tell better the story of American business, which he believed was becoming ever more ethical. Canham said at the time, "Too many people — both at home and abroad — do not realize the degree to which American business has accepted social accountability to its customers, its employees, its stockholders and the entire community." He also observed that business was "its own worst salesman."

Canham headed the American Society of Newspaper Editors in 1948 and served as commentator and moderator on Boston radio and television programs. He was known for his unique brand of soft-spoken, genteel humor and strong ethical views. After Canham's death in 1982, Robert P. Hey, managing editor of the *Monitor,* said, "He had quite an extraordinary gift for combining the big broad canvas, in terms of national and international coverage, with the importance of the individual, no matter what his job. He made it his business to know something about and to care about you."

Canham wrote and spoke openly about turning to his religion for physical healing, as well as for professional and moral guidance: "I have met with many physical problems, and any that could have kept me from my work have been swiftly healed." He remarked, however, that his need for glasses to correct nearsightedness had not been helped. He offered no excuses but expressed his belief that this problem, too, could be overcome. He was also willing to submit to the inoculations required for his foreign travels, but, like other Christian Scientists, he sought exemption from compulsory medication on grounds of religious conviction whenever the exemption was recognized not to jeopardize "the supposed protection of others." While embarking on one trip to the Far East, he was told that because he had no exemption in writing, he had to take the shots then and there or not board the plane. He did and credited his faith that he had "not the slightest perceptible reaction to any of the injections."

Erwin Canham died at seventy-seven, two weeks after undergoing abdominal surgery in Guam. He and his second wife, the former Sue (Patience Mary) Daltry, had maintained homes on Saipan – where he had served as resident commissioner of the Northern Mariana islands in the 1970s following his retirement from the *Monitor* – and at Cape Cod, Massachusetts. He was also survived by two daughters, Carolyn and Elizabeth, from his first marriage to the former Thelma Whitman Hart, who died in 1967.

Among the many tributes to Canham that his wife received following his death was a cable from Carlos S. Camacho, governor of the Northern Marianas at the time. It read in part: "We shall ever remember Erwin Canham with gratitude and high regard for the way he shaped and prepared the people of these islands for the responsibility of common-wealth government and then demonstrated his faith in us by making his home with us, and in his own quiet way, practicing exemplary citizenship every day of his life: on the streets, in our homes, in our churches, on the radio, in the newspapers and our committees. . . . These intense memories will endure . . . for they are true monument of a great man."

References:
"The Canham Example," *Christian Science Monitor,* 4 January 1982, p. 24;
"Canham of *The Monitor*," *New York Herald Tribune,* 15 January 1961, II: 3;
William Dicke, "Erwin Canham, Longtime Editor of Christian Science Monitor, Dies," *New York Times,* 4 January 1982, p. 10;
Obituary, *Newsweek,* 99 (18 January 1982): 96;
Obituary, *Time,* 119 (18 January 1982): 89;
"Readers Write on Erwin D. Canham," *Christian Science Monitor,* 20 January 1982, p. 22;
"Tributes to Mr. Canham," *Christian Science Monitor,* 5 January 1982, p. 2.

Papers:
The archives at the First Church of Christ, Scientist, in Boston contain extensive material on Canham.

Hodding Carter, Jr.

(3 February 1907 – 5 April 1972)

Jean Folkerts
George Washington University

MAJOR POSITIONS HELD: Night manager, New Orleans bureau, United Press International (1930); manager, Jackson, Mississippi, bureau, Associated Press (1931–1932); founder, editor, and publisher, *Hammond* (Louisiana) *Daily Courier* (1932–1936); founder, editor, and publisher, *Greenville* (Mississippi) *Delta Star* (1936–1938); editor and publisher, *Greenville* (Mississippi) *Delta Democrat-Times* (1938–1962); editor, Cairo edition of *Stars and Stripes* (1943–1945); editor, *Yank* (1943–1945).

BOOKS: *Civilian Defense of the United States,* by Carter and Ernest Dupuy (New York & Toronto: Farrar & Rinehart, 1942);

Lower Mississippi (New York & Toronto: Farrar & Rinehart, 1942);

The Winds of Fear (New York & Toronto: Farrar & Rinehart, 1944);

Flood Crest (New York: Rinehart, 1947);

Southern Legacy (Baton Rouge: Louisiana State University Press, 1950);

Where Main Street Meets the River (New York: Rinehart, 1953);

Robert E. Lee and The Road of Honor (New York: Random House, 1955);

So Great A Good (Sewanee, Tenn.: University Press, 1955);

Marquis de Lafayette: Bright Sword for Freedom (New York: Random House, 1958);

The Angry Scar: The Story of Reconstruction (Garden City, N.Y.: Doubleday, 1959);

The South Strikes Back (Garden City, N.Y.: Doubleday, 1959);

Gulf Coast Country, by Carter and Anthony Ragusin (New York: Duell, Sloan & Pearce, 1961);

Doomed Road of Empire: The Spanish Trail of Conquest (New York: McGraw-Hill, 1963);

First Person Rural (Garden City, N.Y.: Doubleday, 1963);

Hodding Carter, Jr.

The Ballad of Catfoot Grimes and Other Verses (Garden City, N.Y.: Doubleday, 1964);

So the Heffners Left McComb (Garden City, N.Y.: Doubleday, 1965);

The Commandos of World War II (New York: Random House, 1966);

The Past as Prelude: New Orleans, 1718–1968 (New Orleans: Tulane University Press, 1968);

Their Words Were Bullets: The Southern Press in War, Reconstruction, and Peace (Athens: University of Georgia Press, 1969);

Man and the River: The Mississippi (Chicago: Rand, McNally, 1970).

SELECTED PERIODICAL PUBLICATIONS –
UNCOLLECTED: "Kingfish to Crawfish," *New Republic,* 77 (24 January 1934): 302–305;
"Chip on Our Shoulder Down South," *Saturday Evening Post,* 219 (2 November 1946): 18–19, 145–148;
"The Civil Rights Issue As Seen in the South," *New York Times Magazine,* 21 March 1948, pp. 15, 52–55;
"A Wave of Terrorism Threatens the South," *Look,* 19 (22 March 1955): 32–36;
"A Double Standard for Murder?," *New York Times Magazine,* 24 January 1965, pp. 20, 22, 24, 27, 30;
"The Old South Had Something Worth Saving," *New York Times Magazine,* 4 December 1966, pp. 50–51, 170–179.

William Hodding Carter, Jr., exemplified the image of a country editor with a national reputation, an editor who loved and fought for his community, a writer of recognized ability, and a spokesman for moderate change. Carter – steeped in southern tradition, educated in the North, and cognizant of the importance of national unity as well as southern progress – was among those editors and writers categorized as southern liberals, but known more accurately as southern moderates.

Carter was also a crusading newspaper editor who took seriously the role of editor as reformer or advocate of change. His parents, William Hodding and Irma Dutatre Carter, were prominent residents of Hammond, Louisiana. Because his mother taught him to read when he was four, he entered the fourth grade when he was only seven and graduated from high school at sixteen. He was graduated from Bowdoin College in Brunswick, Maine, in 1927. He did postgraduate work at the Columbia University School of Journalism from 1927 to 1928 and studied at Tulane University the following year, where he was a teaching fellow. He married Betty Werlein on 14 October 1931. They had three sons: William Hodding III, Philip Dutatre, and Thomas. In 1939 Hodding, Jr., was awarded a Nieman Fellowship at Harvard University.

Carter began his newspaper career in 1929 in New Orleans as a twenty-five-dollar-a-week reporter for the *Item-Tribune,* and in 1930 he assumed duties as night manager for the city's United Press International bureau. He moved to Jackson, Mississippi, in 1931 to manage the Associated Press bu-

reau there. A year later he was dismissed with a letter that indicated that while he had good qualities, he "would never make a newspaperman, and . . . ought not to waste any time getting into another business." He then went home to Hammond, where he took over a throwaway mimeographed advertiser and made it into the successful *Daily Courier.* Carter published the first issue on 18 April 1932 and continued until 1936, when he sold the newspaper and moved to Greenville, Mississippi.

Carter's first flirtation with national prominence came with his opposition to Huey "Kingfish" Long, a Louisiana demagogue who appealed to the poor with attacks on the rich and who, while expanding state services, operated according to the rule that the ends justify the means. Carter was one of the few southern journalists to attack Long, and he was soon writing for national magazines as well as editorializing in the *Courier.* Carter called Long the "Crawfish," "the most arrant thiever of votes since the carpet-bag Reconstructionists." Carter accused him of fomenting class hatred and appealing to the "arrogant ignorance" of poor whites at the expense of "the taxpaying and articulate opposition." During the spring of 1934, when Long controlled nearly the entire state government, Carter acknowledged in the *Courier* that Louisiana's poor had reason to seek redress. Supporting Franklin Delano Roosevelt's New Deal, Carter sympathized with the fact that "national wealth, power, and labor have been ill-distributed," but he argued that Long, unlike Roosevelt, offered only promises, not results.

Carter's courage engendered personal attacks, and Long had Will Carter, the editor's father, removed as a trustee of Southeastern Louisiana College. Long also created a state printing board with the power to approve or reject any newspaper as the official journal of a town, school district, parish (county), or other political subdivision. The *Courier* was the only paper rejected for public printing, a severe strike not only against Carter personally, but against his balance sheet as well. In September 1935 the crusade against Long ended abruptly with Long's assassination, although Carter continued to fight against the Long forces. The assassination angered Carter, however, and produced an editorial example of the tolerance he would promote for the rest of his life. Five days after the assassination, Carter encouraged the people of Louisiana to "work toward the goal of democracy" so that "the tragedy of political assassination as a means of political freedom may never be re-enacted." Later that fall Carter ran for the state House of Representatives, but the Long machine prevailed, and Carter sold his newspaper the following spring and left the state.

Carter's attacks on Long had created an interest among a group of paternalistic, although reform-minded, Mississippians, who provided him with the capital to start a newspaper in Greenville. Among those encouraging his move were William Alexander Percy and David Cohn, who hoped Carter would show the same attitude toward corrupt Mississippi politicians that he had shown against Long. In 1936 Carter established the *Delta Star,* and on 1 September 1938 the paper merged with the *Democrat-Times* to become the *Delta Democrat-Times.* Carter remained at this paper for the remainder of his career and referred to it as "my" newspaper even after his son Hodding III took over the editorship in 1962. Hodding, Jr., edited the paper as a local voice, but he also created a national platform, particularly after he won a Pulitzer Prize in 1946. In the first issue of the *Delta Democrat-Times* Carter promised to publish the truth and be tolerant. He also said he "hoped" to be kindly and fearless. "We mean," he wrote, "to study the problems of this town and of this delta of ours and of this nation we love. We trust the results of our study will give us wisdom enough to be helpful. . . . We aspire to be in time the spokesman for the best that is thought and done in our section of the South."

During his first ten years in Greenville, Carter established himself as an active member of the community, serving on the boards of the local Chamber of Commerce and the city library, and the Boy Scout club council. He represented the well-educated, conservative, entrepreneurial, Delta planter faction, although his attitude on race relations placed him to the left of the majority of this group. The *Delta Democrat-Times* contained standard rural newspaper content, including church and wedding announcements, sporting events, and social notices. Carter represented the style of editor who believes that journalists belong to a community and have a responsibility to move the cultural and business climate toward cautious, but progressive, reform.

Although Greenville served as Carter's home base, he quickly became a national figure, in part for the campaign he ran against Long in Louisiana and later for one against Sen. Theodore Bilbo in Mississippi. As a Nieman Fellow at Harvard in 1940, which he recalled fondly as "the most satisfying time of my life as a newspaperman," he met Ralph Ingersoll, soon to be the publisher of *PM,* a New York tabloid created with the financial backing of business magnates such as Marshall Field III and designed to be devoid of advertising. In his autobiographical *Where Main Street Meets the River* (1953), Carter says he did not believe a newspaper without advertising could succeed, but he was, as were most of the other fellows in his class, intrigued with the idea. Ingersoll persuaded him, Carter wrote, in a way that made everything seem too good to be true: "*PM* would be 'against people who pushed other people around.' It would be completely departmentalized. Out the window would go the abused who-what-when-where formula for writing news stories; out all other stereotypes, all hackneyed phrases, all that spelled impersonal dullness and useless convention and superficial treatment. *PM* would be personal, and it would insist on the why; it would dig for the reason and expose for the reader whatever lay beneath the casual surface . . . *PM* would be a beautiful newspaper. . . . It would be the journalistic dreamboat."

In mid May, Carter left Harvard and went to New York to work for Ingersoll, but he remained only a few months, quitting in August to return to Greenville. Once *PM* surpassed the conceptual stage, problems multiplied, and Carter noted, "I am sure that a dreary, humorless, consecrated insistence upon conformity to a fixed and condescending liberalism contributed more to *PM*'s failure than did the clever, busy Communist minority itself, or the incredible mismanagement that even I could see from the cellar level, or the persistent jealousies and the professionally irreconcilable ideas as to what kind of paper *PM* should be." Carter did not stay in Greenville long. He had joined the National Guard in 1938, and he went on active duty in November 1941. He served with the War Department and from 1943 to 1945 edited Middle East editions of the serviceman's magazine *Yank* and the weekly newspaper *Stars and Stripes.*

On Carter's release from the army in 1945 he was awarded a Guggenheim Writing Fellowship, which he said "made me think for the first time that maybe I might become a pretty fair writer." In 1946 he won a Pulitzer Prize for "editorials on racial, religious, and economic intolerance." The editorial selected as representative of Carter's views on tolerance chastised Americans for not treating Japanese-American soldiers fairly as they returned from the war. Carter noted that he had been writing books before the Guggenheim was awarded, and that he "had been protesting editorially against racial and religious injustices" long before the Pulitzer Prize was awarded. But the prize induced more people "at home to concede that there might be some merit in what we were saying." Not all people at home agreed, however. Greenville residents were engrossed in a dispute over erecting a memorial to World War II servicemen, and the project had stalled over the issue of race. Some prominent residents were willing to stop the project if names of blacks were to be included. Carter chided his fellow townspeople in the *Delta Democrat-Times*:

> And then we might ask ourselves this: How in God's name can the Negroes be encouraged to be good citizens, to feel that they can get a fair break, to believe that here in the South they will someday win those things which are rightfully theirs – decent housing, better educational facilities, equal pay for equal work, a lifting of health standards, and all the other milestones along an obstacle-filled road – if we deny them so small a thing as joint service recognition?

Carter continued his progressive stance in editorial attacks against Bilbo, who in 1946 was running for reelection to the U.S. Senate. Bilbo shot back with race-baiting comments. He even attacked Carter's Pulitzer Prize: "No self-respecting Southern white man would accept a prize given by a bunch of nigger-loving, Yankeefied Communists for editorials advocating the mongrelization of the races." In June 1946 Bilbo intensified his charges, claiming that "Since I have been the outspoken defender of the white South, the white race and our white American civilization on the floor of the Senate in opposing all efforts to destroy our American way of life and integrate the negro race into the social and political life in the Deep South, he [Carter] has joined hands with negroes, Communists, and foreigners in a studied and determined effort to smear and destroy me."

Carter's editorials contained no such inflammatory rhetoric, but rather represented a reasoned call to give just due to those who fought in the war. On 27 August 1945 Carter's editorial was titled "Go For Broke":

> The loyal Nisei have shot the works. From the beginning of the war, they have been on trial, in and out of uniform, in army camps and relocation centers, as combat troops in Europe and as frontline interrogators, propagandists, and combat intelligence personnel in the Pacific where their capture meant prolonged and hideous torture. And even yet they have not satisfied their critics.
> It is so easy for a dominant race to explain good or evil, patriotism or treachery, courage or cowardice in terms of skin color. So easy and so tragically wrong. Too many have committed that wrong against the loyal Nisei, who by the thousands have proved themselves good Americans even while others of us, by our actions against them, have shown ourselves to be bad Americans. Nor is the end of this misconception in sight. Those Japanese-American soldiers who paraded at Leghorn in commemoration of the defeat of the nation from which their fathers came, will meet other enemies, other obstacles as forbidding as those of war. A lot of people will begin saying, as soon as these boys take off their uniforms, that "a Jap is a Jap," and the Nisei deserve no consideration. A majority won't say or believe this, but an active minority can have its way against an apathetic majority.

While Carter's return to Greenville was on a high intellectual note, his lack of business acumen as a publisher had put his newspaper in distress. During 1941 and 1942, while he was in the army, Carter worried about the management of his newspaper, so he sought a good business manager who would be interested in buying out some of the stock of the original directors. He found a fellow officer with sizable newspaper holdings to buy out some of the Greenville directors, as well as some of Carter's own stock, and the two men operated the paper with each having 50 percent control. Their contract included a buy-and-sell clause that dictated that at the end of two years if either partner wanted to buy out the other, he could make an offer. The other partner had the choice of either selling at the offered price or buying instead at the same price. Carter neglected to note that the buy-or-sell clause also included a phrase dictating that the purchaser must buy the "entire creditor position" of the seller for cash. During the next two years Carter's partner acquired a strong creditor position – annual payments to the original stockholders, preferred stock, a mortgage, and notes on a newspaper press – that totaled about eighty-four thousand dollars. When the buy-and-sell clause came due, the partner notified Carter that he wanted to sell. Only through loans from the friendly Greenville bank and some friends was Carter able to save the paper.

The status of the Pulitzer Prize and the Guggenheim Fellowship, combined with publication of his first novel, *The Winds of Fear* (1944), gave Carter a wider national platform from which to express his views. The postwar era was a period in which a national platform would prove essential in responding to federally mandated change. World War II had paved the way for change not only in the South, but in the nation as a whole. Widespread institutional discrimination in the armed forces embittered blacks who enlisted to serve their country; black leaders forged a "Double V" campaign, arguing for victory at home as well as abroad. As they fought the Nazis and the Japanese, black leaders fought for the principles of equality to be enforced in the fields and factories of their home country. From 1945 to 1960 a group of black leaders emerged to lead the sit-ins and the marches of the 1960s as a response to demands for equality was delayed.

Amid such an era of social change, Carter and other literary figures and newspaper editors, such as Virginius Dabney, James Dabbs, Jonathan Daniels, William Faulkner, and Ralph McGill, cast themselves as southern liberals arguing for selective change, moderation, and equality without the dismantling of segregation. Anthony Lake Newberry, in a 1982 study of southern liberals, cast the period as the "seedtime of the South's second attempted Reconstruction." Carter's group had what Newberry characterized as a love-hate relationship with the South, a sincere commitment to social justice and an emotional attachment to their native land. Such attachment barred any thought of federal intervention, which only recalled southern hatred of the first Reconstruction. When President Harry S Truman sought legislation requesting a Fair Employment Practices Commission, a federal antilynching bill, an anti-poll-tax measure, and an end to discrimination in interstate transportation facilities, Carter responded: "There is no Blueprint for Brotherhood. Legal action which bears on the folkways of nearly one-fourth the nation's population cannot become effective unless the affected group is largely willing to abide by it."

Carter, like the intellectual planter William Alexander Percy, who had brought Carter to Mississippi, held dear, as William C. Havard has written, "those features of the South that are usually identified as establishing the region's distinctiveness — its individualism, personalism, emphasis on family, sense of history and place, love of the land and closeness to nature, good manners, unyielding religious commitment, distrust of the abstract, and awareness of the elements of spatial and populational scale that make for humane social relationships." Carter supported segregation, but his liberalness of the time was reflected in demands for separate but equal treatment and for his condemnation of politicians such as Bilbo, who exaggerated racial stereotypes and fears in his political campaigns. Carter firmly believed that change must be channeled or it would destroy the South, just as federal intervention and forced change had created furor rather than progress during Reconstruction.

What might be better termed a moderate, rather than liberal, position was expressed in a *Delta Democrat-Times* editorial on 26 January 1947, when Carter explained his position to those who challenged him. He said he did not advocate any movement for social equality, terming it "unrealistic and dangerous" to the course of improved race relations. However, he supported equal justice, the condemnation of bigots, and raising the educational and economic standards of the Negro. He also noted that, in what was to be a continuing theme of the importance of national unity in a postwar world, a sense of Christian responsibility to fellowmen had real meaning in a world threatened by communism.

In a 1948 article for the *New York Times Magazine,* Carter described the civil-rights issue as seen in the South. He covered this subject for the next fifteen years, writing for various magazines including the *Post* and the *New York Times Magazine.* In 1948 Carter still expressed a good deal of optimism that the South would solve its own racial disputes. He recognized the importance of what happened in small southern towns in a 5 July 1946 editorial in the *Delta Democrat-Times*: "What we do here is noted in remote places, in places which may yet be the dying ground for your sons and ours." America, he wrote in December 1946, was "on trial before the world," as foreigners faced a choice between communism and democracy. As Carter sought to encourage Mississippians to move slowly but deliberately toward racial justice, he sought to quiet southern reactionaries as well as those espousing federal intervention. He wrote in the *Post* that "much change, unrelated and largely impervious to legislation, must come in the South, gradually and with the consent and participation of the white Southerners who are the principal present inheritors of a yet unsolved problem." Change had to come from within, and because of that, it would be gradual. Carter noted, however, that the Supreme Court had expressed a willingness to tolerate separate facilities only if they were indeed equal, and he charged that southerners must "act at once" to equalize the Jim Crow system, out of moral obligation as well as legal responsibility.

Carter was a voice out of the wilderness in Mississippi. The *Brown* v. *Board of Education* decision in 1954 energized the reactionaries, and Carter continually called for caution. He chided those who sought to destroy the public-school system as a means of avoiding desegregation, and he argued that "if ever a region asked for such a decision, the South did through its shocking, calculated and cynical disobedience to its own state constitutions which specify that separate school systems must be equal. For seventy-five years we sent Negro kids to school in hovels and pig pens. . . . And if we are to effect a workable and fair compromise at the local Southern levels we have to spend dollar for dollar all down the line, for every educable child. . . . Most Negroes want only the same opportunities for their children as we white people want for ours." Nevertheless, Carter viewed immediate integration as impractical, arguing that most southerners were not ready for the reality of integration at the public-school level.

Citizen's councils formed across the South in the fall of 1954, determined to prevent federally mandated change. Carter viewed the development as reactionary and dangerous, and in March 1955 he wrote an article for *Look* magazine, "A Wave of Terrorism Threatens the South," condemning the citizen's councils as a reactivation of the Ku Klux Klan. Reaction to Carter's position was definite and swift, and leaflets dropped over Greenville featured this doggerel:

> There was a young man named Fodding Harder
> Who with his scrawlings replenishes his larder
> He is world renowned by the liberals and pinks
> But with his homefolks, my he stinks.

In late March the Mississippi House of Representatives passed a formal resolution by a vote of eighty-nine to nineteen (with thirty-two not voting) that Carter had lied, slandered his state, and betrayed the South. Carter told the legislators in a response published in *Look* that they could go to hell and wait there for him to back down. "They needn't plan on returning," he added. Carter was later investigated by a state committee that accused him of being a member of Communist groups.

Events in the late 1950s and early 1960s dismayed Carter; he believed black militancy and white separatism were driving the races apart. He opposed boycotts across the board, charging that "it is neither American nor Christian to seek to destroy financially a person or group of people because of a difference of opinion or policy." Carter continued to speak out for legal justice, and in a 1965 *New York Times Magazine* article he noted that "never in the state's history has a white man been found guilty of first-degree murder, and only rarely of manslaughter, when the slain person was black." The prejudice went deeper, he claimed, to regarding black life so casually that white juries failed to punish blacks in intraracial crimes as well. Carter's article came the year after four civil-

rights workers were murdered in Philadelphia, Mississippi. When he wrote the article, no one had been brought to justice.

In his opposition to black militancy, Carter looked to the past, reviving memories of relationships between blacks and whites that he regarded as more Christian: "Too many spokesmen for the new Negro say the black man's Southern legacies just aren't so, meaning that they are so but that the Negro intends to erase them from American folkways and even from American memory. If they were to succeed, some values that are tender and rich and irreplaceable will disappear. And the disappearance will not serve to bring closer together the denier who is black and the denied who is white. Why this goal should be sought is a philosophical concept beyond my understanding." He recalled traditional relationships between the races in the Deep South as "brutal and loving, poignant and wry and ecstatically comical, wrong in the basic premise of superiority and inferiority and so right in a basic affection that made the abuses less bitter to the soul and less heavy upon the heart." Such sentiments gained few accolades in the years following the assassinations of Martin Luther King, Jr., John F. Kennedy, Robert Kennedy, and Medgar Evers.

In 1967, when seven men were convicted in federal court in Meridian, Mississippi, of killing the civil-rights workers in 1964, the *Delta Democrat-Times* carried an editorial championing the decision. "For the first time," it read, "a jury of white Mississippians has demonstrated it can convict white men for a crime involving civil rights. The long, shameful record of acquittals of obviously guilty men for no other reason than they were white and their victims were unpopular enemies of segregation has been shattered."

Carter relinquished control of his beloved *Delta Democrat-Times* to his son Hodding III in 1962. The newspaper was sold in 1980. The aging editor became a writer-in-residence at Tulane University in New Orleans and an adviser to the campus newspaper. During the last ten years of his life, he suffered repeated bouts of depression and lost most of his sight. Yet, with the help of his wife, he continued to write. He resigned from his position at Tulane in 1970 because of ill health; he died of a heart attack on 5 April 1972. Along with the Pulitzer Prize and the Guggenheim Fellowship, he received many awards, including the Southern Literary Award (1945) and the William Allen White Foundation National Citation for

Journalistic Merit (1961). He also received honorary degrees from many institutions, including his alma mater, Bowdoin College, and Tulane. In addition to his editorials and magazine articles, he was author or coauthor of twenty books.

References:

Garry Boulard, "'The Man' versus 'The Quisling': Theodore Bilbo, Hodding Carter, and the 1946 Democratic Primary," *Journal of Mississippi History,* 51 (August 1989): 201–207;

William C. Havard, "The Journalist as Interpreter of the South," *Virginia Quarterly Review,* 59 (Winter 1983): 1–21;

John T. Kneebone, "Liberal on the Levee: Hodding Carter, 1944–1954," *Journal of Mississippi History,* 49 (May 1987): 153–162;

Kneebone, *Southern Liberal Journalists and the Issue of Race, 1920–1944* (Chapel Hill & London: University of North Carolina Press, 1985);

Harry D. Marsh, "Hodding Carter's Newspaper on School Desegregation, 1954–55," *Journalism Monographs,* no. 92 (May 1985);

Anthony Lake Newberry, "Without Urgency or Ardor: The South's Middle-of-the-Road Liberals and Civil Rights, 1945–1960," Ph.D. dissertation, Ohio University, 1982;

James E. Robinson, "Hodding Carter: Southern Liberal, 1907–1972," Ph.D. dissertation, University of Mississippi, 1974;

Anne Waldron, *Hodding Carter* (New York: Workman, 1993).

Papers:

Carter's papers are at Mississippi State University. His literary manuscripts are in the Mississippi Department of Archives and History. Some of his correspondence is available in these collections: Josiah George Chatham Papers, Amistad Research Center, Dillard University, New Orleans; Sarah (Patton) Boyle Papers and Maud (Carter) Clement Papers, University of Virginia library, Charlottesville; Walter John Lemke Papers, University of Arkansas library, Fayetteville; and Lewis Gannett Papers, Houghton Library, Harvard University.

Turner Catledge
(17 March 1901 – 27 April 1983)

Edward E. Adams
Ohio University

MAJOR POSITIONS HELD: Editor, *Tunica* (Mississippi) *Times* (1922–1923); managing editor, *Tupelo* (Mississippi) *Journal* (1923); editor in chief, *Chicago Sun* (1942–1943); assistant managing editor (1945–1951), executive managing editor (1951), managing editor (1951–1964), executive editor (1964–1968), *New York Times*; vice-president (1968–1970), director (1968–1973), New York Times Company.

BOOKS: *The 168 Days,* by Catledge and Joseph Alsop (Garden City, N.Y.: Doubleday, Doran, 1938);
My Life and the Times (New York & London: Harper & Row, 1971).

Turner Catledge accepted a position as reporter with the *New York Times* in 1929, when it was still considered inferior to Joseph Pulitzer's *New York World.* During his more than forty years with the *Times,* the paper became one of the most prominent in the world. The Mississippi-born Catledge rose to an unprecedented power with the *Times* in 1964, when all new activities were centralized under him as executive editor. From 1960 to 1961 he served as president of the American Society of Newspaper Editors, a group that included the top editors of newspapers nationwide. He helped to build the *Times* into the greatest American newspaper of its time.

Catledge was born on 17 March 1901 near New Prospect, Mississippi, the second child of Lee Johnston and Willie Anna (Turner) Catledge. When Turner was three, his family moved to Philadelphia, Mississippi, where two of his mother's brothers were opening a hardware store. Other brothers in the Turner clan soon moved to Philadelphia and eventually started a market, a drugstore, and an automobile dealership. Turner worked for his uncles at various stages of his teenage years, and the Turner brothers' benevolence and industriousness had a lasting impact on him. Lee Catledge did not have consistent employment

Turner Catledge

but did serve two terms as mayor of Philadelphia. His father's love of politics influenced Turner, while his mother impressed upon him the importance of organization and hard work.

Catledge decided to attend college, but the best one in the state, the University of Mississippi at Oxford, was too expensive, so he chose Mississippi A&M, now known as Mississippi State. He earned money his first two years there by serving meals in the school dining room. Catledge took classes in literature, history, government, and languages, although he was a business major. During his junior year he became secretary to a professor who helped him get a job as assistant to the school's agricultural editor, who produced bulletins on agricultural topics for the state's farmers. After he was graduated from Mississippi A&M in 1922, Catledge worked as a wholesale hardware clerk in Memphis and a door-to-door salesman of aluminum pots and pans in middle Tennessee, and in various jobs for his Turner uncles in Philadelphia. Then he was offered a job as a newspaperman on the weekly county paper located in Philadelphia, the *Neshoba Democrat*.

Catledge had worked at the paper during the summer between his junior and senior years at college, soliciting subscriptions, gathering news, writing articles, and operating a press. In the summer of 1922 the paper's owner, Clayton Rand, offered him an editor's position with the *Tunica* (Mississippi) *Times,* a weekly he had purchased. Tunica was the county seat of Tunica County, which had a population of twenty-five thousand, approximately twenty-three thousand of whom were black. Rand's newspapers were the only ones in Mississippi to fight the Ku Klux Klan. Some of the prominent merchants in Tunica were Klan members who refused to advertise in the paper. Rand blamed Catledge for the lack of ad sales, but with every editorial by Rand against the Klan, advertising decreased. He became anxious to sell the *Tunica Times,* and the local merchants were successful in locating a buyer. Catledge then headed for the *Tupelo* (Mississippi) *Journal,* serving three months as managing editor and mechanical supervisor. He then decided to try what he called "the big leagues of Southern journalism – Memphis."

In February 1924 Catledge secured a reporting job with the *Memphis Press.* His first assignment was to get an "add" (addition) on a story about the blizzard that had hit the city that day. Catledge confused the word "add" with "ad" and proceeded to sell three advertisements to local coal companies. The following week he received word that his father was failing, but by the time he reached Philadelphia, his father had died. Turner returned to Memphis, and after three more weeks he was released from the *Press.* The managing editor, Walter Morrow, told him, "I think you'd do better at the *Commercial Appeal.*" Catledge did not need to hear more, since he had dreamed of working with the *Memphis Commercial Appeal.* As a young boy he and his father had read the paper. Catledge secured a position after barging into the office of editor C. P. J. Mooney and relating his ordeal at the *Press.* After several weeks of general-assignment reporting, Catledge began covering local government. He had made friends easily while growing up in Philadelphia, and he made them just as easily in Mem-

phis. He was assigned several difficult stories and built up quite a few contacts, including Mayor Edward Crump. Most of the articles about Crump in the *Commercial Appeal* were not favorable, yet Catledge maintained a good relationship with him. On one assignment Catledge checked into possible voting irregularities and was pushed into the gutter by some of Crump's colleagues. Even though the incident caused some contention, the two men remained friends. Years later, when Crump served in Congress and Catledge was a Washington correspondent, the politician became one of Catledge's best sources.

A terrible 1927 flood in Mississippi afforded Catledge an important journalistic opportunity. His familiarity with the state and the river helped him to get the assignment to cover the flood and the resulting visit of Secretary of Commerce Herbert Hoover. Catledge covered the flood primarily by airplane. Hoover was so impressed with Catledge's knowledge and assessment of the river that he wrote a letter to Adolph Ochs, owner of the *New York Times,* suggesting that he ought to meet the young reporter. Catledge did not immediately land a job with the *Times,* but he did know he had to move on. Mooney had died in 1926, and the family had sold the newspaper to a group in Nashville. Catledge became concerned that his job was in jeopardy because of the new ownership's concern for profit.

Through a new friend, W. A. S. Douglas, Catledge secured a position as a features writer and reporter with the *Baltimore Sun* in the summer of 1927. During the presidential campaign of 1928 he was assigned as a Washington correspondent. Catledge was with the *Sun* for two years when he received a telegram from the managing editor of the *New York Times,* Frederick T. Birchall, inviting him to come to New York to work as a reporter. Catledge viewed the *Times* as a dull, stodgy newspaper, but New York was the mecca of the newspaper business, and on 11 August 1929 he started his career with the *Times.* In December of that year he became a Washington correspondent for the *Times.* Even though he maintained his relationship with Hoover, who was then president, he was assigned to the House of Representatives. He also knew George Akerson, Hoover's press secretary, who referred him to two important politicians, John Nance Garner, the Democratic leader in the House, and Pat Harrison, a leading Democratic senator from Mississippi. The power in Congress lay with a veteran contingent from the South, and Harrison was at the forefront of the group, which included Sam Rayburn, James F. Byrnes, Cordell Hull, and Alben Barkley. This group provided many story leads that helped advance Catledge's career. The Washington assignment allowed Catledge to resume a courtship with Mildred Turpin, whom he had dated while in Washington with the *Baltimore Sun.* They were married in New York on 19 March 1931.

In January 1932 Arthur Krock became the bureau chief of the *Times* Washington bureau. He promoted Catledge to chief Capitol correspondent and assigned him to cover the 1932 presidential election. Catledge was on Hoover's train during the campaign, and he could see by the angry mobs assembled in cities such as Detroit that it was not going favorably. Hoover was soundly defeated by New York governor Franklin Delano Roosevelt. One week before the election the first of Catledge's two daughters, Mildred Lee, was born. The other, Ellen Douglas, arrived four years later.

The New Deal period brought new importance and demands to Catledge's job. Legislation was rapidly introduced in Congress: the Economy Act, Civilian Conservation Corps, Federal Emergency Relief Act, Tennessee Valley Authority, Agriculture Adjustment Act, and other measures kept Catledge and his colleagues sorting and reporting on the meaning of the New Deal fervor. The excitement that permeated Congress, however, did not carry over to the Supreme Court, which found nine of Roosevelt's New Deal programs unconstitutional by the beginning of 1937. Roosevelt planned on fighting this with the "court-packing" bill, which would allow the president to appoint a new justice, up to a total of fifteen, for every justice who refused to retire at full pay within six months of reaching age seventy. This would affect six of the nine seated justices. Catledge pursued the progress of this bill from its inception on 5 February 1937 to its death 168 days later, following the story seven days a week and filing every *Times* story on the bill except one.

In 1936 Joseph Alsop, a Capitol Hill correspondent for the *New York Herald Tribune,* and Catledge began collaborating on magazine articles, including several for the *Saturday Evening Post* on the drama surrounding the "court-packing" bill. They expanded their *Post* articles into a book, *The 168 Days* (1938). They were offered a syndicated political column with the North American Newspaper Alliance. Alsop was excited at the prospect, but Catledge felt more confident with reporting and declined. Catledge followed the campaign trails of Alfred M. Landon in 1936 and Wendell Willkie in 1940. His assignments on Capitol Hill and as roving political correspondent put him in touch with the most powerful politicians in the country.

Senator Pat Harrison of Mississippi answering questions from Catledge during the 1930s, while Catledge was a Washington bureau reporter for the New York Times *(from Turner Catledge,* My Life and the Times, *1971)*

From 1 October 1941 to 1 May 1943, Catledge worked for the *Chicago Sun.* He began as chief political writer and roving correspondent based in Washington. Within a few months he was named editor of the paper, which he found embroiled in confusion. Prior to his arrival as editor, the *Sun* had attacked Col. Robert McCormick, publisher of the *Chicago Tribune.* McCormick responded by persuading news dealers not to sell the *Sun,* which kept the paper from obtaining the Associated Press wire service. Catledge never felt comfortable at the *Sun,* so he accepted a standing offer to come back to the *Times.* After his return to the Washington bureau with the newly created title of national correspondent, he learned of war plans for a cross-Channel Allied invasion of Europe. In November, Catledge began a four-month tour covering the Red Cross in the Western war zone, including Naples, Algiers, Tripoli, and Cairo.

Catledge returned to Washington in mid March 1944 and resumed his assignment as national correspondent. He covered the presidential campaign that year between Roosevelt and Thomas E. Dewey. On 13 November 1944 he departed on a five-week tour of the Pacific war theaters with *Times* publisher Arthur Hays Sulzberger. There were two purposes for the trip: Sulzberger, a member of the central board of the Red Cross, wanted to discuss Red Cross operations with military commanders; he also wanted to observe the war in order to give *Times* readers a better understanding of it. The trip took them to New Guinea, the Philippines, and several islands in between. On the island of Peleliu they were fired at by a Japanese sniper; in Leyte they stayed with Gen. Douglas MacArthur, who had Gen. Richard K. Sutherland brief them on plans to recapture the Philippines. During the trip Catledge was informed that he would not return to the Washington bureau; instead he would be the new assistant managing editor in New York.

The first problem Catledge saw that needed to be resolved in New York was a lack of communication between the day and night editors. The two shifts rarely had contact with each other. The managing editor, Edwin L. (Jimmy) James, and the night managing editor, Raymond McCaw, often went for weeks without conferring. Both men were key members in the production of the *Times,* and both made decisions independently. The problem was not limited to shifts but was also evident between departments. Editors who had worked a floor apart for years did not know each other. Catledge began to resolve the dilemma by instituting daily late-afternoon planning meetings. Another administrative nightmare was the coverage of news stories along jurisdictional lines. For instance, the city desk covered Camden, New Jersey, but the national desk covered Philadelphia, which was across the Delaware River from Camden. If a story originated in Philadelphia and moved to Camden, the national reporter would cover the story until it came to Camden, and it then would be picked up by a city desk reporter. Catledge implemented guidelines to cover stories topically rather than by jurisdictional boundaries and worked at expanding national coverage. He felt there was too much focus on Washington, and he wanted to include more reporting from around the nation. This new dimension of reporting involved not just looking at new bills or laws but the effect they would have on the American people. He also expanded foreign coverage to include Latin American countries.

The family relationships at the *Times* also posed some problems. When publisher Adolph Ochs died in 1935, the job went to his son-in-law,

President John F. Kennedy with Catledge in April 1961, after the unsuccessful Bay of Pigs invasion (from Turner Catledge, My Life and the Times, 1971)

Sulzberger. The business executive of the *Times* was Gen. Julius Ochs Adler, Ochs's nephew. Sulzberger and Adler became close friends, yet they were two very different individuals. Cyrus Sulzberger, nephew of the publisher, was chief foreign correspondent, and he did not like interference in his position and resented any editing of articles by him or other foreign correspondents. Catledge decided early to walk through every part of the *Times,* go in every office, and shake every hand he could. By the time he finished, he felt he knew the operations at the paper better than any other editor.

Not long after his arrival in New York, Catledge was visited by an army captain who summoned him to Washington about a matter concerning *Times* science reporter William L. Laurence, who was on loan to the army for a secret project. In Washington, Catledge was informed of the atomic-bomb program, the Manhattan Project. Gen. Leslie Groves, head of the project, briefed Catledge on the New Mexico test and its devastating nature. He also told Catledge that one or more of these bombs would be dropped on Japan. Groves sought assurance that the *Times* would

Catledge using opera glasses to view picket lines of New York Times *employees during a 1962–1963 strike that lasted 114 days (from Turner Catledge,* My Life and the Times, *1971)*

report a full and accurate account of the bomb's development and use following the attack on Japan, which occurred four days later, on 6 August 1945.

Catledge continued to enlarge the role of assistant managing editor. Sulzberger would often come to him for advice before going to the managing editor. Catledge's early years in this position were not without personal trials. In 1949 his wife sought a legal separation, and they divorced nine years later. The late 1940s also brought other job prospects. The Marshall Plan administrators asked him to be Averell Harriman's public-relations adviser in Paris. *Houston Chronicle* owner Jesse Jones asked him to be publisher of that paper. The *Cleveland Plain Dealer* offered to triple his salary to become editor. Catledge turned all of them down. His satisfaction with the *Times* and the bad experience in Chicago with the *Sun* made his decision easier.

In May 1951 Catledge accepted the newly created position of *Times* executive managing editor, intended to help bridge the gap between the day and night editors. However, he was still subordinate to the managing editor. James died on 3 December 1951, and the next day Catledge became the new managing editor. James had been an old-style editor, familiar with editing a paper but not managing it. Under James's editorial leadership the *Times* grew in prestige and public acceptance, yet administratively the company was filled with holes. Catledge immediately set out to establish a stronger chain of command. Information started flowing through editors to their respective staffs. Catledge worked closely with Sulzberger and his successor, Orvil Dryfoos, to resolve the problems of running a top-rated newspaper. Catledge worked to change the writing style of the paper. The *Times* had become known for its long sentences, which dated back to Ochs's tenure, when the paper paid reporters by story length. Catledge named E. Clifton Daniel as an assistant managing editor. Daniel, a well-known correspondent in London and Washington, married Margaret Truman in the spring of

1956. During the 1950s Catledge received honorary degrees from Southwestern at Memphis (now Rhodes College), Washington and Lee University, and the University of Kentucky.

As managing editor, Catledge expanded the obituary column, and Alden Whitman became chief obituary writer. The obituaries would not just announce the death, but would reflect the person's life. During the 1950s and 1960s the *Times* opened or expanded bureaus in San Francisco, Detroit, Boston, Hollywood, Los Angeles, Chicago, Des Moines, Houston, Atlanta, and New Orleans. A transition to carry news analysis was made during Catledge's editorship, breaking an old *Times* tradition of using only hard news. He felt that readers needed interpretation of what the news meant and how it applied to them. Political and economic stories were oriented to the consumer, not the politician or economist. Some of Catledge's best work was among people. His promotion decisions helped the *Times* to evolve into a stronger paper. The new organization became filled with talented managers and editors, including James (Scotty) Reston, Harrison Salisbury, Frank Adams, and Abe Rosenthal. On 19 February 1958 Catledge married Abby Ray Izard, a widow from New Orleans, in Las Vegas.

When publisher Orvil Dryfoos died in 1963, the *Times* followed tradition and Arthur ("Punch") Sulzberger, Ochs's grandson, became publisher. He was thirty-seven years old and had few contemporaries at the paper to help him adapt to this position, so Catledge assisted him in the transition. On 1 September 1964 Catledge was named executive editor, and he served in this capacity for four years, building up the prestige of the *Times* Washington bureau and clarifying coverage of the Vietnam War. On 1 June 1968 he became a vice-president of the New York Times Company; he resigned this position on 1 January 1970 but remained on the board of directors until 1973. During Catledge's service he had seen the *Times* go from a ranking below other New York papers to one of the most powerful in the world. Following his retirement Catledge and his wife moved to New Orleans, where he died on 27 April 1983.

References:

Thomas Harrison Baker, *The Memphis Commercial Appeal: The History of a Southern Newspaper* (Baton Rouge: Louisiana State University Press, 1971);

Meyer Berger, *The Story of the New York Times, 1851–1951* (New York: Simon & Schuster, 1951);

Richard Kluger, *The Paper: The Life and Death of the New York Herald Tribune* (New York: Knopf, 1986);

Harrison Salisbury, *Without Fear or Favor: The New York Times and Its Times* (New York: Times Books, 1980);

Gay Talese, *The Kingdom and the Power* (New York: World, 1969).

Norman Chandler
(14 September 1899 – 20 October 1973)

and

Otis Chandler
(23 November 1927 –   )

Terry Hynes
California State University, Fullerton

MAJOR POSITIONS HELD: **Norman Chandler:** Assistant to the publisher (1929–1934), assistant to the general manager (1934–1936), vice-president and general manager (1936–1941), president and general manager (1941–1945), president and publisher (1945–1960), *Los Angeles Times*; director (1938–1973), president (1941–1944), chairman (1944–1960), chairman and chief executive officer (1961–1968), chairman of the executive committee (1968–1973), Times Mirror Company.

Otis Chandler: Assistant to the president (1957–1958), *Mirror-News*; marketing manager (1958–1960), publisher (1960–1980), *Los Angeles Times*; vice-chairman (1968–1980), editor in chief (1980–1985), chairman (1981–1985), chairman of the executive committee (1986–   ), Times Mirror Company.

The *Los Angeles Times* and its parent company, Times Mirror, are, by professional journalistic and business standards, major examples of the successful urban-national newspaper and media conglomerate, respectively, in the late twentieth century. For most of its history, however, the *Times* was as far from being a "newspaperman's newspaper" as fool's gold is from the real thing. Then, in the period from 1960 to 1969, it was transformed into a world-class newspaper, identified by the end of that decade as a publication in the same rank as the *New York Times* and the *Washington Post*. At the same time its parent company began to imitate the major

33

corporations of that era by expanding and diversifying its holdings.

The metanoia of the *Times* and Times Mirror in the 1960s occurred for several reasons, including changes that were taking place in the newspaper industry and in society as a whole. Chief among the causes of the transformation of the *Times,* however, was the new leadership of its young publisher, Otis Chandler. And a key factor that enabled Otis to move as quickly as he did in guiding the paper to the front ranks of the industry was the stable financial base that his father, Norman, had restored to the family business after the Depression. In addition, Norman made Times Mirror a diversified corporation, able to survive in a highly profitable manner even if one of its most profitable holdings could not.

Born 14 September 1899, Norman was the third child and eldest son of Harry and Marian Otis Chandler. Marian, with whom Harry had six children, was his second wife. Harry also had two daughters, Franceska and Alice, with his first wife. Norman's grandfather Harrison Gray Otis was a fiery editor and publisher who used his frontier newspaper as a personal vehicle for sounding off about every public issue that concerned him and as a public tool for the shaping – literally – of southern California.

By Norman's generation, the major political battles of city growth, land grabbing in the San Fernando Valley, and water stealing from the central California Owens Valley – as well as the role of the *Times* in each event – had been accomplished. The newspaper and other media holdings did not make the family rich in the beginning. Harrison Gray Otis and Harry Chandler earned their wealth the old-fashioned way in California: by buying and selling real estate. By the 1920s Harry's wealth was estimated to be at least $200 million.

Given the era in which he lived and his father's expectations for his eldest son, it is not surprising that Norman was groomed from an early age to be publisher of the *Times.* He began his career in the composing and stereotype rooms while he was still a student at Hollywood High School, from which he was graduated in 1917. During part of World War I, Norman served in the Reserve Officers' Training Corps. In 1918 he became a student at Stanford University, but he quit the university in 1922, a semester before he would have earned his bachelor of arts degree. Three decades later his only son, Otis, followed an almost identical path.

At Stanford, Norman met Dorothy "Buff" Buffum, daughter of a department-store owner in Long Beach, California. A year behind Norman at Stanford, Buff gave up college after her third year and married him on 30 August 1922. After their marriage Norman accepted a sixteen-dollar-a-week job on the *Times,* delivering newspapers in a Ford Model T. The Chandlers' real living expenses, however, were met by the income from the fifty thousand dollars in hotel stock that Harrison Gray Otis left as his legacy to his grandson.

From 1922 to 1929 Norman worked in almost every department of the paper as a kind of publisher-in-training – another pattern that would be repeated by Otis in the 1950s. Norman focused on the business side of the paper during his apprenticeship and displayed little interest in journalism per se or in the operations of the newsroom itself. After serving briefly as secretary to his father, he was made assistant to the publisher in 1929, then assistant to the general manager in 1934. By 1936 Norman was the virtual publisher of the paper, although he did not receive that title until after his father died in 1944. During the late 1930s to the early 1940s Norman served as vice-president and general manager (from 1936), then president and general manager (from 1941).

In 1938 he was elected a director of the Times Mirror Company, the family enterprise named for both the *Los Angeles Times* and the *Mirror,* an advertising newspaper of the 1870s that had been published by three print-shop owners. They rescued the *Times* from an early demise shortly after it began on 4 December 1881 by accepting the paper as payment for a printing debt and continuing to publish it as part of their operation.

From its early connection with the *Mirror* and the close ties between that paper's owners and local businesses, the *Times* developed strong ties to the business structure of the region, a relationship reflected to some degree in the high volume of advertising in the paper. Harry had particularly strong ties to the business community of Los Angeles; but his neglect of the newspaper in his later years, combined with cutbacks in advertising by local businesses during the Depression, resulted in an emaciated *Times* advertising section. Norman set out to salvage the newspaper's profits. When he became president and publisher in 1945, the *Times* ranked thirty-fourth in ad linage among the nation's daily newspapers; six years later it ranked third.

The effort to increase the newspaper's profits began in the early 1930s, when, at Norman's insistence, a Chicago efficiency expert, Col. Guy T.

Visknisski, was hired to make the staff more productive and the newspaper more appealing to a wider readership. Visknisski fired many longtime employees and replaced them with younger, college-educated individuals, who were paid much less for their work. His cost-cutting measures included monitoring phone calls to be sure they were business-related and ordering the staff not to change typewriter ribbons.

The *Times* had never been known for the quality of its news pages. Otis's penchant for fulminating in print earned him a scathing diatribe from California senator Hiram Johnson of San Francisco: "We have nothing so vile . . . nothing so infamous in San Francisco as Harrison Gray Otis. He sits there in senile dementia, with gangrened heart and rotting brain, grimacing at every reform, chattering impotently at all things that are decent; frothing, fuming, violently gibbering, going down to his grave in snarling infamy."

This emotional eruption was no more extreme than some of those by Otis in the *Times*. After Otis died in 1917, the tradition of diatribe and vitriol lived on in the newspaper. Harry, after all, was not much interested in the editorial side of the paper; what mattered most to him was the commercial strength of this family enterprise and its value in increasing his business influence. The cost cutting of the early 1930s helped the *Times* improve its news content and become what Norman hoped would be a more modern-looking and readable paper. Under his direction the paper's columns were widened, more pictures were included, and headlines became bolder.

Like his father and grandfather, Norman was antiunion, anticommunist, and a conservative Republican. With a tradition of political conservatism already entrenched at the *Times,* Norman could remain aloof from most of the day-to-day decision making and operation of the newspaper without fear that his or his family's views would be contradicted in the paper's news or editorial pages. The family's conservative Republican loyalty was ably underscored by the work of *Times* political reporter Kyle Palmer, who by the 1940s wielded dual power. He was a broker of political careers as a Republican party insider, and he was a publicizer and endorser of politicians as political editor for one of the state's most powerful newspapers. In 1946 he helped launch the political career of a then-obscure young Republican, Richard M. Nixon. As anti-Japanese sentiment began to develop after the bombing of Pearl Harbor, the *Times* became one of many California newspapers that supported the relocation of

Otis Chandler (Los Angeles Times *photograph)*

Japanese to detention camps for the duration of World War II.

In an odd coupling for the historically antilabor *Times,* the newspaper became a codefendant with International Longshore Worker's Union leader Harry Bridges in a freedom of speech and press case during the late 1930s. The case began when the *Times* published the text of Bridges's telegram denouncing a local judge's injunction against union picketing. The *Times* was cited for contempt when it insisted editorially that a newspaper had a right to comment on the conduct of courts and court trials. The case was finally decided in 1941 by the U.S. Supreme Court in a five to four decision in favor of Bridges and the *Times*. Justice Hugo Black wrote for the majority: "The assumption that respect for the judiciary can be won by shielding judges from published criticism wrongly appraises the character of American public opinion. . . . It is a prized American privilege to speak one's mind, although not always with perfect good taste, on all public institutions. And an enforced silence, however limited, solely in the name of preserving the dignity of the bench, would probably engender resentment, suspicion, and contempt much more than it would enhance respect."

In 1942 the *Times* won its first Pulitzer Prize, for meritorious public service, because of its role in supporting freedom of speech and the press in this case. The paper also received Pulitzer Prizes in 1946 (for editorial cartoons) and 1955 (for photography). Being on the winning side of a free-press court decision could not obscure the fact that the *Times* was regarded by many major journalists as one of the "least fair and reliable" papers in the country. Leo Rosten's 1937 book, *The Washington Correspondents,* based on a survey of ninety-three Washington journalists, ranked the *Times* third worst in this regard, surpassed only by William Randolph Hearst's newspapers and the *Chicago Tribune.*

The changes in the *Times* that Norman initiated or supported during the 1940s were intended to broaden the paper's readership base to a larger part of the lower-middle class. With its deeply embedded antipathy toward unions and its corresponding bias toward the concerns of business owners, the paper was not very successful in this effort. In post–World War II Los Angeles, with its influx of industrial-working-class men and women, the image of the *Times* as a conservative Republican paper inhibited its ability to reach this new audience.

Norman solved the problem of reaching the new working class in Los Angeles by creating the *Los Angeles Mirror.* Named for the advertising sheet of the 1870s, whose legacy remained in the corporate title of the company, this paper was introduced as an afternoon publication on 11 October 1948 after an intense promotional campaign by the J. Walter Thompson advertising agency. It was one of the most ill-timed introductions of an urban daily paper. Few metropolitan dailies had been successfully launched in the preceding two decades. Moreover, with the automobile supplanting public transportation in the sprawling Los Angeles basin and people driving home from work increasingly to watch a newfangled invention called television, the emerging southern California popular culture of the second half of the twentieth century would not be supportive of afternoon newspapers.

The *Mirror,* however, fit Norman's post–World War II plans for expanding the Chandler family empire. He had already bought a local television station, KTTV, and had joined with the Mormon church to invest in forest lands and pulp and paper companies in Oregon. As Norman structured it, the new paper's losses could be used as tax write-offs. Thus, if it could splinter the audience for the two newspapers that already appealed to working-

class readers, Hearst's *Herald-Express* and the *Daily News,* the *Mirror* would indirectly benefit the *Times,* even if it lost money.

Much of the style and content of the *Mirror* was typical of the tabloids it was designed to imitate, but in its political endorsements the paper generally followed the lead of the *Times.* Occasionally, as in its support of Dwight D. Eisenhower for the Republican presidential nomination in 1952, endorsements by the *Mirror* seemed to reflect Buff's, rather than her husband's or other Chandler family members', preferences. She may have used the *Mirror* to move the family's reputation away from rabid anticommunism and extreme cultural conservatism. Although Norman did not really approve of the sensationalism and screaming headlines that characterized the *Mirror,* he seems to have allowed the paper a good deal of autonomy, especially during its early years under managing editor Ed Murray.

Norman imitated earlier publishers, such as Hearst and Joseph Pulitzer, in introducing the *Mirror* as a five-cent paper, while the *Herald-Express* and *Daily News* each sold for seven cents. The lower price helped attract readers, especially away from the *Daily News,* and advertisers soon bought more space in the *Mirror.* By 1954 circulation of the *Mirror* reached 224,438. That year, working anonymously through a broker, Norman bought the "name, goodwill, and features" of the *Daily News,* leaving the city without a Democratic newspaper. The *Mirror* became the *Mirror-News.* By 1956 circulation was more than 300,000.

By 1954, however, Norman's tolerance for the racy style of the *Mirror* had ebbed, and he authorized a change to a standard eight-column format, which managing editor Murray called a "grand mistake . . . transforming a hot tabloid into an anemic, non-character standard size paper." Three years later *Mirror* publisher Virgil Pinkley, former United Press bureau chief for Europe, was fired. *Times* city editor Hugh "Bud" Lewis was brought in as publisher. Otis Chandler was made assistant to Lewis and charged with reporting to the *Times* board of directors on options for the future of the *Mirror.* More conservative format changes were made to the *Mirror:* its picture page was eliminated; the zoned editions Murray had pioneered to reach the sprawling Los Angeles readership were dropped; and fewer long features – a hallmark of the *Mirror* – appeared. After Murray was forced out as managing editor in 1960, the *Mirror* struggled along with a disheartened staff until it ceased publication on 5 January 1962.

By 1958 Norman had accomplished a great deal to make the *Times* and the Times Mirror Company stable financial enterprises. The paper's total revenue had increased almost annually from 1944 onward; its circulation lead on its nearest rival, Hearst's *Examiner,* was more than 100,000. By the mid 1950s the *Times* had become the nation's leading newspaper in its volume of advertising. In 1955 its circulation had reached 440,394 on weekdays and 839,400 on Sunday. But the paper's editorial content continued to be a predictable mix of what *Times* historian Jack R. Hart called "civic boosterism, Republican conservatism, and . . . traditional establishment morality."

No one was more offended by the low regard in which the *Times* was held by other newspaper professionals than Buff. She played a major role in shaping the image of the *Times* while working as her husband's assistant and in seeing that Otis was prepared to mold the paper into something of which she and others could be proud. By Norman's generation the Chandler family had moved to Pasadena, home in the early twentieth century of the nouveau riche of greater Los Angeles. Some family members had a somewhat inflated sense of self-importance, reflected in a disdain toward Buff, the daughter of a merchant. In the first years of their marriage, she and Norman lived in Hollywood. After the birth of their daughter Camilla in 1926, they moved to larger quarters in Pasadena.

Buff felt constrained by the rules of acceptable behavior in Pasadena social circles and, having reached an emotional breaking point in 1932, entered a psychiatric hospital in Pasadena where she remained almost exclusively for six months. This action was indicative of both the extremity of her emotional state and of her great courage. The sanitarium experience helped her to recognize her strengths and to accept the Chandlers' differences without feeling diminished by them. Her determination grew to apply her talents to transforming the reputations of both the city of Los Angeles and the family newspaper.

During World War II, Buff became Norman's assistant at the *Times* and was responsible for the paper's corporate image. She had an office and an apartment on the newspaper building's top floor. After the war she took a course in journalism at the University of Southern California and became even more actively involved in the *Times.* She took charge of the women's pages and fortified the society coverage. In 1950 she originated the *Times* Women of the Year Award, which is presented annually to southern California's leading women in art, literature, science, and other areas of accomplishment.

Norman Chandler congratulating his son, Otis, on being named the fourth publisher of the Los Angeles Times, *April 1960*

In 1948 Buff was named administrative assistant to the president of the Times Mirror Company, and in 1955 she was named a company director. Just as two earlier generations of Chandlers had shaped the geographic landscape of southern California, Buff became a leading architect of its cultural landscape. When she successfully marshaled business leaders to help the Hollywood Bowl overcome a financial crisis in 1951, she learned the power and satisfaction of winning a cultural battle for the city. She used her influence to help rid Los Angeles of its reputation as a "cultural desert." After she and Norman traveled in the Soviet Union in 1955, she appeared before a House of Representatives subcommittee of the Committee on Education and Labor to urge adoption of a more liberal cultural exchange program between the two countries. A few years later she was a key leader in bringing the Bolshoi Ballet and Moiseyev Dancers to Los Angeles, a particularly controversial move in the rabidly anticommunist Chandler family as well as the city at large.

In the 1950s and 1960s Buff was the central force in the fund-raising drive for what became the Los Angeles Music Center. In recognition of her efforts the center's largest pavilion was named in her honor. So strong was her cultural power in the city by the early 1960s that her championing of a young musician from India, Zubin Mehta, led to Georg Solti's resignation as conductor of the Los Angeles Symphony Orchestra. With Buff's backing Mehta was appointed conductor of the orchestra in early 1961. In 1956 President Dwight D. Eisenhower appointed her to the U.S. Committee on Education Beyond the High School.

By the late 1950s Otis was already moving through various positions at the paper in a management apprenticeship that paralleled his father's ascendancy to publisher thirty years earlier. According to the timetable informally agreed to among Norman, Buff, and Otis, the son would replace his father as publisher by the late 1960s. This schedule was disrupted when in 1958, while on vacation in Hawaii, Norman became seriously ill. Fearful that if he died the publisher role would pass to Norman's ultraconservative brother, Philip, Buff hired a management consulting firm, McKinsey and Company, ostensibly to conduct an organizational study of the Times Mirror Company but also as a means for neutralizing Philip's influence.

McKinsey and Company recommended that a successor to Norman should be in place for at least fifteen years in order to stabilize the company during an era of corporate change. That would effectively eliminate Philip, age fifty-one, because of the company's mandatory retirement age of sixty-five. Having reviewed the declining fortunes of the newspaper industry nationally, the consultants doubted the *Times* would continue to be profitable and also recommended that the timetable for Otis's succession be sped up so Norman could give more time to the umbrella company.

The consultants made several other recommendations that, when adopted, would result in the dislocation of Norman's generation of Chandlers from their positions of power in the Times Mirror Company. Diversification of corporate holdings and becoming a public corporation were among several elements designed to bring the staid family operation into the major leagues of U.S. businesses. All of this was profoundly unsettling to the power holders of Norman's era, but Buff's negotiating skills and tenacity effected the transition.

Her maneuvering climaxed in spring 1960, when major California political and cultural leaders were invited to the Biltmore Bowl auditorium on 11 April for "an announcement of great importance." Few of the several hundred guests – including a former governor; the lieutenant governor; the mayor of Los Angeles; county supervisors; education, industrial, and banking leaders; and publishers and editors – had a clue about what was in store. Norman made the announcement: effective immediately, Otis was publisher of the *Los Angeles Times*. Norman would give all his attention to Times Mirror.

Within a few weeks of Otis's appointment as publisher, the *Times* received its second Pulitzer Prize for meritorious public service. The 1960 Pulitzer was for an eight-part series on illegal drug smuggling from Mexico to the United States. The series was written by Gene Sherman, one of those hired by Visknisski during the reorganization of the early 1930s. In the two decades that Otis remained publisher, the paper received six additional Pulitzer Prizes, including a third "meritorious public service" gold medal in 1969.

But none of the earthshaking change that was to come during Otis's tenure as publisher was apparent at the time of his appointment. On the day after the announcement at the Biltmore, Otis wrote in a *Times* editorial, "No changes are in the offing. A continuation of the successful Times format of an unbiased, informed and responsible press is in order." As Hart noted, Otis "took exceptional pains to create an impression of unexcited continuity." At thirty-two, Otis in 1960 had a modest record of achievement. In 1946 he was graduated from an elite private school, Andover Academy in Massachusetts. In 1950 he earned a bachelor of arts degree from Stanford University, where he excelled as an athlete. He married Marilyn "Missie" Jane Brant, daughter of another wealthy southern California family and granddaughter of Otto Brant of Title Insurance and Trust Company, on 18 June 1951. They had five children – Norman, Harry, Cathleen, Michael, and Carolyn – before they divorced in the late 1970s. During the Korean War, from 1951 to 1953, he served in the air force.

Otis had no fierce loyalties to the family's conservative ideological heritage. After he left the air force, he began as a printer's apprentice on the *Times* in 1953, the first step in learning the technical complexities of the paper's mechanical production. His publisher's apprenticeship included three years on the mechanical side, then almost a year as a general assignment reporter for the *Times*, followed by a few months in a similar position at the *Mirror*. Otis then moved to the *Times* circulation department, then to the advertising department, until his appointment as special assistant to the president in 1957. With few emotional ties to the past, he would eventually be in a perfect position to help the family maintain its power by following his mother's lead,

Dorothy, Norman, and Otis Chandler in 1961 (Collection of Otis Chandler)

expanding the power structure to include a newer generation of players.

By the 1960s the new mix of power players in Los Angeles required a more sophisticated journalism than the old *Times* provided. The provincialism of the city's early years had already been superseded by more cosmopolitan interests. The social, economic, and political changes that had occurred in Los Angeles were part of national, post–World War II realliances at various levels. In the midst of the rapid economic expansion that followed the war, the mass media of communications, too, had undergone significant change. Newspapers, for example, were losing circulations. Television was becoming a major competitor for people's leisure time. Rising production costs were outstripping the ability of most newspapers to keep up with them, and new technologies would exacerbate the problem before the 1960s were over.

At the *Times* in 1960 the editorial staff was top-heavy with veteran employees who, as Hart wrote, "long accustomed to paternalistic job security, carefully avoided the development of energetic potential successors. . . . The result was stifling provincialism." Yet some change had already begun on the *Times* editorial side before Otis was made publisher. In 1958 Norman had appointed Nick Boddie Williams, then a twenty-seven-year *Times* veteran, to re-

place longtime editor Loyal Durant "Hotch" Hotchkiss in the senior management position. Williams would remain editor until 1971. He began making changes, shifting staff internally and hiring people he hoped would help move the paper in a different direction. He cut back on some traditional beat assignments, especially coverage of the central city, in order to free some reporters for new features. With a fine-tuned negotiating skill Williams proved to be a key link between old-guard staffers and family members who wanted little or no change and new staff members who were impatient for it.

In some respects Otis's contribution to the changes that Williams had started was that of facilitator, rather than driving force. With more than three thousand employees in 1960, the *Times* may have been too big and complex for any single person, even the publisher, to have a pervasive effect. But it was a matter of personal pride with Otis – as with his mother – that he be publisher of a great newspaper. His ambition in this regard was the equivalent of a driving force. Achieving the goal meant the *Times* had to change, and this required money and a sense of direction. As publisher, Otis could provide the capital. In addition, he recognized what he did not know about the *Times* and was prepared to listen to informed advice. Editor Nick Williams found him accessible and receptive.

The new *Times* was to offer well-researched, informative, and lengthy stories geared to an upscale readership of college-educated suburbanites in the expanding sprawl of southern California. The assumption was that this audience received its local news from community papers – thirty-three daily newspapers in southern California in 1960 – so the *Times* would concentrate on larger issues and trends as well as on regional, national, and international news. This approach fit well with increased calls in the 1960s for changes in journalistic practice. Journalists had been sharply criticized in the aftermath of McCarthyism for purporting to practice an ideal of "objectivity" that was humanly impossible to achieve. The "new journalism" of the 1960s called in part for more explanatory, interpretive reporting that could be done best in the style proposed for the *Times*.

Creating the new *Times* required new talent. Williams hired *Time* magazine's West Coast bureau chief Frank McCulloch in fall 1960 as one of two new managing editors for the paper. Wholesale firing of veteran staffers followed, the first such cuts at the paternalistic *Times* in decades. By the mid 1960s McCulloch was gone, and the paper had an almost entirely new staff, including editorial cartoonist Paul Conrad, who was wooed from the *Denver Post* after he received a Pulitzer Prize in 1964.

During the early 1960s Otis dealt effectively with competitive threats from outside the paper. When the *New York Times* withdrew its wire service from all West Coast clients in late 1961 as a prelude to publishing its own West Coast edition, Otis formed a syndicated news service in conjunction with the *Washington Post,* thus strengthening *Los Angeles Times* coverage of national and international news. When the *New York Times* western edition began in October 1962, it never garnered the readership or advertising needed to stay afloat. Less than fifteen months later, $2 million in the red, it folded. Although Otis later insisted that the East Coast competition in no way changed his timetable for his own paper, Williams, McCulloch, and other editorial staffers saw it differently. In their view the competitive threat from the New York–based paper enhanced their ability to get the resources needed and speed up improvements at the *Los Angeles Times*.

In early 1961 the *Times* published a thorough, factual series on the right-wing John Birch Society that so offended Philip Chandler and his wife, who was a member of the society, that Philip resigned as vice-president of the Times Mirror Company. With two lengthy series in 1963 on Mexican-Americans and African-Americans, the *Times* took a modest step toward dealing with major tensions affecting the lives of local readers. In 1965 the smoldering frustrations of the African-American community broke out in the Watts riots. The *Times,* which did not have an African-American reporter at the time, remained the least-trusted news medium in the region as late as 1969 among members of the African-American community.

Meanwhile, the changes wrought at Times Mirror – still under Norman's leadership and following the advice of the McKinsey consultants – were more surefooted. In the winter of 1960 it became the first family newspaper company to be taken public. Almost six million new shares of Times Mirror stock were issued. In June 1960 the company acquired New American Library (NAL), a large paperback-book publishing company established in 1947, marking the first time a publishing house had been purchased outside the book-publishing field. Several months later Times Mirror bought Four Aces, a British paperback publisher.

In January 1962 the company purchased its first suburban newspaper, the Newport Beach/Costa Mesa *Daily Pilot.* When Times Mirror bought the *San Bernardino Sun* in June 1964, the Justice Department sued the company for violation of antitrust laws. The ensuing legal battle resulted in a 1968 U.S. Supreme Court decision that forced Times Mirror to divest itself of the *Sun.* In 1963 the company bought World Publishing of Cleveland, Ohio, a major publisher of dictionaries and Bibles, and, as it had done with Four Aces, integrated it with the NAL operation in New York. In 1973 much of the World operation was sold or discontinued.

In May 1964 Times Mirror was listed on the New York Stock Exchange. Through diversification the overall percentage of the company's newspaper assets (75 percent of Times Mirror assets were in the newspapers of the company's name in 1960) was to be reduced. As the company diversified, each purchase was supposed to fit its self-definition as a "communications company" interested in firms related to the "knowledge industry." Although all the purchases did not fill precisely these elements, they did fit the overall goal to make the company more profitable.

Most of the purchases were accomplished by issuing new Times Mirror stock. Under its subsidiary, Publisher's Paper Company, Times Mirror added to its newsprint, paper mill, and forest holdings in northern California, Oregon, and Washington. Publisher's Paper had been started in 1947 in partnership with the Mormon church. In 1965 Times Mirror bought out the church's interest. In

The block-long city room of the Los Angeles Times, *1983 (photograph by Penni Gladstone,* Los Angeles Times)

1963 Times Mirror had $9.1 million in profit out of total revenues of $175 million. By 1969 its profit was $38.6 million out of $466 million in revenues. Its long-term debt had risen to $50 million.

One of Times Mirror's biggest business deals was its merger with the Times Herald Company of Dallas, Texas, in 1970. In this deal, Times Mirror acquired the *Dallas Times Herald,* two radio stations (which were later sold because of FCC cross-ownership regulations), television station KRLD, two subsidiaries that published advertising and newspaper circulars and supplements, 50 percent of the Hill Tower corporation, and various real-estate holdings. In all, the price tag on the purchase was estimated at $90 million.

The *Dallas Times Herald* was hardly a distinguished or major newspaper. Yet it would be considerably strengthened in subsequent years under the leadership of its new editor, W. Thomas Johnson, who came to the newspaper in 1973 after selling former president Lyndon Johnson's Austin station, KTBC, to Times Mirror. In 1975 Johnson was named publisher of the Dallas paper. In May 1977

he became president of the *Los Angeles Times,* second in power only to Otis Chandler.

In 1970 Times Mirror purchased the Long Island, New York, newspaper *Newsday* and several Long Island cable companies, which were formed into a new Times Mirror subsidiary, Long Island Cable Vision. For a brief period the company also owned the *Denver Post* and the *Allentown* (Pennsylvania) *Morning Call.* In 1979 Times Mirror bought the *Hartford* (Connecticut) *Courant.* In 1986 the company arranged for the sale of the *Times Herald* and bought the *Baltimore Sun* and *Evening Sun.* This deal also included two television stations.

When Otis became publisher of the *Times* in 1960, the paper had one foreign correspondent and a small bureau in Washington, D.C. The Washington bureau was improved dramatically when Robert Donovan, Washington bureau chief for the *New York Herald Tribune* and one of the most respected journalists in the capital, was made *Times* bureau chief in late 1963. By the early 1980s the paper had thirty-four foreign and domestic bureaus. By 1992, even in the midst of a serious international recession, it had twelve domestic bureaus – with 36 staff members in Washington, D.C., alone – and twenty-seven international bureaus.

From 1955 until the early 1990s the *Times* was the nation's leader in total advertising volume as well as in help-wanted ads. Because of a deepening recession, the paper's help-wanted ads fell 50 percent between October 1989 and October 1990. To forestall further hemorrhaging, the *Times* stopped its San Diego edition in late 1992. Despite such problems even the paper's critics acknowledged that it remained a major leader among U.S. newspapers.

In 1968 the *Times* opened the first satellite printing facility for a U.S. metropolitan newspaper when it started its Orange County edition in Costa Mesa, thirty-seven miles from Times Mirror Square in Los Angeles. During the 1980s the Orange County edition was in a fierce competition with the *Orange County Register*. The San Diego edition was also printed at the Costa Mesa site. In the mid 1980s the company opened another satellite printing plant in the San Fernando Valley.

Changes at the *Times* in the 1960s did not include the advancement of women. In 1970 the paper still had no women executives, no women in production, and only one woman in the city room. A few women worked for the transformed society section, renamed "View." Most women employed at the *Times* – as at Times Mirror–owned *Newsday* and most newspapers throughout the country – occupied secretarial positions. In addition, leaders of some of the newer women's organizations in the early 1970s felt the paper's coverage of women and women's issues was demeaning. External pressures from the National Organization for Women and the Fair Employment Practices Commission, as well as internal pressure from women in classified advertising and the editorial women's caucus, resulted in some modest changes at the *Times* by the mid 1970s. But in Los Angeles, as at the Long Island paper, progress came slowly and only through the women staffers' persistent pressure.

After twenty years as publisher of the *Times*, Otis gave up the position in 1980. For the first time since 1882 the position went to a nonfamily member, W. Thomas Johnson. He remained publisher until 1989, when he was succeeded by David Laventhol, who had come to the paper from *Newsday* in 1987. In 1989 Shelby Coffey III became editor of the paper. Under his leadership the *Times* began featuring sharper, tighter stories and a sleeker, easier-to-read design that guides readers with graphics, news summaries, and subheads. By 1990 the *Times* – with a daily circulation of 1.2 million and

Otis Chandler, circa 1984 (photograph by Anthony Di Gesu)

1.6 million on Sundays, over an area the size of Ohio – was the nation's largest metropolitan daily.

In 1980 Otis assumed the newly created position of editor in chief, and in 1981 he became chairman of the board of Times Mirror. On 15 August 1981 he married Bettina Whitaker. At the end of 1985 Otis gave up his Times Mirror positions and became chairman of the company's executive committee, thus relinquishing direct involvement in the company. The new chairman was Robert Erburu, a Times Mirror general counsel since 1961. Since 1985 Otis has devoted his time to working with disadvantaged children, traveling, and pursuing hobbies, including a museum-quality collection of muscle cars. During two generations of family leadership, Norman, Buff, and Otis Chandler succeeded in making their flagship newspaper, the *Los Angeles Times,* and their media conglomerate, the Times Mirror Company, world-class leaders in the media industry.

References:

Jonathan Alter, "Cruising Speed in L.A.," *Newsweek,* 107 (26 May 1986): 58;

David Barry, "Muscle Car Magnate," *Auto Week* (17 July 1989): 21;

Front page of the Los Angeles Times, *5 May 1970*

Peter Bart, "The New Look at the *Times,*" *Saturday Review,* 48 (12 June 1965): 68–71, 79;

Ivan Benson, "The *Los Angeles Times* Contempt Case," *Journalism Quarterly,* 16 (March 1939): 1–8;

Marshall Berges, *The Life and "Times" of Los Angeles: A Newspaper, A Family and A City* (New York: Atheneum, 1984);

William Bonelli, *Billion Dollar Blackjack* (Beverly Hills, Cal.: Civic Research Press, 1954);

Mitchell Gordon, "The Chandlers of Los Angeles," *Nieman Reports,* 19 (December 1965): 15–19;

Robert Gottlieb and Irene Wolt, *Thinking Big: The Story of the Los Angeles Times, Its Publishers, and Their Influence on Southern California* (New York: Putnam's, 1977);

David Halberstam, *The Powers That Be* (New York: Knopf, 1979);

Jack R. Hart, *The Information Empire* (Washington, D.C.: University Press of America, 1981);

John Hohenberg, *The Pulitzer Prizes* (New York: Columbia University Press, 1974);

"How To Build an Empire," *Newsweek,* 69 (2 January 1967): 41–45;

Alex Jones, "Reshaping the *Los Angeles Times,*" *New York Times,* 18 June 1990, p. D1;

"*Los Angeles Times* Revises Its Image to Reach Changing Market," *Business Week* (19 November 1960): 118–126;

John M. Mecklin, "Times Mirror's Ambitious Acquirers," *Fortune,* 78 (1 September 1968): 99–103, 155–157;

"Midas of California," *Newsweek,* 24 (2 October 1944): 80–81;

"A New Edition in Los Angeles," *Business Week* (20 November 1971): 27;

"No Comment," *Time,* 95 (23 March 1970): 38;

"Norman Chandler: Heir to an Empire," *Look,* 11 (27 May 1947): 78, 80–81;

"A Publishing Giant Takes a Long Step," *Business Week* (14 March 1964): 72–78;

Frank Riley, "The Changing Direction of the *Times,*" *Los Angeles* (June 1966): 29;

Leo Rosten, *The Washington Correspondents* (New York: Harcourt, Brace, 1937);

Jack Star, "L.A.'s Mighty Chandlers," *Look,* 26 (25 September 1962): 107–112;

"The Ten Best American Dailies," *Time,* 103 (21 January 1974): 58–61;

"Times Mirror Acquires Harry N. Abrams, Inc.," *Publisher's Weekly,* 189 (11 April 1966): 28;

"Times Mirror Company: Spreading into the Knowledge Industry," *Newsweek,* 69 (2 January 1967): 44–45;

"Times Mirror Expands Again," *Time,* 89 (10 March 1967): 47.

Gardner Cowles, Jr.

(31 January 1903 – 8 July 1985)

Herb Strentz
Drake University

NEWSPAPERS OWNED: *Des Moines Register* (1946–1985); *Des Moines Tribune* (1946–1982); *Minneapolis Star* (1946–1982); *Minneapolis Tribune* (1946–1982); *San Juan* (Puerto Rico) *Star* (1959–1970); *Gainesville* (Florida) *Sun* (1962–1971); *Lakeland* (Florida) *Ledger* (1963–1971); *Rapid City* (South Dakota) *Journal* (1964–1985); *Great Falls* (Montana) *Tribune* (1965–1985); *Suffolk* (Long Island, N.Y.) *Sun* (1966–1969); *Palatka* (Florida) *Daily News* (1969–1971); *Leesburg* (Florida) *Daily Commercial* (1969–1971); *Jackson* (Tennessee) *Sun* (1972–1985); *Waukesha* (Wisconsin) *Freeman* (1978–1983); *Minneapolis Star-Tribune* (1982–1985).

BOOK: *Mike Looks Back* (New York: Gardner Cowles, 1985).

To judge from his life, no one ever told Gardner (Mike) Cowles, Jr., that being a newspaper editor and publisher should not be fun. If anyone had, Cowles would have asked so many questions, told so many stories, and exhibited such a joie de vivre that the adviser, not Cowles, would have been the one with second thoughts. Although loyal to family traditions in responsible, public-spirited, and innovative journalism, he also enjoyed working with the young George Gallup to determine reader interests and was a pioneer in photojournalism. He mingled with celebrities, measured the earthshakers of his time, and still had the whimsy to own for a few years the Cardiff Giant – the carved-gypsum man created for a successful 1869 hoax.

The Cowles family brought to American newspaper journalism a tradition of innovation, newsroom independence, and community service that typically is part of the definition of the family-owned, regional newspapers of an almost bygone era in journalism history. As *Fortune* magazine noted in 1950: "There is nothing in the Cowles' record to indicate that the family ever lusted after power or profits. They were a dyed-in-the-wool newspaper

Gardner Cowles, Jr.

family with an urge, above all, to produce a paper that would honor their craft."

In 1903, in response to a plea from Harvey Ingham, Gardner Cowles, Sr., invested the family's life savings into the *Des Moines Register and Leader* – part of a successful effort by Ingham to protect his interest in the paper from a planned sale. (The *Leader* was dropped from the paper's name in 1916.) Ingham and Cowles then bought the *Des Moines Tribune* in 1908 and completed domination of Iowa's capital city by buying the rival *News* in 1924 and the *Capital* in 1927.

Gardner Cowles, Jr., was born on 31 January in the year of the *Register* purchase, and he died on

8 July 1985, just one week after the *Register* was sold to Gannett after eighty-two years of Cowles family ownership. Gardner, Jr., was the third son and the last of six children born to Gardner, Sr., and Florence Call Cowles. His brother Russell became a well-known painter and muralist, and his brother John became Gardner, Jr.'s compatriot in many publishing ventures. His three sisters were Helen Cowles LeCron, Florence Cowles Kruidenier, and Bertha Cowles Quarton.

Gardner, Jr., was called Mike from the time he was a day or two old. His father "took a good look at me and announced, 'He looks like an Irishman. Let's call him Mike.'" (Mike kept that family practice alive by dubbing his son Gardner Cowles III "Pat.")

Family ancestors from Scotland settled in upstate New York, where Mike's grandfather William Fletcher Cowles was born in 1819. His career as a Methodist minister moved him through a series of pulpits in Missouri and Iowa, and he settled for a time in Oskaloosa, Iowa, where Gardner, Sr., was born on 28 February 1861. President Abraham Lincoln appointed William Fletcher Cowles as Iowa district collector of U.S. revenues, and his commission hangs in the home of a fifth generation of the family.

While Mike never met his grandfather, he appreciated at least three of the parson's characteristics that shaped Cowles family history. First, William Fletcher was said to be "a patriarchal figure right out of the Old Testament," complete with a long gray beard and a booming voice. Such a father convinced Gardner, Sr., that "it was up to me alone if I succeeded in business." Second, the family's travels from one church to another in Iowa gave Gardner, Sr., a background that would serve him well in developing a regional newspaper. And third, the Methodist minister was a civil-rights advocate calling for freedom for blacks while a clergyman in Missouri, at the risk of personal injury.

At age twenty-one, after receiving undergraduate and master's degrees at Iowa Wesleyan College, Gardner, Sr., became superintendent of schools in Algona, Iowa. He hired Florence Call, a grade-school teacher, to help develop a high-school program. She was one of the first women graduates of Northwestern University in Evanston, Illinois, and the daughter of Ambrose Call, a banker who with his brother had founded Algona. Gardner and Flora, as he called her, were married three years later.

At that time Gardner had already been involved in controversy with his future partner

Ingham. Within a year of moving to the town, Cowles had purchased a half interest in a local weekly, the *Algona Republican.* Ingham, editor of the competing *Upper Des Moines,* called for Cowles's ouster as superintendent of schools, saying a person should not hold two such jobs at once. Nevertheless, the dispute resulted in a mutual respect that developed into friendship between Cowles and Ingham. Cowles soon left the *Algona Republican* because of a dispute with the other owner. He devoted his time and interests to politics, serving two terms in the Iowa legislature, and to business and banking, joining his father-in-law in enterprises that produced enough revenue to finance the 1903 venture with Ingham and the family's move to Des Moines.

The purchase of the *Register and Leader* came at a time when newspapers were changing from commitments to political parties to commitments to public service. It also came at a time when such ventures could be profitable. Within eight months of assuming ownership, Gardner had the *Register and Leader* in the black. In a few years the Cowles family had one of the most elaborate homes in the city. Visitors ranged from evangelists Billy Sunday and Aimee Semple McPherson to politician William Jennings Bryan and presidents William Taft and Herbert Hoover. All contributed to the children's informal education and to stories that were to entertain Mike's listeners — such as when McPherson bested future vice-president Henry Wallace in a test of biblical knowledge, or when Bryan, after consuming a huge meal, asked Mrs. Cowles to make him a sandwich to stuff in his jacket pocket, or when a chair collapsed under the weight of the corpulent Taft when he was in the neighboring Wallace home.

Mike attended public schools in the city until he was fifteen, when he enrolled in Phillips Academy in Exeter, New Hampshire. At Exeter, he was editor of the school's weekly paper, the *Exonian.* At Harvard University, from which he was graduated in 1925, he was editor and president of the student daily newspaper, the *Crimson.* He joined the staff of the *Des Moines Tribune* soon after graduation and then switched to the *Register.* Almost as far back as he could remember, he had been associated with the family papers. When he was eight, his father paid him twenty-five cents for each editorial he proofread, and he had worked as a *Register* reporter during summers off from Harvard.

One of his first assignments as a full-time reporter was covering the legislature and the *Register* campaign to "get Iowa out of the mud." In 1920 the state had about 25 miles of paved highways; by

Gardner Cowles, Sr., with his sons: John, Russell, and Gardner, Jr.

1930 it had 3,272. The precise measure was recorded on a map outside Gardner, Sr.'s office on which each new paved mile was colored in crayon. These not only got Iowa out of the mud, but also enhanced Gardner, Sr.'s efforts to circulate the *Register* throughout Iowa.

Mike said his mother was the greatest influence on his life, through her liberal social views, humor, and soft-spoken nature. He and his brother John learned the newspaper business well from their father, but much of the influence on Mike as an editor came from Ingham. Mike said he had Ingham in mind when he spoke about what makes a great editor in 1955: "The greatest editors I know are just like the greatest educators and are successful for the same reason. They are thoughtful men with scrupulous regard for the truth. They are men who strive to stir the best in the human race, not pander to the worst. They are men who dare to lead, even when the direction is temporarily dangerous and unpopular."

Mike sounded a similar theme in a 1949 commentary at an Iowa centennial banquet:

The only answer to ignorance is education and more education. And I mean more than just the formal education in more and better schools, colleges, and universities. I mean more adult education, more public forums, more discussion groups. But above everything else, I mean better newspaper and magazine editing, better news and discussion and debate programs on the radio. And I mean the use of the powerful new medium of television to make people understand and think. Too much thinking nowadays goes on in a bath of noise, because life is so busy, so complex . . . leaving the common man appallingly confused and misinformed.

His concept of education mirrored a personal ethic of learning that was built on meeting people and asking questions. Friends and acquaintances who characterized him invariably spoke of an insatiable curiosity that would figuratively drain people of information, and a gregarious nature that relished meeting new people and sharing ideas and stories. His most noted questioning episode came in 1959, when he irritated Soviet leader Nikita Khrushchev by persisting in a question about freedom of expression in the USSR. In a speech at the

Economic Club of New York, Khrushchev had called for Americans and Soviets to become better acquainted. "That being your feeling," Cowles asked, "... why do you insist on censoring the dispatches of Americans in the Soviet Union?"

In the late 1920s and early 1930s Mike moved through various newsroom executive positions, apparently informally and fast enough so that his own recollections and newspaper records just list the positions in succeeding years as city editor, news editor, associate managing editor, managing editor, executive editor, and associate publisher. He also listed the title of publisher along the way. He was *Register* and *Tribune* president from 1943 to 1971 and chairman of the board from 1971 to 1973.

His innovations and impact upon journalism were more important than the newsroom titles he carried. His father, who would be publisher until his death at eighty-five in 1946, gave him some latitude. In fact, Mike and John are often credited with more than doubling *Register* and *Tribune* circulation in the 1920s, from 110,000 to 243,000 daily for the two papers and from 86,000 to 206,000 on Sunday. Under Mike's leadership, the Sunday *Register* circulation rose from 168,271 in 1928 to 376, 372 in 1941.

In the late 1920s Mike, about twenty-five, teamed up with a doctoral student from the University of Iowa, George Gallup, about twenty-seven. Gallup, who was teaching at Drake University in Des Moines at the time, conducted some of the nation's first readership studies for the *Register* and the *Tribune*. What he found confirmed Mike's interest in photojournalism. Gallup showed that any use of graphics would increase readership of news items and that readers preferred a series of photographs on a related subject more than photographs on different topics. Based on this research and his own passion for pictures, Mike greatly expanded the use of photographs in the *Register* and the *Tribune,* and he pointed with pride to a finding that in one six-day period the *Tribune* carried more photographs than any other leading newspaper in the nation. He credited the rotogravure section in the Sunday *Register* with helping get the newspapers through the Depression. Graphics and visual communications would become newsroom buzzwords thirty years later, but many newspapers even then still trailed in the use of photographs, maps, and charts compared with the *Register* and the *Tribune* of the 1930s and 1940s.

Despite the lean economic times of the 1930s and the fact that the papers were barely breaking even, Mike chose Richard Wilson, then twenty-eight and the *Register* city editor, to open a *Register* and *Tribune* news bureau in Washington, D.C., in 1933. An editorial noted that such a Washington outpost was needed because "it is the obligation of these papers to the state to give such news service from every quarter ... and that applies with particular force to Washington news with an Iowa slant." That philosophy was consistent with the *Register* slogan that it was "The Newspaper Iowa Depends Upon," and it was also consistent with the nature of the family-owned newspaper to have priorities other than the bottom line. Over the years Washington bureau reporters won five Pulitzer Prizes for the *Register,* including one for Wilson in 1954. From the Pulitzer Prize won by cartoonist Jay (Ding) Darling in 1924 to the one won by Jane Schorer in 1990, the *Register* has won sixteen Pulitzer Prizes, including seven for national reporting, more than any other newspaper for that category except the *New York Times.*

Cowles combined two of his passions, photography and aviation, with the development of aerial photography. As early as 1928 the *Register* had its own airplane, named the *Good News* in a reader contest. The aerial photography with a "machine-gun" camera – developed by photographers George Yates and Charles Gatschet in 1935 for rapid exposures – made the *Register* and the *Tribune* national leaders in photojournalism. The availability of the *Good News* improved *Register* and *Tribune* news coverage of the region, especially on fast-breaking stories. Mike also increased sports coverage in the papers and, thanks to Yates and Gatschet's camera, provided readers with pictures of key plays in football games. Aerial photography for the *Register* was developed to its fullest extent under Don Ultang, a pilot and photographer for the paper from 1946 to 1958.

Cowles recognized the onset of the aviation age and urged airport development in Des Moines, arguing that the city had missed opportunities to be part of the railroad age and needed to assure itself a place in transcontinental aviation. In 1936 he spent his own money to assure that land would be available for airport expansion in Des Moines when the city had the public authorization and funds to do so. The 160 acres that he purchased for seventy thousand dollars were transferred to city ownership at cost. His leadership in airport development continued into the 1940s.

In the 1930s Mike's career began to parallel rather than follow that of John, and by the mid 1930s they and their father realized that the town was not big enough for both of them – a decision

Gardner Cowles, Jr., and his brother John as managers of the Cowles family newspapers

not borne of bitterness or jealousy, but rather out of respect and the recognition that each wanted to have his paper. In 1923, within three years of his graduation from Harvard, John became vice-president, general manager, and associate publisher of the Register and Tribune Co. — a move that Mike, in his memoir *Mike Looks Back* (1985), said reflected respect for his reporting achievements in international affairs and his business acumen. While looking for a newspaper property that would afford opportunities comparable to those offered by the *Register,* Des Moines, and Iowa, the Cowles family focused on the *Star,* Minneapolis, and Minnesota. The *Star* was the weakest of three papers in Minneapolis, a paper with potential and a reasonable price. In 1938 John moved to Minneapolis to take over as full-time publisher while Mike stayed in Des Moines to "look after the *Register* and *Tribune* and to develop my plans for *Look* magazine."

Based on response to the photo coverage in their newspapers and the sale of photo features to other newspapers, Mike decided in 1936 to start a national picture magazine, *Look,* a name suggested by his mother. Upon hearing that Henry Luce had similar plans for a magazine to be named *Life,* the Cowles brothers met with Luce and Roy Larsen of *Time* to compare notes. The plans for *Life* to be a weekly with a news orientation and for *Look* to be a feature-oriented monthly were different enough so that the brothers thought there was room in the market for both. They decided to see how *Life* fared before entering the magazine field, so the first issue of *Look* was published on 5 January 1937.

The Minneapolis and Des Moines newspapers emphasized newsroom independence from advertising and political pressures. Soon after Cowles ownership was assumed in Minneapolis, the business community there became upset when the *Star* refused to join its two competitors in ignoring the news about a well-known executive arrested for violating hunting laws. The Des Moines papers occasionally suffered economically from advertising boycotts in protest of news coverage.

In part, the Cowles brothers argued that the monopoly ownership they enjoyed in both cities — after 1927 in Des Moines and after 1941 in Minneapolis – enabled them to resist pressures to sensationalize or censor the news. But resistance to advertising, personal, or political pressures – including those of the railroad and liquor interests – was established early in the leadership of the senior Cowles and Ingham. In 1915 Ingham wrote:

Two avenues of popularity are open to the newspaper. The first is to yield to flattery, to cajole. The second is to stand for the right things unflinchingly and win respect.... A strong and fearless newspaper will have readers and a newspaper that has readers will have advertisements. That is the only newspaper formula worth working to.... After making all allowances the only newspaper popularity that counts in the long run is bottomed on public respect.

At family-owned newspapers, newsroom and family traditions are frequently intertwined. David Kruidenier, who in 1971 succeeded his uncle Mike as president of the Register and Tribune Co., said newsroom independence "is bred into one. I come off this heritage." As a child, Kruidenier said, he heard of the lore of the newspapers as his uncles had, like how grandfather did not knuckle under to advertising pressures. Such lessons found believers in the newsroom too. In a rare instance where the senior Cowles might suggest that a story be played inside the paper instead of on page 1, the newsroom had the confidence that it could play the story on page 1 and not hear a word about it.

Kenneth MacDonald, himself a newsroom leader as editor and publisher during his fifty years with the Register and Tribune Company, thought that one root of the newsroom independence stemmed from Gardner, Sr.'s respect for Darling, *Register* cartoonist from 1906 to 1949, except for a fling in New York from 1911 to 1913. Politically, Darling was far more conservative than Ingham, and Cowles devoted considerable time to keeping peace between them. To bridle Darling might mean losing him, so he remained an independent cartoonist who contributed two Pulitzer Prizes to the *Register,* in 1924 and 1943. Mike continued that tradition of newsroom independence, relying on editors such as MacDonald and editorial-page editors such as Bill Waymack, Forrest Seymour, and Lauren Soth – all Pulitzer Prize winners, in 1938, 1943, and 1956 respectively – to set the newspaper's agenda.

At a dinner marking MacDonald's retirement in 1977, Mike shocked editors and longtime staffers by noting that he never did agree with the editorial policy on agriculture in the *Register,* and then spelling out what he thought the policy should be. Some of those present thought that maybe Cowles was

overstating his disagreement – but the point was made: a paper could, perhaps should, have editorial stands different from its publisher's. That point was also made when Gilbert Cranberg was editorial-page editor of the Des Moines papers in the 1970s and early 1980s and opposed a downtown-business development plan supported in part by then-publisher Kruidenier. To Des Moines business interests such policies were puzzling; to the Cowles family it was the way to run a good newspaper.

Not that Mike and John Cowles were political wallflowers in their communities. Their fascination with politics, Mike said, included a "belief that it was our duty as citizens to be involved." Their strong support for Wendell Willkie's candidacy for president in 1940 was so public and impassioned that on a swing by Willkie through Minneapolis and Des Moines, the news coverage in the Cowles papers was almost fawning. A review of correspondence and the news stories suggests that the favorable coverage was not at the overt direction of either of the Cowles brothers, but at the perception of the reporters that this was the bosses' candidate. Correspondence between Mike and Willkie indicates that the former did wield a heavy hand, however, in *Look,* giving Willkie a strong boost.

The Cowles brothers were intimate advisers of Willkie during his drive for the Republican nomination and his campaign against President Franklin Roosevelt, and they remained so after the election. They hoped to lay the groundwork for another Willkie bid in 1944 – an effort with little hope of fruition at the outset and no hope ultimately because of GOP disaffection with the liberal politician and then an illness that incapacitated Willkie in mid 1944 and led to his death that October. The largest single memorial to Willkie was a gift of $125,000 from the Gardner Cowles and Florence Call Cowles Foundation to establish Willkie House, a black community center in Des Moines, a memorial that reflected both Willkie's and the Cowleses' concerns with civil rights and race relations.

The links between the brothers and Willkie were forged even stronger after the 1940 campaign. John accompanied Willkie to England in January 1941 in a bipartisan journey requested by President Roosevelt, who wanted to rally congressional support for the U.S. Lend-Lease program to provide the Royal Navy with more ships in its war against Nazi Germany. Willkie's testimony before Congress helped assure approval of Lend-Lease. Almost two years later Mike accompanied Willkie on his forty-nine-day "One World" tour, a trip again supported by Roosevelt to assure U.S. allies of the

The Minneapolis STAR

Tuesday, Nov. 4, 1969   XCI—No. 298   Four Sections   •   Single Copy Price 10c   Lower Price for Carrier Delivery

"Our answer will be half a million people in Washington demanding immediate and total withdrawal"—Antiwar organizer Rennie Davis, commenting on the planned protest next week in light of Mr. Nixon's address.

Nixon 'shares youth concern'

WASHINGTON, D.C. (P)—Assuring them he has a "plan for peace," President Nixon aimed a brief portion of his Monday night speech at youth.

"I would like to address a word to the young people of this nation who are concerned about the war.

"I respect your idealism.

"I share your concern for peace.

"I want peace as much as you do.

"There are powerful personal reasons I want to end this war. This week I will have to sign 83 letters to mothers, fathers, wives and loved ones of men who have given their lives for America in Vietnam. It is very little satisfaction to me that this was only one-third as many as I signed during my first week in office. There is nothing I want more than to see the day come when I no longer must write any of these letters.

"I want to end the war to save the lives of those brave young men in Vietnam.

"I want to end it in a way which will increase the chance that their younger brothers and their sons will not have to fight in another Vietnam someplace in the world.

"I want to end the war so that the energy and dedication of our young people, now too often directed into bitter hatred against those they think are responsible for the war, can be turned to the great challenges of peace, a better life for all Americans and for people throughout the world.

"I have chosen a plan for peace. I believe it will succeed."

Nixon 'dismays' protest heads

WASHINGTON, D.C. (P)—Leaders of antiwar demonstrations scheduled later this month ridiculed President Nixon's war policy speech as disappointing and insulting, predicting that his comments will only drive more protesters into the streets.

"I think in a sense the speech is a clear impetus to our efforts to bring large numbers of people to Washington," said Sid Johnson, a leader of the New Mobilization Committee to End The War in Vietnam (New Mobe). That group is sponsoring a Nov. 13-15 march on Washington.

"People perhaps who were uncertain they would come here are now convinced that the only way they can have any effect is to come here," Johnson said.

Dave Hawk, one of the coordinators of the Oct. 15 Vietnam moratorium, said "I anticipate that the reaction will be one of dismay and the people who were active on Oct. 15 will see the need to continue and intensify their efforts."

Hawk's group is sponsoring another moratorium Nov. 13-15. He said moratorium leaders were hoping Mr. Nixon would "make public a new peace initiative."

"The American people want the war to end. It's apparent that the President has not gotten that message and we shall have to continue."

Homeward bound Against the gray November sky, a cow stands alone on a barren hill and looks toward the barn, a shelter from the chilling breeze. The scene is not as bleak as it looks. Otto and Tom Arens, father and son, find farming the good life just one mile north of Loretto. (Details, other photos, Page 1C.)

Hanoi and Cong condemn talk, see prolonged war

PARIS, France (UPI)—North Vietnam and the Viet Cong officially condemned today President Nixon's peace program as a maneuver allegedly designed to prolong the war in South Vietnam.

The delegations of both Hanoi and the Viet Cong at the Paris peace talks issued statements denouncing the chief executive's policies as set forth in his speech.

The Viet Cong said Mr. Nixon displayed in his speech a desire "to prolong and intensify the American war of aggression in South Vietnam."

Soon afterward, the North Vietnamese issued a statement saying Mr. Nixon's speech "clearly shows that his administration follows and always prolongs more obstinately the war of aggression, and reveals the warlike and perfidious nature of his administration."

An American delegation spokesman said Henry Cabot Lodge's peace negotiating team was "disappointed" they have made little snap characterization. We hope they'll take the time to study the text of the President's speech more carefully because there's a bit in it for them."

The Viet Cong, while condemning Mr. Nixon's policies and upholding unchanged their own negotiating stand, announced they will go on striving for a settlement here. This remark ruled out any Communist walkout from the parley, observers said.

The Viet Cong accused Mr. Nixon of having repeated in his Vietnam policy statement his already-stated policies.

Although the Communist negative answer to Mr. Nixon's speech was largely expected, its harshness and virulent tone nevertheless surprised observers.

'The silent majority' 'overwhelms' Nixon

By LOUIS CASSELS

WASHINGTON, D.C. (P) — President Nixon said today he was overwhelmed by an outpouring of public support for his plan to extricate the United States from the Vietnam War.

On the morning after his broadcast saying he had worked out with Saigon a plan for complete withdrawal of all American forces from Vietnam, Mr. Nixon met briefly with reporters sitting behind stacks of telegrams on his desk.

"It's very important in our quest for peace to realize the country is behind you," he said some 13 hours after appealing for public support for his plan to wind down the war.

He added: "I would put it this way very flatly — the demonstration of support can have more effect on ending the war sooner than the most skilled diplomacy, military tactics or training of South Vietnamese forces.

In the speech to the nation — and the

world — Monday night from the same desk where he displayed the wires, Mr. Nixon had asked the "silent majority" of Americans to support him in his plan to get out of Vietnam.

He did not for a timetable for pulling out all troops, saying it would be a graduated process which could be accelerated as South Vietnam was able to take over more and more of its own defenses.

Press Secretary Ronald L. Ziegler said the outpouring of wires of support — he said the unexpected number was in "the high thousands" — appeared to be a direct, quick response from the "great silent majority" supporting the President's course.

Ziegler said a White House spokesman whose tenure dated back to the Truman era reported he had never seen the like of the flow of messages.

Mr. Nixon, displaying the wires which were sweeping real wide told reporters: "This can be most effective in bringing the war to an end."

In obvious good spirits, he opened a few of the wires which reporters and photographers gathered around. He said the major theme of all was "We are silent Americans who are behind you.

"About 50 percent and the term silent Americans," he said.

He also held up a long yellow roll of paper he described as "the longest wire in history." He said it came from "some fellow in Colorado" who got 22,000 signatures on it pledging support to Mr. Nixon.

In his speech, Mr. Nixon seemed to challenge hopes of a peace breakthrough at the Paris talks, but he told reporters today "the diplomatic track" is still open. He added that "The train would move on that track on a much faster pace in direct relation of the support of the people of the United States.

In his speech, he said "no progress whatever has been made except agreement on the shape of the bargaining table," despite the Paris talks and a series of "secret intiatives," including a summer exchange of letters between Mr. Nixon and the late Ho Chi Minh.

The other side, he said, has not shown "the least willingness to join in seeking a just peace."

The Nixon approach was sharply criticized by most of his previous critics and praised by his supporters Sen. J. William Fulbright, D-Ark., said today he would schedule new Vietnam hearings soon by his Senate Foreign Relations Committee. (Details: Page 3A.)

N. Viets launch heavy attacks

SAIGON, South Vietnam (P) — North Vietnamese troops launched their heaviest ground attacks in two months Tuesday, some 12 hours before President Nixon said that a "significant" increase in enemy activity might force him to stretch out his timetable for withdrawal of U.S. troops.

However, an official U.S. source said the current upsurge in enemy attacks, which began last weekend in the central highlands, didn't appear to be sufficient to slow the withdrawal program.

U.S. and South Vietnamese headquarters reported at least 45 enemy rock-

et and mortar attacks during the night, and infantry assaults on four American bases north of Saigon, an American night bivouac in the central highlands, and two South Vietnamese positions in the southern central highlands.

The enemy lost heavily in the ground attacks, with

the allied commands claiming 160 killed, while allied casualties were four American and five South Vietnamese killed, 45 Americans and 12 South Vietnamese wounded, plus 23 Americans wounded in the shellings. The Americans captured seven North Vietnamese in the fighting north of Saigon.

"I think what the President is talking about is whether or not they launch something that would be relatively large scale," said the U.S. source. "We've said all along we anticipated that in the immediate future they would continue the campaign idea, a low level of action with periodic peaks, as opposed to a

sustained offensive. I think President Nixon is thinking in those terms.

"The latest action isn't significantly different from what has been going on. Periodically there are days in which attacks pick up."

The attacks were the heaviest since the night of Sept. 5-6, when the enemy shelled more than 100 bases and towns and launched several ground attacks. This was during the final "high point" of the enemy's fall campaign.

The Saigon government reported 47 Vietnamese civilians were killed, 107 were wounded and 47 were kidnapped by Viet Cong terrorists in the week ending Oct. 26.

UNITED PRESS INTERNATIONAL
PRESIDENT RICHARD NIXON

Thieu 'completely agrees' with Nixon

U.S. soldiers' reactions to President Nixon's speech are split: Page 2A.

SAIGON, South Vietnam (P)—President Nguyen Van Thieu expressed total agreement today with President Nixon's speech on the Vietnam war.

Thieu in a statement said:

"The people of Vietnam want nothing more than to gradually take the responsibility to preserve their own independence and freedom with the efficient assistance of the allied countries, especially that of the people of the United States, with a view to achieving the self-sufficiency and self development which I have affirmed many times."

Thieu termed the speech "one of the most important and greatest addresses of a president of the United States."

"I believe that this policy to end the war and restore a genuine peace to Vietnam, which President Nixon has recalled in his address today, is the right policy which conforms with our just position," the official English translation of Thieu's statement said.

"This policy is one which President Nixon and I have completely agreed upon," Thieu said.

New York spurns U.S. gift of $10-million fair building

By WALTER R. MEARS

WASHINGTON, D.C. (P)—The government claims it's a marvelous building, despite a sagging, leaking roof, but they can't give away the $10-million U.S. pavilion at the New York World's Fair.

In an appropriations bill is before the Senate to provide $350,000 to tear it down and clear the site where little more than four years ago fairgoers stood in line to ride a motorized train through scenery from American history.

Vacant since the spring of 1966, the

pavilion now has been officially spurned by the city in which it stands, and Mayor John V. Lindsay wants it cleared away.

When Larry A. Jobe, an assistant secretary of commerce, brought the word to the Senate Appropriations Committee, Sen. John L. McClellan, D-Ark., was incredulous.

"It is a structure of permanent nature," he said. "It seems to me they could find some use for it. And they are demanding now that it be removed, they have no use for it?"

"Yes, sir," said Jobe. "When the World's Fair closed we entered into negotiations with the city seeing if in a marvelous building, can't you use it? We drew up an agreement handing it over to the city free. No deal.

While the pavilion was made of concrete, Jobe said, the roof wasn't so durable. "It was not made for permanent use and it has begun to leak and sag."

The pavilion is on city-owned land, the World's Fair Corp. is out of business and the Commerce Department says demolition is now a federal responsibility.

"It is the old story, the government is always liable," complained Sen. Margaret Chase Smith, R-Maine. "We are always expected to pick up the tab."

Pakistan troops again fire on battling mobs

DACCA, East Pakistan (UPI) — Pakistani soldiers fired for the second successive day Monday at battling mobs of Bengali and Indian refugees.

The fighting has killed at least nine by official count but unofficial reports placed the dead at 25 or more. Soldiers patrolled the streets to enforce a curfew that has closed all schools and public places.

The violence erupted in a dispute over the use of the Urdu and Bengali languages on electoral forms.

'70s will be a time for femininity

Roy Swan's photos: Page 6C

Editorials, Page 4A	Weather, B Section
Business, B Section	Books & Arts, B Section
Comics, Pages 4, 5C	Theaters, Page 5D
TV, Radio, B Section	Women's, Pages 6-7C
	Sports, Pages 1-3D

STAR TELEPHONES   News, General 372-4141   Circulation 372-4343   Want Ads 372-4242

Dow Jones Averages

(Noon N.Y.)	Avg.	Chg.
30 Industrials	849.13	-3.41
20 Rails	190.83	-.59
15 Utilities	118.29	-.48
65 Stocks	296.29	-1.41
Noon sales, 5,240,000 shares		

Nixon, Ho Chi Minh letters: Page 4A
Text of Nixon speech: Page 6D

Front page of the Minneapolis Star, *4 November 1969*

strong bipartisan support in the United States for the war effort. The "One World" tour carried the unity theme to Allied leaders in Africa, the Middle East, Russia, and China from late August to mid October.

The trip, which Mike called the highlight of his life, included potentially major news items that never gained much attention except in Mike's storytelling and in his memoirs. These were privately published "for the benefit of my children, grandchildren, a few of my closest friends and business associates" in 1985, the year of his death. One such story deals with a meeting in Syria at which a French woman asked Cowles to forward to Allied leaders her proposal that she arrange for the assassination of Gen. Charles de Gaulle in exchange for recognition of her husband as the new French military leader.

Mike's joie de vivre extended to his ownership of the Cardiff Giant, the nineteenth-century hoax that was taken as evidence of biblical accounts of a superrace when it was found buried – planted would be a better word – just north of Syracuse, New York. Since it was created from gypsum quarried in Iowa, Mike bought the Giant for forty-five hundred dollars when a circus exhibiting it went bankrupt. He displayed it in his home during the 1930s to guests, including H. L. Mencken. In 1945 the Giant was donated to the New York State Historical Society for exhibit in the Farmer's Museum in Cooperstown.

The "One World" journey came soon after Cowles had been appointed to wartime duty as assistant director of the Office of War Information (OWI), where he directed a domestic news bureau, coordinating information from nonmilitary government agencies. He took the job in response to a brief request from President Roosevelt – a note that read: "Dear Cowles, *Please* do! FDR." Cowles served in the OWI under the leadership of Elmer Davis for about a year and then returned to Des Moines with an accolade as "one of the forces of sanity in the OWI" domestic programs.

While the Cowles brothers came up short on Willkie's 1940 candidacy, they both urged Gen. Dwight D. Eisenhower to return to public life and seek the presidency in 1952. They supported his election and his reelection in 1956, but the Cowles papers were critical of the Eisenhower administration, particularly with what was regarded as a "moralistic" approach to international relations, epitomized by Secretary of State John Foster Dulles.

Cowles's interest in international issues and in aviation led to occasional around-the-world tours and frequent trips to Europe, one of which included a flight home aboard the Nazi airship Hindenburg a year before its 7 May 1937 explosion in Lakehurst, New Jersey. But, as with the Willkie trips, there was little news coverage in the Cowles papers about such journeys. As a matter of newspaper policy and what they saw as journalistic decorum, the Cowles family shunned news that might be viewed as self-promotion. "We covered Mike's divorces, but not his trips," is how MacDonald put it, and the three divorces were front-page news in the *Register*.

Cowles was married four times. He said that his first marriage, to Helen Curtiss, was unfortunately driven in part by his brother John's suggestion that perhaps Helen was too sophisticated for him. They wed in November 1926 and were divorced in May 1930. His May 1933 to August 1946 marriage to Lois Thornburg resulted in four children: Jane Cowles, Gardner III, Lois Cowles Harrison, and Kate Cowles Nichols. The third marriage was to Fleur Fenton, from December 1946 to November 1955. He was married to Jan Hochstraser (also known as Jan Streate Cox) from May 1956 until his death; they had a daughter, Virginia.

The *Register* and *Tribune* also covered Mike's speeches to community business and educational groups when he spoke about political trends. In a May 1938 talk to the Des Moines Chamber of Commerce, he commented on Adolf Hitler's cementing of power in Germany, France's lack of unity, and England's lack of preparation for war, including his observation that the "Chamberlain government will go to any length to prevent one." A dozen years later, reflecting on the onset of McCarthyism in the United States and the fear of Russia, Cowles told the chamber, "I would prescribe for the United States more confidence in ourselves, less hysteria about Russia and a big dose of restraint and patience.... Of course we would like to see the Soviet dictatorship overthrown tomorrow, but more likely that hoped-for event is a score of years off.... I doubt if Communism can be killed with a gun."

In the post–World War II years, Cowles's business and personal interests moved him to New York, fulfilling a boyhood dream, he said, that began while on his first trip to the city at age twelve, when his father gave him five dollars and turned him loose. Mike navigated the subway system and the rides at Coney Island all day, returning to the hotel and a relieved mother in the early evening.

In New York he directed *Look* and undertook other publishing and broadcast ventures while maintaining his leadership at the *Register* and *Tribune*. By the mid 1950s the Sunday circulations of the Des Moines and Minneapolis newspapers totaled more than one million, covering Iowa and Minnesota and circulating into neighboring states. The peak Sunday circulation of the *Register* was about 550,000, and the paper circulated in each of the state's ninety-nine counties, helping to set a statewide agenda.

Look was also a success, becoming a bimonthly. The publication reached a peak circulation of about nine million before trailing off as a result of television, higher postal costs, and other forces that spelled doom for many mass-circulation magazines. The most difficult day of his life, Cowles later said, was 16 September 1971, when it was announced that *Look* would cease publication on 19 October 1971.

Other magazine ventures by Cowles included *Quick,* a pocket-sized weekly newsmagazine that was started in 1949 and suspended in 1953, after it had reached a circulation of 1.3 million. Although the smaller size was not attractive to some advertisers, the main reason *Quick* was killed was that its subscribers, if transferred to *Look,* would help *Look* maintain an important subscription edge in a critical circulation battle with *Collier's. Flair,* a magazine pressed upon Mike by Fleur Fenton, had so many special design elements that, although interesting – *Time* called it "avant gaudy" – it lost about seventy-five cents per copy and was suspended one year after its debut in January 1950. *Venture,* a travel magazine, was published from 1963 to 1967 and featured a three-dimensional photograph on each month's cover.

Mike Cowles held honorary degrees from eleven colleges and universities, including seven in Iowa. He served on the Columbia University Advisory Board on Pulitzer Prizes and the boards of directors of the American Society of Newspaper Editors, the Magazine Publishers Association, and the National Association of Broadcasters. He was also on the boards of directors of the New York Times Co., R. H. Macy and Co., and United Air Lines.

In New York, Mike saw the opportunity for a daily newspaper serving Long Island and started the *Suffolk Sun* on 21 November 1966. The *Sun* survived for almost three years, with publication suspended on 18 October 1969. A longer-lasting venture was the *San Juan* (Puerto Rico) *Star,* established 2 November 1959 and sold to Scripps Howard on 12 August 1970. The *Des Moines Tribune* was among the afternoon newspapers falling almost like dominoes in the early 1980s, and its last issue was put out on 25 September 1982. In the frenzy of newspaper buying during those years, a bidding war for the *Des Moines Register* resulted in its sale to Gannett for about $160 million, leaving the *Minneapolis Star-Tribune* as the primary Cowles presence in the Midwest. The publisher of the *Register* under Gannett was Charles Edwards, a nephew of David Kruidenier, the fourth generation of the Cowles family to head the paper, but the first without family ownership.

References:

"The Cowles World," *Time,* 72 (8 December 1958): 55–58;

George Mills, *Harvey Ingham & Gardner Cowles, Sr.: Things Don't Just Happen* (Ames: Iowa State University Press, 1977).

Papers:

Cowles's papers are at Drake University, Des Moines, Iowa. His correspondence is also on file in the presidential libraries of Herbert Hoover in West Branch, Iowa, and Dwight D. Eisenhower in Abilene, Kansas. Correspondence with Wendell Willkie is at the Indiana University Library, Bloomington.

James Middleton Cox

(31 March 1870 – 15 July 1957)

and

James McMahon Cox

(27 June 1903 – 27 October 1974)

Gregory C. Lisby
Georgia State University

DAILY NEWSPAPERS OWNED: *Dayton* (Ohio) *Daily News* [formerly *Dayton Evening News* and *Dayton Journal Herald*] (1898–1974); *Springfield* (Ohio) *News-Sun* [formerly *Springfield Press-Republic* and *Springfield Sun*] (1903–1974); *Miami* (Florida) *Daily News* [formerly *Miami Metropolis*] (1923–1974); *Canton* (Ohio) *News* (1923–1930); *Atlanta Journal* (1939–1974); *Atlanta Georgian* (1939); *Atlanta Constitution* (1950–1974); *Palm Beach* (Florida) *Daily News* (1969–1974); *Palm Beach* (Florida) *Post* (1969–1974).

BOOK: James Middleton Cox, *Journey Through My Years* (New York: Simon & Schuster, 1946).

James Middleton Cox, a twenty-eight-year-old former schoolteacher, began the company that is today Cox Enterprises when he purchased the *Dayton* (Ohio) *Evening News* for twenty-six thousand dollars in 1898. Cox Enterprises has grown to become the thirteenth-largest media company in the United States, based on estimated revenue reports from *Ad Age* in 1991. The company has properties ranging from twenty-five newspapers, to twenty-one radio and television stations, to twenty-three cable television systems. Other Cox properties include automobile auctions, paper manufacturers, and cattle ranches.

The youngest of Gilbert and Eliza Cox's seven children, James Middleton Cox was born and raised on a farm in Butler County, some twenty miles south of Dayton, Ohio. As a youth he worked as a janitor in the public school and later as a sexton in the United Brethren church, which his family attended. After two years of high school he dropped out, but he later passed the teacher's certification

James Middleton Cox (photograph by Underwood & Underwood)

examination, thanks to tutoring from his brother-in-law, John Q. Baker. Cox began teaching in 1887 at age seventeen.

He subsequently worked as a printer's devil and as a reporter for the *Middletown* (Ohio) *Signal*, where he scored a major scoop about a train wreck, which led to a job with the *Cincinnati Enquirer* in April 1892. He covered the railroad route, which was – in his words – "magnificent training" for a young newspaperman. He married Mayme L. Harding of Cincinnati in 1893; they had three children – James, John, and Richard – but were divorced in 1910. In 1895 Cox accompanied Ohio congressman Paul J. Sorg to Washington, D.C., where he served as his private secretary until 1897.

Backed primarily by a six-thousand-dollar loan from Sorg, the twenty-eight-year-old Cox – who later described himself then as "too young to be running a newspaper" – "took advantage of the opportunity Dayton provided for metropolitan journalism" and purchased controlling interest in the struggling *Evening News*, because it had an Associated Press franchise and because Dayton was "a growing city." "Looking back on those days," he wrote in his autobiography, *Journey Through My Years* (1946), "I cannot but feel that the gods were kind."

As publisher, Cox adopted wire services for all national and international developments, used photographic services, charged all advertisers uniform rates, guaranteed advertising results, and added a female society editor. He developed a reputation for aggressive, reform journalism, characterizing the *News* as "the People's paper." He also took a high-minded attitude toward his competition. Even when other Dayton newspapers began spreading negative rumors about him in an attempt to gain a competitive advantage, Cox directed his circulation and advertising departments "not to discuss competitors." By the end of 1900 the *Mail Order Journal*, a national trade magazine for advertisers, listed the *News* among the top one hundred newspapers in the country. "After the red ink disappeared from our ledger," Cox formed the News League of Ohio in 1905 with the *News* and the *Springfield* (Ohio) *Press-Republic*, which he had purchased in 1903.

Cox was twice elected to represent Ohio's Third Congressional District, serving from 1908 to 1912. He resigned after winning the governorship of Ohio in 1912, at the height of the state's progressive movement. He served three two-year terms (1912–1914; 1916–1920) – the first Ohio Democrat to do so – and left a legacy of reform legislation that included a direct-primary law, public-school and prison reforms, state-court reorganization, extension of the civil-service law, authorization of a budget commission and a roads program, a model workman's compensation law, a mother's pension law, and a minimum wage and nine-hour-day limit for women workers. Cox was awarded the Red Cross Gold Medal of Merit for his vigorous response to the tragic 1913 Ohio River flood. In 1917 Cox married Margaretta Parker Blair of Chicago; they had two children, Anne and Barbara.

At the 1920 Democratic National Convention in San Francisco, he was chosen the party's nominee for president on the forty-fourth ballot. Cox and running mate Franklin D. Roosevelt were defeated decisively by Republican Warren G. Harding after Cox strongly endorsed Woodrow Wilson's League of Nations and based his campaign on that issue. Cox resolved "never again to seek or to accept a public office. I had my newspapers. The procession of events interested me deeply, and our own publications gave me the outlet for my convictions. And so I turned back content to my private affairs, confident that civilization would in time be compelled, if not by conviction, then by sheer necessity for self-preservation, to join together the nations of the world as a protective instrument."

Business success enabled him to acquire the *Miami* (Florida) *Metropolis* – in a city that Cox once called "America's greatest human dry dock" – and the *Canton* (Ohio) *News* in 1923. He sold the Canton paper in 1930 after a gang-organized murder of its editor; it had won a Pulitzer Prize in 1927 for its fight against municipal government corruption. Cox purchased the *Springfield* (Ohio) *Sun* in 1928.

After assuming control of the *Metropolis*, which he later renamed the *Daily News*, Cox revealed his philosophy of public service combined with community boosterism:

> Any city growing . . . needs a vigilant press. The public interest must always be paramount. The function of a newspaper carries a grave responsibility. It is the agency of information and the utmost care should be taken to publish the truth. Its news columns should give all sides of an issue of general concern, regardless of the convictions which the paper has. A journal without conviction is of little use to a community. Influence of public opinion should be sought in the fairest manner. Either misrepresentation or suppression of essential facts profanes the tradition of a great profession. Every useful interest should be treated fairly, but it must be remembered that individual and corporate designs sometimes trespass upon the rights of the public. These interests are organized and they employ their own representatives while the people without organizations must look to an honest and courageous press for protection. And yet the press should go no further than measures of restraint against chartered interests. They are essential to the growth of the city.

"It was the rounding out of a dream," Cox said when he bought both the *Atlanta* (Georgia) *Journal* and the *Atlanta Georgian* in 1939. He had hoped for many years to purchase a property in Atlanta, because of its "rare opportunity for service and development" and not, as popular lore has it, to gain tickets to the Atlanta premiere of *Gone With the Wind* a few days later. The city, he foresaw, would become "the geographic terminus for northern and southern economic interaction, and the leading city in the Southeast." He closed the *Georgian* immediately, leaving the *Journal* as the dominant newspaper in the state for forty years. The purchase would prove to be "the most important step in building the communications empire which has become Cox Enterprises," for, in his words, "running water never grows stagnant."

Cox's conception of the role of newspapers in society was further developed in the first edition of the *Journal* under his ownership. A newspaper, he wrote, "should tell the truth as only intellectual honesty can discern the truth. It should do what is in conscience needful and right. To try with vague and pointless preachment and evasion to please everyone is bad faith. Persisted in, it pleases none and exposes a lack of character which the people will soon appraise."

The Atlanta purchase also made him a significant player in Georgia politics, even though he was never a candidate for state office himself. Generations of rural Georgia politicians campaigned against Cox as the "Yankee owner of them lying Atlanta newspapers," although it never seemed to hinder the papers' financial success. Cox wrote that "it had never been my intention to create a highly centralized form of 'chain journalism.' Now that I had newspaper properties in Ohio, Georgia, and Florida, each journal was encouraged to maintain its own personality under its own staff." Still, readers of his Atlanta papers "swore at them and by them."

In 1934 Cox entered the broadcasting business when his son James McMahon Cox, Jr. – who was not really a "junior" although listed as such in *Who's Who in America* – established the first radio station in the Dayton area, WHIO. J. Leonard Reinsch, hired as WHIO's first manager, later became head of Cox Broadcasting.

Cox acquired the *Dayton* (Ohio) *Journal Herald* in 1948 and the *Atlanta* (Georgia) *Constitution* in 1950, which provided him with a monopoly in the Atlanta newspaper market. James McMahon Cox is generally recognized as having built the Cox broadcasting empire. The father was at first reluctant to

James McMahon Cox (courtesy of Cox Enterprises)

get into television, but his son supported the gamble.

Atlanta became the core of Cox's media operations in 1939 when he acquired WSB – the South's first radio station when it began broadcasting in 1922 – as part of the *Atlanta Journal* purchase. WSB, whose call letters stand for "Welcome South, Brother," was licensed to the *Journal* on 15 March 1922 by the U.S. Department of Commerce. On 24 September 1948, after years of experimenting and meeting licensing requirements, the counterpart of "The Voice of the South," "The Eyes of the South" – WSB-TV – went on the air.

In 1933 Cox accepted President Franklin Roosevelt's appointment as a member of the American delegation to the London World Monetary and Economic Conference, which was organized to halt the consequences of the spreading world depression. Thereafter, however, he steadfastly refused all job offers from the Roosevelt and Truman administrations, which ranged from ambassadorships to head of the Federal Reserve System to an appointment to the U.S. Senate in 1946. An avid sportsman and reader, he kept close business control of his media companies, coupled with editorial leeway – even going so far as promising he would never enter either the *Journal* or *Constitution* newsrooms – believing that individuality and competition for news could thus be preserved.

Not long before his death in 1957, he remarked, "We all want to contribute something to our time and it just so [happened] that I [have been] more useful in the newspaper business." James McMahon Cox inherited control of most of his father's $10 million estate and succeeded him as head of Cox businesses on 31 July 1958. In his will Cox directed that his newspapers be operated "in accord with the principles of Thomas Jefferson" and urged their "devotion to the best interests of those communities wherein [they] are located." He asked his heirs to recognize the "debt" they owed to "the working people" who read his newspapers, to continue to be "champions of the rights of the weak," but "never be pressed to an encroachment on the just rights of anyone."

The younger Cox – named for his father's trusted friend John A. McMahon, although always known to close friends as "Jim, Jr." – was born on 27 June 1903, graduated from Yale University in 1928, and became a police reporter the following year on the *Dayton Daily News*. In 1930 he married his first wife, Helen Rumsey. After her death he married Jan Streate; they were later divorced. In 1958 Cox married Betty Gage Lippitt; they had no children.

Cox worked his way up the Dayton corporate ladder from general manager in 1931 to assistant publisher, vice-president, president, and vice-chairman of Dayton Newspapers. He was given the job of getting WHIO radio on the air and later guided the company's purchase of WSB; WSOC in Charlotte, North Carolina; and WIOD in Miami, Florida. In 1942, at age thirty-nine, Cox joined the Naval Air Corps as a lieutenant – against his father's wishes – and served until 1945, when he left the corps as a lieutenant commander.

Cox generally continued his father's newspaper policies of decentralization and editorial independence, except in the 1972 presidential race, when he sent a memorandum to Cox newspapers recommending editorial support for Republican Richard Nixon over Democrat George McGovern. Two years later the Atlanta newspapers themselves became news when editor Reg Murphy was kidnapped by the American Revolutionary Army. Forty-nine hours later Murphy was released after Cox paid the seven-hundred-thousand-dollar ransom. An Atlanta-area resident and his wife were arrested for the crime, and the ransom money was recovered.

Problems with the organizational differences in Cox's broadcasting properties became apparent in the mid 1960s. Some stations had newspaper associations, including WSB radio and WSB-TV, which had been properties of the *Atlanta Journal* for forty and fifteen years, respectively. Some stations were not associated with newspapers. The entire mass-communications industry was growing and becoming more complex. Governmental and regulatory problems, along with threats of antitrust actions, were also becoming more acute. In a move to realign operations, Cox established Cox Broadcasting Corporation in 1964 to operate the radio and television properties. After the reorganization Cox Broadcasting began trading on the New York Stock Exchange on 17 July 1964.

The first acquisition of the newspaper group, the *Evening News*, is now the *Dayton Daily News* and is still owned by the Cox Newspapers division of Cox Enterprises. The company has daily newspaper properties in thirteen other cities across the country. The *Atlanta Journal* and the *Atlanta Constitution* are the group's flagship papers, with a combined daily circulation of more than 500,000 and a Sunday circulation of more than 680,000. The Atlanta papers are followed in size by the *Dayton Daily News*, the *Austin* (Texas) *American-Statesman* (acquired in 1976), the *Palm Beach* (Florida) *Post*, and a newspaper group, Cox Arizona, which consists of four daily papers – the *Mesa Tribune*, the *Tempe Daily News Tribune*, the *Chandler Arizonan Tribune*, and the *Gilbert Tribune*, acquired in 1977, 1980, 1983, and 1990 respectively – in the suburban Phoenix area. Smaller Cox-owned papers are located in Texas, Arizona, and Colorado.

Cox Enterprises was established in 1968 as a private newspaper company headquartered in Atlanta, with James McMahon Cox as chairman. His death in 1974 left his two sisters, Anne Cox Chambers of Atlanta and Barbara Cox Anthony of Honolulu, in control of 95 percent of the privately owned company, although neither has ever held an operational or managerial position with the company. In 1991 *Forbes* magazine estimated that the sisters, listed as the third richest women in the world, share an estimated $4 billion fortune. In 1974 administrative control of Cox Enterprises was passed to Garner Anthony, Barbara's husband. Anne was named chairwoman of Atlanta Newspapers, and Barbara became chairwoman of Dayton Newspapers. Anne was appointed U.S. ambassador to Belgium by President Jimmy Carter in 1977.

In the most significant and far-reaching decision of his tenure as Cox chairman and chief executive officer, Anthony completed a $1.3 billion buyout/merger of Cox Communications in September 1985 and transformed the separate newspaper and broadcasting companies into one of the largest media conglomerates in the nation, ending the twenty-one-year history of public ownership of Cox Communications. In 1988 James Cox Kennedy, son of Barbara Cox Anthony, was named chairman and chief executive officer of Cox Enterprises.

At the end of 1991 Cox Enterprises consisted of seventeen daily newspapers, seven weekly newspapers, seven major television stations, fourteen radio stations, and an enormous cable empire with more than 1.6 million subscribers. It has some twenty-five thousand employees and annual revenues of more than $1.6 billion. Yet each operation has by and large retained its individuality, so that Cox Enterprises is essentially a conglomerate of small businesses. The corporation's success, according to Kennedy, is a result of its commitment to "embrace new ideas, rather than fight them."

References:

Roger W. Babson, *Cox – The Man* (New York: Brentano's, 1920);

James E. Cebula, *James M. Cox: Journalist and Politician* (New York: Garland, 1985);

Millard Grimes, *The Last Linotype: The Story of Georgia and Its Newspapers Since World War II* (Macon, Ga.: Mercer University Press, 1985);

Irving Stone, *They Also Ran: The Story of the Men Who Were Defeated for the Presidency* (Garden City, N.Y.: Doubleday, 1964).

Papers:

James Middleton Cox's gubernatorial papers are at the Ohio Historical Society, Columbus.

Jonathan Daniels
(26 April 1902 – 6 November 1981)

David A. Copeland
University of North Carolina

MAJOR POSITIONS HELD: Washington correspondent (1926–1929), associate editor (1931–1933), editor (1933–1942, 1948–1968), editor emeritus (1968–1981), *Raleigh* (North Carolina) *News and Observer*.

BOOKS: *Clash of Angels* (New York: Brewer & Warren, Payson & Clarke, 1930);
A Southerner Discovers the South (New York: Macmillan, 1938);
A Southerner Discovers New England (New York: Macmillan, 1940);
Tar Heels: A Portrait of North Carolina (New York: Dodd, Mead, 1941);
Frontier on the Potomac (New York: Macmillan, 1946);
The Man of Independence (Philadelphia: Lippincott, 1950);
The End of Innocence (Philadelphia & New York: Lippincott, 1954);
The Forest Is the Future (New York: International Paper, 1957);
Prince of Carpetbaggers (Philadelphia: Lippincott, 1958);
Mosby: Gray Ghost of the Confederacy (Philadelphia: Lippincott, 1959);
Stonewall Jackson (New York: Random House, 1959);
Robert E. Lee (Boston: Houghton Mifflin, 1960);
Thomas Wolfe: October Recollections (Columbia, S.C.: Bostick & Thornley, 1961);
The Devil's Backbone: "The Story of the Natchez Trace" (New York: McGraw-Hill, 1962);
They Will Be Heard: America's Crusading Newspaper Editors (New York: McGraw-Hill, 1965);
The Time Between the Wars: Armistice to Pearl Harbor (Garden City, N.Y.: Doubleday, 1966);
Washington Quadrille (Garden City, N.Y.: Doubleday, 1968);
Ordeal of Ambition: Jefferson, Hamilton, Burr (Garden City, N.Y.: Doubleday, 1970);
The Randolphs of Virginia (Garden City, N.Y.: Doubleday, 1972);

Jonathan Daniels (Raleigh News and Observer *archives*)

The Gentlemanly Serpent and Other Columns from a Newspaperman in Paradise: From the Pages of the Hilton Head Island Packet, 1970–73 (Columbia: University of South Carolina Press, 1974);
White House Witness: 1942–1945 (Garden City, N.Y.: Doubleday, 1975).

Jonathan Daniels served as editor of the *News and Observer* in Raleigh, North Carolina, from 1933 to 1942 and from 1948 to 1968. After his retirement in 1968 he served as editor emeritus until his death in 1981. As editor, Daniels continued the paper's tradition as a southern liberal democratic organ, a practice begun by his father, Josephus, who bought the paper in 1894 and served as its editor and publisher until his death in 1948. As the dominant voice in eastern North Carolina, the *News and Observer* was influential in politics, and the Daniels family used the newspaper as its platform to push for reform in the state.

Jonathan was more than a newspaperman, although that is what he considered himself first and foremost. He wrote twenty-one books between 1930 and 1975 as well as many periodical articles. During World War II he served as an administrative assistant and press secretary to President Franklin Roosevelt. Following Roosevelt's death, Daniels served briefly as Harry Truman's press secretary and as a Democratic national leader in Truman's 1948 campaign for the presidency. He was a member of the Democratic National Committee (1949–1952), the Economic Cooperation Administration and the Mutual Security Agency (1948–1953), the Federal Hospital Council (1948–1953), the United Nations Subcommission for the Prevention of Discrimination and Protection of Minorities (1947–1952), and the U.S. Advisory Commission on Information (1960s).

Jonathan Daniels was the third of four sons born to Josephus and Addie Worth Bagley Daniels. Josephus was both a newspaperman and a public servant. His life provided a model for his sons, and Jonathan followed closely in his father's footsteps. Born in 1862 in Washington, North Carolina, Josephus began working for a newspaper at age twelve. By the age of nineteen he was owner and publisher of the *Wilson Advance* in Wilson, North Carolina. After receiving a law degree from the University of North Carolina, he moved to Raleigh, where in 1885 he obtained controlling interest in the *State Chronicle*. Josephus changed the newspaper's format in 1890, making it a daily rather than a weekly. In 1894 he bought the *News and Observer* and soon combined the two morning dailies under the flag of the *News and Observer*.

Josephus entered public service during the administration of Grover Cleveland, working in the Department of Interior, but he was best known for serving two terms as secretary of the navy under Woodrow Wilson, and as ambassador to Mexico from 1933 to 1942. Josephus returned to Raleigh in 1942 and continued as editor of the *News and Observer* until his death in 1948.

Because of his father's appointment as secretary of the navy in 1912, Jonathan's childhood years were spent in North Carolina and Washington, D.C. He attended public school in Raleigh, then Saint Albans School in Washington, and matriculated at the University of North Carolina at Chapel Hill. He finished his bachelor's degree in three years and was graduated in 1921. While at UNC he became friends with novelist Thomas Wolfe, also a student, and worked with the *Daily Tar Heel*, the campus newspaper, eventually becoming its editor. In addition, he worked during the summers as a cub reporter for the *News and Observer*.

After graduation Daniels accepted a reporter's position with the *Louisville* (Kentucky) *Times*, but he stayed with the newspaper for only a short period. By 1922 he was once again enrolled as a student at Chapel Hill, and he received a master's degree in English the same year. Following the advice of his father, Daniels then enrolled in law school at Columbia University. New York – more specifically, Broadway – proved to be more interesting to Daniels than his law books. He returned to Chapel Hill after failing all of his courses at Columbia.

The excursion to New York did not deter Daniels from earning a law degree. Back in Chapel Hill he spent eight weeks studying eighteen hours a day and passed the bar examination. He went to court only once and got his client out of an assault charge. In a 1981 *News and Observer* interview, Daniels remarked that after the case he had the good sense to "quit while I was ahead."

In September 1923 Daniels married Elizabeth Bridgers. He also became sports editor for the *News and Observer*, a position he held until he was named the paper's Washington correspondent in 1926. During that year a daughter, Elizabeth, was born to the couple. Late in 1929 Daniels's wife died, and in 1930 he left the *News and Observer* to become a writer for *Fortune* magazine in New York. While there he completed his first novel, *Clash of Angels* (1930), a satirical work depicting the successful struggle of Lucifer against God's angels. The novel demonstrated how Daniels sought to emulate his father by not being afraid to speak out on controversial issues while at the same time displaying that he was his own man. In a letter to his father he wrote, "I know that you won't agree with the ideas in the book. And please feel free to say vigorously to everyone that you do not. I hope that you will see the literary ability in it. I am sure that it has that."

The literary quality of *Clash of Angels* could not be disputed, and Daniels earned a Guggenheim Fellowship for creative writing after its publication. He spent sixteen months in Europe doing research, then returned to New York in 1931 as a writer for *Fortune*. He married Lucy Billing Cathcart in April 1932. The couple had three daughters – Lucy, Adelaide, and Cleves – and Daniels's second wife served as his critic, researcher, and counselor until her death in 1979.

When Josephus accepted the ambassadorship to Mexico in 1932, the affairs of the *News and Observer* were turned over to Jonathan and his two

Political cartoon depicting North Carolina governor William Kerr Scott and Daniels controlling U.S. senator Frank Porter Graham. This cartoon was circulated by Graham's opponent, Willis Smith, during Graham's unsuccessful 1950 campaign to regain his Senate seat.

brothers, Frank and Josephus, Jr. They assumed control of the business end of the operation, and Jonathan left New York and *Fortune* to move into the editor's chair.

As editor, Daniels continued to fight many of the battles first engaged by the *News and Observer* under his father, but he was not afraid to refute his father, especially on issues of religion, sex, race relations, and alcohol. Daniels – who liked good bourbon and was known to buy moonshine or even mix

his own drinks from chemicals while a college student – actively pursued a repeal of Prohibition once he moved into the editorship, in direct opposition to his father's position on drink. Josephus wrote to his son from Mexico, complaining about the newspaper's position on the Eighteenth Amendment. If the *News and Observer* could not support Prohibition, the ambassador to Mexico believed the newspaper should not work for its repeal. Jonathan felt the issue was not worth a face-off with his father, so he relinquished writing editorials concerning alcohol during the pre–World War II period.

However, the two firmly agreed that it was their duty to champion the causes of the common people and the less privileged. Jonathan demonstrated this commitment following the 1929 Gastonia textile strike. In editorials he spoke of the rights of unions, Communists, and the "little fellow." The "little fellow" in this case was Communist organizer Fred E. Beal, who, along with six others, was sentenced to seventeen to twenty years for the murder of the Gastonia chief of police. Daniels questioned whether anyone in America cared for justice, saying that Beal was innocent. Because Beal was not a "cause" for liberals, Daniels said, he had been "buried alive" by the American legal system and the intolerance of the nation toward the rights of minorities.

When Europe erupted into war in 1939, Daniels saw no way that the United States could avoid entering the fray and said so in an editorial. He was concerned for the loss of life that would be involved and for the loss of First Amendment freedoms that would no doubt accompany war. "If I understand freedom of the press," he wrote, "it does not belong to either the editors or the officials but the people."

Daniels realized that some self-censorship of the press might have to take place if war occurred, but he wrote an "open" letter to Secretary of Interior Harold L. Ickes in Washington, urging him to keep President Roosevelt from placing limitations on the press. "Personally," Daniels wrote, "I would rather take my chances on the American press even with the possibilities of Roy Howard being crazy in ownership and Colonel McCormick being wicked in possession than on any other press in the world."

In 1942 Daniels stepped down from the editorship of the *News and Observer*. His father had returned from Mexico after America's entry into World War II, and Jonathan, who had met Roosevelt in the 1920s just after he had been stricken with polio, accepted his old acquaintance's offer to serve as one of six administrative assistants during Roosevelt's unprecedented third term. Daniels continued in this position until 1945, when he became Roosevelt's press secretary. After the president's death Daniels remained on the White House staff as Truman's press secretary. In the spring of 1945 he returned to Raleigh and worked part-time for the *News and Observer*, devoting the majority of his time from 1945 to 1948 to writing and lecturing.

Josephus died in January 1948, and Jonathan assumed control of editorial activities at the *News and Observer*. As editor of a family-owned newspaper, Daniels enjoyed free rein with the editorial page and did not have to worry about conflicts on issues with the publisher. He let his personal opinions and liberal views run free. Because Daniels spoke his mind and often chastised his readership for not supporting liberal causes, the paper earned the nickname "The Nuisance and Disturber."

One of the liberal causes supported by "The Nuisance and Disturber" was the 1950 campaign of Frank Porter Graham for the U.S. Senate. Graham, president of the University of North Carolina system from 1933 to 1949, had been appointed to fill a vacant Senate post by Governor William Kerr Scott. An outspoken liberal, Graham had supported the integration of the state's university system, and his opponent focused on racial hatred and growing fears of communism. Daniels used Graham's candidacy to remind his readership of the devotion of the paper and his father to the causes of the common people. Nevertheless, his editorials could not elect Graham. The editor, however, did not give up his civil-rights efforts, pushing even harder for them in the following decade.

The quest for civil rights had always been a goal of Daniels and his father. Josephus had advocated equal educational opportunities for blacks, and his son continued the fight and enlarged its sphere throughout his life. On 10 April 1933 Jonathan had unleashed his opinions on the decision in the *Scottsboro* case, where seven blacks were sentenced to death for raping two white women. In his editorial Daniels said it was inconceivable that the verdict could be allowed to stand and that all southern justice would be "discredited by the shocking verdict."

In the period before World War II, however, Daniels advocated segregation along with his non-discrimination policy. A 29 September 1936 editorial aptly described his position: "Separation of the races was one thing but another thing was permitting the provision of inferior, run-down, uncomfortable and often unclean facilities for Negroes while providing altogether different facilities for whites." In addressing the economic plight of blacks before World War II, he said that the nation was slowly squeezing blacks out of working opportunities: "The one right of the Negro which has been steadily destroyed while other rights have grown has been the right to earn a living by the use of his skill."

Daniels advocated opportunities for blacks in all economic and educational strata in the nation. Paraphrasing Booker T. Washington, he warned his readers that the only way to keep a Negro in a ditch was to stay there with him. Daniels bemoaned the fact that a black could earn a Ph.D. but could

Daniels speaking at a dinner for North Carolina Democrats, 1950

not find work as a plumber. He explored the situation in his 1938 book, *A Southerner Discovers the South.* A young southern black, the valedictorian of Abraham Lincoln High School, speaks of his success during his graduation pronouncement. Daniels contrasted that hope with the reality of the 1930s South: "He grabbed confidently at the old familiar rungs on the ladder of success. . . . And all his learning merely led back to the broom and the shovel, the plow and the hoe. . . . The shining promises were rusty and dull."

Daniels believed that justice should equally serve both races. One of his common editorial themes during the 1930s advocated judicial equality for blacks. From 1934 to 1936 he repeatedly told his readership that crime was not racial. He supported equal treatment for blacks by white law-enforce-

ment officers and judges. In 1933 he sarcastically commended a Greensboro judge for acquitting a white policeman for murdering a black man charged with assaulting the officer. An autopsy report had revealed the black man had been shot in the back of the head.

Daniels's sense of equality in law was mixed with his view that segregation was not all bad. Blacks were not allowed to serve on North Carolina juries, and Daniels saw no problem with that position. He opposed blacks voting because he felt that many poor, uneducated voters could be manipulated by politicians. His plans to educate and to elevate blacks economically would make them, in his eyes, capable of voting.

During the 1948 presidential election civil rights became the pivotal issue in the South. Southern politicians formed the Dixiecrat party to oppose new civil-rights legislation coming from Washington. Daniels upheld Truman's bid for election; "separate but truly equal" was still Daniels's theme. "Where separation exists and equality does not, the South is untrue to itself and acting in violation of its own laws," he wrote in the *News and Observer* on 6 March 1948. Truman carried North Carolina and the nation, and Daniels responded with a challenge for his state and region. He urged his fellow southerners to accept Truman's requirements on civil rights, including laws against lynching and poll taxes, as well as integration of interstate transportation.

The 1950s brought the question of race and education to the forefront. "Separate but equal" was still Daniels's message, but his understanding of the doctrine truly emphasized equality. He chided one North Carolina school district's fifty-fifty spending on black and white schools when nearly three-fourths of the students were black, calling it "gross favoritism to the white schools." When separate-but-equal conditions did not exist, the editor advocated integration, exactly what the University of North Carolina at Chapel Hill law, medical, and graduate schools did in 1951. Daniels said that North Carolina would always act "in good faith" to provide equal educational opportunities for both races. "The word 'equal' has now and will continue to be applied," Daniels declared in a 26 April 1951 editorial concerning the education of North Carolina's students.

In 1954 *Brown* v. *Board of Education* provided more fuel for the fire of southern race relations. Daniels steered an impartial course in the aftermath of the Supreme Court decision by publishing letters on both sides of the issue. He called the Greensboro school system "courageous" for voting to comply with the court's decision. He also advised the state not to ignore the ruling. In the wake of national uproar about the decision, President Dwight Eisenhower proposed a constitutional amendment to permit segregation. Daniels opposed the president's recommendation, saying that if segregation continued, it must be " 'voluntary' separation of races in schools." Instead of forced segregation or integration, he proposed "free choice schools," a policy adopted in the South until mandatory desegregation occurred during the late 1960s.

As Daniels moved for equal educational opportunities, he continued his efforts for equal justice, advocating strong punishment for whites who used violence against civil-rights workers. Trials should have "nothing to do with race," he said in the 27 June 1963 *News and Observer*. On 27 March 1965 he wrote that the Ku Klux Klan was a "bunch of hoodlums" that had to work underground, equating Klan members with criminals and stating that they would "smell and act as bad" no matter what they were called.

Perhaps the most significant racial incident in North Carolina during the 1960s occurred when four black university students entered Woolworth's in downtown Greensboro on 1 February 1960 and took seats at the lunch counter reserved for the store's white clientele. Their requests for cups of coffee were denied, and the nation's first sit-in began. Daniels, supporting the students' actions, said that if a store took blacks' money in one of its departments, it had no legal right to refuse them service in another. Daniels went on to support the civil-rights legislation of 1964 and 1965, equal employment practices, and the formation of biracial committees to solve the racial and economic problems facing North Carolina and its capital city in the latter half of the 1960s.

Although the *News and Observer* editorial page often reflected Daniels's liberal views, especially on race relations, many of the newspaper's daily activities were left to a managing editor. This left Daniels with time to write books. During his first tenure as editor, from 1933 to 1942, he sent three books to press. From 1948 to 1968 Daniels delivered twelve different titles to publishers, including *The Man of Independence* (1950), a biography of Truman. One series of works during this period dealt with southern Civil War heroes, while a second group focused on the Washington that Daniels discovered when he worked as an assistant to Roosevelt.

Under Daniels the *News and Observer* solidified its position as the major newspaper in eastern North Carolina. In 1955 the *News and Observer* bought out the *Raleigh Times*, its primary competition in the capital city. The *Times* was an afternoon newspaper, and Daniels promised after the acquisition to keep both newspapers "separate and distinct." The *Times* was discontinued in 1990.

During the 1950s the *News and Observer* instituted a fight against secrecy in government, believing that legislative decisions should not be reached behind closed doors. The newspaper's battle to create an open-door policy for the press spanned three decades. It intensified during the late 1960s, and in 1971 the North Carolina Open Meetings Law was ratified.

In 1968 Daniels stepped down as editor of the *News and Observer*, but he continued to contribute columns to the newspaper. One of his chief causes in these later years was the coastal regions of North and South Carolina. He vacationed at Hilton Head Island in South Carolina during the 1960s and moved there shortly after retirement. He saw the rapid beach development along the coasts of the two states as environmentally destructive. In December 1979 he wrote in his *News and Observer* column that he feared the "New Jerseyfication" of the coasts would soon be complete.

After moving to Hilton Head, Daniels helped establish the *Island Packet*, a weekly newspaper designed to serve the residents of the island. He wrote a column for the *Packet* each week, and many of these were collected in *The Gentlemanly Serpent* (1974). His last book, *White House Witness: 1942–1945* (1975), recounted events within the Roosevelt White House that he recorded in diary form during those years.

Daniels died at Hilton Head on 6 November 1981 after a period of declining health. Barry Bingham, chairman of the board of the Louisville Courier-Journal and Louisville Times Company, remarked that Daniels "was a great American editor. His wit, his charm and his fine writing skill were at the service of a lively social conscience. His career gave honor to the journalistic profession." James B. Hunt, then governor of North Carolina, praised Daniels for devoting the *News and Observer* "to policies of equality and justice to the underprivileged." Hunt went on to say that Daniels "did it with wit and humor, with compassion and conviction that could only have come from genuine concern about the poor, the uneducated, the hapless, the voiceless people in our society. . . . Perhaps no single individual did more in modern times to help win and keep a place for North Carolina as a progressive, enlightened political forum in the South and the nation than Jonathan Daniels."

References:

Charles W. Eagles, *Jonathan Daniels and Race Relations: The Evolution of a Southern Liberal* (Knoxville: University of Tennessee Press, 1982);

Julian M. Pleasants and Augustus M. Burns III, *Frank Porter Graham and the 1950 Senate Race in North Carolina* (Chapel Hill & London: University of North Carolina Press, 1990);

Thad Stem, Jr., *Tar Heel Press* (Southport: North Carolina Press Association, 1973).

Papers:

Daniels's papers are in the Southern Historical Collection at the University of North Carolina, Chapel Hill.

Mark Ethridge, Sr.

(22 April 1896 – 5 April 1981)

Morgan David Arant
Memphis State University

MAJOR POSITIONS HELD: Managing editor, *Macon* (Georgia) *Telegraph* (1925–1933); assistant general manager, *Washington Post* (1933–1934); general manager (1934–1935), general manager and publisher (1935–1936), *Richmond* (Virginia) *Times-Dispatch*; general manager (1936–1937), vice-president and general manager (1937–1942), publisher (1942–1961), *Louisville Courier-Journal* and *Louisville Times*; chairman of the board, Louisville Courier-Journal and Louisville Times Company (1961–1963); vice-president and editor (Long Island, N.Y.) *Newsday* (1963–1965); professor, University of North Carolina at Chapel Hill (1965–1968).

BOOK: *America's Obligation to Its Negro Citizens: An Address* (Atlanta: Conference on Education and Race Relations, 1937).

SELECTED PERIODICAL PUBLICATIONS – UNCOLLECTED: "Ethridge Calls for Investigation of FCC," *Broadcasting*, 20 (19 May 1941): 15–17;

"Ethridge Sees Postwar Years Challenge to Press," *Editor & Publisher* (13 October 1945): 9, 84.

Mark Ethridge, Sr., December 1946 (courtesy of the Louisville Courier-Journal)

By making editorial excellence his priority in the management of the *Louisville Courier-Journal,* publisher Mark Foster Ethridge was able to turn the newspaper into one of the most respected dailies in the country. By focusing resources on the news-editorial content of the newspaper, he transformed the *Courier-Journal* and *Louisville Times* from money-losing ventures into excellent and profitable newspapers. His commitment to journalistic excellence, his courage in championing liberal causes in the segregated South in the first half of the twentieth century, and his participation on the national and international political stage made Ethridge one of America's best-known newspaper executives. A 1944 *Chicago Sun* editorial described him as "one of the most forceful, intelligent and progressive newspapermen in America."

Born in Meridian, Mississippi, Ethridge was one of nine children of William Nathaniel and Mary Howell Ethridge. Growing up in the South, Mark witnessed scenes of white mobs lynching blacks. William, a lawyer whose practice consisted of almost as many black clients as white, successfully defended blacks in a white-dominated legal system. William died when Mark was fourteen, but he instilled in Mark an interest in the law, the profession to which he aspired.

Ethridge's work with newspapers began the summer before his junior year in high school, when he stuffed papers together for the *Meridian Star*. During his senior year he got what he called "his first fatal smell of printer's ink" working as the high-school correspondent for the *Star*. In addition, the sports editor recruited him to write a column. According to Ethridge, the editor gave the feature, "Baseball Bubbles by Fannie," a woman's byline so that no reader would suspect that a regular staff member had written it.

Upon graduation from high school, Ethridge worked for a year as a court reporter for the *Meridian Star* to save money to go to the University of Mississippi. With a year's earnings he was able to attend the university beginning in September 1913, but after a year he had to return to Meridian to support the family and help put three younger sisters through school. At age nineteen Ethridge took a job as reporter at the *Columbus* (Georgia) *Enquirer-Sun* and also wrote a regular column, "Shoes and Ships and Sealing Wax." After only three months at the *Enquirer-Sun*, he moved to the *Macon* (Georgia) *Telegraph*, where he made twenty-five dollars a week, an increase of five dollars. In Macon he met the woman who would become his wife, Willie Snow, a star on the Lanier High School girls' basketball team.

In April 1917 the United States entered World War I, and a month later Ethridge joined the navy. At war's end he became the city editor for the *Macon Telegraph*. The paper had hired four women during the war when male employees were scarce. Among the women working there was Snow, who was also attending Wesleyan College in Macon. Of the female employees, Ethridge said, "I kept one, I fired one, I made a woman's editor out of one, and I sacrificed myself beyond the call of duty by marrying one." He and Snow were married on 12 October 1921, and she gave birth to their first child, Mary Snow, on 20 November 1922. Their second child, Mark Foster, Jr., was born 29 July 1924. The third child, Georgia Cubbedge, was born 19 April 1926. Their fourth child, David, was born more than a decade later, on 2 December 1938.

After three years as city editor, Ethridge joined the Consolidated Press in Washington and a few months later moved to the *New York Sun* as reporter and rewrite man. He covered mostly politics for the paper but also wrote weekly full-page features for the *Atlanta Journal Sunday Magazine*. In late 1924 *Telegraph* owner and editor W. T. Anderson enticed him to return to the paper as managing and associate editor. In this role Ethridge wrote most of the editorials. In an unpublished biography of her husband, Willie wrote, "The editorial page was —

and still is — his first love." Under his leadership for eight years, the *Telegraph* crusaded on many social, economic, and educational fronts but focused on ridding the state of the Ku Klux Klan. The campaign against the Klan became so heated that Ethridge took his vicious German shepherd when he went to the office in the evenings, and Anderson carried a sawed-off shotgun. The paper's stance against the Klan and poor labor conditions in cotton mills, as well as its general excellence, gained national attention. In addition to his newspaper duties, Ethridge taught journalism courses at Mercer College.

He also had the good fortune of meeting interesting and important people. At the University of Mississippi, he encountered William Faulkner. While at the *Telegraph* he and his wife became friends of Franklin Delano Roosevelt, who in 1924 had begun regular trips to Warm Springs, Georgia, for recuperative treatments after his attack of polio. Ethridge even got Roosevelt to write a series of columns on conservation and soil erosion for the *Telegraph*. One Sunday afternoon in October 1928, while Willie was visiting the Roosevelts and Mark was working at the paper, he got a call from the *New York Sun* asking him to find out whether Roosevelt would accept the nomination for governor of New York. Ethridge tried to get through to Roosevelt by phone but was put off by a secretary who said that he was in conference. When Willie returned that evening, Ethridge learned that she had spent the afternoon with Roosevelt discussing whether he would accept the nomination. Roosevelt was elected governor that fall. Other notables whom the Ethridges got to know while in Georgia were authors Margaret Mitchell of Atlanta and Sherwood Anderson, who wintered in Macon.

As the national reputation of the *Telegraph* grew in the late 1920s and early 1930s, Ethridge became a popular speaker on the lecture circuit. In January 1931 he spoke at the Seventh Annual Newspaper Institute at the University of North Carolina. In his lecture, "Inside of the Newspaper," Ethridge shared his operating principles as a managing and associate editor: "The prescription I give for publishing a paper that will be read is to have the resources for collecting news, the intelligence to handle it and the courage to comment upon it frankly, unafraid, unawed and unsubsidized." First, he believed that a newspaper must focus on its own constituency. He hinted that William Randolph Hearst had failed miserably in his Georgia newspaper venture, the *Atlanta Georgian*, because he tried to publish a big-city newspaper in big-city style in a predominantly agricultural state. Ethridge said that the contract the newspaper has with the reader is to provide the news of the day, and the reporter is "a photographer with words whose only function is to give . . . an honest, truthful and accurate picture of what transpires in the world."

He warned against pandering to the prejudices and passions of the paper's lowbrow readers by filling it with sensational stories of crime and violence instead of providing a diet of news that reflects what is going on in the world. Because newspapers need intelligent reporters in the news departments, Ethridge advocated paying reporters better wages. He believed that the editorial page gave the newspaper its distinctiveness. Readers should expect the utmost honesty from the editorialist, who should write under no obligation except that to the highest truth. Ethridge said that an editor who speaks out bravely will enhance his own self-respect and the character of his newspaper. Several years later he noted that one problem with the rise of chain ownership was that editorials of chain newspapers did not mean as much as when newspapers were family owned and spoke with a single voice. "Their voices have been neutralized and they no longer blast like a trumpet," he wrote.

In April 1931 Ethridge accepted an offer as a special writer at the *New York Sun* for a much larger salary than he was making at the *Telegraph*. In order to keep Ethridge in Macon, Anderson offered him a free hand in running the paper and promised that he would receive half ownership of the *Telegraph* at Anderson's death. Ethridge decided to stay. In the 1932 presidential election the *Telegraph* supported Roosevelt.

In 1933 Ethridge took a leave of absence from the *Telegraph* and went to Europe on an Oberlaender Fellowship to study political and economic conditions in central Europe, particularly social-security measures and the ramifications of the Versailles Treaty. Ethridge and his wife landed in Bremen on 6 March 1933, two days after Roosevelt was inaugurated and one day after Adolf Hitler came to power in Germany. They observed the Nazi hysteria sweeping Germany, which Ethridge described in a *Telegraph* column: "There is nothing quite like it except when a successful revivalist has a crowd in the hollow of his hand."

The Ethridges saw Hitler's symbolic crowning later that month at Potsdam and witnessed the start of the persecution of the Jews when Nazis instituted boycotts against Jewish businesses in early April. In what he regarded as one of the worst misjudgments of his newspaper career, Ethridge concluded that the German people were too sensible to put up with Hitler for long. In an article datelined 19 August 1933, Associated Press writer Francis Jamieson wrote, "Six months in Germany have convinced Mark Ethridge, southern newspaper editor, that the luster of Hitlerism is rapidly wearing off."

While the Ethridges were in Germany, Anderson began publishing editorials criticizing Roosevelt's New Deal legislation. From Germany, Ethridge wrote to Anderson that he needed to clarify the positions of his recent editorials and reassure the readers of the paper's progressive stance. In response, Anderson invited Ethridge to leave the paper anytime he wanted. Ethridge resigned immediately and gave up any claim to a share of the *Telegraph*. He received several offers of employment. Ivy Lee, who handled public relations for John D. Rockefeller, Jr., offered him a job, but Ethridge decided to stick with newspapers because he "didn't want to spend the rest of my life perfuming skunks."

Instead, he joined the Associated Press for a brief time. Then Eugene Meyer offered him a position as associate editor of the *Washington Post*. After three months in this position, Ethridge was promoted to assistant general manager in charge of the news and editorial department and the mechanical department. He wrote editorials and news stories in his spare time. Among them was a story that appeared on 7 October 1934, just as criticism of Roosevelt and his New Deal legislation was intensifying. Ethridge's article, which compared the histories of social legislation in the United States and England, provided needed support for Roosevelt's programs just prior to the November elections. The day after the article appeared, Ethridge was invited to the White House to receive Roosevelt's congratulations. The Democratic candidates received overwhelming voter support in November.

In December 1934 Col. Sam Slover, owner of the *Richmond* (Virginia) *Times-Dispatch,* asked Ethridge to become the paper's general manager and promised him that within five months he would be named publisher. Slover assured him that he would have a free hand in operating the *Times-Dispatch,* and Ethridge took the job. He led the paper in strong support for New Deal reform. Powerful Virginia senator Harry Byrd, an opponent of Roosevelt's economic programs, tried to pressure Ethridge to abandon the paper's New Deal support. Byrd appealed to the paper's advertisers and owner Slover, but Slover sided with Ethridge. The editorial stand remained firmly pro-Roosevelt.

During his time at the *Times-Dispatch,* Ethridge improved news and editorial content and reduced

President Franklin D. Roosevelt in August 1941 with members of the Fair Employment Practice Committee: Chairman Ethridge, Earl B. Dickerson, John Brophy, Milton P. Webster, David Sarnoff, and Lawrence Cramer (courtesy of the Louisville Courier-Journal*)*

circulation promotional expenses. He disliked a practice common among newspapers of offering subscriptions as premiums to purchasers of insurance policies, believing that publishers could make more money by producing better newspapers. Instead of putting money into circulation gimmicks, Ethridge raised the salaries of the news and editorial writers. He wanted good reporters who had a broad understanding of world affairs and domestic economic and social measures. Within two years the *Times-Dispatch* surpassed the circulation of the rival *Richmond News-Leader* for the first time.

Ethridge tried to find out the interests of his readers by surveying them twice a year to determine what kind of features they wanted. He believed that a newspaper manager in the 1930s could no longer publish papers filled with only news and editorials, which were the primary content of the papers he had read as a child. Instead, Ethridge regarded the newspaper as a daily magazine. His polling of people in his circulation area revealed the dramatic change brought about in newspapers by graphics. One survey showed that of the fifteen leading features, thirteen had visual rather than content appeal. He also found that while men pre-

ferred political news, sports, and market reports, women favored health, style, food, society, and fashion features.

In 1936 Ethridge met Barry and Mary Bingham at a Richmond dinner party. Barry was the son of Judge Robert Worth Bingham, owner of the *Louisville Courier-Journal* and the *Louisville Times,* who at this time was U.S. ambassador to Great Britain. Barry had heard of Ethridge's excellent management of the *Times-Dispatch* through Mary's family, who lived in Richmond. He invited Ethridge to Louisville to discuss the newspapers. On his return from London in 1936, Judge Bingham called on Roosevelt and mentioned that he was looking for a new general manager. Roosevelt recommended Ethridge. Determined to reorganize his newspapers, the judge asked his top executives to resign, and he put Barry in charge of the two papers. When the judge suggested Ethridge as general manager, Barry said he was considering the same man.

In a 1950 article about the history of the *Courier-Journal* published in the *Reporter,* Llewellyn White wrote that "the acting editor-publisher [Barry Bingham] laid siege to this fellow [Ethridge] who was coming to be known as the greatest newspaper doctor in the land." White described Ethridge as having "a very sharp nose and a very persuasive drawl," and as "a genuine liberal." In April 1936 Ethridge became general manager of the Louisville newspapers. Later that month a Frankfort, Kentucky, banker, Lisle S. Baker, Jr., was named company secretary. In October 1936 the rival *Louisville Herald-Post* discontinued publishing after substantial financial losses. That left the *Courier-Journal* and the *Times* as Louisville's only dailies.

When Judge Bingham died on 18 December 1937, Barry became president and publisher and Ethridge moved up to vice-president and general manager, while Baker added the duties of treasurer. Ethridge was in charge of the news, and Baker handled business affairs. Both reported to Bingham. When Bingham went into the navy in 1942, Ethridge was named publisher and left in full charge of the papers. The *Courier-Journal* also lost its editor, Herbert Agar, to the navy. When Bingham returned, he assumed the title of editor in chief and left Ethridge as publisher, a position he would hold for nineteen years. Ethridge and Bingham, who thought alike on most issues, set the policy for the editorial writers.

Upon his arrival in Louisville, Ethridge set out to transform the newspapers. In his study of the Louisville daily press for *PM* in 1945, Kenneth Stewart wrote that the *Courier-Journal* had become "a paper with a personality – and this time it is the personality of Mark Foster Ethridge [who] descended on Louisville like a tornado." Just as he had done in Richmond, Ethridge sought to invigorate the papers by emphasizing the news and editorial departments and terminating costly circulation promotions. First, he raised the salaries of the editorial staff. In a 1945 *Editor & Publisher* article, Ethridge wrote, "if we want to get out good newspapers we have to pay for news and editorial brains."

Next he took aim at the newspapers' schemes of selling low-premium accident and life insurance and, as Ethridge described it, "throwing the paper in like a stick of candy with a side of bacon." He cut out all the circulation gimmicks and put all available money into getting and publishing the news, under the premise that people will pay for a good newspaper. He increased news content from the 1935 average of 90 columns daily to an average of 121 daily by 1939 and had a news-advertising ratio of fifty-seven to forty-three. During this period circulation increased by more than forty thousand. In 1944 the two dailies had one of the highest ratios of news to advertising in the country. During the war the *Courier-Journal* and *Times* turned down millions of dollars in advertising rather than displace space allocated for news coverage.

By working to stimulate Louisville's overall business climate, Ethridge established a strong base for advertising revenue. When he first arrived there, he researched local business conditions. From government commerce studies he discovered that retail sales were flat at Louisville department stores compared to sales in cities of comparable size. Because weak retail sales limited the level of newspaper advertising revenue, Ethridge sought to correct what he considered causes of the problem: too many bad roads and toll bridges into the city and general rural antipathy for the city. The newspapers promoted better roads and reduction of toll bridges and reached out to the surrounding rural communities. The newspapers sponsored farm- and home-improvement campaigns and initiated tours of Louisville for all graduating high-school students.

Ethridge also built a strong relationship with Louisville advertisers by abolishing a policy requiring them to buy space in both dailies. He said that he faced only one occasion in which an advertiser tried to dictate the newspapers' editorial policies. A local Sears manager attempted to organize an advertiser boycott of the *Courier-Journal* in order to force it to change its stand backing a proposed city sales tax. At an advertisers' meeting Ethridge told businessmen that nobody except the editors fixed editorial policy. The advertisers did not boycott, and the Sears manager was soon replaced.

In order to extend excellence to all aspects of the newspapers' operations, Ethridge gathered a talented staff. He hired a new art director to improve the appearance of the papers and new personnel for circulation, advertising, and production. He employed the best writers he could find. In the *Reporter,* White wrote that the policy of hiring the best writers available paid off "in a quality of writing, particularly on the editorial pages, not to be matched by any newspaper today." Ethridge also employed good leaders. He hired Jim Pope, former managing editor for the *Atlanta Journal,* as managing editor of the *Courier-Journal.* Pope would later become executive editor of both papers. In 1951 Ethridge recruited Norman Isaacs as managing editor.

Among other changes in the paper were the addition of easier-to-read type, an extra editorial page, and a locally edited Sunday magazine supplement, along with the practice of jumping stories from page 1 to the back page of the front section. Ethridge created the second editorial page for background and think pieces from the Washington and

Frankfort (Kentucky) bureaus and a column by conservative Republican Frank Kent "as an antidote for the paper's liberal leanings." On Saturday mornings, the *Courier-Journal* op-ed page would feature writers debating controversial issues, such as birth control. Begun in 1942, the paper's "Roto Magazine" was one of the first locally edited Sunday magazine supplements, a four-color insert for feature-story presentation. The "Roto Magazine" also rescued the company-owned Standard Gravure Corporation, a rotogravure printing firm that had struggled to make a profit. Impressed by the *Courier-Journal* magazine, several other newspapers launched similar efforts and employed Standard Gravure to print them.

Under Ethridge's leadership the *Courier-Journal* became one of the most liberal papers in the South, especially in its advocacy of racial justice and in its support of the social legislation of the Roosevelt and Truman administrations. The paper opposed the use of poll taxes and white primaries to disenfranchise blacks. In a 1937 speech to a Louisville civic club, Ethridge urged that the nation provide the black citizen "full protection of his rights and person under the law, opportunity for professional and trade advancement and a more equitable distribution of public monies to provide him better educational advantages and a greater measure of public health protection." In another 1937 speech, *America's Obligation to Its Negro Citizens,* Ethridge said that though the laws of southern states called for "separate but equal" facilities, "it was the rarest exception when accommodations were anything like equal."

Although ahead of most of his peers on race issues, Ethridge remained a child of the South. He stopped short of calling for radical steps to establish social equality: "I have nowhere mentioned the abolition of segregation or so-called 'social equality,' because I have nowhere found these steps to be among the Negro's aspirations." In a 1940 Senate hearing Ethridge offered testimony for a federal antilynching bill. Then in June 1941 Roosevelt created a Fair Employment Practice Committee to investigate racial discrimination in the government and defense industries and appointed Ethridge its chairman. Ethridge's committee findings led to an executive order requiring federal departments and agencies to hire without regard to race or religion. At a 1944 Atlanta meeting of the Committee of Editors and Writers of the South, he led the committee in condemning poll taxes and other devices to exclude blacks from voting. He called for economic opportunity for blacks and maintained that integration could only be accomplished through education, not legislation.

Because Barry and Mary Bingham also owned the largest Louisville radio station, WHAS, a fifty-thousand-watt CBS affiliate, Ethridge became active in broadcasting. In 1938, in response to a musicians' union strike on radio stations that prevented them from playing the musicians' copyrighted music, Ethridge organized the Independent Radio Network Affiliates to negotiate an agreement. With the support of his independent radio associates, Ethridge pushed the National Association of Broadcasters to reorganize as a more powerful political voice for broadcasters and to establish a strong, paid presidency. The NAB established a powerful presidential office and selected Ethridge for this new position of "radio czar." Ethridge took it on an interim basis, until his Louisville friend Neville Miller was named president.

In 1941 Ethridge was called again to broadcast duty by President Roosevelt, who appointed him to investigate the controversy between the NAB and the Federal Communications Commission. The FCC wanted to break up the radio monopolies of the big networks. Within a month of Ethridge's appointment, just as the publisher was about to launch a survey of radio-station owners to find out whether they were oppressed by network domination, FCC chairman James Lawrence Fly issued a report calling for the breakup of the monopoly of radio stations by the two big chains, CBS and NBC.

In a 26 May 1941 article on the NAB convention in Saint Louis, *Time* magazine reported that "Ethridge, liberal, sense-making general manager of the *Louisville Courier-Journal,* the industry's keyman and ex-radio tsar . . . in a scourging speech resigned from making his radio survey, suggested that the President was deceived . . . and bitterly denounced the attempt to regulate the radio industry by bad temper, impatience and vindictiveness." Ethridge charged that the commission under Fly had exceeded its power, and he called for a congressional investigation. Ethridge's contributions to broadcasting, in particular his efforts in reorganizing the NAB, were recognized in 1956 when the NAB named him its "man of the year," making him the third person to receive the award after David Sarnoff of RCA and William Paley of CBS.

After World War II, Ethridge engaged in diplomatic duties for the U.S. government. In the fall of 1945 Secretary of State James Byrnes appointed him as his special investigator to observe the general elections in Bulgaria and Romania, whose Moscow-backed governments had not been recognized

Ethridge, Lisle S. Baker, Jr., and George Barry Bingham in 1961. They made the Louisville Courier-Journal one of the top ten U.S. newspapers during the 1950s (photograph by James N. Keen; courtesy of the Louisville Courier-Journal).

by the United States. During the assignment Ethridge visited Moscow for meetings with Andrey Vyshinsky, deputy commissar for foreign affairs. In his report to Byrnes, Ethridge concluded that the Bulgarian and Romanian governments were not broadly representative of the people and that Soviet influence on these countries must be resisted.

In December 1946 President Harry Truman asked Ethridge to be the U.S. representative on the United Nations Balkan Commission, which was to investigate charges by Greece that its neighbors were aiding the Communists in its civil war. Ethridge's cables predicting the imminent fall of the pro-Western Greek government played an important role in persuading Truman to ask Congress for economic and military assistance for Athens. By his urgent appeals for aid to Greece, Ethridge played a part in the formulation of the Truman Doctrine. During the remainder of the Truman administration, he served on several government panels, including a 1948 appointment as chairman of the U.S. Advisory Commission on Information to guide the State Department in such operations as Voice of America broadcasts, and a 1949 appointment as the American repre-

sentative to the United Nations Conciliation Commission for Palestine.

Throughout his career Ethridge was recognized for his contributions to the newspaper industry and to society at large. He was awarded honorary degrees by Harvard, Tulane, and other universities. In 1960 he was honored by Columbia University as "distinguished journalist," an award made only twice before, to J. N. Heiskell of the *Arkansas Gazette* and Arthur Hays Sulzberger of the *New York Times*. Ethridge served as a trustee of the Ford Foundation.

In 1961 Ethridge faced a standing rule that *Courier-Journal* employees had to retire at age sixty-five, a rule that he had introduced. He reluctantly gave up the duties of publisher to Barry Bingham, and the board of directors of the Louisville Courier-Journal and Louisville Times Company elected him chairman of the board. As chairman, Ethridge had mostly honorary duties. In the fall of 1963 he retired from this position and made plans to join the faculty of the School of Journalism at the University of North Carolina at Chapel Hill. Two of Ethridge's children, David and Mary Snow, were living in North Carolina. Before he could make the move, however, Harry F. Guggenheim, chief executive of Long Island's *Newsday,* recruited him as the newspaper's editor and vice-president. Ethridge replaced Alicia Patterson, Guggenheim's wife, who had died unexpectedly that summer. Friends of the Ethridges for years, the Guggenheims were horse-race fans who often visited them on trips to Louisville. The University of North Carolina deferred Ethridge's appointment, and he agreed to a two-year editorship at *Newsday.*

On the day of his departure from the *Courier-Journal* and *Times,* Ethridge posted this note on the bulletin board: "I'll always be proud of these papers – the best combination dailies in the United States – of WHAS with its record of public service and civic consciousness, and of Standard Gravure, which has been a real pioneer in the field of local magazines and color printing, and of all of you who made the 'corner' what it is. Sometime when your voices are well lubricated, I hope you will take one more and then sing for me: 'Adieu kind friends, adieu, I can no longer stay with you; I will hang my harp on a weeping willow tree, and may the world go well with thee.'"

In 1965, after two years in New York, Ethridge retired as editor of *Newsday.* He became a full-time resident of North Carolina and served on the faculty of the School of Journalism of the University of North Carolina at Chapel Hill until he retired from teaching in 1968. He and his wife built a house on a 192-foot bluff overlooking the Rocky River in rural Chatham County, North Carolina. At age seventy-nine, Ethridge had the first of a series of debilitating strokes. He died at his home on 5 April 1981. A *Raleigh* (North Carolina) *News and Observer* editorial observed that in his fifty-five years of newspapering, Ethridge, "one of the greats from journalism, never lost his love for the printed word or his zeal for a solid news and editorial product."

Jim Pope, executive editor of the *Courier-Journal* and the *Times,* said that while Ethridge was a great publisher and managed to make the papers profitable, he "never managed to be thought of as a publisher by the newspaper fraternity . . . what mattered is that he was recognized as a great newspaperman." One of the best summations of Ethridge's abilities as a publisher was written in 1950 by White for the *Reporter:* "In addition to knowing as much about how to produce an attractive, salable newspaper as anyone ever employed by the *Chicago Tribune* or the *New York Daily News,* and as much about how to sell it as any Hearst man, Mark Ethridge happens to be a genuine liberal."

What elevated the *Courier-Journal* to its national stature was the newspaper's distinctive, liberal editorial voice to a region struggling to escape a bankrupt, racist past for a progressive and prosperous time for all its people. What made Ethridge an outstanding newspaperman was that he possessed both a keen business acumen and an unwavering conviction that the rule of law protected all the people and that it was the newspaper's responsibility "to explain what the issues in the world are." And despite the personal costs, Mark Foster Ethridge had the courage to speak and live his convictions "frankly, unafraid, unawed and unsubsidized."

Interview:

Donald McDonald, *The Press: Interviews by Donald McDonald with Mark Ethridge, Louisville Courier-Journal and Times, and C. D. Jackson, Life Magazine* (Santa Barbara, Cal.: Fund for the Republic, 1961).

References:

"Radio v. New Deal," *Time,* 37 (26 May 1941): 17;

Llewellyn White, "Papers of Paradox: The *Louisville Courier-Journal* and *Times* Confound Critics of Press Monopolies," *Reporter,* 2 (31 January 1950): 24.

Papers:

Ethridge's papers are in the Southern Historical Collection, Wilson Library, University of North Carolina at Chapel Hill, along with Willie Snow Ethridge's unpublished biography, "Cherubic Devil: A Biography of Mark Ethridge."

Katherine Fanning

(18 October 1927 –   )

Aralynn Abare McMane
University of South Carolina

MAJOR POSITIONS HELD: Editor and publisher, *Anchorage Daily News* (1971–1983); editor, *Christian Science Monitor* (1983–1988); president, American Society of Newspaper Editors (1987–1988).

SELECTED PUBLICATION: "Katherine Woodruff Fanning," in *New Guardians of the Press: Selected Profiles of America's Women Newspaper Editors,* edited by Judith Clabes (Indianapolis: Berg, 1983), pp. 59–72.

Katherine Fanning built the *Anchorage Daily News* into the winner of a Pulitzer Prize. She later became one of the few women in the 1980s to lead a major American newspaper, the *Christian Science Monitor,* and the first woman to head the American Society of Newspaper Editors.

Katherine Woodruff Fanning, the only child of Frederick William and Katherine Bower (Miller) Woodruff, was born in Chicago on 18 October 1927. She spent most of her early years just outside Joliet, Illinois, where her father was the third generation in a line of bank presidents. She credits him with inspiring in her an interest in the world and its events and a sense that there were no limitations on what she could do. She went to school at home with nine other children because there was no private school nearby, and her parents felt the public schools were inadequate. In seventh grade she was driven thirty miles daily to attend a private, progressive junior high school.

She attended Joliet High School for a year before going to boarding school, where she "spent four miserable years unpopular and convinced of my own mediocrity." She credits that experience with helping to give her what she considers a useful outlook for a newspaper person, "a lifelong empathy with the underdog." At Smith College she took every possible writing course, wrote a play that was later produced, and cowrote and produced two musical comedies. She also wrote for an alternative

newspaper. She was graduated in 1949 with a B.A. in English literature and dreams of becoming a magazine writer in New York. She recalls that her mother persuaded her to return home instead. She married Marshall Field IV a year later, joining a family that had owned department stores and still had the *Chicago Sun-Times.* In 1951 Field became editor and publisher of the paper, and Katherine's newspaper training began.

"I was closely associated with the effort behind the scenes, a once-removed education in all aspects of a metropolitan newspaper," she recalls. "Marshall brought home his journalist associates, and also his problems, which we would work on together." She concentrated on volunteer work and raising her son, Frederick ("Ted"), and two daughters, Katherine and Barbara. The couple was divorced in 1963.

The next two years brought many changes, some despair, and much self-examination. She and her children moved into Chicago's Old Town area, carefully removed from the wealthy Gold Coast where she had lived as a society matron. She became involved in the civil-rights movement and other social causes. She went through a personal crisis that she later characterized as akin to a runaway cable car on a San Francisco hill. She credits her survival with the "inner spiritual self," developed during her years at boarding school, that emerged and took hold. She gave up smoking and drinking and converted from the Presbyterian church of her upbringing to Christian Science.

The emphasis Christian Science places on the essential goodness of humanity and the power of scientific prayer to solve problems was part of the appeal. "Christian Science made sense to me," she said later. "It helped me take the teachings of Jesus and form my life around them." She also began looking for a place to start anew, a wholesome place to raise her children and, for the first time, to have

74

Katherine Fanning, 1983

her own career. She visited friends in Anchorage, Alaska, found she liked it, and decided to take her children there. She stayed for eighteen years. "In Alaska, no one seemed to care who you had been or what you had done before you migrated north. Total equality. A classless society. A chance to begin again," she observed.

She arrived in Alaska in August 1965. There were two newspapers in Anchorage. One was the thirty-thousand-circulation, firmly established *Anchorage Times,* owned by the Atwood family under publisher Robert Atwood. The other, the *Anchorage Daily News,* had been started as a weekly in 1946 by Norman and Blanche Brown. The paper had become an afternoon daily in 1947. By the time Fanning arrived, it was a twelve-thousand-circulation morning and Sunday broadsheet. She went to work for the *Daily News* as a two-dollar-an-hour librarian. The paper occupied a dingy warehouse on Post

Road in the industrial section of town where it was written by a news staff of eight and produced on a seventy-five-year-old press.

However, her interests turned to reporting. She had never learned how to write a news story, so she read other newspapers and tried to copy their style. In the next Alaska Press Club contest, she won two first-place awards: best spot news for a story about three university students who had frozen to death on a glacier and best series for a set of stories on the problems of promoting birth control among natives in the Alaskan bush. Her work on birth control had caused some controversy when it appeared on the front page – with a picture of a hand holding a contraceptive – the same day Alaska's first Roman Catholic archbishop arrived.

In 1966 Katherine married Larry Fanning, former editor of the *San Francisco Chronicle, Chicago*

Sun-Times, and *Chicago Daily News.* They planned to sell her house in Alaska and move to the lower forty-eight, but not back to Chicago. Instead, he, too, became captivated by Alaska. The next year, against all the advice they sought, the two bought the *Anchorage Daily News* for $450,000. At first, Larry was editor and publisher, with Katherine doing a smattering of other duties: reporting, selling ads, producing a Sunday magazine, writing a column, and, on occasion, running the accounting department.

The paper constantly faced financial difficulties. The previous owner had kept the only profitable part of the business, the commercial printing operation. The paper itself had always hovered on oblivion, and the deficit mounted. The Fannings had to upgrade all the equipment, adding six linotype machines and replacing the antique press with a "new" thirty-year-old Goss Tubular.

The financial difficulties were compounded by highly unpopular editorial stands. In a state where most people owned at least one firearm, the Fannings advocated gun control after presidential candidate Robert Kennedy was shot and killed in 1968. In a state that was generally ecstatic about the economic prospects of the impending Trans-Alaska Pipeline, they published in 1968 an award-winning thirty-two-part series, "Oil on Ice," in which reporter Tom Brown explored the potential dangers of laying eight hundred miles of pipeline to carry hot oil across permafrost. The paper was denounced from the podium of the Anchorage Chamber of Commerce for its support of a movement to give Eskimos, Indians, and Aleuts title to or compensation for their ancestral lands. Years later one prominent Anchorage banker admitted to Fanning that for a decade he had refused loans to any client who advertised in the *Anchorage Daily News.*

The mounting financial burden became solely Katherine's when her husband died of a heart attack in 1971 at age fifty-six. "At first I was uncomfortable behind Larry's big desk," she said. "Whenever a man came in to meet with me, I would sidle around the desk, pulling my chair to the side. I knew I was moving into a job usually held by a man, but I had always enjoyed being a woman. I vowed to cherish my womanhood, to make it as effective and decisive as necessary but never to become like a man." She readily acknowledged, however, that she patterned much of her own management style after that of her late husband: "He literally loved his reporters. He understood that talented people were special and must be treated according to their own individual needs."

In November 1974 the Justice Department gave Fanning approval to enter into a Joint Operating Agreement (JOA) with the *Anchorage Times.* It was the nation's first such agreement between separately owned newspapers under the Newspaper Preservation Act of 1970, which had been designed to ensure the survival of two editorial voices in cities dominated by one paper. Unlike later agreements of this sort, a separate entity was not set up to run the business affairs of both companies; instead, the *Times* performed that function. The agreement meant the *Times* would print the *Daily News,* plus sell advertising for it and handle the distribution. The *Daily News* also moved into a new building built for it by the *Times.* The *Daily News* gave its Sunday paper to the *Times.* Unlike later JOAs of that time, this agreement did not include profit sharing.

The JOA allowed Fanning and her staff to concentrate on editorial excellence. In the summer of 1975 three of the staff's eight reporters devoted full attention for three months to investigating rumors that the Alaska Teamster's Union was controlling the state through financial and political clout as the $8 billion Trans-Alaska Pipeline was becoming a reality. Fanning's *Daily News* team of Howard Weaver, Bob Porterfield, and Jim Babb traveled more than three thousand miles within Alaska, interviewed at least one hundred people, listed and cross-indexed more than 250 corporations and three hundred individual incorporators to trace Teamster fund investments, and examined nine hundred deeds, mortgages, and land records.

The team was well into its investigation when the *Los Angeles Times* sent four reporters to cover the same story. The less-detailed *Times* version came out first. "There was a temptation to rush our series into print before it was ready, but we refrained in order to present a complete, thoroughly documented account," Fanning stated. The restraint paid off, as the fifteen-part "Empire: The Alaska Teamster Story" won the *Daily News* the 1976 Pulitzer Prize for public service over, among others, the *Times* series.

Meanwhile, the money problems continued, with a loss for 1975 of about $750,000. There was no income from the revenue departments operated by the *Times,* and all of Fanning's own resources had been put into the paper. Two of the three Pulitzer Prize winners had gone to better jobs, and the remaining *Daily News* staff was reduced by half to

Fanning (center) at the Christian Science Monitor *in 1983, with editor in chief Earl Foell (left) and John Hoagland, Jr., manager of the Christian Science Publishing Society*

twelve. Circulation sank from about eleven thousand to less than eight thousand. Four months after the Pulitzer, the paper announced on page 1 that it would have to stop publishing if financial help was not immediately forthcoming. Reaction to this statement prompted Fanning to say later that the experience of going publicly broke may have been as rewarding in its way as the Pulitzer Prize. More than one hundred people crowded into the newsroom and formed the Committee for Two Newspapers. "The *Daily News* does not speak for my point of view at all, but we need two newspapers," explained one of the leaders, Susan Overby, a conservative Republican. "We desperately need two newspapers. This is a key state up here – we're sitting on the future mineral wealth of the whole United States."

Members of the committee stood on street corners to sell subscriptions, pressured businesses to advertise, and helped seek major funding. The Bristol Bay Native Corporation provided a low-interest loan of $70,000 in gratitude for the paper's longtime support of land claims against the U.S. government by it and eleven other native corporations. When that loan ran out, Fanning traveled around the country seeking aid from individuals, corporations, and foundations. Actor and environmentalist Robert Redford held a re-

ception at his New York apartment for potential investors. A midwestern woman provided loans of more than $250,000. Others made loans of $50,000 or more. The total came to three-quarters of a million dollars. Three years later all the loans were repaid with interest.

Despite the help, financial difficulties continued. By then, Fanning's son, who was president of the *Daily News,* had put the last of nearly $5 million into the paper. The relationship with the *Times* was deteriorating. In February 1977 Fanning filed a $16.5 million suit, claiming antitrust actions and contract violations. In October, Atwood of the *Times* responded by announcing that he would end the agreement because the *Daily News* owed the *Times* $300,000 and because the lawsuit had interfered with his paper's ability to manage the agreement. That November a U.S. district court judge handed down a ruling that forced the *Times* to continue to publish the *Daily News* under federal-court injunction until the lawsuit was settled through arbitration.

Ultimately, the *Times* had to pay the *Daily News* $750,000 and give the paper until 1 April 1979 to move to a new plant before ending the JOA. The ruling "launched a scramble as threatening as anything we had faced before," Fanning said later. "With the help of the Fairbanks paper to the north, I ordered a press and computer production system even though we had no plant to put it in, no personnel to operate it and no clear idea of how we were going to pay for it." The solution came in January 1978 with Fanning's sale of 80 percent interest in the paper to the California-based McClatchy Newspaper group. She retained 20 percent, and McClatchy provided her with a contract to manage the paper with complete editorial independence. The move brought a million-dollar building in which sixty employees were operating a new computer system and press and putting out a redesigned newspaper with a circulation of 12,000 by the 1 April deadline. By October, circulation had grown to more than 20,000. By March 1980 it was up to 30,500. In October 1982 it surpassed the *Times,* with more than 50,000 weekday readers. By the end of the decade, weekday circulation neared 60,000.

Fanning said in 1990 that she thought the paper's survival made a difference in the way Alaska had developed: "In the early seventies, the *Daily News* was dubbed by some as 'Pravda North' because of its perceived 'left wing' stands on preserving the environment. Now, environmental concerns are in the Alaskan mainstream – especially since the [March 1989] oil spill of the Exxon *Valdez.*" In 1979 Fanning was awarded an honorary doctorate from Colby College for her work in Alaska, the first of seven she would be given by 1992, including one from Harvard University. In 1980 she received medals of honor from the University of Missouri School of Journalism and from her alma mater, Smith College.

Fanning's 1983 move to the *Christian Science Monitor* came quickly and unexpectedly. She was invited to Boston with other Christian Scientists for an update on the activities of the paper and the church. Two *Monitor* board members asked her to come to Boston. She thought they meant to consult and replied that while there was still much to do in Alaska, she might be available occasionally to help. When they told her the job was as editor, she was dumbfounded: "I tried to explain to them that I wasn't qualified, and they kept insisting that they thought there were things that I could do for the paper. The net result was that two weeks later my name was on the masthead and I was back in Alaska packing up and moving to Boston."

She had reason for doubt. Her newspaper experience had been confined to a regional Alaska newspaper, and she was becoming editor of a major

U.S. publication that had been explaining the world to its nationwide audience for three-quarters of a century. The *Monitor* was begun on 25 November 1908 by Mary Baker Eddy, the originator of Christian Science. Eddy said the paper's purpose was "to injure no man, but to bless all mankind." In order to do that, explained the paper's first editor, Archibald McLellan, it would "publish the real news of the world in a clean, wholesome manner, devoid of the sensational methods employed by so many newspapers."

Erwin Canham, editor of the *Monitor* from 1942 to 1974, argued that "clean" did not mean naive. "To describe the *Monitor* as a 'clean' newspaper is correct but incomplete," he wrote in his 1958 history of the paper, *Commitment to Freedom.* "It also strives to expose whatever needs to be uncovered in order to be removed or remedied. It seeks to put the news in a sound perspective, giving greatest emphasis to what is important and reducing the merely sensational to its place in the accurate system of values." By the time Fanning arrived, the paper had won five Pulitzer Prizes, two for international reporting.

However, by 1983 the *Monitor* was in need of a quick infusion of new ideas. Circulation for the five-day-a-week tabloid had declined from a peak of 217,000 in 1971 to about 140,000. As had been the case since the early 1960s, the paper was losing money. One estimate put losses at at least $10 million a year. "I wanted to preserve the great qualities of this paper, but make it easier to read, make it more lively," Fanning told *Advertising Age* a year later. "I thought the paper could be a little more active, more immediate than it had been, and that a lot could be achieved by changing the layout."

In October 1983, four months after Fanning became editor, the paper unveiled a major redesign by consultant Robert Lockwood. There was also an aggressive advertising and circulation plan devised by John Hoagland, Jr., who had joined the staff in 1983 as manager of the Publishing Society. Meanwhile, the paper continued to produce thoughtful journalism. During Fanning's tenure more than a dozen reporters were added to news bureaus. The paper ran weekly updates on the disastrous Ethiopian famine of the mid 1980s long after it was off the front pages of most newspapers. Fanning sent Kristin Helmore to about a dozen countries in Africa, Asia, and Latin America for a series about women in the developing world, "The Neglected Resource." Another series during Fanning's tenure, "Children in Darkness," exposed the way children were being exploited as prostitutes, factory workers, and soldiers. By 1986 the paper's readership had risen by twenty thousand.

In 1987 Fanning became the first woman to head the one-thousand-member American Society of Newspaper Editors (ASNE), having served as a board member and chair of its ethics committee. She felt welcome and supported by her male colleagues but very much in a spotlight: "The ranks of newspaper editors was very much an old boy's club if ever there was one, and so I felt quite a responsibility to my gender to do a decent job." Under her leadership the society created a committee to study the future of newspapers, reflecting her belief that editors were not paying enough regular attention to why readers were defecting to television and other sources of information. She also intensified efforts to encourage the hiring and promotion of minority journalists.

As had been the case in Alaska, Fanning's management style at the *Monitor* called for a calm, team approach. Weaver, who had become editor of the *Alaska Daily News,* argued that Fanning's faith had a great deal to do with how she managed people: "The Christian Science was a kind of background music for everything – that tone of quiet, moderate rationality. She believes at the bottom of her soul that if people talk calmly they can solve anything – in the newsroom or the U.N." Fanning credits her gender: "I think that women do tend to take a team approach, do tend not to be autocratic. I know of men who manage that way, too, but I think that women tend to have a more collegial style and I think that's an effective kind of management."

At the *Monitor* she met with top editors weekly to work out decisions for the whole news operation, including the editorial page. Fanning acknowledged that the approach was less successful outside the newsroom: "We tried very hard to build a sense of team with advertising and circulation and mechanical parts of the paper. That was more difficult because of the way it was organized, and that difficulty in the end really led to our departure."

The same year that she was ASNE president, Fanning was working to rescue her own paper. Circulation was continuing to rise, but it was also continuing to lose money, and the church wanted to move more heavily into broadcasting. With the consent and support of the church's board of directors and the head of the Publishing Society, Fanning set up a task force to create a plan that would reduce costs for the *Monitor* but "preserve its editorial integrity, its claim to be an international paper of import-

ance." Her task force worked out a five-year plan to reduce the *Monitor* deficit to $10.6 million by cutting some feature coverage and limiting the size of the paper to twenty-eight pages. During the summer of 1988 she learned that former managing editor Richard Nenneman had been appointed to head a separate task force working with management consultant NEK of Boston.

In November 1988 recommendations of both task-forces were presented to the church's board of directors. Nenneman's plan called for cutting staff, shrinking the paper to sixteen pages, removing advertising, and appointing a new business executive to oversee the editors, who previously had reported directly to the board of directors. The board accepted that plan, and Fanning resigned. Managing editor David Anable and assistant managing editor David Winder joined her. By the following year forty reporters and editors had resigned. "I love the newspaper and I love the church," Fanning told the *Boston Globe* at the time, "but we had to take a stand on principle. The new format cannot be a vital, world class newspaper."

Nevertheless, Fanning stayed close to newspapering. Within a year after her resignation she addressed American publishing groups and university students as well as a symposium sponsored by the *Times* of India in New Delhi – the starting point of a two-month vacation in Asia with her husband, Amos Matthews, a retired army engineer and Alaska natural-gas-pipeline executive whom she had married in 1984. She joined the board of directors of the parent company of the *Boston Globe*. She continued work she had begun with journalists in Eastern Europe. She became a visiting professor at Northwestern University's Medill School of Journalism and taught a course on journalistic ethics at Boston University.

Fanning saw idealism in her journalism students that she wanted to encourage in her teaching. "I think some of the bottom-line journalism of the 1980s put would-be journalists off quite a bit," she said in 1992. In Eastern Europe she saw journalists struggling to avoid exchanging the tyranny of government for tyranny of the marketplace. She argued that perhaps the most important thing American journalism can do for the emerging peoples is to keep reminding them of the ideals of a free press, and that those ideals are worth a fight: "To set a proper example, we in this country should be clear about what our own free press is and what it is not."

Fanning was clear and critical in her assessment of American newspapering. She argued that there was an overemphasis on profit and packaging by U.S. papers. In a 1989 speech she expressed concern about the changes some papers had made in the 1980s in order to compete with television: "Newspapers have felt compelled to increase their emphasis on appearance, packaging, color and graphics, all of which can be useful and make newspapers more attractive and compelling. But the danger is these considerations may supplant substantive coverage. The 'celebration of surface,' one observer calls it." She saw a future in which the daily newspaper would have an increasing role of synthesis and explanation to "provide a footpath through the maze of modern communications." She saw promise in efforts to make papers more connected to their readers by greater community involvement in sponsoring community meetings and topical forums.

In a 1992 interview Fanning said that she felt fulfilled by her multiple roles, but she did not totally rule out a return to daily newspapering: "From my point of view, with the *Anchorage Daily News,* which was a tremendously exciting challenge on the frontier, and the *Monitor,* with its exciting challenge on a different kind of frontier, I've had the best jobs in newspapering. So I think it is unlikely unless there were some way that I could become involved again with the *Monitor.*"

References:

Jonathan Alter, "Crisis of Faith at the *Monitor,*" *Newsweek,* 112 (28 November 1988): 81;

"*Anchorage News* sues *Anchorage Times,*" *Editor & Publisher,* 110 (26 February 1977): 10;

Alex Beam, "After a 10-year Nap, the *Christian Science Monitor* Wakes Up," *Business Week,* no. 2896 (27 May 1985): 114–118;

Beam, "Monitor Editor Resigns," *Boston Globe,* 15 November 1988, p. 1;

Bruce Butterfield, "Kay Fanning, a Risk Taker," *Boston Globe,* 15 November 1988, p. 47;

Stuart Emmrich, "There's Kay Fanning, out on a New Frontier Again," *Advertising Age,* 55 (2 January 1984): M4–M5, M21;

Debra Gersh, "Using Research to Build Readership," *Editor & Publisher,* 119 (27 December 1986): 16;

William A. Henry III, "Giving Rebirth to the *Monitor,*" *Time,* 122 (10 October 1983): 57;

Alex Jones, "Woman Is to Head Editors' Society," *New York Times,* 11 April 1987, p. 7;

Andrew Radolf, "Another Editor Resigns," *Editor & Publisher,* 121 (19 November 1988): 9–10;

Carla Marie Rupp, "Pulitzer Gold Medal Won by *Anchorage Daily News,*" *Editor & Publisher,* 109 (8 May 1976): 24;

Arlie Schardt, "The Press War in Alaska," *Newsweek,* 95 (31 March 1980): 72;

Suzanne Wilding, "The Lady Is a Newspaperman," *Town & Country,* 140 (January 1986): 114–116, 166–167;

Laurence Zuckerman, "Who's Running the Newsroom?," *Time,* 132 (28 November 1988): 88–89.

Marshall Field III

(28 September 1893 – 8 November 1956)

Marshall Field IV

(15 June 1916 – 18 September 1965)

Marshall Field V

(13 May 1941 –   )

Mary Ann Weston
Northwestern University

MAJOR POSITIONS HELD: **Marshall Field III:** Owner and publisher, *PM* (1940–1948); owner and publisher, *Chicago Sun* (1941–1948); president, Field Enterprises, Inc. (1944–1956); owner and publisher, *Chicago Times* (1947–1948); owner and publisher, *Chicago Sun-Times* (1948–1950).

Marshall Field IV: Editor and publisher, *Chicago Sun-Times* (1950–1965); president (1956–1965), chairman of the board (1964–1965), Field Enterprises, Inc.; president and publisher, *Chicago Daily News* (1959–1965).

Marshall Field V: Publisher, *Chicago Sun-Times* (1969–1980); publisher, *Chicago Daily News* (1969–1978); chairman of the board, Field Enterprises, Inc. (1972–1984).

BOOK: *Freedom Is More Than a Word,* by Marshall Field III (Chicago: University of Chicago Press, 1945).

Marshall Field III, IV, and V, heirs to the fortune of the first Marshall Field, a retailing magnate, were important figures in the newspaper world of Chicago and, in the case of Marshall Field III, of New York. Marshall Field III, grandson of the founder of the department store that still bears the family name, was the first of the family to engage in journalism. He used tens of millions of dollars from his inheritance to publish newspapers that would advance his idealistic liberal philosophy, but he was reluctant to take a direct hand in their editorial di-

rection. All three Marshall Fields were considered gentlemanly and rather reticent; all three felt keenly the responsibility of having inherited great wealth.

Marshall Field III, one of the world's richest men during his lifetime, entered newspapering in 1940, when he was forty-six. He invested two hundred thousand dollars in the venture that was to become *PM,* a liberal New York newspaper that accepted no advertising. In October of that year Field bought out the struggling paper's other investors and became its primary financial backer. The following year he launched the *Chicago Sun,* conceived as an independent newspaper that would serve as a counterweight to the reactionary and isolationist *Chicago Tribune,* then the city's only morning newspaper. For Field, journalism was the culmination of a remarkable personal transformation that took him far from the role expected of one of his lineage – a sheltered life of wealth and privilege – to the unabashed liberalism that led some, according to author John Tebbel, to brand him a "traitor to his class."

Marshall Field III was born in Chicago, the son of Marshall Field II and Albertine Huck Field. His name and the fortune that accompanied it not only gave him the wherewithal to make a mark in the world but also burdened him with the responsibility of passing on one of the world's great fortunes to future generations. As a young child Field was taught by private tutors; he later attended the Colter School in Chicago. When he was twelve, two tragedies struck that were to change his life. His father died of a self-inflicted gunshot wound, possibly a suicide. Two months later his grandfather died of pneumonia.

Field had been closer in some ways to his grandfather than to his melancholy father. His grandfather, the severe and taciturn merchant prince, had sat up nights with young Marshall when he was ill.

Soon after these deaths Albertine took Marshall, his brother, and his sister to England. Field was educated at Eton and at Trinity College, Cambridge. At Eton he "discovered, by way of *noblesse oblige,* what social conscience was," though "he never realized that until twenty years had passed," according to his biographer Stephen Becker. Field returned to America when he was twenty-one.

When the United States entered World War I, Field prevailed upon the commander of the First Illinois Cavalry to allow him to enlist, despite a childhood history of rheumatic fever. He entered as a private in the unit, which later became the 122d Field Artillery, 33d Division. He served as a field artillery captain in France, where he participated in the Saint-Mihiel and Meuse-Argonne offensives and was awarded the Silver Star for gallantry in action. Robert J. Casey of the *Chicago Daily News* wrote that Field was "probably the most unobtrusive millionaire who ever curried a horse for thirty dollars a month."

After the war he "led a life common to well-bred, well-educated multi-millionaire men of fashion," as the *New York Times* commented in his obituary. He engaged in hunting, yachting, and riding; established an English-style estate, Caumsett, on Long Island; and acquired a thirteen-thousand-acre "quail lodge" in South Carolina. A 1934 article about him in *Country Life* magazine was titled "Full Length Portrait of a Country Gentleman." Field had married Evelyn Marshall in 1915, and the couple had three children: Marshall IV, Barbara, and Bettine. They were divorced in 1930; Field married Audrey James Coats the same year. That marriage ended four years later.

Partly because of these personal disappointments and partly because of the social and economic chaos he saw around him during the Depression, Field came to question himself and his way of life. In 1934 he turned to psychoanalysis as a means of finding answers. His analyst was Dr. Gregory Zilboorg, a native of Russia who had been in the United States since 1919. Field emerged from analysis a genuinely changed man, with new direction and faith in himself. In 1935 he left the investment-banking firm of Field, Glore and Company, of which he was senior partner, and by 1936 he was an ardent New Dealer with an interest in liberal causes. In 1936 he was also married a third time, to Ruth Pruyn Phipps, who took an active interest in his

Marshall Field III

causes. The couple had two daughters: Phyllis and Fiona.

Both his social concern and, perhaps, his naiveté were revealed in 1941 when he remarked, "I happen to have been left a great deal of money. I don't know what is going to happen to it, and I don't give a damn. If I cannot make myself worthy of three square meals a day, I don't deserve them." The quote brought Field considerable ridicule, and it was not until two years later that he explained that the statement had been taken out of context. His point had been that he would not encourage fascism in order to keep his fortune.

PM, the brainchild of Ralph Ingersoll, was editorially liberal and journalistically exciting, though erratic. The newspaper emphasized photography and assigned news stories to departments, as did *Time* magazine, of which Ingersoll had been publisher. While its contentiously left-leaning policies and occasionally brilliant writing earned *PM* a core of loyal readers, it was not large enough to sustain the tabloid without advertising. And Ingersoll was berated for having Communists on the staff.

In October 1940, when the paper was four months old, circulation hovered just above one hundred thousand, less than half of what was needed to break even. Field stepped in and bought out the other investors at twenty cents on the dollar. Though he visited the paper often, he did not try to influence it editorially. Some of the paper's stances were undoubtedly more radical than those Field would have taken, but he did not intervene. Only once did he take a hand in the paper's operation, when Ingersoll, who had fervently advocated American intervention in World War II, was called up for the draft in 1942, a move that was seen by some as discriminatory because other editors were being given exemptions. Without Ingersoll's knowledge, Field wrote Gen. Lewis Hershey, director of Selective Service, requesting an exemption, which was granted at the last moment. Ingersoll, who did not help his case by crusading on his own behalf in *PM*, eventually enlisted.

Before the *PM* experiment ended in 1948, Field poured some $5 million into the paper and was labeled by *Time* as "the sugar daddy of New Deal journalism," but he saw the venture as more than a journalistic fling by a rich man. In his book, *Freedom Is More Than a Word* (1945), he wrote of the importance of *PM* as a crusader for justice: "The American public learned that *PM* is the place where people can get a hearing if they have a just cause. This is true whether they represent racial or religious minorities, pro-labor groups, independent businessmen fighting the monopolists, consumers, or individuals deprived of civil liberties in one way or another. *PM* became and remains the focus of whatever cries out for courage against injustice."

If Field remained detached from the editorial operations of *PM,* he was far more involved in his next journalistic venture, the creation of a morning newspaper in Chicago to compete with Col. Robert R. McCormick's *Tribune,* described as "outrageously right-wing, and often unforgivably vicious toward its political antagonists" by Turner Catledge in *My Life and "The Times"* (1971). The confrontation between the newspapers of these two rich and powerful men was described as "Homeric" by the *New York Times.* Legend had it that Marshall Field I had loaned money to Joseph Medill, McCormick's grandfather, to buy control of the *Tribune* in 1874. Field's paper, the *Sun,* first appeared on 4 December 1941. It was printed on the presses of the afternoon *Daily News,* then owned by Col. Frank Knox, President Franklin D. Roosevelt's secretary of the navy.

The masthead on the editorial page carried this pledge: "The news columns shall be fair and accurate; the editorial columns shall be honest and just in the expression of conscientious opinion." It was not only a declaration of Field's journalistic intentions but an implicit jab at the *Tribune,* whose news columns were often outrageously slanted. De-

Marshall Field III and his wife, Ruth (foreground), with executives of PM, *1944*

spite Field's wealth and good intentions, the early months of the *Sun* were disappointing. The haste with which the paper was put together was a major source of its early difficulties. Field wanted to rush his paper into production in order for it to be a voice for intervention in the European war against Adolf Hitler and for support of the Roosevelt administration against the fulminations of the *Tribune.* The first cause evaporated three days after the *Sun* appeared, when the Japanese bombed Pearl Harbor and America entered the war. Nevertheless, Field insisted that the paper was not founded solely on the issue of intervention and that Chicago needed an independent morning paper.

There were other problems with the new venture. It lacked local roots and tradition in a town with a long, lusty newspaper history. Many of the top staff were out-of-towners, among them the publisher, Silliman Evans from the *Nashville Tennessean,* who was not only unfamiliar with Chicago but also considerably more conservative than Field. Other staffers knew the city but were not in tune with Field's liberal views. Finally there was Field himself. Diffident and self-effacing, he hovered in the background and let the men he hired take charge, feeling he did not have enough newspaper experience to direct the operation.

Catledge, onetime editor of the *Sun,* wrote in his memoir that Field "should have become an active, deeply involved publisher. His lack of newspaper experience could have been overcome by his good instincts, his intelligence, and his intimate knowledge of Chicago. But deep involvement was not Field's style. He was a shy, modest, self-effacing man. . . . I liked and respected Field, but he lacked the temperament to be a great newspaper publisher." Becker wrote that the *Sun* "suffered not from the presence of a bumbling owner, but from the reserved modesty of its very capable owner. What the newspaper needed for the next ten years was not less Field, but more."

Curiosity and pent-up demand for an alternative to the *Tribune* brought the *Sun* first-day sales of nearly nine hundred thousand. However, circulation dropped to less than a third of that figure. Part of the problem was the new paper's difficulty in getting newsstands to carry it and getting the local carriers association to distribute it. Though the *Tribune* was by far the dominant newspaper in Chicago, with a circulation of more than a million in 1941, McCormick did not ignore his new rival. Two incidents epitomize his clash with Field. In 1942, during the controversy over Ingersoll and the draft in New York, McCormick attacked Field as a "slacker. He is of age to volunteer [for military service]," he wrote in the *Tribune.* "The term to fit to him and to all the herd of hysterical effeminates is coward." Field, a decorated World War I veteran, replied to this astounding charge in a one-line editorial: "You are getting rattled, Colonel McCormick."

More damaging than hysterical editorials was denial to the *Sun* of use of the Associated Press wire service. The AP, a cooperative organization, was by far the country's largest news-gathering agency. In 1941 its bylaws provided that a new newspaper could acquire an AP franchise only if all other member newspapers in the same city agreed. This put McCormick's *Tribune* in a position to veto its rival's application for AP membership. At the time such a veto could be overridden only by a four-fifths vote of the members. Even if it succeeded in overriding the veto, the new newspaper would have to pay an amount equal to the cumulative annual assessments of all the newspapers in its city since 1900. In the case of the *Sun,* this would have amounted to about $330,000 over its annual assessment.

Field's lawyers filed a complaint with the government that the AP was in violation of antitrust laws; the Justice Department began a civil action against the AP in 1942. Joining in the defense of the AP were many newspaper publishers, the vast majority of whom were members of the wire service. They argued that subjecting the AP to antitrust laws was an unconstitutional interference with freedom of the press, and that it was not a monopoly because other wire services were available. In 1945 the Supreme Court decided, five to three, for the Justice Department, opening the way for the *Sun* and other papers in similar circumstances to become members of the AP. In his majority opinion Justice Hugo L. Black wrote, "The First Amendment affords not the slightest support for the contention that a combination to restrain trade in news and views has any constitutional immunity."

The *Sun* had been printed on the presses of the *Daily News* for a low annual rent that started at two hundred thousand dollars. When John S. Knight bought the *Daily News* in 1944 after Knox's death, he greatly increased Field's rent. Field could have afforded the higher charge: when he reached his fiftieth birthday on 28 September 1943, he came into the remainder of the fortune his grandfather had left, some $75 million. Nevertheless, after his experience with *PM,* Field had determined that his Chicago newspaper venture would eventually pay its own way. Such thoughts led him to the *Chicago Times,* described by *Time* magazine as a "peppy, popular and money-making" afternoon tabloid. It had been the only newspaper in Chicago to support Roosevelt and the New Deal consistently and enthusiastically. Its founder and publisher, Samuel Emory Thomason, died in March 1944, and the paper passed to its able and respected editor, Richard Finnegan.

In August 1947 Field bought the *Times* for $5,339,000 and assumed its $2.5 million debentures to International Paper Company. Because the presses at the *Times* were configured for tabloid production, the *Sun* became a tabloid, much to the outrage of some of its readers, who thought such papers lacked dignity. After several months of trying to put out the *Sun* in the morning, the *Times* in the afternoon, and a combined edition on Sundays, the two papers were merged into a morning tabloid, the *Sun-Times,* in 1948.

By 1950 Field was ready to retire from the *Sun-Times* and turn its operation over to Marshall IV. The paper was still losing money; Field reportedly poured some $25 million into the venture before it eventually became profitable. Increasingly, Marshall Field III spent his time in New York, though he continued to be active in Field Enterprises, the corporation he established in 1944. In addition to the *Sun-Times,* its holdings included *Parade,* a Sunday magazine supplement; Simon and Schuster and Pocket Books; World Book Encyclopedia; Childcraft children's books; and radio stations. He was also active in many philanthropies, including the New York Philharmonic Society, the Metropolitan Opera Association of New York, the Chicago Museum of Natural History (later named the Field Museum), and the University of Chicago. In 1940 he set up the Field Foundation to administer grants in the areas of race relations and child welfare. He was one of the founders of Roosevelt University in Chicago.

Marshall Field III died of a brain tumor at age sixty-three on 8 November 1956 in New York. His nature and English schooling made him a true gentleman, reserved and civilized in his dealings. He became a man of lofty ideals who sincerely tried to use his wealth for the betterment of society as he saw it. These qualities, however admirable, are not those required to win in the rough-and-tumble of newspaper wars. While Field's liberal outlook and deep pockets assured his *Sun-Times* a modest success, his diffident nature forestalled the kind of greatness a more forceful publisher might have achieved.

Marshall Field IV, who for most of his life was known as Marshall Field, Jr., was born in New York City on 15 June 1916 to Marshall Field III and Evelyn Marshall Field. Marshall Field III was a good, if indulgent, parent who taught his three children by this first marriage to ride, shoot, fish, and play bridge and chess in the 1920s. Though the children lived a luxurious life at the family estate, Caumsett, their "education was serious and disciplined," according to Becker.

Marshall, Jr., an excellent student, was educated at the Fay School in Southboro, Massachusetts, and St. Paul's School in Concord, New Hampshire. He was graduated magna cum laude from Harvard University in 1938 with a B.A. in English. His senior honors thesis, "Tears of Eternity," was an analysis of A. E. Housman's poetry. In 1941 he was graduated third in his class from the University of Virginia Law School, where he was president of his class and an editor of the law review. After law school he clerked for Armistead M. Dobie, judge of the Fourth U.S. Circuit Court of Appeals. The summer before Field entered Harvard, he left the sheltered confines of his youth and spent five weeks working in a steel mill under the name Mike Farley. Later, his father returned to the company the seventy-seven dollars the younger Field had earned, to be given to an unemployed steel worker.

In 1938 Field married Joanne Bass. They had two children, Marshall V and Joanne, before the marriage ended in divorce in 1947. Though he was married and a father, Field volunteered for the navy after the bombing of Pearl Harbor. He turned down an ensign's commission to enlist as a midshipman but was later recommissioned as an ensign. He served aboard the USS *Enterprise* as a gunnery officer and was wounded twice during the Battle of Santa Cruz in October 1942. He was in a dozen battles in the Pacific and was awarded the Purple Heart, the Silver Star, and a Presidential Citation.

His brushes with death in battle changed Field and made him focus on future priorities, which shifted from the law to journalism. In a publication for his Harvard class's twenty-fifth anniversary, he wrote, "The war made a lot of things look different. My basic interests were unchanged, but it seemed to me that I could bring whatever interest I had in government and politics to bear better through journalism and mass media than through the law."

After the war he went to Chicago to learn newspapering from the bottom up at the *Sun-Times,* selling classified advertising and helping load papers onto delivery trucks. He later covered the police beat and reported from the paper's Washington and London bureaus. Within four years he had worked his way through most of the paper's departments into management. In October 1950 he became editor and publisher of the *Sun-Times* when his father retired.

Marshall Field IV moved the paper in a more conservative editorial direction, moderating if not abandoning the liberalism that was the cornerstone of his father's beliefs. Only once did the elder Field take public issue with his son's policies. In 1952, when the *Sun-Times* became an early supporter of Dwight D. Eisenhower for president, Marshall Field III wrote a letter to his son that was published in the paper's letters column on 9 October. In it the elder Field politely differed with his son's choice and declared his own support for Adlai Stevenson. "This letter is, of course, in no way intended as an effort to influence your attitude. But I did wish to clear up the confusion which I know exists, and I am certain that you respect my independence as I admire yours," he concluded.

Marshall Field IV was perhaps the most avid newspaperman of the three generations of Fields who engaged in journalism. In 1962 he told an interviewer, "This is what I'd like, above all else, to earn for my tombstone, 'He was a good newspaperman.' " Marshall Field V, in an interview for the Northwestern University Journalism Oral History Project at the Chicago Historical Society, said his father "loved the newspaper business. He lived for the newspaper business." Marshall Field IV's conservative management put the *Sun-Times* in the black, and his editorial guidance, though he left day-to-day decisions to others, won his papers a respected place in Chicago journal-

Marshall Field IV

ism. Yet emotional problems sometimes kept him from active leadership of the enterprise.

If his father was an unapologetic idealist, Marshall Field IV tempered his idealism with a sharp eye on the ledger book: "We're in this as a public service, and not primarily to make a profit. However, our profit picture is satisfactory." He worked to make the *Sun-Times* attractive to a politically moderate "class and mass" audience. "I hope the paper will appeal to and will be read by independents and the liberal elements of the Republican party as well as the Democratic party," he told *Editor & Publisher* in 1950. Field described himself as a "sensibly conservative Republican" who nevertheless, after agonizing privately over his decision, endorsed a Democrat, Lyndon B. Johnson, for the presidency in 1964. Writing in the *Saturday Review,* Kenneth McArdle, associate editor of the *Chicago Daily News,* said Field made the *Sun-Times* "one of the hardest-hitting, brightest-reading, yet most responsible and serious newspapers in the nation" while building its circulation and advertising.

Field was generally described as being soft-spoken and unpretentious. *Time* said he had "the mild, diffident mien of a church usher." He worked in shirtsleeves in the office and was on a first-name basis with many staff members. When Field was touring the city room of the *Chicago Daily News* shortly after buying that paper in 1959, a columnist complained to him about the "disreputable" condition of his typewriter. The next day Field lugged in his own typewriter for the columnist.

In 1950 Field married Katherine Woodruff, daughter of a Joliet, Illinois, banker. The couple had three children: Frederick Woodruff, Katherine Woodruff, and Barbara Woodruff. They divorced in 1963. During the mid 1950s Field suffered several heavy emotional blows. In late 1955 ground had been broken for a $21 million building to house the *Sun-Times.* While construction was under way, Field engaged in grueling but unsuccessful dealings to buy the Hearst afternoon newspaper, the *American,* losing out to the *Tribune.* While negotiating for the purchase of the *American,* Field was flying nightly to New York to be at the bedside of his dying father. The accumulated grief at his father's death, added responsibility for stewardship of the family fortune, and disappointment at the failed newspaper negotiations resulted in Field's hospitalization for six months for what was then called a nervous breakdown.

In 1959 Field bought the *Chicago Daily News* from Knight for $24 million. He partially financed the transaction by selling *Parade.* His father had coveted the distinguished *Daily News,* a Chicago institution since 1876, but ended up purchasing the *Times.* The sale was somewhat controversial, because the profits for the *Daily News* were slim, and prospects

Chicago Daily News *executive editor Basil "Stuffy" Walters, columnist Jack Mabley, and Marshall Field IV, 1960. When Mabley complained about his typewriter in a column, Field gave him his.*

for afternoon newspapers were not bright. In a January 1959 interview with *Advertising Age,* he defended the acquisition: "I'm enormously interested in public service, and I'm sentimental about Chicago. But I'm not running a sentimental operation here. I insist on making a profit, and from that standpoint I think we got a good buy."

Field enlarged the editorial staffs of both newspapers and increased the news holes. In 1963 the *Daily News* won its twelfth Pulitzer Prize and went on to win three more under Field ownership. The sale left Chicago, which had had five major daily newspaper publishers in 1946, with two: the *Tribune* with its morning *Tribune* and afternoon *American,* and Field Enterprises with the morning *Sun-Times* and afternoon *Daily News.*

When his father died, Marshall Field IV became president of Field Enterprises and was named chairman of the board in 1964. In addition to the two Chicago newspapers, the corporation still owned World Book Encyclopedia and other educational publications; a television station; Publishers Newspaper Syndicate, which distributed news, features, and comic strips to daily and weekly newspa-

pers; and a paper manufacturing company. Field was also active in civic and philanthropic organizations, serving as a trustee of the University of Chicago, the Chicago Natural History Museum, the Art Institute of Chicago, and Presbyterian–St. Luke's Hospital.

The mental illness that caused Field's hospitalization at the time of his father's death continued to plague him in later years. As *Time* put it in October 1965, "Since 1963 he had been less and less able to exercise command." The management of Field's newspapers and other enterprises was in the hands of corporate executives during that period. However, he married in 1964 for a third time, to Julia Lynne Templeton. The couple had a daughter, Corinne Templeton.

On 18 September 1965 Field died at age forty-nine at his home in Chicago. An autopsy showed the cause of death as acute congestive heart failure complicated by a viral infection of the heart lining. Under terms of a trust set up by Marshall Field III, most of the stock in Field Enterprises was to be divided equally between his two grandsons, Marshall Field V

George B. Young, Marshall Field V, and Edward I. Farley, 1965

and Frederick Woodruff Field, when each turned twenty-five. Marshall Field V was twenty-four when his father died; his half brother was thirteen.

When his father died, Marshall Field V was working in the circulation department of the *New York Herald Tribune*. The younger Field came to Chicago immediately and prepared to step into the family business, even though, as he later remarked, "I never saw Chicago until my father died. . . . I couldn't have told you where State Street was." He was the third and last generation of Fields to direct the Chicago newspapers. An affable and direct man, he presided over what was perhaps the peak of circulation and prestige for the *Sun-Times,* closed the *Daily News,* and later sold the *Sun-Times* to Australian publisher Rupert Murdoch.

Marshall V was born on 13 May 1941 in Charlottesville, Virginia, the son of Marshall Field IV and his first wife, Joanne Bass Field. He was educated at St. Albans School in Washington, D.C., and Deerfield Academy in Deerfield, Massachusetts. He was graduated from Harvard University in 1963 with a degree in fine arts and served on active duty with the army from July to December 1964. His first excursion into journalism was at Harvard, where he worked on the *Lampoon.* One summer during college he worked in

the editorial department at the *Boston Globe,* and after graduation he took a job at Random House, the New York book publisher, before going to the *Herald-Tribune.* In 1964 he married Joan Best Connelly; they had a son, Marshall Field VI. The marriage ended in divorce in 1969.

In Chicago, Field was supposed to undergo a five-year, department-by-department training program to prepare him to lead the Field newspapers. He completed the training in four years and in 1969 was named publisher of the *Sun-Times* and *Daily News.* At twenty-eight he was the youngest publisher of a major newspaper in the United States. At the time Field described himself as a "very liberal Republican," more so than his father but less so than his grandfather.

Field, who admitted he was an "abysmal" writer, preferred to manage his newspapers rather than engage in journalism himself. He entrusted the day-to-day operations to his editors, particularly James Hoge, who became editor in chief of the *Sun-Times* and the *Daily News* in 1976. In 1980 Field relinquished the post of *Sun-Times* publisher and named Hoge to the position. Hoge was the first non-Field publisher in the paper's history. Under Field's ownership the *Sun-Times* won six Pulitzer Prizes and became a well-respected newspaper with a national reputation. In 1977 the paper embarked on one of

CHICAGO
SUN-TIMES

WEATHER
Mostly sunny and continued cold Thursday. High 6 to 12. See Page 96.

. 1963 by Field Enterprises, Inc.

FINAL
TURF EDITION

Vol. 16, No. 275   Phone 321-3000   THURSDAY, DECEMBER 19, 1963   120 Pages—7 Cents.

We're Frozen

7 Days Of It; 3 More To Go

A two-dimensional record for a December freeze was set in the Chicago area early Thursday as below-zero temperatures marked the weather's turn from cold to colder.

It was the longest and deepest December freeze in these parts, said the weather bureau —seven straight days of zero or subzero temperatures. The previous such record for the month was five straight days in 1945.

With the mercury still on the early morning descent Thursday, the temperature was 9 below at O'Hare Airport and 7 below at Midway Airport, where the official reading is taken. Lower readings were reported in suburbs, where the weather bureau expected the mercury to reach 15 below.

There were prospects that the record might be extended indefinitely.

A long-range forecast envisioned low temperatures near zero for Friday, Saturday and Sunday.

While Chicagoans cranked

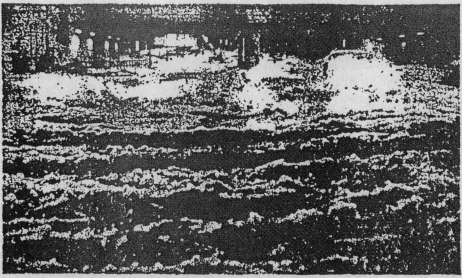

Sea of ice greets motorists on Cicero Av. near 55th after water main break. (Sun-Times Photo by Larry Nocerino)

Other pictures on Page 2

ed with the cold's deepening bite, Muskegon, Mich., struggled through a 24-hour storm that dumped 34 inches of snow and threatened to pile up at least three more inches.

Mountainous drifts rose in near-blizzard conditions to block streets and create emergencies in the Lake Michigan industrial-port city's area of 100,000 residents.

Muskegon Fire Chief Deni-als Ward urged special precautions against fire because of the difficulty of moving fire-fighting equipment. Snowplows kept Muskegon's main arteries passable, but few side streets were cleared.

With the storm, Muskegon's December snowfall records for one hour, 48 hours and one week were rewritten.

In the Chicago area, the cold was blamed for the bursting of two water mains.

A break in a 30-inch main under 55th, between Cicero and Laramie caused the Chicago Transit Authority to re-route bus traffic in the flooded area.

Water pressure was reduced in a one-mile radius as city crews sought to repair the break. But no water shortage developed anywhere in the area served by the mains, said Thomas Allen, acting assistant

Turn to Page 2

SURPLUS OF MINUSES

Unofficial temperatures in suburban communities early Thursday:

Arlington Hgts.	-5	Hinsdale	-2	Naperville	-6
Aurora	-6	Highland Park	-10	Oak Lawn	-8
Barrington	11	Hinsdale	-7	Oak Park	-5
Batavia	-7	Homewood	-7	Park Forest	-9
Blue Island	-8	Joliet	-10	Park Ridge	-10
Calumet City	7	LaGrange	-14	River Grove	-9
Des Plaines	-9	Lake Forest	-6	Skokie	-7
Downers Grove	-8	Libertyville	-12	West Springs	-7
Elgin	12	Maywood	-14	Wheeling	10
Gary	-6	Morton Grove	-9	Wilmette	-7
Glenview	12	Mount Prospect	-8	Zion	-6

How 'Perfect' Kidnaping Failed

By Sandy Smith
Sun-Times Correspondent

LOS ANGELES—The Federal Bureau of Investigation has learned that Barry Worthington Keenan, 23, planned the $240,000 ransom kidnaping of Frank Sinatra Jr. as a perfect crime.

An FBI probe revealed the abduction was plotted over the last six months by Keenan, son of a Los Angeles stockbroker.

An obsession for money impelled Keenan to polish his plans for the kidnaping until

he believed the crime was so perfect that he never would be caught, The Sun-Times learned.

Several times since June, Keenan and his co-conspirators stalked the 19-year-old singer in an attempt to kidnap him.

In one instance, they were prepared to snatch Sinatra when he appeared at a night club here. For undisclosed reasons, their plans went awry.

Keenan finally put his plan into action Dec. 8, kidnaping Sinatra from a motel at Lake Tahoe, on the California-Nevada border.

The abduction showed flashes of cunning but it was far from perfect. The FBI seized Keenan and his partners, Joseph C. Amsler, 23, and John R. Irwin, 42, soon after they collected the ransom from film star Frank Sinatra Sr.

Young Sinatra was released unharmed Dec. 11. Within 48 hours, all of the ransom except $6,000 was recovered, and the three conspirators were jailed on kidnaping charges.

A wrangle among the Sinatra kidnapers over the $240,000

Turn to Page 43

Front page of the Chicago Sun-Times, *19 December 1963*

journalism's most controversial investigations when it bought a Chicago tavern, the Mirage, which was run by a team of undercover journalists. The resulting series of stories documented the corruption among city employees that victimized small-business owners.

In July 1974 *Time* described Field as a "tough, profit-minded executive." This toughness was tested in 1978 when Field decided to close the 102-year-old *Daily News,* which was renowned for its staff of foreign correspondents and for its writers and reporters, such as Georgie Anne Geyer and Mike Royko. Field personally took responsibility for the decision, explaining that the afternoon paper's circulation and advertising had been declining and that the paper had lost $11 million in its last year of publication.

Field married in 1972 for a second time, to Jamee Beckwith Jacobs. The couple had three daughters: Jamee Christine, Stephanie Caroline, and Abigail Beckwith. In 1972 he assumed the title of chairman of the board of Field Enterprises. Under Field's leadership the corporation sold World Book Encyclopedia and ventured into real estate and other areas.

When Frederick (Ted) Field reached age twenty-five in 1977, the voting stock in Field Enterprises was split equally between him and Marshall V. The arrangement "creates a deliberate deadlock that forces us to get along whether we want to or not," Marshall Field told the *Wall Street Journal* in 1978. The half brothers ran the corporation jointly until 1983, when Frederick sought its liquidation. The *Sun-Times* and other Field Enterprises assets were sold in early 1984 to Murdoch for about $100 million.

The sale to Murdoch, who had a reputation for sensationalism, led Hoge and other *Sun-Times* staff members – including Royko, who had moved to the *Sun-Times* when the *Daily News* died – to leave the paper. About two years later Robert E. Page, installed by Murdoch as publisher of the *Sun-Times,* led a group of investors that acquired the paper from Murdoch for $145 million. In 1988 Page was forced out, and the following year the investors brought in Sam McKeel, formerly of the *Philadelphia Inquirer,* as president and chief executive officer. Dennis A. Britton, formerly of the *Los Angeles Times,* was named editor. During its changes in leadership the paper drifted editorially and lost circulation.

Marshall Field V, in deciding with his half brother to sell the *Sun-Times* and liquidate Field Enterprises, indicated that his greater responsibility was to the family, not its newspapers. This was a view he often expressed. "The only real tradition in my family," he told *Newsweek* in September 1969, "is that each successive generation shouldn't blow it. If you can leave the family fortune a little bigger than you found it, well, that's what counts."

Biography:

Stephen Becker, *Marshall Field III: A Biography* (New York: Simon & Schuster, 1964).

References:

George A. Brandenburg, "Field Jr. Moves Ahead as Vigorous Publisher," *Editor & Publisher,* 94 (25 November 1961): 13, 52, 54;

"Chicago Inheritance," *Time,* 86 (1 October 1965): 69;

Edwin Darby, *The Fortune Builders* (Garden City, N.Y.: Doubleday, 1986);

"Field at Fifty," *New Yorker,* 19 (13 November 1943): 20–21;

"Field Bids to Fan Chicago Newspaper War," *Business Week,* no. 1539 (28 February 1959): 56–63;

"Field Times," *Newsweek,* 30 (4 August 1947): 82–84;

Frederick C. Klein and Harlan Byrne, "Brothers Share Control of Field Enterprises Through Unusual Pact," *Wall Street Journal,* 17 August 1978, pp. 1, 17;

"Marshall Field Dies at Age of 63," *New York Times,* 9 November 1956, p. 29;

Kenneth McArdle, "Behind the Image," *Saturday Review,* 48 (9 October 1965): 72;

Dan Rottenberg, "Crackup," *Chicago* (September 1983): 179–185;

John Tebbel, *The Marshall Fields: A Study in Wealth* (New York: Dutton, 1947);

"Two Soldiers," *Time,* 40 (10 August 1942): 51;

"We're in This as a Public Service," *Printers' Ink,* 272 (26 August 1960): 40–42;

Willson Whitman, "Marshall Field: The Native's Return," *New Republic,* 105 (3 November 1941): 581–583.

Papers:

Material on Marshall Field III, IV, and V is in the archives of the Field Corporation, Chicago.

Wes Gallagher

(6 October 1911 –)

Douglass K. Daniel
Ohio University

MAJOR POSITIONS HELD: General executive (1951–1954), assistant general manager (1954–1962), general manager (1962–1976), president and general manager (1972–1976), Associated Press.

BOOK: *Back Door to Berlin: The Full Story of the American Coup in North Africa* (Garden City, N.Y.: Doubleday, Doran, 1943).

OTHER: "Perspective Reporting Versus Humbugability," in *The Press and the Public Interest,* edited by Warren K. Agee (Washington, D.C.: Public Affairs Press, 1968), pp. 208–216;

Ralph S. Izard, Hugh M. Culbertson, and Donald A. Lambert, eds., *Fundamentals of News Reporting,* foreword by Gallagher (Dubuque, Iowa: Kendall/Hunt, 1973), pp. vii–ix.

SELECTED PERIODICAL PUBLICATION – UNCOLLECTED: "The Newsman: Society's Lonesome End," *Saturday Review,* 51 (13 January 1968): 114–115.

For nearly forty years Wes Gallagher helped shape the news reports of the Associated Press (AP), joining the wire service in 1937 as a newsman and retiring in 1976 as its president and general manager. Whether the event was the Allied invasion of Europe or the growing involvement of the United States in Vietnam, Gallagher was active in defining the role of the world's largest news organization in American journalism. As an AP executive he expanded its news coverage and completed its evolution in an age of electronics. While a strong proponent of press freedom, Gallagher also recognized the shortcomings of his profession. In a speech upon his retirement in 1976, he warned his colleagues that the public was becoming "turned off" by the press.

James Wesley Gallagher was born in San Francisco on 6 October 1911 to James and Chispa

Wes Gallagher, 1946 (Associated Press)

Gallagher. He was raised in Santa Cruz, California, by his mother and grandmother after his father, a barber, died during the influenza epidemic of 1917, which killed millions of Americans. Chispa worked at various jobs, including real estate and insurance, during her son's youth. The family moved to nearby Watsonville when Gallagher entered high school.

He played football for Watsonville High School, but the 160-pound teenager suffered a broken bone each season. When an English teacher started a newspaper at the high school, Gallagher turned his attention to journalism. Writing and reporting gave him satisfaction, as they would for the next two decades, and he also believed that journalism served the public. As a high school senior he covered sports as a stringer for the *Watsonville Register-Panjaronian.*

After graduating from high school in 1929, Gallagher wanted to study journalism. He won a football scholarship to Saint Ignatius College, now the University of San Francisco, and played end for the college team during his freshman year. After suffering yet another broken bone, Gallagher gave up football. He worked as a stringer for the *San Francisco Daily News* during his sophomore year.

Short of money amid the deepening Depression, Gallagher left college in 1931. He was hired as both sports editor and janitor at the Watsonville paper, remaining there for the next two years. In addition, he sometimes worked in orchards near Santa Cruz for fifteen cents an hour. He also found part-time jobs at the local YMCA and through the Works Progress Administration.

After saving enough money to return to college, Gallagher and a friend boarded a bus for Baton Rouge, Louisiana, in 1934. His decision to attend Louisiana State University was based as much on the hope of covering important news stories as studying journalism at a prestigious school. Huey Long, the dictatorial Louisiana politician, had become a national figure as both governor and a U.S. senator. Gallagher thought that Long's state would be an interesting place for a journalist, and he also wanted to see a different part of the country. The decision proved to be a wise one for a young man hungry for experience.

While attending school Gallagher worked part-time as a telegraph editor for the *Baton Rouge Advocate and State Times.* The job included delivering a noon newscast on WJBO-AM, a radio station owned by the newspaper, but Gallagher preferred reporting and writing for newspapers. He also became a stringer for the International News Service (INS) during sessions of the Louisiana legislature.

He was reporting on a routine session of the legislature on 8 September 1935 when Long visited the capitol. Long walked by Gallagher on his way out of the chamber, and moments later an assassin's gunfire erupted in the hallway. Gallagher did not sleep for the next four days, covering for the INS both Long's two-day struggle to survive and his funeral.

Long had also brought about Gallagher's first major brush with government interference with the press. He had been working for the *Louisiana State Reveille* for only a few months in the fall of 1934 when a student wrote a letter to the editor that was critical of Long's appointment of an LSU football

player to the state senate. Long ordered state troopers to shut down the student press and seize the papers that had been printed. The biweekly paper was not printed the following week, and student editors refused to allow a censor to approve each issue. Gallagher was among the students who spoke against the crackdown at a rally.

The university's president, James Monroe Smith, eventually expelled five student editors. Twenty-six other students who protested the expulsions were suspended for two weeks. Gallagher and another student escaped expulsion and suspension when the university administration passed over them by mistake. Five years later, to Gallagher's satisfaction, Smith went to prison for embezzling university funds.

After graduating in 1936 with a B.A. in journalism, Gallagher was hired by the *Rochester* (New York) *Democrat and Chronicle.* He spent the next two years as a traveling reporter-photographer for the newspaper. However, Gallagher became impressed by the glamour of foreign reporting and the opportunity it offered to cover major news events. He decided to seek a job with a wire service, which at that time was the best avenue for an overseas assignment.

In 1937 he joined the staff of the AP bureau in Buffalo, New York. At that time Kent Cooper was revitalizing the eighty-nine-year-old wire service, a mission he had begun when he was appointed general manager in 1925. Cooper had reorganized the AP's system of international news gathering and continued to modernize its reporting, including the establishment of its Wirephoto service in 1935.

The two years Gallagher spent in Buffalo introduced him to the workings of the wire service. He also left Buffalo with an anecdote, which he would repeat many times, that pointed out the AP's strict rules of attribution in a news story. On 27 January 1938 ice collapsed the Falls View International Bridge over the Niagara River. When Ed Fales, the correspondent who oversaw the Buffalo bureau, checked in during a trip away from the office, a colleague of Gallagher's informed Fales that the bridge had fallen. "Who says it did?" asked Fales. "Well, now, Ed," the reporter replied, "I walked over to the window and it just ain't there no more." As an executive of the AP, Gallagher would relax such hard-line rules about attribution.

In 1939 Gallagher moved to the AP bureau in Albany to cover the New York legislature, but he stayed there only a few months. The AP was seeking volunteers for the potentially dangerous assignment of covering the war that was breaking out in

Associated Press staff writers Boots Norgaard, Louis Lochner, Wes Gallagher, and Dan De Luce at the war-crime trials in Nuremberg, Germany, December 1945 (Associated Press)

Europe. Being a war correspondent, he later determined, was the ultimate job in journalism. There was always a story to be written, and he enjoyed autonomy in deciding what to cover and how to cover it. The catch, of course, was the strong possibility of becoming a casualty. But war promised to provide the elements of a good story – drama, heroes, and villains. Single and approaching his twenty-eighth birthday, Gallagher had never been out of the United States. He volunteered for an overseas assignment and eventually became a key war correspondent for the AP, covering every aspect of the European theater for hundreds of AP–member newspapers.

Gallagher was dispatched to Finland in February 1940 to report on the Finnish-Russian war. The German army arrived before Gallagher, and he went instead to Copenhagen. When the Germans invaded both Denmark and Norway in April 1940, press operations were quickly shut down. Gallagher then moved on to Stockholm to report on the Norwegian campaign. During the summer of 1940 he

worked out of the AP's Budapest bureau, covering the war in the Balkans. As the German army moved into the region, Gallagher traveled through Romania, Hungary, Bulgaria, Greece, and Yugoslavia.

He was vacationing in Belgrade when Italy invaded Greece, and he took the first train to Athens. Part of the journey was made by handcar when the engineer refused to travel beyond the Greek border. He covered the Albanian front on foot, by mule, and in a roadster for the next four months. After recovering from jaundice, Gallagher reported the invasion of Greece by the Germans. He and another American reporter remained in Athens as the German army approached, and Gallagher's dispatch on 27 April 1941 was the first news that Athens had fallen.

German authorities refused to allow Gallagher to leave Athens for the next two months. He gained a visa to depart on 21 June 1941, the day Germany attacked Russia, but he was placed under arrest by the Gestapo when he arrived in Vienna. Gallagher was released after twenty-four hours and eventually traveled to Lisbon on a refugee train. After three months of reporting on refugees passing through the port city, he arrived in London. He remained there after Pearl Harbor was attacked on 7 December 1941, shifting the focus of his reports from the European governments in exile to the buildup of U.S. forces in England.

When troops under Gen. Dwight D. Eisenhower invaded North Africa in November 1942, more than thirty reporters and photographers accompanied them. Gallagher led the AP field crew and began a six-month assignment that involved both battles and policy developments. In one reporting coup he had an exclusive interview with Adm. Jean Darlan, the controversial Vichy commander who had been designated high commissioner for French North Africa. Eight days later, on 24 December 1942, Gallagher reported Darlan's assassination. He also covered the Casablanca conference in January 1943, during which President Franklin Roosevelt met with other Allied leaders.

Gallagher's assignment in North Africa ended abruptly on 8 May 1943. The jeep in which he was riding outside of Bizerte, Tunisia, swerved to avoid a bicyclist and overturned, pinning him underneath. His back was broken, and he observed the remainder of the campaign from a field hospital before being sent home to recuperate. He later accepted a thirty-five-hundred-dollar advance to write a book about his experiences in North Africa. First, though, Gallagher returned to his overseas duties in the fall of 1943, following troop movements in Italy. As his book's deadline approached, he spent twelve days in a hotel in Morocco writing *Back Door to Berlin: The Full Story of the American Coup in North Africa.* Published that year, it was based largely on his AP dispatches but was neither noteworthy nor a success.

In London, Gallagher began preparing the AP coverage of the Allied invasion of Europe. As other correspondents accompanied troops headed for Normandy on 6 June 1944, Gallagher wrote the AP's lead story. His seventeen-hundred-word dispatch on the beginning of the invasion was carried by newspapers across the United States. The following month he crossed the Channel to collect information for the AP for further invasion coverage. He later reported on the Allied advancements during that autumn, then the Battle of the Bulge in December 1944, continuing to cover the war until the German surrender in May 1945.

He was awarded a Certificate of Merit in June 1945 by Lt. Gen. William H. Simpson for exceptionally meritorious service in coverage of the

Betty and Wes Gallagher after their wedding in Carmel, California, 1 June 1946 (Associated Press)

Ninth Army. In the same year Gallagher was named one of the outstanding young men in the United States by the U.S. Chamber of Commerce. He was thirty-three, and despite nearly five years of covering the war in North Africa and in Europe, he had not lost his taste for overseas reporting.

Cooper asked him to return to the United States to run a domestic bureau. Gallagher, however, was adamant about remaining in Europe. He was named Paris bureau chief for the AP in 1945 and, a few months later, began directing the wire service's coverage of postwar Germany. At the time of his assignment to Germany, *Time* magazine described him as the AP's "cocky, capable" foreign correspondent. In the years that followed he covered the trial of war criminals in Nuremberg, the blockade of Berlin, and West Germany's slow recovery from war.

He also began a new role as husband and father. During his recuperation from the jeep accident, Gallagher had gone on a blind date in New York with actress Betty Kelley. They remained in touch for the next three years. While Gallagher was home on leave from the AP, they were married on 1 June 1946 in Carmel, California. The couple eventually had three children: Bryan and Jane were born

President Lyndon Johnson (bottom row, sixth from left) and Gallagher (bottom row, fourth from left) at an Associated Press luncheon in New York City, 20 April 1964 (Associated Press)

in Germany, and Christine was born after their return to the United States. They made their home in Rye, New York, during Gallagher's years at AP headquarters in Rockefeller Plaza in New York City.

By 1951 Gallagher had spent more than a decade as a foreign correspondent, working in twenty-six countries during and after the war. He felt that he had no other challenges as a writer and decided it was time to try something different, yet he wanted to remain with the AP and move up in the organization. He returned to New York and began a new career in the administration of the wire service when he accepted an offer by the AP's general manager, Frank J. Starzel, to become a general executive in charge of personnel.

Of all his duties with the AP, Gallagher liked dealing with personnel matters the least, particularly the negotiation of contracts with the employees' union. More enjoyable duties were added, however, when he was put in charge of AP Newsfeatures and Wide World Photos. He was named AP's assistant general manager in 1954, but his responsibilities did not change significantly during the eight years that followed.

Gallagher hoped that his next move with the news cooperative would be to executive editor.

Under Starzel's tenure as general manager, the executive editor directed news operations while Starzel looked after the business operations. Starzel announced on 9 October 1962 that he was retiring after fourteen years as general manager. Gallagher, assuming the board of directors would replace Starzel with assistant general manager Harry T. Montgomery, did not expect to be offered the top post.

On the day following Starzel's announcement, however, the board named Gallagher general manager. Twenty-five years after joining the AP, Gallagher, at fifty-one, became its ninth chief executive since the wire service was founded in 1848. (The title of president was added in 1972 to make AP titles more consistent with those of executives elsewhere.) The first major news story of his tenure as general manager, the Cuban missile crisis, began on the next day.

Although he assumed control of a multitude of AP operations and services, Gallagher remained primarily interested in the production of the news reports. His approach to the delegation of responsibilities was nearly opposite to that of Starzel. Within a month of being named general manager he created a new position, deputy general manager, and appointed Montgomery to it. Montgomery would specialize in the business and membership activities of the wire service, allowing Gallagher to focus on the news operations.

Gallagher also decided that when Alan J. Gould retired as executive editor the following January, he would assume those duties as well. He was a tough, demanding boss. In a profile written at the time of Gallagher's retirement, AP writer Saul Pett described him as "King Kong with a crew cut" but added that Gallagher inspired his staff and often dealt with problems with humanity and sensitivity.

As general manager, Gallagher's primary mission was in three areas. First, he ensured that the wire service produced the best news reports possible. Second, he created an atmosphere within the company that encouraged the staff to do its best work, which mainly involved keeping peace between writers and editors. Finally, he protected the staff from outside influence and pressure, whether from publishers or the people and institutions the reporters covered. Gallagher would tell a writer if he had done a poor job rather than allow a publisher or news source to do so.

He met daily with department heads at the AP headquarters in Rockefeller Plaza to discuss the news of the day and how it would be covered. Since he had been involved with decision making on the executive level for the previous ten years, there was no transition period when he became general manager. Nor did he institute a plan for changes within the organization, believing that the best way to manage the AP was to respond to whatever challenges were presented by the news.

Keeping pace with new systems of distributing the news was a constant challenge, and Gallagher ensured that the AP remained at the front of developments in news gathering and dissemination. During his tenure the AP completed its move from mechanical to computerized delivery of news reports. The wire service began transmitting news stories, as well as stock-market tables, by computer in 1963, and a year later the AP became the first press association to compose its wire copy by computer.

In 1970 the AP introduced cathode-ray tubes and facsimile to its computer system, allowing reporters to compose stories on computer terminals and transmit them to other bureaus. Two years later it completed a transition to a nine-city system of regional computer centers and placed computer terminals in nearly all bureaus. By 1974 the AP had developed its Laserphoto system, improving the delivery of photographs. Its DataStream system boosted transmission of news reports from the teletype speed of sixty-six words per minute to twenty words per second via computer.

While fostering such technological developments, Gallagher focused more of his attention on the news reports, believing that what was distributed was more important than the method of distribution. "It is the journalist – the newsman – who is the master of these new communications," Gallagher wrote in a 1969 Saturday Review article. "It is his responsibility to see that these scientific miracles serve mankind to bridge gaps, not create them. This is a tremendous responsibility."

Gallagher considered his most important contribution as AP general manager the greater freedom he allowed its writers. Where there had been restrictions on the length of stories, Gallagher allowed longer pieces to tell stories properly. The AP increased its use of the question-and-answer format, surveys, roundups, and special series that explained changes in society. A special desk that planned and supervised features also was developed under Gallagher's leadership.

As the issues of the day – Vietnam and racism, among others – became more complicated, Gallagher pushed for more analysis by AP writers and the production of multipart series that could deal with issues in greater depth. He created an eleven-member team of investigative reporters in Washington to improve coverage of the federal government. The AP, recognizing that its audience of younger readers was growing, also instituted a Living Today department to produce stories aimed at readers between eighteen and thirty-five.

A book division was developed in late 1963 with the production of The Torch Is Passed, which commemorated the life and death of President John F. Kennedy. Offered exclusively through member newspapers, the book sold more than 4 million copies in the United States and abroad. The wire service later began a series of news annuals that highlighted the previous year's events. It continued to produce news-related books, including a hardcover version of the Warren Commission report on the Kennedy assassination in 1964.

As head of the largest press association, Gallagher was an important supporter of press freedom and responsibility. Early in his tenure he warned that reckless behavior by the press could turn people against it. "Mass reporting of some major news events is becoming so unruly that it puts all media in a bad light," he told AP members in his annual report in 1964. "The profession badly needs a solution and is groping for one." Yet when press restrictions grew tighter during the Vietnam

The top Associated Press managers at a November 1965 meeting in the office of General Manager Wes Gallagher (center): Samuel G. Blackman, Robert Eunson, Robert R. Booth, Harry T. Montgomery, Keith Fuller, Dan De Luce, and Stanley M. Swinton (Associated Press)

War, Gallagher criticized government efforts to suppress the news media. In a statement to the *New York Times* published on 18 March 1965, Gallagher said: "News restrictions imposed by the Pentagon raise serious questions as to whether the American people will be able to get a true picture of the war in Vietnam."

Gallagher's experience as a World War II correspondent helped him direct the AP's coverage of the Vietnam War. He understood as well as anyone the importance of giving reporters in the field a free hand as well as support at home when they were criticized by officials. He made four trips to Vietnam to gain a better understanding of the challenges faced by his reporters and photographers. Although he had tolerated censorship during World War II, Gallagher bristled at efforts by the government to control the news out of Vietnam. The difference, he believed, could be found in the controversial nature of U.S. involvement in Southeast Asia versus the wholehearted support of the fight against Adolf Hitler.

One instance of censorship came when AP correspondent Peter Arnett was accused by military officials of having invented a story about a U.S. raid on a Vietnamese village. The officials retreated from their allegations when Gallagher showed them pictures of the raid taken by the AP. Within days Gallagher and AP president Paul Miller were invited to lunch with President Lyndon Johnson. Instead of criticizing the wire service's coverage, Johnson complimented them. However, the pressure from the Johnson administration on how to report the war never changed. Vietnam also provided Gallagher with a lesson in the dangers of self-censorship. When Arnett reported that American troops had entered a Cambodian village and looted it, Gallagher decided to hold the story. Within days he admitted he had made a mistake.

In a case that ended with a crucial expansion of press protections, Gallagher presided over five years of litigation surrounding a libel suit filed by Edwin A. Walker against the AP. The former major general sued the AP for falsely reporting that he had led a charge of student rioters against federal marshals at the University of Mississippi in 1962 when a black man, James H. Meredith, was admitted to the university. Gallagher refused to settle the suit, although attorneys suggested that doing so would be more economical than taking the case to court.

When a Texas jury awarded Walker eight hundred thousand dollars in a 1964 libel judgment, Gallagher favored an appeal of the decision. In 1967 the Supreme Court overturned the award by a seven to zero vote. The Court, linking the Walker case to the landmark 1964 *New York Times* v. *Sullivan* decision, ruled that public figures come under the same standards as public officials in libel actions. Both have to show actual malice or reckless disregard for the truth, the court ruled, which further protected the news media as they reported controversial issues.

Recognition of Gallagher's contributions to the profession followed his first years as general manager. Awards included a national citation for journalistic merit from the William Allen White Foundation at the University of Kansas, 1967; the George Polk award from Long Island University, 1969; the John Peter Zenger Freedom of the Press award from the University of Arizona, 1969; the Carr Van Anda award from Ohio University, 1969; election to Sigma Delta Chi's Deadline Club Hall of Fame, 1975; and the Medal of Honor from the University of Missouri, 1976.

In accepting the White award on 10 February 1967, Gallagher told an audience at the University of Kansas: "If we, as journalists, use the tools we have at our disposal to put the news in perspective, then the news will have that ring of authenticity, and we won't have to fear any credibility gap. . . . The public will have confidence in the journalist not only as a conveyer of vital information, but as the principal guardian of its freedom as well."

Gallagher reached the AP mandatory retirement age of sixty-five in October 1976. However, he already had turned over the operations of the wire service to his deputy general manager, Keith Fuller, when the board of directors named Fuller as his successor during its annual meeting in May. Gallagher spent the remaining months of his career with the AP as supervisor of the 1976 elections coverage. He and his wife then moved to Santa Barbara, California.

Determined to stay out of AP affairs despite forty years with the wire service, he devoted much of his time to golf and other sports and leisure pursuits. Yet he did not remain out of journalism completely. Two weeks after his retirement from the AP, he was elected to the board of directors of the Gannett Company. He served on the Gannett board for eight years and was among the supporters of Al Neuharth's proposal to publish a national newspaper, *USA TODAY*.

One of Gallagher's sharpest commentaries on the profession in which he worked for almost a half century came in an address to the American Newspaper Publishers Association on 3 May 1976, the same day his retirement was announced. He used the occasion to issue a stern warning to his colleagues about the dangers of his profession's excesses. A binge of investigative reporting had resulted from the Vietnam War and Watergate, he contended, and many readers were viewing the press as "a multi-voiced shrew nitpicking through the debris of government decisions for scandals but not solutions."

He cautioned the publishers that irresponsible use of the First Amendment could result in controls that could permanently damage the free press: "Emphasis and tone are all important to us. Strident, accusatory, and shrewish tones undermine our credibility. Investigative reporting, yes, but on the important subjects that threaten society. It seems to me we need to lower our voices."

Like other general managers in the history of the AP, Gallagher had moved up from the ranks of writers and editors. Moreover, he maintained the writer's perspective when making decisions as an executive of the wire service, largely leaving the details of membership and technological changes to others while concentrating his efforts on the quality of the news reports. Gallagher promoted reporting in depth and with analysis as issues in society warranted more than merely printing official statements and opinions. His preference for developing higher standards in the news reports of the world's largest news organization served the profession of journalism well as it entered the troublesome decades of the 1960s and 1970s.

References:

"The AP Deploys," *Time,* 46 (3 September 1945): 63;

John Consoli, "Gallagher Cautions Press," *Editor & Publisher,* 109 (8 May 1976): 14;

"Newsmen Report U.S. Imposes Curbs on Coverage in Vietnam," *New York Times,* 18 March 1965, p. 4;

Saul Pett, "He Came in Like a Lion. He Goes out Like a Lion," *AP World* (1976): 3–10;

"Report of the General Manager," *Associated Press Annual Report* (1964): 3–23;

"Wes Gallagher of AP: An Extensive Newsman," *Broadcasting,* 85 (9 July 1973): 57.

Edward King Gaylord

(5 March 1873 – 30 May 1974)

and

Edward Lewis Gaylord

(28 May 1919 –)

Carol Sue Humphrey
Oklahoma Baptist University

MAJOR POSITIONS HELD: **Edward King Gaylord**: Part-owner (1897–1901), editorial writer (1901), *Colorado Springs Telegraph;* business manager, *St. Joseph Missouri Gazette* (1902); founder, Oklahoma Publishing Company (1903); general manager, (1903–1918), editor and publisher (1918–1974), *Daily Oklahoman;* owner, *Oklahoma City Times* (1916–1974).

Edward Lewis Gaylord: Executive vice-president and business manager (1954–1974), president and general manager (1974–), Oklahoma Publishing Company; editor and publisher, *Daily Oklahoman* (1974–); owner, *Oklahoma City Times* (1974–1984); chairman of the board, Gaylord Broadcasting Company (1974–1991); chairman of the board, Gaylord Entertainment Corporation (1991–).

For more than ninety years the Gaylords, father and son, have dominated print journalism in Oklahoma. The *Daily Oklahoman* – initially under the leadership of Edward King Gaylord and now under the guidance of Edward Lewis Gaylord – has grown into the leading newspaper throughout the state. Staunchly conservative in their politics and overall outlook on life, the Gaylords, particularly E. K., were progressive in their business activities. Their Oklahoma Publishing Company has been a leader in adopting the latest journalism technology, and the Gaylords successfully promoted the growth and development of Oklahoma and its capital city.

The Gaylords' impact on Oklahoma's development began prior to its admission to statehood in 1907. E. K. Gaylord became part-owner of the *Daily Oklahoman* in Oklahoma City and established the Oklahoma Publishing Company in 1903. He was born on a farm in Muscotah, Kansas, on 5 March 1873 to George Lewis Gaylord and Eunice Edwards Gaylord. E. K. was six years old when his family moved to Colorado. He first became involved in the newspaper business while attending Colorado College in Colorado Springs. During his first two years there he served as the business manager and then the editor of the student newspaper.

In 1897 E. K. and his brother Lewis bought controlling interest in the *Colorado Springs Telegraph,* using money borrowed from a Springfield, Missouri, banker. At first E. K. was not directly involved in the newspaper, choosing to study law at night and to serve as a deputy clerk of court in Cripple Creek, Colorado. However, he joined the staff of the paper in early 1901, serving as advertisement salesman and editorial writer as long as he and Lewis owned the paper. In late 1901 the Gaylord brothers sold the paper, and Lewis purchased the *St. Joseph* (Missouri) *Gazette.* E. K. did not invest in this paper, but he served as business manager for several months prior to moving to Oklahoma.

E. K. was attracted to Oklahoma because of a newspaper story describing the territory as "the land of opportunity." In December 1902 he moved to Oklahoma City, which was still a rough frontier town. In 1903 Gaylord joined with Roy E. Stafford, Ray Dickinson, and Roy McClintock to organize the Oklahoma Publishing Company and to publish the *Daily Oklahoman.* The *Oklahoman* – founded in 1894 by the Reverend Sam W. Small, originally from Georgia – had managed to survive but had not grown much in the eight years of its existence.

Edward King Gaylord

Gaylord served as general manager and was in charge of the advertising, business, and circulation departments, while Stafford controlled editorial operations. Gaylord worked diligently to improve the newspaper and to increase its circulation from 6,732 in 1903 to more than 31,000 at the end of 1908. He directed the paper's move to a new building and its purchase of a new sixteen-page, two-deck press. He also changed the emphasis from commercial printing to the newspaper itself, often calling the printers off of commercial jobs in order to publish news extras.

The extras gained the *Oklahoman* a good reputation in the region and provided the basis for the paper's elevation to a place of prominence and influence. Nicknamed the "Redheaded Daily" because of its practice of printing headlines in red ink, the *Oklahoman* became one of the best-produced papers between Dallas and Kansas City. Gaylord became both editor and publisher of the *Oklahoman* in 1918, when Stafford sold his shares in the Oklahoma Publishing Company.

The use of extras also provided the means for the first major achievement of the *Oklahoman* under Gaylord's leadership – an enormous scoop in 1904.

In February of that year Gaylord ordered a seventh day of Associated Press reports, even though the paper did not publish on Mondays, because he thought the lack of coverage resulted in a gap that might need to be filled quickly at some point in the future. The gamble paid off that very month, for the *Daily Oklahoman* soon published a Sunday-night extra announcing the beginning of the Russo-Japanese War and detailing the disastrous Baltimore waterfront fire. No other paper in the area covered these stories immediately, and the pressrun was triple the normal amount. The paper's reputation was firmly established.

The *Oklahoman* became the leading paper in the state following the demise of the *Guthrie Daily Capital* and the purchase of the *Oklahoma City Times*. The Guthrie paper claimed a circulation of twenty thousand, but Gaylord questioned that figure. He wrote to *Printers' Ink*, stating that the circulation was actually closer to six thousand. Advertisers complained, and D'Arcy Advertising of Saint Louis sent an agent to investigate Gaylord's charges.

The investigator, having been refused access to the records at the *Capital*, came back at night to watch the pressrun and to ascertain the amount of paper and number of mailbags used. His report confirmed the charges. As a result of the ensuing public embarrassment, the *Capital* soon ceased publication. In 1916 Gaylord purchased the *Oklahoma City Times* at a sheriff's auction for thirty thousand dollars. The *Times*, an evening paper, continued to publish, but the *Oklahoman* became the principal newspaper in the area. The two papers merged in 1984.

Although never officially committed to any political party, the *Oklahoman* has always taken a conservative stance. Even though Oklahoma is a predominantly Democratic state, the paper has generally supported the Republican party (the paper has not endorsed a Democratic presidential candidate since 1932). Gaylord was proud of his conservative leanings. He strongly supported the Eighteenth Amendment, and he continued to support Prohibition in Oklahoma after its national repeal in 1933.

Gaylord used his newspaper to drive gamblers and prostitutes out of Oklahoma City. He opposed deficit spending for any reason but also supported a powerful national defense. He strongly opposed labor unions and worked to undermine any union efforts in his company. The few times that unions called strikes against his newspapers, Gaylord always won by breaking up their organizations.

Throughout his involvement in the journalism business Gaylord led the way in innovation. From the purchase of the first two-deck press in 1903, he pushed the *Oklahoman* toward becoming a progressive newspaper in the area of technology. As a ninetieth birthday present to Gaylord, the 5 March 1963 edition of the *Daily Oklahoman* was the first newspaper to be produced entirely with computerized typesetting.

During the Depression, Gaylord faced circulation problems as the railroads cut back service in order to deal with the economic crunch. Rather than fail to deliver the newspaper to its 104,000 subscribers, the Oklahoma Publishing Company developed its own delivery system. The Mistletoe Express, founded in 1931, originally carried only the Oklahoma City newspapers. However, the company slowly became involved in transporting other goods, and by the late 1960s, 75 percent of the trucking company's cargo was in other merchandise. In 1988 the Mistletoe Express was sold to Red Stone Carriers of Colorado.

Gaylord also provided leadership in efforts to develop the paper-mill industry in the South. While serving as president of the Southern Newspaper Publishers Association in 1935, he led a move to study the possibility of manufacturing newsprint from southern pine, previously considered unusable for such a purpose. The first paper mill in Texas was established three years later, with southern publishers guaranteeing to purchase all of its output. Since that time many other mills have been established throughout the southern states.

Gaylord envisioned journalism as more than just the production of a daily newspaper and sought ways to broaden its impact and appeal. In 1911 he founded a farm paper, *The Farmer-Stockman,* which the Oklahoma Publishing Company produced for more than sixty years (it was sold to its employees in 1972). Gaylord entered the broadcasting business in 1928, using the profits from a company oil well to buy Oklahoma City radio station WKY. Originally founded in 1922 and the oldest radio station west of the Mississippi, WKY lost money for several years but soon became a profitable investment. In 1948 WKY received its television license, and it remained the NBC affiliate in the state capital for many years.

The promotion of Oklahoma City was vital to the well-being of Gaylord's newspapers. His efforts in this area first began in 1906 when Gaylord led the fight for the creation of one state out of the Oklahoma and Indian territories and the establishment of its capital at Oklahoma City, rather than at nearby Guthrie, the territorial capital. He continued to trumpet the potential of Oklahoma City throughout his life. He also backed the construction of a massive state highway system, most of which now leads to Oklahoma City. He used the *Oklahoman* to lead a campaign for the construction of several lakes to provide Oklahoma City with an adequate water supply.

His last major success in the economic development of his hometown was the move to locate Tinker Air Force Base near Oklahoma City. The base has grown into one of the largest military installations in the country, a community in and of itself, as well as the state's biggest employer. Because of his tremendous influence in the state, Gaylord became a power to be reckoned with, and his support almost guaranteed success in any venture. Upon the occasion of his one-hundredth birthday in 1973, Gaylord addressed a joint session of the Oklahoma legislature, the first time such an invitation had been extended to a private citizen.

Gaylord represented one of the last of a particular breed of newspapermen: a paternalistic owner/publisher who remained heavily involved in the daily operations of the publication. Even when the employees of the Oklahoma Publishing Company numbered one thousand, E. K. Gaylord knew many of them by name. He developed a reputation for taking a personal interest in the lives of his employees, staging several parties each year for his workers. He always took an active interest in the *Oklahoman,* particularly its editorial section; the proceedings of his company; and the growth and development of his home state. After putting in a full day at the office, he died in Oklahoma City on 30 May 1974 at the age of 101.

E. K. Gaylord had married Inez Kinney, a national secretary for the YWCA, on 29 December 1914. They had three children: Edith Kinney, Edward Lewis, and Virginia Elizabeth. Inez died on January 1974. Following his father's death in 1974, Edward Lewis Gaylord became editor and publisher of the *Oklahoman* as well as president and general manager of the Oklahoma Publishing Company and all of its subsidiaries. E. L. had served as executive vice-president and business manager for the company for twenty years, so he smoothly took over the operating reins of the business empire created by his father.

Under his leadership the Oklahoma Publishing Company has become one of the most successful media companies in the country, consistently ranking in the top twenty in annual revenues. E. L. has greatly expanded the holdings of the Oklahoma Publishing Company, venturing further into the broadcasting industry through the purchase of additional outlets and the creation of a film-production company. He also bought the rights to the television show *Hee Haw* and the Opryland theme park in Nashville, Tennessee. He has attempted to buy controlling interest in several other business ventures, including the Texas Rangers baseball team. E. L. Gaylord married Thelma Feragen on 30 August 1950. They have four children: Christine Elizabeth, Mary Inez, Edward King II, and Thelma Louise. E. L. is one of the wealthiest men in Oklahoma and one of the most financially successful newspaper publishers in the country, but he is a reclusive man and avoids public scrutiny. A prime example of his desire to preserve his privacy occurred in the mid 1980s, when he attempted to buy the Texas Rangers. The *Oklahoman* was forced to carry articles on the story from a Dallas paper because Gaylord refused to grant an interview to his own paper.

While still maintaining much of the influence of his father in Oklahoma affairs, E. L. has not been able to create the same level of public popularity. E. K. Gaylord, while not liked by everyone, was widely respected. E. L. Gaylord has not been so fortunate. He has continued to encourage economic development in Oklahoma, helping to entice a General Motors assembly plant as well as a major horse-racing track to the Oklahoma City area. The GM plant has been popular, but the establishment of Remington Park has been more controversial, opposed by many in the state's conservative contingent.

E. L. Gaylord continues to serve as both editor and publisher of the *Oklahoman,* but his day-to-day involvement in the newspaper is less than that of his father. Recent estimates of the value of the Gaylord conglomerate range from $200 million to $300 million. Besides the *Oklahoman,* its holdings include radio and television stations in Tennessee, Texas, Washington, and Wisconsin; several ranches in Texas and Colorado; and many other business and industrial ventures. In the fall of 1991 Gaylord created the Gaylord Entertainment Corporation, which includes all of his entertainment-related properties (Opryland, the Nashville Network, and the radio and television stations). Gaylord Entertainment is listed on the New York Stock Exchange. The rest of Gaylord's holdings, including the *Oklahoman,* are still part of OPUBCO (the Oklahoma Publishing Company), which remains privately owned.

References:

Ben Berger, "E. K. Gaylord Marks 50 Years in Business," *Editor & Publisher,* 86 (28 February 1953): 9, 61;

"E. K. Gaylord, 101-year-old Publisher, Dies," *Editor & Publisher,* 107 (8 June 1974): 20;

Toni Mack, "His Father's Son," *Forbes,* 129 (24 May 1982): 104, 107;

"Oklahomans Fete Gaylord, Communications Centenarian," *Advertising Age,* 44 (26 March 1973): 91;

"Profile: Centenarian Gaylord, a Pioneer Broadcaster," *Broadcasting,* 84 (5 March 1973): 73;

"Publisher Gaylord's Climb to Success Began in Rowdy Oklahoma City in 1902," *Manufacturers Record,* 125 (July 1956): 20–21;

Jean Truman Richardson, "The Oklahoma Press and the New Deal, 1932–1936," Master's thesis, University of Oklahoma, 1951;

Kathryn Sederberg, "Story of Oklahoma's Publisher, Gaylord, Now 96, is Saga of State," *Advertising Age,* 40 (2 June 1969): 3, 34–37;

"Survival of the Fittest," *Time,* 91 (3 May 1968): 53–54;

"This Is OPUBCO," special supplement, *Sunday Oklahoman,* 20 October 1963;

Lenora Williamson, "Week-long Birthday Party to Fete Gaylord on His 100th," *Editor & Publisher,* 106 (3 March 1973): 13.

Philip Graham
(18 July 1915 – 3 August 1963)

and

Katharine Graham
(16 June 1917 –)

Maurine H. Beasley
University of Maryland – College Park

MAJOR POSITIONS HELD: **Philip Graham:** Publisher, *Washington Post* (1946–1961); president and chief executive officer, Washington Post Company (1961–1963).

Katharine Graham: President (1963–1973), chief executive officer (1973–1991), chairman of the board (1973–), Washington Post Company; publisher, *Washington Post* (1969–1979).

SELECTED PERIODICAL PUBLICATION – UNCOLLECTED: Katharine Graham, "Women and Power," *FOLIO: The Magazine for Magazine Management* (July 1984): 128–131, 146.

Katharine and Philip Graham, 1956
(United Press International)

Both Philip and Katharine Graham played vital roles in making the *Washington Post* – purchased at a bankruptcy sale in 1933 by Katharine's parents, Eugene and Agnes Ernst Meyer – into the base of an influential media empire. Today the Washington Post Company consists of diversified media holdings including the news magazine *Newsweek*; four television stations; cable television systems; an on-line information service; newsprint manufacturing and distribution operations; and ownership interests in the Los Angeles Times–Washington Post News Service, the *International Herald Tribune,* and Cowles Media Company. Its keystone, however, remains the *Washington Post,* considered one of the leading newspapers in the world, known particularly for its role in exposing the Watergate scandal that led to the resignation of President Richard M. Nixon in 1974. Its present standing is attributed largely to the leadership of Katharine Graham, a timid housewife who uncertainly took charge of the Washington Post Company after the death of her husband in order to keep it in her family.

In terms of their backgrounds and upbringing, Philip and Katharine Graham led vastly different lives prior to their marriage at the Meyer family estate in Westchester County, New York, on 5 June 1940. She was born on 16 June 1917 in New York City into a wealthy family oriented to public service. Her father – the son of a well-to-do Jewish merchant and banker who had emigrated from France to Los Angeles – acquired a fortune on Wall Street and in international finance before marrying her mother, the daughter of German Lutheran immigrants.

The fourth of five children, Katharine experienced only limited emotional support from her mother, who resented the demands of domestic life and sometimes left the family to take trips abroad in pursuit of cultural and literary interests. A woman known for her intellectual interests, Agnes Meyer wrote a book on Chinese painting and published translations of the works of German author Thomas Mann, her close friend. She considered Katharine her inferior in terms of intellect and social aptitude.

Philip Graham had a much different start in life. He was born on 18 July 1915 in Terry, South Dakota, one of four children of Ernest Graham, a mining engineer and agricultural manager, and Florence Graham, a former schoolteacher. As a child he moved with his family to the Florida Everglades, where his father experienced initial difficulties in making a living. For a while the family lived on a houseboat, but even in the midst of poverty Florence Graham subscribed to quality magazines, such as the *New Yorker,* and made her children aware of books and the theater. Philip attended public schools in Miami. Eventually Ernest Graham, a stern, hard-driving individual, became a prosperous dairy farmer, a member of the state senate, and an unsuccessful candidate for governor.

At the University of Florida, Philip breezed through his studies, making As with little effort. He moved on to Harvard Law School, where he was elected president of the law review and attracted the attention of Professor Felix Frankfurter, who subsequently was named to the Supreme Court. Tall and thin with a countrified, homespun manner, Graham ranked tenth in a class of four hundred when he was graduated in 1939. Because of Frankfurter's influence Graham was appointed to an unprecedented two terms as a law clerk to two Supreme Court justices, first Stanley Reed, then Frankfurter.

Upon arriving in Washington in the summer of 1939, Graham reveled in the New Deal political atmosphere, living with a group of bright, well-connected young bachelors in a Virginia residence called Hockley House. One of the residents, John Oakes, then a reporter for the *Washington Post* and later editor of the *New York Times* editorial page, brought Katharine Meyer, known as Kay, to a party at Hockley House, where she met Graham. As she recalled it, he soon told her that he was going to

marry her, but that he did not want her father's money. Instead, according to her recollection, he said that they would move to Florida; he would go into politics; and they would be so poor she would have only two dresses.

The brilliant, energetic Graham immediately captivated Katharine, a serious-minded, shy young woman, and the couple were married shortly after their meeting. As the daughter of a multimillionaire, she had been given a sizable trust fund, but she valued achievement and ability over money. She was educated in private schools in the Washington area, graduating from the exclusive Madeira high school, where she edited the newspaper. After attending Vassar College for two years, she transferred to the University of Chicago, a center of radical thought in the 1930s, receiving a B.A. in history in 1938. Years later her father told friends that of his children, "Kate's the only one like me. She's got a hard mind. She'd make a great businessman." Because she was a woman, however, he did not see her in this role. Neither did she see herself in it.

After graduation she had no desire to return to Washington and work for her father. However, journalism intrigued her, as she wrote her sister in 1937:

> What I am most interested in doing is labor reporting, possibly working up to political reporting later. As you can see, that is no help to Dad. He wants and needs someone who is willing to go through the whole mill, from reporting, to circulation management, to editorial writing, and eventually to be his assistant.... I detest beyond description advertising and circulation, and that is what a newspaper executive spends most of his time worrying about.... I doubt my ability to carry a load like the *Washington Post* and ... I damn well think it would be a first-class dog's life.

Using her father's influence she obtained a job on the *San Francisco News,* where she was a reporter for seven months, covering a strike on the waterfront. When her father suggested, however, that she take a job on the *Post,* she agreed. At first she handled the "Letters to the Editor" department for twenty-five dollars a week. She soon began writing editorials, turning out about a hundred in 1939. During this period she met Graham.

Following their marriage she realized that she did not know how to cook and suggested that she give up her job in order to concentrate on being a housewife. According to Chalmers M. Roberts, author of an official history of the *Post,* Graham discouraged her, answering, "My God, I don't think I

Katharine Graham and Washington Post *executive editor Benjamin Bradlee after the U.S. District Court in Washington, D.C., ruled that the* Post *could publish the Pentagon Papers, June 1971 (Wide World / Bettmann Archives)*

could stand having you wait around with a pie for me to come home from the Court." So she stayed with the newspaper, writing features for the Sunday department and also preparing thoughtful articles on the pre–Pearl Harbor struggle between isolationists and interventionists.

As the United States became involved in World War II, Philip worked as a lawyer for the Lend-Lease Administration and then the Office of Emergency Management. He joined the U.S. Army Air Corps as a private in 1942. A year later he was commissioned and served in military intelligence, working to break Japanese codes. In 1944 he went to the Southwest Pacific as a staff officer, picking bombing sites in the Philippines. He was discharged as a major in 1945 after having been awarded the Legion of Merit.

Before Graham departed for the Pacific, Eugene Meyer had asked him to promise to take over the *Post* at the end of the war. Meyer wanted the paper to remain in his family, but none of his children except Katharine had any interest in it, and Meyer could not imagine leaving a woman in charge. Graham hesitated before giving an answer. He still harbored dreams of a political fu-

ture, but he acceded to Meyer's request, although over the years he apparently regretted his decision to move directly out of politics. On 1 January 1946 Graham became associate publisher. Six months later he was named publisher. In 1948 Meyer placed the *Post* squarely in the hands of Philip and Katharine Graham by transferring five thousand shares of voting stock to the couple, giving him thirty-five hundred and her fifteen hundred on grounds that a husband should not work for his spouse.

Meyer's decision seemed in line with the subordinate role that Katharine played in her family's life. After Pearl Harbor she helped in the circulation department of the *Post,* fielding complaints from subscribers and recruiting carriers, but her husband was her main interest. She followed him to a military post in South Dakota in 1943 and then to intelligence school at Harrisburg, Pennsylvania, before he left for the Pacific. She gave birth to four children: Elizabeth (Lally) and Donald during the war, William and Stephen afterward. After Graham moved to the *Post,* she stopped working there, devoting herself to her family, although she did write a Sunday digest column on magazines from 1947 to 1950. According to friends she seemed overshadowed in the presence of the outgoing, witty Graham.

When he took over the *Post,* he found it an uneven newspaper that barely broke even. Eager to make a reputation independent of that of his father-in-law, Graham led the newspaper more squarely into the liberal political camp, making it an instrument of social change in the city of Washington as well as a voice in Democratic politics. During the McCarthy era he wrote an editorial against "witch-hunting" and "the mad-dog quality of McCarthyism," which was a key element in the courageous campaign by the *Post* against anti-Communist hysteria.

An individual of many talents, Graham "could out-sleuth the paper's star reporters, out-think its sagest pundits, out-wit its most genial spoofers and out-write its fanciest – or most fancied – stylists," according to Alfred Friendly, the managing editor under Graham. He backed integration in Washington and home rule for the city. He had a broad view of the role of politics in bringing the world closer together in an era of nuclear arms.

For example, on 16 April 1961, in one of a series of occasional articles he wrote for the *Post,* he attacked the idea that scientists should be the key decision makers because of their technical expertise: "Great politicians, such as Lincoln, know that patience and wisdom are the watchwords of hope. At their best, politicians (then called statesmen) know only Truth. They know that Truth is a great single thing which cannot be fractured into 'engineering' or 'statistical' truth."

Graham distrusted technical experts in general. He found flaws in "readability formulas" and other efforts to draw readers to newspapers. "What I am feeling, rather than thinking, is that the press is stale and disoriented," he told a University of Minnesota seminar in 1960. "Not in techniques, for we are encased in and fascinated by techniques. Our staleness and our disorientation are caused rather by our basic assumptions. They are shallow, out of date and almost entirely unexamined because we all of us spend all of our time with techniques."

Graham's main preoccupation, however, was to make the *Post* profitable – a feat that Meyer had been unable to accomplish. He sensed that broadcasting would have an enormous impact in the years ahead, so he bought into radio and television stations, including network TV affiliates in Washington, D.C.; Jacksonville, Florida; and later Miami and Hartford, Connecticut. He presided over construction of a new building for the *Post* in downtown Washington. He instituted stock-option and profit-sharing plans to reward employees, since the *Post* had no money to raise salaries. As one of four newspapers in the nation's capital, it trailed behind both the morning *Times-Herald* and the venerable afternoon *Star,* the city's leading newspaper in both circulation and advertising.

Fortunately for the *Post,* in 1954 Col. Robert R. McCormick, the isolationist publisher of the *Chicago Tribune* and owner of the *Times-Herald,* decided to sell his Washington property. Graham had dreamed of buying the *Times-Herald* after the death of its publisher, Cissy Patterson, in 1948, but instead McCormick, Patterson's cousin, had acquired it. In spite of his political differences with Meyer and Graham, McCormick agreed to sell them the money-losing *Times-Herald.* He recognized that his brand of anti-intellectual journalism did not suit Washington and that the capital could not sustain more than one strong morning newspaper. The merger of the *Post* and the *Times-Herald* insured the success of the *Post* as an influential newspaper and allowed it to challenge the supremacy of the *Star.*

During the next decade Graham became a Washington power broker. He acted as a top adviser to and promoter of Lyndon Johnson, and as an unofficial lobbyist for civil-rights legislation. He put together the John F. Kennedy-Johnson presidential ticket in 1960, according to David Halberstam. Kennedy appointed Graham chairman of the incorporators of the Communications Satellite Corporation.

He also pulled off one of the most successful business deals in American journalism history – buying *Newsweek* in 1961 for only seventy-five thousand dollars in cash as part of a stock trade. Graham soon enhanced the prestige of *Newsweek* by employing Walter Lippmann, considered the nation's leading philosopher-journalist, to write a monthly column. Graham added to the reputation of the *Post* by establishing the successful Los Angeles Times–Washington Post News Service.

Yet Graham was not stable. He suffered from recurring bouts of mental illness marked by manic depression, during which he threatened to divorce Katharine and take the Washington Post Company away from her and their children. He embarrassed her by an affair with a young woman whom he said he intended to marry.

Philip committed suicide by shooting himself on 3 August 1963 at his farm near Marshall, Virginia. He had been taken there by his wife on a weekend furlough from a private psychiatric hospital where he had spent the previous six weeks. At

Front page of the Washington Post, *21 July 1969*

his death prominent political leaders, including Kennedy and Johnson, paid tribute to his achievements in business and public affairs. He had been a director or trustee of various organizations, including the University of Chicago, George Washington University, the Advertising Council, the Committee for Economic Development, the RAND Corporation, and the American Council to Improve Our Neighborhoods.

Left in control of the Washington Post Company, Katharine – perceived as an awkward and insecure figure – lost little time in putting to rest rumors that she intended to sell the company. In spite of painful shyness she met with the newspaper's board of directors on the day of her husband's funeral and assured it that she would retain the company for the benefit of her children. She moved rather quickly from a caretaker's role to that of an assertive publisher.

After becoming aware that the *Post* was considered a parochial newspaper by leading journalists, she decided to make major changes. In 1965 she replaced Friendly, although he was one of her closest friends, with a new editor. She brought in Benjamin C. Bradlee, then Washington bureau chief for *Newsweek,* to run the newspaper. Under his editorship it attracted talented young reporters and gained increased national and international recognition for its lively, aggressive news coverage.

In 1971 the *Post* followed the example of the *New York Times,* which it aspired to rival, and printed the Pentagon Papers, a secret account of the Vietnam War, in spite of a legal restraining order barring publication on grounds of national security. The right to publish them was later upheld by the Supreme Court. Katharine personally decided that the *Post* should run the Pentagon Papers.

This decision came only two days after a cash flow problem forced her to turn the family-owned company into a public corporation. At first the stock did poorly, so she endeavored to show Wall Street that a woman could run a media corporation. She overcame her reluctance to speak publicly and addressed a group of analysts on why her newspaper represented a good investment; within days the stock began to rise.

The following year Graham supported Bradlee's position that the *Post,* unlike most of the other media, should investigate a burglary at the Democratic National Committee headquarters in Washington's Watergate complex. The trail of the burglars, followed by Bob Woodward and Carl Bernstein, two young *Post* reporters, eventually led to the White House and President Nixon.

In spite of heavy-handed pressure from the administration to silence it, the willingness of the *Post* to pursue the story resulted in journalistic accolades for the newspaper, including a Pulitzer Prize for public service.

Determined to make the *Post* more profitable and attractive to investors, Katharine took a tough position against striking pressmen and their supporters in 1975. During a 139-day walkout by pressmen, who vandalized the pressroom before they left, she continued to publish the *Post.* Eventually she hired nonunion pressmen, effectively breaking a union in spite of complaints that this violated the newspaper's liberal editorial policy.

The Washington Post Company's financial picture brightened markedly in 1981. That year the newspaper attained unquestioned preeminence in Washington when the *Star,* then owned by Time Incorporated, ceased operation, a victim of declining revenues in the dwindling afternoon market. The *Star* had previously absorbed its tabloid competitor, the *Daily News.* After the demise of the combined afternoon newspapers, the *Post* quickly reached a 55 percent penetration rate of Washington households on weekdays and a 75 percent rate on Sundays. Stockholders saw their investments soar in value. For example, a $10,000 investment in *Post* stock when the company went public in 1971 was worth $185,329 in 1985. In 1989 *Fortune* magazine recognized the company as one of the twenty most profitable major corporations in the United States during the preceding decade.

In 1979 Katharine stepped down as publisher, turning that position over to her son Donald, a Harvard graduate who had been groomed to take charge. Katharine, however, kept control of the corporation. As chairman of the board, she was routinely referred to as one of the nation's most influential women, one who had mastered the intricacies of profit margins, strategic planning, and executive compensation. During her tenure she increased the size and influence of *Newsweek*; purchased more television stations; and diversified into other areas, from cable television and cellular-phone operations to ownership of the Stanley Kaplan Educational Center, which offers courses to prepare students for academic and licensing examinations.

Not all of the company's ventures made money. It was forced to sell the *Trenton Times* in New Jersey to cut its losses there, although it successfully operated another small newspaper, the *Herald,* in Everett, Washington. In general Katharine's management made the company bigger, better run,

Truman Capote and Katharine Graham at the masked ball he gave in her honor at the Plaza Hotel in New York City,
29 November 1966 (Associated Press)

more lucrative, and more highly regarded than when she took over. According to a personal friend and mentor, Warren E. Buffett, the billionaire chairman of Berkshire Hathaway and a large stockholder in the Washington Post Company, "She's made an enormous contribution. In 1963 it was a fairly equal race between the *Post* and the *Star.*"

Her management style, however, has not engendered universal praise. Some observers saw high-handedness in her treatment of key executives, particularly in the early years of her leadership. In his book *The Pillars of the Post,* Howard Bray quotes one staff member as saying, "There is the good Queen Kate and the bad Queen Kate. It all depends on how she's feeling that day."

Minorities and women have made complaints concerning their treatment by the *Post* organization. The newspaper's coverage of the predominantly black city of Washington has proven controversial. In 1981 the newspaper was forced to return a Pulit-

zer Prize awarded to Janet Cooke, a reporter who had made up a story about an eight-year-old heroin addict. According to Roberts, Bradlee said at the time that he knew nothing about the inner-city area where the child was supposed to live. When the newspaper's redesigned Sunday magazine appeared in 1986, it led to a thirteen-week protest on grounds that the initial issue portrayed blacks as criminals. Bradlee subsequently apologized.

Some in the feminist ranks have been disappointed in Katharine as a role model for young women. When in 1979 she became the first woman elected president of the American Newspaper Publishers' Association, she did not choose to address women's issues. The *Post* was cited for sex discrimination by the Equal Employment Opportunity Commission in 1974 and has sought and promoted women since then, but some have complained about a lack of support for working mothers. "We certainly have not succeeded in doing anything about day care," Katharine told *Working Woman* in 1989, explaining, "but I don't know that I think companies can. It's terribly expensive and very complex to run." As for her own views on feminism, she said, "I was so in the old mold that it was really long after I went to work that I changed."

She spoke on "Women and Power" at a Women in Communications luncheon in 1984, giving her philosophy in regard to women in top management. She warned against "artificial aids or special deals": "The simple fact is this: people are interested only in results. To get to the top, women – like men – will simply have to put their careers and companies first for some part of their working lives. Their families and children may suffer to some degree, as may their friendships. I know mine have. But men in power have always been willing to pay this price."

Like other chairmen of boards of large corporations, Graham has received handsome compensation. In 1991 her total pay, including base income, cash bonus, and long-term compensation, came to $497,474. This amounted to a decline of 56.3 percent from her total 1990 compensation of $1,138,486, a decrease in line with her decision to step down as chief executive officer in May 1991, to be succeeded by Donald Graham. She remains board chairman.

In addition to her board responsibilities, she is a cochairman of the *International Herald Tribune* and an independent trustee of the Reuters Founders Share Company. A noted hostess who entertains leading society and governmental figures at her home in Washington's elite Georgetown area, she participates in various civic and professional organizations. A former board member of the Associated Press, she is vice-chairman of the board of the Urban Institute and a member of the Council on Foreign Relations and the Overseas Development Council. She is cochairman of the Circle of the National Gallery of Art and a member of its collectors' committee. A fellow of the American Academy of Arts and Sciences, she is also a member of the independent D.C. Committee on Public Education.

On Graham's seventieth birthday in 1987, some six hundred notable guests – all personal friends representing the three branches of government, the media, industry, the arts, and the diplomatic corps – gathered in Washington at a government auditorium to honor her. According to the *Post,* President Ronald Reagan toasted her as a "sensitive, thoughtful and very kindly person," while humorist Art Buchwald declared that the group had assembled because of "fear" of her power. Reporter Mike Wallace of *60 Minutes* commented, "She is a woman who in effect, I suppose, came to the job unprepared and turned out to be one of the giants of journalism in the last quarter century."

In what perhaps represented a symbolic merger of the political and media spheres that dominate Washington, the *Post* reported that the guest of honor was seated between President Reagan and her tennis partner, Secretary of State George Shultz. She said little, according to her newspaper, except that she would just as soon forget her age although the evening had made her birthday memorable. She is a woman who changed roles at age forty-six from a dutiful housewife to a hard-driving business executive. Her success testifies to her extraordinary competence. She proved to be a stronger corporate head than either of the two men who molded her earlier life – her father and her husband.

Biographies:

Deborah Davis, *Katharine the Great: Katharine Graham and the Washington Post* (New York: Harcourt Brace Jovanovich, 1979; revised and enlarged edition, Bethesda, Md.: National Press, 1987);

Carol Felsenthal, *Power, Privilege and the Post: The Katharine Graham Story* (New York: Putnam's, 1993).

References:

Howard Bray, *The Pillars of the Post: The Making of a News Empire in Washington* (New York: Norton, 1980);

David Halberstam, *The Powers That Be* (New York: Knopf, 1979);

"Publisher Philip Graham," *Time,* 67 (16 April 1956): 64–72;

Chalmers M. Roberts, *The Washington Post: The First 100 Years* (Boston: Houghton Mifflin, 1977); revised and enlarged as *In the Shadow of Power: The Story of the Washington Post* (Cabin John, Md.: Seven Locks Press, 1989);

Larry Van Dyne, "The Bottom Line on Katharine Graham," *Washingtonian* (December 1985): 128–133, 185–213;

Judith Viorst, "Katharine Graham," *Washingtonian* (September 1967): 32–35, 80–86.

Papers:

The papers of Katharine and Philip Graham are in the personal possession of Katharine Graham at her home in Washington, D.C. Some material related chiefly to Philip Graham is in the Agnes and Eugene Meyer papers at the Library of Congress.

Edward Holmead Harte

(5 December 1922 –)

and

Houston Harriman Harte

(15 February 1927 –)

John M. Coward
University of Tulsa

MAJOR POSITIONS HELD: **Edward Holmead Harte:** Editor, *Snyder* (Texas) *Daily News* (1950–1952); president, *San Angelo* (Texas) *Standard-Times* (1952–1956); vice-president (1956–1962), publisher (1962–1987), *Corpus Christi Caller-Times.*

Houston Harriman Harte: Partner (1950–1952), editor (1952–1954), *Snyder* (Texas) *Daily News;* president, San Angelo Standard, Inc. (1956–1962); vice-president, Express Publishing Co. (1962–1966); president (1966–1972), chairman of the board (1971–), Harte-Hanks Communications.

Harte-Hanks Communications – the San Antonio-based media company with major holdings in newspapers, television, advertising shoppers, and direct marketing – was taken over on 11 September 1984 after a twelve-year run on the New York Stock Exchange, which included fifty consecutive quarters of earnings-per-share growth. A team of company insiders, among them Edward and Houston Harte, consolidated control over the media company cofounded by their father, the late Robert William Houston Harte. It was a move that might have pleased the elder Harte, a Missouri-born newspaperman who began his publishing empire in the western Texas town of San Angelo in the 1920s.

The 1984 buyout and subsequent sell-off of some of Harte-Hanks major media properties were another phase in the evolution of a fifty-year-old media empire started by the elder Houston Harte and Bernard Hanks, rival newspaper publishers who formed a partnership during the 1920s to acquire Texas newspapers. As it had been from the 1930s to the 1960s, Harte-Hanks after the buyout

Edward Holmead Harte (courtesy Harte-Hanks Communications)

was largely in the hands of the Harte and Hanks families, anchored in Texas towns such as Abilene, Corpus Christi, and San Angelo. In effect, the return to private ownership in 1984 marked a shift away from the company's aggressive growth and

111

rising presence on the national stage to a more scaled-down and tightly controlled organization. This, too, might have pleased the Harte patriarch.

The elder Houston Harte was nothing if not ambitious. He was only twenty-seven when he purchased the *San Angelo Standard,* but it was the third paper he had owned. He was born on 12 January 1893 in Knob Noster, Missouri, to Edward and Lizzie Houston Harte. He worked as a reporter for the *Los Angeles Examiner* in 1911 while a student at the University of Southern California. He became a publisher for the first time in 1913 – a year before he was graduated from the journalism school at the University of Missouri – when he bought the weekly *Knob Noster Gem.*

In 1916 he became publisher of the *Central Missouri Republican* in Boonville, taking time out for army duty during World War I. In May 1920 he sold the Missouri paper and moved to Texas to publish the *San Angelo Standard.* Two months later he doubled the news staff by hiring – sight unseen – a University of Missouri graduate, Dean Chenoweth, to edit the paper. Despite their political and religious differences – Harte was a Democrat and a Presbyterian, Chenoweth a Republican and a member of the Christian (Disciples) Church – the two became fast friends, and Chenoweth stayed in San Angelo the rest of his life. The San Angelo paper, later called the *Standard-Times,* prospered under Harte's leadership and became the cornerstone of his newspaper empire.

The Harte-Hanks partnership soon prospered too, though it was not necessarily a natural arrangement. Hanks published the *Abilene Reporter,* only ninety miles from San Angelo, and the two papers were rivals, especially in overlapping circulation areas. "The San Angelo vs. Abilene rivalry was one of the most important things in Harte's life, literally," Ed Harte has said of his father. "Every ten years he went through several months of nervousness wondering whether San Angelo would have grown more than Abilene did. He lost that war, but not for lack of trying."

According to Ed, his father often blamed San Angelo's troubles on the Santa Fe Railroad, which failed to provide the level of service he thought the town deserved. Harte was also critical of West Texas Utilities for its reluctance to take three-phase power all over town, a move that could have helped local businesses. To Harte, the Abilene-based electric company was clearly biased against San Angelo. Although the elder was critical of the railroad and electric monopolies, Ed has said that his father was a monopolist himself: he published the only paper

in San Angelo and was a principal owner of the town's largest radio station. "But," Ed has noted, "that never stopped him from helping other monopolies 'tell right from wrong' as he put it."

Despite their newspaper rivalry, Harte and Hanks liked each other immediately. By the mid 1920s the partnership began to buy other Texas papers, including the *Corpus Christi Times,* purchased in 1928 and still one of the company's principal newspapers. The Harte-Hanks partnership was unwritten and informal – but it worked. "They usually bought major interests, maybe 65 or 70 percent, and they would invite the publisher or editor of the paper to buy an interest," said Andrew B. (Stormy) Shelton, Hanks's son-in-law. "They usually bought on credit, with the seller often carrying the note." A company history of the partnership states that Harte provided the editorial strength, Hanks the business acumen. According to Shelton, Harte sometimes wanted to take a chance on a newspaper venture, but Hanks would say no: "If either didn't want to go [into an acquisition], they didn't."

If Hanks was considered the businessman in the partnership, this did not diminish the extraordinary energy and drive that motivated Harte. "To say that Houston Harte was totally absorbed in business would be an overstatement; he was only 99 percent absorbed in business," according to Ed Harte. "But 'business' to him meant not only his own business interests, but everybody else's as well." Harte knew that his newspaper's prosperity depended on that of San Angelo, and he made it his business to know the business of western Texas. "He was minutely interested in what went into the paper," Ed Harte said.

He promoted San Angelo as a center for ranching, agriculture, and even tourism, but it was the oil business that first transformed the city. The *Standard* reported the opening of the western Texas oilfields during the 1920s, and the paper made oil news a major part of its coverage. Even after the oil business moved from San Angelo to Midland, Ed recalled, the *Standard* had several thousand readers there because of its oil-industry reporting. Agricultural and ranching news were major parts of the newspaper's editorial formula. Ed believes that his father was ahead of his time in his emphasis on business reporting. This emphasis paid off with readers: the newspaper's circulation extended into more than forty counties in western Texas.

With the newspaper as his platform and abundant energy and an outgoing personality as his method, Harte worked to make San Angelo a good place to live. For him this meant that the city needed a college – Abilene, after all, had three. But the state of Texas had little interest in opening a new campus in western Texas, and the idea had powerful opponents in Austin, the state capital. "Harte was undeterred," Ed has written, "and the existence of Angelo State University is due in large part to Harte originality and drive."

With an energetic newspaper publisher as father and role model, Harte's two sons were expected to go into the newspaper business, though their father did not pressure them to do so. "It never occurred to me to think of anything else to do," young Houston has said. "Everything pointed my life that way." Edward Holmead Harte was born on 5 December 1922 in Pilot Grove, Missouri, to Houston and Caroline Isabel McCutcheon Harte. He began working summers at the *Standard-Times* when he was about nine. Houston Harriman Harte, born on 15 February 1927 in San Angelo, has said, "Ed and I worked there every summer. I think we mostly started on the switchboard as kids in short pants. Then we worked in classified, collections, some circulation work. I worked in the pressroom one summer." In the newsroom Houston wrote sports stories, farm news, and obituaries: "Obituaries were something very special with my father. Obituaries, he felt, were a chance for you to make a person's whole family feel good about something and perhaps weld a loyal subscriber to you for the rest of his or her life."

The elder Harte also expected his boys to do well in school. That was no problem for Ed, who spent a year at a boarding school in Mexico City, became fluent in Spanish, and began a lifelong interest in Mexico. However, Houston struggled: "My father sent me away to 'Bad Boys School' – Texas Country School in Dallas." After high school Ed went off to Dartmouth College, though World War II interrupted his studies. He enlisted in the Army Air Corps in 1943 and left the service in 1946 as a staff sergeant. He returned to Dartmouth, completed a degree in English, and was graduated in 1947. He worked for two years as a reporter for the *Claremont Eagle* in New Hampshire, and then another two years at the *Kansas City Star*. "Everybody wants to prove himself in another non-family environment even if he intends to go into the family business," Ed has said about this time in his life.

His younger brother finished high school in Dallas and attended New Mexico Military Institute before enlisting in the navy in 1944. After the war Houston studied journalism and business at Washington and Lee University in Virginia and was graduated in 1950. Later that year the Harte broth-

Houston Harriman Harte (courtesy Harte-Hanks Communications)

ers teamed up with Stormy Shelton to publish the *Scurry County Times* (later the *Snyder Daily Times*) in Snyder, Texas. The area, just west of Abilene, was experiencing an oil boom, and the young newspapermen worked to convert the weekly into a daily. Ed was editor, while Houston worked in circulation and advertising. The partnership worked and helped cement the bond between Shelton and the Harte brothers.

In 1952 Ed left his younger brother in Snyder and moved to San Angelo to work directly for his father for the first time in his career. Ed covered the legislature, served as editor, and soon became president of the *Standard-Times*. Young Houston stayed in Snyder until 1954, when he left Texas and the family fold to work in the promotion department of the *Des Moines Register* and *Tribune*. In 1956, when Ed left the *Standard-Times* for the Corpus Christi paper, Houston returned to San Angelo to work for his father, by then an important publishing figure in Texas. "He was a great man to work for," Houston has said. "You never felt he was sitting on you, making you do exactly what he wanted done, and yet he didn't hesitate to go down to the newsroom and tell them exactly how things should be done."

In 1962 Ed was named publisher of the *Corpus Christi Caller-Times,* a job he held until his retirement in 1987. Founded in 1883, the *Caller-Times* became the dominant media institution in the city, and Ed, following his father's example in San Angelo, used his position to promote Corpus Christi, its economy, and a host of favorite causes. He once served, for example, as chairman of the Chamber of Commerce Military Facilities Committee, a group dedicated to supporting the Corpus Christi Naval Air Station and protecting four thousand jobs at the Army Depot. An avid ornithologist who was chairman of the national board of the Audubon Society, Ed also worked to protect the coastal environment in southern Texas. He was a founding member of the city's Bay Drilling Committee, which wrote the first municipal offshore drilling regulation ever enacted in any state. He also chaired the chamber of commerce group that supported the creation of the Padre Island National Seashore.

Ed Harte has also used his energy and influence to support such causes as the Corpus Christi Symphony Society and the Corpus Christi Museum. He and his wife, Janet, have also traveled widely. His special passion has been Mexico, an interest that led him to join the Inter American Press Association in the 1950s and to work for greater press freedom throughout Latin America. He served as president of the IAPA in 1986 and has written about Mexican politics for years in a weekly column in the *Caller-Times.*

While Ed found a home in Corpus Christi, young Houston remained in San Angelo until 1962, when he moved to San Antonio to become an executive at Harte-Hanks's newest properties, the *San Antonio Express* and *News,* acquired along with KENS, the CBS affiliate in San Antonio and the company's first television station. The *Express* and *News,* the company's largest newspapers, were in competition with the Hearst-owned *San Antonio Light.* Although the papers were the company's largest single revenue producers, direct competition, union relations, and a host of other problems kept their profits low.

Moreover, by the late 1960s company managers were facing some new conditions. Harte-Hanks Newspapers was a loosely run organization of thirteen newspapers, all in Texas. But with the elder Harte in increasingly fragile health, questions about the succession of family ownership arose. Bruce Meador, managing trustee of the Hanks estate following Bernard Hanks's death in 1948, was running

Harte-Hanks at the time, and he sought outside advice. Consultants identified three options: sell out, go public, or do nothing. The latter option, company managers were warned, might lead to a breakup of the organization. Harte-Hanks managers decided to go public, although the move did not please the elder Harte. The stock offering was made in 1972. Robert William Houston Harte died on 13 March that same year.

The public offering was carried out by an ambitious young newspaper executive who had joined the company in 1970 from the Copley Newspapers chain. Robert G. Marbut proved to be a visionary manager. After receiving an MBA from Harvard University, where he edited the business-school student paper, Marbut worked as a vice-president for engineering at Copley for seven years. In 1970 he asked Harte-Hanks to back him and another Copley executive, Charles Wahlheim, in their own publishing venture. Instead, Harte-Hanks managers, already planning to take the company public, asked the pair to handle the transition.

The match between Marbut and Harte-Hanks soon proved successful. Although Wahlheim left the company in 1973, Marbut thrived in San Antonio, partly because the Harte brothers genuinely liked him. Marbut followed the established Harte-Hanks formula of buying the only newspaper in a small but growing market, beginning an ambitious expansion plan in the early 1970s. Unlike the company founders, however, Marbut looked well beyond Texas, buying papers in such places as Hamilton, Ohio; Ypsilanti, Michigan; Anderson, South Carolina; and Yakima, Washington. In October 1972 Harte-Hanks moved into California, acquiring nineteen weekly and twice-weekly publications and a printing facility in San Diego. In order to finance more purchases and to unload its troubled urban newspapers, the company sold the San Antonio papers to Australian publisher Rupert Murdoch in 1973 for about $19 million. With Houston H. Harte as chairman of the board, Marbut as chief executive officer, and Larry D. Franklin as Marbut's executive vice-president, Harte-Hanks continued to grow throughout the 1970s, buying small dailies and weeklies in places where operating expenses were low, but profits – or potential profits – were high.

A new, revitalized Harte-Hanks soon began to emerge. Not only was the company more geographically dispersed, but it also became substantially more diversified. It moved into television broadcasting, for example, especially in the Sun Belt. In 1975 the company purchased WTLV, the NBC affiliate in Jacksonville, Florida. Two years later

Harte-Hanks acquired another television station, WFMY in Greensboro, North Carolina, and, two years after that, the company purchased KYTV in Springfield, Missouri. Harte-Hanks moved into radio broadcasting in a major way in 1978, buying Southern Broadcasting's stable of AM and FM stations, mostly located in the South. The company also changed its name to reflect Marbut's expanding vision: Harte-Hanks Newspapers became Harte-Hanks Communications. By 1980 Harte-Hanks owned twenty-nine daily newspapers, sixty-eight weeklies, four VHF television stations, eleven radio stations, four cable television stations, two trade publications, three market research firms, and a network of free-circulation advertising shoppers and other companies devoted to alternative distribution and marketing.

However, in the image-conscious world of publishing and broadcasting, it was a decidedly pedestrian portfolio. Most Harte-Hanks newspapers were small; the company's flagship newspaper, the *Corpus Christi Caller-Times,* had a circulation of eighty-five thousand. The company's free-circulation shoppers, moreover, were not considered journalism at all and held very little status in publishing circles. Glamorous or not, Marbut's management of Harte-Hanks was profitable, and that counted both in San Antonio and on Wall Street, where the company's growth and consistent performance had not gone unnoticed. Throughout the 1970s the management team led by Marbut, Franklin, the Harte brothers, and Shelton pushed hard to keep expenses low and earnings high. Revenues rose from about $100 million in 1975 to more than $260 million in 1979. Net income also rose steeply during that period, and the company joined the Fortune 500.

Under Marbut's leadership Harte-Hanks also developed a reputation for innovation. He was especially interested in new ways to deliver advertising messages. By 1980 the company's fastest growing division was its Consumer Distribution Marketing Group, which offered an assortment of marketing services, direct-mail operations, and alternative delivery systems reaching millions of households in a variety of markets. Harte-Hanks managers encouraged their newspapers to look for new publishing opportunities. Instead of simply putting out a single newspaper, Harte-Hanks papers became "community information centers," launching new information and advertising publications.

In Anderson, South Carolina, for example, the Harte-Hanks daily produced a special tabloid, the *Orange and White,* to reach ten thousand sports fans

of nearby Clemson University. In Gatlinburg, Tennessee, the Harte-Hanks community newspaper revamped and expanded its tourist publication, the *Mountain Visitor,* to reach more travelers at the Great Smoky Mountains National Park, and launched a free shopper, *Bert's Bargain Bonanza,* to offer local advertisers total market coverage. While not all of these projects succeeded, many did, fulfilling Marbut's expanded marketing philosophy.

While this philosophy paid off in financial terms, the Harte-Hanks newspapers were sometimes criticized for their lack of journalistic vigor. Although they were editorially autonomous, most of them were small and – to some critics – undistinguished. Newspaper analyst John Morton, for one, complained to the *New York Times* that "the only paper of any distinction would be the Corpus Christi paper, which is run in an aggressive journalistic fashion. Generally, the papers are not ones that attract much attention." Despite such criticism, Franklin, head of newspaper operations during the late 1970s, pushed for improved journalism at the company's papers.

Whatever the journalistic judgment, Marbut's forward-thinking policies and the company's financial success won him a following among financial analysts. A 1980 *New York Times* headline described the "Rise of an Information Empire" and quoted Morton: "They are a small, rapidly growing version of Gannett." But unlike Gannett and other newspaper groups, Morton continued, "Harte-Hanks is much less newspaper-oriented than the other newspaper companies. It's more interested in information transfer. It's much more financially oriented." In 1983 *Forbes* focused on Marbut's no-nonsense approach to the communications business: "Forget Glamour, He Will Deliver the Mail" was the magazine's headline. In short, the aggressive expansion and financial successes of the 1970s gave rise in the 1980s to the image of a tightly run and innovative company.

But the expansion did not last. Indeed, the economic forces of the early 1980s shifted Marbut's strategy and took Harte-Hanks out of the national spotlight. In the merger-mania climate of that period, it was one of many media companies vulnerable to a hostile takeover. Faced with that possibility and the increasing pressure to perform on the stock market, Marbut and the Harte-Hanks management team moved to go private, "to take better advantage of opportunities without the pressure for consistent and predictable quarterly earnings per share," as a 1984 company announcement put it. It was a calculated risk that turned out have both positive and negative consequences. On the positive side, it kept the company largely in family hands, with the Hartes and Shelton each owning about 20 percent of the stock. Marbut and Franklin were the two other major stockholders; about thirty other managers were also involved in the buyout. The insiders secured financing from a group of sixteen banks, the investor group itself, and an institutional investor, Teachers Insurance. The company sold its nine radio stations in September 1984 for about $80 million, including about $36 million from Gannett for an AM-FM combination in Houston.

But the buyout saddled the company with nearly $1 billion in debt. To make matters worse, the Texas economy went sour during the mid 1980s. Harte-Hanks managers, operating as HH Holding, responded by simplifying the company's organizational structure and concentrating company resources in its largest and most attractive markets, a strategy that helped pay off the debt. In the process Harte-Hanks sold three of its four television stations, keeping only its flagship station in San Antonio. It also sold many of its small newspapers, including those in Corsicana, Big Spring, and Del Rio, Texas. However, the company continued to operate its cornerstone newspapers in Abilene, San Angelo, and Corpus Christi; those in other middle-sized markets; and its advertising shoppers and direct-marketing companies.

By 1990 Marbut and the Harte-Hanks insiders had re-created the company. Although they had substantially reduced its debt, they had also diminished its diversity as well as its national stature. The new Harte-Hanks was dedicated to three principal businesses: newspapers, advertising shoppers, and direct marketing. A 1991 company profile lists it as the owner of nine daily newspapers and about forty nondaily publications, including community newspapers and supplemental publications. Its only broadcast property was KENS, San Antonio's number one television station. The company reported that its free-circulation shoppers, zoned in 465 separate editions, reached 5.8 million households in five major markets each week. In the area where Harte-Hanks made its reputation as an innovator, direct marketing, the company retained a variety of services, including direct-mail systems, computer services, research and telemarketing services, a commercial printing and graphics network, database ap-

plications, and alternate delivery and transportation of advertising materials.

By 1992 Marbut had left Harte-Hanks to pursue other interests. His longtime colleague Franklin became chief executive officer, while Ed Harte and Shelton remained on the board, and Houston Harte continued to serve as its chairman. Ed married Janet Frey on 8 February 1947; they had four children: Christopher, Elizabeth, William, and Julia. Houston married Carolyn Esther Hardig on 17 June 1950; they had three children: Houston Ritchie, David Harriman, and Sarah Elizabeth. With stock holdings divided between the Hartes and Shelton, the controlling families once again face a succession problem. In 1992 Houston suggested that Harte-Hanks might become a public company for the second time in order to raise new capital for expansion and to facilitate the placement of the company's rising managers.

References:
"Harte-Hanks Gets Slightly Higher Bid from Investor Group," *Wall Street Journal,* 2 May 1984, p. 22;
"Harte-Hanks Moves to Take Company Private," *Broadcasting,* 106 (2 April 1984): 32–33;
"Harte-Hanks out of Radio to the Record Tune of $76 Million," *Broadcasting,* 107 (24 September 1984): 32;
"Houston Harte, Publisher, Dies; Led Paper Chain in Southwest," *New York Times,* 14 March 1972, p. 46;
Alex S. Jones, "Harte-Hanks Obtain Trading Halt," *New York Times,* 27 March 1984, p. D6;
Jones, "A Media Industry Innovator," *New York Times,* 30 April 1984, pp. D1, D12;
Jones, "$717 Million Buyout Bid for Harte-Hanks," *New York Times,* 29 March 1984, p. D3;
"Journalism Life Is 'Fascinating,'" *San Angelo Standard-Times,* centennial edition, 1984, p. 6;
Thomas O'Donnell, "Forget Glamour, He Will Deliver the Mail," *Forbes,* 131 (11 April 1983): 166, 170;
"Portability Still a Newspaper Plus," *San Angelo Standard-Times,* centennial edition, 1984, p. 7.

Papers:
Private papers and company documents concerning the Harte family are located at the *Corpus Christi Caller-Times* and at Harte-Hanks Communications in San Antonio.

William Randolph Hearst, Jr.

(27 January 1908 –)

Michael J. Dillon
Pennsylvania State University

MAJOR NEWSPAPERS OWNED: *Albany* (New York) *Times-Union* (1951–); *Baltimore News-Post and American* (1951–1986); *Boston American* [becomes *Boston Record* (1961), becomes *Boston Herald-American* (1972)] (1951–1982); *Chicago Tribune* (1951–1956); *Detroit Times* (1951–1961); *Los Angeles Examiner* (1951–1962); *Los Angeles Herald-Express* [becomes *Los Angeles Herald-Examiner* (1962)] (1951–1989); *Milwaukee Journal* (1951–1960); *New York Daily Mirror* (1951–1963); *New York Journal-American* [becomes *New York World-Journal-Herald* (1966)] (1951–1968); *Pittsburgh Sun-Telegraph* (1951–1960); *San Antonio Light* (1951–); *San Francisco Call-Bulletin* [becomes *San Francisco News-Call-Bulletin* (1959)] (1951–1964); *San Francisco Examiner* (1951–); *Seattle Post-Intelligencer* (1951–); *Albany* (New York) *Knickerbocker-News* (1960–1988); *Plainview* (Texas) *Daily Herald* (1979–); *Huron* (Michigan) *Daily Tribune* (1980–); *Midland* (Michigan) *Daily News* (1980–); *Midland* (Texas) *Reporter-Telegram* (1980–); *Edwardsville* (Illinois) *Intelligencer* (1982–); *Beaumont* (Texas) *Enterprise* (1984–); *Laredo* (Texas) *Morning Times* (1984–); *Clearwater* (Florida) *Sun* (1985–1990); *Houston Chronicle* (1987–).

BOOKS: *Ask Me Anything: Our Adventures with Khrushchev,* by Hearst, Frank Conniff, and Bob Considine (New York: McGraw-Hill, 1960);
The Hearsts: Father and Son, by Hearst and Jack Casserly (Niwot, Colo.: Roberts Rinehart, 1991).

William Randolph (Bill) Hearst, Jr., struggled to gain his famous father's respect, confidence, and legacy. Promoted often in title and rank within the Hearst Corporation, young Hearst was kept from real power by his father and the executives whom the elder Hearst hired to run his enterprises. After a successful but largely undistinguished career as a reporter and publisher in the news operation, Hearst inherited, upon his father's death in 1951, a publicly prominent but limited role in the faltering, though

William Randolph Hearst, Jr. (courtesy of the Hearst Corporation and Mr. and Mrs. William Randolph Hearst, Jr.)

still vastly wealthy, Hearst Corporation. He presided over the decline of what was once the most powerful, innovative, and influential newspaper empire in the United States.

After acting as publisher of the *New York American,* Hearst, Jr., covered World War II as a correspondent for the paper and then resumed his career as a publisher, heading the *New York Journal-American* until 1960, when he was named chairman of the board of the Hearst Corporation, a position he held until 1973. Despite the fact that Hearst, Sr., left control of his company largely in the hands of longtime executives instead of his five sons, Bill Hearst carved a niche for himself in the organization and went on to share a 1956 Pulitzer Prize for reporting on the Soviet Union. The ten years that followed his father's death were stormy ones for the corporation, but, as its newspaper operations atrophied, its magazine, broadcast, and syndicate ventures thrived.

More than his Pulitzer Prize, Bill Hearst's strident promotion of anti-Communist senator Joseph McCarthy marks his place in the history of journalism. With a stable of fanatical anti-Red columnists given free rein to smear and insinuate, and with Bill himself aiding McCarthy with his witch-hunt, the Hearst papers faced libel suits, political disfavor, and diminished credibility.

The sensationalism, vitriolic commentary, and anticommunism that once underpinned the Hearst empire were – by the time Bill Hearst ascended to the upper echelons of the corporation – outdated and increasingly resented by readers and contemporaries in the news business. Although the company by no means came close to folding, its preeminence as a news-gathering leader and editorial voice diminished, and the period from 1955 to 1966 saw the closing, sale, or merging of a dozen Hearst newspapers, including the flagship *New York Journal-American*.

Hearst, Jr., tried desperately to please his father and live up to the legend he had created. The son of the rags-to-riches mining magnate and U.S. senator George Hearst, William Randolph Hearst, Sr., used his father's fortune to revive the failing *San Francisco Examiner* and then to build a New York–based press empire that would make him wealthier and more influential than his father. Hearst was one of the most enigmatic and controversial figures in modern newspaper history and a founding father of "yellow journalism." He built one of the largest private fortunes in early-twentieth-century America, became an important collector of art, and wielded great power in politics, aspiring at one point to the presidency.

Hearst's every undertaking was on a grand scale – symbolized best by San Simeon, the great estate he built on the Pacific Coast of California – but his sons were to find that they could match neither his accomplishments nor his expectations. Although all five filled various roles in the family business, only Bill managed to achieve a significant level of success on his own terms.

William Randolph Hearst, Jr., was born on 27 January 1908 into a world of privilege and wealth. "None of us knew the meaning of financial need," he wrote in his 1991 autobiography, *The Hearsts: Father and Son.* "We asked and things appeared." Hearst and his four brothers (George [1904–1972], John Randolph [1910–1958], Randolph Apperson [1915–], and David Whitmire [1915–1986]) lived two childhoods: a frenetic one in their father's huge, bustling Riverside Drive apartment complex in New York City where newspaper cronies, states-men, and political fixers came and went at all hours; and a quiet, idyllic one at the sprawling California hacienda of their grandmother, Phoebe Apperson Hearst.

Hearst saw little of his sons, sending them copious letters and telegrams full of orders, advice, and criticism. He brought them to New York when it fit his schedule or his goals, especially for his many abortive campaigns for state and national office. Hearst prodded his sons to work hard, at the same time satisfying their every whim. Bill tried hardest to adopt his father's work ethic, but he could not overcome the fact that he was a Hearst, a title that carried perquisites and rewards whether one worked or not. If the Hearst sons fell while climbing the corporate ladder, there was a wide net to catch them.

While growing up the boys saw more of their mother, Millicent Hearst – the daughter of a vaudeville hoofer – whom Hearst married in 1903, but she believed the New York life-style was not suitable for children and encouraged their frequent extended stays with their grandmother. Bill attended a variety of private and military schools before enrolling at the University of California, Berkeley, to study liberal arts. With the encouragement of his father – himself a college dropout – Bill left Berkeley halfway through his sophomore year to take a job on the *New York American,* where he planned to work his way through the ranks before joining his father at the top of the organizational chart as the heir apparent.

Hearst, Jr., relished the chance to become a newsman. He started on the city-hall beat, covering flamboyant mayor Jimmy Walker. He then moved to the police beat and tagged along with veteran police reporters, playing a small role in the coverage of the Lindbergh-baby kidnapping. However, he was unsuccessful in disguising himself as a telegram-delivery boy in order to gain access to Charles and Anne Lindbergh's house.

His plan of mastering the newspaper business from the bottom up was short-lived. By 1931 he found himself president of the *American,* a figure-head executive bypassed in the decision-making process between his father and other top executives. In 1936 he was named publisher. In an interview with authors Michael Ciepley and Lindsay Chaney, Hearst said that being pushed up the corporate ladder before he was ready stunted his development as a newsman: "It was all way too fast . . . I was upstairs, in management, before I knew what a newspaper was all about – and some of those editors had been around from the day Pop bought the place. There was bound to be trouble."

Hearst's tenure at the *American* – which declined during the Depression and merged with its sister paper, the *New York Journal,* in 1937 – set a pattern that continued throughout much of his career at the company: short on experience, naive in office politics, and unsure of his own ability, Bill depended upon the tutelage and kindness of a senior Hearst executive. During periods in his life when no such mentor appeared, he lost ground in the company and, ultimately, his chance to control it.

Hearst, Sr., who was seldom with them, nevertheless watched his sons' lives closely. George, he concluded, was a "flop," while John was a lazy playboy; Randy and David, in Hearst's judgment, simply did not have the vision or energy to merit the Hearst legacy. Hearst also kept up private correspondence with his executives, criticizing his sons and insisting that they not move up in the company because of their name. The pressure, embarrassment, and mixed messages they received from their father kept all but Bill from giving a full effort to a newspaper career; however, in later years Randy would also blossom into a productive Hearst executive.

Hearst laid out his policy toward his sons in a letter to Tom White, general manager of the Hearst newspapers, in 1935: "Regarding the boys, I would like to make their admission to the board of directors conditional on a record of hard work and actual achievement. . . . I think that Bill can be speedily admitted on this basis, but I do not think that John can, and I do not propose to appoint him until he has proved he has something of value to contribute." Most executives took Hearst to mean that his sons were not sharp or energetic enough to succeed in the company and, with Hearst's blessing, treated them accordingly, as inferiors.

Eager to prove his worth as a newsman and move out from under his father's gaze, Bill departed for the European theater of war in 1943 as a correspondent for the *Journal-American.* The war years were the most exhilarating and satisfying of his journalistic life. He covered the Italian campaign and later followed the push from Normandy to Paris. He developed a camaraderie with, and was accepted by, his peers. The war opened his eyes to the brutality of human affairs, but he later delighted in telling war stories, including one about being knocked cold by Ernest Hemingway in a French hotel lobby.

In the field Hearst had greater access to military and political leaders than his colleagues be-

Hearst as publisher of the New York Journal-American, *1939. Behind him is a photograph of his father as a young man (courtesy of the Hearst Corporation and Mr. and Mrs. William Randolph Hearst, Jr.).*

cause of his famous name, but he was also determined to endure the same hardships his peers did. Away from the front he lived a much different life, staying at exclusive hotels and occasionally sharing rooms with movie star Clark Gable. His stories about the war were competent but not distinguished, and editors cringed at his chatty, rambling dispatches from liberated Paris. Still, the war gave Hearst confidence and a determination to increase his status in his father's eyes – and in the corporation.

By 1947 Hearst, Sr., had begun to withdraw from public life. He was eighty-four years old and preferred the quiet company of his longtime mistress, actress Marion Davies, to New York or even to the grand San Simeon, which he had abandoned for Beverly Hills. Although Hearst, sometimes through Davies, communicated often with top executives, a fight was shaping up for control of the company.

Bill was confident that he would take the helm of the corporation. But Hearst executives did not plan to give up power easily – nor did Hearst, Sr., intend them to: his will stipulated that a thirteen-member board of trustees, comprised of eight nonfamily executives and five family members, would control the power and money he left behind until his last grandchild died. With the family in the minority on the board, Richard Berlin, company president since 1943, assumed full control and quickly demonstrated that he would be giving the orders, often lording his authority over the family and telling cronies that he appeased the Hearsts by "tossing them a bone" occasionally. During a 1963 shake-up at the company, an anonymous family member told the *New York Times* that Berlin treated the Hearst brothers as if they were "congenital idiots."

While Bill had been building his confidence and reputation as a newsman during World War II, Berlin had been consolidating his position within the Hearst hierarchy. A career Hearst man, Berlin had helped to preserve many of the company's holdings – as well as San Simeon – after they had been placed in the hands of a bank-appointed trustee during the Depression.

During the late 1940s the senior Hearst slowly withdrew from the corporation because of declining health, and more and more decisions were left to Berlin. Bill seemed to all the world an heir apparent, and he expected to replace his father as the guiding authority of the corporation. Newspapers and trade publications touted his ascendancy, and he became, in many respects, the public face of the corporation, appearing frequently in news and society columns as he glided through Broadway nightspots, hobnobbing with celebrities and politicians. Berlin, however, was the real power within the corporation. With the allegiance of the majority of the trustees and the titles of president and chief executive of the Hearst Corporation, Berlin thwarted Bill's ambitions.

The fight for corporate control lost, Hearst, unable to follow his father as a media magnate, focused his energies on living up to his father's legend as a newsman. As publisher of the *Journal-American* and untitled director of Hearst editorial operations, Bill carried on his father's crusade against communism. Although milder and more cautious than his father in most matters, Bill's campaign to aid McCarthy was as frenzied and vituperative as any of his father's crusades.

Bill Hearst makes only two fleeting references to McCarthy in his autobiography, but biographers and historians describe his role in the McCarthy witch-hunt as deliberate and vicious. With Hearst's

Joseph Kingsbury-Smith, Hearst, and Frank Conniff in Moscow, 1955. They won a Pulitzer Prize for coverage of this trip (courtesy of the Hearst Corporation and Mr. and Mrs. William Randolph Hearst, Jr.).

blessing, columnists such as Walter Winchell, Westbrook Pegler, and Louella Parsons launched scurrilous and sometimes libelous propaganda campaigns against suspected Communists, and enemies of the Hearst organization. In addition, Hearst newspaper editorials attacked the Fifth Amendment, urged widespread government wiretapping, and even proposed the construction of detention centers in a "remote part of Wyoming for subversives in the event of war with the U.S.S.R."

Hearst later described Winchell as a "real bastard" who "swallowed the whole hook" of Red-baiting sources such as McCarthy counsel Roy Cohn. However, Hearst gave Winchell free rein to lie and smear, and assigned a team of reporters to help McCarthy ferret out Communists after the senator admitted to him that the notorious list of 205 purported Communists in the State Department that McCarthy had brandished in 1950 at a public rally in West Virginia did not even contain one name. Hearst later told interviewers: "Joe gave us a call not too long after the speech. And you know what – he didn't have a damned thing on that list. He said,

Hearst, 1984 (courtesy of the Hearst Corporation and Mr. and Mrs. William Randolph Hearst, Jr.)

'My God, I'm in a jam. . . . I shot my mouth off. So what am I gonna do now?' Well, I guess we fixed him up with a few good reporters."

Many newspapers besides Hearst's sided with McCarthy, but Hearst remained dogged in his support of the junior senator from Wisconsin and his "noble experiment" long after it became clear that he had lied, bullied, and subverted the democratic process. When McCarthy's colleagues in the Senate censured him and news organizations turned on him, the Hearst papers claimed a Communist conspiracy was afoot to discredit a great patriot. These irrational and shrill tirades further dimmed the credibility of the chain's newspapers.

Other factors worked against the chain's viability. Hearst, Sr., had kept such a tight rein on all of the papers and editors that leaders of individual papers did not know how to act flexibly and independently when Bill tried to decentralize control during the early 1950s – a policy that rival John S. Knight was using successfully to build his growing chain. In addition, where Hearst papers had once led in technological innovation and implementation, by the 1950s their equipment was outdated and inferior.

Along with directing news operations, Bill continued to build his reputation as a reporter and commentator in the years after his father's death. With Joseph Kingsbury-Smith and Frank Conniff, Hearst traveled to the forbidding Soviet Union in 1955 to report on the transition of power following Joseph Stalin's demise. Despite Hearst's rabid anticommunism, the Hearst name still carried weight in international circles and no doubt gained the reporting team extraordinary access to the Soviet people and their leaders, including Nikita Khrushchev, Vyacheslav Molotov, and Nikolay Bulganin.

Kingsbury-Smith and Conniff were by far the more experienced newsmen, but Hearst emerged as the voice of the team and gave interviews to Hearst news organizations and the major broadcasting networks back home. When the trio was awarded the Pulitzer Prize for International Reporting in 1956, Hearst could boast that he had finally reached a journalistic summit that neither his father nor any of his star reporters had achieved. The *Journal-American* announced the coup in a big headline: "Pulitzer Prize to W.R. Hearst Jr." In much smaller type at the top of one column, the paper mentioned that "Conniff and Smith Share."

In *Ask Me Anything: Our Adventures with Khrushchev* (1960), which recounts the assignment, Hearst, ever the zealous anti-Communist, reports that nervous Hearst executives feared he might rush into the Moscow streets to denounce Marxism. He left the Soviet Union with his deep hatred of communism intact, but also with an enhanced reputation as a newsman and as an expert in foreign affairs. He briefed President Dwight Eisenhower on the Soviet Union and continued to cover big political assignments, describing himself as a "president watcher." In recognition of his growing stature, in 1955 he was officially named editor in chief of the Hearst Newspaper Group, a position that had gone unfilled since his father's death.

The timing of the long-overdue appointment was ironic. With Berlin at the helm, the corporation began a policy of closing, selling, or merging unprofitable newspapers and focusing its energies on the more lucrative fields of specialty-magazine publishing and broadcasting. The *Chicago Tribune* was sold in 1956; in 1959 the *San Francisco Call-Bulletin* was merged with a rival Scripps-Howard afternoon paper. Between 1960 and 1962 closings and mergers followed in Pittsburgh, Detroit, Los Angeles, and Boston. In addition, the small but scrappy International News Service was absorbed by United Press in 1958.

Hearst, Jr., opposed many of the closings in principle but could not deny that his father's policy of keeping newspapers going, whether they made money or not, could not continue in an age of declining readership and tighter corporate accountability. In several clashes over the fate of faltering newspapers, Hearst's pleas that the company make a good-faith attempt to salvage them met with Berlin's scorn. In the midst of the closings during the early 1960s, Berlin told the *New York Times:* "Personally, I would sell everything but the wife and children if the proper price were offered." Bill was becoming an editor in chief without a news operation.

The Hearst flagship newspapers were dying, but many of them had lost money for years. While they fell, the company regained its health. The magazines continued to gain market shares and profits, but it was clear that while Hearst would remain a communications empire, it was no longer a major force in shaping the nation's news.

The Hearst family increased its control of the company during the late 1960s. By the time Berlin, ailing with Alzheimer's disease, retired in 1973, Bill was firmly entrenched as news director and a member of many boards of the corporation and its myriad subsidiaries. During his career Hearst held many prominent positions within the corporation, including chairman of the board, but the real power in the Hearst empire remained with the board of trustees and the executives Berlin had tutored to replace him.

Although the Hearst family gained power and increased access to corporation profits during the late 1960s – and a new generation of Hearsts carved reputations as newsmen and executives – in 1979 Berlin protégé Richard Bennack was appointed chairman of the board, a position he still holds. (In a 1987 speech recounting the history of the corporation, Bennack praised the "brilliant will" that left Berlin in control of the company; he made only a passing reference to Bill Hearst.)

Despite his activities in aiding McCarthy and the destruction that the senator caused with his anti-Communist crusade, there is little to suggest that Hearst was malicious or vindictive. For Hearst, the fall of the Communist bloc was final vindication of his stance during the McCarthy years. In dealing with subordinates he was fair and compassionate but did not exhibit the tendency toward the grandiose that was his father's trademark. Associate Harry Bull once described Bill as "kindly, bumbling in appearance, tall, puffy and popeyed with balding, slightly crinkly sandy hair. I've never heard anyone speak highly of his ability or badly of him as a man."

Hearst has married three times and divorced twice. His relationships with his own sons (by third wife, Austine) – William Randolph III, publisher of the *San Francisco Examiner*, and Austin, a Hearst executive – have been warm and open. Nevertheless, he told them at an early age the same thing his father had told him: that their success in the family business would be determined by their initiative and not their name.

Newspapers are but a small part of the Hearst empire as it navigates the 1990s, although the corporation did engage in the buying and selling of some dailies and several weeklies during the 1980s. The corporation continues to operate fifteen newspapers – only three in major urban markets – but the magazine division reaps the lion's share of the corporation's profits, estimated at $1.2 billion in 1987. Hearst magazine holdings include *Cosmopolitan, Esquire, Good Housekeeping, Harper's Bazaar, Popular Mechanics,* and *Redbook.* That division may be eclipsed as the Hearst Corporation, one of the largest diversified media companies in the United States, continues to expand into the field of electronic communications, operating both television stations and cable ventures. The corporation also has extensive timber and real-estate holdings.

Hearst lives near the grounds of the family's former estate, San Simeon, which was donated to the state of California as a park in the 1950s. His autobiography indicates that he was still, at the age of eighty-three, contemplating his stormy relationship with his father. At many points in the book he comes back to San Simeon as a metaphor for all the daring and folly that made Hearst, Sr., both revered and infamous as a public figure and hard to please as a father: "That was Pop – a man whose unexpected leaps into the unknown were buttressed by an unquenchable optimism. Unfortunately, none of us was blessed with such an adventurous spirit, although I tried to adopt one.... In retrospect, I don't believe any of us could have filled the shoes of our father."

References:

Frank Bennack, *The Hearst Corporation: 100 Years of Making Communications History* (New York: Newcomen Society, 1987);

Charlene Canape, "The New Money Makers at Hearst," *New York Times,* 6 March 1983, III: 1;

Michael Cieply and Lindsay Chaney, *The Hearsts: Family and Empire – The Later Years* (New York: Simon & Schuster, 1981);

"Estate of Hearst Near Settlement," *New York Times,* 2 December 1956, p. 55;

Geraldine Fabrikant, "Hearst's Eight-Year Buying Spree," *New York Times,* 26 April 1987, III: 4;

Charles Grutzner, "Death of Mirror Focuses Attention on Vast Hearst Corp.," *New York Times,* 20 October 1963, III: 10;

Grutzner, "Hearst Newspaper Chain, Part of Corporate Empire, Now a Third its Former Size," *New York Times,* 16 October 1963, p. 30;

Thomas C. Reeves, *The Life and Times of Joe McCarthy: A Biography* (New York: Stein & Day, 1982);

W. A. Swanberg, *Citizen Hearst: A Biography of William Randolph Hearst* (New York: Scribners, 1961).

John Heiskell

(2 November 1872 – 22 December 1972)

John De Mott
Memphis State University

MAJOR POSITIONS HELD: Editor, (1902–1970), co-owner (1902–1972), chairman of the board (1970–1972), *Arkansas Gazette.*

During the sixty-eight years that he edited the *Arkansas Gazette,* John Netherland Heiskell made that newspaper nationally known for its courageous stand against lawlessness and for its devotion to journalistic integrity. Although known as the South's "Old Gray Lady" as a result of its plain makeup and graphics, the *Gazette* earned international acclaim for Heiskell's condemnation of southern resistance to the Supreme Court's 1954 school desegregation order.

One hundred years old at the time of his death, Heiskell was born on 2 November 1872 to Carrick White Heiskell and Eliza Ayre Netherland Heiskell at the Rogersville, Tennessee, home of Eliza's father, John Netherland, a prominent lawyer. The future editor's father, also a lawyer, had served as a Confederate army officer during the Civil War. Shortly after John's birth the Heiskell family moved to Memphis, where he was reared.

While still a boy, Heiskell exhibited a taste for serious reading, preferring encyclopedias to novels, and magazines such as *Scientific American* to publications designed for children. He displayed an intense interest in news, reading the morning *Memphis Appeal* and the evening *Public Ledger* regularly. He also enjoyed the cartoons in the British humor magazine *Puck.*

At the age of ten Heiskell created a neighborhood newspaper, the *Jolly Fellowship,* containing news about his family and its neighbors. Priced at five cents, copies of the paper were peddled on Beale Street in downtown Memphis and in nearby areas. "In politics," the young editor notified his readers, "this paper will be strongly democratic." The deep interest in politics continued to characterize Heiskell's journalism throughout his life and became a major factor in the evolution of the involve-

John Heiskell

ment of the *Gazette* in efforts to foster better government in Little Rock and throughout Arkansas.

The early age at which Heiskell began to display such interest reflected his family's political character. In Memphis his father served as city attorney and as a circuit judge for Shelby County. During the Civil War he was a colonel in the 19th Tennessee Infantry. One of John's uncles served as a member of the congress of the Confederate States of America.

Heiskell's interest in journalism also had antecedents in his family background. A grandfather,

124

Frederick S. Heiskell, was a printer; he had a brother, John Heiskell, who published a newspaper, the *Winchester Gazette,* in Virginia. Frederick worked for his brother and in 1816 established a newspaper in eastern Tennessee, the *Knoxville Register.*

Perhaps as a result of his family's ties to eastern Tennessee, John enrolled at the University of Tennessee in Knoxville upon completion of his schooling in Memphis. He had distinguished himself – and received a gold medal – for an essay about William Shakespeare and his works. While studying at the university, Heiskell covered a football game – a sport still new at that time – between his own university and the University of the South (Sewanee). He received two dollars for the story, which was published in the *Knoxville Tribune.*

Heiskell was graduated from the University of Tennessee at the head of his class in 1893, after only three years. He then obtained a nine-dollar-a-week job as a news reporter for the *Knoxville Tribune.* While at the *Tribune,* Heiskell carried out one assignment in a manner that foreshadowed the firm stand that he would take against the violence advocated by many opposed to the integration of Little Rock's schools in the 1950s.

After returning from the hanging of a Negro in Knox County, Tennessee, Heiskell wrote an account that he headlined "Allen Cousan Dies Bravely." Over Heiskell's objection, the newspaper's editor changed the headline:

> By the Neck and By the Law
> Allen Cousan Dies.

Shortly afterward, Heiskell left the *Tribune* for the *Knoxville Journal,* which offered him twelve dollars a week to be its city editor.

He then returned to Memphis, where he took a fifteen-dollar-a-week job on the *Commercial Appeal.* He reported local news there until 1899, when he joined the Associated Press in Chicago. After only a year in the Chicago bureau, Heiskell was transferred by the AP to Louisville, Kentucky, where he served as bureau chief until he and other members of his family acquired control of the *Arkansas Gazette* in 1902. They invested fifteen hundred dollars, which included money John had saved during his years with the AP. For the remaining financing the family went into debt for eighty thousand dollars.

John become editor in chief of the newspaper, while his brother Frederick became its managing editor. Frederick William Allsopp, who had been a part of the previous management, was named busi-

ness manager. Judge Heiskell was not involved in the paper's operation. In 1922 Allsopp recalled the significance of the Heiskells' takeover:

> The most important change in the history of the newspaper with which I am connected occurred in June 1902, when a controlling interest in the property passed from W. B. Worthen to C. W., and J. N. and Fred Heiskell and myself.
>
> The Heiskell brothers, J. N. and Fred, have impressed the newspaper world with the fact that they are two of the most brainy and conscientious journalists in the South.
>
> The business relations with these gentlemen have been pleasant and profitable. For twenty years we have worked together, and handled the different departments of the newspaper, each pursuing his own line of endeavor, without a single disagreement or the semblance of an angry word.
>
> J. N. Heiskell is a worthy successor to W. B. Worthen and the long list of illustrious editors who have edited the *Arkansas Gazette.* While a newspaper is partly conducted to make money, the first consideration with him is to make a meritorious newspaper, and no amount of patronage could swerve him one way or the other.

Many years later Harry Ashmore – who served as chief editorial writer and executive editor of the *Gazette* during its battle against its state's defiance of court-ordered school desegregation – wrote: "When Mr. J. N. crossed over from Tennessee in 1902 to invest most of his family's modest fortune in Little Rock's venerable but shaky morning daily, he offered the usual announcement that he considered the newspaper a public trust ... generations of assorted Arkansas demagogues discovered that this was not a self-serving advertisement but an irrevocable statement of fact."

Heiskell, explaining the reorganized paper's mission in an early editorial, stated: "Instead of devoting itself to the exploitation of persons, it aims to be a clearinghouse of news and opinions." He made efforts from the beginning of his career as an editor to prevent the business function of the *Gazette* from influencing its editorial policy. In 1971 Heiskell recalled some of his early attempts to make news the paper's top priority: "I finally got the ads down below the centerfold ... later I got 'em all off page one, and gradually we built the paper up."

Heiskell married Wilhelmina Mann on 28 June 1910. They had two daughters, Elizabeth and Louise, and two sons, John, Jr., and Carrick. Both sons were killed in service during World War II. Early in Heiskell's career as editor of the *Gazette,* he became engaged in a struggle to break the power of

Jeff Davis, a U.S. senator who controlled Democratic politics in Arkansas around the turn of the century. What turned out to be a long battle against Davis and his supporters ended in 1913, when the senator died. Heiskell was appointed Davis's interim successor. He served for twenty-two days, during which he attempted to improve his state's reputation through a speech deploring the way Arkansans were frequently dubbed "rednecks" or "hillbillies."

Balancing the reputation of his state against its periodic need for political and social reform continued to challenge Heiskell throughout his seventy-year career in Little Rock. Loyal to his state and its people, he nevertheless addressed – as politely as practical, but always forthrightly – issues that he considered important to the continuing improvement of Arkansas. Aware of the press's power as a molder of public opinion during the early years of the twentieth century, Heiskell dedicated his paper's news-editorial policies to social causes, including most of those promoted by America's Progressive movement.

Heiskell championed social order, civility, culture, and education. He deplored lawlessness, bad manners, and ignorance. In 1910, commenting upon the opening of a library, he asked, "Why do people who go to a library leave dusty on the shelves the works of the master minds of all ages while they devour the cheap and tawdry tales of the loves of man and womankind." The editor later served as president of the Little Rock public library system's board of trustees.

Despite his sensitivity toward the mistreatment of blacks in the South, Heiskell approved of racial segregation and defended it on many occasions. When President Theodore Roosevelt closed a post office in Mississippi because its patrons refused to accept a black postmaster, Heiskell severely criticized the president. The editor deplored the influence of twentieth-century "carpetbaggers" representing interests outside the South, and he observed in 1907 that "the Negro is gradually coming to realize that his real friend is the Southern White man." Heiskell accepted the "separate but equal" premise of the Supreme Court's 1896 decision in *Plessy* v. *Ferguson*.

Irritated by a Negro's effort to join a segregated club in Little Rock, Heiskell ridiculed the issue as a test of one's "inalienable right to life, liberty and the pursuit of a golf ball." Moreover, he once even recommended that the Fifteenth Amendment be repealed. He reflected the racist attitudes of his early years as an editor in observing that no

Heiskell near the end of his seventy-year career with the Arkansas Gazette

amount of education, position, or financial status could put blacks "on the plane of equality with the higher race." Despite that attitude and his approval of segregation, Heiskell advocated education for blacks. The better their education, he reasoned, the better service they would be able to provide society.

Heiskell's lifelong commitment to the orderly administration of justice compelled him to oppose lynching. The *Gazette* endorsed a proposed statute providing for the removal of any Arkansas official who allowed the lynching of anyone in his custody. Heiskell pointed out that "lynching can be put down if we kill a few lynchers by process of law." His devotion to law and order prompted him to advocate the execution of draft resisters during World War I. However, he saw African-American soldiers as a threat to public safety.

In his support of education – as well as in his criticism of political corruption, violence, inadequate public services, and the dearth of cultural opportunities – Heiskell consistently argued that the state's shortcomings constituted a significant handicap in its quest for economic gain and general prosperity. He believed that prosperity and social enlightenment were inseparably linked. Consequently, he deplored public intoxication and even jazz, which he saw as a degenerate style of music condemned to "wither and die." Heiskell served on the board of directors of Little Rock's Chamber of Commerce, urged farmers to abandon their over-dependence on cotton in favor of crop diversification, and advocated making the Arkansas River navigable.

Although Heiskell believed that the University of Arkansas campus should be moved from Fayetteville to the state's capital, the *Gazette* supported its programs. The university awarded him an honorary doctorate in 1938. He also received honorary degrees from Little Rock College in 1929 and Arkansas College in 1934.

As his name and influence became known to other newspaper editors around the country, Heiskell was offered attractive positions elsewhere. Such propositions — even one by Arthur Brisbane, editor of the Hearst chain's flagship paper, the *New York Journal* — proved unpersuasive. Heiskell was elected a vice-president of the AP in 1926.

In 1927 a sensational racist-inspired miscarriage of justice outraged Heiskell's deep sense of law and order. Reminiscent of the hanging that he had covered in his early years as a reporter, this event involved the murder of a Negro by a lynch mob that dragged the body around the streets of Little Rock and then burned it. The *Gazette* reported the incident under an eight-column head-line:

With Officers Making No Attempt at Restraint
Mob Burns Negro's Body and Creates Reign of Terror

On the editorial page Heiskell observed, "The City of Little Rock suffered last night the shame of being delivered over to anarchy. Little Rock and Pulaski County must demand an accounting from the officers who have failed us." As in other situations of like kind, the chief emphasis of the *Gazette* was upon the maintenance of law and order.

As the shades of two world wars and the Depression faded away, Heiskell and his newspaper found themselves approaching a crisis that would sharply define the editor's philosophy. As a result of the Supreme Court's decision in *Brown* v. *Board of Education,* much of the South found itself in turmoil. Hard-line segregationists in such states as Georgia, Alabama, and Mississippi decided to resist the court's ruling. Others were concerned that any violence resulting from such resistance might cripple the South's effort to attract more industry and otherwise play a more important part in national affairs.

As the emotional atmosphere became more and more tense, Gov. Orval Faubus decided to resist the federal courts by taking over Central High School in Little Rock with troops from the state's national guard. Ashmore later summed up Heiskell's reaction to this event:

> The Gazette had been skirmishing with the militant segregationists for some years, but now we faced total war and the odds were long against us. He had to realize, I told him, that we would stand alone; the politicians and civic leaders were already running for cover, and the opposition *Arkansas Democrat* would play it safe and grow fat on our blood.
>
> Neither he nor I had any doubt what his answer would be; he reminded me that he had never been willing to stand aside while scoundrels and mountebanks took charge of his city and his state, and at eighty-five no one could reasonably expect him to change his mind, or The Gazette's stand.
>
> In the bruising years that followed, I would man the bridge along with Hugh Patterson and draw some of the shot and shell. But it was J. N. Heiskell who had to watch the substance he had gathered for his family drain away under boycott and bitter, constant abuse — well over a million dollars irrevocably lost before circulation and advertising hit bottom and began the slow crawl back. He had to bear with prudent friends who came to warn him that he had passed beyond considerations of financial loss, and that his newspaper faced extinction. If he felt panic, or entertained doubt, none of us on the firing line ever knew it.

On 23 September 1957 a mob stormed a protective detachment of police, and the Negro children being admitted to Central High School had to be removed for their own protection. Calling that day a tragic one in the nation's history, a *Gazette* editorial, "The High Price of Recklessness," observed, "In one sense we rolled back our history to the Reconstruction era when federal troops moved into position at Central High School to uphold the law and preserve the peace. Yet there was no denying the case President Eisenhower made in solemn words on television last night. Law and order had broken down here. The local police could not restore the peace with their own resources."

The *Gazette* pointed out that the governor had refused to use the state guard to enforce the law, but rather had used it to defy the federal court's order. The newspaper asserted that Faubus had made "inevitable" the president's use of federal troops to restore order. "And so," the editorial concluded, "the reckless course the governor embarked upon three weeks ago has raised old ghosts and tested the very fiber of the Constitution. And, the greatest irony of all, he has by his acts and words dealt a major and perhaps a lethal blow to the cause of segregation which he purported to uphold."

The federal government's restoration of order in Little Rock did not, however, avert a near-disaster for the *Gazette*. There came a new wave of racially inspired emotion. Heiskell recalled the situation:

> Reprisals against The Gazette took the form of cancellation of subscriptions. For day after day the "stops" came so fast that our usually efficient circulation department could not keep up with them. Our circulation fell from 100,000 to 83,000, and some of our small advertisers became so uneasy that we lost their business.
>
> In their bitter campaign against our newspaper, militant foes of desegregation resorted to a circular letter which called for a boycott. We obtained a copy and published it on the front page. We thought that right-minded people would agree with us that this was the best way to make the attack recoil upon itself.

Nevertheless, the *Gazette* continued to press its campaign against resistance to integration.

In recognition of its sacrificial battle against lawlessness, the *Gazette* in 1958 received a Pulitzer Prize for Public Service "for demonstrating the highest qualities of civic leadership, journalistic responsibility, and moral courage in the face of mounting public tension." The newspaper's "fearless and completely objective news coverage, plus its reasoned moderate policy, did much," the Pulitzer awards panel pointed out, "to restore calmness and order to an overwrought community."

At the time of Little Rock's school crisis, Heiskell was eighty-five, an age at which most publishers, if they are fortunate enough to be living, have retired and gone globe-trotting or settled down to compose their memoirs. However, Heiskell retained the editorship of the *Gazette* until 1970. During these years he received many awards, including a medal and citation from Syracuse University's School of Journalism, the University of Arizona's John Peter Zenger Award, the University of Missouri's distinguished service medal, an award from Columbia University's School of Journalism, and the Freedom House Award. In accepting the latter, Heiskell observed:

> Every newspaper must come to judgment and accounting for the course that forms its image and character. If it is to be a moral and intellectual institution rather than an industry or a property, it must fulfill the measure of its obligation, even though, in the words of St. Paul, it has to endure affliction. It must have a creed and a mission. It must fight the good fight. Above all, it must keep the faith.

Interviewed about a month before his hundredth birthday, Heiskell restated the creed by which he had edited the *Gazette* throughout the seventy years of his tenure: "The role of the newspaper is to print the news as fully as it can, and to print it impartially. It can be as loud as it pleases in its editorial columns, in opposing the other side, but it should be absolutely factual in its news columns."

Following Heiskell's death the *Gazette* continued to be a leading newspaper under the direction of his son-in-law Hugh Patterson. Nevertheless, competition from the *Democrat* took a financial toll on the *Gazette,* which was sold to the Gannett Company in 1986. WEHCO Media, which owned the *Democrat,* and Gannett struggled against one another for control of the Little Rock market, until Gannett sold the *Gazette* to WEHCO in 1991. The final issue of the *Gazette* was published on 18 October 1991. It then merged with the *Democrat,* becoming the *Arkansas Democrat-Gazette*.

References:

Fred W. Allsopp, *Little Adventures in Newspaperdom* (Little Rock: Arkansas Writer, 1922);

Harry Ashmore, "J. N. Heiskell," *American Library Association Bulletin,* 51 (October 1957): 691–692;

Abraham S. Chanin, *The Flames of Freedom* (Lanham, Md.: University Press of America, 1989), pp. 28–37;

"John N. Heiskell Is Dead at 100; Oldest Active Newsman in U.S.," *New York Times,* 29 December 1972, p. 28;

Wesley Pruden, "Mr. J. N. and a Legend at the *Gazette,*" *National Observer,* 3 (28 September 1964): 1, 17;

John Thompson, "Gentleman Editor: Mr. Heiskell of the *Gazette*: The Early Years, 1902–1922," Master's thesis, University of Arkansas at Little Rock, 1982.

Lee Hills
(28 May 1906 –)

Alf Pratte
Brigham Young University

MAJOR POSITIONS HELD: Chief editorial writer and associate editor, *Indianapolis Times* (1936–1937); editor, *Oklahoma News* (1938–1939); associate editor, *Memphis Press-Scimitar* (1939–1940); news editor, *Cleveland Press* (1940–1942); managing editor (1942–1951), executive editor (1951–1966), *Miami Herald*; executive editor (1951–1969), publisher (1963–1979), president (1967–1973), *Detroit Free Press*; executive editor (1959–1966), executive vice-president (1966–1967), president (1967–1973), Knight Newspapers; chairman and chief executive officer (1974–1979), editorial chairman (1979–1981), Knight-Ridder Newspapers.

BOOK: *Facsimile* (New York: McGraw-Hill, 1949).

As a reporter, editor, and executive with both the Scripps and Knight-Ridder organizations, Lee Hills worked to bring about the transition from the personal newspaper chains of the pre– and post–World War II periods to modern media companies. Along with other journalist-managers Hills helped to shape the old-fashioned newspapers of the past into those that define newspaper ownership today: chain ownership, local monopolies, joint-operating agreements, cross-media ownership of newspaper and television stations in the same city, and media conglomerates.

Hills was one of the most important of the post–World War II editors who brought about fundamental and often radical changes in newspapers, accommodating daily journalism to the increased tempo of modern living. He emphasized writing that was terse, colloquial, and designed to explain complex issues in terms that could be grasped quickly by readers with heavy demands on their time. He redesigned newspapers to give them greater eye appeal through the increased use of bold headlines, white space, and pictures. He strongly believed that newspapers could better serve the public by providing usable information and realigning themselves through the results of reader surveys. He also advocated better interpretive

Lee Hills

and investigative reporting, believing that newspapers often fail to get at the facts underlying a news development because of their "obsession with objectivity."

Despite being overshadowed by his boss, John S. Knight, Hills helped introduce or refine such management techniques as recruitment and personnel testing. Indeed, many of his ideas were continued through such Knight-Ridder leaders as C. A. (Pete) McKnight, Don Shoemaker, Allen H. Neuharth, James K. Batten, Bill Baker, Rolfe Neill, Eugene Roberts, and David Lawrence, Jr. Hills's influence was further enhanced by court cases fought by the Knight group. In addition, he served as president of four of journalism's major professional groups – the

Associated Press Managing Editors, the Society of Professional Journalists, the Inter-American Press Association, and the American Society of Newspaper Editors. Hills also served as a pioneer in such areas as newspaper facsimile broadcasting and the establishment of journalism education in South America.

Hills was born on 28 May 1906 in a farmhouse at Egg Creek near Granville, North Dakota, the son of Lewis Amos and Lulu Mae (Loomis) Hills. His ancestors were English and Scottish immigrants who moved from New England to Iowa and then to North Dakota where they homesteaded in the Minot area just south of the Canadian border. When he was three, the family moved to Salt Lake City and later to the mining community of Price, Utah, where Hills's father went into the insurance business. The family also lived for a short time in Grand Junction, Colorado. There Hills got his first feel for journalism by pecking out short neighborhood stories and mimeographing them in a newsletter. "I was fascinated by news from an early age," he later recalled.

At fourteen Hills got a job after school and on Saturdays with the *Price News-Advocate,* doing whatever chore came up: sweeping the floor, writing school news, printing the paper, and selling advertising. After the death of the owner in 1923, Hills helped run the weekly. In 1924 he enrolled at Brigham Young University in Provo, Utah, but left after his father was stricken with a serious illness. Hills returned to Price and worked full-time with the *News-Advocate* to help support the family.

The 1920s were turbulent, news-filled years for the young reporter. Among the major stories he covered were the Castle Dale mine disaster, which killed 171 men, and a rare event in the West, the lynching of a black miner who had violently murdered a police officer. In 1927 Hills enrolled at the University of Missouri School of Journalism. During his last year there he was hired by Walter M. "Skipper" Harrison, editor of the *Oklahoma City Times.*

In addition to reporting city and state politics, writing an occasional editorial, and helping on the copydesk, Hills took night classes at the Oklahoma City University School of Law, received a law degree, finished in the top 10 percent on the bar examination, and was admitted to the Oklahoma bar. He later remarked that the training in disciplined and analytical thinking helped him in assuming management duties: "It increased my confidence that I could do well in another field if I had to. It also taught me to recognize when I need a lawyer and how to pick one." Despite offers from law firms, he decided to stick with journalism. He resolved that if he did not obtain a top job in the

newspaper business by the time he was twenty-nine, he would abandon the profession. In 1932 he went to work as a political writer for the *Oklahoma News,* a Scripps-Howard newspaper. "Scripps just provided me with much greater opportunities," he recalled in 1992. Hills worked for the Scripps group for the next ten years.

In contrast to the newspaper chain owned by William Randolph Hearst, the Scripps papers supported labor unions, collective bargaining, and employee stock buying. Despite his identification with the working people, however, Scripps was still most comfortable as a capitalist. His employees were poorly paid, and after his death in 1926 his chief manager, Roy Howard, slowly shifted the group toward a more economic-oriented middle ground. Hills quickly became the star reporter at the *News,* covering the George "Machine Gun" Kelly trial, the activities of Charles "Pretty Boy" Floyd, and the colorful doings of Gov. William H. "Alfalfa Bill" Murray.

From 1932 to 1942 Hills worked in a wide variety of jobs for Scripps-Howard in Oklahoma City, Cleveland, Indianapolis, and Memphis. His experience with the chain had a profound effect on what he achieved later in helping to lead the transition of the family-owned Knight Newspapers into the largest publicly owned newspaper group in the nation, Knight-Ridder. Hills enumerated the lessons he learned through Scripps-Howard:

> How to serve a mass circulation constituency. The importance of the separation of church and state [editorial and business operations]. Central financial controls are necessary, but the best people thrive and do their most creative work with a degree of local autonomy. Compassion, especially for those who suffer through no fault of their own. Sensitivity. Be careful not to hurt or embarrass people unnecessarily. Get both sides. Get specific details. Don't cut corners. Get it right, especially direct quotes. Write so clearly that it cannot be misunderstood.

His work in Oklahoma drew attention from top Scripps-Howard officials in New York. Among others, Robert Scripps, son of founder E. W. Scripps, stopped in Oklahoma to interview and encourage Hills. In 1935 Scripps editor in chief George "Deac" Parker offered Hills a choice of going to Washington, D.C., as a correspondent and possible future columnist, or to Cleveland, the historic base of the Scripps penny press, to train as editor. Hills liked both ideas but deferred to Parker, who steered him to the *Cleveland Press.*

The paper still had some of the early Scripps traditions: language aimed at the average reader,

As managing editor of the Miami Herald, *Hills campaigned against illegal gambling and organized crime with articles such as the lead story above.*

forthright editorials, human interest, and local crusades. In 1936 Hills was sent to the *Indianapolis Times,* where he ran the editorial page. Because Hills had worked in Oklahoma, Scripps-Howard management asked him to go back to the money-losing *News* in 1938. He returned at age thirty-two, the youngest editor of a major metropolitan paper in the country.

Hills was able to reduce losses but concluded that the paper was too far-gone to save it and recommended that it be sold or closed. He stayed on several weeks during which all the staffers who wanted jobs and were willing to move were placed. Scripps was about to move its two newspapers in Memphis into one combined plant operation, and management asked Hills to go there.

Despite his rise to executive level in the Scripps-Howard group, Hills wanted out of the organization. His mentor at the *Cleveland Press,* Louis B. Selzer, referred him to Jack Knight, who was looking for help in expanding his family-owned newspapers from Akron, Ohio, and Miami, Florida. After a Sunday afternoon interview during which Knight's wife advised, "Don't let that young man get away," Hills was hired to run the news operations of Knight's *Miami Herald* in 1942. With World War II causing

loss of staff and cutbacks in newsprint, the thirty-six-year-old Hills had his hands full.

Nevertheless, his confidence and his instincts as a newsman prevailed even during the bleakest days of the war. He helped turn a crisis into a major turning point for the *Herald* in November 1943. The aggressive *Miami News* was competing fiercely for dominance in the market. Circulation boomed as 150,000 servicemen jammed the Miami area for training. Newsprint was strictly rationed. Knight told Hills that his plea for ration relief was denied and the *Herald* would run out of paper in two weeks. Hills urged that they cut out all circulation outside the immediate area and eliminate all paid advertising for the full month of December, except for classifieds related to the war effort. He suggested giving advertisers free space on one page for condensed messages. Knight was shocked at the idea but agreed. The *News* filled much of its scarce space with advertising, while the *Herald* filled its pages with war news. The *Herald* took a financial beating but built respect and loyalty. It quickly gained the upper hand in the market, an advantage that propelled it into the top ranks of American publishing. The *News* was never again a serious competitor.

At the end of World War II, Hills took a leave of absence, serving as a foreign correspondent for

Paul Miller, Vermont Royster, and Hills with Soviet premier Nikita Khrushchev in Moscow, 1962

both the *Herald* and the then-famous *Chicago Daily News* Foreign Service, which Knight had acquired along with the *Daily News*. He wrote about bombed cities and the stench of Adolf Hitler's death camps, as well as the war-crimes trial at Nuremberg, Germany. With information obtained during his European travels, Hills wrote one of the few interpretive articles on the development of the atomic bomb, which appeared in the *Herald* the day after Hiroshima was leveled.

Miami was already being talked about as the gateway to Latin America when Hills arrived there from Cleveland in 1942. He joined a group of North Americans at Havana in 1943 for the second meeting of the Pan American Congress. He worked with the organization through the turbulent period to 1950, when it was reorganized as the Inter-American Press Association at a meeting in New York City. As soon as the manpower pinch permitted, he assigned reporters to cover Latin America, and the *Herald* became known for its authoritative coverage of the region.

In 1946 he became one of the first North American newspapermen to be awarded the Maria Moors Cabot Prize by Columbia University for "outstanding contributions to better Inter-American relations." Under Hills's leadership the *Herald* be-

came one of the most cosmopolitan newspapers in the United States. In 1945 Hills inaugurated an international air-express edition of the *Herald* that was circulated in thirty-two Latin American countries. It was delivered by noon on the day of publication as far south as Santiago, Chile.

In 1947 Hills and Carl W. Ackerman, dean of graduate studies at the Columbia University School of Journalism, were invited to visit Venezuela and advise on the establishment of a school of journalism at the University of Caracas. The school was established along the lines they recommended. The *Miami Herald* has been the dominant U.S. English-language newspaper in Latin America for almost fifty years.

In 1951 Hills was given the dual responsibility of being executive editor of both the *Miami Herald* and the *Detroit Free Press,* which at that time was trailing its competitors in advertising and circulation. As head of both operations Hills had to shuttle between the cities.

One of the major stories covered by the *Herald* during the post–World War II boom in Florida was the influx of mobsters from the North, including Meyer Lansky and the Purple Gang from Toledo. Hills carried out his crusade against the gangsters by using the *Herald* to exchange information on known criminals with northern newspapers and

Hills with President John F. Kennedy in Miami, four days before Kennedy's assassination on 22 November 1963

law-enforcement officials. Some of the information in the newspaper bank was used in stories about the efforts of a county prosecutor to shut down gambling clubs. When some judges blocked his efforts, the *Herald* ran an editorial and cartoon critical of them. The judges in turn cited the paper for contempt and interference of justice. After its appeal to the Florida Supreme Court was rejected, the *Herald* took its case all the way to the U.S. Supreme Court, which on 3 June 1946 threw out the original conviction in a landmark victory. This proved to be the first in a line of expensive legal battles that the Knight group would pursue on behalf of journalistic principles.

In 1951 Hills directed the *Herald* to a Pulitzer Prize for Public Service for its series against organized crime and racketeering in Dade County. FBI chief J. Edgar Hoover is supposed to have said, "If I could stretch a net over 23rd and Collins on Miami Beach, I could end crime in America." One of the most imaginative aspects of the campaign was the "Know Your Neighbor" series that Hills inaugurated, featuring pictures of mansions and yachts belonging to notable gangsters in the Miami area. "I woke up the town," he recalled. Hills and other Miami leaders also

brought about the formation of the Greater Miami Crime Commission, and he later served on its board of directors.

In 1955 Hills stepped out of his editor's role at the *Free Press* to start digging into the United Auto Workers' contract negotiations over a guaranteed annual wage. In awarding him the Pulitzer Prize for his reporting, the judges cited his "aggressive, resourceful, and comprehensive coverage of the labor negotiations." Frank Angelo, the managing editor who worked closely with Hills on editing the series, stated, "Hills literally lived in his fourth-floor office at the *Free Press* for a week at a time."

Under Hills's direction the *Free Press* became a "bright, highly readable newspaper, adding to its reputation as a vehicle of solid coverage. The paper became known for its aggressive coverage of the growing suburban area, including questionable government practices in some communities," according to Angelo. The relationship between Hills and John S. Knight flourished. Knight called him "one of the finest newspapermen in the nation. . . . No other newspaperman I have ever known has possessed the sum of Lee Hills' qualities of judgment, wisdom, energy, perseverance and genuine feel for people." Hills's esteem for Knight as a role model was equally complimentary. "He gave me the job of recruiting the best talent I could find at both the entry level and middle-management stages," Hills stated in a 1990 interview.

Hills has been married three times. He wed Leona Haas in 1933; they were divorced in 1944. They had a son, Ronald Lee Hills. Lee Hills married Eileen Whitman in 1948. After her death he wed Argentina Schifano Ramos in 1963.

In *On Guard: A History of the Detroit Free Press* (1981), Angelo remarks that while there was never any doubt about the primacy of the news function, Hills also devoted considerable energy and talent to the business side of the newspaper – and to its competitive strategy. "The circumstances in Detroit suited Hills well for he had a winning instinct – and great impatience with those who didn't. He was quick to delegate authority, yet always managed to keep a hand in whatever was going on." In addition to sharing his journalistic skills and business abilities with the Knight papers in Miami and Detroit, Hills helped bring new life to the *Charlotte* (North Carolina) *Observer* – purchased in 1954 for $7 million – supervising the revamping of the paper and its staff.

Other publishers attempted to lure Hills away from the Knight organization. In the late 1950s John Hay Whitney wanted him to shore up the failing *New York Herald Tribune*. Hills declined a generous offer from Whitney, who considered him the key to saving the publication. He was offered a thirteen-year contract calling for a hundred-thousand-dollar annual salary, ample expenses and benefits, and an option on 10 percent of the *Herald Tribune* stock at an inside price. Hills enjoyed strong job satisfaction in a situation that would lead to the top of the nation's largest newspaper chain.

During the 1960s Hills was one of the executives who urged Knight to adopt modern management practices and better controls of the company's business side. They persuaded Knight to bring E. J. Thomas on the board. Thomas, the chief executive officer who helped build Goodyear into the world's largest tire company, recommended financial and management reforms that were soon adopted. Knight saw what newspapers should be editorially, but he scoffed at some business-school teachings until his friend Thomas convinced him to change.

In 1967 Hills became the first person outside of the Knight family to be named president of Knight Newspapers. The company went public two years later. Hills was one of the major architects of the merger with Ridder Publications in 1974 and was named the first chairman and chief executive of Knight-Ridder Newspapers. The combined opera-

tions included thirty-five daily and twenty-three Sunday newspapers. In combined circulation – 3.8 million on weekdays, including Saturdays, and 4.2 million on Sundays – Knight-Ridder was the largest newspaper group at that time. The new company also operated a national news and feature service, plus a commodity news service.

Hills summed up some beliefs he tried to foster at Knight-Ridder:

> The importance of thorough, authoritative reporting. Try to make your paper essential to the readers. Provide services and information that help people with their daily lives. The watchdog role is only part of it. A stubborn conviction that quality and profits can go hand in hand. A first-rate business operation is essential. Stay solvent. Create a climate in which people can do their best and give them freedom to do it. Try to be creative, innovative. Getting satisfaction vicariously through the accomplishments of others. A confrontational style of interviewing may be good TV show business but it doesn't produce the best factual reporting.

On 28 April 1981 Hills retired as editorial chairman of Knight-Ridder, giving up positions on both the operating and executive committees of the company. He remained a member of the Knight-Ridder board of directors.

Notwithstanding his rise to the top of journalism's corporate hierarchy, Hills continued to think of himself as a reporter and an editor: "I'm very proud of both of these titles. It is more fun being a reporter than anything else in the business; there is no more satisfying job. And there is no more important position than being an editor." When he phased out of top management duties, he took the title of editorial chairman, and then editorial chairman emeritus. David Halberstam, speaking to the American Society of Newspaper Editors in 1990, said, "The quality and ethics of journalism cannot be better than the values ingrained in the institutions themselves. . . . At the Knight-Ridder papers, the ethics of Lee Hills live on. It is a sense of obligation, of putting back as much as one takes out."

References:

Frank Angelo, *On Guard: A History of the Detroit Free Press* (Detroit: Detroit Free Press, 1981);

Richard Kluger and Phyllis Kluger, *The Paper: The Life and Death of the New York Herald Tribune* (New York: Knopf, 1986);

Neal Shine, "He's Master of News Arts in Shirtsleeves," *Editor & Publisher,* 95 (21 April 1962): 17, 60;

Nixon Smiley, *Knights of the Fourth Estate: The Story of the Miami Herald* (Miami: Seemann, 1974).

William Hobby

(26 March 1878 – 7 June 1964)

and

Oveta Hobby

(5 January 1905 –   )

Charles H. Marler
Abilene Christian University

MAJOR POSITIONS HELD: **William Hobby:** Managing editor (1903–1907), publisher and president (1932–1955), *Houston Post;* editor (1907–1914), publisher (1907–1931), *Beaumont* (Texas) *Enterprise;* lieutenant governor of Texas (1915–1917); governor of Texas (1917–1921); publisher, *Beaumont* (Texas) *Enterprise-Journal* (1922–1931); president, *Houston Post-Dispatch* (1922–1932).

Oveta Hobby: Parliamentarian, Texas House of Representatives (1926–1931, 1939, 1941); assistant editor (1937), executive vice-president (1938–1952), coeditor and publisher (1952–1955), president (1955–1964), editor (1955–1983), chairman of the board (1964–1983), *Houston Post;* chief, Women's Interest Section, U.S. War Department Bureau of Public Relations (1941–1942); commander, Women's Auxiliary Army Corps (1942–1945); director, Federal Security Administration (1953); secretary, U.S. Department of Health, Education, and Welfare (1953–1955); president, Houston Post Company (1965–1983); chairman of the board (1978–1983), chairman of the executive committee (1983–   ), H&C Communications.

BOOKS: Oveta Hobby, *Mr. Chairman: Rules, and Examples in Story Form, of Parliamentary Procedure Written Expressly for Use in the Elementary Schools and the Junior High Schools* (Oklahoma City: Economy Co., 1936);
Oveta Hobby, *Around the World in 13 Days* (Houston: Houston Post, 1947).

The twentieth-century version of Texas publisher-politico was pioneered by William Pettus "Will" Hobby, governor of Texas from 1917 to 1921 and president of the *Houston Post* from 1932 to 1955, and his second wife, Oveta Culp Hobby, secretary of the U.S. Department of Health, Education, and Welfare from 1953 to 1955 and editor or top executive of the *Post* since 1955. They were each born into families rich in public-service heritage, and each came early to journalism and politics.

Will's journalism involvement began in 1894 at age sixteen in the circulation department of the *Post;* at age nineteen Oveta also started work there. Politics was a game Will was content to observe from the sidelines as editor and publisher of the *Beaumont* (Texas) *Enterprise* from 1907 to 1914, when he agreed to file as a candidate for the Democratic nomination for lieutenant governor. "I can't tie a string cravat. I don't even own a swallow-tailed coat," he observed.

When Will ran for governor in 1918, Oveta, then thirteen, and her sister were told by their mother, "You'll have to can the peaches, girls; I'm going out to campaign for Will Hobby." Oveta's father, Isaac Culp, served in the Texas legislature in 1919 while Will was governor, and Isaac took her to every session. In 1925 she was appointed parliamentarian for the new legislative session, and she served in this role until 1931, then again in 1939 and 1941. She later wrote a widely used parliamentary textbook, *Mr. Chairman* (1936).

Will Hobby was born in the sawmill village of Moscow, Texas, on 26 March 1878, to Capt. Edwin E. and Eudora Adeline Pettus Hobby, of Virginia descent. Edwin – an antebellum immigrant to Texas from Florida and Georgia, and a Confederate officer – served three terms as a Texas state senator and as a district judge in Livingston, near the settlements of the Alabama and Coushattas Indian tribes. The elder Hobby, an expert in constitutional and land law, failed in his 1892 reelection bid as district judge. He then accepted a partnership in a Houston law firm, and the Hobby family moved to McKinney Avenue near the business district; the city's population was about fifty thousand.

Next door to his schoolhouse on Congress Avenue stood the *Houston Post;* Will often hovered near the doorway to journalism and a broader world. In this milieu he met reporters and their sources – Governor Jim Hogg; Gentleman Jim Corbett, the boxing champion; and Geronimo, the Apache war chief who was being transferred to an Atlanta prison.

The magnet of journalism outpulled law, politics, and a more formal education. When G. J. Palmer, business manager of the *Post,* offered Will a job in the circulation department at eight dollars a week, the die was cast. The *Post* carried the full text of William Jennings Bryan's "Silver Manifesto" speech on Will's first day at the job, 2 March 1895, Texas Independence Day.

A year later he was promoted to cashier; in two years he was working in the advertising department. Yet Will's goal was the editorial room, where the fascinating editors and writers worked. His favorite was Sydney Porter, a quiet, good-looking columnist in his early thirties, the quintessential storyteller. Will frequently fetched coffee and sandwiches for Porter and listened to his tales – material for the short stories for which Porter became famous as O. Henry.

Will turned twenty-one in 1899, borrowed one thousand dollars that April to buy ten shares of *Post* stock, and stood to defend the *Post* against political attack and to plead for party unity in the Harris County Democratic Convention, typical of the performances that prompted biographer James A. Clark to call Hobby "the tactful Texan." Watching Will's development was *Post* editor Rienzi Johnston, a former Confederate officer and a good friend of John Henry Kirby, law partner of Will's father. Kirby had made a fortune in lumber and was on the verge of completing a $30 million deal to form the Houston Oil Company, an effect of the 1901 Spindletop boom eighty miles east of the city.

Marcellus Foster, who would soon start the *Houston Chronicle,* the paper that would survive as the competitor of the *Post,* called Will into his office and asked him if he could do a complete biography of Kirby. The story was so good that Foster was promoted to managing editor, and Will gathered enough courage to say, "Mr. Foster, I want to be a reporter." The $22.50-a-week business-and-markets beat fulfilled Will's dream of a job in the newsroom. His performance earned him a 1902 promotion to city editor; a few months later when Johnston, pre-

William Hobby, 1920s

occupied with politics, left the managing editor's post, Will effectively assumed that job.

One of the biggest stories of his life erupted on 24 April 1905 at a prohibition rally in Hempstead that left Congressman John M. Pinckney and three others dead after about thirty shots were fired. The Texas Rangers were called in to prevent further bloodshed. Will directed the coverage, devoted all of page 1 to the sensational details, used graphics to illustrate a second-day story, earned new respect among Texas editors, and at age twenty-six was officially named managing editor by Johnston.

By the time of the financial panic of 1907, Will had become secretary of the state Democratic Executive Committee and had met Walter Joshua Crawford of Beaumont, one of five men who wanted to rescue the collapsing *Beaumont Enterprise.* They hoped Will would become editor, manager, half owner – and eventually full owner – of the *Enterprise.* On the advice of Johnston and Kirby, he took the opportunity at two hundred dollars a week, borrowed five thousand dollars to buy half of the stock, and became the partner of the five Beaumont leaders. Will was twenty-nine when the deal was announced on 11 June 1907 in the evening *Enterprise.*

Five years later he was president of the Beaumont Chamber of Commerce, a consequence of his making the *Enterprise* a champion of a deep-water channel to open the city as an inland seaport, similar to a ship channel projected for Houston. The *Enterprise* also advocated completion of the Intracoastal Canal, municipal development of land along the Neches River, the first countywide drainage survey in Texas, and rail connections to Waco, the trade and agricultural center of the Brazos valley.

The interconnected interests of Waco and Beaumont led Will and his brother Edwin to buy a small Waco paper, the *Morning News,* in 1913. This speculative property was not as successful as the Beaumont paper because of competition from the afternoon *Times-Herald.* They sold the *Morning News* a year later to Artemus Roberts, who wanted to run a prohibition paper in predominantly Baptist Waco. The Hobby brothers made ten thousand dollars on the venture.

On 31 May 1914 a chance meeting in Dallas with Democratic party friends changed Will's life. At its conclusion he agreed to file for the party's nomination for lieutenant governor against a prohibitionist candidate, state senator B. B. Sturgeon. James E. Ferguson – a Bell County farmer, lawyer, and banker – was a candidate for governor and had promised voters he would leave intact the state's local-option liquor law, which permitted precincts inside "wet" counties to vote "dry." Will said he agreed with Ferguson, because prohibition had obscured more important issues in Texas.

This team of unofficial running mates was up against prohibitionists Tom Ball for governor and Sturgeon, both of whom were political veterans. Will was a new type in Texas politics – "quiet, almost retiring," "modest and unpretentious," "warm and sincere," according to Clark. Will was also an uncomely man – short, large-eared, and jowly. Yet on the stump he spoke forcefully and effectively with a mellow,

Oveta Hobby

pleasing voice. His platform included benefits for laborers and tenants, home-ownership assistance, unambiguous laws, educational improvements, flood control, campaign-contribution reform, and a neutral position on prohibition. Ferguson upset Ball, but Hobby received more votes than Ferguson.

The new lieutenant governor was inaugurated on 19 January 1915 and presided in the senate chamber during the Thirty-fourth Legislature of Texas with a judicial dignity inspired by his father's presence on the district court bench. Ferguson and Hobby delivered their campaign promises and inspired the legislators to lay aside, if only for a little while, prohibition and controversy. After fulfilling his duties in Austin, Will returned to the *Enterprise,* hiring Alfred Jones, of the *Houston Telegram,* as his editor.

Within a few weeks the Beaumont publisher had married the blond, blue-eyed Willie Chapman Cooper, daughter of Samuel Bronson Cooper, a former U.S. congressman from New Orleans and longtime family friend. The couple had met in Washington, D.C., during one of Will's business trips. Her political interests and Washington society experience was an asset to the Hobbys' official duties. In 1915 his Beaumont friends often came to call the publisher "Governor," rather than his preferred "Will," and the Texas Associated Press Managing Editors Association elected him president. He urged the AP editors to develop a fast, accurate system of gathering and reporting the unofficial Texas election returns, a suggestion that resulted in the Texas Election Bureau.

The raging European war formed the background for more pleasant events in Will's life during 1916. The arrival of the Italian steamer *Lampo* initiated Beaumont's role as a seaport. The publisher came to believe that women should be given the right to vote. He ran unopposed and was reelected lieutenant governor. Ferguson also was reelected but sustained charges that led to his impeachment.

Ferguson's opponent, East Texas banker Charles H. Morris, accused him of malfeasance, which provided a bed of discontent upon which Ferguson picked a no-win battle, attempting to dismiss six University of Texas faculty members. The quarrel led him to veto university appropriations, and a Travis County grand jury indicted him on charges of misapplication of public funds, embezzlement, and diversion of a special fund – the old Morris charges.

Another controversy emerged that would scar later relationships between Ferguson and Hobby. A board was named to choose a location for a new agricultural and mechanical college in West Texas, and the Ferguson-appointed board secretary announced that Abilene, the site favored by Ferguson, had been selected. Hobby, one of the board members, revealed in a speech that he had voted for San Angelo; the Speaker of the House and the commissioner of agriculture also announced that they had not voted for Abilene. Hobby suggested that the board reconvene to solve the controversy and apparent error. The reconsideration of the site led to the eventual selection of Lubbock for Texas Tech University.

Ferguson called a special session of the legislature in August to consider university appropriations, during which the lawmakers adopted twenty-one articles of impeachment of the governor related to the grand-jury indictment. Constitutionally, Hobby became acting governor on 14 August 1917, barely four months after Congress had declared war on Germany and in the midst of a state drought. On 25 September 1917 the state senate announced that Ferguson was to be removed from the governorship and prohibited from ever holding office in Texas. Before the action was final, Ferguson resigned and declared that he would run for a third term in 1918. Hobby automatically became governor upon the senate's action.

During Hobby's brief first term as governor he used the Texas Rangers to control bandit raids along the Rio Grande; forged a plan under which the federal government agreed to aid drought-stricken farmers; reformed the new Texas Highway Commission to "get the farmers out of the mud"; urged the legislature to approve ten-mile "dry" zones around all state military training areas; led the fight to ratify the Eighteenth Amendment; submitted and supported passage of woman suffrage in Democratic primaries; and helped reform the primary system to allow for runoffs. Hobby's behind-the-scenes management of the legislature made him the dominant leader in Texas politics. On 6 January 1918 he announced that he would be a candidate for governor.

Hobby declined friends' encouragement to seek court action to enforce the legislature's ban of Ferguson from the governor's race, because he believed that "the people should have an opportunity to express their preference." Hobby's hopes were strengthened by his success with the legislature and his support of the war effort, the Texas press, and the newly franchised women who could vote in Texas Democratic primaries. Ferguson's crusade for self-redemption was marked by intemperateness and attacks on Hobby as a "weakling" and a "political accident."

By May the emotional Ferguson and the rational Hobby were at it. The former governor described his opponent as "a misfit whom God had failed to endow with the physical attributes that make up a man." Hobby opened his campaign at McKinney, answering, "I will admit that the Supreme Being failed to favor me with physical attributes pleasing to Governor Ferguson, but at least He gave me the intelligence to know the difference between my own money and that which belongs to the state."

The West Texas college-site controversy figured significantly in the campaign rhetoric. In Abilene a Fergusonite, Judge Fred Cockrell, claimed that Hobby said, "I will never vote for Abilene for it is the biggest witch-burning prohibition town in Texas. I will favor San Angelo because it is the only wet town offering." A few days later in Abilene, Hobby said, "I denounce the statement as absolutely false." Ferguson's ad hominem attacks backfired, and Hobby won more Democratic primary votes than any opposed candidate for office in Texas history, carried 234 of 254 counties, and garnered more than double the impeached governor's vote. In the November general election he defeated his Republican opponent by a margin of six to one.

Hobby's elective term as governor was highlighted by the passage of his "free textbook" constitutional amendment in the general election; his unprecedented release of all contributions to his campaign; ratification of the Nineteenth Amendment for woman suffrage, making Texas the ninth approving state and the first in the South; clarification of the state libel law, including the principle of privilege; and a comprehensive oil and gas conservation law. The Hobby administration maintained good relationships with newspapers, with the exception of the attempted arrest of a Houston editor who was critical of Texas National Guard martial law during a violent Galveston labor dispute. Hobby counted the capitol press corps among his personal friends, and he appointed several journalists to key Austin jobs.

Hobby initially found his postgubernatorial period at the *Enterprise* still exhilarating and bought out his afternoon competitor, the *Beaumont Journal,* in 1921. The morning-evening combination experiment of Hobby's *Enterprise-Journal* soon became the norm for many papers in Texas and elsewhere. The size and resources of Beaumont, however, imposed limits upon Hobby's ambitions, and in mid 1922 he returned to Houston, leaving his *Enterprise-Journal* interests in the hands of Jim Mapes, who later acquired the papers.

Houston offered a more expansive market for the publisher, and he found that Roy Watson had displaced the old trio at the *Post* of Johnston, Palmer, and H. F. MacGregor. Watson's newspaper policies cost him the support of staff and readers, but he refused to sell the paper to Ross Sterling, president of the Humble Oil and Refining Company. Sterling, who was lining up a run at the governorship, started a new paper, the *Houston Dispatch.* Advertising did not materialize for the *Dispatch* because of always-denied charges that it was begun as a Ku Klux Klan organ. But in mid July 1922 Watson made a surprise sale of the *Post* to Sterling, who offered Hobby the presidency, a directorship, and stock in the combined *Post-Dispatch.*

Hobby announced that he would publish "an independent newspaper" and prefaced his first edition of the *Post-Dispatch,* on 1 August 1922, with this promise: "The object and purpose is to make it possible for Houston to have one morning newspaper measuring up to the best standards of journalism of the best American cities." Ironically, this stance was soon tested in the gubernatorial election.

The Democratic nominee was Ma Ferguson, wife of Jim Ferguson. The *Post-Dispatch* supported Republican George Butte, a law professor who had crafted the oil and gas utilities regulations that Hobby had backed as governor. Ma Ferguson won the governorship, and the *Post-Dispatch* often reminded her husband that her election was not an approval of Jim's policies and the acts for which he had been impeached.

Hobby and Sterling again opposed Fergusonism in 1926 and helped Dan Moody, a successful prosecutor of the Ku Klux Klan, win a landslide victory. Moody installed Sterling as full-time chairman of the highway commission, which meant that Hobby had unparalleled power in Texas media: president of the *Post-Dispatch,* and publisher of the *Beaumont Enterprise-Journal,*

as well as control of radio station KPRC, which Sterling bought and activated on 9 May 1925 from the roof of the *Post-Dispatch* building.

The next major turn in Hobby's life was the death of his wife on 15 January 1929. Within two years Sterling was elected governor in a bruising battle with Ma Ferguson. The *Post-Dispatch* publisher assumed office in January 1931, during the worst of times. The newspaper had published a comment in its "Houston" column at the outset of the race: "The *Post-Dispatch* will not deviate from its fixed policy of treating all candidates fairly."

In February 1931 Hobby was two hundred thousand dollars in debt, because an insurance company in which he was a partner fell victim to the Depression. He needed the understanding and companionship of a strong woman and found the answer in his marriage on 23 February to Oveta Culp, daughter of I. W. and Emma Hoover Culp of Temple. He was fifty-two and she, twenty-six. Intelligent and beautiful, Oveta, too, was marked for command. She had served as the Texas chairman of the League of First Voters in 1928 at the Democratic National Convention in Houston, executive secretary of the Women's Democratic League of Houston, and assistant to the Houston city attorney. She ran a close but unsuccessful race for the Texas legislature from Harris County in 1930.

The *Post-Dispatch* was purchased by insuranceman J. E. Josey on 8 December 1931. William Pettus Hobby, Jr., was born in Houston on 19 January 1932, also the birthdate of Robert E. Lee and then an official holiday in Texas, Confederate Heroes Day. "I had no idea babies were so popular," the new father told Oveta, "or I would have had them in my platform." The son would be reared to serve in government and would do so as lieutenant governor of Texas from 1973 to 1991. Josey made Hobby president of the company and publisher of the newspaper. Hobby quickly dropped the hyphenated name for his preferred *Post,* which alleviated the objections of the *St. Louis Post-Dispatch.*

The Hobby team backed Franklin D. Roosevelt for president in 1932 and helped lead the fight in Texas to repeal prohibition. Hobby signed the National Recovery Act plan and announced a forty-hour workweek and thirty-five-dollar minimum weekly pay plan for *Post* employees. Oveta, who had attended Mary Hardin-Baylor College, became book-page editor and worked in the campaign to help assure the success of the National Recovery Act.

Fergusonism collapsed in 1934 with the help of the Hobbys and the *Post,* who backed James V. Allred in his successful run for the governorship. The Hobbys went to Dallas in June 1936 as members of Roosevelt's party during his visit for the Texas centennial. On their return to Houston in a small, single-engine plane with Houston financier Jesse Jones, a fire broke out in the aircraft south of Dallas. The pilot kept the plane under control until it went into a steep dive, leveled as it hit the ground, skidded, and came to rest in a cotton field. As the motor fell out and flames shot from the cockpit, Jones and the Hobbys escaped. Shaken, the Hobbys never flew together again.

Oveta advanced to the position of assistant editor of the *Post* in 1937, retained her role as book-page editor, and gave birth to daughter Jessica Oveta on 19 January 1937. The *Post* directors promoted Oveta to executive vice-president in March 1938. Onlookers assayed the strengths of the Hobby team: the governor provided dignity, experience, and wisdom; Oveta gave it ideas, initiative, and charm. Together they bought the *Post* in the fall of 1939.

By the end of the next year, the Depression behind them, the Hobbys had thoroughly injected their economic and political philosophy into the *Post* editorials, built a new plant, installed a new press, improved the newspaper's appearance, invigorated the content, and increased the advertising rates. They opposed Roosevelt's third-term effort, helped Wendell Willkie without endorsing him, but threw the total support of the *Post* behind Roosevelt's national unity and preparedness program once he won reelection.

In July 1940 a call came from Washington asking Oveta to become the dollar-a-year head of the women's section of the War Department's Bureau of Public Relations, a preface to her May 1942 commission as a colonel to run the Women's Auxiliary Army Corps. Will attended her swearing-in as WAAC chief, and George Dixon of the *New York Daily News* wrote, "If ever a man looked as if he was saying to himself what-the-hell-am-I-doing-here, it was Mr. Hobby." The focus of fame shifted to Oveta in Washington and elsewhere, while Will ran the wartime *Post,* and the children split their time between Houston and Washington.

The five-foot-four Oveta, who as a civilian was known for her pretty yet sometimes wacky hats, donned a Lord and Taylor–designed WAAC cap dubbed the "Hobby hat," an olive-drab uniform, sheer stockings, and Cuban-heeled shoes, and plowed into the job with the energy of a Jeep. She included forty black women in the first contingent of officer candidates. The colonel declared that WAACs should wear "inconspicuous" makeup, civilian clothes on leave, and girdles if they had unmilitary bulges. She

Oveta Hobby as commander of the Women's Auxiliary Army Corps during World War II

ordered khaki underwear to quiet complaints about pink underthings flapping on barracks clotheslines.

When the army wanted to give dishonorable discharges to out-of-wedlock pregnant WAACs, the generals collided with her argument that the guilty men should likewise be dishonorably discharged. Afterward, pregnant WAACs were honorably discharged. She nudged the list of congressionally approved WAAC jobs from 54 to 239, saying, "We are only supposed to have noncombatant duties, but it is difficult to know where fighting begins or ends." Her husband once said, "Anything she does is all right with me. We're all proud of her. She's doing her duty."

The wartime pace of the Little Colonel, as she was sometimes known, took its toll by July 1945, when, physically exhausted, she resigned as chief of the WAACs. She was awarded the Distinguished Service Medal, the first military woman and the seventh woman ever to win the nation's third highest recognition. Will hurried to Washington, checked her into a hospital for recovery, and took her home

Oveta Hobby as secretary of the U.S. Department of Health, Education, and Welfare, circa 1954

to their twenty-seven-room Georgian mansion filled with her silver and rare-book collections.

Houston welcomed her home with a dinner at which Oveta referred to Will as "my partner, my friend, my husband." She was soon back at the *Post* and covered the March 1946 United Nations Security Council meeting in New York, calling it "something like watching a chess game between powerful antagonists." The *Post* was enthusiastic about the United Nations and warned that Russia's minor aggressions might lead to major ones.

During the postwar period the Hobby team continued to serve as newspaper, civic, and political leaders. The Southern Newspaper Publishers Association named Oveta its first woman president in 1949, and she was appointed to the 1948 UN Conference on Freedom of Information and the 1948 Hoover commission on governmental reorganization. In 1949 the *Post* won four first-place awards for news-editorial achievements from the Associated Press, which confirmed their belief that the newspaper was fulfilling its slogan: "Written and Edited to Merit Your Confidence." The newspaper company, which had been an early entrant into radio with

KPRC, also purchased KPRC-TV, Houston's first television station, in 1949.

"Mr. and Mrs. Texas," as Governor Allan Shivers referred to the Hobbys, chose an un-Texan political path in 1952 when they sided with Dwight Eisenhower, the Republican presidential candidate, because "he is in favor of state ownership of the tideland against the federal grab of the submerged oil reserves." The former colonel pitched into the campaign for the former general with a "political primer" that helped cast the outcome for Eisenhower in the Texas Republican precinct conventions, and the former governor pushed him in editorials. Oveta became a leader in the national Citizens for Eisenhower organization, and Will focused on the Texas Democrats for Eisenhower campaign.

The triumphant "Ike" soon named Oveta as federal security administrator. Congress expanded the scope of her duties under the Department of Health, Education, and Welfare. The president appointed her its first secretary with cabinet status; she was the second woman cabinet member after Frances Perkins, Roosevelt's secretary of labor. While Oveta served in the Eisenhower administration, the Post

Company opened a new television center for its NBC affiliate and built the fifth home for the *Post,* one of the largest plants in the South, to produce papers for two hundred thousand subscribers.

Oveta's Washington challenge was formidable: how to create a welfare program and avoid a welfare state, concerns about what the Republicans would do with the social security system designed by the Democrats, and how to cope with the American Medical Association's fears about federal health schemes. The charm and intelligence of the Texas lady with the steel-gray hair calmed the naysayers. She disliked obscurely written law and bureaucratic delay and worked long days. "We are not looking for trouble," she said, "but, where we have a law to enforce, we'll enforce it. If the law is bad, that's the affair of Congress – not ours." *Business Week* magazine commented that observers "can make two mistakes about Mrs. Hobby, either of them fatal. They can figure that, as a woman, she doesn't really know much about business. Or they can get the idea, for the same reason, that she can be pushed around."

Back in Houston, Will, seventy-seven, became ill from the pace he was keeping during the closing phase of the new plant construction and opening, and in August 1955 Oveta resigned her cabinet position to return to him. He recovered quickly, and, in order for the team to function at full speed, he became chairman of the board and Oveta, president and editor. The *Post* emerged as Texas's largest daily newspaper in 1957, the year he underwent surgery for a hemorrhaging ulcer, which began a seven-year period of failing health. Oveta was at his side when he died on 7 June 1964 at age eighty-six.

She was given the National Publisher of the Year award in 1960. After her husband's death she led the paper as chairman of the board and editor until 1983. From 1978 to 1983 she served as chairman of the board of H and C Communications; she has been chairman of the board's executive committee since 1983. She also ran the family's broadcast properties, which came to include KPRC-TV and KPRC-AM (Houston), KVOA-TV (Tucson, Arizona), WESH-TV (Daytona Beach-Orlando, Florida), KCCI-TV (Des Moines, Iowa), and KSAT-TV (San Antonio, Texas). Daily circulation of the *Post* during the early 1990s was about 320,000.

Hobby, Texas – named after Will Hobby – is in Fort Bend County, southwest of Houston, where his maternal grandfather, Dr. John Pettus, settled in 1858. The Hobby Airport and Hobby Elementary School in Houston are also named after the gover-

nor. The library at Central Texas College in Killeen is named for Oveta. Honorary doctorates have been bestowed upon Oveta by more than a dozen colleges and universities, including Smith College, the University of Pennsylvania, and Columbia University. She was the recipient of an Honor Medal from the University of Missouri School of Journalism in 1950. A campaign to promote the eighty-seven-year-old colonel to brigadier general in 1992 was managed by U.S. senator Lloyd Bentsen of Texas, who wrote President George Bush, urging him to "honor a hero . . . and recognize the special contribution which women made to our victory." The White House declined the request.

Interview:

"Interview with Mrs. Oveta Culp Hobby," *U.S. News & World Report,* 33 (26 December 1952): 44–48.

Biography:

James A. Clark, *The Tactful Texan: A Biography of Governor Will Hobby* (New York: Random House, 1953).

References:

"Among Presidential Appointees," *Independent Woman,* 32 (January 1953): 7, 32;

"Generalissima," *American Magazine,* 134 (September 1942): 73;

William P. Hobby, Jr., "William Pettus Hobby," in *The Handbook of Texas,* volume 3 (Austin: Texas State Historical Society, 1976);

"Hobby's Army," *Time,* 43 (17 January 1944): 57–62;

"Major Hobby's WAACs," *Time,* 39 (25 May 1942): 72;

"More Eisenhower Team," *Newsweek,* 40 (8 December 1952): 21–22;

"Oveta Culp Hobby's New Job," *Business Week,* no. 1237 (16 May 1953): 116–121;

"Promotion Sought for Oveta C. Hobby," *Dallas Morning News,* 8 May 1992, pp. A1, A31;

"WAAC: U.S Women Troop to Enlist in Army's First All-Female Force," *Life,* 12 (8 June 1942): 26;

"William P. Hobby, 86, Is Dead; Governor of Texas, 1917 to 1921," *New York Times,* 8 June 1964, p. 29;

"With the First Lady and the First WAAC," *Newsweek,* 20 (9 November 1942): 45.

Palmer Hoyt

(10 March 1897 – 26 June 1979)

Jeffrey B. Rutenbeck
University of Denver

MAJOR POSITIONS HELD: Editor and publisher, *Portland Oregonian* (1938–1946); director, domestic branch of the Office of War Information (1943); editor and publisher, *Denver Post* (1946–1970).

SELECTED PERIODICAL PUBLICATION – COLLECTED: " 'Gone Wrong' Does So at the Pendleton Round-up," in *News Stories of 1933,* edited by Frank Luther Mott (Iowa City: Iowa City Press Club, 1934), pp. 168–172.

During a period when metropolitan newspapers were falling into the grasp of major newspaper chains and coming under fire for ignoring their community and social responsibilities, fiercely independent Palmer Hoyt resurrected the *Portland Oregonian* and the *Denver Post,* elevating them to national prominence. Hoyt's strategy was simple: separate news from opinion and reestablish the newspaper's connection with its community. His eight years at the *Oregonian* and twenty-four years at the *Post* established Hoyt as a leader in the struggle for credibility and viability in American journalism.

Edwin Palmer Hoyt was born on 10 March 1897 in Roseville, Illinois, the son of Edwin Palmer, a Baptist minister, and Annie Marie Tendler Hoyt. His father died of pneumonia in 1910, when Hoyt was thirteen. In the fall of the next year Hoyt's mother sent him to Baptist-sponsored William Jewell College Preparatory School in Liberty, Missouri. After finding out that many of his teachers smoked and chewed tobacco, she moved her son to another Baptist school, McMinnville College, in McMinnville, Oregon. He enlisted in the Oregon National Guard and was sent to France during World War I with the American Expeditionary Force, advancing from private to corporal, sergeant, and finally sergeant major.

After his discharge in 1919 he married Cecile de Vore on 18 May 1921 in Vancouver, Washington. He and his wife moved to Eugene, Oregon, where he enrolled in the University of Oregon with the intention of becoming a writer. Soon he became

sports editor of the school paper, the *Daily Emerald,* and sports correspondent for the *Portland Oregonian.*

In 1922 he took a job as copyreader at the *Oregonian,* and in 1923 he was graduated from the university with a degree in journalism. His first child, Edwin Palmer Hoyt III, was born on 5 August 1923. This was also the year that Hoyt was to begin full-time his long career in journalism; he became telegraph and sports editor of the *East Oregonian* in Pendleton. He soon found himself in charge of making up the paper, reading proofs, covering sports, and writing editorials.

Hoyt was also pursuing his dream of becoming a published fiction writer. His short stories spanned many genres: sports, horror, Westerns, and detective stories. He sold his first piece in 1926 and had about fifty short stories published in pulp-fiction magazines. However, his budding career as a writer was soon overshadowed by his natural management ability.

Hoyt entered the world of metropolitan journalism as he steadily worked his way up the ladder at the *Oregonian* as a movie reviewer and reporter from 1929 to 1931. According to *Denver Post* historian Bill Hosokawa, Hoyt was mulling over the idea of quitting the newspaper business at this time and writing fiction as a vocation. Then he was offered a promotion to night city editor at fifty-five dollars a week. He chose steady income over literary potential and accepted the position, which he occupied until he was named executive news editor in 1932. He was promoted to managing editor in 1933. Hoyt received some professional recognition as a journalistic writer when his story " 'Gone Wrong' Does So at the Pendleton Round-up" was printed in the book *News Stories of 1933,* compiled by Frank Luther Mott and twenty-seven other journalism educators as representative of the best news and feature writing for that year.

In 1938, at the age of forty-one, Hoyt became one of the youngest editor-publishers of a metropolitan daily in the country and undertook to resurrect the *Oregonian* much as he would do the *Denver Post* less than a decade later. Hoyt restored the paper's viability using an assortment of strategies, the most important

Palmer Hoyt

of which was separating news from opinion in the newspaper's columns. Hosokawa quotes from an unpublished manuscript by Supreme Court Justice William O. Douglas, who wrote that when Hoyt became editor of the *Oregonian,* "he launched a revolution in newspaper circles by taking editorial comment out of news stories and putting it on the editorial page. It was a sad reflection on the press that such a move was a revolution."

The paper's stature rose steadily under Hoyt's leadership, receiving the University of Missouri citation for distinguished service in journalism in 1940. His stature rose with the newspaper's, and in 1943 he was asked by Elmer Davis, director of the Office of War Information (OWI), to head up the office's domestic division. In June, Hoyt took a six-month leave from the *Oregonian* to serve his country during wartime. Davis expressed his pleasure with Hoyt's acceptance of the position: "Mr. Hoyt is a competent, experienced newspaperman who enjoys the respect of newspapermen throughout the country. He knows particularly well the problems and point of view of the West, which should be helpful to all of us here in Washington."

Davis and the policies of the OWI had been sharply criticized for exerting excessive control over what the press, radio, and motion-picture companies could do with news of the war. Most cogent of all criticisms were those directed at the office's inefficiency.

Many newspaper editors and publishers, including Hoyt, had attacked the OWI for its failure to coordinate news and for incomplete and inaccurate reporting of the war.

Just before Hoyt arrived in Washington, the House of Representatives voted to abolish the domestic branch of the OWI, so Hoyt faced more than minor obstacles in his new post. At his first press conference he asserted the need for a domestic branch to be run in accordance with the free standards established by American journalism. On 29 June 1943 an appropriations subcommittee voted to reverse the decision of the House and give the domestic branch of the OWI $3 million, which was later cut to $2.25 million – almost one-quarter of the budget originally requested by the division.

On 6 July Hoyt began his campaign to reform the OWI by appointing nine newspaper editors and managing editors, many of whom had been critical of the OWI, to act as an advisory committee. He then reorganized the domestic branch, asking for cooperation from government agencies and media corporations to show the horrors of the war, a move he believed would boost the home-front morale by making the public feel informed. Years later, Mortimer P. Stern, one of Hoyt's managing editors, observed that what Hoyt had done was to apply "much the same principle he had established at the *Portland Oregonian* and which he would later establish at the *Denver Post* – keeping news and opinion separate – and as the year 1943 ended, the press of America generally showed that it appreciated the effort."

As Hosokawa points out, Hoyt was a national figure when he returned to the *Oregonian*. He was mentioned for an appointment to the Senate seat of minority leader Charles L. McNary, who had died. He also was mentioned as a candidate for the presidency of the Curb Exchange (now the American Stock Exchange), a vice-presidency with the American Broadcasting Co., the editorship of the *Chicago Daily News,* and other positions.

Yet Hoyt's future with the *Oregonian* seemed unduly limited. He had not been permitted to acquire equity in the paper, and the ownership was wary of his personal motivations in apparently promoting his own accomplishments more than he promoted the paper's. About two years after returning to the *Oregonian,* Hoyt received a letter from Ernest Ray Campbell, chief executive officer of the *Denver Post,* concerning the editor-publisher position at that paper. After a brief negotiation period in which Campbell and owner Helen Bonfils agreed to his every demand, Hoyt accepted the position without much hesitation.

He arrived in Denver in 1946, facing perhaps the biggest challenge of his life. The atmosphere at the *Post* during the late 1930s and early 1940s was described by Lawrence Martin, then its managing editor, as a "doldrum time when imagination and initiative were becalmed, and progress was mere circumnavigation of old ideas, on a troubled sea." University of Colorado journalism professor A. Gayle Waldrop wrote in 1951, "Like Denver, the state of Colorado, and the Rocky Mountain Empire, the *Post* in 1945 stood at the crossroads. Each was almost entirely complacent with the status quo, at an hour when the West, the nation and the world were being jet-propelled toward change by war and postwar forces."

While the newspaper had enjoyed some success under Bonfils and Harry H. Tammen, who had taken over the paper in 1895, the *Post* had lulled itself and the Denver area into a conservative, shortsighted, isolationist funk. Denver and its sleeping newspaper were ripe for an editor and publisher with Hoyt's talents for resurrection. The weaknesses of the *Post* in 1946 played right into Hoyt's strengths – it was to be a propitious partnership.

Hoyt's move to the *Post* attracted much attention within the newspaper industry. As Stern notes, within a few months after Hoyt took charge of the *Post,* national magazines were publishing articles about the "miracles" he had performed upon the paper and the organization. He appeared on the

Denver Post *vice-president Ernest Ray Campbell, Palmer Hoyt, and* Post *business manager Fred W. Bonfils examining a stereotype plate for their new Headliner presses, 1950*

cover of *Business Week* on 15 March 1947 and seemed to enjoy almost immediate "savior" status.

Hoyt's most significant accomplishments at the *Post* came during his first decade as its editor and publisher. He did surprisingly little in the way of restructuring the newspaper and weeding out old staff to make way for his handpicked transplants, as was typical of most newspaper revitalizations of the era. No one was fired, but he brought several key players in his success at the *Oregonian*. He achieved changes primarily by instilling his editorial vision in the many experienced writers and editors that already worked at the paper.

Hoyt's plan of action for strengthening the *Post* was relatively simple: he sought to restore the newspaper's respectability, credibility, and vitality. His first significant move in this direction was the reintroduction of the editorial page, which had been eliminated by Bonfils and Tammen in 1911. The top of the page read, "Dedicated in perpetuity to the service of the people, that no good cause shall lack a champion and that evil shall not thrive unopposed." The *Post* also promised to publish letters from readers, not just on Sundays, as was customary in many newspapers at that time, but every day.

The Post *building in downtown Denver; Hoyt orchestrated the relocation of the paper to this facility in 1950.*

Hoyt balanced this zealous approach to publishing diverse opinions with a firm commitment to publishing news *without* opinion. In an effort to take away the temptation to slant the news, Hoyt issued a standing invitation to reporters to submit editorials. He believed it was a newspaper's responsibility to inform the public as completely and honestly as possible, and toward that end he more than doubled the editorial staff and directed his reporters to pay close attention to the story behind the story, not only on local and regional matters, but also on national and international trends. Stern comments that the *Post* addressed the "whys" of such complicated issues as urban blight, earthquakes, tax measures, race relations, campus revolutions, the New Left, the "Far Right," and just about every issue in the foreign-policy field.

The invigorated *Post* took the lead on several community crusades, including the election of a new mayor, a shake-up of the state penitentiary, the revelation of Denver's unsanitary and inefficient system of trash and garbage collection, campaigns for highway safety and civil rights, and the support of improvements in Denver's mass-transit system. In 1946 Hoyt was ahead of the times in constantly reminding newspapers of their "social responsibility," an approach that was to be validated a year later with the report by the Commission on Freedom of the Press, chaired by Robert M. Hutchins. In a 1946 interview with the *New Republic,* Hoyt stated: "The trouble with

most of our larger papers is that they're big business and they're too apt to go along with big business instead of getting down to the grass roots and listening to the people . . . . Too many papers talk about freedom of the press and too few of them live up to their responsibility to the people."

Part of Hoyt's social responsibility, as he saw it, was to boost the region's self-image, not only locally, but nationally. According to Hosokawa, the *Post* had done little to promote the state before Hoyt's arrival: "Denver's narrow interests were pitted against those of the rest of Colorado and the newspapers of the state were aligned virtually unanimously against the *Post.*" He changed the newspaper's motto from "The Best Newspaper in the U.S.A." to "The Voice of the Rocky Mountain Empire." He also reformed the paper's Sunday magazine, *Rocky Mountain Empire Magazine* (shortened to *Empire*), in 1950 and used it to help foster new interest in the West.

Hoyt also engineered the dealings that led to the 1950 move of the *Post* into state-of-the-art printing and office facilities. Within days of his arrival in Denver he began planning the construction and move to a new plant. The old *Post* facility had been occupied since 1907, and its presses and typesetting machinery were vintage turn-of-the-century. After signing contracts to purchase new presses at a cost of about $1 million, Hoyt led the quest to find a suitable downtown Denver location. In the spring of 1950 the *Post* had a new $6-million-dollar home.

Politically, Hoyt was a liberal Republican and an impassioned anti-Communist. He believed that a newspaper's endorsement of a presidential candidate should be undertaken with great care, considering all of the available facts and not owing to any political party. "Political parties are not matters of men alone but also matters of principles and collective ideals," a 27 July 1948 editorial read. While in 1948 the *Post* supported Thomas Dewey for president, the Republican candidate for the U.S. Senate, and a Democrat for governor, it operated in its traditionally Republican caste until 1960, when it endorsed John F. Kennedy for the presidency – the first time the paper had endorsed a Democratic presidential candidate since Woodrow Wilson. Hoyt went on to support Lyndon Johnson in 1964 and Hubert Humphrey in 1968.

Although Hoyt openly expressed his abhorrence of communism, under his direction the *Post* emerged as one of the first newspapers in the nation to criticize Senator Joseph McCarthy; it was also one of several papers on McCarthy's "left-wing list." Edwin R. Bayley notes in *Joe McCarthy and the Press* (1981) that a 21 February 1950 *Post* editorial warned readers "there are many traitors among us." However, Hoyt grew suspicious as McCarthy's vague charges continued and his numbers of Communists kept changing. He quickly decided that what the Senator was doing was outrageous and "jumped into the fight with both feet."

According to Bayley, Hosokawa, and others, the *Post* under Hoyt enjoyed a lasting reputation as a courageous critic of McCarthy. Bayley states that the *Post* is known best in industry circles for a memorandum by Hoyt in February 1953 that described how a newspaper could avoid being "used" by McCarthy. The memo advised precautions against "loose charges, irresponsible utterances and attempts at character assassination" and instructed reporters and editors to evaluate the sources of charges and provide the point of view of the accused.

Hoyt also advised newspaper staff to "apply any reasonable doubt they have to the treatment of the story" if they knew the charges were false, and pointed out that such stories could be played down or put into sharper perspective by headlines and placement. The memo was widely circulated in the nation's newsrooms, debated at many newspaper editor meetings, and came under attack from the American Civil Liberties Union. Bayley claims that the memo "stands as one of the milestones in the evolution from purely 'straight' reporting to interpretive reporting."

Hoyt's notoriety during his last years at the *Oregonian* and his early years at the *Post* had as much to do with his service in Washington at the OWI and as a member of President Harry Truman's Air Policy Commission (1946) as it did with his accomplishments in journalism. Hosokawa claims that during much of this period Hoyt was regarded as a more prestigious figure in Washington than in Denver, a prestige that was to culminate with his close relationship with President Johnson in the 1960s. But through the 1950s and 1960s Hoyt's name was synonymous with the *Denver Post*. The civic crusades sponsored by the paper led Denver and the state into a new age of modernization and economic development. They also led the *Post* into financial difficulties that were to unseat Hoyt in 1970.

With his editorial vision firmly established, his new newspaper-production facilities in place, and his reputation solidified, from the late 1950s onward Hoyt devoted his attention to day-to-day business concerns, speaking engagements, and a wide range of professional and civic involvements. Hoyt experienced some tumult in his personal life. In June 1949 his wife filed for divorce. On 7 November 1950 he married Helen May Taber, former wife of the wildlife and ecology writer at the *Post*.

As Hosokawa notes, during the early 1950s "some of the fire, the verve, the exuberant enthusiasm that causes newspapermen to call their profession a game seemed to go out of the *Post* as Hoyt became increasingly concerned with fiscal burdens." In the latter years of his administration the *Post* was devoting more space to news and editorial material than any other afternoon newspaper in the United States. While such an approach to journalism had steadily increased the paper's gross income, it was an extremely costly path to follow in the long run. By 1970 the paper's after-tax profits dwindled to a mere .5 percent, compared to about 26 percent when Hoyt had taken over twenty-four years earlier.

Much of Hoyt's energies during the latter years of his tenure as editor were devoted to a prolonged effort to prevent the *Post* from becoming another link in the growing newspaper chain of S. I. Newhouse. Hoyt steadfastly opposed chain ownership, and his heartfelt belief that a newspaper should be tied to its community prevented him from advocating chain ownership as a solution to the financially weakening position of the *Post*. As Richard H. Meeker notes in *Newspaperman: S. I. Newhouse and the Business of News* (1983), Hoyt and Newhouse shared a "sufficiently adversarial" relationship, especially after Newhouse succeeded in taking over Hoyt's old paper,

Front page of the Denver Post *on Hoyt's first day as editor and publisher in 1946 (left) and on his last day in 1970*

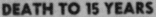

| Pentagon Offers Aid to Lockheed | Haywood Signs with Seattle | Detective's Bullet Stops Truck |
| Story on Page 8, Front Section | Story on Page 35, Section D | Photos and Story on Page 17, Section B |

DEATH TO 15 YEARS

2 Russ Jews Spared In Skyjack Plot Case

Restrictive Confinement Is Decreed

MOSCOW—(AP)—The Soviet Union Thursday spared the lives of two Jews convicted of treason in the Leningrad hijack case. One of them will serve his labor camp sentence under substitution conditions which friends described as "slow death."

The Supreme Court of the Russian Federation ordered Josef Mendelevich, 24, and Mark Dymshits, 43. It decreed tightly restrictive conditions—including a reduced diet—for Kuznetsov.

6 Sentences Upheld

It also reduced the labor camp terms given to Leningrad to three other defendants, but upheld the other six sentences.

The trial and sentencing of the Jews set a storm of protests in Western Europe, Israel and the United States, and a number of foreign governments and leaders appealed to the Soviet government for clemency.

The appeals court reversed the death sentence in less than 24 hours after Generalissimo Francisco Franco, the Spanish chief of state, commuted the death sentences of six Basque separatists, and Russians sympathetic to the Latins' great deterrent said the Russian court undoubtedly was influenced by Franco's actions.

The 11 defendants—nine Jews and two gentiles—were convicted in June as they planned to board a small Soviet airliner in Leningrad for Finland.

Treason Charge

At the trial, which began Dec. 15 and concluded Dec. 24, the Jews admitted planning to hijack the plane because the Soviet government refused to let them emigrate to Israel. They were charged with treason.

In completing their appeals, the Soviet agency Tass reported the Supreme Court proceeded from the fact the hijack attempt was snuffed in time, and that under the Soviet law the sentences are too severe.

Continued on page 4

Front Bears Snow Threat

A Pacific cold front is expected to bring lowering cloudiness, lower temperatures and possibly snow over Friday to Colorado, the National Weather Service said.

Most of any snow will be in the mountains along the Continental Divide, with warming Thursday and a colder trend in northwest Colorado on Friday tomorrow and...

Denver's history of precipitation Friday was rated at 28 per cent.

Cloudy skies were expected in the state and along the Eastern Slope Wednesday and were Thursday. Snow reached to areas as wide as Squaw Mountain and Monte Springs. Snow up to 30 to 8 inches, with Wednesday afternoon at the Soil Weather Service station at Steamboat Springs reported...

Temperatures Wednesday were in the 30s in Pueblo, Colorado Springs, minus 3 mile to 24 in and the first the past few Thursday in and...

Price Declines Take Lead On N.Y. Stock Exchange

NEW YORK (AP)—Also Wednesday's session prices stock declines was mixed Thursday in brisk trading...

THE WEATHER ☁

Disaster Brings Tears

A sobbing woman is comforted by relatives and friends as they watched wait for the fate of 38 men killed by a shattering explosion in a coal mine Wednesday, near Hyden, Ky. Tragic news one knows emerged from the sky shift after the blast which killed underground coal shafts, and said that dynamite gas had caused recovery of the bodies. (STORY PAGE 4)

FTC Says Motorists Given 'Ride' on Gas

WASHINGTON—(AP)—The government estimates the average American motorist annually pays an extra $6 to $9 through the gas for a more powerful gasoline than but not need.

And, in an effort to curb drivers names, cut down on engine damage and reduce air pollution, the Federal Trade Commission said FTC has ordered the nation's major gasoline sellers to begin posting octane ratings on their pumps in 30...

The use of gasoline which is too rich in octane rating but had particular octane levels in result in excessive engine noise which contribute to air pollution, the FTC said.

Opposed by Industry

On the other hand it added, use of gasoline with too low an octane rating can result in extended period of very costly damage.

The order, scheduled to take effect June 30, is intended to help consumers spend no longer by buying cheaper and lower octane gasolines which do not put part of its fuel to achieve uniform publish each year.

The ruling does not apply to the other half of the gas issue. Industry—the small independent-owned businesses.

Posting does not apply to use manufacturers, though the FTC hopes they will follow suit and publish octane ratings of their own national branding on behind sold new methods...

IN TODAY'S POST

Ann Landers	76	Bally
Bridge	19	Horoscope
Classified	34-36	Movies
Comics	28	Obituaries
Crossword	9	Society
Drama	12-13	Sports
Editorials	18	TV, Radio
Financial	30-32	Women
Fire Calls	36	World News

Sports Scores

Library

Teletypewriter

Dial 297-1521

To Place Want Ad—Dial 297-1030

WORK REQUIREMENT INJECTED

Food Stamp Bill Passed

By NICK KOTZ
Copyright 1970, Denver Post-Washington Post

WASHINGTON—Congress Thursday had passed a new food stamp bill that contains several liberalizing features and a new restrictive measure—the work requirement.

Food aid advocates failed Dec. 16, to strike the work requirements in the House Wednesday. This would bar an entire family from food stamp aid if one adult member refused to accept offered work.

Senate approval of the House bill came Thursday.

Features Detailed

The measure sets the following features in the program for the hungry poor:

—A national uniform eligibility requirement, expected to be $4,900 annually for a family of four, to replace the present state requirements. Many states, particularly in the South, now bar eligibility at far less than $4,900 annual income.

—A provision of free food stamps for families with less than $30 monthly income. Other families would pay up to 30 per cent of income for food stamp benefits.

—A provision that food stamps can be used in "meals on wheels" programs for the elderly.

—Provisions permitting the operation of both food stamp and commodity distribution programs in a county, permitting food stamp recipients to buy less than a full monthly stamp allotment of the beginning of a month and recovering that food stamp purchases be offered at least once two weeks.

Work Clause Debated

Congressional debate centered on the controversial work provision, which requires all family members age 18 to 65, except mothers and students, to accept any work offered at a minimum wage or $1.30 an hour. The requirement makes no provision for substitute of work or for payment of the prevailing wage.

In an emotional speech, Rep. Thomas Foley (D-Wash.) called the new requirement "coercion."

He questioned why Congress would approve with some increase of food aid to meet the hungry in foreign countries but not with effectively approving food aid for the American poor.

If any part made why poverty should be punished because an absolute father, either loafers or some refuses to take a job...

Stating, both are members of Congress would be against the new section he said. The ethical intention to reinstate this private intention in our public employment...

Pakistani Airliner Crashes

DACCA, East Pakistan—(AP)—A Pakistan airliner with 33 persons aboard crashed Thursday the third earthquake in Dacca, killing seven passengers. The Boeing included the fourteen number in the airline's fleet was...

The Water May Get Colder Friday

One of the waterfowl enjoyed the unusually warm weather and swells were out at Denver City Park Lake Wednesday. Sunlight glints off the water and the coolness of ice that may disappear with Thursday's expected high of 48, promising cloudiness and slight chance of snow or flurries for Friday.

Scenic Wall Calendars Going Way of Dodo Bird

By WILLIAM ENDICOTT

Just as indicators of the economy as a profit-and-loss statement, in a fairly type, California and lots these calendars, Re used to deliver 12 or 15.

Right Mr. Egan Heppe has told us is no particularly boring, according to calendars, which include illustrations of these scenes to...

the *Oregonian,* in late 1950. The two had met at American Newspaper Publishers' Association meetings in the early 1940s and quickly developed a "healthy disregard for each other." Meeker writes that just after Newhouse purchased the *Oregonian,* he instructed newspaper broker Smith Davis to deliver a message for him in Denver on his way back to New York: "You tell Ep Hoyt that he made the *Oregonian.* And I stole it from him!"

Newhouse was able to take advantage of a family squabble between sisters May and Helen Bonfils to acquire May's 15.67 percent of *Denver Post* stock in 1960. His conquest would end there. After almost ten years of unsuccessfully trying to obtain a majority interest in the paper through business means, Newhouse filed a lawsuit claiming that the owners and managers of the *Post* had conspired improperly to prevent him from acquiring control. The case was finally decided in 1972, two years after Hoyt's departure. The attorney for the *Post,* former Supreme Court justice Arthur Goldberg, claimed that the *Post* was "a great newspaper." If it were to fall into Newhouse's hands, Goldberg argued to the Court of Appeals, it would most certainly lose that distinction. The Court found in favor of the *Post,* but the costs of the battle were high – legal fees alone exceeded $1 million. Combined with falling profits, the legal costs and failing morale among the paper's managers prompted its October 1980 sale to the Times Mirror Company of Los Angeles.

At the age of seventy-three Hoyt retired as editor and publisher of the *Post* on 31 December 1970. Although he was certainly battle weary, he considered himself capable of directing the *Post* for many more years. But the faltering fiscal performance of the newspaper, combined with a cooling of his relationship with majority stock owner Helen Bonfils, prompted a change at the helm. He was succeeded by Charles R. Buxton, who had been with Hoyt since the *Oregonian* days.

The mark Hoyt made on the paper, the city of Denver, and the greater world of journalism was, indeed, indelible. Waldrop compared Hoyt's success at the *Post* with Adolph Ochs's resurrection of the *New York Times* in the 1890s – a truly monumental achievement. His successors were "his men," thus the *Post* after Hoyt greatly resembled the *Post* under Hoyt. In retirement he was given an office in a downtown building, a secretary, and a lifetime job as consultant to the *Post* at fifty thousand dollars per year, plus his normal pension.

Hoyt died on 26 June 1979 at the age of eighty-two. He was survived by his wife; three sons, Edwin Palmer Hoyt III, Charles Richard Hoyt, and Lincoln Hoyt; and three sons adopted after his second marriage, Monty, Gregory, and Wesley Hoyt. In addition to his editor-publisher positions at the *Oregonian* and the *Post,* he served as national president of the Society of Professional Journalists (1941–1943), a director of the Associated Press (1944–1945), president of the Oregon Newspaper Publishers Association (1943–1945), and on the U.S. Advisory Commission on Information (1965–1971). He received honorary doctor of laws degrees from Linfield College (1938), Whitman College (1942), William Jewell College (1955), and the University of New Mexico (1965). He was a founding member of Radio Free Europe.

In 1954 Hoyt was chosen as the recipient of the University of Arizona's first annual John Peter Zenger Freedom of the Press Award. At various times he also served on the executive committee of the Conference of Christians and Jews, on the Pulitzer Prize board, as director of the Advertising Federation of America, as head of the Denver Community Chest campaign, and on the Freedom of the Press Committee of the American Newspaper Publishers Association.

References:

Edwin R. Bayley, *Joe McCarthy and the Press* (Madison: University of Wisconsin Press, 1981);

Business Week, no. 915 (15 March 1947): 8;

William H. Hornby, *Voice of Empire: A Centennial Sketch of the Denver Post* (Denver: Colorado Historical Society, 1992);

Bill Hosokawa, *Thunder in the Rockies: The Incredible Denver Post* (New York: William Morrow, 1976);

Richard H. Meeker, *Newspaperman: S. I. Newhouse and the Business of News* (New Haven: Ticknor & Fields, 1983);

Mortimer P. Stern, "Palmer Hoyt and the *Denver Post*: A Field Study of Organizational Change in the Mass Media of Communication," Ph.D. dissertation, University of Denver, 1969;

A. Gayle Waldrop, "A Chinook Blows on Champa Street," *Journalism Quarterly,* 24 (June 1947): 109–115;

Waldrop, "Reborn Denver 'Post' Has Prestige and Power," *Journalism Quarterly,* 28 (Summer 1951): 327–336;

Allan M. Winkler, *The Politics of Propaganda: The Office of War Information, 1942–1945* (New Haven: Yale University Press, 1978).

Ralph Ingersoll

(8 December 1900 – 8 March 1985)

Daniel W. Pfaff
Pennsylvania State University

MAJOR POSITIONS HELD: Managing editor, *New Yorker* (1925–1930); associate editor and managing editor, *Fortune* (1930–1935); vice-president and general manager, Time Incorporated (1935–1938); publisher, *Time* (1937–1939); founder, editor, and publisher, *PM* (1940–1946); president, R. J. Company (1949–1959); president and director, New England Newspapers (1957–1975); president, Capital City Publishing Company and General Publications (1957–1975); president, Mid-Atlantic Newspapers (1959–1975); vice-president and director, Central States Publishing (1961–1975).

BOOKS: *In and Under Mexico* (New York & London: Century, 1924);
Report on England, November, 1940 (New York: Simon & Schuster, 1940);
America Is Worth Fighting For (Indianapolis & New York: Bobbs-Merrill, 1941);
Action on All Fronts: A Personal Account of this War (New York & London: Harper, 1942);
The Battle Is the Payoff (New York: Harcourt, Brace, 1943);
Top Secret (New York: Harcourt, Brace, 1946);
The Great Ones: The Love Story of Two Very Important People (New York: Harcourt, Brace, 1948);
Wine of Violence (New York: Farrar, Straus & Young, 1951);
Point of Departure (New York: Harcourt, Brace & World, 1961).

Ralph Ingersoll

Ralph McAllister Ingersoll, educated in science and engineering at Yale and Columbia Universities, entered the work world in 1921 as a goldminer in California. A gifted writer, he shifted to journalism within three years and was actively employed in the field for more than fifty years. He began in 1924 as a reporter for the *New York American,* became managing editor of the *New Yorker* in 1925, and five years later moved to Time Incorporated, where he rose through several high-level editorial and managerial positions, becoming publisher of *Time* magazine in 1937. In 1939 he left *Time* to found *PM,* an adless New York newspaper that he edited and published until 1946; it failed in 1948. Following service during World War II he was a buyer and seller of newspaper properties in the northeastern United States until his semiretirement in 1975.

In addition to those activities, Ingersoll wrote seven nonfiction books and two novels, married four times, had love affairs, suffered a mental breakdown, and had five years of psychoanalysis. He made and lost much money and many friends, but shortly before he died at eighty-four in 1985, he expressed overall satisfaction with his life's course and said he would change little. "He was an intense man – he wanted to know everything about everything," said Roy Hoopes, author of Ingersoll's 1985 biography.

Ingersoll was born in New Haven, Connecticut, on 8 December 1900, the fourth child and only son of Colin Macrae Ingersoll and Theresa McAllister Ingersoll. On his father's side he was descended from a line of prominent politicians, lawyers, statesmen, and at least one businessman. His father was a consulting engineer who supervised the construction of the Manhattan and Queensboro bridges over the East River.

He expected his son to follow in his professional footsteps. Accordingly, Ralph was educated at the Sheffield Scientific School at Yale University, from which he was graduated in 1921, followed by training in engineering at Columbia University. He worked as an engineer in California, Arizona, and Mexico until 1923, turning some of those experiences into his first book, *In and Under Mexico* (1924).

The *New York American* hired him as a reporter that year, largely on the strength of the book, and within a matter of months he was reporting for Harold Ross's *New Yorker*. He became the newly founded magazine's first managing editor in 1925 and held that post until 1930, when Henry R. Luce hired him to be associate editor, and then managing editor, of *Fortune*. Luce elevated him to vice-president and general manager of Time Incorporated in 1935, allowing Ingersoll to set his own annual salary: forty-five thousand dollars.

Ingersoll filled several key roles in the founding of *Life* magazine in 1936, including the negotiation of the rights to its title for ninety-two thousand dollars, from the owners of a failing magazine of that name. In 1937 Luce appointed him publisher of *Time* magazine. Ingersoll was thirty-six and "probably the most powerful journalist in New York" but was also "struggling, quite frankly, to move outside the shadow of Henry Luce," according to Hoopes.

After he began psychoanalysis that same year, Ingersoll attributed this struggle to a "good old Oedipus complex." As Hoopes explains it, Ingersoll had submerged this tendency in his relationship with his biological father "but did not remain a model of correct behavior when he went out into the world of men. When he encountered a father figure – such as Ross or Luce – he felt a 'demonic need' to challenge and destroy him." *Time* editor in chief John Shaw Billings, who observed Luce and Ingersoll up close, said of the latter: "He blew his own horn in the most outrageous way. What a conceited egoist. He's been a snake-in-the-grass in this organization for years and yet, funny thing, he's the

only fellow in the company that Luce really seems to want to be 'palsy-walsy' with."

The Luce-Ingersoll relationship changed during the last years of the decade into a showy struggle over who would have ultimate editorial control over *Time* and the other Luce publications, with Luce inevitably prevailing. One incident illustrative of their contention occurred when Ingersoll unilaterally replaced a Luce-selected, flattering cover portrait of Adolf Hitler as the 1938 *Time* "Man of the Year" with a black-and-white drawing depicting Hitler as a torturer. This enraged Luce, yet there never was a total break between the two.

When Luce died in 1967, Ingersoll wrote an almost totally laudatory obituary for the *Washington Post*, stating that his main flaw was that "getting so rich confused him." Ingersoll also mined his intimate knowledge of Luce in writing his first novel, *The Great Ones* (1948), the story of Sturges Strong, head of the publishing company Facts Incorporated, and highly successful Letia Long, an actress and painter whom Strong marries after divorcing his first wife. The parallel between Luce and his second marriage, to editor and playwright Clare Boothe Luce, was powerfully evident. In the novel Ingersoll identifies Luce as a rival of Strong's and describes Letia as "a woman even more beautiful than Clare Luce and even more talented." Clare Luce had never liked Ingersoll, and publication of the novel no doubt intensified her distaste for him.

Ingersoll resigned from *Time* in April 1939 to launch the venture for which he is best remembered, *PM*, an adless afternoon tabloid. The first issue was published on 18 June 1940 following what Hoopes calls "the most frantic, confused and overpublicized publication launching in the history of the country." Many ideas and assumptions – most of them drawn from Ingersoll's experience on magazines – guided its creation. The newspaper was to be brilliantly written and edited by the most talented staff ever assembled. Its prospectus, which has become one of the most widely quoted documents in the history of American journalism, began: "On the one hand: there exists in all men, but particularly in men of intelligence and education, an inordinate desire to know what is going on in the world today. This desire is not satisfied by the existing daily press. On the other hand, there exists today all the facilities necessary to produce a daily paper which would satisfy this curiosity. They simply wait to be organized into a profit-making venture."

The almost manic enthusiasm with which he approached this project caused Ingersoll's father

Ingersoll (second from left) leading a staff meeting of PM, *the newpaper he founded and edited*

and, more important, his revered psychoanalyst, Dr. Gregory Zilboorg, to advise against it. His father believed Ralph was overreaching his truly remarkable talents; Zilboorg saw in the undertaking the overpowering desire in Ingersoll to prove that he was an even greater publisher than Luce. The psychoanalyst predicted that the venture would fail because it was driven by a self-destructive component in Ingersoll's makeup that would cause him to arrange his own defeat.

Whether or not that analysis was valid, the doctor was correct with respect to *PM*. Ingersoll insisted upon absolute control of the publication, but he could not have begun it without substantial financial backing. He therefore sought the support of individuals to whom he referred as "VRM" (Very Rich Men), although some of them were women. Among the most generous backers were Marian Rosenwald Stern, daughter of the founder of Sears, Roebuck and Company, and Chicago publisher Marshall Field III, who, unbeknownst to Ingersoll at the time, also had been psychoanalyzed by Zilboorg and believed the experience had changed

his life. Investors purchased one or more of the one-hundred-thousand-dollar units Ingersoll was selling in the venture, and he rapidly acquired more than the $1.5 million needed to proceed.

He attracted financial support largely through the circulation of a twenty-eight-page digest of his sixty-page prospectus, which was written by William Benton, a former advertising copywriter regarded as the best in the country. Benton's aim in the "Blue Book," as the digest was called, was to convince prospective investors that *PM* would make money for them. It described a publication intended to revolutionize newspapers by the wide use of color and photographs. The writers would be well known and well paid, and their stories would not be broken up or "jumped" throughout the paper, but would run continuously.

PM was promoted, in many ways, as was *USA TODAY,* the Gannett Company venture launched in 1982, with one major difference – *PM* carried no advertising, relying on sales for its support and profits. A circulation of 200,000 was calculated as the break-even point at five cents a copy, and a phenomenally successful prepublication promotion sold 150,000 charter subscriptions. When the first issue appeared, interest was so intense that dealers were able to sell copies for five and six times the cover price. More than 450,000 copies were sold that day, but in the excitement the charter subscribers were forgotten.

As expected, circulation declined within days, but it remained strong for about two weeks, enough time to convince Ingersoll that he had succeeded. But as sales continued to drop, he knew that changes would be necessary, and he began moving writers, editors, and others around in the organization in order to achieve the formula he believed would work. This never happened, and while he tried, there was criticism that *PM* was both dull and confused in philosophy and appearance. "*PM* is gotten out by a bunch of young fogies," quipped Ingersoll's former boss at the *New Yorker,* Ross.

Despite its problems, the paper was in many ways brilliant and innovative. Its writing was its greatest strength, with labor covered by Leo Huberman and James Wechsler, the press by Hodding Carter, Jr., and movies by Cecilia Ager, and with a fine sports section edited by Joe Cummiskey. It boasted a "living section," edited by Elizabeth Hawes, that set a standard in consumer reporting some believe was not again equaled until the 1970s. Among the bylines in the paper's first years were those of many eventual notables, including Sidney Margolius, Erskine Caldwell, I. F. Stone, Theodor Seuss Giesel (Dr. Seuss), and Max Lerner.

In the last analysis, however, the paper failed either to achieve a clear focus or to strike a chord of sufficient acceptance to catch hold. Ingersoll had hoped *PM* would find its largest readership among the lower middle class, who would be attracted by a brand of liberalism he described as being "against people who push other people around . . . whether they flourish in this country or abroad. We are against fraud and deceit and greed and cruelty and we will seek to expose their practitioners."

Instead, the paper stirred controversy and was attacked by the religious Far Right and, most damagingly, by militant anti-Communists, who assailed some of the paper's key staffers as members of, or sympathizers with, the Communist party. Ingersoll could neither understand nor dispel this, and by August 1940 circulation was down to thirty-one thousand. In an important respect Ingersoll's experiment had failed in only three months, but, sustained by his patient backers, he continued the struggle for two years before events shifted his preoccupation to the conflict in Europe.

With the outbreak of World War II, Ingersoll became a reporter, a role in which he was happier. He was drafted into the army in 1942. Editorially, he called this an act of persecution, but he soon adapted to military life and rose from private to lieutenant colonel. He favored U.S. entry in the war against Hitler well before the idea gained wide acceptance. His book on army training, *The Battle Is the Payoff,* was published in 1943.

Though insolvent, *PM* survived the war, thanks largely to Field, but when Ingersoll could not get the operation into the black after the armistice, the paper's major investors asked him to step down to the role of consultant. In 1946 Field decided that the paper had to accept advertising, and Ingersoll resigned. There were many expressions of regret. "I don't feel as strongly as you about the advs.-no-ad thing," E. B. White wrote him, "but . . . I am always stimulated by the sight of somebody hanging on to a principle (like a thrown rider to the bridle)." The *New Yorker* observed: "One of the odd things about advertising . . . is that the public rather counts on it. We found that out during the war, when we sent an edition overseas with no ads. The boys complained that they were being shortchanged." Advertising did not change the paper's fortunes, however, and it went out of business in 1948.

There are a variety of assessments of what went wrong, but in Hoopes's view, "Ingersoll was trying to do the impossible in 1940 – that is, to publish a newspaper by magazine standards. There was just not enough talent around at the time to do that on a daily basis; and after the war, when there was more talent, it was too expensive and he did not have the money." At the same time, according to Hoopes, *PM* did promote substantial changes in newspapering by expanding coverage into such areas as labor, the press, and consumer news, and by introducing magazine techniques in reporting, writing, layout, art, and photography that were widely adopted. He describes Ingersoll as "a catalyst – the one who made things happen," noting that this had been the case when he was working at the magazines and that in creating *PM,* "he made things happen to the American newspaper."

As he disengaged himself from *PM,* Ingersoll produced two more books. *Top Secret* (1946) describes the invasion of Europe from the vantage point of one who has access to the top levels of command, including the planning of the Normandy invasion. *The Great Ones* was also written during this period.

Ingersoll had married Mary Elizabeth Carden on 18 November 1926. He would marry three more

Ingersoll's newspaper announced that the United States was involved in World War II in May 1941,
after President Franklin D. Roosevelt declared a state of national emergency.

times: to Elaine Keiffer Cobb, on 9 August 1945; to Mary Hill Doolittle, on 25 November 1948; and to Thelma Bradford, on 16 July 1964. He and Elaine had two sons: Ralph II and Ian.

Ingersoll's life entered a new phase in 1949, when he and Charles Marsh, an eccentric millionaire he had met through *PM,* established R. J. Company, a newspaper investment firm, with Ingersoll as president. This was shortly after Ingersoll's second wife, Elaine, died unexpectedly following the birth of their second son, Jonathan Ingersoll VIII (who later changed his first name to Ian). As he had not before, Ingersoll now felt the need to make money, primarily to raise and educate his sons, but also because wealthy people and the process of becoming rich had always fascinated him. R. J. Company – named for Ralph II and Jonathan – was established with fifty thousand dollars that Ingersoll inherited from the estates of his wife and his father, who died eight days after Elaine, and fifty thousand dollars from Marsh.

Ingersoll arranged a kind of apprenticeship with Marsh, whom he regarded as being even smarter than he was; Marsh saw in Ingersoll a man who could help him add to the newspaper holdings he had in the Southwest and the East. Marsh was a master at acquiring "OPM" (Other People's Money) to make his purchases. Ingersoll was knowledgeable about newspapers and had a low-key way of convincing the owners of family properties that their newspapers would not be changed significantly under the new ownership he would arrange. By 1952, with R. J. Company worth $1 million and his health failing, Marsh decided to dissolve the partnership on a fifty-fifty basis. Ingersoll's half was the *Middletown* (N.Y.) *Times-Herald,* then making about one hundred thousand dollars a year, a handsome return on his fifty-thousand-dollar investment.

Aided partly by persistent rumors that Ingersoll was a Communist, a new paper broke into the *Times-Herald* monopoly, substantially curtailing its profits. After a three-year battle for newspaper supremacy in the community, Ingersoll gave up and sold the paper to the Ottaway chain in 1959. That transaction left him with one hundred thousand dollars to invest. He used the money to reinforce an alliance he had established in 1957 with television game-show producers Mark Goodson and William Todman and their accountant, Seymour Schneidman, to operate newspapers purchased largely with their funds. The first of these was the *Pawtucket Times* in Rhode Island, followed by the *Elizabeth Journal* in New Jersey. He soon added the *Trentonian,* also in New Jersey, and the *Delaware County Daily Times* in Pennsylvania.

From that point until his semiretirement in the 1970s, Ingersoll worked as a newspaper manager, running General Publications with mostly Goodson-Todman money and his own expertise. By 1967 the group owned seventeen newspapers, eight of them weeklies, as Ingersoll continued to scout for more properties. In most cases Goodson and Todman each owned 45 percent of the newspaper, while Ingersoll and Schneidman each had 5 percent.

However, Ingersoll was the only visible partner, with many believing he was the sole owner. He had virtually total control, because, as Hoopes puts it, "the key to the success of the operation was Ingersoll's reputation, and everyone involved knew it." The small and medium-sized papers he acquired usually had been in the hands of one family for several generations, making it important for him to understand the emotional relationships involved. "Every single newspaper I ever bought or tried to buy eventually put me in possession of enough material for a solid novel, none of which was ever written," he commented. He was most adept at convincing owners that the paper under his direction would retain the character it had long held. He also kept existing employees – if they were good. His management style was to put editorial control in the hands of others and to leave them alone as long as they did capable work. If they did not, he replaced them.

As with virtually all of his emotional ties, Ingersoll's relationships with his sons were complex and difficult. He was by turns loving and generous, then harsh almost to the point of cruelty. He was willing to train both boys in the newspaper business so they could strike out on their own if they so chose, not so they could succeed him. Ralph II was

more like his father and had both interest in and aptitude for the business. After service in the Vietnam War, Ian went his own way, becoming successful as a cabinetmaker.

Like his father, Ralph II had a prominent ego. By 1975 he decided that he had become more adept at the business than his father and moved to gain greater control. He proposed changes in his father's arrangements with Goodson and Todman that required the formation of a new company, Ingersoll Publications, with himself in control and his father holding a 49 percent share. The father was agreeable; the changes would give him more time to write, and the financial arrangements were generous. Ralph II became a successful publisher with a reputation for toughness.

By 1982 the father's share of the income exceeded $1 million annually. He had become a "VRM," dispelling lingering traces of the failure of *PM.* However, his philosophies of publishing did not mesh with his son's, and the senior Ingersoll left Ingersoll Publications in 1982. He died on 8 March 1985 of complications following a stroke.

References:

Wolcott Gibbs, "A Very Active Type Man – I," *New Yorker,* 18 (2 May 1942): 19–28;

Gibbs, "A Very Active Type Man – II," *New Yorker,* 18 (9 May 1942): 21–29;

Roy Hoopes, *Ralph Ingersoll: A Biography* (New York: Atheneum, 1985);

Robert Lasch, "*PM* Post-Mortem," *Atlantic Monthly,* 182 (July 1948): 44–49;

Robert D. McFadden, "Ralph Ingersoll, Editor and Publisher," *New York Times,* 9 March 1985, p. 16;

James Thurber, *The Years with Ross* (Boston: Little, Brown, 1959);

Loudon Wainwright, "Life Begins," *Atlantic Monthly,* 241 (May 1978): 56–73.

Papers:

Ingersoll's papers are in the Boston University Memorial Library.

Jenkin Lloyd Jones

(1 November 1911 –)

Carol Sue Humphrey
Oklahoma Baptist University

MAJOR POSITIONS HELD: Managing editor (1936–1938), associate editor (1938–1941), editor (1941–1988), publisher (1963–1991), publisher emeritus (1991–1992), *Tulsa Tribune.*

Jenkin Lloyd Jones worked for his family's newspaper in Tulsa, Oklahoma, for almost sixty years, beginning as a reporter for his father, Richard Lloyd Jones, in 1933 and rising through the ranks to become publisher of the *Tulsa Tribune* in 1963. Jones used the pages of his newspaper as well as a syndicated weekly column to discuss pressing concerns in the modern world.

Jenkin Lloyd Jones was born in Madison, Wisconsin, on 1 November 1911, the son of Richard Lloyd Jones and Georgia Hayden Jones. He was named after his paternal grandfather, theologian Jenkin Lloyd Jones. His family moved to Oklahoma in 1919 when his father bought the *Tulsa Daily Democrat,* changing its name to the *Tulsa Tribune.* Richard Lloyd Jones, a native of Chicago, Illinois, had been active in journalism, working as a writer for the *Washington Times* and as an editor for the magazines *Cosmopolitan* and *Collier's Weekly.* He had owned and edited the (Madison) *Wisconsin State Journal,* which he sold prior to relocating to Tulsa. After the establishment of the *Tribune* in 1920, Richard Lloyd Jones served as its editor until 1941, then as its publisher until his death in 1963.

From his early years onward Jenkin Lloyd Jones took an interest in his father's business. Both he and his older brother, Richard Lloyd Jones, Jr., eventually became heavily involved in the *Tribune,* Richard directing production and advertising while Jenkin concentrated on reporting and commentary. Jenkin attended the Tome School in North East, Maryland, and then matriculated at the University of Wisconsin, from which he was graduated in 1933 with a degree in journalism. After receiving his degree Jones searched for a newspaper job in Wiscon-

sin. He failed to find one because of the Depression and returned to Tulsa to work for his father.

Jones's entire journalistic career was spent at the *Tribune.* He began as a reporter in 1933, moving up to become managing editor in 1936, and then associate editor in 1938. In 1941 he became the paper's editor, a job he held until 1988. He took over as publisher in 1963, a position held until 1991, at which time he became publisher emeritus. This post allowed Jones to continue to write and travel without the hindrance of administrative duties. Jones has claimed that he will continue "to write as long as I think I make sense, or, perhaps, as long as a reasonable number will read me."

Jones worked for the *Tribune* throughout his entire adult life, except for a few periods during which he filled other positions. During World War II he served in the Pacific theater as a communications officer aboard the USS *Makassar Strait.* For a brief period in 1953 he served as special assistant to Secretary of the Navy Robert Bernard Anderson, helping to set up the navy's Office of Analysis and Review. In 1969 he became president of the U.S. Chamber of Commerce, which required him to travel as the official spokesman for American business. Aside from these interludes Jones's center of operations was the editorial room of the *Tribune.*

Jones credits his success as a journalist to both talent and his family connection: "I became editor at 27 because of my ability and the fact that my father was publisher." Because he was so young to be the editor of a metropolitan daily newspaper, Jones sometimes did not know how to deal with irate readers. He admits that he was often mistaken for an office boy or a reporter. When asked, "Where's the editor?" he would claim that the editor was out to lunch. Yet Jones took an active interest in the daily operation of the paper, particularly the editorial stance on all issues, whether international, national, state, or local in nature.

Jenkin Lloyd Jones

He worked to report news objectively in his paper, but also to use the *Tribune* to guide readers. In Jones's estimation failure to attempt to provide leadership and guidance, whether the readers respond or not, reduces a newspaper to only a news summary with no clear purpose. As a result of this outlook the *Tribune* always took a strong, vigorous stand in elections, even though it was a Republican newspaper in a predominantly Democratic state. Nevertheless, Jones believed that "it's less ruinous to be beaten often than to be neutral."

Jones also emphasized the importance of communication between editor and staff. For him, "the newspaper business is a creative industry," and the "newspapers are created by the reporters." He worked hard to maintain contact with the staff members of the *Tribune,* allowing the reporters, in rotation, to sit in on the morning editorial conferences and to contribute ideas and opinions. He feared that the growth of the paper would interfere with the maintenance of good communication between newsroom and editor. Besides writing editorials for the *Tribune,* Jones produced a weekly syndicated column, "An Editor's Outlook," in which he addressed such subjects as the presence of American military bases in the Philippines, AIDS education in public schools, and the language of computer technology. The column, distributed by the Los Angeles Times Syndicate for more than thirty years, ceased publication in September 1992.

In many ways Jones is "the last of a breed of newspaper owners — more journalist than businessman, more comfortable behind a typewriter than in a corporate boardroom." He has worked hard to remain informed, not only about the "news" but also about overall world developments. This desire for knowledge is reflected in his love for travel. While on a trip to Mexico in the late 1980s, Jones — in his late seventies — accompanied a military-helicopter raid against drug warlords hiding out in the mountains. When asked what should be done if he failed to return, Jones said that his son Jenkin, Jr., should be told that Jones "went in facing the sun."

Jones's active journalism career ended with the final appearance of the *Tulsa Tribune,* on 30 September 1992. The *Tribune* had been published since 1941 under a joint-operating agreement with the *Tulsa World,* in which the two papers maintained separate news and editorial departments but shared

Jones in his office at the Tulsa Tribune

the costs of advertising, production, and circulation. At the time of its negotiation the joint-operating agreement between the *World* and the *Tribune* was one of the first of its kind, and it set a standard followed by other morning and afternoon newspapers. However, decline in readership of afternoon papers produced increasing strains that even a widely respected paper such as the *Tribune* could not withstand. Since the owners of the *World* had indicated that they would not renew the joint operating agreement when it expired in 1996, the executives at the *Tribune* chose to cease publication in 1992, after seventy-three years. It joined a host of other evening newspapers that had found it impossible to continue publication.

As the *Tribune* approached its last day of publication, Jones continued to emphasize the importance of doing a good job of covering the news, no matter what the future held for the newspaper. He challenged the staff to continue to produce a quality publication: "We come to work every day striving to exceed the quality of the day before. We want the last paper to be the very best we have published.

When Ted Williams ended his Hall of Fame career, he hit a 450-foot home run and stepped out of the game. That's what we'd like to do." In his last editorial for the *Tribune,* Jones remembered the good and the bad in the paper's history, which he described as "memorable. We gloried in our fights, not all won." He concluded with praise for the paper's staff, who continued to work diligently until the end: "They rode *The Tribune* under with its sails set and its colors flying."

The *Tulsa Tribune* was always a family business. First published by Jenkin's father, Richard, the paper then passed to the leadership of his sons and his daughter, Virginia Lloyd Jones Barnett. In later years another generation became involved in the publication.

Jenkin Lloyd Jones married Juanita Rose Carlson on 12 November 1935. They had three children: Jenkin Lloyd, Jr., David, and Georgia. All three worked on the *Tribune:* Jenkin, Jr., as editor and publisher; and David and Georgia as columnists. Jenkin, Sr.'s nephew Howard G. Barnett, Jr., served as president of the *Tribune,* while his grandson Landon (son of Jenkin, Jr.) was a sports reporter.

Jones has taken an active interest in the business of journalism, being a member of the Inter-American Press Association, the International Press Institute, and the American Society of Newspaper Editors. In 1956 he served as president of the latter organization; during the same year his brother, Richard, served as president of the American Newspaper Publishers' Bureau of Advertising. Jenkin has also become well known as a world traveler and commentator on foreign locales. He has journeyed around the globe, visiting 120 countries and both the North and South Poles. His favorite mode of transportation is by rail, and he has attempted to ride on every major train in the world.

Throughout his career Jones has sought to find purpose in his actions, whether writing editorials or traversing the continents. His philosophy of life emphasizes its cyclical nature: "My theory that human history is like a point on the rim of a wheel – an endless series of downs and ups, accompanied by forward progress, has saved me from the cynicism, if not despair, characteristic of many journalists. The lesson of fallen civilizations is that all good things decay, and the lesson of nature is that out of decay new life springs."

References:

Tony Case, "*Tulsa Tribune* to Fold," *Editor & Publisher,* 125 (8 August 1992): 16;

Bob Foresman, "Globe-trotter from Tulsa," *Editor & Publisher,* 89 (28 April 1956): 23, 140;

Jean Truman Richardson, "The Oklahoma Press and the New Deal, 1932–1936," Master's thesis, University of Oklahoma, 1951;

"Thinking the Unthinkable," *Nation's Business,* 57 (May 1969): 50–57.

Samuel Kauffmann

(24 February 1898 – 12 January 1971)

Wendy Swallow Williams
American University

MAJOR POSITIONS HELD: Director (1927–1963), treasurer (1941–1949), business manager (1944–1948), vice-president (1948–1949), president (1949–1963), chairman (1963–1968), (Washington, D.C.) Evening Star Newspaper Company.

BOOK: *The Evening Star: 1852–1952, A Century at the Nation's Capital* (New York: Newcomen Society, 1952).

Samuel Hay Kauffmann was the last long-term president of the Washington Evening Star Newspaper Company to come from the three-family dynasty that built the newspaper into one of the leading papers of its day. "The Gray Lady of Pennsylvania Avenue," as the paper was known in Washington, D.C., in the mid twentieth century, was rich and politically conservative when Kauffmann was named president in 1949. It had dominated the Washington market for many years and ranked fifth nationally in classified advertising. Kauffmann, who had worked in every mechanical and business department at the newspaper during his years of being groomed for the top position, was a member of a privileged, genteel, insider class that ran Washington through strong personal ties.

Yet during Kauffmann's tenure as president of the *Star,* Washington changed from a southern city of powerful families into a complex and massive bureaucracy peopled by a younger, more liberal generation. Kauffmann ultimately failed to understand the impact these changes would have on his newspaper as well as the strength of the competition from both the *Washington Post* and television. When he took the helm, the paper was Washington's preeminent news organ. When he left, the paper had lost its dominant position in advertising and circulation, and the three-family dynasty was beginning to look for a buyer.

Kauffmann was the grandson of the first Samuel Hay Kauffmann, an Ohio publisher who, along with four other men, bought the *Washington Evening Star* in 1867 from William Douglas Wallach. In

fourteen years Wallach had built the *Star* from a four-page tabloid into a politically independent newspaper committed to covering local events as well as the federal government, a rare vision among the shrill, partisan publications of the day. Wallach's vision was shared by his editor, Crosby Stuart Noyes, a native of Maine who came to Washington in 1847 looking for a warmer climate.

When Wallach decided to retire at age fifty-five, he offered Noyes the paper. Noyes, together with Kauffmann and three others, bought the paper for one hundred thousand dollars. One of the original purchasers dropped out soon afterward, leaving the paper in the hands of Noyes; Kauffmann; George W. Adams, a former correspondent for the *New York World*; and Alexander R. Shepherd, a businessman and local political leader. The Evening Star Newspaper Company was formed under a charter granted by special act of Congress in 1868. At the first company meeting Noyes was formally named editor, and Kauffmann was made president.

Over the next several decades the paper grew in influence and, through a series of editorial campaigns, promoted the rebuilding of the District of Columbia after years of neglect during the Civil War. Shepherd became powerful in local politics during this period and pushed through – with the help of the *Star* – a $22 million public-works program that swept away the ramshackle Civil War capital and laid the groundwork for the federal city of today. The program bankrupted the District, however, spelling the end of the fledgling territorial government and Shepherd's power.

Shepherd left Washington, and the *Star* pushed for the federal government to agree to finance 50 percent of the District's budget in the future, an editorial position it retained for almost a hundred years. In 1881 the paper moved from its quarters at the southwest corner of Pennsylvania Avenue and 11th Street across the avenue to a narrow, marble-fronted, four-story building that it quickly outgrew. By 1900 the company had redeveloped the site, building a tall, ornate, beaux arts–style structure that blended with the architecture of the "city beautiful" movement of the day.

Victor Kauffmann, the youngest son of Samuel H. Kauffmann I, started at the paper as a cub reporter in 1889. While the leading families of the *Star* practiced nepotism, they were also careful to reward and promote talent among their progeny. Victor's older brother, Rudolph, became managing editor in 1893, and two of Noyes's three sons emerged as the driving forces behind the paper during the early part of the twentieth century: Theodore W. Noyes, who became editor after his father died in 1908; and Frank B. Noyes, who was named president of the company a year after the death of Samuel Kauffmann I.

The period between 1910 and 1930 saw the greatest growth at the *Star,* and the paper evolved from a prosperous small-town business into a major metropolitan enterprise. The paper gave its employees many benefits, including a noncontributory employee pension fund and a home-purchase plan offering mortgages through payroll deduction. This paternalistic care of employees helped create an atmosphere of mutual loyalty between management and labor that was unusual in its day. Victor served as Sunday editor of the *Star* (the Sunday *Star* was first published in 1905 with fifty-six pages) and treasurer of the company.

Samuel Hay Kauffmann II, son of Victor and Jessie Christopher Kauffmann, was born into the dynasty during the time that the *Star* reigned supreme among Washington's newspapers. He attended public schools in the District, then the Washington Collegiate School and the Lawrenceville School in New Jersey. He entered Princeton, his father's alma mater, in 1916 but left two years later to serve as a cadet in the Naval Reserve Flying Corps during World War I. After the armistice he returned to Princeton, where he was a member of the crew team, the Triangle Club, Theatre Intime, the University Glee Club, and the University Cottage Club.

After graduation in 1920 he returned to Washington and joined the staff of the *Star,* starting as a clerk behind the classified-advertising counter at twenty dollars a week. He became assistant mechanical and building superintendent several years later. In 1926 he was named assistant advertising manager. He joined the paper's board of directors in 1927, and he was named assistant business manager in 1929.

He worked directly under Fleming Newbold and Frank B. Noyes, learning his leadership style from them. Newbold had married into the Noyes family and was business manager of the paper until 1948. Noyes served as president of the company from 1910 to 1948. His tenure as president was distinguished by his belief in three basic editorial concerns: first, that District residents should be given the right to vote for president and be represented in the House and Senate; second, that the American taxpayer should help support the District; and third, that the *Star* should report the news without partisan or political bias.

In 1895 the *Star* had begun a campaign to clean up advertising within its own pages, under the slogan that "ads should be fit to be read by every member of the family." The paper also campaigned for the government to police the claims of patent-medicine doctors, whose potions were often advertised as having miraculous curative powers. In 1912 Newbold, as business manager, invited readers to report any misleading or untrue statements in the paper's advertisements and promised to eliminate such statements in future ads, or ban the advertiser.

The majority of the paper's advertising came from small concerns, allowing it an independence from being pressured by any one advertiser that few other papers of the day could boast.

By 1941 the *Star* was so successful that it had led all the newspapers in the country in total advertising linage for ten years. Its 1941 linage volume far surpassed that of the *New York Times,* and none of the other three newspapers in Washington came anywhere close. The *Star* had 39 million lines of advertising in 1941, 40 percent of the total Washington market. The *Washington Post* had 25 percent of the market, the *Times-Herald* had 23 percent, and the tabloid *Washington Daily News* had just under 12 percent.

As Kauffmann developed under the guidance of Newbold and Noyes, he exhibited an instinct for salesmanship. He believed in the personal touch, often visiting advertisers to seal a deal. He was a well-built, handsome man, with gray eyes, shaggy eyebrows, and wavy red hair. The older generation at the *Star* believed that he had a quick grasp of detail and a sixth sense for figures, as well as a loyalty to the company and employees, and a thoroughness in his business dealings.

As assistant business manager in the mid 1930s, Kauffmann persuaded the board to invest in a local radio station, so the company purchased WMAL and established the Evening Star Broadcasting Company, a wholly owned subsidiary of the paper. Kauffmann considered the radio company his particular responsibility. He served as its president from 1938 until his death, expanding the AM station into FM and television, and acquiring another station, WSVA, in Harrisonburg, Virginia. At the time of Kauffmann's death in 1971, WMAL was one of three major radio-television enterprises in Washington.

In 1936 he was named assistant secretary-treasurer of the Evening Star Newspaper Company. He was promoted to treasurer in 1941 and business manager in 1944. When Noyes resigned because of ill health in 1948, Newbold was named president and Kauffmann was named vice-president. Newbold lived only one more year, and Kauffmann succeeded him as president of the company in 1949. He was fifty-one years old and had worked for the company for twenty-nine years.

As president, Kauffmann carried on the traditions he had learned from Newbold and Noyes. He believed in honest advertising, sincerity and integrity in business dealings, and truthfulness in journalism. He dressed informally because he believed it helped him "get in and conduct business." Kauffmann personally knew all the top merchants in the District and retained advertising through these connections. He would often call his best advertisers to notify them of increases in the advertising rates.

The paper had a history of separation between the editorial and business sides – in fact, the division was prescribed in the paper's bylaws – yet the editorial vision reflected Kauffmann's training and heritage and dovetailed with his business practices. As a prominent Washingtonian of the privileged class, Kauffmann served on civic and business boards that extended his personal connections among the Old Washington aristocracy. The *Star* was considered the paper of record for Old Washington. It covered local politics in detail and often dictated policy from the editorial pages. Indeed, all the release times for news stories from city offices were arranged to give the *Star* an advantage.

However, the financial and political strength of the *Star* at mid century perhaps sowed the seeds of its own destruction. In a 1952 speech to the Newcomen Society of North America celebrating the paper's centenary, Kauffmann revealed the corporate arrogance that would soon lead the paper into a series of misjudgments about the Washington market and the competition. He reviewed the history of the *Star* in this largely congratulatory discourse, concluding that the paper's code of public service remained the simplest and most successful business practice of all:

> Our whole experience leads us to the conviction that so long as our first concern remains the welfare of our readers, the success of our business operation should be assured. We have faced a lot of competition in our time. The powerful, rich and clever of the newspaper world ... have made their way to our city and tried their hands here. We are always glad to see them come. And we are always sorry to see them go. And so, tonight, not only are we looking back over the past hundred years with a feeling of honest pride: we also are looking forward to the next hundred years with an equally strong feeling of hope.

The public that the *Star* strove to serve was changing, and Kauffmann failed to change his paper to meet the times. The *Star* was staunchly conservative on the editorial pages, and its news columns were dull. It campaigned to retain segregation and had largely ignored Franklin Roosevelt and the New Deal. Yet after World War II the city was flooded with a younger, more democratic group of bureaucrats. They wanted a livelier, more liberal

Front page of the Washington Sunday Star, *28 May 1961*

newspaper, and they had the buying power to attract advertisers.

One of the younger generation that Kauffmann underestimated was Philip Graham, son-in-law of Eugene Meyer, owner of the *Post*. When Meyer bought the *Post* at a public auction in 1933, it was forty-seventh among morning papers nationally in total weekday advertising linage. By 1943 the *Post* was ninth. But for the next decade, as Meyer and Graham tried to overtake the *Star,* the *Post* remained caught in an unwinnable competition for morning readers with the *Times-Herald,* owned by Col. Robert R. McCormick. As long as both morning papers survived, neither would be able to compete with the afternoon *Star.*

McCormick, a midwestern publisher who felt unwelcome in Washington, had invested several million dollars in new machinery but still was losing between $500,000 and $1 million a year on the *Times-Herald.* Meyer, prodded by Graham, pressed his old friend McCormick to sell him the paper. McCormick had outbid Meyer and Graham ten years earlier when the previous publisher of the *Times-Herald* had died, but McCormick's health was failing and he had no heirs. He finally agreed to sell, and in March 1954 the *Post* bought the *Times-Herald* for $8.5 million. The *Star* never made an offer.

According to industry analysts, there were several preconditions for failure in place at the *Star* when the *Post* merged with the *Times-Herald.* The *Star* had a provincial interest in local coverage, rather than a national or regional focus; it was by then in an isolated editorial position with its strong conservatism; and it had no vision of future market performance, particularly in regard to the competition that television posed for afternoon papers. The *Star* also failed either to expand its enterprise at the time of the merger or to move to publish a morning edition, which could have helped support its position. At the same time there were several preconditions for success in play at the *Post.* The paper had bold, nationally prominent editorial views on its op-ed page; bold, energetic leadership at the top; and an understanding of the changing market of the Washington area.

In March 1954 the *Times-Herald* – which published several editions a day – led in circulation, with a daily total of 262,803 and a Sunday total of 304,840. The *Star* was second, with a daily total of 238,600 and a Sunday total of 274,014. The *Post* was third, with a daily total of 204,237 and a Sunday total of 208,243. While the *Star* was second in circulation, it still dominated in advertising, running two to one against the *Post* in linage, partly be-

cause it was successful enough to keep ad rates artificially low. The advertising director at the *Star* later said, "In those days all we had to do was open the transom and let the business in. The feeling was we were invulnerable."

Some of the executives at the *Star* estimated that the *Post* would gain 80,000 in circulation from the *Times-Herald* merger, but Kauffmann is reported to have said he believed this figure would be only 5,000. But the *Post* exceeded all predictions, including Meyer's and Graham's. Within a year its daily circulation stood at 383,495, and its Sunday total was 395,022. At that time the *Star* had a daily circulation of 247,368 and a Sunday total of 276,810. Where the readers went, advertising soon followed.

By 1959 the *Post* had edged past the *Star,* with 43.5 percent of the Washington market in advertising linage against the 43.3 percent of the *Star.* And by the time the Kauffmann and Noyes families sold the paper in 1974, its share of the market had dropped to 33.3 percent. When Time Incorporated, the last owner of the *Star,* bought the paper in 1978, linage had dropped to 28 percent of the market. Time Incorporated sank millions into the *Star,* but the paper never recovered, and that corporation shut down the presses in 1981.

Ironically, as the *Star* began to lose advertising after the *Post* and *Times-Herald* merger, the news product flourished under Benjamin M. McKelway, the first editor hired from outside the ranks of the Noyes family. In 1958, 1959, and 1960 the paper won a Pulitzer Prize each year, all for local reporting, which continued to be its strength. Official Washington and reporters representing out-of-town newspapers read the evening edition of the *Star* to find out what had happened in Congress or the White House, but that role was increasingly being usurped by nightly television news.

In December 1958 the paper suffered its first strike in the history of the Washington Newspaper Guild, which shut down the paper for three days, further weakening it financially. In 1959 Kauffmann oversaw the paper's move from its historic but cramped quarters on Pennsylvania Avenue to a modern $15 million plant at Third Street and Virginia Avenue Southeast, one of the big projects of his tenure as president. Newbold Noyes, Jr., a fourth-generation descendant of the cofounder Noyes, became the new editor, and the *Star* pursued the goal of being a "tighter, brighter paper" in order to fight the growing strength of the *Post.*

By this time Kauffmann was sixty years old; he had had a lung removed in 1953 and later, through complications from the operation, became completely deaf. But he still led an active business and social life. His civic work extended back to 1932, when he was named a trustee of the Washington Community Chest. He later served as president of the Emergency Hospital and guided the plans for the merger of Emergency, Episcopal, and Garfield hospitals into the Washington Hospital Center. In 1951 he was elected honorary permanent life member of Children's Hospital, which his grandfather had helped found in 1870. He also served as a trustee of the American Cancer Society's District Divison and of American University, and as a director of the American Red Cross, the Riggs National Bank, and the Acacia Mutual Life Insurance Company.

He was active in many professional organizations, including the American Newspaper Publishers Association. From 1932 to 1938 he chaired ANPA's mechanical committee, and in 1943 he was appointed a member of the committee in charge of ANPA's Bureau of Advertising, serving as director of the bureau from 1946 to 1951. He also served as secretary of the Washington Newspaper Publishers Association.

Kauffmann, always interested in local affairs, served as chairman of the Federal City Council's Urban Renewal Committee during the early 1960s, playing a leadership role in the redevelopment of southwest Washington and the Washington waterfront. He also served as a director of the American Council to Improve Our Neighborhoods, part of the National Council of Good Cities.

Kauffmann and his wife, the former Miriam Georgia Hoy of Albany, New York, whom he married in 1920, were prominent in Washington social life. In 1953 the Kauffmanns were selected by Dwight Eisenhower's inaugural committee to represent official Washington in greeting the Eisenhowers at the inaugural ball. The Kauffmanns had four children: Samuel Hay Kauffmann III, John Hoy Kauffmann (who followed his father as president of the *Star*), Jessie Kauffmann Hollands, and Joan Kauffmann Lamphere. By the time he died in 1971, Kauffmann had twenty grandchildren.

Kauffmann stepped down as president of the Evening Star Newspaper Company in 1963, but he served as chairman of the board until 1968. He continued as a board member until he died of pneumonia and complications from emphysema on 12 January 1971. He was characterized in a *Star* editorial at the time of his death as a "formidable competitor, in business, intellectual jousting or on the golf links" and honored as a perfectionist who demanded the same high standards, ethics, and performance of his staff as he demanded of himself.

References:

David Halberstam, *The Powers That Be* (New York: Knopf, 1979);

"Samuel Hay Kauffmann Dead; Led Washington Evening Star," *New York Times,* 13 January 1971, p. 40;

"Samuel Kauffmann of the Star Dies," *Washington Star,* 13 January 1971, p. A1;

"S. H. Kauffmann Dies, Star Head," *Washington Post,* 13 January 1971, p. C11;

Washington Star, centennial edition, 16 December 1952;

Washington Star, final edition, 7 August 1981.

Bernard Kilgore

(9 November 1908 – 14 November 1967)

James Bow and William Herbert

MAJOR POSITIONS HELD: Washington bureau chief (1935–1939), managing editor (1941–1942), vice-president and general manager (1942–1943), *Wall Street Journal*; vice-president (1943–1945), president (1945–1966), chairman of the board (1966–1967), Dow Jones and Company.

BOOK: *Do You Belong in Journalism? Eighteen Editors Tell How You Can Explore Career Opportunities in Newspaper Work,* edited by Kilgore and Henry Gemmell (New York: Appleton-Century-Crofts, 1959).

Bernard Kilgore guided the emergence of the *Wall Street Journal* into a national daily newspaper of more than a million readers by the time of his death in 1967. Known to his colleagues as "Barney," Kilgore spent his postcollege career working for the *Journal* and its parent company, Dow Jones. He was a columnist who explained complex economic questions in simple language, and a company president who campaigned in the newsroom for clear, uncomplicated prose.

Kilgore was a quiet man but a generator of ideas. Under his guidance the *Journal* launched its practice of two "leader" (major) articles, on the left and right sides of the front page. He also established the *National Observer,* a general-interest newsweekly published from 1962 to 1977. The Kilgore years also saw the expansion of other Dow Jones properties, including *Barron's Weekly* and the Dow Jones News Service, a national and international distributor of business and financial news. In the late 1950s Kilgore started the Dow Jones Newspaper Fund, which provides internships on American newspapers and other programs designed to encourage college students to enter journalism.

Colleagues have described Kilgore as mild-mannered but energetic, restless with new ideas and diplomatic about setting them into motion. Andrew Heiskell, former chairman of the board of Time Incorporated, said that he highly respected Kilgore

Bernard Kilgore

but the newspaperman was hard to get to know. In the newsroom it was easier to get to know Kilgore, who was plainspoken but sometimes witty. As president of Dow Jones he "was a strong and forceful character," recalled Warren Phillips, who served as copy editor, reporter, and foreign editor during the Kilgore years. Phillips was chief executive officer of Dow Jones from 1975 until 1991. He remarked that Kilgore's "force was the force of his contribution to the *Journal.* Everybody had a lot of respect and affection for him. He built the *Journal* from a thin stock-market sheet." According to Phillips, Kilgore's new concept of the *Journal* was the redefinition of news so that it did not just include what happened the day before, the livening of business news to appeal to the consumer, and Kilgore's recognition that the paper did not need a geographic base. Its base was the "vocational community" of business people.

Kilgore's management style included comment and criticism – after the fact. Phillips has noted that Kilgore read the morning *Journal* every day on the way in to work from Princeton, and he marked up the pages to show to editors. However, he avoided getting involved in daily news and editorial decisions. Kilgore was once shown a page proof of a major editorial on the Vietnam War, but he did not read it, adding, "I'll read it in the paper." (The paper's editorial-page policy, then directed by Vermont Royster, included an appeal for the United States to get out of Vietnam.)

While Kilgore's criticism of the paper seemed to come only after publication, his comments could be sharp. He scanned the *Journal* carefully and once sent a note to an editor who had let the word *upcoming* appear in the paper. In a memo reported by Winthrop and Frances Nielson in 1973, Kilgore dispatched that word's bothersome and unnecessary use with the threat, "If I see 'upcoming' slip into the paper once again, I'll be downcoming and someone will be outgoing." His changes in the *Journal* simplified language and broadened readership to a national business and financial community beyond Wall Street and the Pacific Stock Exchange in San Francisco. The *Journal* also became a newspaper for general-interest readers who wanted in-depth reporting along with the opportunity to keep abreast of business and financial news.

Kilgore described himself simply as a "newspaperman," although he assumed the presidency of a corporation at age thirty-six. His newspaper interests extended to Princeton, New Jersey, where he lived with his family. He bought and ran a local weekly, the *Princeton Packet,* separately from his Dow Jones association. Kilgore eventually owned six New Jersey weeklies, which offered him an opportunity to experiment with typography and layout. He also took up photography as a hobby, an outlet unavailable on the *Journal,* which did not use photographs. He influenced photographic techniques at the *Packet* and the *Observer,* and picture-taking sessions with colleagues gained him their jocular designation as "Staff Photographer for the *Wall Street Journal.*"

Kilgore's early mentors at the *Journal* included fellow alumni from DePauw University in Greencastle, Indiana. He was hired by the *Journal* in 1929

and soon was transferred to San Francisco to train under Indiana-reared Deac Hendee, editor of the then-new West Coast edition. Kilgore's New York boss was Kenneth Craven "Casey" Hogate, then managing editor and later president of Dow Jones. Hogate had launched the San Francisco edition in 1929, shortly before the stock-market crash, an inauspicious time for new business ventures.

A native of Danville, Indiana, Hogate was graduated from DePauw, where he edited the student newspaper, as Kilgore was to do later. In 1928 Hogate hired Charles Robbins, Kilgore's college roommate. During Kilgore's years as managing editor of the *Journal,* it was reported – convincingly – that a DePauw degree was a helpful asset for being hired or promoted at the newspaper. The small-city Indiana background of many *Journal* reporters and editors in the 1930s and 1940s underscored Kilgore's aims for the newspaper to cover not only Wall Street and worldwide business but to make it meaningful to the small-town reader.

Leslie Bernard Kilgore was born in Albany, Indiana, near Muncie, to a father of Scottish descent and a mother of Pennsylvania Dutch–farm background. Kilgore later dropped his first name, because he did not like it. Tecumseh Kilgore, his father, was a school superintendent in Albany, but he moved his family to South Bend and went into the life-insurance business. Kilgore's mother was the former Lavinia Elizabeth Bodenhorn.

Reports of Tecumseh's business success vary, but the family needed scholarship aid to finance Bernard's education at DePauw. After Kilgore entered college, he considered becoming an engineer and working in South America. He earned a Phi Beta Kappa key, but he never made it to South America as an engineer. Robbins urged him to join the campus newspaper staff, and Kilgore, by then a political-science major, became editor of the student newspaper, the *DePauw,* as well as editor of the college yearbook. Because of these positions the college allowed him to keep a Model T on campus, and he gave rides to students for five cents.

Robbins was graduated a year ahead of Kilgore and sent out letters to prospective newspaper employers, landing a job on the *Indianapolis Star* before going to the *Journal.* Kilgore took a supply of the *DePauw* letterhead with him when he was graduated and sent out a multitude of job inquiries. He worked for the father of a girlfriend until Hogate summoned him. Kilgore quit his job, said goodbye to his girlfriend, and headed for the *Journal.* He was twenty years old.

After he was sent to San Francisco, Kilgore's duties under Hendee varied, and the new staffer spent part of his first day in the pressroom on a mechanical assignment. Kilgore became news editor of the San Francisco *Journal* two years later, and he was transferred back to New York in 1932. In San Francisco he began a column in which he explained complex economic problems. In the form of a letter to "Dear George," it attracted enough response from West Coast–edition readers to convince New York editors to feature "Dear George" on the editorial page of the main edition. The column ran without Kilgore's byline, because these were not used then for most *Journal* writers.

In 1935 Kilgore was named Washington bureau chief. The *Journal* struggled for survival during the Depression years. Kilgore was not the only writer and editor at the newspaper seeking new ways to attract readers. In 1928 the newspaper's circulation was fifty thousand; it shrank to about half that during the Depression, a time when millions of Americans felt betrayed by the financial markets that comprised a major portion of the publication's coverage. Despite the down-to-earth prose in Kilgore's column, the *Journal* continued to publish for business and financial audiences whom the newspaper assumed should be addressed in the jargon of Wall Street, without translation for the average reader.

Later, as managing editor, Kilgore noted a story about sugar trading that used the term *Bombay Straddle* to describe a form of speculation. He was unable to get a definition from his staff and grew angry, telling reporters that the *Journal* was written for readers beyond those who knew the commodities market. His crusade to simplify language, broaden readership, and add subject matter was resisted by many older staff members but was preceded by a foundation laid by other *Journal* executives.

In 1939 Hogate, then Dow Jones president, said he wanted the newspaper to grow from a financial paper into a more general business publication. He had launched a column, "What's News," a series of briefs for busy readers that was written by Kilgore when he worked in New York during the 1930s. Hogate had noticed that other newspapers were taking stories from the *Journal* and rewriting them as briefs, with livelier language. At the same time William Henry Grimes, managing editor before Kilgore, campaigned for higher professional ethics for reporters.

When Kilgore joined the *Journal,* several reporters had been playing the stock market on mar-

gin in the weeks before the 1929 crash. Grimes ordered that no *Journal* reporter could own stock in a company he was writing about, and he fired violators. He also ended the practice of allowing, or encouraging, reporters to sell advertising. He asked Hogate to fire Robbins for selling an ad to Monsanto Chemical in Saint Louis. Hogate refused to sack Robbins but warned him to choose between the news side and the business side of the newspaper.

Through Hogate and Grimes the *Journal* matured as a newspaper during the 1930s, although its circulation was low and its writing often turgid. Long before he held executive power in New York, Kilgore seemed to be a catalyst, or a gadfly, to people such as Grimes. The managing editor often resisted the suggestions Kilgore sent to New York from Washington. However, Kilgore did institute a new column of briefs, "Washington Wire."

Kilgore was a political conservative, in line with the editorial page of the *Journal.* Nevertheless, its Washington coverage showed some neutrality. The *Journal* defended the New York Stock Exchange after the 1929 crash and was generally opposed to strong regulation of the securities markets. After President Franklin Roosevelt was elected, Hogate ordered a moratorium on any political-party allegiance by the newspaper. The *Journal* backed the Emergency Banking Act to reopen closed banks, the creation of a Farm Credit Administration, and the Truth-in-Securities Act, although it supported amendments to the act a year later. Kilgore, while certainly aware of the newspaper's editorial positions, distanced himself from any major role in editorial-page policy.

Kilgore's writing helped to pave the way for his credibility in Washington. In 1934, while Kilgore was still in New York, President Roosevelt was asked at a press conference about a complicated Supreme Court decision concerning the National Recovery Act. Roosevelt responded, "Read Kilgore in the *Wall Street Journal,*" because he had written "a good piece" on the subject. The *Journal* ran a story the next day headlined, "President Tells Reporters to Read Kilgore Article." Roosevelt read the *Journal* every day, while most other newspapers were reviewed by secretaries.

Kilgore set out to become known personally in the nation's capital. He rented an apartment in northwest Washington, hired a cook and general servant, and joined the party circuit, using social events to make contacts. He became the first *Journal* staff member to be elected to the select Gridiron Club of Washington journalists. In 1941 he was

Vermont Royster (second from left), Kilgore, and William Kerby in the Wall Street Journal *composing room, circa February 1962*

called back to New York to serve as managing editor. This was when the "Kilgore revolution," as historians of *Journal* history depict his administration, began in earnest. His role as the newspaper's chief news executive, with day-to-day management responsibilities, was not to last long before he was moved up the ladder again, in 1943, to Dow Jones vice-president.

As managing editor and vice-president, Kilgore faced the technical problems of making the *Journal* a truly national newspaper, delivered at the same time all over the country. News was transmitted for the San Francisco edition so that much of the content would be the same. Photographs could not be transmitted easily at that time, and the newspaper has avoided their use ever since. The challenge of synchronized delivery between the coasts was resolved with innovations in technology that Kilgore pushed through after World War II.

In his executive role Kilgore expressed three major goals for the *Journal*: comprehensive national news coverage; in-depth reporting beyond immediate news; and broader subject matter, in which economic news was defined in the widest possible terms. Kilgore became vice-president and general manager of the *Journal* through the influence of Grimes. Hogate had become seriously ill, and Grimes invited Kilgore and William Kerby, deputy

managing editor, to his home. Grimes told them that he would voluntarily step aside to allow Kilgore to become general manager and Kerby, managing editor. Grimes would continue to run the editorial page, however.

In 1945 Hogate, having suffered a stroke four years earlier, named Kilgore to his job and moved up to chairman of the board – with the consent of the descendants of Clarence Barron, late owner of Dow Jones. Kilgore had been nominal head of the company during Hogate's extended absence, and in those wartime years circulation had risen to a point higher than its peak in the 1920s.

As president, Hogate had worked with Dow Jones's principal owner, Jane Waldron Bancroft, who possessed 80 percent of the company's stock. The Barron-Bancroft family avoided direct administration of the newspaper, and before she died, Jane Bancroft had her lawyers streamline the corporation, creating a board of directors from a board of trustees. Her two daughters later sat on the board, following the policy of their mother to play a role in choosing a company president, but then to give him a free hand. Kilgore was thus blessed in his presidency with a tradition of family noninterference, along with a modernized corporate structure.

Although Kilgore's twenty-two-year presidency of Dow Jones began in 1945, it was shaped by

The front page of the Wall Street Journal is shown, with headlines:

THE WALL STREET JOURNAL.

War With Japan—

U. S. Industry's Sole Objective: Arms Production Speedup; Congress Prepares To Act; Tax Bill Will Be Rushed; N. Y. Stock Exchange To Open As Usual Today, Says Schram

Front page of the Wall Street Journal, *8 December 1941, the day after Japan bombed Pearl Harbor, Hawaii*

an edition of the *Journal* four years earlier, when he was the paper's managing editor. In 1941 Kilgore had argued that the main problem of the then-financially ailing *Journal* was that it had not defined its constituency. He told skeptical peers that economic news did not have to be dull, or to occur within the previous twenty-four hours. On 7 December 1941 Japanese planes bombed Pearl Harbor, Hawaii, and Kilgore seized the chance to push his views.

Journal staff members who assembled that Sunday put out a Monday-morning paper and, in the process, gave the somewhat "Tired Old Lady" of Wall Street a new lease on life. On 8 December the newspaper published detailed coverage of what Japan's attack would signal for American business and its economy. Financial news went to the back of the paper, and business, Washington, and world news to the front. Before, the *Journal* had been reliable and thorough with financial news; now it was brief, brisk, human, and even humorous. The Pearl Harbor edition demonstrated that the *Journal* was a *news*paper that covered business and financial subjects, not a financial business publication that was capable of handling general news only as a peripheral service.

During Kilgore's presidency the *Journal* became a national newspaper in a country that had never produced a successful one. The changes did not please everyone: some staff members thought the new *Journal* belonged to auto dealers in the hinterlands. But Kilgore could reply with a midwestern image of his own: "If you are publishing in Elkhart, Indiana, you have got to edit for the Elkhart reader. The business community is our Elkhart." That quotation apparently was cited often around the *Journal* when Kilgore was in charge.

Readers around the nation seemed to agree with the shift in emphasis. In 1941 there were 33,000 subscribers; by 1947 there were 102,000. By 1959 circulation had climbed past 500,000. By 1967, when Kilgore died, it was at 1.1 million.

Under Kilgore's leadership Dow Jones established a research department in the late 1940s, and out of this came a device crucial to plans for a national paper. The patented Electro-Typesetter allowed type to be set at such diverse points as Chicopee Falls, Massachusetts; Cleveland, Ohio; Chicago, Illinois; Dallas, Texas; Palo Alto, California; Silver Spring, Maryland; and Highland, Illinois. All of this could be done using news copy and layout produced in New York and transmitted electronically to all the printing plants in order to publish an edition at each location every weekday. The regional editions, then and now, are basically

the same, with some changes to incorporate more news of each region. A. Kent MacDougall, *Journal* reporter during the last five years of Kilgore's tenure, remarked that Kilgore put the stamp of "his Hoosier personality" on the paper: "For Barney, every story had to be simplified and sugar-coated for the auto dealer in Elkhart." He also noted Kilgore's daily involvement with *Journal* news operations during his years as Dow Jones president: "Besides serving as a one-man quality control panel, Kilgore contributed infectious enthusiasm for the *Journal* and an intense drive to improve it."

The newspaper often has defied simplistic designations, except on the editorial page. Although the *Journal* supported Republican Dwight Eisenhower over Democrat Adlai Stevenson — a favorite of many American intellectuals — for president, it was called "the intellectual's darling" by *Harper's* magazine. And while the paper could hardly be described as anticapitalist during the Kilgore years, it gave up $250,000 of annual General Motors advertising in a dramatic demonstration to the automotive giant that it could not influence *Journal* editorial policy. In its investigations and coverage of American business, the *Journal* won Pulitzer Prizes for stories dealing with business ethics, a salad-oil scandal, President Lyndon Johnson's wealth, and gambling in the Bahamas.

When Kilgore retired as company president in 1966, ill with incurable cancer, Dow Jones had annual sales of $83 million and a net income of $14 million. Kilgore was given a lump-sum payment of $3,503,678 that bought out his contract, signed in 1946. He was elected chairman of the board and given a consulting contract. In his 1983 autobiography Royster cites three people who, in his lifetime, made "original and lasting contributions to publishing": Kilgore, Henry Luce of Time Incorporated, and DeWitt Wallace of the *Reader's Digest*.

Kilgore died at Princeton on 14 November 1967 at age fifty-nine. He was survived by his wife, the former Mary Louise Throop, of Greencastle, Indiana. She and Kilgore were married on 1 October 1938, while he was Washington bureau chief. They had three children: a daughter, Kathryn, and two sons, John and James.

Kilgore had long been active in the Society of Professional Journalists, serving as treasurer and honorary president. He was a member of the American Society of Newspaper Editors and a director of the Inter-American Press Association. He was a member of the board of trustees of the Princeton Theological Seminary and of the *Daily Princetonian* student newspaper.

Kilgore was elected posthumously to the Business Hall of Fame in 1984. He was awarded several journalism honors and honorary degrees during his lifetime. These included the Elijah Lovejoy Award from Colby College and the Distinguished Service in Journalism Award from the University of Missouri. He also received a special honor from his home state of Indiana, which named him Hoosier of the Year for 1960.

References:

"Bernard Kilgore Dies; Made a National Daily of Wall Street Journal," *Wall Street Journal,* 16 November 1967, pp. 1, 10;

"DePauw-Trained Hoosiers Play Key Roles in Rise of Business Publisher Dow Jones to National Fame," *Indiana Business & Industry* (August 1965): 8;

"Dow Jones President Bernard Kilgore Displays Early Skills As Writer, Orator," *Indiana Business & Industry* (August 1965): 9;

William F. Kerby, *A Proud Profession: Memoirs of a Wall Street Journal Reporter, Editor and Publisher* (Homewood, Ill.: Dow-Jones Irwin, 1981);

"Kilgore, 59, Is Dead; Led Wall Street Journal," *New York Times,* 15 November 1967, pp. 1, 31;

A. Kent MacDougall, "Up Against the *Wall Street Journal,*" in *Stop the Presses, I Want to Get Off! Inside Stories of the News Business from the Pages of More,* edited by Richard Pollak (New York: Random House, 1975), pp. 271–294;

Winthrop Nielson and Frances Nielson, *What's News — Dow Jones, Story of Wall Street Journal* (Radnor, Pa.: Chilton, 1973);

Jerry M. Rosenberg, *Inside the Wall Street Journal: The History and the Power of Dow Jones & Company and America's Most Influential Newspaper* (New York & London: Macmillan, 1982);

Vermont Royster, *My Own, My Country's Time: A Journalist's Journey* (Chapel Hill, N.C.: Algonquin, 1983);

Edward E. Scharff, *Worldly Power: The Making of the Wall Street Journal* (New York: Beaufort, 1986);

Lloyd Wendt, *The Wall Street Journal: The Story of Dow Jones & the Nation's Business Newspaper* (Chicago: Rand, McNally, 1982).

Clayton Kirkpatrick

(8 January 1915 –)

Louis W. Liebovich
University of Illinois

MAJOR POSITIONS HELD: Day city editor (1958–1961), city editor (1961–1963), assistant managing editor (1963–1965), managing editor (1965–1967), executive editor (1967–1969), editor (1969–1979), *Chicago Tribune*; vice-president (1967–1977), executive vice-president (1977–1979), president and chief executive officer (1979–1981), chairman of the board (1981), Chicago Tribune Company.

Clayton Kirkpatrick is generally credited with ushering the *Chicago Tribune* into the modern newspaper era. A career-long reporter and editor with the *Tribune,* Kirkpatrick was named overall editor in 1969, eventually remaking the appearance and redirecting the goals of the newspaper. Under his guidance the *Tribune* shed its image as a parochial midwestern publication, the right-wing tool of longtime editor and publisher Col. Robert R. McCormick, who died in 1955.

Kirkpatrick emphasized hard-hitting, objective journalism. The son of a small-town auto mechanic, Kirkpatrick envisioned a wide-ranging appeal to sophisticated, urbane, modern readers and reoriented the *Tribune* to fit that vision. Between 1971 and 1976 the newspaper won three Pulitzer Prizes and changed its tone, both on the editorial and news pages.

McCormick and his cousin Joseph Medill Patterson became president and chairman of the board respectively of the Tribune Company in 1911. When Patterson assumed the leadership of the fledgling *New York News* in 1919, McCormick soon became the sole driving force behind the *Tribune.* The Colonel – so designated for his army rank during World War I – eventually assumed the titles of editor and publisher, dictating editorial and news policies at the *Tribune* until his death. For more than a decade after McCormick died, his successors remained loyal to his ideas, keeping the pages of the *Tribune* devoted to ethnocentric, conservative views.

Clayton Kirkpatrick

That changed when Kirkpatrick became editor in 1969.

Kirkpatrick was born on 8 January 1915 in Waterman, Illinois, about sixty-five miles west of Chicago, to Clayton Matteson and Mable Rose Swift Kirkpatrick. He lived all his early years in the rural northeastern Illinois community, where most of the townspeople were retired farmers. The senior Kirkpatrick was a mechanic who repaired farm implements and then automobiles in his later years. The Kirkpatrick ancestors settled in De Kalb County in 1854, coming from Pennsylvania to homestead some of the world's richest farmland.

Kirkpatrick's mother nurtured her only son's writing interests, while his father urged him to become a farmer. Neither Clayton's older sister, Doris, nor his younger sister, Betty Jane, displayed the same flair for writing. Mable wrote poetry, served as librarian in Waterman, and organized the annual Waterman history pageant that commemorated the community's pioneer days. She passed on her passion for the arts to her son.

After being graduated valedictorian from Waterman High School in 1933, Kirkpatrick enrolled at the University of Illinois in Urbana. He was graduated Phi Beta Kappa with a bachelor's degree in English in January 1937. He yearned to write fiction but sensed that he needed life experience. He hitchhiked to Cincinnati, hoping to write about a major flood, but the waters had abated before he arrived. His odyssey took him to Nashville, New Orleans, Seattle, a logging camp in northern California, and then Washington, D.C., before he returned to Illinois. Along the way he wrote advertising copy for a radio station, hauled carcasses in a meat-packing plant, sold cast-iron stovetops door-to-door, waited on tables in a mess hall, wrote a promotional booklet for an aircraft-manufacturing firm, and heard President Franklin Roosevelt deliver a stirring speech.

Back in Chicago after his yearlong sojourn, Kirkpatrick decided he needed a practical outlet for his talent. He sent résumés to all the newspapers in Chicago. Only J. Loy Maloney, managing editor of the *Tribune,* answered his inquiry. Maloney told Kirkpatrick that he needed experience in the City News Bureau, a low-paying reporter's pool on which all the city's newspapers relied for routine local stories.

The bureau offered Kirkpatrick a brief introduction to the hectic world of Chicago journalism. He covered police news on the city's West Side, hanging around the precinct station, picking up tips, and reading police reports. Maloney called a year later. Kirkpatrick joined the *Tribune* staff in late 1938 as a general-assignment reporter, earning a pay increase from $19.50 a week at the City News Bureau to $30 a week at the *Tribune.*

"I found the *Tribune* to be a good newspaper with a lot of good people on it," he recalled fifty years later. "But if I had my choice I would have gone to the *Daily News.* It was a writer's paper. I was impressed with their foreign staff, the quality of their coverage, and the quality of their writers." However, he stayed with the *Tribune,* even turning down an offer of better pay from the newly formed *Chicago Sun* in 1941. Maloney learned of the offer and waited ten weeks to see what the young re-

porter would do. Maloney rewarded Kirkpatrick's loyalty with a ten-dollar-a-week raise.

Under McCormick the *Tribune* evolved into the dominant morning newspaper in Chicago and a midwestern voice for conservative traditional American values. A raw, brawling, hardworking city in the 1920s and 1930s, Chicago was populated by working-class, ethnic neighborhoods and controlled by ambitious entrepreneurs, rough-and-tumble politicos, and corrupt public policies. McCormick preferred polo to boxing and a horseback ride through the country to a poker game. His attitudes and ideas mixed peculiarly with the gamey atmosphere of Chicago during his reign at the *Tribune.*

Still, many Chicagoans continued to cling to the nineteenth-century, laissez-faire values that had provided a foundation for the nation's rise to greatness and found comfort in McCormick's philosophy. The *Tribune* was a regional newspaper, and it remained the bible of small-town, midwestern conservatism. In addition, many people just did not care about the newspaper's philosophy; they read the *Tribune* because it was the most complete newspaper in the Midwest.

Despite his parochial attitudes, McCormick was a business genius who knew how to put out a distinctive product. The city's many newsstands were crowded with a half-dozen to a dozen local newspapers vying daily for the public's hard-earned wages. After only a few years of McCormick's control, the *Tribune* was at the top of the heap – the best-selling newspaper in Chicago. "I think he was a much better businessman than he was a newsman," Kirkpatrick observed many years later.

The feisty publisher made the *Tribune* a personal vehicle for his ideals, using it to further his political influence. He actively supported his favorite local and statewide candidates. His staff weighted the newspaper's editorial pages with glowing words about favored Republicans while vilifying opposing candidates. This bias spilled over to the news pages. McCormick demanded a front-page political cartoon every day. *Tribune* editors made sure that preferred local officials received careful attention. Stories quoted them often, usually on the front page, while opposition politicians found their quotes buried far inside the newspaper, except when they were implicated in scandal or corruption.

McCormick attended Republican National Conventions, pushing his favorite candidates during presidential election years. His attempts at kingmaking often failed, and he flailed at the party itself in frustration. Near the end of his life, in August 1952, McCormick lashed out at the Republicans for nominating Dwight Eisenhower, whom he viewed as a tool of the eastern, moneyed interests in the Republican party. The Colonel angrily called for the creation of a third major political party but backed off after editorial writer Leon Stolz and managing editor Donald Maxwell counseled caution.

Throughout the 1920s and the 1930s McCormick used the *Tribune* to express his abhorrence of foreign entanglements. He felt that America had been hoodwinked into World War I, and he wanted no more involvement in Europe's problems. Most of America shared this attitude. The *Tribune* trumpeted isolationism in the face of Japanese militarism in the Far East and Adolf Hitler's spiraling aggression in Europe. Even after the Japanese attack on Pearl Harbor, McCormick bore bitter resentment about America's entry into the war, suspecting that Roosevelt had surreptitiously brought the United States into the conflict.

McCormick hated Roosevelt; he despised the New Deal and Roosevelt's spending programs. The *Tribune* daily attacked Roosevelt in less-than-polite language, and its editorial writers recoiled in horror at the social programs created during the Depression. As Roosevelt's popularity grew, McCormick's despair over the country's direction mushroomed. He offered his advice and counsel to Roosevelt's presidential opponents – Alf Landon in 1936 and Wendell Willkie in 1940, but to no avail. The newspaper's attitude toward the president distanced it from the public, which remained enamored with the charismatic leader. This was the atmosphere at the *Tribune* when Kirkpatrick joined the staff in late 1938. From 1939 to 1942 he served mostly as a general-assignment reporter covering routine affairs in city neighborhoods for the newspaper's zoned sections. He wrote stories out of the federal building for several months before enlisting in the U.S. Army Air Corps in 1942. During World War II he served in Great Britain as a chief clerk of a group-intelligence section, advancing to the rank of master sergeant and earning the Bronze Star.

In 1943 Kirkpatrick married Thelma Marie Mott. Over the next eleven years they had four children: Pamela Marie, Bruce, Eileen Bea, and James Walter. None of them became journalists.

After the war Kirkpatrick returned to general-assignment reporting, often writing lengthy articles about municipal problems and political corruption. Reporters almost never spoke directly with McCormick, although the colonel frequently sent cryptic messages to editors about stories that he wanted researched. The editors would pass on the messages to befuddled reporters, who tried to determine what the

publisher wanted. Those who guessed wrong often met with rebukes and stern warnings to get the story right.

In one such instance McCormick, a Civil War buff, wanted Kirkpatrick to trace Gen. Ulysses S. Grant's campaign from Cairo, Illinois, to Vicksburg, Mississippi:

I could not understand the assignment and the city editor could not explain it either. So I did something no other reporter would do. I took the elevator to the 24th floor and asked to see the Colonel. He explained that he wanted me to take his airplane – it seated 20 people – and fly back and forth along the Mississippi River trying to trace the march the soldiers took and to find Island No. 10, a sand bar in the Mississippi that apparently had had some strategic value during the Civil War.

Well, I took my father, who was retired by then, and a couple of secretaries and I spent a week trying to follow the path taken by Grant's Army. I never did find that Island No. 10. I reported that it must have been covered by the river and that seemed to satisfy the Colonel. I wrote a very lengthy article. About six months later, I asked Maloney why I was asked to fly that airplane to New Orleans. He said, "The Colonel was having a hard time proving to the IRS that the plane was a journalistic tool." So I guess that was why he had a raggedy-ass reporter using his airplane.

On another occasion, as Kirkpatrick visited the publisher's office, the door slammed shut behind him. McCormick controlled the door by a button installed on his desk. When he turned to leave, Kirkpatrick discovered that the closed door blended with the richly paneled wall. He could not find the exit, so he returned to stand in front of McCormick's desk. Without looking up the publisher grunted, "Kick the brass plate!" Kirkpatrick pushed a plate at the bottom of the wall with his toe, and the door flew open.

Kirkpatrick's climb to the top of the *Tribune* editorial staff was swift by major news-organization standards. The mechanic's son – who worked his way up from the City News Bureau to become chief executive officer of one of the nation's most influential newspapers – offered a stark contrast to the well-heeled, opinionated McCormick, who inherited his position at the newspaper from the Medill-McCormick-Patterson family. Kirkpatrick was passionately in favor of objectivity and public-affairs reporting. He believed that the news should be presented without comment, and as editor he created an op-ed page called "Perspective," which was open to a variety of opinions.

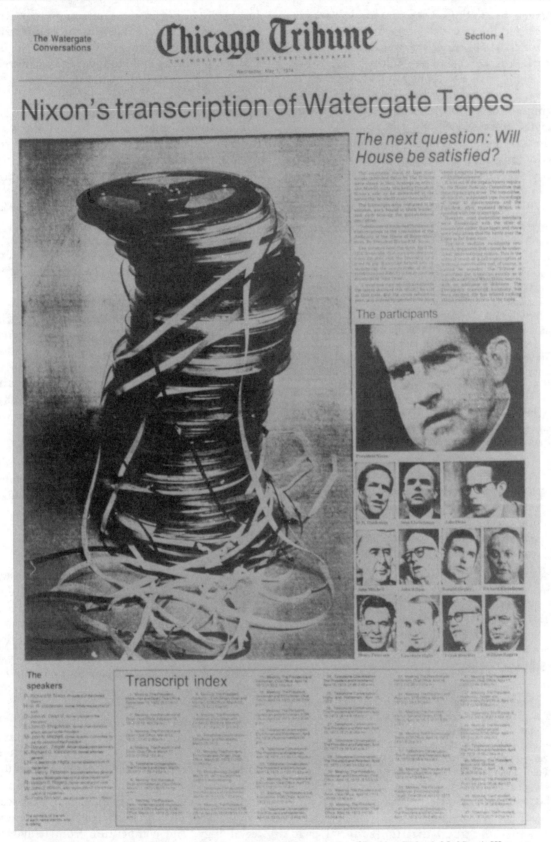

The Chicago Tribune *was the first newspaper to publish a complete transcript of President Richard M. Nixon's Watergate tapes, 1 May 1974.*

After a brief stint on the copy desk, Kirkpatrick succeeded the retiring George Schreiber as day city editor in 1958, three years after McCormick died. Kirkpatrick became city editor in 1961. For the next eight years he climbed quickly up the *Tribune* hierarchy to assistant managing editor (1963), managing editor (1965), executive editor (1967), and, finally, editor (1969).

He also became a member of the Tribune Company executive leadership. He was named a company vice-president in 1967, executive vice-president (1977), president and chief executive officer (1979), and chairman of the board for six months in 1981 before he retired. Kirkpatrick commented on his ascent within the organization:

> I never thought of being an editor when I was a reporter. Like most reporters, I didn't have too much respect for editors. But I guess a lot of those promotions were luck. I think also it had to do with the fact that I was in a class which was a little bit scarce. The Colonel insisted on taking back to his staff every person who had served in the military. For the first five to ten years after the war, we were way over-staffed. Promotion at the *Tribune* did not look like a good prospect. A lot of people my age drifted away. I believe someone had made the decision [in 1958] that I could rise at least to managing editor, though. I think I must have had some partisans over on the business side.

The *Tribune* had carried a front-page editorial cartoon every day for decades under McCormick and thereafter. In 1968 Kirkpatrick began to take the cartoon off the front page occasionally. By the time he was editor, the newspaper was free of front-page cartoons, a signal to its readers that a clearer distinction between editorials and news was being forged. The ethnocentric slogan "An American Newspaper for Americans" also disappeared from the editorial page of the *Tribune*. In 1971 the long-time masthead logo on the front page, "World's Greatest Newspaper," also was removed. Kirkpatrick recalled:

> People around the *Tribune* were very cautious about change. Often, at meetings, they would ask, "What would the Colonel do?" when some policy decision came up. My theory was that changes should be made, but very quietly, evolutionary rather than revolutionary. I didn't want to start a jarring revolution that would make the readers think that everyone at the tower had lost his senses.

However, he knew that the editorial page alienated readers, especially young people raised during the comfortable, post–World War II days.

Just before he assumed his duties as editor, Kirkpatrick commissioned a survey by the Lou Harris polling organization. Readers indicated that the *Tribune* was too pompous and stodgy. Many believed that its biased presentation of the news and one-sided editorial page damaged its credibility.

The survey results created a rift between the old guard, particularly editor Donald Maxwell, and the reformers, headed by Kirkpatrick. Maxwell disregarded the findings, but many Tribune Company executives reviewed them and were impressed. When Maxwell retired, he wanted an editorial writer from the McCormick era to take over as editor, but the Tribune Company board appointed Kirkpatrick. Maxwell and Kirkpatrick hardly spoke to each other again, but Maxwell remained on the board, railing against each change that Kirkpatrick instituted, to no avail.

"People don't remember, but the Colonel was a reformer, himself, when he was young," Kirkpatrick said. "He was a Bull-Moose Progressive. It's just that in his later years, he was too inflexible. The newspaper had to change." Soon after Kirkpatrick became editor, the promotion department wanted to announce that a new *Tribune* was being printed, but he insisted that changes be instituted quietly.

Every aspect of the newspaper came under scrutiny. The line-ruled, eight-column format disappeared in favor of a six-column, flexible layout with a smaller page size. Block headlines changed to upper and lower case, and the type style was altered. Special life-style sections were created, with stories that appealed to younger readers. Layouts emphasized imagination and creativity.

In 1969, after astronaut Neil Armstrong's walk on the moon, the front page featured only about sixty words in large type over a page-long background picture of the moon landscape. "Sometimes, we just did some things for shock value," Kirkpatrick said. "We had to get the message across that the *Tribune* was changing, but we could never say that publicly."

Kirkpatrick credited managing editor Maxwell McCrohon and city editor Bill Jones with much of the newspaper's success in making its transition during the 1970s. McCrohon eventually succeeded Kirkpatrick as editor, and Jones moved up to managing editor. In that period many newspapers fell on hard times. Archaic management practices, the rising cost of newsprint, increased costs of updated technology, and competition from television cut into newspaper profits, sometimes causing papers to fold. The *Tribune*-owned *Chicago American,* later called *Chicago Today,* ceased publication in September 1974. Four years later the city's only other afternoon newspaper, the *Daily News,* also died. During Kirkpatrick's editorship the thriving Chicago newspaper market shrank drastically to just two publications, the *Tribune* and the *Chicago Sun-Times.* Both had been morning newspapers, but both converted to twenty-four-hour publications after their afternoon counterparts failed. They returned to morning-only editions a few years later.

While drastically overhauling the *Tribune,* Kirkpatrick was also forced to oversee the newspaper's transition to a daylong publication. This required major changes in publication schedules, news-editorial operations, and circulation patterns. He had to reorganize the *Tribune* staff to accommodate many people who transferred from the newsroom of *Chicago Today.* Through it all the *Tribune* maintained a steady circulation rate. "But it didn't go up much," Kirkpatrick said. "That was always a disappointment to me. A lot of subscribers just stopped reading newspapers."

In 1979 publisher Robert Hunt left Chicago to assume leadership of the troubled *New York Daily News,* then owned by the Tribune Company. Kirkpatrick was nearing retirement age, but board chairman Stanton Cook asked him to assume Hunt's duties as president and chief executive officer. When Charles Brumbaugh moved from the Tribune Company's *Orlando Sentinel* to become *Tribune* publisher in 1981, Cook asked Kirkpatrick to take over as chairman of the board for a few months. In late 1981 Kirkpatrick retired to suburban Glen Ellyn, Illinois.

In 1977 the University of Kansas honored Kirkpatrick with the William Allen White Award. Colby College presented him with the Elijah Parish Lovejoy Award in 1978, and the National Press Club named him its Fourth Estate Award recipient in 1979. He addressed a UNESCO conference on freedom of the press in Nairobi, Kenya, in 1976, telling delegates not to endorse a Soviet-sponsored resolution supporting Soviet-style controls on Third World news organizations. "The Third World countries were ready to go along with them," Kirkpatrick said. "I don't think it would have affected

newspapers in this country or in other democratic nations, but there could have been much less free expression around the world. I've always taken an interest in press freedom. Without it, you can't have democracy. I believe that." The resolution was defeated.

In reflecting on the changes at the *Tribune,* Kirkpatrick pointed to a 9 May 1974 editorial, which he cowrote, as the turning point in the newspaper's history. Entitled "Listen, Mr. Nixon," it denounced the Republican president and called on him to resign. Kirkpatrick said that the editorial had much to do with President Richard M. Nixon's decision step down three months later. On 1 May 1974 the *Tribune* accomplished the extraordinary feat of publishing the entire transcription of Nixon's White House tapes the morning after they were released.

Kirkpatrick has decried many newspapers' trend toward briefer, less complete stories, which developed during the 1980s following the establishment of *USA TODAY* by the Gannett Company. "I don't think those newspapers are very satisfying at all," he commented. "They miss the primary function of a newspaper: establishing a dialogue and climate for major decision making."

References:

Jerome Edwards, *The Foreign Policy of Col. McCormick's Tribune, 1929–1941* (Reno: University of Nevada Press, 1971);

Philip Kinsley, *The Chicago Tribune: Its First Hundred Years* (New York: Knopf, 1943);

John J. McPhaul, *Deadlines & Monkeyshines: The Fabled World of Chicago Journalism* (Englewood Cliffs, N.J.: Prentice-Hall, 1962);

H. L. Mencken, *The Bathtub Hoax, and Other Blasts & Bravos from the Chicago Tribune,* edited by Robert McHugh (New York: Knopf, 1958);

Frank C. Waldrop, *McCormick of Chicago: An Unconventional Portrait of a Controversial Figure* (Englewood Cliffs, N.J.: Prentice-Hall, 1966);

Lloyd Wendt, *Chicago Tribune: The Rise of a Great American Newspaper* (Chicago: Rand, McNally, 1979).

William Loeb

(26 December 1905 – 13 September 1981)

Margaret A. Blanchard
University of North Carolina at Chapel Hill

NEWSPAPERS OWNED: *St. Albans* (Vermont) *Daily Messenger* (1941–1981); *Burlington* (Vermont) *Daily News* (1942–1961); *Vermont Sunday News* (1943–1977); *Manchester* (New Hampshire) *Union Leader* (1946–1981); *New Hampshire Sunday News* (1948–1981); *Haverhill* (Massachusetts) *Journal* (1957–1965); *Connecticut Sunday Herald* (1966–1974).

When William Loeb died in 1981, the *Boston Globe* said, "Not since the free-wheeling days of William Randolph Hearst Sr. has the United States seen a newspaper mogul as controversial and choleric as William Loeb." A year or so before his death that Hearstian image also appeared in a *Washington Post* feature that told readers of "the San Simeon of the Atlantic" – Loeb's thirty-room mansion on an estate that covered seventy acres of oceanfront land in Prides Crossing, Massachusetts. Visitors were welcomed by a German shepherd and a Doberman pinscher, which augmented a high-tech security system.

Although there seems to be no record of just what Loeb thought of such comparisons to Hearst, they were indeed apt in view of his career. Even though Loeb's newspaper empire was much smaller than Hearst's, the power that Loeb wielded over his territory – and over the nation – was almost as great. That power came primarily from his ownership of the *Manchester* (New Hampshire) *Union Leader,* purchased in 1946, and the *New Hampshire Sunday News,* purchased in 1948.

As publisher of these papers, Loeb had a stranglehold on a small but important American audience: the people of New Hampshire. His were the only statewide media available to New Hampshire readers. Print competition was limited to small regional publications; broadcast competition was almost nonexistent because of the state's geography. By the late 1960s an entire generation of New Hampshire readers had grown up on the peculiar editorial views of publisher William Loeb – most

William Loeb

often expressed through front-page, signed editorials.

Loeb took a strong interest in New Hampshire politics and determined to make or break any and all politicians who strayed into his bailiwick. A conservative Republican, he had an outstanding success rate, especially given the importance of New Hampshire's "first in the nation" presidential primary. The adage that a candidate cannot win the

Oval Office without first winning in New Hampshire is not of recent vintage, although it has recently been disproven in the case of Bill Clinton. It was accepted wisdom when Loeb was churning out his front-page vitriol and tagging national politicians with such names as "Dopey Dwight," "Calamity Jack," "Snake Oil Lyndon," "Tricky Dicky," and "Jerry the Jerk" – referring to Presidents Eisenhower, Kennedy, Johnson, Nixon, and Ford.

He is most famous for derailing the presidential aspirations of Edmund Muskie in 1972 and for going after that "incompetent liberal masquerading as a conservative," George Bush, when he sought the Republican presidential nomination in 1980. Muskie's ambitions were destroyed in a snowstorm one New Hampshire winter's day; Bush's dreams were sidetracked in the Ronald Reagan avalanche, of which Loeb fully approved.

Loeb was the only child of William Loeb, Sr., and Catherine Wilhelmina Dorr Loeb. As a young man, his father learned stenography to augment the family's income. That led Loeb, Sr., to part-time stenographic work in his hometown of Albany, New York, and eventually to assignments for the state's governor, Theodore Roosevelt. As Roosevelt rose in power, so did Loeb, Sr., until he became the president's personal secretary. Roosevelt and his wife served as godparents for Loeb, Jr. His father's importance in Roosevelt's administration and the Republican party led to a term as collector of customs of the Port of New York, and to a modest fortune earned off investments.

Loeb, Jr., was sent to the best schools. He disliked the Allen-Stevenson School in New York City and transferred to the Hotchkiss School in Lakeville, Connecticut, when he was thirteen. Following graduation from Hotchkiss he enrolled at Williams College in Williamstown, Massachusetts, and later attended Harvard Law School. He was his parents' pride and joy. When important people visited Loeb, Sr., his son was on hand to join in the conversations. He grew up with impeccable manners, expensive tastes, the habit of getting his own way, and a bad tendency at best to mislead his parents and at worst to lie to them outright.

While he was a student at Williams, he became attracted to Elizabeth V. Nagy, an instructor in philosophy at Smith College. Although Nagy was eight years older than Loeb, the two were married on 29 May 1926. She was not introduced to the family until the spring of 1928, and his parents promptly consigned her to a lodging house in Oyster Bay, Long Island, rather than allowing her to stay at the family home.

Nevertheless, the marriage lasted a few more years, and as would prove true in his other marriages, he let his wife help support him while he continued on with his life. She obtained another teaching position while he attended Harvard Law School; his parents also provided financial assistance. After two years he left Harvard, returned home, and filed for an annulment. Elizabeth countered with a suit against his parents for alienation of affection, and one against him for divorce. The Loebs ultimately paid five thousand dollars to settle the suit against them, as well as their son's alimony judgment of thirty dollars a week until Elizabeth remarried.

During the 1930s Loeb, Jr., dabbled in business, became enmeshed in a few minor international issues, and seemed destined to make little of himself. Looking back on this period of his life from the perspective of 1971, he told a *New York Times* reporter that he had learned to hate Communists during these years: "That time is when my principles were refined, and they haven't changed. I guess seen from the viewpoint of that age I was an idealist, but seen from the viewpoint of today, I'm called reactionary. . . . You are supposed to adjust, and if you don't you are called a reactionary. I just haven't changed much from those days."

His life changed dramatically when his father died in 1937. He dropped the "Jr." from his name and played on his father's reputation for honesty. He also manipulated his mother's inheritance, because, although Loeb was not mentioned in his father's will, he was to keep half of the net profits that he earned from managing her estate.

Loeb later claimed that he became bitten with the newspaper bug by working for the *New York Times* during this period. He also claimed at various times to have worked for Hearst's International News Service, the *New York World,* the *Springfield* (Massachusetts) *Union,* the *Springfield* (Massachusetts) *Republican,* and the Paul Block newspapers. Exhaustive investigation by his biographer, Kevin Cash, shows that at best he may have written a few articles as a stringer for the *Union* and the *Republican* in 1929. Other than that, there seems to be no truth to any Loeb assertions that he had newspaper experience before he began at the top – by becoming owner and publisher of the *St. Albans* (Vermont) *Daily Messenger* in 1941. The paper was purchased through a loan from his mother, and Loeb remained its owner until the paper's death a few months before his own in 1981.

His experiences at the St. Albans paper typified his later newspaper career. Signed, front-page editorials displayed Loeb's propensity for backing God, country, and conservative political ideas. According to his highly critical biographer, Loeb almost immediately alienated the St. Albans audience by proclaiming in his first front-page editorial that "Vermont Stands For Victory," which ignored the fact that Vermonters had been joining the armed forces for months before Loeb appeared on the scene. Such a lack of connection with his constituents became a trademark of Loeb's newspaper career. It was his job as publisher to convert readers to the proper way of thinking – his own.

That attitude caused him particular problems in New England, where newcomers often are looked at with a good deal of suspicion. Vermonters were better prepared to fend off Loeb's advances, because they had access to rival media. Although residents of New Hampshire would have much the same reaction to Loeb's techniques, they formed a captive audience.

Front-page editorials followed when he took over ownership of the *Burlington* (Vermont) *Daily News* in February 1942. Once again Loeb offended the sensitivities of Vermonters when his first editorial concluded, "We feel that in the unity of happy families and with the support of Almighty God, Vermont can yet be the greatest State in the greatest nation on earth." Vermonters already felt that their state was the greatest in the Union.

The Burlington venture, which was never prosperous, served as the backdrop for another Loeb courtship. He married Eleanore McAllister, who taught riding at a private girls' school, in September 1942. She returned to her position at the Foxcroft School in Middleburg, Virginia, after the ceremony, told no one of her marriage, and sent Loeb most of her five-thousand-dollar annual income. Loeb had told her that he had only forty-seven dollars in the bank at the time of their marriage. "I felt sorry for him," she later told his biographer.

Although Loeb would later have harsh words for those who tried to evade the draft during the Vietnam War, Cash says that Loeb aggravated his duodenal ulcers by heavy drinking in order to avoid serving during World War II. He was thirty-six when America entered the war, and with his medical history he likely would have been exempted from the draft anyway. Nevertheless, Cash uncovered letters from Loeb to his new wife outlining his plan to avoid service. In 1971 Loeb banned all news of the Muhammad Ali–Joe Frazier heavyweight-championship fight from his newspapers, because Ali had been convicted for draft evasion and

was free on bail pending appeal. When readers complained of the boycott, Loeb responded, "I do not want to do anything to help make money for a convicted draft dodger while our boys are fighting and dying in Vietnam."

The war years also saw the first publication of the Loeb baptismal certificate in one of his newspapers. Loeb always was unhappy when people assumed that, because of his name, he was Jewish. When he got into the publishing business, he found a way to defuse such critics: he simply would publish the baptismal certificate issued by the Episcopal bishop of Washington, D.C. – complete with the signature of the Roosevelts as godparents – to prove that he certainly was not Jewish.

Loeb's first confrontation with newspaper labor unions also occurred during the war years. When the International Typographical Union tried to organize at the St. Albans paper, Loeb simply moved all printing operations to the Burlington plant, which was safely nonunionized. Although he later proclaimed his support for workers and labor unions, one of his first confrontations with organized labor resulted in a union-busting campaign and the loss of several jobs at the St. Albans paper.

As the war was ending, two events occurred that would change the publisher's life. The first was personal: he met Nackey Scripps Gallowhur, an heir to the Scripps newspaper fortune, and started seeing her socially even though both of them were still married to others. The second event was professional: both owners of the *Manchester Union Leader* died in 1944, and the paper went on the market. Marshall Field III of Chicago tried to buy the *Union Leader*, as did the growing Gannett chain, but Mrs. Frank Knox – widow of the secretary of the navy who had been one of the owners – favored Loeb. Both Knox and Loeb's father had been associated with Theodore Roosevelt, and Mrs. Knox and Mrs. Loeb were friends. In addition, Loeb offered the highest price.

That price, however, was the result of creative financing. His mother thought that she had helped to purchase the Manchester paper, but the money really came from the Ridder Brothers. Bernard, Victor, and Joseph Ridder loaned Loeb $1.1 million to complete the deal – 50 percent of the cost for 50 percent interest in the newspaper. As it turned out, the Ridders actually put up 90 percent of the money for 50 percent interest in the *Union Leader*. The contract included a buy-out clause, and within six months Loeb had maneuvered the Ridders into a position where they were ready and willing to sell out. Loeb found the money to complete the deal and assumed total control of the publications.

When he purchased the Manchester newspaper operation, he got the morning *Manchester Union* and the afternoon *Manchester Leader*. Shortly after the sale he changed their names to the *New Hampshire Morning Union,* which was aimed at a statewide audience, and the *Manchester Evening Leader,* which served the city. He purchased the *New Hampshire Sunday News* in 1948, giving him total control over the state's most important print-media outlets.

In 1966 a *Columbia Journalism Review* writer reported that the *Union Leader,* as an all-day paper, had a total circulation of 53,800 in a state with a population of 607,000. Some 30,000 of these newspapers were sold in Manchester. The *Sunday News* had a circulation of 45,700 in 1966.

The combined New Hampshire sales of three Boston papers topped Loeb's circulation figures. The *Globe, Herald,* and *Record American* sold a total of 58,700 copies daily and 102,400 on Sundays in the state. Their influence in New Hampshire, however, was minimal, because they did not cover the state's politics. New Hampshire also had eight regional daily newspapers, all published in evening editions, which had a total circulation of 82,000; however, none of them had a statewide circulation.

The lock on statewide circulation and coverage was in place when Loeb purchased the papers, and it was all he needed to run rampant through New Hampshire – and national – politics. When he took over the Manchester papers, he announced that his watchword would come from Daniel Webster, a nineteenth-century New Hampshire hero: "There is nothing so powerful as truth." As many critical journalists discovered after the Muskie affair in 1972, the truth according to Loeb did not necessarily equal the truth as others saw it.

Over the years Loeb generally found that he could dictate the candidates for statewide office from New Hampshire's weak Democratic party and influence who would be named as Republican nominees for various state offices. He successfully blocked repeated efforts to introduce income and sales taxes in New Hampshire while promoting "sin taxes" in general and a state lottery in particular. In 1960 he convinced a politically obscure pen manufacturer from Chicago, Paul Fisher, to enter the Democratic presidential primary against John F. Kennedy. Fisher, who scarcely visited the state, garnered 13 percent of the vote with Loeb's backing.

Readers of the Manchester papers grew accustomed to Loeb's selective version of the truth. People and ideas of which Loeb approved received cov-

erage; those of which he disapproved were either ignored or poorly reported in his newspapers. A *Columbia Journalism Review* study of the coverage of Republican candidates in the 1964 New Hampshire presidential primary reveals that Barry Goldwater, Loeb's choice, received 694 column inches of space inside the newspaper as opposed to 252 column inches for Nelson Rockefeller, whom Loeb disliked heartily. Front-page pictures of Goldwater filled 214 column inches, while those of Rockefeller filled 44 column inches.

Upon the death in 1957 of one of his heroes, Senator Joseph McCarthy, a Wisconsin Republican, Loeb thundered: "Joe McCarthy was murdered by the Communists as surely as if he had been put up before a wall and shot." McCarthy, who had been censured by the U.S. Senate, had died of hepatitis at Bethesda Naval Medical Center. The front-page, signed editorial was bordered in black and carried on with the murder theme, concluding, "FINALLY WE COME TO THAT STINKING HYPOCRITE IN THE WHITE HOUSE [Eisenhower], WHO RECENTLY BECAME SO SMALL THAT HE ASKED EVERY OTHER SENATOR AND REPRESENTATIVE TO HIS RECEPTION EXCEPT JOE M'CARTHY."

The editorial led a New Hampshire state senator to introduce a resolution to censure the publisher of the *Union Leader.* The resolution said that "the right of free speech and free press does not grant the privilege of degrading the highest elective office in the nation" and called on the state senate to condemn "the unbridled use of such vicious and irresponsible language in the public press." It looked as if the resolution might pass, but by the time the statement progressed to a third reading, wary state senators had abandoned their challenge.

John F. Kennedy was another favorite target of Loeb, because, according to Cash, Joseph P. Kennedy would not loan money to the publisher, who was chronically in dire financial straits. Just before the 1960 election Loeb editorialized, "It is just plain nonsense to say that Senator Kennedy whose father has a half a billion dollars and whose family has $40,000 weddings can understand the problems that face the average citizen in the United States."

When Kennedy won the presidency a few days later, he responded, "I would like to have the *Union Leader* print in a headline that we carried New Hampshire." The president-elect continued, "I believe there is probably a more irresponsible newspaper . . . in the United States but I've been through 40 states and I haven't found it yet. . . . I believe that there is a publisher who has less regard for the

STATE OF NEW HAMPSHIRE
· CONCORD 03301

WALTER PETERSON
GOVERNOR

December 5, 1969

Mr. William Loeb, Publisher
Manchester Union Leader
Manchester, New Hampshire

Dear Mr. Loeb:

I am writing you instead of one of your employees because I know that no attack such as the one on my daughter Meg that appeared in this morning's issue is published in the Manchester Union Leader without your knowledge and approval.

You will also note that I write you not only as Governor of New Hampshire, but also as a private citizen who is the father of two teenage children in the public schools, and as a parent who is as seriously concerned with the problems of youth as anyone could be.

Any thoughtful reader of your newspaper is aware of your continued efforts to destroy me politically through distorted news stories and vicious editorials. You and I know, Mr. Loeb, that this campaign against me is caused by your inability to force me to dance to your tune. I respect your right to attack me and my programs to improve the quality of life in New Hampshire. I shall leave it to the people of New Hampshire to assess my performance.

I must object to your despicable tactic of attacking my 15 year old daughter Meg as a means of getting at me. This morning's story distorting the truth is a new low in journalism, even for your newspaper. I am fair game, Mr. Loeb, but I must ask you to stop picking on my 15 year old daughter who, after all, is only a young girl with many years of life ahead.

Why not pick on someone your own size.

Walter Peterson
Walter Peterson
Governor

(This space has been paid for by Walter Peterson, Peterborough)

Letter from New Hampshire governor Walter Peterson to Loeb, as it appeared on the front page of the Manchester Union Leader, *6 December 1969. Peterson was upset with the coverage of his teenage daughter in the paper, which stated that she condoned the use of marijuana.*

truth than William Loeb but I can't think of his name."

Loeb's newspaper carried Kennedy's comments but gave the publisher twice as much space to reply to the slurs on his reputation. In his front-page editorial Loeb called Kennedy a "liar" and a "spoiled brat." The publisher remained an avowed enemy of the new president. The rest of the Kennedy clan also suffered from his editorials, with Ted Kennedy becoming a favorite target after the Chappaquiddick incident. Loeb once wrote of the youngest Kennedy brother, "Senator Kennedy certainly has a great deal of gall criticizing the daring U.S. rescue mission for our prisoners in North Vietnam when he couldn't even rescue a girl from the bottom of the pond at Chappaquiddick bridge."

Any New Hampshire politician or public official was a natural target of Loeb's editorials and his version of investigative reporting. When Thomas N. Bonner was named president of the University of New Hampshire in 1971, Loeb sent a reporter to Cincinnati, where Bonner had served as vice-president and provost of the University of Cincinnati. There followed a multipart series that subjected Bonner to a spotlight previously unexperienced by any person named to head a major public educational institution. Among the charges levied at Bonner was that he had, in some way, sponsored "allnight drinking parties, marijuana parties, the sharing of showers by male and female students, and around-the-clock sex."

As with everything in New Hampshire, Loeb felt he had a proprietary interest in the state's educational facilities. Unable to exert much influence on Dartmouth College, a private school, he concentrated on the University of New Hampshire, carefully monitoring its selection of presidents. In some circles that office was seen as the most undesirable in the nation, and its occupants did not last long if Loeb took a dislike to them. In Bonner's case, his politics were suspect. He had been an aide to South Dakota senator George McGovern, and the attack on Bonner coincided with the 1972 presidential primary and campaign, in which McGovern became the Democratic standard-bearer.

Perhaps the most reprehensible of his attacks was that against Meg Peterson, fifteen-year-old daughter of Walter Peterson, the Republican who was then serving as governor of New Hampshire. Loeb and Peterson were at political odds, and the publisher regularly looked for ways to discredit the politician. When Peterson's daughter was invited to a conference on drugs in the nation's capital, Loeb found his chance. A reporter cornered her and some

other teenagers at the conference and asked them about drug use in their schools. The United Press International story that was printed in the *Union Leader* quoted Peterson as saying, "I don't think there is anything wrong with smoking pot myself," and adding that a teacher had once brought a lighted marijuana cigarette into her classroom.

That article led to more stories and to editorials, including some by the publisher himself. The governor responded by taking out a front-page advertisement in the *Union Leader,* in which he called on Loeb to "stop picking on my 15 year old daughter, who, after all, is only a young girl with many years of life ahead." "Why not pick on someone your own size?" the governor asked. As a result of this incident, Meg Peterson suffered an emotional breakdown and had to be hospitalized.

The publisher's life-style was not above reproach. In 1946, for instance, Eleanore Loeb left her job at the girls' school in Virginia and joined her husband in Vermont. Whether or not he wanted her there is unclear. In any event, he finally took her to meet his mother in 1947 – five years after they were married. The announcement of the marriage that appeared in newspapers soon thereafter sounded as if the couple had been married that year. In October 1948 Loeb's first child, Katharine Penelope, was born.

By that time, however, Loeb's affections had been won by Gallowhur. He divorced Eleanore to marry Gallowhur, creating a scandal in the process. He was briefly jailed in lieu of a $150,000 bond on charges of alienation of affection brought by Gallowhur's husband. He was arrested while he and Nackey were visiting his mother's home; police officers were trying to serve her with divorce papers at the same time. He distracted the officers while she slipped out a back window. The story of the publisher's arrest appeared several days after the fact in his newspaper, with Loeb helping to write the account.

Years later he used the *Union Leader* to condemn New York governor Nelson Rockefeller for "wife swapping" after he divorced his wife of many years and remarried. Even though the governor's actions paled in comparison to Loeb's, the publisher had an easy rationalization. "I'm not running for president. I make no claim for personal virtue," he told a *Washington Post* reporter, "but I don't want somebody just like me in the White House. I want somebody brighter, somebody better."

The Eleanore-Nackey-William triangle produced substantial hard feelings within the family. Loeb's mother liked Eleanore and Penelope and thought her son had treated them abysmally. Although she had bankrolled many of his business ventures in the past, his personal life had become too much for her. She cut her son out of her will and made Penelope her sole beneficiary. Upon his mother's death Loeb contested the will for several years. He finally took a modest settlement from Penelope and her mother, who, by the time the litigation ended, had lost almost half of the bequest.

Upon his marriage to Gallowhur, the granddaughter of E. W. Scripps, Loeb became even more of an absentee publisher. He set up legal residence in Reno, Nevada, but spent most of his time at his estate in Prides Crossing, Massachusetts, fifty miles from Manchester. Critics said that he chose Nevada as his legal residence to avoid Massachusetts taxes and that he picked Massachusetts for his New England headquarters because he could not safely venture into Vermont for years. Eleanore tried to serve him with legal papers demanding support within that jurisdiction.

He was eventually ordered to make seven-hundred-dollar-a-month payments to support his daughter, but he never did. His attention was fixed on his new family, and he soon adopted Nackey's daughter by her first marriage, Elizabeth. The couple also had a daughter of their own, Edith. Loeb's obituary in the *Union Leader* listed only Nackey, Elizabeth, and Edith as survivors.

His personal life settled down with his marriage to Nackey. They had much in common. Both enjoyed the outdoors and spent hours playing tennis at their Massachusetts estate and riding horses at their Nevada home. They often carried pistols, and Loeb was an officer in the National Rifle Association. Their sporting came to a halt, however, in late 1977, when their jeep skidded on a patch of black ice on an isolated Nevada road and overturned. Both were pinned under the vehicle; Loeb escaped with relatively minor injuries, but Nackey was paralyzed from the waist down.

Loeb was constantly in financial trouble. His Burlington paper was a special drain, and he began to siphon money from the Manchester operation to prop up the failing *Daily News*. When the paper did obtain some degree of financial stability, its publisher refused to give its employees a raise. He used *Daily News* revenues to finance a bid for the *Toronto Star*. The effort to buy the Canadian paper failed – and so did the *Daily News*, which went out of business in May 1961.

Loeb generally took good care of the only cash cow in his stable of newspapers – the *Union Leader*. Although he had troubles with employees at

his other newspapers, he set up a profit-sharing operation with those who worked at the *Union Leader*. However, the profit sharing stopped abruptly when Loeb started a paper in Haverhill, Massachusetts, in 1957.

Union printers had struck the *Haverhill Gazette,* just across the state line from Manchester, shortly before Christmas 1956. Several Haverhill merchants asked Loeb to start a paper in which they could advertise. He launched the *Haverhill Journal* as a weekly shopper and quickly turned it into a daily newspaper. Loeb put out a fairly good newspaper and hired the striking printers to get it on the streets. When the strike against the *Gazette* was settled, the printers went back to their old jobs, and the *Journal* was produced by *Union Leader* printers. Overtime replaced profit sharing.

The strike had sapped the reserves of the *Gazette,* and Loeb saw it as ripe for the picking. He made several offers to buy it in 1958, all of which were rejected, in part because of his interference in the strike. As a result of the offers, several publishers established the Newspapers of New England, Inc., in December 1958 and purchased the *Gazette* to keep it out of Loeb's hands. Loeb filed a $4.5-million antitrust suit against the Newspapers of New England, and that corporation filed a $3-million countersuit.

As the case progressed, Loeb admitted that he had made an agreement with several Haverhill merchants to start the *Journal* and to pay each set fees for their cooperation. The *Columbia Journalism Review* reported that the court case revealed that the merchants were to get a minimum of five thousand dollars apiece for the first ten years and seventy-five hundred dollars apiece for the next ten years "if and when the *Haverhill Journal* or any newspaper controlled by Loeb became the sole daily newspaper in Haverhill."

Both parties were found guilty of discriminatory advertising practices. Only Loeb was found to have violated the antitrust laws. After five years of legal maneuvering, the Union Leader Corporation agreed in April 1965 to pay the *Gazette* $1.25 million in an out-of-court settlement. The *Haverhill Journal* went out of business one month later.

In order to pay the costs encountered by the Haverhill experiment, Loeb struck up a long-term relationship with the Teamsters Union, which tapped its pension fund for a $2.2-million loan to the New Hampshire publisher. This was the second loan to him underwritten by union funds; the first came in 1963. The pension fund took a twenty-year mortgage on the *Union Leader* in return for the sec-

Senator Edmund Muskie and his wife, Jane, *holding a copy of the* Manchester Union Leader *announcing the senator's victory in the 1972 New Hampshire primary (United Press International)*

ond loan. The publisher became an ardent supporter of the union and its president, Jimmy Hoffa.

For the next several years Loeb's editorials often dealt with how wonderful Hoffa was, and how despicable the federal government was in trying to railroad the union leader into jail. "Obviously," read one editorial, "the purpose behind all this is to try to break the spirit of the one labor leader in the United States who will not knuckle under to Mr. [Robert] Kennedy." When Hoffa was sent to prison, Loeb's goal then became to free him. He threatened to withhold his support from Richard Nixon in the 1972 New Hampshire primary unless the union leader was released. Hoffa was freed from federal custody in December 1971.

Having to push Nixon to free Hoffa was only one of a series of events that made Loeb question the president's politics and loyalty to conservatism. Although Nixon became the first president to invite the Loebs to dinner at the White House, he also became the first president to visit the People's Republic of China, which the New Hampshire publisher denounced. "I had high hopes for Nixon," Loeb told a *New York Times* reporter in 1971, "but I've been disappointed, in part because of his foreign policy, but mostly I'm offended by the evidence of

his petty duplicity. . . . It has marked everything he does, trying to play both sides of the street on every issue, and it is repugnant. He has tried to deceive both sides, and that is not good for the nation. I'm just interested in getting someone in the White House who makes some sense. With Nixon we are dealing with someone with no fixed philosophy and who is not terribly bright." Despite that assessment, after Nixon freed Hoffa, Loeb put his reservations aside and supported the incumbent's reelection campaign.

Loeb gained most of his national notoriety as a result of the 1972 New Hampshire presidential primary. Reporters learned a lot about him that year. For decades journalists had gone into New Hampshire for the quadrennial show and had basically reported surface events without searching for a possible manipulative hand behind them. During the 1972 primary they sought and found that hand in Loeb.

Muskie and Loeb had had a running feud for months by the time primary season rolled around. When the Maine senator seemed to devote more time to primaries in other states than to New Hampshire, Loeb charged that Muskie was taking the state for granted. Rather than ignoring the publisher, Muskie challenged Loeb to a debate. Angry rhetoric increased in intensity, and soon Loeb printed the "Canuck" letter, in which an alleged correspondent from Florida charged that Muskie cared little for French-Americans, who comprised New Hampshire's largest minority group. The letter was later discovered to have been part of Nixon's dirty-tricks campaign that led to Watergate. Loeb published many letters to the editor and seldom checked on any writer's identity.

Muskie was not mortally wounded by the letter, but soon thereafter Loeb reprinted a short item from a December 1971 issue of *Newsweek* that was critical of the senator's wife. *Newsweek* had pulled quotes from a *Women's Wear Daily* article in which Jane Muskie, who was on tour in a bus full of women reporters, was quoted as saying, "Let's tell dirty jokes," and "Pass me my purse – I haven't had my morning cigaret yet."

Irate at this treatment of his wife, Muskie went to the *Union Leader* offices, where he mounted the back of a flatbed truck and, in a driving snowstorm, denounced Loeb as a "liar" and a "gutless coward." The senator said, "This man doesn't walk, he crawls. . . . He's talking about my wife. . . . It's fortunate for him he's not on this platform beside me!" The senator tried to continue, and veteran reporters saw tears run down his cheeks.

The reporter for the *Union Leader* told readers of the senator's behavior. While the writer covering the story did not say directly that Muskie had cried, Loeb, in his front-page editorial, had no such compunctions: "Senator Muskie's excited and near-hysterical performance again indicates he's not the man that many of us would want to have his finger on the nuclear button."

Loeb may well have been an unwilling participant in the Nixon campaign's dirty-tricks operation insofar as the "Canuck" letter was concerned, but he had decided that Muskie was not equipped to sit in the Oval Office. His paper knowingly used the story about the senator's wife to hit Muskie in his most vulnerable spot. Muskie barely defeated McGovern in New Hampshire – 36.4 percent to 33.4 percent – but he lost the nomination.

As a result of the attack on Muskie, Loeb became the target of many journalists who sought to expose his unhealthy influence in New Hampshire. His staff fought back. Tom Muller, an assistant city editor for the *Union Leader,* wrote a lengthy, highly complimentary biography of his boss that was published in *Editor & Publisher,* the newspaper industry's leading trade publication. Muller praised Loeb's ac-

tive involvement in the *Union Leader,* attempting to debunk claims that he was an absentee publisher.

The *Editor & Publisher* article did bring out some of the strong points of Loeb's *Union Leader* operation. The paper ran more letters to the editor than almost any other newspaper in the nation–more than sixty-five hundred in 1971. Sometimes whole pages full of these letters appeared in print. The *Union Leader* devoted full pages each week to labor news, veterans' affairs, and medical news. It also employed a full-time farm editor.

Of Loeb's front-page editorials, Muller wrote, "Full credit must go to Loeb for their conception and authorship. Every one of them is dictated, off the cuff, for maximum effect. Loeb feels this is the way to get the conversational style necessary for maximum impact on the average reader. While the editors may punctuate and emphasize the type faces in the final version, every one of those editorials is 100 percent Loeb – and are NEVER ghost written."

Loeb was closely involved in the paper's daily operation – even if from the comfort of his mansion in Prides Crossing. "The staff receives daily direction from Loeb in the form of memos, telephone calls and letters," Muller wrote. "Cryptic comments pencilled in red on various articles, columns, clipping[s] and letters convey Loeb's wishes to the editors. He personally chooses many columns which appear on the paper's editorial page."

Whether Muller's laudatory piece was sufficient to rehabilitate Loeb's reputation is open to question. In 1975 Cash, a former *Union Leader* staff member, published a 472-page unauthorized and highly critical biography, *Who the Hell Is William Loeb?*. Eleven publishers refused to touch the book, and three libel-insurance underwriters refused to issue a policy against possible damages. Cash eventually set up his own publishing house, Amoskeag Press, in order to publish his work and came away with a best-seller – at least in New Hampshire, where about fifty thousand copies were sold within the first few weeks of its release.

Loeb retaliated by saying that Cash had been fired from the *Union Leader* in 1959 because of a drinking problem. Cash admitted that but said that he had dried out in order to take on his former employer: "I thought it was about time somebody stood up to this guy," he said in explaining his motivation. Loeb responded by filing a libel suit, which he later dropped. The unhappy publisher also sued the *Boston Globe* about the same time. Its offense, he explained, was saying that "the *Union Leader* is produced 'by paranoids for paranoids' " and running "a cartoon of me with a cuckoo coming out of the middle of my forehead and [captioned] the 'thoughts of Chairman Loeb.'" This case was thrown out of court.

In 1979 Loeb announced that he would place 75 percent of his newspaper stock in a trust fund for his employees. "After I die," he said, "I want the paper to be run by people who share the same philosophy that I do, that of public service." Some critics contended that the move was made to save his reputation in light of two lawsuits charging that he had mismanaged his employees' pension plan.

Although he denied the charges, he sold 25 percent of the paper's stock in order to pay a settlement. The trust, the critics claimed, was Loeb's way to protect his remaining share of the paper from poachers. A Loeb loyalist outbid the *Boston Globe* and other interested parties for the 25 percent that went on the market; Loeb later repurchased it.

Trust provisions named Nackey as administrator until her death or resignation. At that point it was to be taken over by a board drawn from the newspaper's management. After the death of the next to the last trustee, the survivor was to make sure that the stock was distributed among newspaper employees. The trust, however, allowed Nackey to name directors young enough to keep current employees from receiving benefits. The provisions were broken after Loeb's death, with a settlement finally being reached in 1987. It allowed for distribution of stock to certain longtime employees who might otherwise die before they benefited from Loeb's alleged largess.

Loeb's final presidential campaign — that of 1980 — found him firmly in Ronald Reagan's camp. His front-page editorials had lost none of their punch. As he said in 1979, Reagan "understands the spiritual underpinning of western civilization and especially the principles on which this nation was founded and from which we have wandered so far." At the close of his life Loeb found a candidate whom he could support wholeheartedly.

However, Reagan enthusiasts were not so sure that they wanted the publisher's unqualified support. One backer told a *Washington Post* reporter, "The best situation with Loeb is if he's kicking the hell out of the other guy but not editorializing in your favor, just giving you coverage . . . as much straight coverage as Loeb is capable of."

Straight coverage was beyond Loeb's range of capabilities. Little changed as far as the *Union Leader* was concerned after Loeb died of cancer on 13 September 1981. Nackey took over as president and publisher, and under her guidance the newspaper backed Patrick Buchanan in the 1992 New Hampshire presidential primary. The principles remained, and Loeb's name went down in history for his attempts to sway the nation's political course. William Randolph Hearst, Sr., would have been proud to have been identified with William Loeb.

References:

Kevin Cash, *Who the Hell Is William Loeb?* (Manchester, N.H.: Amoskeag, 1975);

"Cashing in on Loeb," *Newsweek,* 87 (12 January 1976): 53;

"The Front-Page Fulminator: William Loeb: 1905–1981," *Time,* 118 (28 September 1981): 30;

Bill Kovach, "Nixon's Too Left-Wing for William Loeb," *New York Times Magazine,* 12 December 1971, pp. 14, 117–121, 124, 126;

"Loeb Blow," *Time,* 107 (12 January 1976): 34;

Myra MacPherson, "Who William Loeb Is and Why He's Saying All Those Mean Things About . . . ," *Washington Post,* 24 February 1980, pp. H1, H5;

Helen Kirkpatrick Milbank, "New Hampshire's Paper Tiger," *Columbia Journalism Review,* 5 (Spring 1966): 8–14;

Tom Muller, "LOEB . . . His Strong Personality Is Imprinted on his Newspaper," *Editor & Publisher,* 105 (2 September 1972): 12–14;

Jules Witcover, "William Loeb and the New Hampshire Primary: A Question of Ethics," *Columbia Journalism Review,* 11 (May/June 1972): 14–25.

Paul Miller

(28 September 1906 – 21 August 1991)

Cecilia Friend
Utica College of Syracuse University

MAJOR POSITIONS HELD: Assistant general manager (1941–1943), Washington bureau chief (1943–1947), president (1963–1972), chairman of the board (1972–1977), The Associated Press; editor and publisher, *Rochester* (New York) *Times-Union* (1949–1972); publisher, *Rochester* (New York) *Democrat and Chronicle* (1951–1971); president (1957–1970), chief executive officer (1970–1973), chairman of the board (1970–1978), Gannett Company.

BOOK: *China Opens the Door* (Rochester, N.Y.: Gannett, 1972).

Paul Miller, an executive of the Gannett Company for twenty-one years, was the architect of a newspaper-acquisition program that made Gannett not only the largest newspaper chain in the United States, but the most widespread geographically. That geographic breadth provided the company with a broad economic base that insulated its profits from regional downturns. It also gave it a national dimension lacking in the nineteen-paper, mostly upstate New York chain that Miller inherited from founder Frank E. Gannett in 1957.

By the time Miller took the company public in 1967, it had twenty-eight papers in five states. When he left it in 1978, it had seventy-eight papers in thirty states, including Hawaii, and two territories, the Virgin Islands and Guam. It had had forty-four uninterrupted profitable quarters since going public. Miller was dubbed "The Great Acquirer," the driving force in a "newspaper acquisition program without parallel in U.S. publishing," as *Editor & Publisher* described him upon his retirement in September 1978.

In 1977 Miller was named one of the five most influential U.S. newspaper executives by *U.S. News & World Report* for the third year in a row, along with Katharine Graham, Benjamin Bradlee, Arthur Ochs Sulzberger, and Abe Rosenthal. While some hailed the scope of Miller's vision, others scored it. He regularly felt the need to defend Gannett's ac-

quisitions and strategy against criticism, including the charge that large chains that operate monopolies in one-newspaper cities stifle diversity, the foundation of press freedom.

Miller's role in the industry went beyond his leadership at Gannett, however, and he held a profound belief in the power of a free press and in the democratic spirit at a time when the nations of the world were pitted in the ideological battle of the Cold War. At no time did he express those beliefs more strongly than during the fourteen years (1963–1977) that he presided over the Associated Press (AP), in what was to be called the Miller Era.

Miller was elected to the top post at the AP sixteen years after leaving as its Washington bureau chief to become Frank Gannett's right-hand man. He was not only chairman of the AP but its champion, defending it against critics and envisioning its worldwide distribution of news and photos as a path to international peace and goodwill. He went to China in October 1972, five months after President Richard Nixon's historic visit, to conclude negotiations on an exchange-of-news agreement between the AP and Hsinhua, China's news agency. It marked the first time in twenty-two years that an American news organization had established a regular news channel with China.

While he was working to open up borders abroad, he struggled with the boundaries of dissent at home. He publicly criticized the 1970s radicals and activists, whom he felt were dragging down the America he loved. Miller knew all eight presidents who served during his newspaper career, from Franklin D. Roosevelt to Jimmy Carter, and counted many leading figures in government, politics, and business among his friends. He said that it was part of a newsman's job to know people in public service, no matter what their politics.

Miller was a newsman first and foremost, even during the time he was the top executive at Gannett and the AP. He started as a reporter and never completely gave up that role, whether filing dispatches

Walker Stone, Paul Miller, President John F. Kennedy, Lee Hills, and Vermont Royster at the White House, 2 August 1962. The four journalists briefed Kennedy after their twenty-three-day tour of the Soviet Union (United Press International).

from around the world – including Berlin during the 1949 airlift and the Soviet Union, where he interviewed Nikita Khrushchev in 1962 – or writing local columns for the Rochester, New York, paper that he edited. "I hope never to lose contact with the people who put out newspapers," Miller told an interviewer as his retirement approached in 1978. "My idea of a place for an office, if I could have it without bothering anybody, would be right between the newsroom and the mechanical department. I just plain like newspaper people, that's all."

Miller was born on 28 September 1906, in Diamond, Missouri, the first of the Reverend James and Clara Ranne Miller's six children. He spent most of his early life in Oklahoma, which he considered home. Miller later called his father a "husky pioneer Oklahoma Protestant minister." The elder Miller encouraged an interest in current affairs, while his wife often read to the family.

At age fifteen Miller started the *Boy Sportsman*, a four-page sheet financed with twenty-five dollars in savings. It only lasted one issue, but it started him on the professional road he would follow for the rest of his life. A year later Miller won a national high-school editorial writing contest. "Inflated by that triumph," he said, "I hung around the

Pawhuska [Oklahoma] *Daily Journal* until they gave me a job." He became a reporter and served briefly as city editor before he went off to college at age eighteen.

At Oklahoma A&M (now Oklahoma State University) he wrote for news bureaus and served as a correspondent for major state newspapers. He quit school at the end of his sophomore year after he ran unsuccessfully for editor of the *Daily O'Collegian*. Raymond Fields hired him as an editor at the *Okemah* (Oklahoma) *Daily Leader* for thirty dollars a week. "I wasn't worth it, of course, and I shall be indebted always to Ray Fields for his reckless confidence," Miller recalled. He described Okemah, populated primarily by ranchers and oilmen, as "a tough town."

"I was my own reporter; my own city editor too," Miller said. "So there was no excuse any time anything got in the paper that somebody didn't like. I couldn't blame it on somebody else. Every reader knew that if it was in there, I wrote it, and edited it, and put a head on it." Readers there were not satisfied to write a complaining letter to the editor. "The phone would ring," Miller said, "and the call always went about like this: 'Is this the editor? Well, get set. I'm coming down to beat the hell out of you.' "

However, Miller took the experience in stride. He put his own twist on Will Rogers's epigram, stating that he never lived in a place or held a job that he did not like. Miller took three other newspaper positions, all in Oklahoma – at Stillwater, Guthrie, and Norman – before returning to college. He was graduated in 1932.

That year he joined the AP, a cooperative news-gathering agency operated for its member newspapers, as night rewrite man in Columbus, Ohio. There he met Louise Johnson, women's editor for the *Columbus Journal*. They were married seven months later. They would have a daughter, Jean, and three sons, Ranne, Paul, Jr., and Kenper, named after Kent Cooper, an AP general manager whom Miller admired and loved. "We had almost a father and son relationship in the later years," Miller said. "Kenper" was Cooper's cable address. Ironically, Kenper was the only one of Miller's sons who would not follow his father into the news business.

Miller's AP work took him to bureaus in New York City; Kansas City, Missouri; and Salt Lake City, where he became bureau chief in 1936. He took charge of AP operations in Pennsylvania the following year. He returned to New York in 1941 as assistant general manager, staying there two years. He became Washington bureau chief in 1943, during World War II.

In Washington, Miller tried to reinvigorate the bureau, calling for sharper interpretation and background for the news and shorter, crisper leads. "Our leads are running too long," read a Miller memo of the time. "Let's keep them down to 30 words wherever possible and an orchid to anybody who can do it in 20." Deadpan bureau writers produced a flock of such war-era samples as "Matches are scarcer" and "Road oil is back." A deskman ribbed Miller with "AP leads are shorter."

For all the kidding, Miller was respected and liked by his Washington staff. From copyboy up, Miller was "Paul." Once when the head of the AP staff at the House of Representatives was short-handed, Miller strolled into the press gallery. "Paul, watch the gallery for me while I get out this story," the House reporter said, and Miller did, according to a *Newsweek* retrospective of his AP years.

He pushed up salaries, backed his workers in jams with the home office, and even entertained them at his home in the stylish Spring Valley section of Washington. Outside the ranks Miller was "known and respected by leaders of both political parties and often called upon to consult with and give advice to presidents," said former attorney general and secretary of state William P. Rogers. Miller was also remembered for approving a thirty-dollar poker loss on a staff member's expense account. After all, Miller argued with his superiors in New York, it was for a good cause – the man who won the thirty dollars was President Harry Truman.

Miller had worked his way through the ranks at the AP in a little more than ten years. In 1947 he was on the short list of those who might succeed his mentor, Cooper, as general manager. But Miller's work had caught the attention of Frank Gannett, who in 1947 asked him to move to Rochester, New York, to become his assistant at the Gannett Company. He would groom Miller to succeed him as chief executive officer.

In 1963 Miller returned to the AP fold as president, the only former AP employee to take its helm. He was elected to this part-time position, the title of which was changed to chairman in 1972. "Paul Miller was not just AP's chairman. He was its champion, always challenging us to do better but never failing to hail a job well done," said Louis D. Boccardi, AP president and general manager in 1991. "He had many interests and many successes but we always knew he loved the Associated Press."

Miller held to an idealistic view of the cooperative that he served for so many years in so many capacities. He saw it as an underpinning to the evolution of America's press freedoms and a bulwark of national identity. "The Associated Press was established on the principle that truth and fairness must be the unqualified aim of those engaged in reporting the news," Miller said in his Sigma Delta Chi Foundation Lecture at the University of Michigan on 1 December 1965. He continued:

> Its founders committed their careers and their fortunes to a successful rebellion; a rebellion against control of the news by a few individuals able to use it for selfish interest or private prejudice.... For the first time, with the founding of The AP [in 1893], news of national and international importance could be distributed over a nationwide network of telegraph wires; the same news could be read on the same day by people in every state. It was a powerful instrument of national unity, a social institution of a non-government character, awaking a new spirit of national consciousness throughout America.... The greatest strength of The AP lies in the cooperative form of its organization and the diversity of views represented in it. Each member is alert to any departure from objectivity. Altogether, they constitute an ever-watchful host.... Truth is our business. There can be no higher calling.

Miller joined Frank Gannett in Rochester as executive assistant to the president in 1947. The seventy-year-old Gannett Company founder left no doubt that he had hired Miller as his right-hand man: "Mr. Miller will have special work of great importance and will relieve me of many of my burdens." In 1949 Miller became editor and publisher of the afternoon *Rochester Times-Union;* in 1951 he became publisher of the morning *Rochester Democrat and Chronicle.* These were Gannett's flagship papers.

He was named Gannett's executive vice-president in 1951, then operating head in 1955 after Gannett fractured his spine in a fall. He succeeded Gannett in 1957 as president of the nineteen-paper chain and head of the Frank E. Gannett Newspaper Foundation (now independent of the company and renamed the Freedom Forum). The Gannett image at the time was that of a "low-budget exercise in small-city publishing, distinguished mainly by a ban on cigarette and liquor ads that reflected Frank Gannett's personal prohibitions," as *Time* magazine described it.

Like his predecessor, Miller had his business managers keep tight control over the finances of Gannett's member papers and made certain they operated at a profit. But he immediately lifted the ban on liquor ads, and he began subtly altering Gannett's policy of local autonomy, making changes that strengthened the ties between the company and its papers. Miller also began a vigorous expansion program. He followed Frank Gannett's pattern of buying papers in small, growing communities, usually without competing papers, and avoiding big cities, where purchase costs were high and prospects for circulation growth limited. However, he envisioned a company far broader geographically than the mostly upstate New York chain that Gannett had assembled.

"I set out 20 years ago to acquire newspapers in small- to medium-sized cities primarily, and with the widest possible geographic range," Miller said in 1977. "Geographical range gives you that much more insurance against anything happening in a particular part of the country. It provides a broad economic base it wouldn't necessarily have if it remained regionally based. [Growth was] not only necessary but fun. Looking back, I guess one of the most interesting of all the acquisitions was our move into the Pacific. It gave us a new dimension, really. . . . It has broadened our thinking. That was thrilling and still is thrilling."

Miller's extensive AP contacts were to be important, even crucial, to some of the early acquisitions he made for Gannett. As president of the AP he came into friendly contact with practically every newspaper owner in the country, giving him easy access when it came time for a deal. "Paul is on a first-name basis with more publishers and editors around the U.S. than anyone else," Miller's then protégé Allen H. Neuharth told the *Wall Street Journal.* Many were Miller's golf partners, and consequently Miller was often the first to know when a newspaper was for sale.

Most owners liked and trusted him. He had a disarming Oklahoma country-boy personality, polished a bit by his stints in New York and Washington. When it came time for a family to sell, "Miller was often the first man many of them thought to entrust their life's work to," said David Shaw, media writer for the *Los Angeles Times.* Miller was personally able to woo several owners and publishers to join Gannett after they had previously refused to sell their properties. Some he would make Gannett officers to sweeten the deal. "You just don't buy a newspaper by going out and writing a check," Miller said.

While some owners sought out Miller, he calculated other moves, such as venturing into the Pacific. And sometimes he acted on impulse. In 1969 he received a routine letter from Louis Weil, president of the Federated Publications newspaper chain. After glancing at the names of the seven papers on the letterhead, Miller promptly phoned Weil. "Look," he said, "I see that you're not in any states where we are, and we're not in any states where you are. Why not talk about a possible merger?" Four months later Gannett agreed to buy out Federated.

"Miller never saw a newspaper he didn't like," Neuharth said in a further twist on the Will Rogers quip. "He wanted to buy everything available [and] really didn't know or care about price. He just wanted to buy." *Time* made a similar assessment: "[Miller] collected dailies for Gannett with the enthusiasm of a kid amassing marbles." Neuharth said that Gannett's financial officials believed that most available newspapers were overpriced, and they often waffled on the deals Miller tried to make.

The increased revenues from the eight papers Miller added during his first ten years as chief executive helped the company's bottom line, but they were not enough to sustain the acquisition program he envisioned. For that, Miller needed outside capital. In 1967 he turned to Wall Street with a plan to take Gannett public. At the time only two newspaper companies were publicly held: Dow Jones, owner of the *Wall Street Journal,* and Times Mirror, owner of the *Los Angeles Times.* The newspaper industry did not look very good from the windows of Wall Street brokers in New York, where four dailies had died during the decade. The city papers that were left, and other big-city papers in the country, were plagued by labor problems and readers fleeing to the suburbs.

Neuharth, then Gannett executive vice-president and Miller's chosen successor, takes most of the credit for "a major propaganda campaign – based on hard facts – that changed Wall Street's perception of the newspaper industry." Gannett set out to convince the money men that small and medium-sized newspapers across the country, with their emphases on local news and advertising, were thriving. Gannett papers in every city but one had no local competition. "Gannett was a dependable profit machine in good times or bad," was Neuharth's message. It was well received.

"Gannett's basic media business is awesome. It is virtually an unregulated monopoly," said John Kornreich of Neuberger and Berman. "Gannett's management lives, breathes, and sleeps profits and would trade profits over Pulitzer Prizes any day," wrote the *Wall Street Transcript*. Miller got his financing and embarked on an unprecedented buying spree. Before going public in 1967, Gannett had 27 papers in five states. Papers were rapidly acquired from coast to coast and beyond, to Hawaii, the Virgin Islands, and Guam, with 21 added between 1968 and 1971. In 1971, its biggest year thus far for acquisitions, Gannett took over the 7-paper Federated Publications and 10 other daily papers. The company bought another 25 papers between 1971 and 1978, when Miller retired, including the 15-paper Speidel Newspaper Group. At the end of 1978 Gannett had 73 dailies in thirty states. Miller had presided over the purchase of two smaller chains and the founding of a newspaper in Florida – the first of 2 papers the company would start from scratch (and each the brainchild of Neuharth). Miller predicted in 1977 that Gannett would have a hundred newspapers "in the foreseeable future." While Gannett maintained its numerical and geographic superiority, its circulation lagged behind those of other newspaper chains because of its penchant for buying in smaller cities and suburbs. Still, circulation rose, from 776,000 in 1957 when Miller took over, to more than 2.3 million in 1973 and 3.56 million in 1980. Revenues soared. The year Gannett went public it had a net income of about $15 million. Profits increased about 20 percent a year, rising to $112 million in 1978, the year Miller retired. The company did not disclose financial information during the sixty-one years before it went public. It still does not publish a breakdown of the profitability of individual papers.

Gannett was able to boost earnings on the family-owned papers it bought. Their earnings were often low, because the families lacked the desire or know-how to streamline operations. Corporate officials could analyze the papers' problems and make suggestions to improve profits. Gannett also had the resources to modernize outmoded printing plants, with mechanization bringing down the number of workers needed. The company could also achieve economy of size, buying newsprint, ink, and other supplies in bulk at a discount.

In 1957 Miller began a twenty-one-week corporate-training program for beginning reporters and retail-advertising salesmen. It was the first of many moves that strengthened the ties between the company and its member papers. Miller was quick to reassure the Gannett editors assembled for the announcement that the program for new employees at company headquarters was not the beginning of centralized control, but it was bound to influence the new recruits. They were not just employees of the Elmira, Utica, or Rochester papers; they were employees of Gannett, getting the same training in what constitutes news and how to collect and present it. Other corporate ties in personnel and administrative policies would develop as Miller added to the newspaper group, as Gannett preferred to call it in order to emphasize the loose association between the corporation and its papers.

Frank Gannett had preached and practiced a strong brand of local autonomy. He was fond of saying that Gannett papers were "local as the town pump," and that local editors were the best arbiters of local policy. He kept a watchful eye on the business offices but otherwise left decisions to local editors. He believed autonomy was both good business – owners whom Gannett bought out and their readers liked the idea – and popular with local editors.

When Miller took over, he reiterated Frank Gannett's philosophy. "The principle of local autonomy is nursed along more carefully and stressed more emphatically in The Gannett Group than in any other newspaper organization I know," Miller said upon becoming president in 1957. "That's why it's called a group, not a chain. A chain is characterized by a dictated policy. There is usually a uniformity of practice, appearance and style. The opposite is true in The Gannett Group."

But as Miller enlarged the group, the appointment and movement of top editors was increasingly centralized. Along with Miller's novice-training program, this centralization encouraged greater company loyalty and a new accountability to the corporation, which began to play a greater role in the internal affairs of each member paper. Miller transferred and elevated those editors whose performances matched his expectation. Some editors were brought to Rochester and promoted to corporate officers. Some Rochester editors, schooled by Miller, were sent to oversee operations elsewhere. Neuharth, who joined Miller at the Rochester headquarters, was sent to Florida as president of a new branch of six papers there.

Miller acknowledged that the expanded central office checked the operations of each newspaper, often sent in personnel to help solve problems, and sometimes replaced editors. "Autonomy must not lead to autocracy" by local editors, he wrote in the *Gannetteer*. Furthermore, Miller established an editorial role – if only as arbiter – for the corporation. In welcoming a new paper to the group, Miller wrote: "The central office will expect to be advised or even consulted in case of a sharply controversial issue in which [a newspaper] becomes involved. But the final decision will rest with that newspaper as [it] works toward a continually improving product."

At the same time, Miller continued to profess local autonomy. To him that meant, at the least, that Gannett would never disseminate the kind of chainwide editorials for which the Hearst papers were known, or dictate editorial stands. "We believe and preach and, I hope, practice the old-fashioned doctrine that each individual newspaper should stand for something," Miller wrote. "A newspaper should stand for everything that is best for its community and vigorously oppose the bad, as the local management sees it."

Yet some critics charged that chains, and Gannett in particular, cared more about profits than improving the quality of their papers. "Some [Gannett] critics note that such detrimental factors as a shortage of local news, sloppy editing, careless typography, and an overabundance of prepackaged special sections crammed with wire-service features and outdated articles would send many readers to a rival paper – if one were to be had," a *Business Week* article stated.

Miller had an editorial philosophy for Gannett papers, a reformulation of Frank Gannett's policy of "clean and decent" papers. Miller's creed was: "Substance ahead of form; balance ahead of speed; completeness ahead of color; accuracy ahead of everything." This blueprint would be gradually abandoned by his successor, Neuharth, beginning with the launching of *Florida Today* during Miller's term and culminating in *USA TODAY,* which some critics have called the classic example of form ahead of

substance, speed ahead of balance, and color ahead of completeness.

In 1962 Miller exhorted his editors to "get closer to your readers," praising the *Danville* (Illinois) *Commercial-News* for conducting a readership survey – a practice that would spread across the industry, especially Gannett, in the late 1970s and 1980s. Gannett papers were automatically made subscribers to the Gannett News Service, begun in 1943 as the Gannett National News Service. During the 1960s it had two bureaus, in Albany, New York, and Washington, D.C., but it was not used to exchange stories among member papers until 1969. By 1974 the GNS was a round-the-clock wire servicing all Gannett papers and other subscribers.

In 1963 Miller conceived a series on the positive aspects of integration that won Gannett the 1964 Pulitzer Prize Special Citation for Public Service, the first awarded to a newspaper chain. That Miller launched this series while running Gannett and overseeing the AP is not so surprising. While he spent most of his career as an executive, Miller always thought of himself as a reporter and seized opportunities to write stories. In 1971, while on vacation in the Far East, he interviewed Eisaku Sato, then prime minister of Japan, and filed a story. It was the practice he followed throughout his newspaper life, whether sending dispatches to readers from around the world or writing a weekly column in the *Rochester Times-Union.*

He reported from Berlin during the 1949 airlift, flying with his wife on a plane loaded with coal. He reported from Guatemala after its 1954 revolution, from London and Cairo during the 1956 Suez crisis, and from Paris during a conference attended by President Dwight Eisenhower in 1956. In 1958 he was writing from Israel.

In 1962 he visited the Soviet Union with twelve other newspaper editors on a twenty-three-day tour climaxed by an interview with Khrushchev. Miller and three of the other journalists gave President John F. Kennedy a firsthand report upon their return. Miller and Walker Stone, editor in chief of the Scripps-Howard papers, also spent two days roaming the streets of Berlin, asking residents whether they would sleep easier if Allied troops were withdrawn. Most said no. They presented Khrushchev with an open letter on their findings.

One of Miller's most eventful trips abroad was in 1972, for a historic agreement between the AP and the Chinese news agency, Hsinhua. He and four other AP executives met with Chinese leaders to conclude negotiations on an exchange of news and photos. It marked the first time in twenty-two years that an American news organization had established a regular news link with China. Miller sent home dispatches of his observations during his three-week stay in Peking and other cities, and wrote more stories and columns in the days following his return. He compiled them into a booklet, *China Opens the Door,* published by Gannett in October 1972.

Miller's political philosophy was generally conservative. He had an abiding faith in the people, at home and abroad: "Nothing was ever truer than [that] the people, given time and necessary information, will decide between right and wrong, between extreme and extreme. And decide right." But he expressed doubts about the rebellion going on at home in the early 1970s.

In his regular Saturday column on the *Rochester Times-Union* editorial page, Miller did not hesitate to assail the radicals, activists, and demonstrators whom he felt were dragging down the America he knew and loved, who were breaking down the traditions of American life as he saw them. In the aftermath of the 1971 Attica Prison riot, the Rochester papers published stories on the origins and handling of the outbreak, full of case histories, sociology, color, funeral orations, penology theories, and accusations. They disclosed that thirty-nine of the forty-three people killed in the riot did not have slashed throats, as reported by prison authorities, but instead were killed by bullets fired by prison guards and police. The *Times-Union* won a Pulitzer Prize in 1972 for the stories.

While these stories were running, Miller was not completely satisfied. He wrote a memo stating that the coverage of the riot itself was good. But he believed that some of the later stories were overplayed, under headlines that were "cockeyed and editorialized." The coverage of a prisoner's funeral was "excessive and unwarranted," he wrote.

Miller did not relinquish control of Gannett easily. He gave up his titles one at a time to his handpicked successor. Neuharth was named president in 1970 and chief executive officer in 1973. However, Miller remained chairman of the board until the end of 1978, after thirty-one years with Gannett. He continued as chairman of the Gannett Foundation until 1980. He retired as AP chairman in 1977.

A year after he stepped down as chairman of Gannett, Miller suffered a stroke. He never regained his speech and had difficulty moving around. He died of cardiac arrest on 21 August 1991 after being hospitalized for pneumonia in West Palm Beach, Florida. He had divided his retirement time between homes in Florida and Pittsford, New York, a Rochester suburb.

Miller was involved with many organizations, in and outside of the media. He served for nine years on the Pulitzer Prize Advisory Board and for five years chaired the advisory board of the American Press Institute of Columbia University. He was national director of the Boys Club of America and honorary president of Sigma Delta Chi (The Society of Professional Journalists). He also served as president of the New York State Publishers Association.

He received many awards from universities for service to his profession, including the William Allen White Award for Journalistic Merit from the University of Kansas, the Syracuse University School of Journalism Distinguished Service Medal, and the University of Missouri medal for distinguished service to journalism. A Paul Miller Scholarship Fund has been established at Oklahoma State University. The Paul Miller Washington Reporting Fellowships for journalists were set up by the Gannett Foundation in 1986.

References:

"Gannett's Financial Leverage in Newspapers: The Field Leader Shows No Signs of Breaking Its Heady Acquisition Program," *Business Week,* no. 2230 (27 May 1972): 62–65, 68;

N. R. Kleinfield, "The Great Press Chain," *New York Times Magazine,* 8 April 1979, pp. 41–44, 48–52, 59–63;

A. Kent MacDougall, "Paper Profits: News: Newspaper Chains Buy More Dailies, Prosper in Monopoly Situations," *Wall Street Journal,* 15 December 1965, pp. 1, 8;

"Miller Moves On," *Newsweek,* 30 (21 July 1947): 54–56;

Allen H. Neuharth, *Confessions of an S.O.B.* (New York: Doubleday, 1989);

"Paul Miller Will Retire from Gannett on Dec. 31," *Editor & Publisher,* 111 (16 September 1978): 13;

Saul Pett, "What Is Paul Miller Really Like?," *Editor & Publisher,* 110 (6 August 1977): 10-11, 26;

"The Rochester Acquirer," *Time,* 99 (22 May 1972): 39–40;

"Training Program for Gannett Staffs," *Editor & Publisher,* 90 (5 October 1957): 13.

Papers:
Miller's papers are at Oklahoma State University.

Rupert Murdoch

(11 March 1931 –)

Marie Myers Hardin
Georgia State University

U.S. NEWSPAPERS OWNED: *San Antonio Express-News* (1973–); *Star* (1973–1989); *Village Voice* (1977–1985); *New York Post* (1977–1988); *Boston Herald* (1982–); *Chicago Sun-Times* (1983–1986).

Rupert Murdoch may be the most famous media baron alive today, and he may be the only one who has had an entire conference devoted to his study, in Sydney, Australia, in 1989. One observation that best summarized the mood at the conference, according to journalist Ben H. Bagdikian, was that Murdoch is "the Magellan of the Information Age, splashing ashore on one continent after another."

Described by journalist Wolfgang J. Koschnick as a "kind of ogre who debases and sensationalizes the press" through his print and broadcast holdings on three continents, Murdoch sparks controversy. His "Murdochian journalism" – a mixture of sensationalism, political bias, and half-truths in a high-gloss, hard-sell package – has faced constant criticism despite its ability to generate high circulation. However, Murdoch – less an enterprising journalist than a shrewd business magnate – has proven himself a fierce competitor and successful gambler in the U.S. media arena.

Murdoch was born on 11 March 1931 in Melbourne, Australia. His paternal grandfather, a prominent Presbyterian minister, had immigrated to Australia from Scotland. Rupert's father, Sir Keith Murdoch, was a famous World War I correspondent and publisher. Sir Keith met Murdoch's mother, Elisabeth Greene, at a party in Melbourne in 1927, and they were married the following year.

Murdoch spent his childhood days at Cruden Farm, the family estate south of Melbourne. At age nine he was enrolled in Australia's prestigious Geelong boarding school, where he spent the next nine years. His interest in politics began at Geelong, where he earned a reputation as a left-wing ideologue. He was graduated from Geelong in 1949 and matriculated at Worcester College, Oxford University, England, in 1950. He studied politics, economics, and history and was graduated in 1953.

Murdoch's entry into the newspaper business began through his father. The elder Murdoch was made managing editor of the Melbourne *Herald* in 1928, and he set out to acquire more influence and papers for the *Herald*. By the end of the 1930s he had gained both; he pioneered the use of radio and radio photography and launched the first domestic wire service in Australia, the Australian Associated Press. He purchased two small newspapers in the provincial cities of Brisbane and Adelaide, but he was unable to revitalize the sagging circulations of either because of his responsibilities with the *Herald*.

Sir Keith introduced his son to the newspaper business by obtaining a summer job for him at the Birmingham (England) *Gazette*. After graduation from Oxford, Murdoch also carried out a short apprenticeship at the London *Daily Express* in 1953 before returning to Australia to take over newspaper responsibilities in the wake of his father's death.

Murdoch, then twenty-two, took over as publisher of the Adelaide *News* and *Sunday Mail,* two of the few assets left after taxes had been paid on Sir Keith's estate. Murdoch, called "The Boy Publisher" in Adelaide, threw himself into production of the daily *News* and weekly *Sunday Mail* with an intensity "that belied most people's previous perception of him as a rich man's indolent son," according to biographer Thomas Kiernan. Murdoch saw no reason to keep his strident socialist views out of his papers; the *News* and *Sunday Mail* were staunch supporters of Australian leftist politics.

After learning the basics of newspapering in Adelaide, Murdoch began building his empire in 1956, acquiring the Perth *Sunday Times* for four hundred thousand dollars. He replaced much of the Perth staff with handpicked journalists from the Adelaide *News* and injected the paper with blaring headlines and a sensationalized tone. This would become a standard Murdoch formula to boost the sagging circulations of the papers he acquired.

Rupert Murdoch (United Press International)

Described by Kiernan as "the exaggerated story filled with invented quotes; the rewriting of . . . wire copy into lavishly sensationalized yarns; the eye-shattering, usually ungrammatical, irrelevant, and gratuitously blood-curdling headline," Murdochian journalism raised the circulation in Perth to a profitable level. In 1960 he bought the Sydney *Mirror* for $4 million. Expected to fail with the *Mirror,* a tired tabloid weakened by circulation wars, Murdoch turned it into Sydney's best-selling afternoon paper. He also acquired the Melbourne *Truth* and the Brisbane *Truth* in 1960, giving him a publication in every Australian state capital.

Publicly Murdoch professed higher journalistic ideals than his papers practiced. "Unless we can return to the principles of public service, we will lose our claim to be the Fourth Estate," he said in 1960. "What right have we to speak in the public interest when, too often, we are motivated by personal gain?"

During the late 1950s Murdoch became interested in the United States, although he continued expansion in Australia and began making media acquisitions in England several years before investing in America. He traveled to the United States in 1958 to learn more about the television industry, meeting ABC television chairman Leonard Goldenson.

On another trip, in 1962, he gained a personal audience with President John F. Kennedy in the White House. Bruce Rothwell, one of Murdoch's longtime editors in Australia, said Murdoch changed his management style after his visits to the United States. "He came back . . . more organized with plans, a bit more commanding," said Rothwell. "I'd say he'd made up his mind to copy the style of lots of the American chief execs he'd met."

In 1964 Murdoch began the *Australian,* described by some as "the other side of Rupert Murdoch." The paper was produced in Canberra, 150 miles southeast of Sydney, then flown to various Murdoch-owned plants across the country for printing and distribution. Except for its obvious political overtones, this national paper seemed to espouse higher standards of journalism than Murdoch practiced at his other publications, but it was a financial liability. Murdoch, however, kept the paper going as a money-losing talisman of what he called his "essential dedication to quality."

One of the reporters sent to Canberra for assignment on the *Australian* was Anna Marie Torv, born in Scotland in 1944. Her family immigrated to Australia in 1954, and after graduation from high school she obtained a job as a cub reporter at the Sydney *Mirror* in 1962. She met Murdoch when she was asked to interview him for an article, and the two soon began dating. (He had just gone through a bitter divorce from his first wife, Patricia Booker Murdoch, whom he had married in 1956.) Murdoch and Torv were married in 1967.

By 1968 Murdoch's holdings in Australian newspapers, magazines, and other media were worth an estimated $50 million. Murdoch, seeking new ground on which to expand, went to England. In a heated bidding war with media magnate Robert Maxwell, he obtained the weekly *News of the World* in 1969 after befriending its chairman, Sir William Carr. Just months after the acquisition, however, he forced Carr out in what became a standard Murdoch tactic.

Murdoch also bought the daily *Sun,* an ailing tabloid, to keep *News of the World* presses busy during the week. The circulation of the *Sun* soared from eight hundred thousand to two million, thanks in part to Murdoch's move in 1970 to post barebreasted pinups each day on page 3. Other circulation boosters at the *Sun* and *News of the World* were daily lottery games, serialized excerpts from romance novels, and scandalous stories.

In 1969 the *News of the World* printed the sensationalized "diary" of a celebrated call girl, which incriminated a British defense minister. Although the "Keeler memoirs" did boost circulation, they put Murdoch in a swirl of controversy and bad publicity. The *Sun* gained notoriety during the 1982 Falklands War between Britain and Argentina, when it trumpeted "GOTCHA!" across its front page after a British submarine sank an Argentine cruiser, killing 368.

During the late 1960s and early 1970s Murdoch's liberal political views took a turn toward the right. He had outgrown the leftist radicalism of his youth. According to Kiernan, much of Murdoch's move to the right is attributable to his disillusionment with the labor movement in Britain, and the murder of a close friend, which Murdoch blamed on Britain's liberal immigration policies. He moved "once and for all into the right-wing camp," according to Kiernan, after he observed what he believed to be abuses by liberal media in the United States during the 1974 Watergate affair.

Murdoch purchased the *Times* and *Sunday Times* of London in 1981 to complete his grip on the English press. He also gained a powerful hold on politics in the United Kingdom; critics charge that he unabashedly used his papers to help Margaret Thatcher become prime minister in 1979. He would be accused of favoring President Ronald Reagan and other conservative American politicians in his publications. However, Murdoch seems to relish such charges; he has boasted of his ability to influence readers in everything from mayoral races to national elections.

By 1973 the "Keeler memoirs" affair and Murdoch's scandalmongering had prompted harsh feelings from the British establishment. "Murdoch of the Mammaries" (in reference to his *Sun* pinups) and "The Dirty Digger" were two names pinned on him by the British press. Murdoch began his media acquisitions in America that year, relying on contacts he had established on earlier visits.

His first project was to launch a weekly tabloid, the *National Star* (changed one year later to the *Star*), to compete with the highly successful *National Enquirer,* although Murdoch claimed his effort would compete with newsmagazines such as *Time* and *Newsweek*. In interviews Murdoch presented the *Star* as a breath of fresh air in what he considered a dull print industry in the United States. He criticized the American press for columns that "no one really cares about," "achingly dull" layouts, and poorly done features and sports.

Murdoch imported several top editors from the *Sun* and hired some American journalists for the *Star*. His strategy was to "outsleaze" the *Enquirer,* with more sensational headlines, more bizarre articles, and racier photos. The formula worked: although initially precarious, the *Star* became the financial linchpin for News America, Murdoch's American holding company, which was formed in 1974.

He also concentrated on obtaining a metropolitan daily in order to air his conservative political views. Murdoch considered purchasing the *Washington Star* but found the asking price of $35 million too steep. Instead, he settled for a pair of papers in San Antonio, Texas, a city with a population of less than one million. Murdoch obtained the *San Antonio Express,* a successful morning paper, and its sister publication, the *News,* a flagging afternoon paper, from the Harte-Hanks newspaper chain for $19 million.

Murdoch left the *Express* (with a circulation of eighty thousand and a reasonable profit) by and large alone, yet he imported a group of Australian journalists to stamp the *News* with his tried-and-true formula of sex, crimes, and sensationalism. Circulation increased from sixty thousand to more than

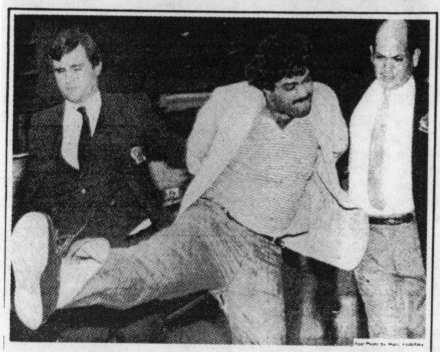

Gunman forces woman to decapitate tavern owner
PAGE TWO

SENATE OKAYS PREZ'S PICK FOR ARMS CONTROL
PAGE FIVE

Koch plans to hire 1,000 more cops
PAGE THREE

TAXING DAY FOR 1 MILLION IN N.Y.

Taken kickin' and screamin'

An angry Juan Emilio Robles tries to kick a photographer yesterday as detectives took him in to be booked for the murder last year of Chase Manhattan exec Kathleen Williams. Robles, a hulking 20-year-old ex-con, is accused of stabbing the 30-year-old victim during a bungled robbery attempt on a stairway in the Waldorf-Astoria Hotel in midtown. Story on Page 14.

Front page of the New York Post, *15 April 1983. The* Post *became known for its sensational headlines during Murdoch's ownership.*

seventy-five thousand in two years. However, Murdoch quickly learned that in the United States higher circulation does not always bring higher revenues. Advertisers stayed away from the *News* because its new readers were at the low end of the city's economic spectrum.

In 1977 Murdoch purchased the *New York Post,* a struggling daily under publisher Dorothy Schiff. Founded in 1801 by Alexander Hamilton, the *Post* is the oldest continuously published daily in the United States. Schiff had controlled it since 1939. The new publisher wasted no time in importing editors schooled in Murdochian journalism, declaring: "Our entire editorial thrust at the *Post* will be to provide New Yorkers with brighter, shorter, more clearly understood stories and to marry the words with better and sharper pictures, better quality printing, and more appealing design." He redesigned the layout and out-sensationalized the main competitor, the *Daily News,* with hysteria-laden scandal and crime stories.

Murdoch's position at the *Post* also gave him the political clout he had been seeking in the United States. In 1977 he used the paper as a mouthpiece for mayoral candidate Edward Koch; after Koch won, Murdoch boasted of having orchestrated his election. The paper supported Reagan over Jimmy Carter in the 1980 presidential race, and Murdoch received personal thanks from Reagan after his inauguration. Another payoff for his role in Reagan's campaign, according to Bagdikian, was a ruling by Reagan's Federal Communications Commission that allowed Murdoch to purchase television stations in a city where he also owned a daily paper.

Murdoch purchased Metromedia's New York and Chicago television stations in 1985, while he still owned the *Chicago Sun-Times* and the *Post.* A few weeks after he acquired the *Post,* Murdoch emerged the victor in a battle with publisher Clay Felker, a former close friend, for control of *New York,* a prestigious weekly magazine covering the arts, popular psychology, and politics; *New West,* a California version of *New York*; and the *Village Voice,* a popular counterculture weekly in New York City.

Murdoch continued his American buying spree. In 1982 he purchased the *Boston Herald.* Although his newspaper formula increased the paper's circulation, advertising did not climb significantly. Neither did the reputation that Murdoch had gained among journalists. He was excoriated for his business and journalism practices.

When he took over the *Chicago Sun-Times* in 1983, more than sixty staff members, including columnist Mike Royko, left. However, the exodus did not phase Murdoch; he sold the *Sun-Times* in 1986 for $145 million, netting a $50-million profit. He made more than $30 million when he sold the *Village Voice* in 1985 for $55 million.

After 1983 Murdoch began to turn his attention toward broadcasting, which he saw as the money-maker of the future. He assumed considerable debt ($8.3 billion by 1991) in his purchase of the 20th Century-Fox motion picture studio and launching of the Fox television network, among other ventures. In turn he sold off the *Village Voice,* the *Sun-Times,* the *Post* (1988), and the *Star* (1989).

Murdoch's News Corporation turned a profit through the mid 1980s. However, his fortunes turned during the latter part of the decade. In a 1991 *Forbes* article detailing the financial difficulties he faced after a late 1980s buying spree that included *TV Guide* and Harper and Row publishers, Murdoch said he had to "swallow a big dose of realism" while he struggled to raise capital to cover his debts.

Murdoch, who owned more than 40 percent of News Corporation common stock in 1991, preferred to finance his acquisitions through borrowing rather than diluting his holding in the company. In order to pay on his debt, he sold eight U.S. magazines, including *New York,* most of which he had purchased earlier in the decade. The financial picture looked better for Murdoch in 1992. News Corporation profits rose 65 percent, and his British Sky Television broke even for the first time since its inception in February 1989.

Despite his economic difficulties, Murdoch still wields media muscle through News Corporation, the parent company of News America. Launched in Australia in 1980, News Corporation operates in North America, Europe, Australia, and Asia and "undoubtedly is the most globalized media company in the world," according to Koschnick. Murdoch, however, expresses no plans to "globalize" many of his media holdings. "There is no such thing as a 'global village,' " he said in a 1989 interview with Koschnick. While Murdoch has consolidated various book publishers into a global operation, HarperCollins, and has spread Fox Film Corporation operations into almost fifty countries, he does not plan to do the same with magazines, newspapers, and television in the immediate future.

Murdoch gives the impression that he will not invest further in the newspaper or magazine industries. He was one of the last publishers in the United Kingdom to equip his newspapers with run-of-press color-printing technology. He remarked in a 1989 interview that he is not sure newspapers will exist in the twenty-first century:

> Will we print a newspaper every day in a plant like the ones we use today?. . . Or will our readers be satisfied with that sort of information on the screen on a 24-hour basis? Or will they want something like that newspaper printed out from the screen? It's far too early to say. Undoubtedly, the coming of television, whether we like it or not, has affected papers, magazines, and there is no doubt that overall reading in our societies is tending to decline.

Murdoch credits his proclivity for empire building to his background. "Part of the Australian character is wanting to take on the world," he remarked in 1987. "It's a hard, huge continent inhabited by a few European descendants with a sense of distance from their roots. They have a great need to prove themselves."

According to a 1990 article in the *New York Times Magazine,* Murdoch has begun delegating executive responsibilities at News Corporation and has tentatively appointed his successor, Andrew Knight, executive chairman of News International, the British subsidiary of News Corporation. He is a former editor of the *Economist* and the *Daily Telegraph.* Murdoch also appointed his wife Anna as a News Corporation board member.

Murdoch became a United States citizen in 1985; he has homes in California and New York. He and his wife have two sons, James and Lachlan, and one daughter, Elisabeth. Murdoch has another daughter, Prudence, by his first marriage.

Murdoch retains his reputation for ruthless journalism, almost giving the impression that he likes it: "They call me 'arrogant Aussie,' 'a shark in the guise of a snake,' 'the Genghis Khan of the media,' 'a sinister force,' 'Murdoch of the mammaries.' I can think of more important things than being loved by everybody."

References:

Ben H. Bagdikian, "Conquering Hearts and Minds: The Lords of the Global Village," *Nation,* 248 (12 June 1989): 805–820;

Roger Cohen, "Rupert Murdoch's Biggest Gamble," *New York Times Magazine,* 21 October 1990, pp. 31–33, 64, 72–75;

Barnaby J. Feder, "Murdoch's Time of Reckoning," *New York Times,* 20 December 1990, pp. D1, D7;

Kathryn Harris, "A Big Dose of Realism," *Forbes,* 148 (2 September 1991): 40–42;

Thomas Kiernan, *Citizen Murdoch* (New York: Dodd, Mead, 1986);

Wolfgang J. Koschnick, "I Can Think of More Important Things Than Being Loved By Everybody," *Forbes,* 144 (27 November 1989): 98–104;

Michael Leapman, *Arrogant Aussie: The Rupert Murdoch Story* (Secaucus, N.J.: Lyle Stuart, 1985);

John Lippman, "Amid the Sheep, Citizen Murdoch," *Los Angeles Times,* 19 October 1990, pp. D1, D11;

"Rupert Murdoch: The Running Man," *Broadcasting,* 115 (11 July 1988): 87;

William Shawcross, *Murdoch* (New York: Simon & Schuster, 1993).

John H. Murphy III

(2 March 1916 –   )

Rodger Streitmatter
American University

MAJOR POSITIONS HELD: Office manager, *Afro-American* (1937–1945); manager (1945–1947), assistant business manager (1948–1956), business manager (1956–1961), president (1961–1974), chairman of the board and chief executive officer (1967–1986), Afro-American Newspaper Company.

John Henry Murphy III is the great-nephew of the founder of one of the country's most influential African-American newspaper empires. A leading force in the Afro-American Newspaper Company from 1937 until 1986, he carefully guided the Baltimore-based newspaper chain, which published editions for a half-dozen cities on the Eastern Seaboard, through an economic roller-coaster ride. The company, like the African-American press in general, enjoyed boom years during the 1940s and 1950s, experienced turbulence during the civil rights movement of the 1960s, and struggled for survival during the 1970s and 1980s.

Throughout the highs and lows Murphy maintained strong fiscal management. He always worked on the business side of the company, having little interest in the editorial content of the newspapers, and his decisions were securely anchored in conservative principles. Even when financial crises became so severe that they threatened the survival of the company, Murphy was unwilling to launch innovative publishing ventures until he was absolutely convinced of their ultimate financial success. His conservative economic planning resulted in consistent annual profits. The fact that Murphy was able to keep his newspapers profitable throughout the third generation of the family-owned business is remarkable considering that, between 1965 and 1985, the combined circulation of the company's newspapers plummeted from 160,000 to 50,000.

Murphy was born in Baltimore on 2 March 1916, the son of Dan Murphy, a typesetter, and Sarah Murphy, a homemaker. When his father died in 1926, John and his mother moved to Philadelphia, where she remarried. John entered the family

newspaper business at the age of twelve, as a paperboy delivering the Philadelphia edition of the *Afro-American*. He joined the company full-time after earning a degree in business administration from Temple University in 1937.

Murphy's great-uncle, John H. Murphy, Sr., and two clergymen founded the politically independent *Afro-American* in Baltimore in 1892. During the next twenty years they built a circulation base of ten thousand. When the senior Murphy died in 1922, editing and publishing responsibilities passed to his son, Carl Murphy. During the following two decades the company expanded to include a semiweekly in Baltimore, weeklies in Washington, D.C., and Philadelphia, and special editions distributed in New England, New York, and Virginia. By 1937 circulation of the *Afro-American* had risen to eighty thousand, making it the largest African-American newspaper operation in the East.

John H. Murphy III first worked as a manager for the *Washington Afro-American*. When the family bought the *Washington Tribune* in 1945, he also assumed management responsibilities for that newspaper, enabling the *Afro-American* to expand to a semiweekly in Washington. Murphy joined the company's board of directors in 1946. He became assistant business manager for the company in 1948.

While in this position Murphy faced one of his first major challenges. During the 1940s the company developed a unique distribution system. Bundles of the Baltimore edition of the *Afro-American* were sent by train to the black schools in various southern communities with large African-American populations. Newsboys then took the newspapers from the schools and sold them in their neighborhoods. Their teachers oversaw the operation, which included collecting the money from the newsboys and sending it to Baltimore.

When desegregation began after the Supreme Court's *Brown* v. *Board of Education* decision in 1954, however, this system could not function because

The National Newspaper Publishers Association helped to sponsor a fact-finding tour of Israel in 1969. This group of journalists included (standing) John Sengstacke, Dick Edwards, John H. Murphy III, Howard Woods, Dale Shields, Kenyon Burke, and John Bogle; (foreground) Thomas Picou, Garth Reeves, and Robert E. Johnson.

many towns no longer had exclusively black schools. Murphy developed a substation system, locating an agent in each town to distribute bundles of the *Afro-American* to newsboys.

Murphy continued to advance in the Afro-American Newspaper Company. In 1961 Carl Murphy passed over older members of the next generation to tap his nephew as president. The early 1960s were years of growth for the *Afro-American,* as well as for other black newspapers. As the civil rights movement emerged, the newspaper gained a national reputation for its willingness to send reporters throughout the South – from Montgomery to Birmingham to Little Rock to Selma – to document the events for black America. In a 1992 interview with Rodger Streitmatter, Murphy recalled: "We were the most liberal black newspaper when it came to sending reporters and photographers where the action was. That was our strength. Black people wouldn't believe what was going on unless they read it in one of their own papers."

In 1967 Carl Murphy died, and John H. Murphy became chairman of the board of directors and chief executive officer. By this time the company was publishing semiweeklies in Baltimore and Washington; weeklies in Philadelphia, Richmond,

and Newark; and a national edition that was distributed to black communities in North Carolina, South Carolina, Georgia, and Florida. Two hundred employees were on the weekly payroll, and the combined circulation had climbed to 160,000.

Growth resulted in change, however, and Murphy was not always comfortable with change, particularly when it meant breaking traditions that had been established as part of the family business for which he had inherited fiscal responsibility. One of Murphy's most difficult decisions came in the late 1960s when advances in technology forced the *Afro-American* to abandon its letterpress printing operation in order to keep pace with its competitors. A generation earlier it had become one of the few black newspapers to rely on its own press and an all-black shop to print its pages. The family took considerable pride in this accomplishment, and Murphy desperately wanted to maintain the tradition. He located a Goss press that would allow the *Afro-American* to print its own pages, along with those of other Baltimore-area newspapers. He then began the formidable task of financing the eight-hundred-thousand-dollar expenditure. He secured loans from three institutions and bought a building to house the three-unit offset press, but he remained two hundred thousand dollars short. Faced with the choice of borrowing more money than he was sure the company could repay or breaking with the family tradition of printing its own newspaper, Murphy opted for security. The Afro-American Newspaper Company hired a West Virginia plant to print its newspapers, and Murphy had to reduce the mechanical-department staff by forty positions.

Circumstances in the larger world also were contributing to financial difficulties for the *Afro-American*. After the Reverend Martin Luther King, Jr., was assassinated in 1968, riots erupted in black neighborhoods of cities throughout the country. In Washington the rioters burned many of the stores that distributed the paper, as well as many of the businesses that advertised in it.

In addition, the assassination and the riots took much of the steam out of the movement for racial reform, giving readers less reason to buy black newspapers. Murphy knew that he had to maintain the company's revenues, but the conservative publisher was reluctant to raise advertising rates, fearing businesses would turn toward the larger-circulation white newspapers that finally had begun to cover news of the black community.

Meanwhile, the editorial side of the newspapers was garnering praise in journalistic circles. The American Society of Journalism School Administrators spotlighted one outstanding newspaper or magazine each year. In 1969 the society honored a black publication for the first time, choosing the *Afro-American* "in recognition of the distinguished record of a newspaper which has served a predominantly black community and which has actively engaged in community service."

Nevertheless, Murphy had to keep the award-winning newspaper in business. After considerable financial analysis and soul-searching, in the early 1970s he launched the most creative publishing enterprise of his career. He borrowed the concept of *Parade* magazine, which many of the country's white newspapers had been inserting in their Sunday editions for twenty years, and introduced a similar weekly supplement for the black press.

Murphy undertook a national campaign to convince the publishers of the country's thirty largest black newspapers to join together in the first cooperative venture in the 150-year history of African-American journalism. After several months of meetings with publishers from Atlanta to Chicago to Philadelphia to Los Angeles, Murphy had sold them on the concept.

Dawn magazine was an immediate success, attracting a circulation of nine hundred thousand –

by far the largest of any publication in the history of the black press. For the first time national advertisers were offered a means by which they could reach black readers throughout the country. The magazine continued to prosper, expanding from its initial sixteen pages to a forty-page format.

Without *Dawn*, the *Afro-American* may not have survived through the 1970s, when many black newspapers ceased publication because of the rising competition from the white press. Murphy always distanced himself from the editorial operations of his newspapers, concentrating on those of the business office. In 1974, however, he made some strong statements about the motivation of the mainstream press in increasing its news coverage of the black community. Murphy told Henry G. LaBrie III, editor of *Perspectives on the Black Press,* that mainstream newspapers were not driven by a desire to provide news coverage for black readers: "It would be almost economic suicide not to consider certainly the activities, and especially the positive activities, of the black community, which they have ignored, I would say almost completely, up until about 10 years ago or, in some cases, a shorter time than that."

By the early 1980s the Afro-American Newspaper Company, thanks in large part to *Dawn,* had annual revenues of six million dollars and annual profits of two hundred thousand dollars. But then external forces again threatened the company's security: the increased health consciousness of the American people and the consequent decline in revenues from cigarette and liquor advertising. *Dawn* depended almost exclusively on advertisements for these products.

As the advertising disappeared, so did the national presence of the *Afro-American.* Rather than jeopardize the company's well-being, Murphy scaled back its operations. He first eliminated the national edition of the *Afro-American,* then the editions published for Philadelphia and Newark. He also dropped back to weekly publication in both Baltimore and Washington. These two weeklies plus the one in Richmond had a combined circulation of fifty thousand.

In the mid 1980s Murphy made another decision that reinforced his career-long theme of valuing fiscal responsibility over what some would call editorial integrity. Many staff members of the *Afro-American* wanted the company to maintain its journalistic professionalism by refusing to publish free-distribution shoppers. But, as the newspapers' circulation continued to decline and the company suffered annual losses – although never more than

Front page of the Afro-American, *21 August 1971*

thirty thousand dollars – during the early 1980s, Murphy insisted that the company find some way to justify its relatively high advertising rates or it would lose its lucrative national advertising.

Despite the opposition of the editorial staff, Murphy created *Every Wednesday,* a free-distribution tabloid that initially focused on home improvement and food. It later expanded to include entertainment-oriented material. The weekly's thirty-thousand circulation allowed the *Afro-American* to maintain its relatively low national advertising rate. In 1992 Murphy remarked, "You do what you have to do to stay in business. That's what we always have been and always will be – a business. We've stayed in operation a hundred years. We must be doing something right." Murphy led the Afro-American Newspaper Company board of directors until 1986, when he retired at the age of seventy, relinquishing his position to his cousin John "Jake" Oliver. Murphy then ceased involvement in the direct operation of the company, although he remains its largest individual stockholder. Since 1987 he has worked as a photographer for the *Baltimore Times,* a free-distribution weekly.

Murphy married Alice Quivers in 1940; they had two children, Sharon and Daniel. After his wife died in 1979, Murphy married Camay Calloway, daughter of musician Cab Calloway, in 1980. They live in Baltimore

During Murphy's career his influence extended beyond the family business into the broader sphere of black journalism. As president and chief executive officer of one of the leading black newspaper companies in the country, he was a strong supporter of the National Newspaper Publishers Association (NNPA), a professional organization of black publishers founded in 1943. Murphy served as president of the NNPA during the 1960s, concentrating his efforts on increasing advertising and circulation for black newspapers. Murphy also served on the board of directors of Amalgamated Publishers, which secured national advertising for some eighty black newspapers.

Murphy's influence also extended into the public affairs of Baltimore. He served on the boards of directors of the Council on Equal Business Opportunities, the National Aquarium at Baltimore, Provident Hospital (now Liberty Medical Hospital), the Baltimore School for the Arts, and the Baltimore City Literacy Commission. He was also a member of the Mayor's Commission to Study Municipal Financing. Murphy's church activities have included membership on the vestry of Saint James Episcopal Church and the Standing Committee of the Episcopal Diocese of Maryland. Murphy has served as a member of the Maryland Advisory Committee of the U.S. Civil Rights Commission; he later served as a member of the commission.

References:

Black Press Information Handbook (Washington, D.C.: National Newspaper Publishers Association, 1977);

Henry G. LaBrie III, *Perspectives on the Black Press: 1974* (Kennebunkport, Maine: Mercer House, 1974);

Carl Murphy, William N. Jones, and William I. Gibson, "The Afro: Seabord's Largest Weekly," *Crisis,* 45 (February 1938): 44–46;

Roland E. Wolseley, *The Black Press, U.S.A.* (Ames: Iowa State University Press, 1990).

Samuel I. Newhouse

(24 May 1895 – 29 August 1979)

Alfred Lawrence Lorenz
Loyola University in New Orleans

MAJOR NEWSPAPERS OWNED: *Staten Island* (New York) *Advance* (1922–1979); *Long Island* (New York) *Press* (1932–1979); *Newark* (New Jersey) *Ledger* (1935–1939); *Long Island* (New York) *Star* (1938–1939); (Long Island, New York) *North Shore Journal* (1938–1939); *Newark* (New Jersey) *Star-Eagle* (1939); *Long Island* (New York) *Star-Journal* [merger of *North Shore Journal* and *Long Island Star*] (1939–1979); Newark (New Jersey) *Star-Ledger* [merger of *Newark Star-Eagle* and *Newark Ledger*] (1939–1979); *Syracuse* (New York) *Herald* (1939); *Syracuse* (New York) *Journal* (1939); *Syracuse* (New York) *Herald-Journal* [merger of *Syracuse Herald* and *Syracuse Journal*] (1939–1979); *Syracuse* (New York) *Post Standard* (1942–1979); (Newark, New Jersey) *Jersey Journal* (1945–1979); *Harrisburg* (Pennsylvania) *Evening News* (1948–1979); *Harrisburg* (Pennsylvania) *Patriot* (1948–1979); *Harrisburg* (Pennsylvania) *Telegraph* [merged into *Harrisburg Evening News*] (1948); *Portland Oregonian* (1950–1979); *St. Louis* (Missouri) *Globe-Democrat* (1955–1979); *Huntsville* (Alabama) *Times* (1955–1979); *Birmingham* (Alabama) *News* (1955–1979); (Portland) *Oregon Journal* (1961–1979); *New Orleans* (Louisiana) *States-Item* (1962–1979); *New Orleans* (Louisiana) *Times-Picayune* (1962–1979); *Springfield* (Massachusetts) *News* (1966–1979); *Springfield* (Massachusetts) *Republican* (1966–1979); *Springfield* (Massachusetts) *Union* (1966–1979); *Mississippi Press Register* (1966–1979); *Mobile* (Alabama) *Press* (1966–1979); *Mobile* (Alabama) *Register* (1966–1979); *Cleveland* (Ohio) *Plain Dealer* (1967–1979); *Bayonne* (New Jersey) *Times* [merged into *Jersey Journal*] (1971); *Newark* (New Jersey) *Evening News* (1976–1977); Booth Newspapers of Michigan: *Ann Arbor News, Bay City Times, Flint Journal, Grand Rapids Press, Jackson Citizen Patriot, Kalamazoo Gazette, Muskegon Chronicle, Saginaw News* (1976–1979).

Samuel I. Newhouse acquired the *Staten Island Advance* in 1922 for ninety-eight thousand dollars,

his first wholly owned newspaper. In 1979, the last year of his life, he still owned it, but by then it was the base of operations for what was at that time the nation's second-largest newspaper chain – a term Newhouse would not use. He preferred "our family of newspapers."

His fifty-seven years as a publisher took Newhouse from poverty to the luxury of Park Avenue. He was born on Manhattan's Lower East Side on 24 May 1895, the first son of Meier and Rose Fatt Neuhaus, both Jewish immigrants – he from Russia, she from Austria. The child was given the name Solomon. Not long after his birth the family moved to New Jersey, where the father Anglicized the family name to Newhouse and his given name to Meyer. Young Solomon began using the name Sammy.

Newhouse finished public grade school in Bayonne, New Jersey, but dropped out of high school to work. He also took a three-month secretarial course at the Gaffney School in Manhattan. He supported himself by ferrying newspapers from New Jersey to New York. On completing the course he sought an office job but was turned down because, he was told, he was too short (he was 5'3"). His father subsequently persuaded Hyman Lazarus, a Bayonne lawyer and city magistrate, to allow the boy to work for nothing for a month in order to prove himself. At the end of the month, Lazarus kept Newhouse on at two dollars a week.

Among Lazarus's interests was the *Bayonne Times,* a money-losing newspaper housed on the first floor of the building in which the judge had his law office. He acquired 51 percent of the newspaper in payment of a debt, but he had little interest in operating it. He made Newhouse, then seventeen, its business manager.

Lazarus wanted the boy to act as a caretaker until he could sell the newspaper, but Newhouse reversed its losses, made it a success, and found a career. The keys were advertising and circulation. He became practiced at helping merchants develop sales campaigns and in devising advertising-rate

Samuel I. Newhouse, 1964

schedules that persuaded them to put their advertising in the *Times.* He improved home delivery. He also studied the newspaper business and, over time, became a walking encyclopedia of facts and figures and of what made successful ventures and what led to failures.

Newhouse juggled his work schedule with legal studies. He took the New Jersey Regents' Examination to enter the New Jersey Law School, from which he was graduated in four years, at the age of twenty-one. He also had substantial family responsibilities. His father had moved to Connecticut, believing that the climate there would be better for his increasingly ill health. With his greater income Samuel became the chief breadwinner of the family. As a result, his mother made him head of the family, which consisted of three other boys and four girls.

Although a lawyer, Newhouse practiced little; the newspaper business absorbed his attention. In 1920 he persuaded Lazarus to help him buy the *Fitchburg* (Massachusetts) *News.* He was unable to make it a financial success, however, and within a year he sold it to the publisher of the rival *Fitchburg Sentinel* at the same price he and

Lazarus had paid for it. In the bargain he acquired a more favorable newsprint contract for the *Times* as well as the equipment at the *News,* some of which he put into service in Bayonne and some of which he sold.

His profit helped him purchase the *Staten Island Advance,* also in partnership with Lazarus, in 1922, while he still managed the *Times* for a healthy salary and a percentage of its profits. On Staten Island, Newhouse perfected the advertising-sales techniques he had developed in Bayonne. He also sought out advertisers in nearby communities, and he offered special discounts to merchants who advertised in both the Bayonne and Staten Island newspapers. He was not above including news-page promotion of Staten Island commerce to advance advertising sales, or using self-promotion to help build circulation, which he expanded through the use of an extensive home-delivery system. The formula was successful, just as it had been in Bayonne.

He brought his brothers and sisters to the *Advance.* Theodore served as business manager; Norman (the only practicing journalist among them) was a reporter and editor; Louis, the mechanical su-

Samuel I. Newhouse (center) in 1976 with his sons, S. I. Newhouse, Jr., and Donald Newhouse, who now control the family's media properties (Wide World/Bettmann Archives)

perintendent; Naomi, the circulation manager; and Estelle, a marketing analyst. As years went on, Theodore and Norman played increasingly important roles in building the business. The publisher's sons, Samuel, Jr., and Donald, were brought in as well; so were the sons of his sisters Gertrude and Estelle, and Norman's son Mark.

When he owned only a handful of properties in the Northeast, Newhouse tried to visit all of them once a week. As the chain grew, the family members were given groups of newspapers to keep tabs on – their "newspaper routes," Norman Newhouse quipped. Samuel still kept in contact with them, but by telephone and occasional visits. He operated his empire, in fact, from his briefcase. He had no office but used a desk at whatever property he was visiting. He kept no files, wrote few letters, and destroyed incoming memos after he acted on them.

Newhouse formed a partnership with his editor and business manager to buy out Lazarus's interest in the *Advance* in 1924. Newhouse continued as business manager of the *Times* until after Lazarus's death in the autumn of that year. In 1927 he bought the interests of his partners. From then on, he and his family held complete control of all

his properties, except on those occasions when he bought a portion of stock on his way to 100 percent ownership.

Newhouse ran the *Advance* so well and made it so profitable that even in the Depression year of 1934 he was able to put down four hundred thousand dollars in cash toward the six-hundred-thousand-dollar purchase price of the *Long Island Press,* which belonged to the publishing brothers Victor, Bernard, and Joseph Ridder. Before the United States entered World War II, Newhouse bought six more newspapers. In 1935 he purchased the *Newark* (New Jersey) *Ledger* and in 1939 the *Newark Star-Eagle,* and he combined them into the *Newark Star-Ledger.* He bought the *Long Island* (New York) *Star* and *North Shore Journal* in 1938 and merged them into the *Long Island Star-Journal.* In 1939 he added the *Syracuse* (New York) *Herald-Journal* to his chain and in 1941, the *Syracuse Post-Standard.*

In the decade following the war, Newhouse extended his "family" across the nation. He bought the *Harrisburg* (Pennsylvania) *Patriot* and the *Harrisburg Evening News* in 1948. Two years later he paid $5.6 million for the *Portland Oregonian.* He acquired the rival, and weaker, *Oregon Journal* for $8 million in 1961, following a two-year strike in which the two newspapers had published as one; the strike continued for another five years.

The *St. Louis Globe-Democrat* became his in 1955 for $6.25 million. It boosted the circulation of his chain past 1.5 million daily and 1.6 million on Sundays for the first time. Later that year he acquired the *Birmingham* (Alabama) *News,* the *Huntsville* (Alabama) *Times,* two radio stations, and a television station in an $18.7 million package deal. That purchase was an extraordinary one for Newhouse: it marked the first time that he borrowed money to buy a newspaper.

Newhouse failed in an effort to purchase the *Denver Post* during the 1960s, but he was successful in buying the Bowles family newspapers of Springfield, Massachusetts, the *Union, News,* and *Republican.* Despite a vigorous, though short-lived effort by minority stockholders to keep him out, he acquired the *New Orleans Times-Picayune* and the *New Orleans States-Item* in 1962 for what was then the highest sum ever paid for newspapers in one city, $42 million. This record stood until he bought the *Cleveland Plain Dealer* in 1967 for $54.2 million. In 1976 he bought eight Michigan dailies and *Parade* magazine from Booth Newspapers for $305 million, the largest amount ever paid in a newspaper transaction.

Newhouse also branched out into magazines, buying holdings in Condé Nast Publications in 1959 for about $5 million (he joked that he bought the company, which published *Vogue,* for his wife, the former Mitzi Epstein, as a present on their thirty-fifth wedding anniversary). A few months later he paid $3.5 million for controlling interest of Street and Smith Publications. Newhouse acquired radio and television stations in some of his newspaper deals. At the time of his death, his company owned WTPA (FM and TV), Harrisburg; WSYE-TV, Elmira, New York; WSYR (AM, FM, and TV), Syracuse; WAPI (AM, FM and TV), Birmingham; and KTVI-TV, Saint Louis. He also acquired cable-television systems.

The growth of the chain was not without difficulties. Labor troubles plagued Newhouse from the start. In 1934 the American Newspaper Guild staged its first strike against the *Staten Island Advance.* Before the end of that year it had staged a boycott against the *Long Island Press.* On 21 February 1959 Guildsmen walked off their jobs at the *St. Louis Globe-Democrat* in a dispute over pensions. The walkout closed the paper for ninety-nine days. During that time additional grievances and complaints were filed against the Newhouse ownership. Among them was a charge that Newhouse had reduced the staff of the paper from four hundred to three hundred in five years. Similar complaints – always disputed by Newhouse – were heard from staffers of other newly acquired Newhouse interests, along with the universal newspaperman's lament of low wages.

Absentee ownership was another charge aimed at Newhouse. Among his critics was the editor James Wechsler, who focused that complaint in saying that the chain was "administered on the frank premise that the owner's concern lies not with the content of his properties but with the returns of the box office; the only common denominator of each of the newspapers acquired by the Newhouse interests is that they are commercial triumphs."

On the other hand, Newhouse and his editors countered that Newhouse was vitally concerned with the editorial integrity and character of his newspapers and left his editors free to make their own decisions. Newhouse himself argued that, unlike William Randolph Hearst, "the newspaper owner must not permit his feelings and his opinions to distort or frustrate the true personality of his paper." He saw the "ideal" owner as one who "has an intense interest in all of the operations of his newspaper but who can top that interest with an even greater degree of self-control."

He tried to maintain the character each newspaper had before he bought it. In several of the cities in which he owned two newspapers, the two had opposing editorial policies, and those policies continued, as did the newspapers' news-gathering competitiveness. His longtime associate, editor Philip Hochstein, said, "Mr. Newhouse gives no orders to his editors, telling them what to do. He may and does argue with them to draw them out. But once he has established confidence in an editor, he wants him to be editorial boss."

In his fight to take control of the Springfield newspapers, their trustees publicly attacked his absentee ownership of newspapers in other cities and told their readers that he would not be good for the community. They pictured him as buying newspapers just as other people collect objects of art. However, the S. H. Bowles family sold their shares in the Springfield newspapers to Newhouse, they said, because they were "entirely certain that as in the case of his other newspapers the Springfield newspapers will be completely autonomous and will continue to operate as community newspapers devoted solely to the interests of Springfield." E. Lansing Ray said that he sold his *Globe-Democrat* to Newhouse because he wanted to assure that the newspaper retained the character he and his family had given it, and Newhouse had a reputation for continuing the original character and direction of each newspaper he bought.

Another criticism was that Newhouse thwarted the traditional role of the newspaper in society because he had no concern for the news, only profits. The critic A. J. Liebling called him a "journalistic chiffonier," and a "rag picker." Newhouse was the archetype of a breed of publishers different from their predecessors in that they were interested in newspapers only as properties. According to Liebling, for Newhouse and publishers like him, business was the main attraction; news was "a costly and uneconomic frill, like the free lunch saloons used to furnish to induce customers to buy beer."

Certainly, his properties were financial successes. In an era in which it became increasingly difficult for newspapers to survive, only two of his failed. The *Long Island Star-Journal* closed in 1968 and the *Long Island Press* in 1977, both victims of changing demographic patterns. The others prospered. At the time of Newhouse's death the "family" included thirty-one newspapers with a circulation exceeding 3 million, two magazine-publishing houses, six television stations, five radio stations, and twenty cable-television systems.

Annual revenues were estimated at $750 million, with three-fourths coming from the newspapers. But his newspapers were not well respected by journalists. When the media review *More* compiled a list of the nation's ten worst newspapers during the mid 1970s, three Newhouse properties were on it: the *Cleveland Plain Dealer,* the *New Orleans Times-Picayune,* and the *St. Louis Globe-Democrat.*

Newhouse made philanthropic contributions of millions of dollars through the Samuel I. Newhouse Foundation. Among the beneficiaries were Rutgers University's S. I. Newhouse Center for Law and Justice and the Mitzi E. Newhouse Theater at Lincoln Center in New York City. He endowed the S. I. Newhouse School of Public Communications at Syracuse University.

Newhouse maintained a close eye on his operations even into his eighties. He was eighty-one when he oversaw the purchase of the Booth Newspapers. Shortly after the deal, however, he suffered a stroke and rapidly deteriorated into senility. He was hospitalized after a second stroke, in 1979, and on 29 August of that year he died at age eighty-four.

References

John A. Lent, *Newhouse, Newspapers, Nuisances: Highlights in the Growth of a Communications Empire* (New York: Exposition, 1966);

Richard H. Meeker, *Newspaperman: S. I. Newhouse and the Business of News* (New Haven & New York: Ticknor & Fields, 1983).

Cecil Earl Newman

(25 July 1903 – 7 February 1976)

William E. Huntzicker
University of Minnesota

MAJOR POSITIONS HELD: Cofounder and coeditor, *Twin City Herald* (1927–1934); founder, editor, and publisher, *Timely Digest* [magazine] (1931–1932); founder, editor, and publisher, *Minneapolis Spokesman* and *St. Paul Recorder* (1934–1976).

Cecil Earl Newman founded Minnesota's most successful black newspapers. Despite many early financial setbacks, Newman believed that African-Americans in Minneapolis and St. Paul could support their own newspapers. While working as a Pullman porter, he contributed both copy and money to an early Minneapolis black paper. He founded the *Minneapolis Spokesman* and *St. Paul Recorder* in 1934 and served as editor and publisher until his death in 1976. Newman's papers covered the social scene of the Twin Cities black community while advocating civil rights and the cases of individuals facing discrimination. Newman also belonged to more than forty professional and civil-rights groups, and he was the first black president of the Minnesota Press Club.

Newman was born on 25 July 1903 in Kansas City, Missouri, the first child of Cora Lee Saunders Newman and Horatio Oscar Newman, who worked as an attendant at a private club. Horatio, whose parents had migrated to free Kansas from Tennessee prior to the Civil War, later became a chef in a Kansas City hotel. Through his parents' encouragement Cecil was an advanced reader by the time he entered first grade. His mother became a domestic worker whose cleaning duties included a home with a large reading room. When its owner died, the man's widow gave Cecil a four-hundred-volume library. "The fact that my parents could not only read and write, but loved books and what they stood for, had much to do with my own strong desire to make something of myself," Newman told his biographer, L. Edmond Leipold.

Cecil, his parents, and his three sisters attended church regularly, and the family managed to survive the Depression without going on relief. A

Cecil Earl Newman

younger brother was born, but he died at the age of eighteen months. The family lived in an integrated, middle-class neighborhood. However, the Kansas City of Newman's youth was segregated in many ways, including "separate but equal" schools. A particularly bitter experience came about when Newman and neighbor Langston Hughes, the future poet, read about a children's party at a public amusement park. The two boys went to the open house only to be told that "niggers aren't included."

Newman began community service, civil-rights work, and journalism studies while in high school. During World War I he quickly rose to captain of one of the four R.O.T.C. companies at his school, yet his and other black units were always relegated to the end of parades supporting the war. As a high-school sophomore Newman wrote an article for the *Call,* a Kansas City black newspaper, protesting the school board's policy of not employing blacks in its central administration. His school principal reprimanded him for the article. Despite his interest in journalism Newman was unable to find training in high school. Black schools had no counselors, and the only work program emphasized manual skills for students who helped support their families. As a result, Newman became a part-time carpenter, a trade for which he lacked interest and acumen. On another brief job he distributed brochures and buttons for local politicians. The only encouragement he received for his interest in journalism came from a fellow student. During this time he began his lifelong observation of the connections between politics and journalism.

Although still a year away from graduation, Cecil married Willa Coleman in 1920, despite his parents' fear that an early marriage would inhibit their talented son; the couple lived with Cecil's parents. His high-school principal, displeased with the marriage of a young role model, removed Cecil from his office as class president; however, the principal relented after the class reelected Cecil to the vacant position. A sophomore when they married, Willa dropped out of school when Cecil was graduated a year later.

Before his graduation Cecil managed a theater concession stand for a year and a half. He was a student manager of athletic teams, and in 1921 he bought a semiprofessional baseball team for one hundred dollars, with a five-hundred-dollar payment due. Yet he soon realized that owners made their teams profitable by betting on them, so, having purchased a losing squad, Newman found his Kansas City Royals a liability. Decades later the American League appropriated the team's name.

Despite his mother's offer to back him on another business venture and a sixty-dollar-a-month job offer in carpentry, Newman thought opportunities would be better in Minneapolis, where his wife's sister lived. The birth of his only child, Oscar Horatio, on 1 September 1921 convinced Cecil to seek prospects where he believed blacks would not be denied access to employment, as well as to theaters, restaurants, parks, and playgrounds. Of course Newman found racism in Minneapolis, even though discrimination was not as formal as in Kansas City. He earned forty dollars a month at his first Minneapolis job – bellhop at the Elk's Club.

He surveyed the newspaper scene, finding two weekly Negro newspapers, the *Northwestern Bulletin* in Minneapolis and the *St. Paul Appeal.* Newman approached the Minneapolis paper, which he felt was on a better footing. He began selling subscriptions to the *Bulletin,* and he was told he could write occasional articles. In addition he worked as a stringer for the *Pittsburgh Courier* and the *Chicago Defender,* at that time two of the nation's leading black newspapers, but this failed to provide reliable income. Editors did not automatically accept his articles, and they shortened those that were published, meaning Newman received less pay. Nevertheless, he found the bylines uplifting. Slowly his confidence, if not his wages, increased, and, two years after he arrived in Minneapolis, his wife and son joined him.

The family still needed a reliable income. Through a friend, Newman obtained a job in 1924 as a porter for the Pullman Company, which furnished sleeping cars on passenger trains. He worked for six years as a porter and traveled into all of the forty-eight states except Louisiana. Although he enjoyed the job, Newman still hankered to be a journalist.

In 1924 he met a black printer, Joshua Perry, who operated a small shop in Minneapolis. The only surviving black paper in St. Paul at the time was the *Echo,* and it was teetering. Convinced that both cities, especially Minneapolis, could support a black newspaper, Newman formed a partnership with Perry, whose business acumen, unfortunately, failed to match his printing talent. Without knowing Perry's precarious financial condition, Newman raised two thousand dollars from a board of directors and investors. Perry's creditors took all but twenty-seven dollars of this capital.

Nevertheless, the four-page first edition of the *Twin City Herald* appeared in 1927, with Newman as editor. At the same time he continued to progress in his main job. He was promoted to porter-in-charge, which gave him more responsibility and income – money he divided between his family and his newspaper. He created an office with a typewriter in the corner of his Pullman car. From there, he wrote editorials crusading against crime and lamenting the number of arrests among black men as well as the arrests for prostitution among black women. While Newman received no pay, the *Herald,* working out of Perry's print shop and later its own office at 242

Staff of the Minneapolis Spokesman *and* St. Paul Recorder, *circa 1935, with Newman seated in the center*

Fourth Avenue South, kept accumulating debt. The *Herald* survived for seven years, but within four years Perry owed Newman five thousand dollars.

In order to settle this debt, Newman convinced Perry to print a magazine geared toward African-Americans. The two launched *Timely Digest,* similar to both *Time* and *Literary Digest,* in April 1931. The foreword to the magazine noted that more than four hundred periodicals were published for blacks, who constituted one-tenth of the U.S. population. The first issue carried a recurrent theme in Newman's work. "Until recent days, not years, little that was creditable appeared in 'white' newspapers and periodicals concerning the Negro," he wrote. "This, despite the fact that most of this group make excellent citizens if given half a chance." He said that white newspapers ignored worthwhile activities of the six million blacks who belonged to forty-seven thousand churches, the nine hundred thousand black home owners, and the more than one million black farmers and ninety thousand black businessmen. Blacks in the United States also boasted 503 institutions of higher education.

The *Timely Digest* folded within a year. Determined to succeed in journalism, Newman set about laying a stronger foundation for his next paper. He called on Ralph Casey, head of the University of Minnesota's journalism school. Impressed by Newman's resilience, Casey gave the young editor seven journalism textbooks, which Newman studied for

several months. He gave up his Pullman job during the Depression to begin his own newspaper on a full-time basis. "I didn't have enough money to begin one newspaper," he recalled, "so I began publishing two." He had tried unsuccessfully to buy out Perry's interest in the *Herald.*

The *Minneapolis Spokesman* and the *St. Paul Recorder* appeared on 10 August 1934. A barber around the corner from the *Herald* shared some of his space with the newspapers for fifteen dollars a month. Although the papers had a nominally large staff, Newman did much of the work himself. He set some type and sold most of the advertising, approaching both white and black businesspeople.

The first issues of both papers featured national news and local editorials. The editorial page also carried reprints from other black newspapers around the nation. An editorial signed "Cecil E. Newman, Northwest Publishing Co., St. Paul Recorder, Minneapolis Spokesman" in the middle of page 1 reiterated Newman's belief that Minnesotans would support "an outspoken Negro organ" in both Minneapolis and St. Paul. "Both publications will be dedicated to the well-being and progress of the Northwestern Negro as a whole," he wrote. He promised to cover local and national news and to support churches, fraternities, and service institutions. "Editorially, both papers will speak out fearlessly and unceasingly against injustice, discrimination and all imposed inequalities, no matter what group or nationality they are visited upon." The editorial concluded with a promise that his news and editorial columns were not for sale: "The only salable space will be the advertising columns that will be open to all bona fide business enterprises."

During World War II, however, at least one business found it was not welcome. The attempted purchase came from one of the four local breweries against whom Newman had organized a boycott for their refusal to hire blacks. Newman asked his readers to stop purchasing the four brands, and he asked the black owners of bars to stop selling them. He even prevailed upon black porters to suggest that railroad patrons purchase other brands. Newman refused a fifteen-hundred-dollar advertisement from one brewery that he considered a blatant bribe. The boycott continued for a year, and Twin City leaders learned that, literally, Newman meant business.

While printing community-building news and editorials, the *Spokesman* and *Recorder* also lobbied for the local black community. "The chief owner of one of the large Minneapolis department stores," a 1934 editorial began, "is a heavy contributor to a Negro college in Florida. His store is the only large one locally which has not a single Negro employee, man or woman." The editorial concluded with the hope that the local philanthropist "has simply overlooked the fact that there is inconsistency in giving people miles away books when the people at home need bread."

The importance of alternative newspapers became a dominant force behind Newman's journalism, as exhibited in a *Recorder* editorial (17 August 1934):

> It is an interesting fact or should be that the big daily papers our people buy by the hundreds seldom carry a word about matters of personal moment to the Negro group, save when some member of the group does something that permits the papers to castigate the race. We may commend the interest we show in keeping in touch with world news and local happenings. We should, however, remember that it is left to the Negro newsgatherer and the Negro publisher to gather and print all other activities of the race. Our progress in every field of endeavor, religious, economic, or political, the men and women who do worthwhile things; our social pleasures and pastimes, these are essential and valuable things and are found only in the columns of the Negro press.

To further strengthen the African-American voice in local affairs, Newman called for more support for the local NAACP and Urban League. He asked these groups to reach out more effectively to young people, and he actively participated in both organizations in Minneapolis and St. Paul. He also became a trustee of the Minnesota board of the United Negro College Fund.

From the start Newman considered his white audience as important as the blacks who read the paper. Within a decade his circulation reached seven thousand at a time when only fifteen thousand African-Americans lived in the Twin Cities. "Back in 1934 when I began publishing the *Spokesman,* most white people didn't even know that there was a Negro problem in Minneapolis," Newman recalled in the late 1960s. "The Negroes were relatively isolated in their own sections of town, and there was little contact between the two groups." Most blacks' contacts with whites were through employment in custodial and domestic jobs.

Late in 1934 C. A. Franklin of the Kansas City and St. Louis *Call* approached Newman with an offer of one hundred dollars a week to breathe new life into his St. Louis paper. For five months Newman worked at this job, living on twenty-five dollars a week and sending the remaining seventy-five dollars back to operate his Twin Cities newspapers. Newman returned to find the business aspects of the Minneapolis office in trouble, so he made an arrangement with P. L. Andersen of the Andersen & Foss Typesetting Company to keep the paper going, despite fifty-two hundred dollars in unpaid bills. While he built his newspapers, Newman's marriage came apart. Although the couple separated by 1936, Newman continued to support his wife and son. One of his part-time employees was DeVelma Hall, a bright and energetic worker who helped put the financial affairs of the newspaper in order. Hall and Newman were married on 11 June 1937.

Newman encouraged young journalists. One of them, Gordon Parks, who became a *Life* magazine photographer and filmmaker, was sixteen years old when he arrived in St. Paul after the death of his mother in the late 1920s. Parks remembered Minnesota's racial climate as much friendlier than the one he had left in Kansas. "Minnesota Negroes were given more, so they had less to fight for," Parks wrote in his autobiography, *A Choice of Weapons* (1966). "Negro and white boys fought now and then in the Twin Cities, but the fights never amounted to much."

On the whole, he wrote, Minnesota blacks seemed apathetic about lynchings and murders farther south, but the newspapers helped increase awareness. "One Negro newspaper existed, the *Minneapolis Spokesman–St. Paul Recorder.* It had a small voice and a small Negro circulation. Its publisher,

Newman (center) outside his Minneapolis newspaper office with Minnesota governor Orville Freeman (left) and County Commissioner George Matthews, circa 1959

Cecil Newman, was as militant as the climate would allow – but the climate wasn't allowing much. My young friends didn't talk about these conditions very often." Although Parks could not support himself as a photographer during the Depression, he found a creative outlet with Newman's newspapers. "There was no pay; I accepted the space for the pleasure of seeing my work published."

World War II brought prosperity to the media and jobs to the black community. Newman's newspapers thrived with increased sales and advertising. The newspaper office moved out of its first barbershop into a larger space in a second barbershop. Newman's papers grew with the Twin Cities black community during the war, wrote George Hage in an essay on twentieth-century Minnesota journalism in *Minnesota in a Century of Change* (1989). The papers combined local and national news with "an editorial voice that spoke eloquently, but never stridently, for human rights. Newman was proud that more than a third of the two papers' combined circulation of twenty thousand went to white subscribers and equally proud that journalist Carl Rowan and photographer and writer Gordon Parks began their distinguished careers on his newspapers."

During the war Newman developed a special relationship with Charles L. Horn, a Twin Cities arms and munitions manufacturer whose grandfather had helped slaves escape through the Under-

ground Railroad. Horn received a government contract for manufacturing munitions for small arms at his plant in the suburb of New Brighton. As the plant grew and integrated, Newman became a personnel director for black employees. His job was to screen potential African-American employees as they moved into job categories in which they had never worked beside whites. Newman endorsed more than a thousand black employees; President Franklin Roosevelt visited the plant and lent his approval. Newman contrasted their success to a Southern plant, which, he said, hired four blacks and then built a thirty-five-hundred-dollar separate toilet for them outside the building.

Newman's newspapers used the increased opportunities brought by the war and prosperity to pressure the Twin Cities to decrease discrimination. DeVelma operated the papers while Cecil engaged in civic and patriotic activities. In a *Recorder* editorial (13 February 1942) he wrote: "We've all got a job to do to win this war. Part of it is to get rid of these petty American Hitlerites who plague the steps of every Negro who tries to live as others. We who must register and perhaps die expect those who govern to free us of the eternal battle of race prejudice from the rear so we can face the common enemy at the front!"

Exposure of abuses, Newman said, was his patriotic duty. He worked outside of journalism to eliminate racial discrimination, especially in dining facilities and jobs. In 1943 twelve African-American organizations sponsored a testimonial dinner attended by Twin Cities dignitaries. The event noted Newman's fortieth birthday and the first time that blacks and whites dined together at a "whites only" hotel.

After the war *Minneapolis Tribune* reporter Geri Hoffner emphasized the multicultural appeal of Newman's newspapers and the risks he took. His editorials attacked anti-Semitism, anti-Catholicism, and Jim Crow laws. "Occasionally Newman's life has been threatened," Hoffner wrote in the *Minneapolis Tribune* (31 August 1947). "In 1940, when he objected to police indifference to prostitution in a neighborhood where there were many school children, his son was mistaken for him and severely beaten."

In 1945 Hubert Humphrey, a moderate Democrat, became mayor of Minneapolis. One of his first moves was to establish the Council on Human Relations, to which he appointed Newman. Within a year the city passed a fair-employment ordinance, and Newman met with a trade association to discuss discrimination in hotels, bars, and restaurants. "Sometimes a personal visit to, say, an employer who discriminates against Negroes does more good than ten thousand headlines," Newman remarked. At this time Newman also served as president of the Urban League.

After the war Carl T. Rowan came to Minneapolis to study journalism at the University of Minnesota, where he completed a master's degree in 1948. In his memoir *Breaking Barriers* (1991), Rowan calls Newman "one of the great and unsung black journalists in the land," who used his newspapers "to hold a sizzling fire to the feet of Humphrey and other Minnesota officials. Newman taught me that age twenty-two was not too early to make a commitment to the NAACP, the Urban League, or other black groups to wipe out bigotry."

In 1948 Newman opposed continuing segregation in the U.S. Army. The opposition, he emphasized, was against a *segregated* army, not against the army. But Newman's actions were not confined to African-American issues. In August 1955 the *Spokesman* called for improved recreation along with job and family counseling for Native Americans: "We have seen our Negro minority in the Twin Cities living in the same terribly bad housing, but we have seen nothing yet compared with the degrading housing conditions under which many Indians living here endure."

Newman began collecting accolades in the late 1940s. The November 1949 issue of *Ebony* magazine

Newman receiving a Doctor of Laws degree from Allen University, Columbia, South Carolina

named him one of the most influential African-American newspaper publishers. In 1952 he became the first black Minnesotan listed in *Who's Who in America*. On 11 August 1954 the *Minneapolis Tribune* noted a twentieth-birthday celebration of the *Spokesman*: "In that time, Newman has provided distinguished leadership in the Negro community and has served the whole city — regardless of race or color — with unselfish devotion."

Cecil and DeVelma Newman were divorced in July 1958. On 3 April 1965 he married Launa Quincy Jackman, the mother of two grown children, Norma Jean Williams and Wallace O. Jackman. Launa, Norma Jean, and Cecil worked together on the *Spokesman* and *Recorder*. The dedication to the Leipold book four years later praised "Launa Newman who has, more than anyone else, motivated Cecil Newman to achieve his life's goals."

In the late 1960s Newman continued bringing down traditional barriers to blacks. In December 1967 he joined the board of directors of Midwest Federal Savings and Loan Association. Editorials stated that the appointment would give blacks more status within the business world; Midwest Federal's chairman said that the appointment made Newman the first black person on the board of a major financial institution. The announcement came while Newman prepared to accompany Vice-President Humphrey on an official trip to Africa. In December 1968 Newman became the first black member of the prestigious Minneapolis Club, which novelist Fletcher Knebel had called "the WASP capital in Minnesota."

Newman remained active in the Minnesota Democratic-Farmer-Labor party. As a delegate to the Democratic National Convention in 1956, he helped keep candidate Adlai Stevenson interested in civil rights by endorsing his opponent Estes Kefauver. Yet Newman took a moderate view on civil-rights issues. In 1956 he opposed New York congressman Adam Clayton Powell's proposed nationwide work stoppage in support of the Montgomery bus boycott led by the Reverend Martin Luther King, Jr. In the late 1960s he attacked violent civil-rights and antiwar protests.

In 1958 the newspaper offices moved into a new building at 3744 Fourth Avenue South in a predominantly black Minneapolis neighborhood. The offices would remain there for more than three decades. By 1975 five newspapers and a magazine competed for the African-American audience and advertising revenue in the Twin Cities. Like Newman's *Spokesman* and *Recorder,* the *Observer* in Minneapolis and the *Sun* in St. Paul were sister papers from the same publisher. They soon folded, but the Twin Cities *Courier* served both cities for twenty years.

Minneapolis Star reporter Jim Jones wrote in August 1975 that advertisers avoided black newspapers because of duplication, rotated their revenue among black newspapers, or supported a favorite for political reasons. Rudy Boschwitz, Republican national committeeman and later U.S. senator, placed his Plywood Minnesota advertising only in the *Observer,* and he denied reports that Republican leaders had financed the Twin Cities *Courier,* edited by former Newman employee Mary J. Kyle. Jones noted that at one time Newman's paper was considered outspokenly liberal, if not militant. "Now it is generally regarded as the establishment black paper," he wrote.

Newman's papers outlasted the others, but the magazine *Insight,* a monthly begun in 1974 and targeted toward predominantly black North Minneapolis, had more staying power. Its editor, Al McFarlane, transformed the magazine into a biweekly newspaper by 1976; it became the weekly *Insight News* in 1978. By 1992 he was cooperating with other minority journalists to create separate publica-

tions for Native Americans, Asian-Americans, and Hispanics as well as African-Americans.

In May 1974 Humphrey presented the seventy-one-year-old Newman with the National Brotherhood Award from the National Conference of Christians and Jews. The award, Humphrey said, recognized forty years of service to blacks. Less than two years later, on 7 February 1976, Newman died of a heart attack. The death was unexpected, *Spokesman* reporter Curtis C. Chivers wrote, even though Newman had not been in good health. He had been working full-time and making plans for the future.

An obituary in the *Spokesman* commented, "In recent years with the growth of a new militancy among younger Blacks, Newman was sometimes called – to his face – an 'Uncle Tom.' His reaction to this was neither indignation nor anger, but rather a kind of compassionate amusement for critics who did not know of or understand the forces which have brought about a climate in which Black militancy can function."

Humphrey was among the dignitaries whose press statements paid tribute to Newman: "He not only inspired, but advised and counseled me, helped sensitize me to civil-rights issues. In fact, he was the first editor to support me when I ran for mayor" (*Minneapolis Tribune,* 8 February 1976). "Calmness and common sense were his trademarks," remarked the *St. Paul Pioneer Press* (11 February 1976), stating that Newman had succeeded through personal effort, talent, and a refusal to recognize the odds against him. "In his time and in his place," wrote the *Minneapolis Star* (10 February 1976), "Newman took his stand. It was for peaceable integration, not divisive hatred, because that was the essence of his being."

References:

Clifford E. Clark, Jr., ed., *Minnesota in a Century of Change: The State and Its People* (St. Paul: Minnesota Historical Society Press, 1989);

L. Edmond Leipold, *Cecil E. Newman: Newspaper Publisher* (Minneapolis: T. S. Denison, 1969);

Gordon Parks, *A Choice of Weapons* (New York: Harper & Row, 1966);

Carl T. Rowan, *Breaking Barriers: A Memoir* (Boston: Little, Brown, 1991).

Papers:

A complete collection of the *Timely Digest,* the *Minneapolis Spokesman,* and the *St. Paul Recorder* is at the Minnesota Historical Society, St. Paul.

James Ottaway

(8 July 1911 –)

Joel Kaplan
Syracuse University

MAJOR NEWSPAPERS OWNED: *Endicott* (New York) *Bulletin* (1936–1960); *Oneonta* (New York) *Daily Star* (1944–1970); *Stroudsburg* (Pennsylvania) *Daily Record* (1946–1970); *Plattsburgh* (New York) *Press-Republican* (1952–1970); *Danbury* (Connecticut) *News-Times* (1956–1970); *Middletown* (New York) *Times Herald-Record* [merger of *Middletown Daily Record* and *Middletown Times Herald*] (1959–1970); *New Bedford* (Massachusetts) *Standard-Times* (1965–1970); *Cape Cod* (Massachusetts) *Standard-Times* (1965–1970); *Sunbury* (Pennsylvania) *Daily Item* (1970).

James Haller Ottaway, Sr., turned his 1936 purchase of a New York semiweekly into a small chain of medium-sized but immensely profitable newspapers that he sold to Dow Jones in 1970 for $37 million in stock. By the 1980s Ottaway's worth had skyrocketed to more than $250 million as he earned a prominent place on the *Forbes* list of the four hundred wealthiest Americans. None of Ottaway's papers was known for exceptional editorial quality – a Pulitzer Prize was never awarded to an Ottaway newspaper.

However, the Ottaway newspapers always strove to be close to the small communities they served, and most turned out to be enormously profitable. After Dow Jones bought the chain, Ottaway began to serve on the company's board of directors, engineering the purchase of ten additional community newspapers. In 1984 Ottaway retired from the board of directors of Dow Jones and Ottaway Newspapers, but he continues to serve as an acquisition consultant to Dow Jones.

Ottaway was born in St. Clair Shores, Michigan, on 8 July 1911, the son of the cofounder of the *Port Huron* (Michigan) *Times-Herald*. Elmer James Ottaway, who died in 1934, had purchased the Michigan daily in 1900. Jim Ottaway cut his teeth at the paper during his high-school and college years, beginning as a paper boy and later serving as the newspaper's classified, and then national, advertising manager.

He attended the University of Michigan in Ann Arbor but decided to transfer south for the climate after suffering from nephritis. Ottaway chose to finish his bachelor's degree at Rollins College in Winter Park, Florida. He majored in journalism and became editor of the college weekly newspaper, the *Sandspur*. While there he met the newspaper's features editor, Ruth Blackburne Hart. Ottaway was graduated in 1933, and the following year he and Ruth were married.

Following his marriage Ottaway spent eighteen months as vice-president and general manager of the *St. Petersburg Times*. His father had acquired a 20 percent interest in the newspaper in 1930 when he agreed to pay off a one-hundred-thousand-dollar newsprint debt owed to the International Paper Company. Elmer Ottaway had also negotiated an option to purchase the entire newspaper, but after his death the family decided to sell their stake. After leaving Florida, Ottaway spent six months working as the classified manager for the *Grand Rapids* (Michigan) *Herald*. The newspaper was owned by U.S. senator Arthur Vandenberg.

Following that stint, Ottaway began building his newspaper empire. Through a series of clever acquisitions bankrolled in large part by his mother, Ruth, he was able to purchase several small and medium-sized newspapers that blossomed under his directorship. The first of these acquisitions was the *Endicott* (New York) *Bulletin*. The selling price for the semiweekly was $56,250. Ottaway and his wife put down $22,500 and agreed to pay the balance to the newspaper's former owner, Harry J. Freeland, at 5 percent interest. At age twenty-five Ottaway became the newspaper's president-treasurer, while his wife became its secretary.

One of Ottaway's first objectives was to boost circulation. That way, he figured, he could turn it into a daily. Ottaway estimated that he needed a paid circulation of at least seven thousand to justify going to a daily. Within a year he met that goal, raising three thousand subscriptions.

James Ottaway with his wife, Ruth, during the early 1950s

"We harped on concise writing," Ottaway wrote years later in explaining the initial success of the *Endicott Bulletin.* "We harped on thorough local news coverage, all the local art that we could get through our ancient engraving department, and an editorial page that spoke out on local, state, national and world issues." Nevertheless, running a newspaper during the Depression, particularly one that was substantially in debt, was not an easy task. And the first two years under his stewardship saw increasing debt. The newspaper survived only because of an influx of cash from a local bank and the willingness of Ottaway's mother to provide the necessary money when the bank ultimately called the note.

By 1939 the newspaper had begun to show a profit, and as the United States prepared for World War II, the Endicott economy began to come alive. Continuing, substantial profits followed for the newspaper until 1960, when Ottaway reluctantly closed the newspaper because it had been overrun by the explosive growth of the nearby *Binghamton Press.*

During World War II, Ottaway was a lieutenant in the U.S. Navy, serving from 1943 to 1945. While stationed in Philadelphia, Ottaway was approached by newspaper broker Allen Kander, who wanted to know whether Ottaway would be interested in owning a second newspaper once the war ended. The paper he had in mind was the nine-thousand-circulation *Oneonta* (New York) *Star.*

The paper, owned by Francis A. Lee, was located in the northwest corner of the Catskill Mountains. Ottaway agreed to put down $50,000 for the newspaper and pay the remainder over the next twenty years at 4 percent interest. Once again, he received most of the money for the down payment from his mother. By the end of the decade, his long-term debt exceeded $350,000.

Kander later approached Ottaway with another deal that looked too good to let go. The owner of the seven-thousand-circulation *Stroudsburg* (Pennsylvania) *Daily Record,* who had purchased the newspaper in 1944, discovered that the federal tax on his investment exceeded his ability to pay, and he had to sell the paper. During the summer of 1946 Ottaway came to his rescue and agreed to purchase the paper for two hundred thousand dollars plus a fifty-five-thousand-dollar bonus to the owner, Edward J. Breece, if he would agree not to start or purchase a competing newspaper. This time Ottaway financed the entire purchase with a combination of long- and short-term loans. As the 1950s began

Ottaway owned three small, but profitable, newspapers. And he carried a substantial amount of debt.

By the end of that decade, Ottaway would purchase four daily newspapers, three in New York and one in Connecticut. His long-term debt would more than triple, to nearly $1.4 million. During the 1950s, Ottaway also began his long-standing association with the American Press Institute (API), an organization based at Columbia University designed to train and teach newspaper executives. That, perhaps, was Ottaway's most significant contribution to the newspaper business. He was always a strong believer in training sessions for his employees and would often hold groupwide seminars. Around that time the API was struggling to expand from an organization that simply trained editorial personnel to one that encompassed all aspects of newspaper operations, from advertising and promotion to circulation.

In 1959 Columbia University president Grayson Kirk appointed Ottaway to the API Advisory Board, a leadership role in the industry he would hold for more than three decades. By 1968 Ottaway had obtained the advisory board chairmanship and thus became instrumental in API's decision to sever its ties with Columbia University, move to Reston, Virginia, and become an independent, nonprofit educational organization.

Ottaway remained as chairman of the advisory board until 1978 and became a major force in raising the $2.6 million needed for the API's new building in 1974. Six years later he led the fund-raising for an additional $1.9 million to enlarge the API headquarters. After stepping down as API chairman, Ottaway remained on the board of directors until 1984 and even in retirement retains close ties to the institution. His leadership in the API, where he still serves as chairman of the Bequest Committee, has not gone unnoticed. Inside the API headquarters lobby is a bronze plaque dedicated to Ottaway, which states, "His foresight, leadership and dedicated effort contributed immeasurably to the construction of this building and to the American Press Institute."

In 1959 Ottaway began negotiation for a medium-sized newspaper that would turn out to be the flagship of his chain. The *Middletown* (New York) *Times Herald* was owned by Ralph Ingersoll, who also owned the nearby *Port Jervis Union-Gazette*. The newspapers were located in Orange County, sixty miles north of New York City. Ottaway became interested in the Middletown newspaper because of the growth potential of the area and the failure of the local newspapers to put out a substantive product.

Ottaway faced only one problem – the competition of the *Middletown Daily Record*. But he was in luck: the owner of the *Daily Record*, Jack Kaplan, had wanted for years to purchase the *Times Herald*. When he failed to acquire it from Ingersoll, he approached Ottaway. Seeing that Ottaway was unwilling to part with his new acquisition, Kaplan agreed to sell him the *Daily Record* for what he had put into it, $1.5 million. Ottaway paid Kaplan three hundred thousand dollars with the remainder to be paid over the next twenty years at 2.5 percent interest. Ottaway remarked, "While the price is high, I do not feel it is an unreasonable price to pay in order to consolidate the newspaper field in the prosperous Middletown market."

The purchase of the *Daily Record* was the lead story in the 19 April 1960 issue of the newspaper, and the fourth paragraph stated: "Mr. Ottaway said that all three Orange County newspapers will continue to publish separately and that – with the exception of several management positions – no changes in personnel are contemplated." But before long Ottaway decided that for efficiency purposes, only one Middletown newspaper could survive, and he decided it should be the *Daily Record*, whose circulation grew to twenty thousand, while *Times Herald* circulation remained at thirteen thousand. The merger took place within five months, and one week afterward circulation of the *Times Herald-Record* stood at twenty-three thousand.

About this time, Ottaway was also looking for a new headquarters for his growing media empire. With the Endicott newspaper about to shut down, he turned his attention to Orange County, which was within a day's drive of all his newspapers. By June 1961 the Ottaways had found the perfect property in Campbell Hall. They paid fifty thousand dollars for the Strasser estate, located on five and a half acres atop a small mountain. The house was built in 1916 and the addition, which became Ottaway's office, four years later. The Ottaways built another addition in 1962, and Ottaway became one of the few executives whose home and business were in the same location.

In 1965 a newspaper broker informed Ottaway about some attractive properties in New Bedford and Cape Cod, Massachusetts, including two daily newspapers, four radio stations, and a 55 percent interest in a television station serving parts of Massachusetts, Connecticut, and Rhode Island. Ottaway was intrigued. The volume of business for those properties exceeded the entire volume for the Ottaway empire. They were well-established, profitable companies that were dominant in their areas.

James Ottaway, Sr., with his son James, Jr., the chairman and chief executive officer of
Ottaway Newspapers

The first offer Ottaway made was for $10.3 million, with $3 million down and the remainder on an installment plan. The offer was rejected; the owner wanted cash.

Ottaway turned to a banker friend and was able to secure a $12 million loan. His final offer was $12.5 million cash for all the properties, excluding the television station. The offer was accepted, and Ottaway was pleased to learn he had beat out the *Boston Globe,* Gannett, and Hearst. He sent his son, James, Jr., who had been associate publisher in Danbury, to take over as publisher and general manager in New Bedford. Other newspapers became available over the ensuing years, but Ottaway's debt had skyrocketed, and his leverage had reached its limit. Ottaway's chain of nine daily newspapers and several radio stations was an attractive target in an industry noted for its explosive growth and profits at that time. During the 1960s Ottaway was approached by at least three other media conglomerates. He turned down the preliminary offer from Whitney Communications as well as a more specific offer from Speidel Newspapers, based in Reno, Nevada. He also rejected overtures from Gulf and Western Industries.

The Dow Jones approach was much different. It did not propose a merger or a takeover. Rather,

President William F. Kerby told Ottaway, Dow Jones was more interested in a marriage. It wanted to develop a different part of its media empire by moving into small and medium-sized markets. The company first approached Gannett, but when that did not work out, it became interested in Ottaway. Ottaway's son was reluctant to enter into any agreement with Dow Jones. He feared that the Ottaway chain would lose its autonomy and that Dow Jones would emphasize profits at the expense of editorial quality. But he also saw a positive side to it – having each family member become an instant millionaire.

Ultimately the elder Ottaway became sold on Dow Jones and its executives; he was willing to merge. For their interest in Ottaway Newspapers, the family received more than 914,000 shares of Dow Jones stock. Based on the market price when the deal was struck, the value of the sale was in excess of $35 million. Dow Jones agreed to maintain Ottaway Newspapers as a separate entity and retain its name and its headquarters at Campbell Hall. James, Jr., would be president of the subsidiary, and James, Sr., would be chairman.

Dow Jones also offered James, Sr., an employment contract. He was to be paid ninety-five thousand dollars a year for six years and then retire. But he was to remain affiliated with the newspapers in a consultant capacity for life and was also given a seat on the Dow Jones board of directors. At the time of the merger, Ottaway was also elected to the Associated Press board of directors, though he was defeated during his reelection attempt two years later.

One aspect of Ottaway's empire that ended with the Dow Jones merger was his radio stations. Along with acquiring nine newspapers before the merger, Ottaway also purchased three radio stations. But Dow Jones did not want to get involved with a regulated medium and specifically said the radio stations could not be a part of the deal. Instead of selling those stations on the open market, Ottaway decided to allow the longtime executives of the stations to purchase them for a special price. He sold the stations for less than half of their market value as a form of thank-you to his employees.

The merger with Dow Jones did not stop the growth of the Ottaway empire. Ottaway was able to use his ability to pick choice newspapers in small markets with impunity. He set his sights in 1971 on the *Sharon* (Pennsylvania) *Herald,* an afternoon daily with a circulation of twenty-six thousand. The price was $4.5 million, but Ottaway engineered a stock exchange. Each share of the newspaper's stock would be exchanged for four shares of Dow Jones stock. The following year, the *Record-Eagle* in Traverse City, Michigan, became the eleventh member of the chain, at a cost of $3.9 million – this time in cash. Of that, $1 million came from Ottaway Newspapers, and $2.9 million was borrowed from Dow Jones.

Soon thereafter, Ottaway moved west, spurred on by a suggestion from a Dow Jones executive that the *Medford* (Oregon) *Mail Tribune* could be had. Of all the newspapers Ottaway had gone after, the *Mail Tribune* had the most illustrious background, having won the Pulitzer Prize in 1934 for public service. This time the price was $7.35 million. Next came the *Joplin* (Missouri) *Tribune* for $12 million in 1976. Two months before that Ottaway retired as chief executive officer of Ottaway Newspapers and was succeeded by his son. That year Ottaway, Sr., also became one of the first two publishers to be installed into the New York State Publishers Association Hall of Fame.

By the mid 1970s Ottaway was in semiretirement, but he remained as chairman of the Ottaway subsidiary, keeping a lookout for interesting properties. In 1977 he spotted a small chain of community newspapers in Essex County, Massachusetts, known as the Essex County Newspapers. They included the *Daily Times* of Gloucester, the *Times* of Beverly, the *Times* of Peabody, and the *Daily News* of Newburyport. Their total circulation was thirty-six thousand. This acquisition cost $10 million. He later consummated a deal for newspapers in southern Minnesota that he had been after for some time and then purchased the *Ashland* (Kentucky) *Daily Independent.*

In the 1980s Ottaway Newspapers turned toward California and purchased the afternoon *Santa Cruz Sentinel.* The Dow Jones subsidiary also purchased a 20 percent stake in the Riverside newspapers, fifty miles east of Los Angeles. In April 1984 Ottaway retired from the Dow Jones board of directors. The following month he stepped down from the board of directors of Ottaway Newspapers. Later that month, without input from Ottaway, his newspaper group acquired the afternoon *Sun City* (Arizona) *News-Sun.*

Although he is retired, Ottaway maintains an office in Campbell Hall. His two sons have carried forth his newspaper tradition. James, Jr., is chairman and chief executive officer of Ottaway Newspapers, and David is a journalist with the *Washington Post.*

References:

William F. Kerby, *A Proud Profession: Memoirs of a Wall Street Journal Reporter, Editor and Publisher* (Homewood, Ill.: Dow Jones–Irwin, 1981);

Charles A. King, *Ottaway Newspapers: The First 50 Years* (Campbell, N.Y.: Ottaway Newspapers, 1986);

Jerry M. Rosenberg, *Inside the Wall Street Journal: The History and the Power of Dow Jones & Company and America's Most Influential Newspaper* (New York & London: Macmillan, 1982);

Lloyd Wendt, *The Wall Street Journal: The Story of Dow Jones & the Nation's Business Newspaper* (Chicago: Rand, McNally, 1982).

Alicia Patterson

(15 October 1906 – 2 July 1963)

Robert F. Keeler
Newsday

MAJOR POSITIONS HELD: Editor and publisher, *Newsday* (1940–1963).

SELECTED PERIODICAL PUBLICATIONS – UNCOLLECTED: "The Case Against Wechsler," *Bulletin of the American Society of Newspaper Editors* (1 September 1952): 1–2;

"This Is the Life I Love," as told to Hal Burton, *Saturday Evening Post,* 231 (21 February 1959): 19–21, 44–45, 50–51.

Alicia Patterson reluctantly became a newspaper publisher in 1940 because her new husband wanted to keep her busy and out of trouble, and because she wanted to show her father that she could be as good a journalist as he was. From that timid start she created the most successful new daily newspaper of the postwar period.

The phenomenal growth of *Newsday* – from a makeshift plant in a former auto dealership to a position of direct competition with the *New York Times* in New York City – depended on two major sociological and managerial factors. One was the stunning population growth on Long Island in the years after World War II, when the combination of returning veterans and astute developers created the archetypal American suburb in Nassau and Suffolk counties, east of New York City. The other was an almost incomprehensible lack of vision by the leaders of the established New York dailies (including Patterson's father), who failed to foresee the dimensions of that growth and took no effective steps to profit from it.

Those factors created the opportunity, and Patterson had the right combination of feistiness and journalistic instincts to take advantage of the opening. So, at its heart, the history of *Newsday* is the story of Patterson's personal growth, from a talented but aimless young woman into a great journalist – a process that depended heavily on her relationship with the two most important men in her

Alicia Patterson, 1942

life: her father, Joseph Medill Patterson; and her third husband, Harry Frank Guggenheim.

It was perhaps inevitable that Patterson would become a journalist, since the driving force in her life was the desire to please her father, and the dominant reality of his family was newspapering. That tradition went all the way back to 1819, when her great-great-grandfather James Patrick set up a small weekly, the *Tuscarawas Chronicle,* in New Philadelphia, Tuscarawas County, Ohio.

Her great-grandfather was Joseph Medill, a Canadian-born lawyer who married Patrick's daughter Katharine. He left the law and took up journalism, starting with the *Coshocton* (Ohio) *Whig,* then the *Cleveland Leader,* and finally the foundering *Chicago Tribune.* From this bully pulpit he espoused the abolitionist cause, trumpeted the virtues of a young country lawyer named Abraham Lincoln, and played a major role in getting Lincoln elected to the presidency. He also served a brief term as mayor of Chicago, after the Great Fire of 1871.

If Joseph Medill was the patriarch of the *Tribune* dynasty, his daughters, Kate and Elinor (Nellie), were the agents of its perpetuation. Kate married Robert Sanderson McCormick, the nephew of Cyrus Hall McCormick, the inventor of the reaper and the owner of the *Chicago Times,* Medill's competitor. Nellie married Robert W. Patterson, Jr., the son of an influential Chicago minister. The younger Patterson had decided against the ministry, gone into journalism, and risen to an influential position at the *Tribune.* With a sharp eye on the future of the dynasty, each sister pointedly named her first son after the patriarch. Kate's was Joseph Medill McCormick, and Nellie's was Joseph Medill Patterson.

From childhood Joseph Medill Patterson felt unworthy of his family's wealth. Riches did not do him much good at Groton, an exclusive prep school, where his classmates poked fun at his midwestern accent and his Little Lord Fauntleroy clothing. But the taunting toughened him and spurred him to rise above his lack of natural athletic talent to play football and baseball and row in the crew. He postponed his entry into college, spending months as a cowboy in Wyoming, then entered Yale in 1897.

Following his freshman year the restless Patterson unsuccessfully sought his father's permission to run off to the Spanish-American War. In 1900 he read about the Boxer Rebellion in China and decided to go, as a correspondent for William Randolph Hearst's papers in New York. By the time he arrived, the rebellion was over.

Upon graduation from Yale in 1901, Patterson went to work at the *Tribune,* covering the police beat and later writing editorials. In late 1902 he married Alice Higinbotham, whose father was a partner in the Chicago merchandising company Marshall Field. As he was preparing for his wedding to the daughter of a society figure, Patterson was campaigning against that society, running as a reformer for a seat in the state legislature.

Patterson took office in 1903. He later decided that his father had arranged the nomination in order to get his increasingly proletarian son out of town and away from the *Tribune.* So Patterson left the legislature and went back to work at the *Tribune,* where his views clashed sharply with his father's.

In 1905 Patterson went to Russia to cover the start of the revolution, and his dispatches to the *Tribune* favored the revolutionaries. Soon after this radicalizing experience, he left the *Tribune* to join the progressive mayoral campaign of Judge Edward Dunne. When Dunne became mayor, he made Patterson his commissioner of public works. Patterson quickly took on Chicago department-store owners over working conditions in poorly ventilated bargain basements. He escalated his war on society when his father-in-law's employer, Field, died with a vast estate, which prompted Patterson to write an article for *Collier's* condemning the rich.

In 1906 Patterson became so disgusted with the establishment that he resigned from office and publicly proclaimed that he was a Socialist. That summer he published "Confessions of a Drone," a detailed account of his views, and announced that he was becoming a farmer. With his wife and his daughter, Elinor, he moved to a farm in Libertyville, near the Chicago suburb of Lake Forest.

At the height of Patterson's Socialist awakening, on 15 October 1906, his second child was born. As soon as he learned that this child was also a girl, his disappointment was so acute that he slammed the door and left the house. His third child turned out to be a daughter as well, Josephine. "He had wanted a boy, instead of three daughters in succession, and that meant one of the Patterson girls would have to be his substitute son," Alicia wrote later. Elinor was too withdrawn, well-behaved, and delicately beautiful, much like her mother. Josephine was too young. That left only Alicia.

So, from her earliest childhood Alicia went through a rigorous indoctrination into the ways of boys: riding horses, diving off high diving boards, fishing – whatever it took to please her father. "Father seemed to get a kick out of having me do dangerous things," she told a *New Yorker* interviewer. "In fact, what with one thing and another, I kept getting so scared that finally I wasn't scared of anything anymore." In a 1959 *Saturday Evening Post* article she said: "Long after I had grown up, father continued to exert an almost hypnotic influence on me. I would have died rather than fail him. . . . Psychiatrists may suggest that pa felt an ambivalence toward me, a mixture of love and hate, a desire to test my nervous system to the snapping point. All I know is that he helped to make me unafraid."

Even before she was five years old, her parents had her doing something that few parents expect of such a young child: studying German in Berlin, along with Elinor. Despite the complication of ear surgery, Alicia survived the experience, but Elinor turned out to be much better at languages. In addition, Alicia felt that Elinor was prettier and more ladylike. "When company came Elinor was dressed up and brought downstairs. I stayed on the nursery floor and peered through the banisters [*sic*] like some little wild animal, watching and hating every minute of the gaiety below," she wrote. Patterson continued:

> Father must have sensed my misery, for one day he saw me sitting on a floor and he asked me if I wouldn't go for a walk with him. It was the most wonderful invitation I had ever had. From that day on, I would have walked around the earth if he had asked me to. . . . I became his slave and I would wait crouched on the top of the stairs when he would come home of an evening. Then with a hoop and a holler I would hurl myself down the steps and into his arms. Obviously my abject devotion pleased him and he began to take an interest in me.

Her father had many other interests during her formative years, however. In 1908 he ran the presidential campaign of the Socialist candidate, Eugene V. Debs. Patterson wrote prolifically from a Socialist perspective, including a novel, *A Little Brother of the Rich* (1908), which became a play in 1909, and another play, *The Fourth Estate* (1909). When he saw how little change socialism brought about, however, he became disenchanted.

In 1910, when his father died, Patterson took control of the *Chicago Tribune,* along with his cousin Robert Rutherford McCormick. The two cousins served in World War I, even though Patterson was an isolationist. After the war ended, Patterson founded the *New York Daily News,* a pioneering American tabloid, on 26 June 1919. Before the end of 1925 its circulation had soared past one million. That year Patterson moved to New York, leaving his wife and daughters behind in Chicago, and leaving the *Tribune* in the care of his cousin.

As Alicia was growing up, she demonstrated that she was her father's daughter in more ways than one. Just as he had gone his own way in school, she exercised her right to be different. She was bright enough, but she seemed to devote more of her energy to getting around the rules than to studying.

She attended the University School for Girls, near Chicago's Oak Street Beach, and later studied at Les Fougères, a boarding school in Lausanne, Switzerland. The students there were not allowed to speak English. Elinor obeyed this rule, but Alicia

was more slipshod. She also got around a rule banning English-language books by asking her father to send them. "There are millions of books I want to read," she wrote him; he sent her what she wanted.

Despite her willingness to break rules, her roommate at Les Fougères thought she was quite talented. "She was intelligent, and she was very well read and very critical and had a very fine sort of analytical mind," Marian Brown remembered. In fact, Brown thought, "she could have really amounted in the academic world to a great deal." While Alicia was at Les Fougères, she began expressing interest in the family business. Her father had mentioned the Columbia University Graduate School of Journalism to her in a letter, and she wrote: "I am awfully interested in that journalism school and would like to go there awfully."

From Les Fougères, her next stop was Saint Timothy's School in Catonsville, Maryland. Her marks were good, but she soon got herself expelled "for general obstreperousness." She then went to Foxcroft, in the hunt country of Virginia, which she enjoyed because she loved riding horses. She adjusted well and was graduated second in her class in 1924.

That fall, just before her eighteenth birthday, she attended a European finishing school, Miss Risser's School for Girls, in Rome. On 4 November she cabled her father: "Complications. Six girls expelled. . . . Cable money for passage. Distressed." She and several of her friends had left the school at midnight, had persuaded Miss Risser's driver to take them to a café for cocktails, and had climbed back over the wall. "I guess I must have some wild blood in my veins," she wrote her father in an apologetic letter.

Once she had been expelled, she wandered the Continent with her mother, her sister Josephine, and a tutor, who took them to see many museums and cultural spots in Europe. The following year, at the age of nineteen, she debuted at a grandiose Chicago coming-out party that marked, in effect, the end of her education and the beginning of the rest of her life. "Her education is rather sketchy," her father wrote. "She has a good enough mind, but put it on bridge and horses."

A few months after her debut Patterson took a typing course and went to work, at the age of twenty, at the *Daily News,* "in the corner clipping out filler items from other newspapers for use in the *Sunday News,*" she recalled. Her responsibilities were slight, but watching her father run the newspaper was useful: "He was geared with invisible antennae that alerted him to the shifting moods of the times.

He changed the *News* so that it reflected and appraised those moods." Her father got out among the people, noticing what interested them and what they were reading, which gave him an accurate sense of what people wanted in their newspaper.

Unfortunately, his example was not enough to save Patterson from making a disastrous mistake. In reporting on a divorce she mixed up the names in the story and caused a libel suit. Her father invited her to lunch in a fancy restaurant, where he fired her – on the theory that this was the best thing for her.

After a brief time at loose ends in Chicago, Patterson received a marriage proposal from James Simpson, Jr., whose father was a Marshall Field executive. From the start she seemed singularly unenthusiastic about marrying Simpson, but she did it anyway, in 1927. Even as she sailed to Europe on her honeymoon, she wrote her father, asking him to join them. In England the newlyweds disagreed so vehemently that she sent for a friend, Janet Chase, to join them. A year later Patterson left Simpson.

Although her honeymoon was contentious, it did help her journalistically. While they were in England, she wrote an article on fox hunting for *Liberty,* a magazine that her father had started in 1924. Later, as she embarked on a series of postmarriage adventures – including learning how to fly and hunting kangaroos in Australia – she wrote about these for *Liberty.* During this period she hunted, set women's speed records in flying, and generally enjoyed life. Then, in late 1931, she married again.

Patterson's second husband, Joseph W. Brooks, was a sportsman and pilot fifteen years her senior. Brooks handled the insurance for the *Daily News,* and he was a hunting and fishing friend of her father, who was responsible for their meeting. They began their marriage with an aerial tour of the South, and while they were away, her father bought land and outfitted a house for them in Sands Point, a wealthy community on the North Shore of Long Island.

Her father also offered her a chance to come back to work at the *Daily News.* He suggested that she try the advertising department. She responded that she preferred the editorial side, but added: "The main thing is I want to learn the newspaper game backwards and forwards. Who knows? I might be a great publisher myself some day."

This marriage lasted longer than the first. Patterson enjoyed hunting and fishing with Brooks and admired his physical courage and charm. In time, however, she began to feel that he was too aimless, and she grew weary of paying his gambling debts. "I began to feel restive about a life based on sports," she said. "Joe and I grew apart." That was when she met and began to fall in love with one of her Sands Point neighbors who was also at the end of a second marriage: Harry Frank Guggenheim.

By the time Alicia met him, Guggenheim had already compiled an impressive list of accomplishments. His family had come to America to escape anti-Semitism in Switzerland and had made a fortune in mining and smelting. Guggenheim had gone into the family business as an executive of Chile Copper, then had served as a naval officer in World War I. After the war his father, Daniel Guggenheim, had expressed a wish to give something back to America, and Harry had guided that philanthropic urge toward the development of the fledgling American aviation industry.

Under Harry's guidance the family's money had set up a model airline and weather service, established six schools of aeronautical engineering, paid for Charles Lindbergh's cross-country tour after his flight to Paris, bankrolled the world's first instruments-only flight, and supported Robert Goddard's rocketry experiments, which later led to the American space program. Guggenheim had also served as ambassador to Cuba from 1929 to 1933. In his lighter hours he had begun to build a thoroughbred racing stable, Cain Hoy, named after his South Carolina plantation, where he raised cattle and timber.

By contrast, Patterson had accomplished little more than a few magazine articles, a handful of women's flying records, some hunting trophies, and two failed marriages. In other ways, too, they could not have been more different. She was a Franklin Roosevelt liberal; he was a Herbert Hoover–Alfred Landon conservative. She was flighty and devil-may-care; he was stultifyingly serious. She had always gotten whatever money she needed from her father and had no real fiscal sense; he was shrewd and cautious with money. He was nearly forty-nine; she was not yet thirty-three.

Despite these differences, in 1939 they divorced their spouses and were married. Immediately Guggenheim began looking for something to keep her busy. Journalism seemed like a natural choice. Her father had told her that he would someday leave her in a position of power at the *Daily News,* and Guggenheim wanted her to run her own newspaper as training for that role. They asked one of her father's friends, *Daily News* circulation director Max Annenberg, to help them find a suitable newspaper to purchase.

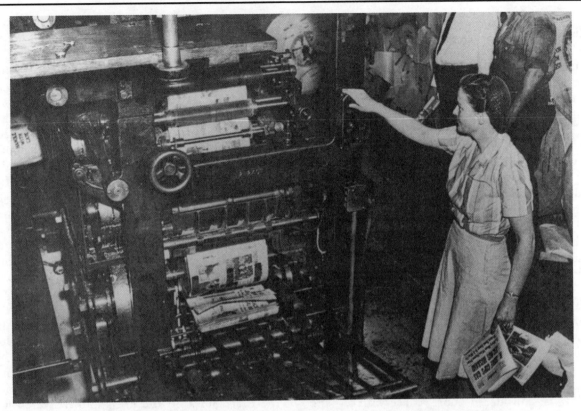

Patterson operating the press on the first day of publication for Newsday, *3 September 1940*

While they were on their honeymoon at Goddard's rocket laboratory in New Mexico, they received a telegram from Annenberg, informing them of the availability of a small newspaper plant in Hempstead, the business hub of Nassau County, just east of New York City. At this time her family was an American newspaper dynasty. Her father ran the *Daily News*. His cousin Robert McCormick dominated the *Chicago Tribune*. His sister, Cissy Patterson, owned the *Washington Times-Herald*. But Alicia Patterson was not ready.

"I had terrible inferiority feelings," she said later. "I didn't think I had anything." At this crucial moment her new husband performed a great service for her by insisting that they go through with the purchase. "I refused to be shaken by her plea to forget all about it," Guggenheim wrote.

They commissioned a survey of Nassau County in order to determine whether it could support a second daily paper, in addition to the *Nassau Daily Review-Star*, a stuffy, lifeless broadsheet whose primary distinction was its slavish devotion to the monolithic Nassau County Republican party. Its publisher, James E. Stiles, was a Republican committeeman and close ally of the county Republican leader, J. Russel Sprague. In fact, Stiles was so loyal

that when Sprague instructed him not to expand the paper's circulation into northern Nassau County, he complied. That left an important territory ripe for potential competition.

William Mapel, a public-relations executive and former journalism professor, conducted the survey with the help of Stanton Peckham, a one-time foreign-service employee with brief journalistic experience. The weakness of the *Review-Star* and the growth potential of Nassau County made them both excited about the prospects for a new newspaper. But Mapel, concerned that their report would sound too optimistic, toned it down. The report, dated 23 January 1940, modestly predicted: "By the end of the second year the paper should have a paid circulation in Nassau County of 15,000 copies daily."

So, on 5 April 1940 Harry Guggenheim agreed to the purchase, for about fifty thousand dollars, which bought a dusty collection of equipment located in a rented building that had been an auto dealership. The plant briefly had been the home of the *Nassau Daily Journal,* the only newspaper ever established by S. I. Newhouse. It had opened on 1 March 1939, but Newhouse had shut it down on 10 March in order to avoid a labor dispute over the distribution of the *Journal* that threatened to spread to his flagship, the *Long Island Press*.

At the time of the purchase neither Patterson's friends nor Newhouse thought that she was likely to stick with the challenge for long. "I thought she'd see it as a toy, something to play with for a while, and that eventually I'd be able to buy it back from her," Newhouse said. But Peckham saw past the "Alicia's toy" theory and into her heart: "The burning ambition she had, all she gave a damn about, was to prove to her goddamn family – and she would call them her goddamn family – that she was just as good a newspaperman as any of them."

Patterson's less-than-serious reputation was not her only obstacle. At the start she had to confront a daunting list of tasks for a woman with no executive experience, such as getting the mothballed plant ready for operation, hiring a staff, finding a name, and designing the paper. On the question of design she faced disagreement with her own father, a proven journalistic genius. "I favored a tabloid despite discouragement from my father, who thought a standard size paper would be more acceptable in a suburban community where the population is considered more conservative," she wrote. That was strange advice, coming from the founder of the most successful tabloid in America. She ignored him and began designing a tabloid with the help of Fred Hauck, a commercial artist who had married her childhood friend Janet Chase.

The design that they chose replaced the traditional vertical format with a horizontal one and eliminated the column rules, giving the paper a brighter, less cluttered look. They also did away with the pyramid system of stacking ads, which packed newspapers with dozens of little fillers, mixing ads and editorial copy in the same column. Instead, they created a cleaner, magazine-style design, with each column containing either all ads or all editorial copy.

As to staff, Patterson hired Mapel as general manager and Peckham as his assistant. Peckham became her factotum, handling details ranging in importance from buying chairs to hiring employees. Some were veterans of other papers, while some were inexperienced, such as copyboys from the *Daily News* who became reporters for the new paper. The staff's strength was its enthusiasm. "In a way," said one young reporter, Norman Lobsenz, "putting that paper together in those days was sort of like Judy Garland and Mickey Rooney sitting around and saying, 'Hey, kids, let's put on a show.' "

Patterson's major personnel decision was the hiring of a veteran *Daily News* editor, Harold Davis,

as the managing editor, on the recommendation of Annenberg. This was just one example of her reliance on help from the *Daily News* in her paper's infancy. During the newsprint shortages of World War II, she often had to borrow rolls of that precious commodity from her father's paper.

At the same time that she was establishing the staff, Patterson had to find a name for the paper. Mapel and Peckham decided to make it a contest, but they nearly despaired of getting any useful entries. Patterson, apparently half in jest, told Mapel about a suggested name that had come from one of her friends, the artist Neysa McMein, who wanted to call the paper the "County Irritant." So Mapel came up with his own suggestion, *Newsday,* and brought it to Patterson. "A light began shining in her eyes," he recalled. Then all they had to do was find contestants who had submitted similar suggestions.

The paper rolled off the presses for the first time on 3 September 1940, filled with typographical errors, misplaced captions, and other glitches. "I'm afraid it looks like hell," Patterson said. Without even noticing the mistakes, Peckham took one of the first copies off the press and delivered it by hand to Joseph Medill Patterson at the *Daily News*.

One of Alicia Patterson's great disappointments in the early years of *Newsday* was her father's apparent lack of interest. Although he allowed his staff to help her in many ways – except for his refusal to let her run *Daily News* comic strips – he did not display much enthusiasm for *Newsday*. At a lunch with Joseph Patterson one of his staff, Hal Burton, asked about her. "He said, 'Oh, she's all right. She's got a little paper out in Hempstead, but it isn't going anywhere,' " Burton said.

In a letter that she wrote her father in 1943 after the *Daily News* abruptly stopped running "Deathless Deer," the comic strip that she and McMein had created for *Newsday,* Patterson complained bitterly about her father's attitudes: "When I started Newsday I thought you would be proud and happy that I was trying to follow your lead. But it took the greatest persuasion to get you even to look at the plant. And you never take any interest anymore in anything I do."

Her relationship with her father was deteriorating for several reasons. One was the birth of her half brother, James Patterson, the son of Joseph and his aide, Mary King, who became his second wife. Once Joseph had a son, his daughter felt that he no longer acted as if he had much need for her, the substitute son. "I know that he is the only thing in your life that matters; that to have a son has always been your one ambition," she wrote, "Well I couldn't help being a girl. And I tried to overcome the handicap." Another source of friction was her marriage to Guggenheim. Joseph Patterson had not been happy when she divorced his friend Brooks, and he had been even less pleased when she married a Jew.

On top of all this, politics came between them. Throughout the Depression, Patterson had steadfastly supported Roosevelt, even when other papers, including the *Chicago Tribune,* attacked him. But at the end of 1940 Roosevelt proposed a lend-lease bill to allow him to provide war supplies to England. This enraged the isolationist Patterson, and he turned on Roosevelt with a vengeance. For much of World War II, Joseph, his sister, and his cousin were known as "the three furies of isolationism" because of their relentless attacks on Roosevelt. But Alicia Patterson stood her ground, and *Newsday* continued to support the president.

In addition to her disagreements with her father, Patterson also faced the often thorny task of negotiating with her exacting husband. Financially Guggenheim was in a position of total power, and she was completely dependent. He had paid the entire purchase price of the paper and advanced money to get it started. Her only equity was a four-thousand-dollar "participation" that he had given her. He was the owner and president, and she was the chief employee. "You will devote your time to the publication of *Newsday* in the capacity of editor and publisher without salary," Guggenheim wrote, in a letter typical of his financial directives to his wife. "In lieu of salary, you are to receive one-half of the net profits to me from *Newsday* that may accrue in any calendar year."

Although he wrote her frequent memos about her fiscal responsibilities, for the most part he left the journalism to her. It was clear, however, that this would always be a difficult balancing act. Within weeks after the first issue of *Newsday,* for example, they wrote opposing columns about the presidential campaign. She supported Roosevelt, and he backed Wendell Willkie. That would not be the only such editorial schizophrenia.

Once America entered the war, the relationship between Guggenheim and his wife changed geographically. He rejoined the navy and was assigned to command a naval air station in New Jersey. That left her to cope with the wartime problems of newsprint and staff shortages. As the government drafted the men, their replacements were often women. Throughout her career she encouraged women at the paper, long before the rise of

Artist Neysa McMein and Patterson working on "Deathless Deer," a comic strip they created for Newsday

feminism – though she never appointed a woman to a top editorial post. "The best thing that ever happened to me professionally was working for Alicia Patterson, a woman who believed that a woman reporter could do anything," said Bonnie Angelo, who came to *Newsday* in 1953.

While Guggenheim was away, Patterson showed on several occasions that she could confidently run the paper on her own. One such instance was her battle with the *Review-Star.* The Republicans had loaded its coffers by awarding it government legal ads, which Stiles made even more lucrative by using larger-than-usual type. *Newsday* argued editorially that this was costing the taxpayer extra money and that *Newsday* could run the ads cheaper. After relentlessly pounding both her rival paper and the ruling Republicans, she broke the *Review-Star* monopoly on the ads, obtaining a share of them for *Newsday.* That was the beginning of the end for the *Review-Star,* which was falling behind *Newsday* in circulation. It folded in 1953.

She also made a significant personnel decision during the war years, revolving around Alan Hathway, a makeup editor at the *Daily News* who was a friend of Harold Davis, her managing editor. Hathway began to do part-time makeup work at *Newsday,* and in 1942 he became city editor. In early

1944 Davis left to go back to the *Daily News,* and Patterson elevated Hathway to managing editor.

Hathway was loud, crude, and often drunk, a figure directly from the 1920s school of high-energy, low-ethics journalism immortalized in the play *The Front Page* (1928), by Ben Hecht and Charles MacArthur. He was a man of egregious excess, and Patterson often failed to rein him in as tightly as she should have. But for the next quarter century, Hathway's energy and doggedness played a major role in lifting *Newsday* above the level of a small country newspaper to exert a profound influence on its community.

In the postwar period Hathway led a crusade to provide adequate housing for veterans. The Republicans saw the veterans as New York City Democrats and were in no hurry to import more of them to Long Island. Hathway joined forces with a developer, Levitt and Sons, which proposed to build cheap, mass-produced housing. They planned to build on slabs, without basements, but the town of Hempstead required basements in all new homes. *Newsday* pounded the drums until Hempstead changed its ordinance, and the Levitts built a community that became known as Levittown, which started the phenomenal growth of Long Island. *Newsday* profited heavily from that growth, selling ads to all the merchants who wanted to sell homes, appliances, and cars to the wave of new residents.

For Patterson, the most profound event that followed the war was the death of her father, who had achieved his caustic wish of outliving Roosevelt, then had descended in a spiral of uncontrolled drinking. He did not, as he had once promised his daughter, leave her a position of power at the *Daily News.* But he did leave her money, which enabled her to write Guggenheim a letter asking him to sell her a share of the paper that she had been running for six years. In reply, he wrote her: "As you know, I desire to retain a controlling interest in the enterprise, and accordingly I am prepared to sell you a 49 percent interest in NEWSDAY, which, on the overall value of $165,000, comes to $80,850."

For the rest of their marriage, that 2 percent was a source of constant contention. Guggenheim's personality required that he have control, and Patterson chafed under his domination. That dispute exacerbated the problems in their marriage. It had been an odd match from the start, and the physical aspect of their relationship had begun to cool within a few years. Then, soon after her father's death in 1946, another complication arose: Adlai E. Stevenson.

Patterson had first known Stevenson when she was a young woman in Chicago. There are even some accounts that he proposed marriage to her. "They enjoyed each other's sprightly minds," said Stevenson's sister, Buffie Ives. "She was one of the first girls he was in love with." But Stevenson had married Ellen Borden, one of Patterson's classmates. He had become a lawyer, worked in the Roosevelt administration, become a leader of the internationalists in the debate over isolationism before World War II, and come to New York in late 1946 as a representative to the first United Nations General Assembly. It was about then that he and Patterson crossed paths again.

In the years that followed — as her marital problems continued and Stevenson's own marriage ended in divorce in 1949 — and for many years after that, Patterson and Stevenson developed and sustained a relationship of great warmth and intimacy. In its early years that relationship seems to have included sexual intimacy. Whether that is true or not, their friendship was remarkable not for its physical dimension, but for its constancy and intellectual depth. Stevenson admired Patterson and relied on her judgment as his career turned from diplomacy to politics, and he contemplated running for governor. In her own marriage her political views contrasted sharply with her husband's, but Patterson's political views were compatible with Stevenson's, and he relied strongly on her advice as he began to navigate Illinois politics.

Over the years the chief obstacle to their friendship was geography. After his brief stay at the United Nations, he was in Illinois, and she was in New York. They managed to meet occasionally — at his farm in Libertyville, near the farm where she had grown up; in Chicago; at the governor's mansion in Springfield; and at her hunting lodge in Georgia. But their primary means of communication was the mail. Although only a handful of Patterson's letters to Stevenson survive, she preserved a large collection of his letters to her. These have been a crucial source for his biographers, partly because they provide a window into his relationship with Patterson, but more significantly because he trusted her so much that he confided in her his deepest thoughts about politics and life.

This profound friendship caused Patterson serious problems during the 1952 presidential campaign. Since shortly after World War II, she had been editorially urging Gen. Dwight Eisenhower to run for the presidency. *Newsday,* in fact, had played a role in a rally on Long Island and another at Madison Square Garden in Manhattan, which finally

Patterson, William McCormick Blair, Jr., and Adlai Stevenson during Stevenson's 1952 presidential campaign

helped persuade Eisenhower to run. But then President Harry Truman decided not to run for reelection and tried to persuade Stevenson to run in his place. Stevenson was torn between remaining governor and seeking the presidency, and he sought Patterson's advice in his letters. It was in a letter to Patterson, in fact, that he first hinted that he might accept a draft.

Once Stevenson decided to run for president, Patterson faced a dilemma. She could hardly back down from her often-repeated support for Eisenhower, but she loved Stevenson. So the *Newsday* editorials reflected this duality: "We feel that the country needs a change of administration, needs a Republican President – in short, needs Eisenhower. Nevertheless, an honest appraisal of Adlai E. Stevenson makes clear that if the nation prefers another Democrat, Stevenson will make a magnificent President."

Throughout the campaign the editorials maintained this evenhanded approach. Although Patterson could not endorse Stevenson over Eisenhower, she did help her friend in other ways. She sponsored a dinner for Stevenson at a New York restaurant, for example, to introduce him to influential publishers. Guggenheim did not attend, but he sent a telegram that made his own position clear: "Tell Adlai how sorry I am not to be able to dine with him. I would like to dine with him anywhere – even in the White House – if we are both guests of Ike."

Soon after the dinner Patterson entered a hospital, and doctors discovered that she had colon cancer. But she was back at her desk when *Newsday* ran the editorial endorsing Eisenhower, closing with a recommendation that, if he won, Eisenhower should appoint Stevenson to run the UN delegation. When Stevenson lost, she sent him a conciliatory telegram. He later responded: "Don't worry about *Newsday*. I had hoped, of course, but I also understand your situation vis a vis Harry." In 1951, when she had told him she was contemplating divorce, Stevenson had counseled her not to be hasty.

When Stevenson ran again in 1956, Guggenheim assumed that his wife would again endorse Eisenhower, and he confidently made that prediction to his friend Leonard Hall, chairman of the Republican National Committee. But she shocked him by endorsing Stevenson. A struggle for editorial control followed at *Newsday;* Guggenheim and Patterson both used attorneys. The legal discussions continued while she was in Africa, on a tour with Stevenson and other friends. At the end of 1957 she typed out a resignation statement:

We have prospered rather than suffered under the theory that journalistic independence and integrity precede balance sheets and business considerations. However in recent months – at the peak of Newsday's success – Harry Guggenheim has increasingly attempted to take control over the journalistic product which he formally can control by virtue of his 51% stock interest.

My choice was painfully simple. I could stay and preside over the gradual disintegration of those journalistic principles which I believe have made Newsday. I have chosen to resign because I cannot be a part of transforming a living newspaper put out by journalists into a balance sheet controlled by businessmen.

In the end, though, Patterson backed down and decided to stay. That decision did not, however, end the friction with her husband. In the next presidential campaign, they once again differed sharply.

Once it was clear that Stevenson could not obtain the Democratic nomination for a third time, Patterson decided to support Senator John F. Kennedy for the presidency. Guggenheim strongly preferred Richard M. Nixon. During the campaign she ran editorials for Kennedy, and he wrote columns for Nixon. At the end of the race the editorial page featured a signed note from Patterson: "The opinions of this newspaper are expressed in the editorial column. Today we endorse John F. Kennedy for President of the United States. . . . In a column on the opposite page my husband, Harry F. Guggenheim, president of Newsday, states his personal endorsement of Vice President Richard M. Nixon for President."

Long Island profited from Patterson's choice. Once Kennedy was in the White House, he invited her and her aide, William Woestendiek, to have lunch with him there. During the lunch she argued against the use of Mitchel Field, a former air force base near Newsday, as a general-aviation airport. At that lunch Kennedy called Najeeb Halaby, administrator of the Federal Aviation Administration, and instructed him not to pursue the use of the base as an airport. Patterson's personal diplomacy with the president made that prime land available for other purposes, such as a campus for Nassau Community College. In the years after that lunch Newsday carried hundreds of stories about the controversies surrounding the use of the land.

That was not the only example of Patterson changing the shape of Long Island. On another occasion she thwarted the plans of Robert Moses to build a road the length of Fire Island. Moses was one of the sacred cows at Newsday, and he originally got support for this road from Hathway, who owned property on Fire Island. But many people felt it would have been an environmental disaster, and they managed to persuade Patterson. Once Newsday turned against the idea, it was dead. "She really did represent Long Island," said her friend Phyllis Cerf Wagner. "She felt so fiercely about it,

as if she'd grown up there. . . . It was her child, as the newspaper was her child."

Patterson was an ever-present parent to that child. She knew most of her employees by name, starting at the little plant in Hempstead and even when they moved into a plant built especially for Newsday in Garden City. She was often in the newsroom, with her glasses perched on top of her head. And when Newsday needed a firm hand, she applied that too. For example, right after the paper won its first Pulitzer Prize – in 1954, for an investigation of corrupt labor leader William DeKoning, Sr. – she refused to let the paper rest on its laurels. Instead, she reached out to hire people with a more cosmopolitan view of the world, such as Time magazine journalist Richard Clurman, who had written the cover story about her and Newsday after the Pulitzer Prize. In that period she pushed to professionalize the paper in many areas, such as the handling of copy at night.

As a journalist she had excellent instincts and a fine sense of a good story. As a manager she showed some strange quirks. She made Clurman her "editorial director," for example, giving him control over the editorial pages and the Washington bureau – an odd construct that in effect narrowed Hathway's power. Hathway had served her well in the paper's early years, but she was apparently reluctant to let him control the paper's national coverage and image. Throughout her career she kept a "palace guard" of journalists who worked closely with her and stood somewhat outside the normal chain of command. She also had some editorial pet concerns, such as protection of the whooping crane. Even though she was a hunter, she was a great lover of animals, and the paper reflected that by running many animal stories.

The one thing that Patterson did not seem able to master was marriage. Her relationship with Guggenheim was strained throughout most of their time together. Still, in his own way he had high regard for her. Despite all their conflicts, he intended to leave her in his will the thing she wanted so much: majority control of Newsday. He had every reason to believe that he would die before she did, since he was sixteen years older. But in 1963 she suffered from an ulcer. Rather than alter her lifestyle, she opted for surgery. After the operation doctors could not stop her bleeding, and she died on 2 July 1963 at the age of fifty-six.

During her lifetime she and Guggenheim agreed that Newsday should remain a Long Island paper and not venture into New York City. But after her death – and after Guggenheim sold the paper to the Times Mirror Company – *Newsday* started a New York City paper, which put it in direct competition with the paper that her father founded, the *Daily News.* She had always wanted to show her father that she could be a good journalist. The irony is that, long after both Pattersons were dead, *Newsday* and the *Daily News* were competing in the same high-stakes game.

"She was the greatest newspaperman I've ever known," said Jack Mann, one of her editors. "I don't know if she could dictate a lead on a fire, or write a 5/42 italic headline, but in spirit, she was the best newspaperman I've ever known."

References:
Joseph Medill Patterson Albright, "Joseph Medill Patterson: Right or Wrong, American," Undergraduate thesis, Williams College, 1958;
Jack Alexander, "Vox Populi," *New Yorker,* 14 (6 August 1938): 16–21; (13 August 1938): 19–24; (20 August 1938): 19–23;
John Chapman, *Tell It to Sweeney: The Informal History of the New York Daily News* (Westport, Conn.: Greenwood, 1961);
Richard Clurman, "Alicia in Wonderland," *Time,* 64 (13 September 1954): 52–58;
John H. Davis, *The Guggenheims: An American Epic* (New York: Morrow, 1978);
Joseph Gies, *The Colonel of Chicago* (New York: Dutton, 1979);
Ralph Hausrath, "The Early Days of *Newsday,*" *Long Island Forum* (July 1975): 128–135; (August 1975): 148–155; (September 1975): 170–178;
Hausrath, "*Newsday*: The Postwar Years," *Long Island Forum* (January 1979): 4–11;
Paul F. Healy, *Cissy: A Biography of Eleanor M. "Cissy" Patterson* (Garden City, N.Y.: Doubleday, 1966);
Alice Albright Hoge, *Cissy Patterson: The Life of Eleanor Medill Patterson, Publisher and Editor of the Washington Times-Herald* (New York: Random House, 1966);
Edwin P. Hoyt, Jr., *The Guggenheims and the American Dream* (New York: Funk & Wagnalls, 1967);
Kenneth T. Jackson, *Crabgrass Frontier: The Suburbanization of the United States* (New York: Oxford University Press, 1985);
Walter Johnson and Carol Evans, eds., *The Papers of Adlai E. Stevenson,* volumes 1–8 (New York: Little, Brown, 1972–1979);

Robert F. Keeler, *Newsday: A Candid History of the Respectable Tabloid* (New York: Morrow, 1990);
Eric Larrabee, "The Six Thousand Houses that Levitt Built," *Harper's,* 197 (September 1948): 79–88;
Milton Lehman, *This High Man: The Life of Robert H. Goddard* (New York: Farrar, Straus, 1963);
Anne Morrow Lindbergh, *Bring Me a Unicorn* (New York: Harcourt Brace Jovanovich, 1972);
Lindbergh, *Hour of Gold, Hour of Lead* (New York: Harcourt Brace Jovanovich, 1973);
Lindbergh, *War Within and War Without* (New York: Harcourt Brace Jovanovich, 1980);
Charles A. Lindbergh, *Autobiography of Values* (New York: Harcourt Brace Jovanovich, 1976);
Milton Lomask, *Seed Money* (New York: Farrar, Straus, 1964);
John Bartlow Martin, *Adlai Stevenson and the World* (Garden City, N.Y.: Doubleday, 1977);
Martin, *Adlai Stevenson of Illinois* (Garden City, N.Y.: Doubleday, 1976);
Ralph G. Martin, *Cissy: The Extraordinary Life of Eleanor Medill Patterson* (New York: Simon & Schuster, 1979);
Leo E. McGivena, *The News: The First Fifty Years of New York's Picture Newspaper* (New York: News Syndicate, 1969);
Porter McKeever, *Adlai Stevenson: His Life and Legacy* (New York: Morrow, 1989);
Gwen Morgan and Arthur Veysey, *Poor Little Rich Boy* (Carpentersville, Ill.: Crossroads, 1985);
Harvey O'Connor, *The Guggenheims: The Making of an American Dynasty* (New York: Covici-Friede, 1937);
Burton Rascoe, *Before I Forget* (New York: Literary Guild, 1937);
John Tebbel, *The Story of the McCormicks, Medills and Pattersons: An American Dynasty* (Garden City, N.Y.: Doubleday, 1947);
Edward Uhlan, *Dynamo Jim Stiles: Pioneer of Progress* (New York: Exposition, 1959);
Frank C. Waldrop, *McCormick of Chicago* (Englewood Cliffs, N.J.: Prentice-Hall, 1966);
Charles Wertenbaker, "The Case of the Hot-Tempered Publisher," *Saturday Evening Post,* 223 (12 May 1951): 36–37, 113–115, 117–118.

Papers:
Patterson's papers are collected at *Newsday.*

Eugene Patterson

(15 October 1923 –   )

Alf Pratte
Brigham Young University

MAJOR POSITIONS HELD: South Carolina bureau manager (1948–1949), New York City night bureau manager (1949–1953), London bureau manager and chief U.K. correspondent (1953–1956), United Press; executive editor (1956–1960), editor (1960–1968), *Atlanta Journal* and *Constitution*; managing editor, *Washington Post* (1968–1971); professor of political science, Duke University (1971–1972); editor and president, *St. Petersburg* (Florida) *Times,* (1972–1988); editor and president, *Congressional Quarterly* (1972–1988); chief executive officer, St. Petersburg Times Company (1978–1988).

Eugene (Gene) C. Patterson is one of a group of southern-born journalists who served as spokesmen for an enlightened South. In his jobs as reporter and bureau chief for United Press in New York and London – and as managing editor, executive editor, editor, and chief executive officer for newspapers in Atlanta, Washington, D.C., and Saint Petersburg, Florida – Patterson helped to promote minority rights, quality writing, ethical awareness, editorial outspokenness, and heightened standing of editors as publishers. A World War II veteran and descendant of Confederate soldiers, Patterson served as a symbol of the editors who demanded an end to the South's segregation laws and influenced opinion on the Vietnam War.

Patterson was born in Valdosta, Georgia, on 15 October 1923, the son of William C. and Annabel (Corbett) Patterson. As a youngster Patterson worked on the family farm, but he was more interested in the *Adel News,* a weekly newspaper in the Cook County seat, where he read proofs and ran errands. He also worked on his high school newspaper.

After graduation from high school he attended North Georgia College in Dahlonega from 1940 to 1942 and was editor of the campus newspaper. He was graduated from the University of Georgia with an A.B. in journalism in 1943. During World War II he served as a tank platoon leader with the

Eugene Patterson

Tenth Armored Division of Gen. George Patton's Third Army. Patterson was awarded a Silver Star and a Bronze Star with Oak-Leaf Cluster for actions during Patton's counterattack at the Bulge and his charge across Europe.

After the war Patterson accepted a commission in the regular army, completed flight training, and became an army aircraft pilot. In 1947 he resigned as an army captain and obtained a job with the *Temple* (Texas) *Daily Telegram.* He soon returned to Georgia where he reported for the *Macon Telegraph,* then joined United Press in Atlanta. In 1948 he was named UP manager for South Carolina, where he met his wife, Mary Sue Carter, a Virginia-born reporter for the *Columbia Record.* They were

236

married on 19 August 1950 and had one daughter, Mary Patterson Fausch.

From 1949 to 1953 Patterson served as the night bureau manager for UP in New York City, where he renewed his friendship with an army buddy, James J. Flood, who had fought with him in Europe and had come home to be a Bronx policeman. "Gene," Flood said, "if you'd have thought to make an honest living – you'd make a good Bronx cop."

Patterson was next assigned to England, where he served three years as UP London bureau chief. He is remembered for the lead he moved when Ernest Hemingway staggered out of a Uganda jungle after surviving a plane crash: "Ernest Hemingway came out of the jungle today, carrying a bunch of bananas and a bottle of gin." Patterson said that he had the good fortune to pluck this journalistic gem out of the detail in a stringer's cable from Entebbe.

Patterson returned to Georgia in 1956 as executive editor of the *Atlanta Journal* and *Constitution*. Ralph McGill at the *Constitution* was a leader of the progressive editors who had been trying to nudge the South toward a more moderate approach to racial integration. In June 1960 Patterson was named editor of the *Constitution* after McGill was appointed publisher. Jack Tarver, then president of the Atlanta newspapers, described Patterson's new job as "playing right field after Babe Ruth."

Despite the handicap, Patterson duplicated McGill's feat of writing a column seven days a week, plus editorials. He covered the final years of Winston Churchill as Britain's prime minister, the first manned spaceflights from Cape Canaveral, and the Democratic and Republican national conventions from 1960 through 1968. In 1965 the London *Times,* in a series on American newspapers, wrote, "Patterson enjoys serving as a lightning rod on what he regards as one of the last great revolutions in the country."

In addition to his newspaper responsibilities, Patterson was active in community, state, regional, and national activities. In 1966 U.S. Secretary of Commerce John T. Connor appointed him as a member of the National Public Advisory Committee on Regional Economic Development. The twenty-five-member committee was set up to provide expert counsel to the department on problems of local and regional development. In announcing Patterson's three-year appointment, Connor said, "His writings have helped millions of Americans better to understand happenings throughout the

world. He is an outstanding leader in journalism and in public service."

The regional appointment was a minor one, however, compared to Patterson's tenure as vice-chairman of the U.S. Civil Rights Commission from 1964 to 1968. Hearings held by the commission and the reports it released played an important role in the adoption of the Voting Rights acts of 1965. Patterson was also one of the leading editors who encouraged newsrooms to become more diverse in hiring. As noted in the ASNE (American Society of Newspaper Editors) proceedings, he aimed "to guide us as a profession in meeting the needs of American minorities, not waiting to be prodded, but acting because it's right."

In 1967 Patterson was awarded the Pulitzer Prize for editorial writing, marking the fourth time the *Constitution* had received the top journalistic honor. It had won in 1931 for its campaign against municipal corruption and twice in 1959, for McGill's editorial writing and for investigative reporter Jack Nelson's campaign for mental health reform.

Patterson was one of the first to protest the Georgia legislature's 1965 refusal to seat Julian Bond. The refusal was not because of Bond's race; other Georgia legislators were black. However, Bond was a dissident, a critic of U.S. policy in the Vietnam War and the Selective Service law.

In one of his prizewinning editorials, Patterson analyzed the critical moment at which the legislature decided to disqualify Bond. As Patterson predicted in the editorial, Bond's case was taken to court. Although the legislature's action was upheld in the lower courts, the U.S. Supreme Court held that Bond was entitled to his seat. At that time Patterson wrote:

> Net results of this controversy, which the Legislature never should have initiated, have been to make Julian Bond famous, spread his views, revive the Student Nonviolent Coordinating Committee and damage Georgia's claims to being a State of wisdom, justice or moderation. That was a mighty poor return on one day's blowoff in the Legislature.

In a 1968 article for the *Masthead* of the National Conference of Editorial Writers, Patterson described the power of editorials and the role of southern editors in breaking down prejudice:

> The race issue in the south was editorially muffled for many years. The primary contribution of editors like Hodding Carter, Ralph McGill and Lenoir Chambers lay not so much in convincing all southerners that segre-

gation was wrong; they obviously failed, had that been their purpose. Primarily, they encouraged people to talk about it – to break the muffling silence, to stop fearing discussion of it, to speak the unspeakable and think the unthinkable, and to realize it was a subject they could argue. This breaking of silent fear, this beginning of talking and thinking, is the goal an editor shoots for in a frozen situation where minds have ceased to question. The editorial doesn't have to be right. But it does get things done.

In addition to being on the cutting edge of the civil rights movement, Patterson was one of the editors who foresaw the space age as one of the most powerful news stories of the twentieth century. As one of five speakers led by Vice-president Lyndon B. Johnson, chairman of the National Aeronautics and Space Council, Patterson addressed his fellow editors at the annual meeting of the ASNE in 1962. He described a world in which a new breed of scientists made calculations in sixty-five ten-millionths of a second.

"To me the greatest story that can be told is to celebrate man when he is, as he so rarely is, worth celebrating," Patterson told his fellow editors. "It is to me the most powerful news story of the 20th century." According to John Strohmeyer of the *Bethlehem* (Pennsylvania) *Globe-Times* Patterson received a standing ovation for his remarks: "Most editors had been emotionally unprepared for the commitment of man in space. This was the day more than any other one became a believer that man was on his way to the moon."

Patterson was also actively involved in the freedom of information movement, which had been led mainly by the ASNE since the end of World War II. In a report of activities on behalf of freedom of the press in the mid 1960s, Patterson told the editors of their responsibility to continue raising the alarm over government intrusion. "When the press relaxes and quits playing Chicken Little, we'd better worry lest we chicken out," he warned.

Patterson also began to have second thoughts about U.S. involvement in Vietnam. In 1967 he traveled to Vietnam as part of a presidential mission. One of his seatmates was another editor, John S. Knight of Knight Newspapers, who described Patterson as "my kind of man, who fears neither the truth nor his adversaries. He is a great editor, a staunch friend, a formidable adversary, and excellent company."

In 1968 Patterson left the *Constitution* for Washington, D.C. where he was named managing editor of the *Washington Post* by owner Katherine Graham and executive editor Benjamin C. Bradlee.

Patterson resigned from the *Constitution* after a dispute with the company president, Jack Tarver, over a column written by B. J. Phillips that was critical of the Georgia Power Company for raising rates. When Tarver denounced Patterson for printing the column, he quit on the spot, later stating that the incident was simply a culmination of several clashes in which he found Tarver "unacceptably abusive."

During his three years in Washington, Patterson did not fall into the plans of Bradlee, however. One editor recalls that Patterson was in an impossible position: "At news conferences, he just stayed on the edge. All he could do was agree with Ben." According to Tom Kelly in *The Imperial Post* (1983), Patterson asked Bradlee to loosen control of him, but that was not the problem. Bradlee just did not give Patterson any authority. In *The Washington Post: The First 100 Years* (1977), Chalmers M. Roberts comments that Patterson never found the rough-and-tumble competitiveness of Bradlee's shop to his taste. As executive editor, Bradlee continued to be, in effect, managing editor. He could find no really different role. Patterson also sensed hostility from others below him who had hoped for the job.

Looking back on his *Post* years, Patterson said, "Bradlee needed a managing editor like a boar needs tits." "That is not quite right," Bradlee responded. "Any editor with brains needs Patterson . . . if only to tell him that the South will rise again, that Agnew had something when he carped about eastern effetes, and that we northern boys can't sing worth a goddamn."

Before leaving Washington, Patterson also gained national attention for modifying his position on Vietnam. Columnist Nicholas von Hoffman described the night that Patterson walked among Vietnam veterans bivouacked on Independence Mall:

> This time they came to march on the Capitol and return the medals by throwing them on the marble steps. Gene, the news man, the editor, the father, the citizen and the old soldier had to go down and talk to those young soldiers spending the night in pup tents and sleeping bags.

Von Hoffman related how Patterson said that he thought the young veterans illegally parked on the mall were making the same fight for peace he wished he had gone on making as a young man. Von Hoffman concluded that he never thought the ASNE, an organization in which Patterson had been active since the 1950s, would make such a fine man its president. "Not that I approve," he added. "Patterson has been misleading the public for years by giving newspapers a better reputation than they deserve."

Patterson was at the *Post* when that paper and the *New York Times* refused to buckle under to threats from President Richard Nixon's administration about publishing the Pentagon Papers. When the Supreme Court threw out a government case against the newspapers, Patterson jumped up on a newsroom desk with the flash: "We win, and so does the *New York Times!*"

In 1971 Patterson moved for an academic year to the faculty at Duke University, where he taught political science. He also directed press studies at Duke's Institute of Policy Science and Public Affairs. In 1972 Nelson Poynter named him as his successor as editor and president of the *St. Petersburg* (Florida) *Times* and its Washington publication, *Congressional Quarterly.* The aging Poynter recalled that Patterson was the only editor whom he felt could make the most of the freedom and independence he had to offer.

Patterson succeeded Poynter as chief executive officer in charge of the companies upon Poynter's death in 1978. In that capacity Patterson became one of the few editors in the country whose publisher reported to him. He had total responsibility for the entire operation but took his title as editor seriously. He conducted editorial conferences most mornings, and on Fridays he closed his door for two hours – the only time he closed it – to turn out a Sunday column that read as if he had spent the entire week crafting it. He composed on a video display terminal, being the first *Times* executive to educate himself in electronic editing – the first step toward computerizing the whole operation.

Executive editor Robert Haiman reported that Patterson "unflaggingly pushed his staff to write better – to restore literary quality to newspapers." Haiman also said that his boss was consistent about professional ethics, conflicts of interest, and conducting the affairs of the newspaper with the openness it demanded of public officials. When Patterson was arrested for driving while intoxicated after a Bicentennial celebration on 4 July 1976, he insisted that a report of it appear on page 1, despite the fact that the paper did not publish such stories there – and local news seldom appeared on the front page of the highly departmentalized *Times.*

Under Patterson, the *Times* won two Pulitzer Prizes, and the Times Publishing Company acquired *Florida Trend* magazine, a business journal, then launched *Georgia Trend* and *Arizona Trend.* In 1978 he directed the *Congressional Quarterly,* which covers the federal government, in starting a new magazine, *Governing,* to cover trends in state and local governments.

From 1977 to 1978 Patterson served as president of the ASNE. At the top of his journalistic agenda he set a goal of minority employment in the nation's newsrooms equivalent to the percentage of minority persons in the national population by the year 2000. He also occupied the leading edge of First Amendment and freedom of information initiatives; enunciated the need for a new dimension in U.S. reporting that would accompany investigative reporting with an emphasis on explanatory reporting devoted to making complex issues comprehensible to the public; supported national dialogues on ethical conflicts between the media and the law; and established the annual ASNE writing awards to emphasize quality writing in newspapers. Today the ASNE writing award is an institution, and a Pulitzer Prize is now awarded for explanatory journalism.

During this period Patterson also became involved in an ethical dilemma with his own newspaper and other publishers. The issue concerned whether newspapers should, contribute to a fund to purchase advertisements opposing casino gambling before a referendum on the question in Florida. Some publishers' and reporters' groups argued that such involvement was inappropriate and would harm the paper's credibility in covering the controversial issue.

Patterson was among the journalists who made a strong case for involvement, holding that the casino-gambling issue was not a political question but an effort to alter the values of Florida society. "I would hate to think newspapers are neutered as citizens by a pacifist mentality when rape is threatened," he remarked. "The magnitude of gambler's financing convinced me this is no time to be spooked by the hobgoblins of little minds. Advertisement of our own virginity scarcely responded to the threat."

Patterson was also the only member of the Pulitzer Prize Board to oppose Janet Cooke receiving a Pulitzer Prize in 1984 for her story of an eight-year-old cocaine user. Patterson told his colleagues that the story did not ring true, and he abstained from the vote. If the board had gone along with Patterson it could have been saved the embarrassment that resulted when the story was revealed to be a hoax pulled on the *Washington Post* editors.

In many speeches around the country, Patterson encouraged editors to begin looking upon themselves as potential publishers, so as to provide such enlightened proprietors as Knight, Poynter, and Otis Chandler with rounded candidates for the top job instead of "ceding it to the bean counters." He disabused editors of fears that they were mathematical illiterates and primed them to rule.

Patterson also worked hard to alter what he described as "the defensive crouch" of editors in regard to publishers and advertising managers and toward assertion of editorial values. He staked out an ASNE role in the Readership Council, which before that time had been only a well-funded entity of the American Newspaper Publishers Association and the National Advertising Bureau. In a letter to press commentator Leo Bogart, who later described him as a "high minded and high-spirited publisher," Patterson said: "A natural evolution of ASNE's interest, spanked along by opportunity and by Mother Necessity, propelled us off the bench and up to bat as self-designated hitters in the Newspaper Readership Project." Working closely with Michael O'Neill of the *New York Daily News* and William Hornby of the *Denver Post,* as well as ASNE project director Pete McKnight and Ruth Clark of the Yankelovich firm, Patterson helped involve editors to a major extent in setting directions of the industrywide improvement project.

In 1988 Patterson retired at age sixty-five from his positions with the *Times,* the Times Company, and all of its affiliated companies, as well as chairman of the board of trustees of the Poynter Institute for Media Studies in Saint Petersburg. In retirement he became a member of the board of trustees of Duke University and the LeRoy Collins Center for public policy at Florida State University. Patterson holds honorary degrees from thirteen institutions, including Harvard, Duke, Emory, Indiana, Oglethorpe, Mercer, Stetson, and Dillard Universities as well as Eckerd, Tusculum, and Roanoke Colleges, Tuskegee Institute, and the University of South Florida.

Patterson found himself in the news again in 1990 when he supported the successful efforts of his successor, Andrew Barnes, to fend off Texas tycoon Robert M. Bass in his attempt to take over the *Times.* According to *Washington Post* reporter Charles Trueheart, the struggle to protect the Saint Peters-burg paper from Bass evoked wide professional solidarity:

> The publisher of the Los Angeles Times, the Washington bureau chief of the New York Times and the national editor of the Washington Post are all former reporters of the St. Petersburg Times. Patterson and Barnes were editors at the Washington Post. Few reporting staffs do not boast at least one alumnus of the many professional seminars the Poynter Institute runs.

A colleague, Joe Parham, summed up Patterson as a "go-go man, a grounded astronaut, living life fully, and savoring every sweet moment. . . . A proud-of-his-home, his wife, his child, his dog man. . . . A gregarious man and come-by-for-a nightcap and don't leave sort of a guy. When his spring gets too tightly wound, he takes off for a Florida lake or a river or the Gulf to do some fishing. How relaxing that really is, though, is questionable." Parham wrote that Patterson is five-foot-seven, "with all hackles raised."

References:

Leo Bogart, *Preserving the Press: How Daily Newspapers Mobilized to Keep Their Readers* (New York: Columbia University Press, 1991);

Norman E. Isaacs, *Untended Gates: The Mismanaged Press* (New York: Columbia University Press, 1986);

Tom Kelly, *The Imperial Post: The Meyers, the Grahams and the Paper that Rules Washington* (New York: William Morrow, 1983);

Chalmers M. Roberts, *The Washington Post: The First 100 Years* (Boston: Houghton Mifflin, 1977); revised and enlarged as *In the Shadow of Power: The Story of the Washington Post* (Cabin John, Md.: Seven Locks Press, 1989);

Charles Trueheart, "A Newspaper Story: A Texas Takeover Tycoon Targets the St. Pete Times," *Washington Post National Weekly Edition* (12–18 March 1990): 9;

Nicholas von Hoffman, "The Night They Wore Old Gene Down," *ASNE Bulletin* (August 1977): 23.

Roger Peace

(19 May 1899 – 21 August 1968)

Mary Elizabeth Padgett
Greenville Piedmont

NEWSPAPERS OWNED: *Greenville* (South Carolina) *News* (1934–1968); *Greenville Piedmont* (1934–1968); *Asheville* (North Carolina) *Citizen-Times* (1954–1968).

While in his mid teens Roger Craft Peace became a newspaper writer, and that pursuit gave him the most satisfaction. His professional life soon centered more on newspaper management than writing, however, as he became the driving force behind the Greenville, South Carolina, newspapers that he had talked his father into buying. He used words precisely and took offense when others used them more loosely. He took pride in the work of others and was credited with molding the careers of many young writers and editors.

When he was twenty-one, Peace was named editor of the *Greenville News*; he became the paper's business manager when he was twenty-five. He ran the newspaper company after his father became ill in 1930, and he was officially named president and publisher of the Greenville News-Piedmont Company when his father died in 1934. He held those positions until his death in 1968, at which time he also held the title of chairman of the board of the newly formed Multimedia corporation.

As a newspaper publisher he was committed to serving his community by reporting the news fairly and completely while editorially and personally working for the growth and development of Greenville. Peace was a behind-the-scenes adviser to governors and senators and a patient confidant of the common man. He filled the unexpired term of U.S. senator James F. Byrnes in late 1941, when Byrnes was appointed to the U.S. Supreme Court.

Rather than pursue a promising political career, Peace chose to return to Greenville to run his beloved newspapers. Except for service in the army and three months in Washington as a senator, Peace spent his entire career in Greenville. He had faith that the South would prosper, and he spurned offers that would have made him a very rich man

Roger Peace (courtesy of Greenville News-Piedmont Company)

by selling the Greenville newspapers. He was adamant that control of the newspapers remain in the region.

Peace moved into the broadcasting field early in his career, when his newspaper company established Greenville radio station WFBC in 1932. A television station was added in 1953, and in 1954 Peace and his business associates bought The Asheville (North Carolina) Citizen-Times Publishing Company, which published the two Asheville newspapers and operated a radio station. Peace's reputation for publishing newspapers dedicated to serving their communities laid the groundwork for the acquisition of the Asheville newspapers. Peace was pleased that larger offers were declined because the Asheville owners were impressed with his community-oriented policies.

By 1968 Peace and his associates were ready to build the foundation for what would become one of the nation's largest and most profitable media companies. Multimedia was formed on 1 January 1968 through the merger of the Greenville News-Piedmont Company, the Asheville Citizen-Times Publishing Company, and Southeastern Broadcasting Corporation, which consisted of the radio and television stations in Greenville, Knoxville, Tennessee, and Macon, Georgia, and an Asheville radio station.

Peace had sown the seeds for a successful media company. A fiscal conservative, he believed in closely managed internal growth and strategic diversification. He also believed in hiring and cultivating key managers. These trusted managers and friends, beginning with J. Kelly Sisk, who immediately followed Peace at the helm of Multimedia, turned that fledgling media company into one of the country's major media corporations, with 1991 revenues of more than $524 million.

Multimedia began acquiring media properties, including more newspapers, almost immediately. From the outset the company's philosophy was to buy blue-chip properties in markets with well-balanced economies. In early 1969 Multimedia bought the *Montgomery* (Alabama) *Advertiser* and the *Alabama Journal.* By the end of the 1960s the corporation owned six daily newspapers, seven radio stations, and three television stations.

The 1970s was a boom decade for Multimedia, which offered its first public stock in 1971. Newspapers were purchased in Arkansas, Florida, Virginia, West Virginia, and Ohio, bringing the company's newspaper ownership to thirteen dailies and twenty-three nondailies. The newspapers have consistently received awards for excellence in their respective state-press competitions. Multimedia newspapers have also won three Pulitzer Prizes. Although the company's flagship newspaper, the *Greenville News,* has not won a Pulitzer Prize, it was a runner-up in 1992 for an investigative series on former University of South Carolina president James Holderman. Multimedia entered the 1990s with twelve daily newspapers and forty-nine nondailies, five television stations, eight radio stations, one hundred twenty cable-television franchises, and an entertainment production/syndication division best known for television talk shows featuring Phil Donahue and Sally Jessy Raphael.

This media giant would never have been founded had it not been for Roger Peace, son of Greenville printer Bony Hampton Peace and Laura Estelle (Chandler) Peace. His family was of Scottish, Irish, and English descent. Although the elder Peace actually bought the *Greenville News,* it was Roger who talked his father into purchasing the financially troubled newspaper.

A native of Tigerville, South Carolina, Bony Peace grew up in Spartanburg County. In 1885, when he was twelve years old, he decided to become a printer. One year later he was working as an apprentice at the *Carolina Spartan.* His skill and hard work attracted attention, and he was quickly promoted to foreman of the *Spartanburg Herald* composing room.

Three years later Peace moved to Greenville, where he obtained a job in a print shop. The elder Peace believed he owed the customer the best printing job at the promised delivery time. When the boss announced that the place would be closed for the Fourth of July holiday, Peace expressed his appreciation but declined the offer, adding, "I couldn't enjoy a holiday for thinking about [the missed deadlines], so I'll work tomorrow." Frank Barnes recalls the confrontation in *The Greenville Story* (1956). An argument ensued between Peace and his boss, and Peace resigned rather than betray his convictions. Instead of working in the print shop that holiday, he negotiated a lease for the job-printing department at the *News.*

At the turn of the century the *News* was struggling to make ends meet, as was its afternoon neighbor a few blocks away. The morning newspaper, founded in 1874 by A. M. Speights, had been owned by a stock company since 1888, of which Capt. Ellison A. Smyth had been the president and largest shareholder since 1903. The *News* continued to lose money, and in 1916 Smyth paid a visit to the enterprising man who operated the on-site printing company quite successfully.

Smyth asked Peace to become the part-time business manager for the newspaper, which Peace reluctantly agreed to do, since he was afraid the added responsibility would take too much time from his printing business. With the elder Peace on board, the *News* began to show a profit, and in 1919 Smyth made him an offer: "You are the only man who has been able to do anything with *The News.* Why don't you buy it?"

Peace detested debt, considered forty thousand dollars a staggering sum, and almost declined the offer. But his oldest son, Roger, filled with youthful optimism and a love for newspapers, urged his father to buy the morning daily. Roger had decided at an early age to pursue a newspaper career. In 1914, while still in school, he became a cub reporter for the *News*. From that time on, newspapers were Roger Peace's life. Upon finishing public schools in Greenville, he continued his education at Furman University but still worked for the newspaper. He was graduated from Furman with a B.A. in 1919, having taken time out following ROTC training in 1918 to be an instructor in the U.S. Army.

The only time Roger ever thought about leaving South Carolina was when his father hesitated at buying the *News*. Bony Peace returned home one night to find his eldest son sitting on a packed truck, ready to take off for faraway places unless his father bought the newspaper. Bony said that if Roger wanted the newspaper that badly, then he would buy it.

Roger became sports editor of the *News* in 1919, and in 1920 – the same year he married Etca Tindal Walker of Greenville – he became editor. He served as editor from 1920 to 1924, when he became business manager. Although he remained active in the editorial direction of the newspaper, Peace increasingly assumed more of the responsibilities for the business side of the operation. Under the Peace family the *News* prospered. By 1923 the newspaper had seen steady growth, becoming a true metropolitan journal, with a daily average of about eighteen pages, a daily circulation of about eighteen thousand, a work force of sixty-seven employees, as well as forty-two correspondents throughout the state serving the newspaper on a part-time basis.

The newspaper began to push for the progressive development of the Greenville community. It often published articles emphasizing the advantages of Greenville's climate and natural resources and proclaiming the community to be the best place in the world to live. The newspaper proved a catalyst for development of the region, including the great strides made in agriculture, the number of railroads built, the development of hydroelectric power, and the growth of textile mills.

Through both his newspapers and his civic activities, such as with the Greenville Chamber of Commerce, Peace worked tenaciously for the development and improvement of his community. While recognizing the importance of textiles, the area's dominant industry, he pushed for economic diversification, so, in the words of one editorial, "our general economy may not be tied solely to the fluctuating economies of one." He advocated a public audi-torium, a regional airport to serve the Upstate, and improvement of highways.

Other Peace sons also played roles in the newspaper company that would become permanently linked to their family's name. Charlie Peace, the second son, was born in 1904. He started as an office boy at the *News,* moving from proofreader to national advertising representative to top management. At his death in 1958 Charlie was vice-president and general manager of the company.

The youngest son, B. H. Peace, Jr., was born in 1906. His first job was delivering papers to soldiers at Camp Sevier during World War I. During the early 1930s he became president of WFBC radio and held that position until a new company was formed to include the television and radio operations. He returned to the newspaper company as an executive and was honorary chairman of the board of the News-Piedmont Company and a director of Multimedia when he died in 1974.

Roger, though, was the driving force behind the Greenville newspapers. In 1927 he talked his father into buying another Greenville newspaper, the afternoon *Piedmont*. At that time the *Piedmont* was struggling while the *News* was thriving. Both newspapers had roughly the same circulation – about 10,000 – when Peace bought the morning paper in 1919. By 1927, however, the circulation of the *News* had soared to almost 25,000, while that of the *Piedmont* had inched up to only 12,338. The afternoon newspaper – which traced its roots back to the Unionist *Greenville Republican,* founded in 1826 to oppose the secessionist movement – was losing money.

Roger credited his friend, colleague, and fellow Baptist, Judson Chapman, with first thinking of buying the struggling afternoon newspaper. Chapman, editor of the *News* and a man Peace described as "somewhat my alter ego," approached Roger about the purchase. Roger knew it would be hard to sell the idea to his father, even though the *News* had not only paid off its debt but also was sitting on a cash reserve of $100,000. The two young friends approached the owner of the *Piedmont,* B. E. Geer, and were told they could buy the afternoon newspaper for $160,000 in cash.

Without consulting his father, Roger went to Charleston to see Robert S. Small, president of the South Carolina National Bank. Peace was told he could borrow $175,000, more than was necessary, to be paid back in fifteen years. With the financing arranged, Peace approached his father about the offer to buy another newspaper. At first the elder Peace balked, but when Roger persisted, his father finally said, "Well, it didn't do me any harm before; so I'll go ahead."

The decision paid off, and much sooner than expected. National advertising was a much greater force in newspapers in those days, and the ownership of two newspapers allowed them to get national ads at a closed rate. The $175,000 loan was paid off in two years. Even the Depression, which came right on the heels of the purchase, did not cut into the profit.

In a signed editorial that appeared on the day of the purchase, the Peace family spelled out its philosophy on what a newspaper should be and what role their papers would play. They wanted to publish "a newsy paper, an accurate paper, an intelligent paper." They wanted the *Piedmont,* like its morning counterpart, to be "a newspaper of Greenville, by Greenville, for Greenville. It will be owned by Greenville men, published by Greenville men and edited by Greenville men. It will strive to be an active, forceful, persuasive instrument in the development of Greenville. It will seek to serve the people of Greenville first and foremost."

By 1930 Bony Peace's health had declined to the point that Roger was running the company. When Peace died in 1934, his eldest son became president and treasurer of the company and publisher of the two newspapers. Improvements took place at the newspapers during the late 1930s. The Broad Street annex to the *News* Building was completed in 1937. It housed the editorial departments, the composing room for both papers, and a large pressroom and mail room. The newspapers also upgraded their wire services.

The newspapers campaigned for better streets and parks, industrialization, and farming diversification. They attacked the growing centralization of the federal government and the waste of federal funds. The newspapers generally reflected a conservative philosophy, though not a predictable one. The *Piedmont,* which had been one of the few newspapers in the state to favor woman suffrage, fought for a divorce law and the right of women to serve on juries.

On the critical issue of racial integration, the Greenville newspapers spoke with what was a moderate voice for those times. Change was inevitable, the newspapers recognized, but it should come slowly, so as not to throw southern communities into chaos. Peace's afternoon newspaper hired a black correspondent in the early 1950s, becoming the second South Carolina newspaper to make that bold move – one that resulted in the *Piedmont* getting more than one bomb threat.

While Peace was building up his newspapers, he also was putting much of his time and energy into helping develop the Greenville community and the state that he so loved. At one time or another he headed every important community organization in Greenville, and he was on the boards of many business and financial institutions. He was a longtime trustee and financial chairman of Furman University. Various family members have contributed a total of $16 million for the construction and operation of Greenville's Peace Center for the Performing Arts.

Peace was also a trustee of the South Carolina Foundation of Independent Colleges, founded in 1954 by several of the state's leading businessmen to promote and raise funds for nine South Carolina private colleges and universities: Coker, Columbia, Converse, Erskine, Furman, Limestone, Newberry, Presbyterian, and Wofford. He was instrumental in organizing the Greenville County Foundation, which has supported many worthwhile causes in that community. He served as president of the Greater Greenville Chamber of Commerce from 1934 to 1935, and in 1936 he was president of the Community Chest of Greenville, the forerunner of the United Way.

Peace was a director of the Peoples National Bank, Greenville Community Hotel Corporation, and Piedmont and Northern Railway. He served as president of the South Carolina Press Association from 1938 to 1939 and was a director of the Southern Newspaper Publishers Association in 1935. His good friend Byrnes said he had never known Peace to ask of him "a favor for himself or his family, [but] now for Greenville, that's different."

In his later years Peace often told friends that of his many honors, there were two things in which he took paramount pride. First was his appointment in 1942 as chairman of the South Carolina Preparedness for Peace Commission. That group was formed to prepare for the state's industrial development following the war and to recommend governmental reforms. In 1945 the commission presented a comprehensive postwar plan for South Carolina, including a recommendation for the formation of the South Carolina Research, Planning and Development Board. By the time of his death the board was responsible for bringing hundreds of millions of dollars in industry to the state.

The other major source of pride to Peace was the establishment of an employee trust fund at the News-Piedmont Company. The fund represented Peace's concern for his associates (he never called them employees). A scholarship fund for the children of employees was established in Peace's name.

In his later years Peace regretted that his business and civic responsibilities had taken him away from his true love, writing. This was a man who, after all, had been neither class president nor class treasurer at Furman, but class poet. Toward the end of his life he often remarked that "no title meant more to me than 'Editor.' "

Etca Peace died in 1965, and their son, Roger, Jr., died in 1951. His second wife, Amy Schwartzenburg Peace, died of cancer in 1967, one year after her marriage to the publisher. Peace was survived by one child, Dorothy Peace Ramsaur, who in 1990 was a member of the Multimedia board of directors.

Upon Peace's death the responsibility for running the Greenville newspapers and the newly formed Multimedia corporation fell to his longtime friend and associate Sisk and his son-in-law Edmund A. (Ned) Ramsaur. Sisk had been involved with the newspapers since 1948, when the Greenville accountant became business manager and treasurer of the News-Piedmont Company and was elected a News-Piedmont director. He became president and chief executive officer of Multimedia shortly after Peace's death. By the time Sisk died in 1980, Multimedia owned eleven daily newspapers, four television stations, eleven radio stations, and several cable-television systems. He helped turn Multimedia into a multistate operation that ranked in size among the top twenty communications companies in the nation.

Ramsaur, a former capital correspondent, state editor, and associate editor of the *News,* became president and copublisher of the Greenville newspapers and was named president of Multimedia when Sisk became chairman of the board. A Greenville native, Ramsaur was director of the Southern Newspaper Publishers Association and a trustee of the Southern Newspaper Publishers Association Foundation. He died in 1976. After Sisk's death Multimedia was headed by Wilson Wearn. In 1992 Walter E. Bartlett was chairman and chief executive officer of the corporation.

In a 1992 speech Bartlett described the philosophy that had guided Multimedia as it had grown from one small, financially unstable morning newspaper into a successful media giant: "The business of communications is a business of constant change, and by recognizing and embracing changes, Multimedia has grown and prospered." That business philosophy emanated from Roger Peace, a newspaperman with keen intelligence, foresight, and business acumen.

References:

Nancy Vance Ashmore, *Greenville: Woven from the Past* (Northridge, Cal.: Windsor Publications, 1986);

Frank Barnes, *The Greenville Story* (Greenville, S.C.: Frank Barnes, 1956);

Mary E. Padgett, "History of the *Greenville Piedmont,*" Master's thesis, University of South Carolina, 1992;

Robert F. Stevenson, "History of the *Greenville News:* 1874–1950," Master's thesis, University of South Carolina, 1990.

Nelson Poynter

(15 December 1903 – 15 June 1978)

David C. Coulson
University of Nevada at Reno

NEWSPAPERS OWNED: *Clearwater* (Florida) *Sun* (1928); *Kokomo* (Indiana) *Democrat* (1928–1930); *St. Petersburg* (Florida) *Times* (1947–1978); *St. Petersburg Evening Independent* (1962–1978).

Nelson Paul Poynter built the small, financially troubled *St. Petersburg Times* into a large, robust daily ranked among the best in the country. He also emerged as one of American journalism's most conspicuous figures – a liberal in a conservative community, an innovator in an industry resistant to change, and a loner in a field increasingly dominated by newspaper chains.

Poynter was influenced by the less strident and more responsible press that began to emerge in earnest with World War I and accelerated with the Depression and World War II. His concept of his responsibility as a newspaper owner is traceable to his lifelong admiration of the idealism exemplified by Woodrow Wilson. Poynter's boyhood recollections carried the "ringing words," as he put it, of the president's doctrine of self-determination. Consequently, the focal point of Poynter's life was turning his newspapers to the causes of self-government.

The younger of two children, Poynter was born into the newspaper business in Sullivan, Indiana. His father, Paul Poynter, was the publisher of a string of ten small papers, including the *St. Petersburg Times*. The elder Poynter was an unrelenting prohibitionist crusader and ardent supporter of William Jennings Bryan. But he could not resist a promising business deal, and after he bought the *Times* in 1912, he devoted as much effort to amassing Florida real estate as to running the newspaper.

While barely in his teens Nelson worked as the sole reporter for the *Sullivan Times* (the other had been drafted because of World War I). He went on to Indiana University, where as editor of the student newspaper he crusaded against the Ku Klux Klan. At the end of his junior year, in 1923, he and Indiana graduate Ernie Pyle worked as reporters on the Scripps-Howard *Washington Daily News*. After

Nelson Poynter

graduation Poynter covered the 1924 Democratic National Convention for the *Indianapolis Star*. He then traveled abroad and worked for a time in 1925 as news editor on the English-language *Japan Times* in Tokyo. He earned a master's degree in economics from Yale University in 1927.

Over the next decade Poynter gained editorial and business experience on seven newspapers in Florida and the Midwest. While assistant general manager of the *St. Petersburg Times,* he bought the *Clearwater* (Florida) *Sun* in 1928 and sold it later that year for a profit. He also purchased the *Kokomo* (Indiana) *Democrat* from his father, but Depression-era debts forced him to sell it to his local competitor in 1930. The following year he went to work again for Scripps-Howard: first as an advertising salesman on the *Cleveland Press* and then once more on the *Daily News,* this time as advertising manager.

The chain promoted him in 1935 to editor and publisher of the *Columbus* (Ohio) *Citizen;* he was fired two years later for supporting President Franklin Roosevelt's "court packing" plan for the Supreme Court. He completed a brief stint as business manager for the *Minneapolis Star* before returning to Saint Petersburg as general manager in 1938. He became editor of the *Times* within a year and took the title of president of the Times Publishing Company in 1953.

Beginning in December 1940 Poynter worked in the federal government's wartime propaganda program – initially as codirector of the press section of the U.S. Communication Bureau in Washington. In the summer of 1941 he was chosen to help activate the new office of coordinator of information. The following year he was divorced by his first wife, Catherine Fergusson, after fifteen years of marriage. They had adopted two daughters, Nancy and Sally, his only children. In August of that year he married government-propaganda coworker Henrietta Malkiel.

A former editor at both *Vogue* and *Vanity Fair* magazines, she became associate editor of the *St. Petersburg Times.* The staff described "a remote figure in long, flowing skirts, dark stockings and large jewelry who periodically strode through the newsroom looking neither right nor left." Her homeliness and sharp intellect evoked comparisons with a controversial contemporary, Eleanor Roosevelt. She demonstrated a keen interest in the newspaper's coverage of politics, women, and culture and gained a detailed knowledge of Congress.

In 1945 she and Poynter cofounded *Congressional Quarterly,* a *Times* subsidiary in Washington, D.C., that sells substantive research and background on Congress to newspapers and other clients. Over the years she devoted much of her talent to its management. Henrietta Poynter died in January 1968 at age sixty-six. Two years later Poynter married Marion E. Knauss, then a *Times* editorial writer, who would continue to serve on the paper's board of directors after his death.

Poynter entered the broadcasting field in 1940 when he bought Saint Petersburg radio station WTSP, which would earn high marks for its public-service programming. However, with the increased popularity of television, he sold the radio station in 1956. Expenses were running high, and the station had begun to lose money.

Poynter made two futile attempts to acquire a television license during the 1950s but lost out to the *Tampa Tribune.* His fierce dedication to the *Times* overshadowed his philosophical reservations about the adverse effects of newspaper-television combination on diversity of media ownership. He feared the financial advantage that his Tampa competitor might gain from the lucrative television market, but his apprehension proved unfounded. In 1971 the *Times* surpassed its cross-bay rival in average daily and Sunday circulation and established itself second to the state's circulation leader, the *Miami Herald.*

Poynter became a reluctant monopolist in 1962 when he acquired his afternoon competitor, the *Evening Independent,* in order to keep it from closing. But the era of independent ownership of the two newspapers had ended. The *Times* – founded on 25 July 1884 in a small office at the rear of a Dunedin, Florida, drugstore – was already a generation old when its rival started publication in 1906. The following year the two weeklies graduated to daily status and entered into a heated battle for readership. After World War II, however, Poynter built the circulation of the *Times* above one hundred thousand at the expense of the *Independent,* which suffered dwindling circulation and rising debts.

Poynter urged the Thomson chain, owner of the *Independent* since 1952, to sell the newspaper to someone else and, only after all such attempts failed, bought the paper for a nominal three hundred thousand dollars. The publisher was convinced that Saint Petersburg would have been better served by competing newspapers under separate ownerships that held up different facets of the city's affairs to scrutiny and clashed in their editorial opinions.

When Poynter gained controlling interest in the *Times* in 1947, he published fifteen "Standards of Ownership." Like much of his writing, the document is wordy and clumsily phrased. But the goals he set are exemplary. They encompass his vows never to sell to, or to form, a chain; to hire above-average employees and pay them above-average wages; and to share the newspaper's profits with its staff. Bothered by his father's real-estate dealings, he wrote that a newspaper "cannot best serve its community if it is encumbered with outside interests." Most media organizations, including the American Society of Newspaper Editors, now have standards of conduct; Poynter's were among the first.

He was also in the forefront of using photos, maps, and other illustrations to break up the monotony of row upon long gray row of type. As television began to invade more and more homes, Poynter sensed that newspapers would have to change dramatically if they hoped to keep readers from defecting to the exciting new medium. "We should be making a more informative, easier to read, better-illustrated newspaper for the man or woman who paid a nickel for it," he said. The *Times* switched to a more attractive page design and began organizing news by sections in order to make it easier to find. In 1955, years before most other papers, the *Times* began printing color photographs and was among the first to convert to the offset method of printing.

Poynter was unique among newspaper publishers because of the active editorial role he played. Before becoming chairman of the board in 1969 – a post he held until his death from a cerebral hemorrhage in 1978 – he often peppered his newsroom staff with story suggestions. Lines of authority were fairly relaxed, and he frequently gave routine news tips directly to staffers. A reporter or editor might look up from his desk to find the boss standing beside him, eager to discuss or impart an idea.

Nevertheless, he could be extremely difficult to work for – stingy with praise, generous with criticism, and "blunt to the point of cruelty in his professional relationships," as his successor, Eugene Patterson, said in 1990. He hated errors and never quit striving for perfection. When the *Times* won its first Pulitzer Prize, in 1964, Poynter briefly joined the celebration, then said: "Now goddamn it, we can't afford to get complacent."

The caliber of the newsroom staff was a major reason that *Time* magazine in 1976 named the Saint Petersburg daily one of the five best in the South. The *Times* boasted Phi Beta Kappas, Rhodes scholars, and Nieman fellows, as well as such respected names as Wilbur Landrey, a former United Press International foreign editor, and Andrew Barnes, a former *Washington Post* metro deputy editor. Poynter lured the two journalists to his newspaper with high salaries and a profit-sharing plan. Another strong inducement was the prospect of working with Patterson, a Pulitzer Prize–winning veteran of the *Atlanta Constitution* and the *Washington Post*.

Poynter took elaborate measures to ensure that control of the *Times* would remain vested in one individual and free from public and chain ownership. Long dedicated to journalism education, he originally planned that the company stock would be placed in a charitable trust, the Poynter Fund, which he had set up in the mid 1950s to provide scholarships for journalism students. But after a change in tax laws the trust was no longer the right vehicle. So he willed most of his stock to the Modern Media Institute (later renamed the Poynter Institute for Media Studies), which opened in Saint Petersburg in 1975.

The nonprofit journalism institute that he created assumed the majority of Times Publishing Company stock when Poynter died in 1978. Under this innovative arrangement the institute owns the business tax free. Most of its nine board members are *Times* executives, but only one, the chairman of the board, can vote the stock in matters relating to the publishing business. "In the final analysis, this means one-man control of the *St. Petersburg Times*," said Patterson, whom Poynter designated to be that man.

Public ownership of newspapers was objectionable to the publisher because of the "inevitable interference" of stockholders. "Even minority stockholders have differences of opinion on editorial policy," he said. Poynter also contended that short-term dividend demands exerted by stockholders could prove financially counterproductive. "I believe more profit will be made over a period of years," he wrote, "if the staff is relieved of the pressures of making good profit showing from month-to-month for the benefit of those who regard a newspaper as just another investment." He deplored the thought of investment analysts looking over his shoulder. "They can divert you from the job of getting out a helluva good newspaper every day," he said.

Poynter believed that there was too much control of Florida's news media by out-of-state individuals and large chains. The chains, he alleged, were mainly concerned with their "bottom lines," not their obligation to a local constituency. He believed that he had something special to offer that the chains did not have – a passionate interest in the welfare of his community.

Chain executives took vehement exception to Poynter's premise. They argued that the difference between their newspapers and one such as the *Times* was that their papers tried to serve their local communities, whereas the *Times* invited national attention by a more global orientation. Poynter was accused of purposefully rejecting the basic character and philosophy of his readership. His paper, it was alleged, was too far out of touch with its readers – too liberal, too intellectual. This lack of rapport was described by *Time* magazine: "So quirkily liberal in a sleepy conservative town that it has been called by readers the '*St. Petersburg Pravda*.'"

At the time of Poynter's death more than 30 percent of the residents and nearly 40 percent of the voters were sixty-five or older – typically, middle-class Republicans from the North living on slim, fixed incomes. Their interest in new schools, public-works projects, and other costly measures was minimal. Nevertheless, the *Times* nearly always backed the bond issues and tax increases placed before the electorate, and its positions managed to prevail more often than not.

Poynter was skeptical of the amount of local autonomy that chain newspapers extended to individual editors to decide their own news play and editorial endorsements. He contended that "chains say they give absolute autonomy to their editor, but he is on a leash." The publisher considered as dishonest the latitude of editorial opinion that chains do permit their member papers. In prohibiting his other newspaper, the *Evening Independent,* from taking positions that differed from those of the *Times,* Poynter said: "We will not be hypocritical and have two different editorial policies."

For nearly forty years under Poynter's leadership, the *Times* championed such causes as civil rights, slum clearance, better welfare programs, low-cost housing, and improved medical care for the aged. He shared Walt Whitman's vision that it is the responsibility of the owner-editor to wield the influence of the newspaper – to lead public opinion, to press "noble reforms," and to school people, perhaps in opposition "to their long established ways of thought."

The Saint Petersburg newspaper led most of the region's press in adamant support of racial integration. Poynter stressed the economic, social, political, and moral burdens that segregation had placed on the South. Basic to Poynter's views was the importance of legal, feasible, southern-based, and moral solutions. His purpose was to convince his readers that the South could learn to live with the social change that he knew was forthcoming. "Our attitude is and has been for many years that segregation violates the American concept, and it was and is inevitable that it be abolished," he said. "Long before the Supreme Court ruled on it, the *Times* opposed segregation."

Poynter believed that the editorial page is the conscience of the newspaper, and to a great extent the conscience of the community in which it is published. He demanded a deliberate effort by his editorial writers to counterbalance national and international offerings with more immediate ones. He wanted them to plow into controversies that affected their state, Saint Petersburg, and surrounding Pinellas County; and to provide insightful editorial items on local politics that would allow voters to discriminate between the municipal candidates and parties on relevant issues. He realized that voters' assessments of local campaign issues become a critical part of public-opinion formulation about candidates, and in partisan elections, about both the candidates and their political parties.

The *Times* editorial page had a great affinity for challenging government agendas, scrutinizing public officials, posing the hard and unpopular questions, and acting as skeptical surrogate of the people. Professor and press critic Irving Kristol deplores such an adversarial stance, citing "the tremendous gap of credibility and mistrust which, in recent years, has opened between public officials and the press." Poynter would have agreed with Patterson's contention that although public officials are not served, the public interest is served by the press's assertion "of the right and duty to question and doubt." When Poynter's newspaper assumed the mantle of opposition, his concern was that it bring reason and good judgment to the issues before the readers.

The newspaper owner exercised firm control over editorial policy. Although he let the editorial board decide on issues to be taken up in each day's editorials, he shaped the views expressed in those editorials. Whenever possible in the early years of his editorship, he saw editorial page proofs before they went to press. If he disapproved of an editorial, he tossed it out or suggested changes, even on deadline.

Poynter conducted periodic editorial conferences in his spacious office on the fourth floor of the Times Building in downtown Saint Petersburg. Once he commenced the meeting, the short, neatly dressed newspaperman with a fancy for bow ties and tweed would step from behind his large desk and walk around the room, gesturing with his glasses toward the editors sitting on two oversized, leather-covered divans. Or he would sometimes stand looking through the large office windows while continuing the discussion.

He was incisive but always punctuated his thinking by soliciting the comments of editors. His method of inquiry artfully avoided betraying his own opinion, and with reason. In a 1974 interview Patterson said: "He'll talk one way and then he'll talk the other. What he is really doing is testing you out to see how you feel. But he doesn't help you along by giving you an indication of how he feels – he may even mislead you just to test you."

St. Petersburg Times

Florida's Best Newspaper

ST. PETERSBURG, FLORIDA, SUNDAY, JANUARY 24, 1971

25 CENTS A COPY

Florida's Courtly Myth: Equal Justice Under Law

Florida's prison sentences vary:

✓ According to where the lawbreaker broke the law, not simply which law he broke.

✓ According to which judge hears his case, and the judge's personal prejudices.

✓ In many cases, according to whether the defendant was foolish enough to insist on his constitutional right to a jury trial.

U.S. Flies War Supplies Into Battered Cambodia

On Sidelines, War Is Cause For Cheering

By PETER S. JAY
Washington Post Service

American Cobra Helicopters Refuel Near Cambodian Border For Sorties Along Route 4

Soldiers 3

Abu Nar, Palestinian Guerrilla

Aron Rosenberg, Israeli Army Private

Emad Ismail, Jordanian Army Private

Tax-Sharing Battle Looms

Modern Children Maturing Earlier

By WALTER SULLIVAN
New York Times Service

Oil Slick Said Moving Into Long Island Sound

L.I. Sound Hit By Oil Spill

on the INSIDE today

Apollo Astronaut In Crash, Safe

Details, 28-A

SECTION A: World and National News
SECTION B: Local and State News
SECTION C: Sports News, Classified
SECTION D: Editorial, Education, Financial
SECTION E: SunDAY Family
SECTION F: SunDAY Leisure and Travel
SECTION G: SunDAY Homes
FLORIDIAN: Magazine
TV DIAL: Magazine
PARADE: Magazine

Reds Expel Protesting Jews

From The Sunday London Times

LONDON —

Front page of the St. Petersburg Times, *24 January 1971*

The point of not telegraphing his own position was both to find out the validity of the other person's viewpoint and to allow himself the flexibility to change his own. Poynter's characteristic pauses and slowness of speech reflected his calculated desire to keep all of his options open. He did not make decisions until he was well informed. However, once he made up his mind on an issue, there was no way he could be shaken from it. "He was so tough he would fight all day on a line of principle even though it cost him money and cost him time," according to Patterson. The *New York Times* dubbed him "tough as a railroad spike" for his editorial grit. But critics, including colleagues in the Florida press, were more blunt, calling him bullheaded.

Poynter asked the simple question, "Is an editorial position right?" When the answer was "yes," he published his opinion regardless of conflicting opinions of readers or special interests. Although it may be argued that calm, judicious interpretation on the editorial page is preferable to a newspaper's taking a one-sided position on a controversial issue, there are occasions when in the public interest a firm and courageous stand must be taken. "My theory is that the overwhelming majority of our readers are with us on 51 percent of the controversial issues," Poynter said. "If we can't have both their friendship and their respect, we'd rather have their respect."

The publisher's editorial moxie and activism evoked the ridicule, but also won the begrudging admiration, of Edward Turville, the leader of his local opposition on many issues. Sizing up his five-foot-five-inch antagonist, the St. Petersburg attorney once commented: "I've found over the years that very small people in high places are like bantam roosters — they can really raise hell. I will say one thing though, Poynter put the fear of God into a lot of public officials. And he sure published a fine newspaper."

Yet Poynter was also a man of apparent contradictions. Despite his endorsement of integration and civil rights, he rarely, if ever, had blacks as guests in his home. His editorial pages called repeatedly for women's equality, yet he saw no conflict in his membership in private clubs that barred women. "Most men have very dull wives," he once explained.

He lamented the ravaging of Florida's fragile environment, yet he contributed to its uncontrolled development by publishing lavish special editions that touted the area's virtues while glossing over its problems. But by the 1970s a rapidly expanding population caused Saint Petersburg residents to become increasingly sensitive to the dangers of overdevelopment. Poynter belatedly acknowledged that his responsibility as publisher was more important than his vested interest in increased circulation and revenues generated by new residents.

Editorially, the *Times* gradually aligned itself with environmentalists and others favoring controlled growth. But this loyalty was not carried over on the advertising pages or in the occasional special sections. Packaged to attract building-industry advertising dollars, the supplements written by *Times* staffers featured articles promising an idyllic life in the sun. Business-side infringement on news-side editorial independence was apparent. Poynter also left his paper open to charges that it had only a token commitment to controlled growth. Not until 1974 did the special sections turn to wooing the tourist trade rather than community development.

Poynter championed labor unions and the right to organize, yet he worked vigorously to keep unions out of his newspaper. Having known discomfiture over this issue, the publisher tried in 1977 to explain the undeniable incongruity. He contended that labor unions had changed substantially since passage of the Wagner Act in the early 1930s: "I think that they have become oppressors in some ways and have not demonstrated sufficient interest in those who do not belong to labor unions." Furthermore, he came to see unions as detrimental to productivity, leaning too much on seniority: "Once a union gets locked in, it's very difficult to get rid of the inefficient worker."

Poynter enjoyed total control over his newspaper and — while admitting that workers in some industries and companies would not realize decent working conditions, fringe benefits, and salaries without union representation — maintained that his organization's employees were always fairly treated. "We have tried to operate the Times Publishing Company in such a way that our staffers do not need a union to gain concessions," he said. "There have been many fine organizations throughout our whole industrial civilization that have never had unions because they behaved in such a way union organizers couldn't improve upon the lot of their employees." However, some staffers resented what they considered Poynter's paternalistic attitude. They felt that management was telling them in effect, "We know what's best, we'll take care of you — just trust us."

Poynter declared that his staff deserved only the best, yet he allowed newsroom salaries to fall below the national average, prompting some of his best reporters to lead an unsuccessful union drive in

1974. In order to escape stricter financial liability, he interpreted their salaries in a narrow, regional context. He argued that the pay range of the *Times* ranked favorably in the Southeast and that it was unfair for staff members to equate their wages with those paid by newspapers elsewhere.

Poynter was a fiercely independent publisher who, in an era of chain ownership, elected to forego any ambitions of amassing great power and wealth. He chose instead to devote himself to providing one city with an outstanding newspaper and succeeded in attracting skilled journalists and gaining their loyalty, despite a tightfisted wage scale. He wanted the *St. Petersburg Times* to assume a leadership role, so he instilled the paper with a strong local voice. The liberal editorial policy of the *Times* was often unpopular with readers, but Poynter sensed that truly distinguished newspapers dare to face public displeasure.

References:

George N. Allen, "Poynters: A Different Kind of Journalism," *Washington Journalism Review*, 1 (January/February 1979): 49;

David C. Coulson, "Nelson Poynter of the *St. Petersburg Times*: An Independent Publisher with Unique Ownership Standards," *Mass Comm Review*, 10 (Winter/Spring 1982–1983): 21–24;

Coulson, "Nelson Poynter: Study of an Independent Publisher and His Standards of Ownership," Ph.D. dissertation, University of Minnesota, 1982;

Coulson, "Nelson Poynter's Editorial Grit," *Masthead*, 35 (Summer 1983): 20–22;

Dennis Holder, "MMI – Nelson Poynter's Anti-Chain Reaction," *Washington Journalism Review*, 3 (October 1981): 19;

Robert Hooker, "The Times and Its Times: A History," *St. Petersburg Times*, 25 July 1984, pp. 37–79;

Susan Taylor Martin, " 'A Great Grudge,' " *St. Petersburg Times*, 25 February 1990, pp. A1, A12–A14;

"Reluctant Monopolist," *Newsweek*, 60 (16 July 1962): 75.

Eugene Pulliam

(3 May 1889 – 23 June 1975)

Michael Buchholz
Indiana State University

MAJOR NEWSPAPERS OWNED: *Atchison* (Kansas) *Champion* (1911–1914); *Franklin* (Indiana) *Evening Star* (1917–1923); *Lebanon* (Indiana) *Reporter* (1923–circa 1946); *Daytona Beach* (Florida) *News-Journal* [merger of *Daytona Beach Morning Journal* and *Daytona Beach News*] (1927–1928); *Washington* (North Carolina) *Daily News* (1927–circa 1929); *Alva* (Oklahoma) *Review-Courier* (1929–1941); *Elk City* (Oklahoma) *Daily News* (1929–1937); *Hobart* (Oklahoma) *Democrat-Chief* (1929–1940); *Mangum* (Oklahoma) *Daily Star* (1929–1939); *Altus* (Oklahoma) *Times-Democrat* (1929–1936); *Clinton* (Oklahoma) *Daily News* (1929–1940); *El Reno* (Oklahoma) *Tribune* [merger of *El Reno Democrat* and *El Reno People's Press*] (1929–1937); *Linton* (Indiana) *Citizen* (1929–circa 1935); *Huntington* (Indiana) *Herald-Press* (1930–1964); *Paducah* (Kentucky) *Sun-Democrat* (1930); *Vincennes* (Indiana) *Sun-Commercial* (1930–1975); *Anderson* (South Carolina) *Daily Mail* (1930–1934); *Quincy* (Massachusetts) *News* (1930–1934); *Bicknell* (Indiana) *Daily News* (1930–1934); *North Jersey Courier* (1930–1934); *Orlando* (Florida) *Morning Sentinel* (1931–1934); *Orlando* (Florida) *Evening Reporter Star* (1931–1934); *Lansing* (Michigan) *Capital News* (1932); *Uniontown* (Pennsylvania) *Morning Herald* (1932–1934); *Uniontown* (Pennsylvania) *Evening Standard* (1932–1934); *Indianapolis Star* (1944–1975); *Muncie* (Indiana) *Star* (1944–1975); *Arizona Republic* (1946–1975); *Phoenix Gazette* (1946–1975); *Muncie* (Indiana) *Evening Press* (1946–1975); *Indianapolis News* (1948–1975).

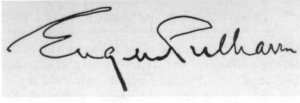

In 1944 Eugene Collins Pulliam bought the *Indianapolis Star* for nearly $2.5 million. It was the first of four major newspaper purchases that would gain Pulliam national attention and bring his brand of right-wing conservatism to the readers of two states. These purchases would be the last in his sixty-three-year career as a publisher, which spanned several states and fifty-one newspapers. His grandson and biographer, Russell Pulliam, called him the "last of the newspaper ti-

tans." But Eugene Pulliam, the son of a Methodist circuit-riding minister, was also criticized for being a kingmaker in the Republican party (an "energetic behind-the-scene GOPoliticker," in the words of *Time* magazine) who slanted his news coverage to help those he supported.

Pulliam grew up on the plains of Kansas. His father, Irvin B. Pulliam, was a salesman for a group of wholesale grocers in Danville, Illinois. He converted to Methodism after attending a series of revivals. He and his wife, Martha Collins Pulliam, moved to western Kansas in March 1888 to bring the word of God to the frontier. Eugene, named for an uncle who had trekked to California to find gold in 1859, was born on 3 May 1889 in Ulysses.

Pulliam's early life was poor and mobile. His father's earnings averaged only a dollar a day, and his calling led to frequent moves. By the time Pulliam was fifteen, he had lived in at least ten towns, working in tamale and popcorn stands and selling the *Saturday Evening Post* and the *Rams Horn* to make extra money. His father was often on the road, and Pulliam found himself the "man" of the house with his mother and two sisters.

But in 1904 Irvin Pulliam was given a church associated with Baker Academy and University in Baldwin City, Kansas, and the Pulliam family settled down to a more normal home life. After a brief and trouble-filled period in the Baldwin City public schools, Eugene Pulliam transferred to the Baker Academy prep school and entered the university in the fall of 1906. In January 1907 he moved with one of his sisters to Greencastle, Indiana, to begin studies at DePauw University, a Methodist school that his mother had attended.

Pulliam quickly became involved in fraternity and journalism activities. He helped start a daily student newspaper and served as its assistant business manager before becoming its business manager. He was also one of the ten founders of Sigma Delta Chi, the organization known today as the Society of Professional Journalists. Pulliam picked up some reportorial experience by working summers for the *Chanute* (Kansas) *Sun* and by stringing for the *Indianapolis Star,* the paper he would eventually own.

However, Pulliam's academic performance at DePauw was mediocre. He did well in English and history but failed some of his other courses. The lure of journalism was stronger than that of a college degree, and Pulliam dropped out in 1909 at the end of his junior year to become a reporter for the *Atchison* (Kansas) *Champion.*

A local dishpan sale gave Pulliam a chance to move up after less than a year at the *Champion.* Women competing for items on sale at a local store became increasingly aggressive, and the competition turned into a fight. Pulliam's story of the brouhaha caught the attention of an editor at the *Kansas City Star,* and Pulliam signed on as a reporter there in 1910 for fifteen dollars a week.

Pulliam worked the night police beat and wrote features at the *Star* under the tutelage of Marvin Creager, the night city editor. Pulliam also fell under the influence of the newspaper's publisher, William Rockhill Nelson, who forever after would be his hero and role model. Pulliam's association with presidential politics also stemmed from his year on the *Star.* While a reporter, he met William Howard Taft, Woodrow Wilson, and Theodore Roosevelt. One of his journalistic coups was an interview with the campaigning William Jennings Bryan, who had become so upset with "misquotations" that he forced Pulliam to write the story on the spot and checked it for accuracy.

Pulliam's pay at the *Star* eventually rose to $20 a week, but that was not enough to marry his DePauw sweetheart, Myrta Smith. And it was not enough to buy a newspaper, which had become his goal. He suffered from appendicitis and left the *Star* in 1911. After the operation he returned to Atchison to work for his father as a secretary. Later that year he landed a job as editor of the *Champion* for $140 a month. As editor, Pulliam had a chance to buy stock in the paper, and after he married Myrta in February 1912, his in-laws bought up the rest of the paper.

Pulliam's competition was the *Atchison Globe,* edited by a man whom he considered a reactionary, Ed Howe. Pulliam by this time was a supporter of Roosevelt, his Bull Moose party, and his Square Deal campaign platform. But Pulliam's running editorial battle with Howe during the 1912 presidential campaign arose from a brief boxing match on the streets of Atchison. Howe was upset about a story in the *Champion* that hinted that his wife had had a better time at a party than she should have had. When he saw Pulliam on the street, he punched him in the nose, and Pulliam returned the blow before companions could separate the two. The battle in the news columns, however, continued, with Pulliam supporting judicial recall, favoring small business over big business, and opposing Taft's nomination to the U.S. Supreme Court. On the local level Pulliam backed public over private ownership of utilities and the commission form of city government over the traditional mayor/council structure.

The *Champion* prospered during Pulliam's first year as editor, with circulation increasing from twenty-one hundred in 1911 to more than five thousand in 1912. But with the defeat of the Bull Moosers, the newspaper began to decline, and, when Pulliam lost the city printing contract in August 1913 with a bid lower than that of the winning

The founders of the Sigma Delta Chi journalism fraternity (now known as the Society of Professional Journalists) in 1934: Leroy H. Millikan, Pulliam, Lawrence H. Sloan, and Paul M. Reddick

Globe, he decided it was time to get out. In 1914 he sold the paper for eleven thousand dollars and some land in Colorado.

The Pulliam family, which included a son, Eugene S. Pulliam, moved in with Myrta's parents in Noblesville, Indiana, while Pulliam began job hunting close to home. He passed up a twenty-dollar-a-week position at the *Indianapolis News* before taking on the managing editor's post at the *Franklin* (Indiana) *Evening Star* for thirty-five dollars a week in January 1915. As managing editor, Pulliam stirred controversy in the small town by pushing for change, such as civic improvements. He also improved the paper by buying a new duplex press to replace the old flatbed model, added wire stories from United Press, and modernized the look of the paper's headlines and gave it an up-to-date layout.

Pulliam almost gave up the newspaper when his wife died in 1917. Myrta suffered a miscarriage in her second pregnancy and died at age thirty after contracting asthma. Pulliam thought hard about becoming a missionary and tried to join the army to get into World War I, but he was rejected because of his weak eyes and recurring intestinal problems. Fearful that Pulliam might leave the *Evening Star,* publisher W. W. Aikens gave him the chance to buy half of the paper for seventeen thousand dollars.

Pulliam, who had teamed with Aikens to buy some weekly papers in Johnson County, used promissory notes to make up his share.

The partnership between Aikens and Pulliam eventually soured as Pulliam continued to make enemies in Franklin with his pushy brand of activism. But an attempt by Aikens and another part-owner, Ray Sellers, to get rid of Pulliam in 1922 backfired. In that year Aikens and Sellers exercised a clause in their partnership contract that effectively forced Pulliam to buy their stock for $20,000 or sell them his. Pulliam, however, persuaded a local banker to loan him the $20,000, and, to his partners' surprise, he bought them out instead. Pulliam finally left Franklin in 1923, selling the paper back to Aikens and sellers for $57,000 and using $38,000 of the proceeds to buy another small Indiana daily, the *Lebanon Reporter.*

Pulliam remarried in 1919, and in 1923 he moved to Lebanon with his wife, Martha; his son, Gene, Jr.; and their daughter, Corinne, born in 1922. Although Pulliam was growing more moderate, he continued to push for progressive reforms in city government by replacing the mayor/council form with the new council/manager form. He called for civic improvements and urged modernization of the one-room schoolhouses that still dotted the countryside. He complained about rich tax dodgers, opposed capital punishment, and continued to rail against the private ownership of utilities.

He also crusaded against the Ku Klux Klan, which controlled state and local government in Indiana during the mid 1920s. In 1924 Pulliam was approached by two local Klansmen who wanted him to run a story about an upcoming march. Blacks, Roman Catholics, and Jews should be instructed to stay off the streets. When Pulliam refused, the men threatened to burn down the *Reporter*. Pulliam grabbed a gun and said that he would kill them both if anything happened to the newspaper. An armed Pulliam spent a tense but uneventful night at his newspaper.

In the latter part of the 1920s Pulliam went on a newspaper-buying spree. He took over the *Daytona Beach* (Florida) *Morning Journal* by assuming its $92,500 worth of debts in September 1926 and merged it with the *Daytona Beach News,* which he bought in 1927 with $50,000 in ten-year bonds. Pulliam also bought the *Washington* (North Carolina) *Daily News* and the weekly *Lebanon* (Indiana) *Pioneer*. Pulliam made a $40,000 profit when he sold the Daytona Beach paper in 1928 for $112,000.

He then turned his sights on Oklahoma, where the growth of towns in the western part of the state had outstripped the growth of their newspapers. He had $145,000 in cash from earlier sales and profits, and the *Reporter* was worth an estimated $150,000. He borrowed more cash from friends, using real estate as collateral, and then used references from his friends to persuade a Tulsa, Oklahoma, bank to underwrite $25,000 in bonds to settle his debts to them. Pulliam expected to pay off the bonds with the profits from the Oklahoma newspapers he planned to buy.

Pulliam moved into Oklahoma and plunked down $175,000 to buy the *Alva Review-Courier,* the weekly *Elk City News-Democrat,* the *Hobart Democrat-Chief,* the weekly *Kiowa County Review,* and two weeklies in Mangum, the *Star* and the *Greer County News*. He converted the Elk City paper into the *Elk City Daily News* and merged the Mangum papers into the *Mangum Daily Star*. Pulliam also bought the *Altus Times-Democrat,* the *Clinton Daily News,* the weekly *Harmon County Democrat,* the *El Reno Democrat,* and the *El Reno People's Press*. The El Reno papers were merged into the *El Reno Tribune*. In the span of a few months, the Oklahoma properties were valued at almost $1 million. In 1929 he added the *Linton Citizen* to his stable of Indiana newspapers.

Pulliam failed to gauge the length and depth of the Great Depression, which started with the stock-market crash of 29 October 1929. The Tulsa bank refused to handle the sale of his preferred stock in the Pulliam Publishing Company, and he turned down the offer of a Kansas newsman to buy part of his holdings, which would have allowed Pulliam to meet his obligations but caused him to lose some of the profits he expected from the papers. Instead, Pulliam decided to try to ride out the Depression, and he sold $150,000 in stock to an Oklahoma City oilman Frank Buttram in January 1930.

Pulliam had met Buttram earlier, but in 1930 Buttram was running for the Democratic gubernatorial nomination. The alliance appeared questionable, even though Pulliam remained in control of policy and management while Buttram controlled the dividends. And even though Buttram's support from the Pulliam papers was spotty, Pulliam's biographer claims that the business deal "gave the appearance of a wheeling-and-dealing financial alliance with a candidate for governor" and that Pulliam had compromised his principles. It was "the only time," Pulliam said later, "I ever let a politician outtalk me." Buttram lost the runoff primary to the eventual winner, William ("Alfalfa Bill") Murray.

In August 1930 Pulliam formed a partnership with a former reporter and editor from Austin, Texas, Charles Marsh, who had become interested in buying and selling newspapers. He was also interested in political influence and had financial interests in oil, real estate, and banking. Pulliam and Marsh formed the General Newspapers corporation. Pulliam contributed the papers in Oklahoma and Indiana to the partnership, and Marsh brought in some of the stock from his chain of Texas newspapers. Together, they ranged all over the country, buying newspapers with bond financing.

Beginning in August, Pulliam and Marsh bought the *Paducah* (Kentucky) *Sun-Democrat,* and they picked up the *Vincennes* (Indiana) *Sun* for $112,500 and the *Vincennes Commercial* for $50,000 and the assumption of its $60,000 debt. The Vincennes papers were merged into the *Sun-Commercial*. By the end of 1930 the corporation had taken over the *Anderson* (South Carolina) *Daily Mail,* the *Quincy* (Massachusetts) *News,* the *Bicknell* (Indiana) *Daily News,* the North Jersey Publishing Company (owner of the *North Jersey Courier*), and newspapers in LaGrange, Americus, and Dublin, Georgia. The purchases continued in 1931 and 1932 with the *Orlando* (Florida) *Morning Sentinel* and the *Orlando Evening Reporter Star;* the *Lansing* (Michigan) *Capital News;* and the *Morning Herald* and the *Evening Standard* in Uniontown, Pennsylvania. In the summer of 1931 Pulliam wrote a friend that General Newspapers owned twenty-three newspapers in seven states.

Some of the newspapers were resold for a quick profit, such as the *Paducah Sun-Democrat,* which turned an $80,000 profit, and the *Lansing Capital News,* which brought a $75,000 profit on a $50,000 investment. But Pulliam, who was more interested in the day-to-day operation of his newspapers and the influence they could bring, grew increasingly skeptical of his burgeoning holdings. He saw himself turning away from the principles he had enunciated in his first Oklahoma editorial:

> A newspaper is a human institution and as such is subject to all the ills and fortunes that man is heir to. It is not like other business chattels that can be bought and sold in cold barter. It is peculiarly human. It takes heart-hold and a spiritual grip on the men and women who produce it day by day. It becomes a part of their very existence. Through it they find themselves giving expression to their highest ideals. It reveals their deepest life interests. The opportunity it affords for satisfying service keeps them in the game when other fields offer more lucrative compensation.

Pulliam saw that he could not run all the papers or provide them all with managers, so he refinanced the Oklahoma properties and in the spring of 1934 began trading stock with Marsh. When he was through, he retained the Oklahoma and Indiana papers and used them to form Central Newspapers. The group turned a collective profit of only $54,977 in 1934, and Pulliam began selling most of them to their managers, a process that took about a decade.

Pulliam continued to keep his newspapers active in presidential politics, but after the death of the Bull Moose Party in the 1912 election he had trouble finding a political home. The Democrats in the 1920s and 1930s, he thought, were too closely tied to state and local political machines, and candidates on the Republican side were, to him, largely uninspiring. In 1924 Pulliam gave the Republican nominee, Calvin Coolidge, only lukewarm support. In the 1928 campaign he had a slight preference for Republican Herbert Hoover over Alfred E. Smith but ended up voting for the Democrat because of the deterioration of the race into anti-Catholic mudslinging against Smith.

He was mostly neutral during the 1932 race but embraced Franklin Roosevelt's New Deal after the election because of its similarity to part of the old Bull Moose program. But by 1940 Pulliam began to believe that the New Deal measures were going to be permanent rather than temporary constructions on the federal landscape, and the growth of government and its cost appalled him. When Roosevelt ran for a third time, Pulliam turned to the Republican nominee, Hoosier candidate Wendell Willkie.

While Pulliam was constricting his newspaper empire in the late 1930s, he was expanding his business interests into radio. With the proceeds from the sale of the Oklahoma newspapers and the outstanding bonds, plus some borrowed cash, Pulliam bought WIRE, the NBC affiliate in Indianapolis for $340,000. With an infusion of funds Pulliam was able to turn the station, the smallest in the city at the time he bought it, into the largest station in Indiana. Pulliam also became part-owner of WKBV in Richmond, Indiana, and KPHO in Phoenix, Arizona, and he started WAOV in Vincennes.

Pulliam's buying sprees in Oklahoma and other parts of the country during the late 1920s and early 1930s – he estimated that he had traveled forty-two thousand miles by car in the last half of 1930 alone – strained his health and his marriage. He was subject to severe headaches and suffered severe back and stomach problems during the Depression. After several hospital stays he had a spinal-fusion operation in 1941. In that year he also divorced his wife, Martha, the mother of two of his three children, after a marriage of more than twenty years. Shortly thereafter he married his longtime secretary, Naomi ("Nina") Mason.

Pulliam's newspaper dealings slowed to a stop after the United States was dragged into World War II. Pulliam was not an isolationist, but neither had he written much on international affairs. Nevertheless, he saw the war coming, and a month before the Japanese attacked Pearl Harbor on 7 December 1941, Pulliam created the Indiana Defense Savings Committee. On 15 January 1942 he organized the country's first statewide rally to sell defense bonds and raised $2 million. (To spark interest in the rally, Pulliam invited movie star Carole Lombard, a Fort Wayne, Indiana, native, to appear at the Indianapolis event. On Lombard's way back to Hollywood, her plane crashed, and the actress was killed.) Pulliam continued to raise money to support the war throughout its duration.

As the war entered its final stages, Pulliam finally got the chance he had been seeking to enter big-time newspapering. John C. Shaffer – who had been editor and publisher of the *Indianapolis Star* since 1911 – died in 1943. The *Star* had been the city's only morning newspaper since 1906, three years after it was launched. Shaffer turned the paper into a money-maker that by 1944 had a weekday circulation of 128,959 and 189,963 on Sundays. It was known as a businessman's newspaper and had led campaigns at the local and state levels for the direct election of U.S. senators and the creation of a state tax board, a conservation department, and a state highway commission.

When the paper came on the market after Shaffer's death, the competition was stiff. Among the contenders were the family of a former vice-president, Charles Warren Fairbanks, which owned the *Indianapolis News;* industrialist George Ball of Muncie, who already owned preferred stock in the *Star;* Roy Howard, a Hoosier who headed up the Scripps-Howard chain and owned the *Indianapolis Times;* chain owner Samuel I. Newhouse; department-store mogul Marshall Field III, owner of the *Chicago Sun;* and Mike and John Cowles, owners of *Look* magazine and several newspapers.

However, the race went to Pulliam, whom *Time* magazine called the "Hoosier Dark Horse." Its report in the 8 May 1944 issue evidenced surprise that Pulliam bought the paper for nearly $2.5 million, because he was "identified more with Hoosier radio than with newspapers." There was even speculation that Pulliam was a front for Field, but *Time* discounted that rumor. "Big, beaming Smith Davis, Cleveland newspaper broker, had arranged and so hidden the deal that no one had seriously suspected Pulliam," according to the article. Actually, Pulliam had borrowed $1 million from the Jefferson Standard Life Insurance Company of North Carolina to make the purchase, which included the *Muncie Star,* Shaffer's other newspaper.

The *Indianapolis Star* was considered a second-rate paper compared to the other two papers in town, but Pulliam moved quickly to make changes. He was the editor as well as the publisher. He added women's pages to pull female readers away from the afternoon dailies, introduced a Sunday magazine, strengthened the sports section, added columns on the editorial page, and increased space for national and international news. He also turned the *Star* into a state newspaper, sending reporters to cover news throughout Indiana. He added a pension plan, medical and life insurance, and a Christmas bonus for his employees; he also developed a recreation area for *Star* employees.

The changes in content – coming on top of editorial campaigns against the Ku Klux Klan and the state Republicans' practice of giving away liquor licenses to their friends – helped to boost weekday circulation to 168,000 by the end of 1946, only slightly behind the *News* at 171,000. By the end of 1947 the *Star* led in the circulation battle.

Pulliam with Dwight D. Eisenhower, 1949

Pulliam was also moving on another front, his longtime vacationland of Arizona. In 1946 Charles Stauffer and Wesley Knorpp, owners of the *Arizona Republic* and the *Phoenix Gazette,* offered to sell Pulliam the papers. Pulliam finally managed to borrow $2.5 million from Jefferson Standard Life and brought in other investors to come up with the $4 million asking price. Among the stockholders were the newspaper broker who helped Pulliam put together the deal, Smith Davis; an ad executive from New York, Bruce Barton; a leader of the Arizona Republican party, author Clarence Buddington Kelland; and Jefferson Standard Life. *Time,* which referred to the purchase as the "Phoenician Invasion," said that the secretary-treasurer of Pulliam's new Phoenix Newspapers corporation was N. G. Mason, who in reality was Naomi Mason Pulliam, the publisher's wife. *Time* called it Pulliam's "biggest deal of all."

Pulliam, much as he had done in Indianapolis, poured money into the Phoenix plant, changed the newspapers' advertising structure, increased the news staff and separated it from the editorial staff, added city editors, and began publishing editorials that avoided walking the political tightrope between the state's dominant Democratic party and the newspapers' leanings toward the GOP. Meanwhile, the competition between the *Star* and the *News* in Indianapolis intensified. By 1948 the *News,* plagued by differences among the Fairbanks heirs about how the newspaper should be run, was facing increased costs, decreasing profits, and the need for new presses and a new building in which to put them. Among the final blows was the loss of an important newsprint contract, and the newspaper went on the market shortly thereafter.

The Cowles brothers, Newhouse, and John S. Knight all expressed interest in the *News,* but Pulliam and Howard outstripped the other competitors and went after the *News* head-to-head. Howard, who was from Indianapolis, had gotten his first newspaper job on the *News,* and he wanted to merge it with his afternoon *Times,* which had a circulation of only ninety-five thousand. But Pulliam wanted to set up a morning-evening combination by merging the *News* with the morning *Star,* and he won out by offering the Fairbanks family something it wanted — a piece of the *News.* The resulting reorganization and stock transfer cost Pulliam $4 million. The new corporation Indianapolis Newspapers grew out of the merger. The Fairbanks family owned one-third of the stock and the long-term bonds. Although he made several attempts before he died in 1975, Pulliam never bought another newspaper.

After the war Pulliam and his wife started a series of worldwide trips that allowed him to see the Cold War firsthand. His observations turned him into a staunch anti-Communist and anti-Socialist, and made him even more leery of big government in the United States. Because of his anticommunism, Senator Joseph McCarthy of Wisconsin attracted Pulliam to the extent that the publisher offered to campaign for him in the 1952 Wisconsin primary. But as the senator grew ever more erratic, Pulliam's attraction began to wane. In 1951 Pulliam met Dwight Eisenhower in Paris and immediately felt comfortable with the general's positions on freedom at home and his internationalist leanings in foreign policy. Pulliam also liked the idea that Eisenhower was not a professional politician and became convinced that Eisenhower could become the first Republican to win the White House in twenty years.

Pulliam worked hard to get Eisenhower the Republican nomination in 1952. He served as an Eisenhower delegate to the Republican National Convention, putting himself at odds with Indiana's two senators, who supported Robert Taft. Before the fall campaign the news columns of Pulliam's newspapers were pro-Eisenhower, and after Eisenhower won the nomination, Pulliam campaigned for him by making speeches and writing front-page editorials. But then Pulliam toned down the news coverage in the *Star,* giving the Democrats front-page space and writing a memo to his editors that the headlines topping the Eisenhower stories were too big.

In Arizona, Pulliam worked to wrest control of the state from the Democrats. Barry Goldwater — who represented the state in the U.S. Senate for many years and who was the 1964 Republican nominee for president — remembers that Pulliam encouraged him to enter politics at the head of a city-government reform ticket in 1949. In 1952 Pulliam supported Goldwater's campaign for the U.S. Senate, and the Eisenhower landslide helped sweep him into office.

However, Pulliam's support for Eisenhower — and eventually his alliance with Goldwater — began to pale. Eisenhower, in Pulliam's mind, had failed to stem the Communist tide abroad and the growth of the federal government at home. Eisenhower's appointment of John Foster Dulles as secretary of state, Pulliam thought, was little better than what the country had under Harry Truman's administration. And Pulliam believed that Earl Warren, whom Eisenhower had elevated to the U.S. Supreme Court, was a socialist.

At the 1956 Republican National Convention, Pulliam served as a delegate and a member of the Platform Committee's foreign-policy subcommittee. Pulliam wanted the nation's foreign-aid program to provide loans, not grants, to foreign countries. His travels had convinced him that governments abroad resented the grant program as a form of American paternalism. Pulliam's advice was rejected, and he left the convention early.

Although Pulliam had supported Eisenhower in 1956, he was attracted to Texas senator Lyndon Johnson in 1960. Johnson had made something of himself out of an impoverished background, which interested Pulliam. He also believed that Vice-president Richard Nixon could win the White House only if he ran an aggressive, conservative campaign. When Nixon chose Henry Cabot Lodge as his running mate and indicated that he would campaign as a moderate, Pulliam began to work in Arizona and Indiana to secure the Democratic nomination for Johnson. Pulliam returned to the Nixon camp when Senator John F. Kennedy became the Democratic nominee.

Although Pulliam criticized the Kennedy administration for what he saw as its liberalism at home on urban aid, civil rights, and Medicare, and

Pulliam in his office at the Indianapolis Star, *1950*

its weakness on communism abroad, he still liked Johnson. The growing distance between Pulliam and Goldwater was made irreversible by Pulliam's support for Johnson in the 1964 presidential campaign, which Goldwater saw as inexcusable.

Part of the rift had its roots in 1954, when Arizona governor Howard Pyle, a Republican, was running for reelection. Goldwater was a strong supporter, but Pulliam was upset when Pyle called out the National Guard in 1953 to quell what he called an insurrection in a Mormon community in the northern part of the state. Pulliam thought the move an overreaction and criticized it in an editorial. He also refused to support Pyle's reelection effort, even though Goldwater pleaded with him to do so for the sake of the party. Frustrated, Goldwater told Pulliam, "We can always start another newspaper."

Another part of the misunderstanding arose from a meeting between Pulliam and Goldwater after Kennedy was assassinated in 1963. Goldwater remembers that Pulliam urged him to seek the presidency to keep the Republican party out of the hands of the liberal eastern wing. But Pulliam said

that he advised Goldwater not to run what obviously would be a failing campaign, setting back the conservative movement several years. Goldwater ran; Pulliam advised and worked for Johnson; and the Democrats won another four years in the White House. An editorial in the *Republic* just before the election urged Arizonans to vote for the home-state candidate, even though he had no chance of winning.

When his newspaper competitors in Phoenix and Indianapolis died in the mid 1960s, Pulliam moved to make his properties more evenhanded editorially. He started op-ed pages in Phoenix and Indianapolis in 1964 and ordered his editors to make the news coverage more balanced. He hired a liberal, J. Edward Murray, to be managing editor of the *Republic*. The changes brought him growing respect in the industry. He was elected to the board of directors of the Associated Press, and he was honored with the John Peter Zenger Award in 1966 and the William Allen White Award in 1970. In a 7 January 1966 article *Time* magazine conceded that Pulliam was not the "intransigent conservative" that he had been painted.

Nevertheless, Pulliam could still revert to form. Hoping to get Johnson back in the 1968 presidential race and stop Robert Kennedy's drive for the nomination, Pulliam ordered his editors to deny Kennedy full coverage. News about Kennedy and another opponent, Senator Eugene McCarthy, was buried, while the candidacy of Indiana governor Roger Branigin, who was expected to throw his support to Vice-president Hubert Humphrey, was played up. The treatment was so slanted that after Kennedy won the Indiana primary, his press secretary called on the American Society of Newspaper Editors to investigate the campaign coverage by the *Star*. In 1969 Pulliam gained national attention when he ordered his newspapers to stop taking ads for X-rated movies. And as he became increasingly hawkish on the Vietnam War, his differences with his managing editor in Phoenix became too great; he fired Murray in 1971.

Although Pulliam was seen as generous toward his employees in times of their personal trouble, he became increasingly dictatorial and less open to differing opinions as his health began to decline in the 1970s. During the last year of his life Pulliam walked with two canes, had problems with his back and stomach, and got more and more of his news from television, because he could no longer read newspapers. Nevertheless, Pulliam refused to retire. On the morning of 23 June 1975, he dictated a memo on unemployment to the editorial-page editor of the *Republic*. That afternoon he collapsed with a massive stroke at his home in Phoenix and died at St. Joseph's Hospital later in the day. Pulliam's will put ownership and control of the Indianapolis and Phoenix newspapers in a ninety-nine-year trust, and they are now published by Indianapolis Newspapers and Phoenix Newspapers, respectively. The controlling stock in both corporations is owned either directly or indirectly by Central Newspapers.

Biography:
Russell Pulliam, *Publisher: Gene Pulliam, Last of the Newspaper Titans* (Ottawa, Ill.: Jameson, 1984).

References:
"Eugene C. Pulliam Dead at 86," *Editor & Publisher,* 108 (28 June 1975): 9, 11;

"Eugene C. Pulliam Dead at 86; Rightist Newspaper Publisher," *New York Times,* 24 June 1975, p. 36;

"Fairness in Phoenix," *Time,* 87 (7 January 1966): 41;

"Hoosier Dark Horse," *Time,* 43 (8 May 1944): 82;

"Hoosier Hotshot," *Time,* 52 (6 September 1948): 55;

"Indiana Warfare," *Newsweek,* 39 (28 January 1952): 84;

Melvin Mencher, "Pulliam's Progress," *Columbia Journalism Review,* 24 (July/August 1985): 62–63;

"Phoenician Invasion," *Time,* 48 (4 November 1946): 79;

"War Whoop," *Time,* 81 (15 March 1963): 67.

Papers:
Pulliam's papers are at Baker University, Baldwin City, Kansas.

Howard Rock
(Siqvoan Weyahok)
(11 August 1911 – 20 April 1976)

Patrick J. Daley
University of New Hampshire

and

Dan O'Neill
University of Alaska at Fairbanks

MAJOR POSITIONS HELD: Founder, publisher, and editor, *Tundra* (Alaska) *Times* (1962–1976).

In 1962 Howard Rock reluctantly embarked on a fourteen-year career as the founding editor and publisher of the *Tundra Times*, a statewide Alaska newspaper concerned with the cultural, political, and economic needs of the indigenous people of that state. For the most part mainstream dailies had not seen Alaska's multicultural natives as part of their audience, often claiming that they were urban papers that did not cover the rural areas inhabited by natives. When the mainstream press did cover or give voice to these people, it did so in trivializing and disparaging ways, or it focused on them as standing in the way of economic progress for a state newly admitted to the Union.

Rock's minority medium began as a crusade against two technological projects that sought to alter or manage nature and threatened the very lives of his fellow Inupiat Eskimos in the process. The first project was an Atomic Energy Commission (AEC) plan to detonate six atomic bombs near Cape Thompson in northwest Alaska, just thirty miles from Point Hope, in order to create a harbor that the AEC claimed would facilitate the transportation of mineral resources. The second project involved the U.S. Fish and Wildlife Service enforcing the previously ignored 1916 Migratory Bird Treaty Act against the taking of eider ducks in Point Barrow. Native subsistence hunters had customarily taken them in order to add variety to their diets after a long winter's reliance on whale meat and caribou.

As the editorial voice behind the *Tundra Times*, Rock's challenge to the Caucasian domina-

Howard Rock

tion of Alaska print journalism — as well as to the political and economic hegemony of the state — began when he was fifty-one years old. In less than

262

a decade, however, his stewardship of the *Tundra Times* was instrumental in loosening white hegemony over the physical, political, economic, and cultural landscape of Alaska and instilling political leadership and unity among Alaska's diverse ethnic minorities. More important, the *Tundra Times* was at the forefront of the united native land claims campaign, which culminated in passage of the Alaska Native Claims Settlement Act (ANCSA), signed into law by President Richard Nixon on 16 December 1971.

While Rock supported ANCSA with its grant of forty-four million acres of land and nearly $1 billion compensation for land irrevocably lost, he was unsure of what it would mean to his people to be caught between their culture and the capitalism into which they were being thrust. ANCSA entitlements were dispensed through a system of regional and village corporations. More than most of his fellow people, Rock had long lived a life in which he moved successfully, yet somewhat uneasily, between his Inupiat upbringing and his Western education, with all of its acculturational force. He was aware as early as 1964 that natives were entering an arena where words — once used to hand down ancient wisdom — would be wielded as weapons in an epic struggle among competing economic and ideological interests.

The record of Rock's early life as pieced together from an authorized biography by Lael Morgan, taped interviews in the years just before his death in 1976, and stories from his "Arctic Survival" column in the *Tundra Times* does not provide many clues to his future journalistic endeavors. However, it does show youthful exuberance and enthusiasm for learning and expanding one's horizons. Siqvoan Weyahok was born on 11 August 1911, the fifth of eight children of Sam and Keshorna (Emma) Weyahok. They lived in Point Hope, an Inupiat village on the Tigara spit jutting out into the Chukchi Sea and thought to be the oldest continually inhabited site in North America.

Rock came from a long line of whale hunters whose skill brought them into contact as early as the mid nineteenth century with capitalist whalers from New England. His father was a devout Episcopalian who had been converted to Christianity by missionaries at an early age. Howard was named after a sixteen-year-old missionary, Howard Caldwell, and the village's Episcopal minister anglicized Weyahok to Rock, apparently a direct translation.

When he was three, Rock began attending the Saint Thomas Mission school in Point Hope. By the time he was eleven, he had shown a facility for the English language, evidencing particular progress under the instruction of Tony Joule, a young Point Hope Eskimo with a U.S. college education. When he was seven, Rock was moved by his mother and father to the sod igloo of his maternal aunt, Mumageena, and her husband, Nayukuk. Apparently his parents' home was too crowded, but they may also have been dissatisfied with his lack of enthusiasm for the traditional subsistence activities of hunting and gathering.

In 1924 Congress passed legislation granting citizenship to Native Americans; that same year William Paul, Sr., a Tlingit Indian from southeastern Alaska, won a seat in the territorial legislature. In 1923 Paul had started the *Alaska Fisherman*, a Tlingit publication with a working-class focus and interest in securing fishing rights in opposition to the predatory practices of Seattle fishermen. While Paul's newspaper was a precursor to the *Tundra Times*, it retained the heavy influence of Presbyterianism, campaigned to obliterate traditional customs, and did not have a territorywide reach. His paper and a like-minded competitor put out by his brother both fell victim to the Depression in 1932. Ironically, many years later Paul would strike a nonaccommodationist stance for land-claims rights in a series in the *Tundra Times*.

In 1926 the Episcopal minister in Point Hope suggested that Rock would be best off, given his disinclination for hunting, attending the White Mountain Vocational School, which was four hundred miles to the south, and Rock's father readily assented. There, Rock's introduction to Western culture was intensified. He and his classmates would often see movies on Saturday nights, and if the atmospheric conditions were right, they would listen to radio programs on their teacher's set. He acquired a love for music and painting from the Renaissance forward, eschewing the popular idols in sports and movies who captivated many of his fellow students.

In addition to exposure to the fine arts, he learned the technical skills necessary to run and repair gasoline engines. He also received a lesson in consumerism when one of his teachers announced that the Sears and Roebuck catalogue was going to be one of their textbooks that semester. None of this instruction elicited outright negative reactions or responses from Rock at the time; however, in retrospect he acknowledged that the schools he attended were modeled after those in New York, Chicago, and Los Angeles and therefore he did not get to study about those things that were important to people in villages such as Point Hope.

In a March 1976 interview he stated that when he was in high school, he realized that the textbooks were not meant for him or his people. He noticed that they tended to belittle Indians. Rock's ethnocentric educational socialization extended to the use of the "proper language." He recalled that some of his classmates had their mouths washed out with brown soap if they used their native Inupiat instead of English. He remembered feeling envious of those who had frame houses even though his own sod igloo was warm and comfortable. The reason for this desire, he believed, rested at the doorstep of what he learned from Western textbooks.

Many years later, as the editor of the *Tundra Times*, Rock would often focus his news-editorial judgment on the issue of native education. The historical record in Alaska is replete with examples backing up his contention that the acculturational influence of missionary schools inculcated a sense of shame among native students toward their heritage and village life. This educational arrangement was not a matter of native choice, for federal and territorial law required native children to travel great distances to attend either missionary elementary schools or secondary schools that did not admit much native influence on their curricula.

Rock's first journalistic effort was on the staff of the White Mountain yearbook, the *Nasevik*, the Eskimo name for White Mountain synonymous with *lookout*. He designed the cover, a panoramic sketch of White Mountain, and also produced the fourteen-page typescript, because he was the most competent typist at the school. In the annual the students clearly recognized that their association with the white man was changing them in ways that were positive, negative, and simply unforeseeable. They needed to keep a broad "lookout."

Given these educational circumstances, Rock was fortunate in finding someone at White Mountain who recognized his talent and love for drawing. Ruby Dingee, a housekeeper, showed him how to mix oil paints, and he was receptive to both her encouragement and criticism. She arranged for him to work in Oregon under Max Siemes, a Belgian-born artist who served as the U.S. Navy's first official photographer during the Spanish-American War.

At age twenty-two Rock left Alaska for Oregon and had his first bus and train rides and his first encounter with a telephone, an instrument that many years later he would still describe in alien terms. After two years under Siemes's tutelage, his mentor arranged a government loan for him to study art at the University of Washington. Rock encountered his first taste of discrimination at age twenty-five as he searched for housing in Seattle. At the completion of his third year, he found that he could no longer afford his art education, despite the fact that he was acquiring a reputation in the field.

The *Christian Science Monitor* published a story on Rock on 18 March 1938 in which he expressed surprise that people wanted to buy his drawings. He added that Northern scenes were his favorite and his goal was to paint his people's way of living. His artistic abilities stood him in good stead, for he obtained work at a Seattle jeweler's where he carved native scenes on ivory. While he made considerable money doing ivory work, he was dismayed at the cookie-cutter approach to art that it entailed. In 1942 he was drafted into the Army Air Corps and hoped that his art training would get him an assignment painting camouflage, or at least put him back in Alaska. Instead he was trained as a radio operator, served in North Africa until the war was over, and then returned to Seattle.

In 1948 Rock visited his family in Point Hope. He also sought out his brother Allen, who had a military job and was living in Fairbanks. Rock's biographer describes this encounter with his brother as a night of drinking during which Allen chastised him for neglecting his family, who had been on welfare for eight years. Indeed, Allen insulted Howard by calling him a *tanik*, a pejorative Eskimo term referring to whites.

Dismayed, Rock returned to Seattle caught between two worlds but still able to make a comfortable living off his artistic skills. He became more and more convinced, though, that he was wasting his talents, an evaluation underpinned by his increasing dependence on alcohol. Art, however, would be the connection that brought Rock back to Alaska in May 1961. He had become friends with an aspiring artist couple who wanted to move to Alaska. He put them in touch with two of his sisters, and plans were made for all of them to visit. While the impending trip made him happy for his friends' sake, he was apprehensive about his relationship with his brother and his equivocal sense of identity as an Eskimo.

When Rock returned home, he found Point Hope villagers upset over a project headed by Edward Teller, a nuclear physicist who had appeared on the 2 January 1961 cover of *Time* maga-

Rock in his office at the Tundra Times *(photograph by Lael Morgan)*

zine as one of fifteen scientists named "1960 Men of the Year." Teller was the driving force behind the AEC's Plowshare program for the peaceful uses of atomic explosives, which had initiated Project Chariot, a plan to explode six atomic bombs in order to create an artificial harbor at Cape Thompson.

Ironically, given Alaskan natives' future entwinement with oil, the genesis of the harbor project can be traced to the 1956 Egyptian blockade of the Suez Canal. Teller and other scientists at the Lawrence Radiation Laboratory had discussed the possibility of cutting another canal through friendly territory with nuclear explosives. While the creation of a new canal became a moot point with the reopening of the Suez, the idea of using nuclear weapons to excavate waterways was very much alive. Teller knew that the preoccupation of the 1956 presidential campaign with the nuclear test ban treaty meant that the public would thenceforth demand better assurances about the risks of fallout. Teller also knew that a demonstration of Plowshare's potential had to take place in a remote area. So, in July 1958 Teller led a contingent of scientists to the urban areas of Alaska to drum up support for the harbor proposal,

promising audiences that two-thirds of the $5 million project would end up in Alaska.

Teller's visit coincided with the passage of the Alaska statehood act, which had an important consequence concerning native Alaskans' land rights. The state was given the right to select 104 million acres of land in order to establish some kind of revenue base. State leaders were more cognizant than ever of the need to develop a sound economic base, a consideration that had been driving the pro-statehood forces for decades. The timing of the AEC's project was therefore opportune. The *Fairbanks Daily News-Miner*, long a supporter of statehood, ran an editorial on 14 July 1958 stating, "We think the holding of a huge nuclear blast in Alaska would be a fitting overture to the new era which is opening up for our state."

However, native Alaskans were not a part of the AEC's public-relations package. A few Point Hope Eskimos had chance encounters with project surveyors in the summer, but residents were not informed about what they were doing there. Don Foote, an independent human geographer under AEC contract who would later become a valuable source for Rock, noted in a 1961 report that Point Hope residents first learned of the plan from a

Kotzebue missionary in April 1959. The missionary was generally supportive of the project, so he did not reveal its magnitude, nor its risks, to the villagers.

Yet, even with favorable publicity and support from politicians and Chambers of Commerce, the AEC changed its experiment and its public-relations face when it became known that touted economic advantages of the harbor were unjustified. In January 1959 the AEC announced that it would be engaged in an experiment to test whether nuclear explosives could create a crater and simultaneously trap radioactivity underground. The AEC knew that it had a new public-relations problem, because the new experiment did not promise long-term economic possibilities for Alaska. As the AEC ratcheted up the pressure, it won the endorsement of the Fairbanks Chamber of Commerce and the Alaska legislature, but lost the endorsement of Sen. Bob Barlett and was challenged by the environmentally conscious Sierra Club.

The *Fairbanks Daily News-Miner*, quoting Teller, played down the threat of radiation and dismissed environmental criticism in a 15 August 1959 story that stated that only the AEC's environmental studies committee could make the final evaluation. The paper also quoted an eminent scientist from the AEC's environmental committee who said that it was conceivable that a rock might hit a caribou in the head but that it was silly to talk about whales being killed. This kind of trivializing reportage, together with the lack of concern by the urban press for those who would be most affected by the blast, prompted natives to discuss the need for a communication medium to support their interests.

More than a year before Rock returned home, the Point Hope villagers were able to query AEC officials directly when Bartlett prevailed upon them to visit the villagers. Foote's report, published a year after this meeting, revealed the distorted picture of the dangers of radiation that AEC officials had painted for the villagers. Residents were assured that fish in the Pacific Proving Grounds were not affected by radioactivity, that no human beings had ever been adversely affected by nuclear tests, and that the Japanese who had recovered from radiation sickness after World War II suffered no further effects.

Faced with this duplicity, Point Hope village council president David Frankson contacted the Association of American Indian Affairs (AAIA). His plea to them for assistance was reprinted in the July issue of *Indian Affairs*: "All and everyone at this village would not like to see this experiment at Ogotoruk Creek at anytime in future or at present — with our earnest desire we have been seeking in someone who would help us to overcome the plan of nuclear experiment." Meanwhile, opposition also came from within the project's recruited ranks as one University of Alaska scientist resigned from the project, citing pressure from the AEC to make his report conform to its apparently predetermined scientific conclusion.

This is the situation that Rock found when he returned to Point Hope in 1961. His personal relationship with the villagers was itself shaky. They chided him for forgetting his language and treated him as an outsider. He was appalled that the AEC had not fully informed them of the dangers involved, and he sought confirmation of the villagers' fears from scientists. Rock was amazed at the sophisticated data that the villagers had at their disposal. Foote verified the accuracy of their knowledge for him and acknowledged the empirical grounding of their fears. On 4 June 1961 the *New York Times* ran a story reporting the work of the Saint Louis Committee for Nuclear Information, headed by Barry Commoner. The article cited the unpublished work of biologists who traced the deposit of radioactive fallout on lichens, which were then absorbed into the natives' food chain.

Another obstacle to the traditional subsistence economy of native Alaskans was thrown in the faces of Point Barrow villagers in May 1961 when a U.S. Fish and Wildlife agent arrested two Barrow natives for killing eider ducks out of season. The agent was enforcing the 1916 Migratory Bird Treaty with Canada and Mexico, which forbade the taking of certain migratory birds between March and August. The treaty essentially meant that native Alaskans could only hunt eider ducks when they were out of state. While this conservation measure made sense in the flyways of the lower forty-eight states and Canada, it interfered with a centuries-old practice of duck taking by the natives as a welcome change in their diet after the relative monotony of their winter food caches.

While it is not clear whether the natives even knew about the treaty, this arrest certainly brought home to them the message that their aboriginal hunting rights and their subsistence economy were hanging in the balance. The agency's effort to manage nature appeared to be an action based on ignorance of these long-standing practices. The July issue of *Indian Affairs* reported the Eskimo response: 138 Eskimos delivered six hundred pounds of eider ducks to game wardens staying at the Top of the World Hotel in Barrow and signed statements indicating their responsibility. The newsletter also reprinted an appeal for assistance to LaVerne Madigan, executive director of AAIA, from Barrow Eskimo Guy Okakok: "We just had a meeting yesterday in school, right after the evening service. We discuss about our ducks, eider and Pacific. We did not know that we can't shoot ducks when they come through our shore. Anyway, please come so that I can let you know everything. It's a long story. . . ."

In the summer of 1961 Madigan and Henry Forbes, a Massachusetts physician who was chairman of AAIA's Alaska Policy Committee, fulfilled Okakok's and Frankson's pleas for help. When Madigan and Forbes met with Point Hope villagers, Rock was in attendance. While the record is not clear, there is some indication that he suggested that Alaska natives in widely scattered villages needed some kind of communication medium to share knowledge about their common problems. What is clear is that Madigan and Forbes were impressed with Rock despite the fact that he kept a low profile. AAIA did agree to sponsor a native political conference in Barrow in November to discuss the problems of Project Chariot and the ban on hunting eider ducks. The Point Hope villagers asked Rock to write to Secretary of the Interior Stewart Udall on their behalf. Rock's letter to Udall requested that the Department of the Interior revoke the Bureau of Land Management's withdrawal of sixteen hundred square miles of land for AEC use in Project Chariot. Rock based his claim on aboriginal land rights not extinguished by the Organic Act of 1884.

Late in the summer of 1961 Project Chariot suffered another setback when a reporter for the *Fairbanks Daily News-Miner*, Thomas Snapp, reversed what a 1986 scholarly article called a "more than two-year-long congratulatory coverage of the proposed project." While Snapp's disclosures were not scoops, they did establish his credibility among the Eskimos. No other reporter in the state had been giving Alaska natives favorable coverage. That fall Rock and Snapp met at a showing of Rock's artwork in Fairbanks, an exhibit sponsored by Ralph Perdue, an Athabascan jeweler whom Rock had met some years before in Seattle. Rock and Snapp discovered that they had a mutual interest in trying to uncover as much material as they could on Project Chariot – Snapp so he could write about it for the *News-Miner* and

Rock so he could present a case to Bartlett to stop it. Their mutual interest drew them to the Inupiat Paitot (People's Heritage) Conference in November at the Top of the World Hotel in Barrow, where they were roommates.

The conference was attended by more than two hundred natives from twenty villages, Madigan, Assistant Secretary of the Interior John Carver, Indian Commissioner Philleo Nash, and Snapp. Since the proceedings were conducted in Inupiat and Yupik Eskimo, Snapp had a translator. In a 1983 interview he recalled that he kept hearing his name and Rock's. Much to his surprise Snapp found out that he and Rock were being appointed to a committee to explore the establishment of a regular newspaper for Alaska Eskimos so that their issues could be given a fair hearing. The Inupiat Paitot conferees also went on record in support of aboriginal hunting rights and against the Bureau of Land Management's licensing of native land for Project Chariot.

While Snapp was taken aback by the magnitude of the charge, he, Rock, Okakok, and Madigan set about exploring how to finance such a venture. Their goal was to put out a weekly paper beginning in May 1962, to be called *Inupiat Okatut*, meaning "The Eskimos Speak." Rock had been thinking of such a newspaper for some time so he was enthusiastically behind the plan. However, he believed that the conferees had erred by not placing enough emphasis on land claims.

When Rock and Snapp returned to Fairbanks, they became involved in organizing Athabascan Indians in the state's interior for a conference of their own. Here the land issue that Rock believed was so important was central to what was happening to the Athabascans' traditional hunting and fishing lands. Madigan urged Snapp and Rock to include Athabascans in their proposed newspaper, since land rights were central to all Alaska natives.

The Athabascan conference was to be held at Tanana, at the confluence of the Yukon and Tanana rivers, and it was to coincide with the revival of Nuch-la-woh-ya, an Athabascan arts and games festival. The conference was called Dena Nena Henash, meaning "Our Land Speaks." Of central concern to the conferees was the encroachment of the state, the oil companies, and the University of Alaska on the traditional lands around the native villages of Minto and Nenana. In the Tanana chiefs policy statement, Chief Frank of Minto expressed what these encroachments meant to the way of life of his people: "White men are all over the land we held by right. For fifteen miles around our village, we hunt rats (muskrats) and moose. We always did. Now there are twenty-four white camps there. Everywhere you turn you are bumping into a white man. . . . Now I hear this summer they are going to build a road into our hunting area. We cannot live when the highway gets to that lake. Without our hunting land, our village is finished."

While Snapp was covering the conference for the *Fairbanks Daily News-Miner*, his copy was distorted and undercut by a front-page editorial lambasting AAIA as outside agitators who wanted to put Indians back on the reservation. Indeed, even Ralph Perdue, Rock's friend and art sponsor, fearing the worst of historic reservation practices, claimed that AAIA was a communistic organization. Rock and Snapp were convinced that they had to move quickly to put out their partisan newspaper to counteract these misrepresentations.

The big stumbling block was money. It would be extremely expensive to cover almost two hundred villages, few of which even had telephones. Other obstacles were high printing costs and distribution of the newspaper over a vast area. Newspapers would have to be delivered by bush planes. Rock and Snapp explored the possibility of obtaining foundation money, but when that proved to be too cumbersome, they sought Madigan's help, asking her for the names of the five wealthiest contributors to AAIA. While she balked at this request on ethical grounds, she later suggested two donors, including Dr. Henry Forbes, whom Rock had met a year before in Point Hope.

Rock wrote Forbes, explaining the need for a native newspaper, and Snapp followed up in late August with a forty-seven-page letter requesting support. In mid September, just as Snapp was packing his bags to return to graduate school in journalism at the University of Missouri, Rock and Snapp received a call from Forbes telling them that he would provide a no-strings-attached grant of thirty-five thousand dollars for the paper on the condition that Rock would be its editor and Snapp would be his assistant. Snapp agreed to stay for a year and a day. A member of the Fairbanks-based Native Rights Association suggested that the paper be called the *Tundra Times* to ensure that its title did not exclude the interests of Athabascans, Aleuts, and the Indians of the Southeast.

On 1 October 1962, almost five thousand copies of the *Tundra Times* were distributed throughout the state. In an emphasis on pan-na-

Rock on a whale hunt at Point Hope, Alaska (photograph by Lael Morgan)

tive unity, the upper corners of the front page addressed the paper's audiences in four languages: "Unanguq Tununktauq" (The Aleuts Speak), "Dena Nena Henash" (Our Land Speaks [Athabascan]), "Utkah Neek" (Informing and Reporting [Tlingit]), and "Inupiat Paitot" (People's Heritage [Eskimo]). Rock's editorial focused on the commitment of the paper to serve the needs and interests of all of the state's native groups. While Rock and Snapp had long agreed that the first issue would feature the threat of Project Chariot, that was no longer necessary, since it had collapsed because of the general ineptitude of the campaign to sell it on economic and environmental grounds. An AEC announcement in August placed the project in indefinite abeyance.

Instead of leading with Project Chariot, Rock chose to focus on the upcoming second Inupiat Paitot conference and to raise the matter of land claims, including the subsistence right to take eider ducks. Unfortunately, Rock also had to report the death of the natives' greatest supporter, Madigan, who had died while vacationing in Vermont. In the second and third issues of the *Tundra Times*, Rock did a long retrospective on Project Chariot. Then, in the first issue of 1963 Snapp pegged the year-and-a-half-long eider duck controversy on a decision by a Canadian judge that upheld aboriginal rights in a similar case. Snapp concluded the story with the announcement that Udall had given the go-ahead for Eskimos to take ducks and geese for food at any time of the year.

From 1963 to 1966 the question of land was the most prominent news and editorial peg in the paper, and Rock used this overriding issue to organize two major statewide conferences that led to a permanent political native organization. The last major land disputes on which Snapp and Rock reported were the claims by some interior Alaska villages, beginning with those of Minto, first voiced at the Tanana Chiefs Conference. Blanket claims had been made by Minto villagers since the 1940s, and a land claim had been filed with the Bureau of Land Management in 1950. These could no longer be accounted for, so Rock and Snapp, with legal assistance, helped the Athabascans to map out new claims. In March the *Tundra Times* headlined a petition asking Udall for a land freeze. In fact, all issues in March centered on the Minto land-claims action, which was not successful, but the paper did succeed in calling attention to the subject of land claims.

Meanwhile, Snapp had held to his promise to teach Rock everything he knew about journalism, but for just one year. Given his artistic past, Rock showed a good eye for design and composition, but he had a harder time grasping how to write a hard-news story. Snapp took responsibility for the controversial stories, but Rock's voice was always evident in news-editorial policy. Besides editorials, Rock devoted much of his early writing to his "Arctic Survival" series, which recounted the traditions, habits, and customs of his people just as he had tried to do with his artist's palette years before. This series won him the Alaska Press Club's acclaim as the top newspaper columnist in the state in 1963 and 1964.

Various native groups throughout the state began to coalesce around the land issues brought to the forefront by Rock. With AAIA sponsorship and organizational work by Rock, the two-day Conference of Native Organizations, representing the entire native population of forty-three thousand, met in Fairbanks in 1964. While this was a onetime affair, it helped make possible the first ongoing statewide native organization, the Alaska Federation of Natives, formed on 18 October 1966. Rock was present when the AFN was established, and he reported on its recommendations, again requesting that the Department of the Interior freeze all disposals of federal land pending a land-claims settlement that Congress was urged to pass with native consultation and assent.

One of Rock's greatest accomplishments did not have to do with land per se, but instead dealt with the achievement of civil rights for Aleuts on the Pribilof Islands, who had been held in semiservitude by the federal government's Bureau of Commercial Fisheries. Dorothy Knee Jones, the author of a historical and sociological study of the Pribilof Aleuts, contends that they were subjected to a case of internal colonialism in which racism was an essential component. Ever since the purchase of Alaska from Russia, the U.S. government had pursued a policy of harvesting Pribilof Island seals for profit by using the labor of the Aleuts in return for often substandard wages supplemented by in-kind payments of food, clothing, fuel, and housing. In the nineteenth century the management program was a combination of government and private enterprise, but in the twentieth century, after conservation measures became increasingly necessary, the government took on the role of imperialist overseer, and the Aleuts suffered from federal cost-conscious market considerations.

In the 1950s conditions improved somewhat as the oppressive federal management regime was criticized by the National Congress of American Indians, the International Labor Organization, and other UN agencies. In a 3 March 1950 *New York Times* articles, the government was accused of holding the Aleuts in semiservitude. Under pressure from Senator Bartlett and because of a change in the program's managers, a slow process of reform was instituted in the 1960s. Rock's eighteen-month investigation accelerated the reform process. He was outraged at the manipulation of Aleut labor and the pathetic state of their civil rights, and his usually understated editorials took on a more strident tone.

One of the more egregious violations of fundamental rights was restrictions on who was allowed to visit Aleuts. When this social segregation extended to political discrimination by denying an Aleut candidate for the state legislature access to the island, Rock assailed the policy in the *Tundra Times* on 23 November 1964. The act was overturned, and Gov. William Egan appointed Rock to the state's human rights commission to investigate the discriminatory practices of what still amounted to a company town. Since earlier reforms had overturned the wardship status of Aleuts and extended federal pension benefits to them for work after 1950, Rock lobbied for extension of coverage for workers prior to 1950 and a change in the reserve status of the island. It took Rock's threat of a minority report to accomplish these goals. From that point on he was an ardent supporter of the subsistence seal-hunting rights of the Aleuts.

Clearly the *Tundra Times* had proved a valuable resource in the movement for native rights and equality, but it always had to struggle financially. As a consequence Rock decided in 1965 to drum up financial support by holding a banquet. While the initial event was a moderate success, it did become an annual institution, and subsequent efforts were quite helpful. Another annual fund-raiser sponsored by the *Tundra Times* was the World Eskimo Indian Olympics. Both fund-raisers resulted from Forbes's desire to pull away from supporting the paper as he aged. In fact, at Forbes's urging, the paper incorporated in 1966 under native control as the Eskimo, Indian, Aleut Publishing Company.

In 1966 Udall announced a freeze on the conveyance of state-selected lands. In 1968 a world-class oil field was discovered on the North Slope of Alaska at Prudhoe Bay. In a comprehensive 1991 history of the oil industry, Daniel Yergin noted that Western governments and oil companies had been keen on exploring for North American oil deposits ever since the Suez crisis. Hence, energy security made the development of Alaskan oil both a corporate and national priority.

Rock and other native leaders realized that oil was the puzzle piece that could bring the land-claims battle to a logical resolution. Environmentalists were also interested in either stopping oil development in the fragile ecosystem or at least ensuring that extraordinary measures would be taken to prevent ecological damage in both the extraction of the oil and its transportation. Environmentalists and native groups were thus the political power brokers who exercised leverage on multinational corporations and the most powerful members of Congress. For native groups this resulted in congressional passage of ANCSA, granting natives forty-four million

acres of land and nearly $1 billion for land irrevocably lost. Since land claims, physical and cultural survival, and subsistence rights had been the centerpieces of Rock's editorial philosophy from the beginning, the *Tundra Times* has been rightly accorded much of the credit for ANCSA.

While Rock rarely hedged on his partisan claims in his paper, he also believed that it should serve as a forum, and he invited opposing positions. Rock was criticized for ANCSA because its corporate structure did not provide sufficient political mechanisms for native self-determination and autonomy. His critics were no doubt right in chiding him for the assimilationist character of the settlement and for the failure of the legislation to protect their traditional resources.

Nevertheless, Rock understood that political pragmatism had its virtues and that any land-claims settlement would necessarily be controversial and complex. He disputed the frequent contention that, with the passage of ANCSA, the raison d'être of the *Tundra Times* no longer existed. He foresaw some of the difficulties the legislation would engender and used the paper to begin the process of enrolling natives in the appropriate regional corporation.

In addition to working to implement this legislation, Rock kept his journalistic spotlight turned on everyday matters of concern to his readers, the most important of which were sanitation and hygiene, housing, and education. He was particularly proud of the fact that the paper was often used as a textbook in native elementary schools. One of the educational concerns of the *Tundra Times* was the farming out of native children to high schools far from their home villages. Long an advocate of a native-influenced curriculum, Rock's work led to the celebrated Molly Hootch case (*Anna Tobeluk* v. *Marshall Lind*), in which a student in 1971 objected to being sent five hundred miles from her native village to high school in Anchorage. As the principal plaintiff in a class-action suit, she charged the state with failing to provide 145 villages having 50 percent or more native students with secondary education nearby. A 1976 out-of-court settlement remedied this situation to the satisfaction of the plaintiffs.

After Rock's decade-long struggle for the resolution of land claims, he was the recipient of many honors. In 1972 he was nominated for the Alaskan of the Year Award, which he shared with Sen. Ted Stevens in 1974. The Alaska Press Club presented him with its highest prize, the 49-er of the Year Award, in 1973. For his continuing efforts to promote the welfare of the native peoples of Alaska, Rock was awarded an honorary doctor of humane letters degree from the University of Alaska in 1974. In 1975 the *Tundra Times* was nominated for a Pulitzer Prize for meritorious public service.

In 1973 Rock was diagnosed with cancer. While his work load decreased, he continued to be a regular contributor to the paper until his death on 20 April 1976. At his request he was interred in the traditional burial grounds outside his village of Point Hope.

Biography:

Lael Morgan, *Art and Eskimo Power* (Fairbanks, Alaska: Epicenter Press, 1988).

References:

Stanley A. Blumberg and Gwinn Owens, *Energy and Conflict: The Life and Times of Edward Teller* (New York: Putnam's, 1976), pp. 395–401;

"The Challenge of Alaska," *Indian Affairs*, no. 42 (July 1961);

Patrick Daley and Beverly James, "An Authentic Voice in the Technocratic Wilderness: Alaskan Natives and the *Tundra Times*," *Journal of Communication*, 36 (Summer 1986): 10–30;

Shirley E. Fogarino, "The *Tundra Times*: Alaska Native Advocate, 1962–1976," Master's thesis, University of Maryland, 1981;

Beverly James and Patrick Daley, "The Development of the Alaskan Native Press in the Movement Toward Self-Determination, 1867–1967," paper presented at the International Association for Mass Communication Research Conference, Prague, Czechoslovakia (August 1984);

Dorothy Knee Jones, *A Century of Servitude: Pribilof Aleuts Under U.S. Rule* (Lanham, Md.: University Press of America, 1980);

Dan O'Neill, "Project Chariot: How Alaska Escaped Nuclear Excavation," *Bulletin of the Atomic Scientists* (December 1989): 28–37;

Daniel Yergin, *The Prize: The Epic Quest For Oil, Money and Power* (New York: Simon & Schuster, 1991), pp. 564–574.

Papers:

Interviews with Rock are located in the Oral History Archive, Rasmuson Library, University of Alaska at Fairbanks.

Vermont Royster

(30 April 1914 –)

Edward E. Adams
Ohio University

MAJOR POSITIONS HELD: Correspondent, Washington Bureau (1936–1941, 1945–1946), chief correspondent, Washington Bureau (1946–1948), editorial writer and columnist (1946–1948), associate editor (1948–1951), senior associate editor (1951–1958), editor (1958–1971), contributing editor and columnist (1971), *Wall Street Journal;* senior vice-president, Dow Jones and Company (1960–1971).

BOOKS: *Journey through the Soviet Union* (New York: Dow Jones, 1962);
A Pride of Prejudices (New York: Knopf, 1967);
My Own, My Country's Time: A Journalist's Journey (Chapel Hill, N.C.: Algonquin, 1983);
The Essential Royster: A Vermont Royster Reader (Chapel Hill, N.C.: Algonquin, 1985).

In 1936, during the Depression, Vermont Royster walked through the door of the *Wall Street Journal* and requested a job. He had only a few months of work experience as an errand boy and reporter, plus a college degree. He started with the *Journal* as monitor of the stock ticker, and twenty-two years later he was editor of one of the two national daily newspapers in the United States.

Vermont Connecticut Royster was born on 30 April 1914 in his grandfather's house in Raleigh, North Carolina, the firstborn of Wilbur High and Olivette Broadway Royster. He was named after his grandfather Royster, whose siblings were also named after states. The boys were Iowa Michigan, Arkansas Delaware, Wisconsin Illinois, and Oregon Minnesota. The girls also had states' names: Louisiana Maryland, Virginia Carolina, and Georgia Indiana. These unusual appellations were listed in "Ripley's Believe It or Not" and found their way into the pages of the *Saturday Review* and *Saturday Evening Post.*

Olivette Royster so admired her father-in-law that she wanted her first son to have his name; however, his brother and sister did not join the legacy of

states' names. His brother, Tommy, was born in 1919 at the height of the influenza epidemic; his sister, Saravette, was born in 1927.

Vermont spent his first years in Chapel Hill, North Carolina, where his father taught Latin and Greek at the University of North Carolina. The family moved to Raleigh in 1920, so his father could help his grandfather in the family candy business. Vermont had an insatiable appetite for reading, which carried over to school. Shortly after starting first grade he was advanced to the third grade.

He had a difficult time fitting in, because he was small for his age and two years younger than his school peers. The *News and Observer,* the morning newspaper in Raleigh, gave Royster his first opportunity for acceptance by his classmates. He became a self-appointed press agent for his high-school football team, writing stories that carried his byline, which made him popular. Royster was graduated from high school in 1929 at age fifteen. He planned on attending the university in Chapel Hill, but his father sent him to the Webb School in Bell Buckle, Tennessee, for two years.

During the summer between his graduation from Webb and attendance at the University of North Carolina, Royster and some friends spent the Fourth of July at a coastal resort town. There he met Frances Claypoole, of New Bern, at a dance. They were married almost six years later, on 5 June 1937.

The preparation at Webb helped him at Chapel Hill. He majored in classical languages and became involved in theater and the campus newspaper, the *Daily Tar Heel.* Over the next four years he became assistant night editor, music critic, and editorial writer. He was graduated Phi Beta Kappa in January 1935.

The degree in classical languages had not prepared him for anything practical, and the only work experience he had was with the campus newspaper. He ventured off to New York City, where he

Royster in his Wall Street Journal *office (photograph by Marvin Koner)*

worked as a busboy in a cafeteria. He then secured a messenger job with Commercial National Bank, which allowed him to move into a new apartment with two college classmates from Chapel Hill. The three launched the Metropolitan News Service, which covered North Carolinians who were visiting or living in New York, as a service to their home-state newspapers. Only a few assignments trickled in, and the venture died.

A promotion to stock-transfer clerk made a career in banking appear imminent. However, on a visit to the New York News Association, Royster was offered a temporary job at less pay as a messenger-reporter. He took it. The association ran an operation similar to the Associated Press, but it covered only New York City as a cooperative venture for New York newspapers. After a few weeks the job was eliminated, and Royster was unemployed.

In February 1936 Royster walked into the office of William Henry Grimes, managing editor of the *Wall Street Journal,* and asked him for a job. After a recitation of his experience, Royster was told to report to Eddie Costenbader, who ran the

Dow Jones News Service. At this time the news service generated the bulk of revenue for Dow Jones, providing financial information to banks, brokerage houses, and similar firms. The *Journal* had a circulation of less than thirty-five thousand, primarily in New York and Washington.

Royster monitored the stock ticker and logged news. In mid March, Grimes asked him if he would like to go to Washington. On 25 March 1936 Royster reported to Bernard Kilgore, the *Journal* bureau chief in Washington. His first assignment was covering the Department of Agriculture and its secretary, Henry Wallace, who would become President Franklin Roosevelt's vice-president and a presidential candidate.

The *Journal* was a small paper, both in circulation and prestige, when compared to the papers of other Washington correspondents. Besides the Department of Agriculture, Royster covered the Departments of Commerce and the Interior. In late 1936 he began serving as backup man for Roosevelt's press conferences, and in the spring of 1937 he covered the Maritime Commission and its

Vice-premier Keng Piao of China with Royster in Peking, 1978 (photograph by Gordon R. Converse, Christian Science Monitor)

chairman, Joseph P. Kennedy. On top of his assignment with the *Journal,* Royster wrote stories for *Barron's,* a Dow Jones weekly financial magazine.

Royster then received a new assignment — Capitol Hill and the Supreme Court. Reporting on both of these areas opened Royster up to the intricacies of law and legal research. While covering the court he received a note from Arthur Krock, Washington bureau chief of the *New York Times,* complimenting him on a series of stories. Krock offered him a position with the *Times,* but Royster did not want to be relegated to writing about the Supreme Court; he favored the flexibility at the *Journal.*

During World War II, Royster served four and a half years with the U.S. Naval Reserve. In 1945 he returned to the job at the *Journal* that Kilgore had promised to hold for him. George Bryant was the new bureau chief. Kilgore had moved up the ladder in the Dow Jones organization. Royster's first assignment was to cover the Treasury and Federal Reserve Board. In midsummer 1946 Bryant left the *Journal;* a few days later Royster became Washington bureau chief.

In early 1948 he went to New York to help on the editorial page, because Grimes was ill. He then returned to Washington, only to receive a call from New York that he was needed on the editorial staff there permanently. He accepted the position of associate editor and an increase in salary. At this time the *Journal* was embroiled in changes to the newspaper and staff. Kilgore was attempting to move the *Journal* toward becoming a national newspaper with printing plants in strategic locations across America. There were some staff changes and promotions that caused internal strife in the New York office.

One year after his arrival in New York, Royster attempted to look elsewhere for a position. An offer came from the *Saturday Evening Post,* but the risk of a short-term position was not appealing to him. He also received an offer from Paul Miller of Gannett Newspapers in Rochester, New York: the editor's position with the Rochester paper and a 30 percent increase in salary.

Kilgore, afraid to lose Royster, tempted him to remain with the *Journal.* Royster received a 50 percent increase in salary and Kilgore's promise to deal with the staff difficulties. In early 1951 Royster was promoted to senior associate editor. That same year

Alan L. Otten, Royster, and President Lyndon B. Johnson in the White House, 1964

he won a Pulitzer Prize for "distinguished editorial writing." It was only the second Pulitzer Prize won by a *Journal* member.

Royster strengthened the staff and brought on capable assistants, which allowed him to work outside the office. Unlike his predecessor Grimes, who was a social recluse, Royster used his position to gain access to important people, including Presidents Dwight Eisenhower and John Kennedy. The *Journal* rose considerably in prestige, power, and popularity. Royster's 1955 editorials pounded away at government spending and the growing national debt. He moved rapidly to establish more credibility on the editorial-policy front. The editorial page won widespread favor for its acute analysis, incisive style, and urbane humor. In 1957 Royster was elected chairman of the National Conference of Editorial Writers.

In 1959 the *Journal* sent him on a round-the-world trip that took him to Vietnam. America had a few advisers in the country, and Royster took the opportunity to interview leader Ngo Dinh Diem. He closely covered the 1960 presidential election between Kennedy and Richard Nixon. In 1962 Royster accompanied a group of journalists invited to meet with Soviet premier Nikita Khrushchev. He reported his impressions to President Kennedy. Royster wrote editorials about Kennedy's involvement in Vietnam, civil-rights policies, and assassination, as well as the 1964 presidential election between Barry Goldwater and Lyndon Johnson. In 1965 Royster was elected president of the American Society of Newspaper Editors. He had been active in the organization for many years and had served as vice-president the year before.

In the fall of 1967 Royster joined a prestigious group of editors called to the White House to confer with President Johnson, who was losing public favor over the war in Vietnam and was seeking answers from the journalists. In November, Kilgore – Royster's boss and mentor in Washington and New York – died. Royster continued to write editorials about presidents, world leaders, wars, and crises. In 1970 he was diagnosed with cancer of the liver. During his convalescence he was offered a chaired professorship at his alma mater, the University of North Carolina at Chapel Hill. In January 1971 he retired as editor of the *Journal* and senior vice-president of Dow Jones, but he remained a director of the company. When he left the *Journal,* its circulation was 1.2 million, a substantial increase over the Depression-era figure when he began with the publication.

Before starting his teaching position in 1972, Royster and his wife spent a year traveling on their boat, *Covenant*. They cruised the waterways between New York and Florida, and then journeyed to the Bahamas. They had two daughters, Frances and Sara, who were born during World War II.

Royster taught journalism and political science at Chapel Hill. Meanwhile, the *Journal* asked him to write a weekly column, "Thinking Things Over." At first he thought this would be difficult, but he found the university's library and faculty great sources of information. He was a regular commentator on public affairs for CBS radio and television from 1972 to 1977. In 1984 he received his second Pulitzer Prize, this time for commentary. He continued his position at the university until 1986.

Royster has received many honorary degrees, including an LL.D. from the University of North Carolina (1959), a Litt.D. from Temple University (1964), an L.H.D. from Elon College (1968), an LL.D. from Colby College (1976), and a Litt.D. from Williams College (1979). He has been the recipient of many awards, including the Society of Professional Journalists' medal for distinguished service in journalism (1958), the William Allen White Award for distinguished service to journalism (1971), the Loeb Memorial Award for contributions to economics and journalism (1975), and the Presidential Medal of Freedom (1986). He was elected to the North Carolina Journalism Hall of Fame in 1980.

References:

American Society of Newspaper Editors, Proceedings (Alexandria, Va.: ASNE, 1965), p. 10;

American Society of Newspaper Editors, Proceedings (Alexandria, Va.: ASNE, 1966), p. 7;

Lloyd Wendt, *The Wall Street Journal: The Story of Dow Jones & the Nation's Business Newspaper* (Chicago: Rand, McNally, 1982).

Dorothy Schiff

(11 March 1903 – 30 August 1989)

Ginger Rudeseal Carter
Northeast Louisiana University

MAJOR POSITIONS HELD: Vice-president and treasurer (1939–1942), copresident and copublisher (1942–1949), owner (1943–1976), president and publisher (1949–1976), *New York Post*.

Dorothy Schiff was, by admission, a wealthy socialite who knew little about business and less about newspapers. She married and divorced four men in forty-five years. She was friend and confidante to presidents and captains of industry.

But it was not until Schiff took controlling interest of the *New York Post* in 1939 that she found her claim to fame. Her acquisition of the *Post* was more than just a business transaction – it was the beginning of a trailblazing publishing career that spanned thirty-seven years. Through her stewardship and leadership one of the nation's oldest newspapers became profitable again – and Schiff became one of America's most influential publishers.

To understand the publishing history of Schiff (she stopped using her husbands' surnames after her third divorce in the late 1940s) it is important to examine the intertwining of her family life, her marriages, and her newspaper. Unlike many newspaper publishers, Schiff did not come from a newspaper family. She was born 11 March 1903 to Mortimer L. and Adele A. (Neustadt) Schiff, both German Jews.

Her paternal grandfather, Jacob Schiff, was a wealthy New Jersey investment banker, head of the firm Kuhn, Loeb and Company. Her parents moved "Dolly," as she was called, and her brother, John, to New York to escape Jacob's New Jersey social scene, although her father (and later her brother) carried on the family business. Her father, among other accomplishments, was national president of the Boy Scouts of America.

Dorothy and John were reared on New York's Fifth Avenue. She attended the Brearley School and, after flunking out of Bryn Mawr College, married Richard B. W. Hall in 1923. The death of her father in 1931 and her mother in 1932 allowed

Dorothy Schiff, 1968

Schiff the freedom – and the funds – to divorce Hall.

In her diary, excerpts of which were published in *Men, Money and Magic: The Story of Dorothy Schiff,* by Jeffrey Potter (1976), Dorothy wrote that after Hall received news of her mother's death, she told him, "My God, I'm rich at last." A few minutes later she added, "And now, I'm going to leave you." Schiff dropped plans to convert to Episcopalianism, Hall's religion. She again took up Jewish-community causes, "returning to my roots," she wrote.

Her 1932 marriage to liberal Democrat George Backer resulted in her alliance with Frank-

277

lin Roosevelt's campaign as a social-welfare advocate, and it marked her divorce from the Republican party. This led to a lifelong friendship with the president, but it did not result in an affair.

Schiff was adamant about the fact that their relationship was platonic. In a statement published for her obituary she said, "President Roosevelt never made a suggestion that I become his girlfriend, and Mrs. Eleanor Roosevelt was just as good a friend as Mr. Roosevelt." Still, she spent much time at Hyde Park, New York, as a guest of the Roosevelts, and she later purchased land from them.

Backer, the catalyst for Schiff's change from Republican to Democrat, also introduced his wife to the Algonquin Round Table set. This appears to have been her earliest interaction with journalists. These journalistic ties and political commitments are believed to be what kept this marriage alive.

Things changed drastically for Backer and Schiff in 1939. He made a commitment to *Post* publisher J. David Stern to purchase the newspaper and keep it alive for the "left-of-center constituency." Backer had no money, but his wife did. He wrote, "I told Dolly about it on account of her having money. She, a wonderful sport, said sure."

Schiff was convinced of the decision because of the paper's history (founded by Alexander Hamilton in 1801 as a Tory information sheet) and President Roosevelt's suggestion that she needed something else to do. She acquired the paper – and all its debts – in 1939. Of the cost of the *Post,* Schiff wrote in her diary, "Stern wrote a book saying he got a check for $500,000 for the stock, but that is not true; I got the controlling stock for nothing." Backer was named president and publisher; Schiff was vice-president and treasurer.

At first her role was titular. In fact, in her diary Schiff wrote of the completion of the deal, "After the signing, I went back uptown to the children. I had only been needed for my signature." She added, "I had no idea what I was getting into or why I was getting it just for debts."

She soon found out. The paper lost $2 million in the first year as circulation plummeted. Schiff tightened her financial belt and considered changes in the *Post.* In spite of her wealth she was firm that the *Post* be self-supporting. "Kept organs are just no good," she said. Her brother told her to "treat it like a racehorse. Determine how much you can pour into it, and make that your limit."

In 1941 Backer was still pleased with the liberal editorial stance, but Schiff's diary noted that he had trouble with the business end. In an interview with the *New York Herald Tribune,* she said she

Schiff and New York Post *pressmen celebrating after the newspaper resumed publication on 4 March 1963 following a 114-day strike*

wanted to make the paper "more popular." Features editor Theodore Thackrey agreed with her, and, working together, they redesigned the newspaper. This moved the *Post* to a tabloid format. Schiff, drawing on her experiences in politics and social work, began to write a column. She and Thackrey also added comics, syndicated columns, plenty of glamour, and scandal.

Her alliance with Thackrey and the drastic editorial changes at the paper led to her divorce from Backer in 1942. Schiff noted in her diary that things were over between them: "George didn't really want the paper anymore. I said, 'Let me go down,' but he said, 'Let's just throw it in the river.' I told him I'd like to see what I could do with it, but he objected. 'I don't want to be married to a career woman. If you go down there, I'm going home to my mother.' I went down on Monday morning and took over. And George did go home to his mother – that very day."

She divorced him and assumed control of the paper that she had purchased for him. Schiff became president and publisher of the *Post,* positions she held throughout the remainder of her ownership of the paper. In 1943 she also married Thackrey, having first promoted him to editor in

Vice-president Lyndon Johnson (center) with Schiff in the New York Post *newsroom, 15 October 1963*

1942. Their marriage was described as more a business union than a relationship; the *Post* continued to increase its circulation and cut its losses.

During the next few years Schiff's journalistic expertise began to expand. She had contributed news copy "from a woman's perspective" when Pearl Harbor was bombed in 1941, and when her friend President Roosevelt died in 1945, she wrote the lead paragraphs for the editorial. With her husband she continued to redesign the paper, launching a three-year plan for change. In 1945 she bought the *Bronx Home News*. (For a while the *Post* was known as the *Post Home News*.)

By the mid 1940s the *Post* had added more features, forty (mostly left-wing) columnists, a syndication service, a foreign bureau, and a Paris edition. It was also in the black financially. But her marriage — and newspaper affiliation — to Thackrey ended in 1949. They disagreed publicly about the 1948 presidential election. Thackrey supported Henry Wallace, a leftist candidate, and Schiff did not. A series of editorials titled "Appeal to Reason" allowed husband and wife to debate the issue. *Editor & Publisher* called them "take-your-choice editorials."

Thackrey's attack on conservative policy in a never-published editorial finally separated the couple. "He was unhappy and miserable, and so was I," she wrote. "He went downstairs, terribly angry, and I followed to say, 'Ted, I'll give you the paper; just get out of here.' He said, 'That's very generous of you. Thank you.' Then he packed a bag and left."

Thackrey was given "control and management" of the paper in the divorce settlement. In only a few weeks he used this to put the paper near bankruptcy. "The paper was very close to dying," said Paul Sann, a former editor. "The accounts receivable had been factored, about one step ahead of the sheriff, and there was legitimate distress over the payroll, week to week."

In addition to the problems at the *Post*, Thackrey had opened a morning paper, the *Compass*. Schiff permanently took back her maiden name, borrowed a half-million dollars from her trust fund, settled the problems, and regained control of the *Post*. Thackrey left the *Post*, and Schiff began to rebuild it.

The 1950s marked a time of renewed dedication for Schiff. She was sole owner and publisher of

Schiff with Rupert Murdoch, to whom she sold the New York Post *in December 1976 (photograph by Nury Hernandez / New York Post)*

the paper, and she cut costs and changed the editorial emphasis, confining news to news pages and editorials to editorial pages. In May 1949 she promoted James Wechsler to editor.

Wechsler served as editor until 1961, in an era known as the golden age of the *Post.* It was also Schiff's golden age – the time when she blossomed as a journalist. Wechsler said he "began to glimpse her emergence as a person with her own sense of journalism." Her "Dear Reader" columns, which began on 30 September 1951, cemented this change. In these columns Schiff addressed the problems of the day.

In her diary Schiff noted that the columns were "the most satisfying thing I've ever done and I'd like to get back to it someday." By the mid 1950s they were running three times a week, featuring, for example, an interview with Albert Einstein at his home. Her political endorsement helped Nelson Rockefeller defeat Averell Harriman in New York's 1958 gubernatorial election.

During this period Schiff married her fourth husband, industrialist Rudolf Sonneborn. She wrote in a "Dear Reader" column, "My husband is very modern in his attitude toward careers for women. He reads the *New York Post* avidly and considers its continuance as the city's only crusading liberal newspaper to be of such vital importance that he is willing to have his wife retain her maiden name professionally and to continue to devote the major portion of her time to its publication." Unlike her three previous husbands, Sonneborn had no involvement in the *Post.* In spite of this, they separated in 1965 and later divorced.

In 1961 Schiff made a decision that permanently divided the paper's news and editorial departments. Wechsler was named columnist and editorial-page editor of the *Post,* and Paul Sann was named editor. According to Sann, the decision was unilateral and rapid. Schiff noted in her diary, "People came to me saying I had to make a change. Circulation was slipping, which was blamed on too much editorializing of the news, and morale was low." The change marked a shift to human interest over crusading.

During the 1960s the *Post* survived a 114-day newspaper strike. In 1965 Schiff began automating the newsroom, renting a computer and a typesetter and "becoming the symbol of the publisher fighting for automation against a union." The *Post* also battled changes in competition. In 1966 a newspaper nicknamed "the Widget" was born when the *New York Herald Tribune* merged with the *New York Journal-American* and the *New York World-Telegram*. "The Widget" (the *New York World Journal Tribune*) lasted one year. About twenty-five hundred people lost their jobs when it folded.

The *Post* survived, the last afternoon paper in New York. Schiff acquired staff from the *World Journal Tribune* when it folded, and she later purchased the *Journal-American* plant on Sixth Street, moving the *Post* there from its West Street home. She completed the paper's automation at that site, and its renovation took up most of her attention during the mid 1960s.

Just before the 1976 publication of *Men, Money and Magic,* author Jeffrey Potter quizzed Schiff on her search for a successor. She said that she had not found a suitable replacement. In December of that year she shocked the publishing world by selling the paper to Rupert Murdoch for $31 million.

Shortly before the sale of the newspaper Schiff wrote, "When I took on the Post, I didn't have much faith in myself or the paper, and I really didn't think I could pull it off. Now, it's part of me – we are part of each other." In a 1988 interview she added, "It [the newspaper] was a terrible headache."

Schiff died in her New York apartment on 30 August 1989. A *Post* official told the *New York Times* that Schiff had been diagnosed with cancer that May but had declined treatment. She was survived by three children: Mortimer Hall, Adele Hall Sweet, and Sarah-Ann Backer Kramarsky. She had fifteen grandchildren and nine great-grandchildren.

References:

"Dorothy Schiff, 86, Ex-Post Owner, Dies," *New York Times,* 31 August 1989, p. A9;

Jeffrey Potter, *Men, Money and Magic: The Story of Dorothy Schiff* (New York: Coward, McCann & Geoghegan, 1976).

John Seigenthaler
(27 July 1927 –   )

Edward Caudill and Betty Farmer
University of Tennessee

MAJOR POSITIONS HELD: Editor (1962–1972), publisher (1973–1991), president (1979–1991), chairman and chief executive officer (1989–1991), *Nashville Tennessean*; editorial director, *USA TODAY* (1982–1991).

BOOKS: *A Search for Justice,* by Seigenthaler, Jim Squires, Frank Ritter, and John Hemphill (Nashville: Aurora, 1971);
The Year of the Scandal Called Watergate (Nashville, 1974).

OTHER: *An Honorable Profession: A Tribute to Robert F. Kennedy,* edited by Seigenthaler, Pierre Salinger, Frank Mankiewicz, and Ed Guthman (Garden City, N.Y.: Doubleday, 1968).

John Seigenthaler's career at the *Nashville Tennessean* has run the gamut from cub reporter to chairman emeritus. He is perhaps most regarded for his commitment to upholding the First Amendment. Throughout his career he has fought for the public's right to know. "There's nothing I could have done that's more satisfying personally and professionally," he has commented.

John Lawrence Seigenthaler was born in Nashville on 27 July 1927 to John and Mary Brew Seigenthaler. He attended Peabody College in Nashville and was later a Nieman Fellow at Harvard University (1958–1959). He married Dolores Watson in January 1955; they have one son, John Michael.

Seigenthaler was willing to challenge the system even at an early age. Jim Squires, of the *Chicago Tribune,* said that his disruptive conduct in a Nashville school was compared to the young Seigenthaler's. As Squires was being reprimanded, the disciplinarian remarked that he was "the most combative, unruly boy we've had since John Seigenthaler." Seigenthaler continued his antics in the newsroom of the *Tennessean,* which he joined in 1949 as a cub reporter. There he established a repu-

tation as "a world-class practical joker." He has been accused of slipping vodka into an unsuspecting colleague's orange juice and describing the religious-news editor in terms of his alleged sexual prowess.

However, anecdotes about Seigenthaler's personality pale in comparison to the accounts of his sometimes dramatic work as a journalist and public servant. In lauding Seigenthaler's instinct for reporting, author and journalist David Halberstam, who worked with him at the *Tennessean,* said: "At best it is the capacity to put yourself in the place of another person, sense how he or she thinks and feels, and thus come up with questions which anticipate what has happened or what that person really thought. At the core of this is the ability to empathize with another person, to get out of your skin and to enter, however momentarily, that of another human being. Looking back, I think John was the first reporter I ever knew who had that ability."

That ability was apparent in Seigenthaler's actions toward other people. As a reporter on the scene of a potential suicide, he tried for about a half hour to talk a desperate man, Gene Bradford Williams, from jumping into the Cumberland River. Just as Williams started to jump, he grabbed him and held him until police could rescue him. Seigenthaler wrote, "I could see in his eyes that he was going to jump." That day Williams told him that he would never forgive him. Three weeks later Seigenthaler received a letter that began, "Dear Friend." Williams thanked him for saving his life, and the two corresponded until Williams died in a nursing home several years later.

A story about a prominent Nashvillian who had disappeared and been declared dead won Seigenthaler national acclaim in 1953. According to a 1989 article by *Tennessean* staff member Frank Sutherland, Thomas C. Buntin had been missing for many years, and his wife had collected one hundred thousand dollars on his insurance policy. However, the insurance company discovered that

Buntin was alive, so they wanted their money back. Buntin agreed to come back if the insurance company and the court protected his new identity. The court agreed and sealed the records.

Seigenthaler, outraged by the court's decision, was determined to find Buntin, tracking him down in Orange, Texas. He had started a new life with his former secretary. "As a result of Seigenthaler's stories, the insurance company got its money back without Buntin's return to court," Sutherland stated. Seigenthaler received the National Headliner Award for Investigative Reporting for this story.

In the early 1960s Seigenthaler left the *Tennessean* for the second time in his career. The first was in 1958, when he served for one year as a Nieman Fellow at Harvard University. The second was to serve as administrative assistant to Attorney General Robert Kennedy from fall 1960 to spring 1962. In the Justice Department, Seigenthaler's work involved civil rights, organized crime, and the judicial-selection process.

He served as the administration's chief negotiator with the governor of Alabama, John M. Patterson, during the 1961 Freedom Rides. While acting in this capacity in Montgomery, Alabama, in May 1961, Seigenthaler was involved in an incident that sent him to a hospital. As he looked on, a crowd of whites attacked a group of students who had chartered a bus to protest racial discrimination in public transportation. He responded by helping two of the protesting students – both women, one white and one black – escape. As Seigenthaler was trying to get them into his car, he was hit on the head. He lay unconscious for about a half hour before he was taken to a hospital. The women, however, escaped unharmed.

Seigenthaler left the *Tennessean* for a third time, in 1968, to support Kennedy's campaign for president, and he was with the Kennedy campaign when the candidate was assassinated. He later coedited *An Honorable Profession: A Tribute to Robert F. Kennedy* (1968). He also collaborated with three other *Tennessean* staff members on *A Search for Justice* (1971). The book reviews the trials of those charged in the assassinations of John and Robert Kennedy and Martin Luther King, Jr. The book points to the flaws in the U.S. justice system and concludes that the courts served the legal system, not the people.

The tensions between the political and legal arenas and journalism were real for Seigenthaler. He has been quoted as saying that his work as a public servant left him more committed to journalism: "I did not want to be a government flak but I was excited about [Robert F. Kennedy] and the

John Seigenthaler

New Frontier. . . . I learned I was more comfortable as a journalist than in government and that for me, the greater public service was as a journalist."

When Seigenthaler was named editor of the *Tennessean* in 1962, he became the youngest person in the United States to hold such a post with a daily, according to a *Time* magazine article. One of his reporters, John Haile, characterized Seigenthaler as a person who believed he could have an impact during the turbulent 1960s: "At the Tennessean, I don't know that many of us set out to change the world. We just found ourselves working for an editor who was convinced his newspaper could. It wasn't long before we were swept up in that purpose."

Under Seigenthaler's leadership *Tennessean* reporters won awards for their undercover stories about the Ku Klux Klan as well as abuses in a nursing home, a mental hospital, and a jail. These stories also prompted reforms. The *Tennessean* won a Pulitzer Prize in 1962 for investigative reporting on undercover cooperation between union and management in the coal industry.

Sending reporters undercover was something Seigenthaler believed should be done only as a last resort – after it was clear that the story could not be told any other way. The best-known undercover exposé under Seigenthaler's leadership dealt with David Duke and his involvement with the Ku Klux Klan. *Tennessean* reporter Jerry Thompson posed as a Klan member for eighteen months and was able to get the story that had previously eluded them. According to Sutherland, Duke had appeared "suave and personable in public," but was believed to be "spouting racial epithets in closed Klavern meetings." Thompson witnessed Duke in action. This information became quite important when Duke was elected to the Louisiana legislature, and when he made an unsuccessful bid for the governorship of that state in 1990. In recognition of Seigenthaler's leadership role in exposing KKK activities, he received the American Jewish Committee's Mass Media Award in 1981.

Seigenthaler has said that the hardest thing about being editor was making the decision "to go with a story when you're threatened with a lawsuit. There are no easy decisions. There are decisions that hurt people, that damage their lives, injure children, relatives and friends. But you have to consider the compelling need of the public to know about those people."

Seigenthaler fought for the public's right to know throughout his career and challenged government rulings that ran counter to the First Amendment. One of his most important challenges dealt with closed legislative meetings in Tennessee. In early 1965 Seigenthaler instructed *Tennessean* reporter Bill Kovach to refuse to leave a closed committee meeting. Kovach, who heads the Nieman Fellowship program at Harvard, cited a state constitutional provision allowing access. The senate responded by barring *Tennessean* staffers from the senate floor. Seigenthaler and Kovach then took the case to court. They sued for access to the closed senate meetings, which had become routine, and they won.

Seigenthaler's most important governmental challenge involved a personal matter. In 1976 he learned that one of his part-time copy editors was serving as an informant for the FBI. He fired the employee and demanded access to his own files through the Freedom of Information Act. He promised he would print whatever appeared in his file.

The story led with the few lines in the file that were still legible: "Seigenthaler had illicit relations with young girls. . . . Source quotes an unnamed source." In his story Seigenthaler criticized the FBI, adamantly denying the charges and demanding a redress. The attorney general apologized, and the er-

roneous statements were purged from his files. As a result of this incident, he received the Sidney Hilman Prize for Courage in Publishing in 1977. The Hilman Foundation stated that Seigenthaler's "handling of this matter met the highest standard of journalism in consonance with the rights and responsibilities of the press under the First Amendment."

Just as he advocated access to government records and meetings, Seigenthaler called for more openness in the editorial process: "We need to open up to the sunshine as much of our own process of news decision-making and editorial opinion-making as soon as possible." In a 1988 interview in *Editor & Publisher,* Seigenthaler said: "We have been preaching openness – that institutions in society should be open. We want governments to be open, corporate boardrooms to be open, open records laws, laws about disclosure . . . and we are more secretive about our own business than any institution we criticize." He added, "We can't sustain arguments that other institutions should be open if we can't do it ourselves."

In a 1989 address to the first National Freedom of Information Assembly regarding the possibility of a reinstatement of the Fairness Doctrine for broadcasters and the ramifications that might have for newspapers, Seigenthaler warned that a free press has never been secure and that journalists need to assume responsibility in assuring that right. "What's the difference between free speech in a newspaper and free press on the air? How can there be free, open, lusty debate in a free, open society if broadcasters are intimidated, harassed or chilled?" he asked. "The First Amendment was in doubt from the outset . . . our freedom will stand or fall on the credibility of an independent press pitted against the self-interest of government and private institutions and those who operate them."

Seigenthaler, who has often spoken on the credibility of the press, has suggested that the public needs to be convinced that journalists are "ethical, responsible, fair, reasonable and open. We need to find ways to explain . . . our positions on journalistic ethics, conflicts of interest, confidential sources – on why we do what we do the way we do it." In an address to Gannett employees at the close of his newspaper career in 1991, Seigenthaler challenged them to "keep the press safe, keep it secure, keep it responsible, make it more so – and keep it free in this last decade of the century so that the freedom will endure 200 years from now."

Seigenthaler has been widely recognized for his commitment to upholding the First Amendment. In 1992 he was named a trustee of the Freedom

Forum, an international organization dedicated to a free press, free speech, and free spirit for all people. A First Amendment Chair of Excellence has been created in his name at Middle Tennessee State University, with the goal of promoting an understanding of the First Amendment in the academic environment.

He was also named chairman of the First Amendment Center at Vanderbilt University in Nashville. The position was created in 1991 by Gannett's Freedom Forum. In making the appointment, Al Neuharth, chairman of the Freedom Forum, declared: "John Seigenthaler is one of the country's strongest advocates of the First Amendment and freedoms it enshrines. He has the creative combination of intellect, experience and passion needed to head a center that will break new ground in promoting free press, free speech and free spirit."

Seigenthaler's relationship with Gannett is a bit ironic. A 1991 article by Frank Ritter describes him as "the foremost authority on the subject" of "the trend toward one-newspaper cities and the growth of newspaper chains." Seigenthaler once testified before Congress in support of a change in newspaper-inheritance laws that would allow the owners of family newspapers to pass on their properties without "punitive, prohibitive taxation." He feared that "without a change in the law, giant chains would soon take over family newspapers," according to Sutherland.

Seigenthaler and Gannett president Al Neuharth publicly debated the newspaper-inheritance laws. The *Tennessean* once competed head to head with Gannett when the chain owned the afternoon paper in Nashville. But in 1979 the debate between Seigenthaler and Neuharth ended: Gannett acquired the *Tennessean*. "I was sold into chains," Seigenthaler remarked about the transition. Gannett recognized his talents and named him president of the newspaper, in addition to his duties as publisher. When Gannett founded *USA TODAY* in 1982, Seigenthaler was named the newspaper's first editorial director.

He divided his time between the *Tennessean* and *USA TODAY,* commuting from Nashville to Washington. Seigenthaler was committed to having a hands-on management at the *Tennessean,* according to Sutherland. He tells the story of how Seigenthaler, on one Saturday afternoon, insisted on working with a young reporter on a story exposing life-insurance problems. Sutherland, the city editor at the time, encouraged Seigenthaler to let someone else work with the reporter, saying, "I know what it takes to fix that story." Seigenthaler replied, "I know you do, but let me do it. This is what keeps me young."

Upon his retirement as publisher of the *Tennessean* in 1991, Seigenthaler remarked, "For me, journalism has been a life calling and a unique form of public service." Seigenthaler's service on boards and committees includes the World Press Institute and the Committee to Protect Journalists. He has served as vice-chairman and a member of the executive committee of the Media and Society Seminars of Columbia University Journalism School, a member of the University of Tennessee College of Communications Board of Visitors, and a member of the Advisory Committee of the School of Communications of American University in Washington, D.C.

He has also served as board member and president of the American Society of Newspaper Editors. He was an associate professor of communications policy at Duke University from 1980 to 1981. In 1984 he was named a Sigma Delta Chi Fellow, the highest honor given by the Society of Professional Journalists. He is also a member of Kappa Tau Alpha, an honorary journalism society.

References:

George Garneau, "Break Up the Old Boy Network," *Editor & Publisher*, 121 (23 April 1988): 40, 145;

Pam Janis, "Seigenthaler Retires after 42 Years," *Gannetteer* (February 1992): 8–9;

Frank Ritter, "A Model and Mentor," *Nashville Tennessean,* 6 December 1991, pp. E1, E4;

M. L. Stein, "Come to the Aid of Broadcasters," *Editor & Publisher*, 122 (18 February 1989): 14, 43;

Frank Sutherland, "Reporter, Editor, Publisher, Role Model: 'Which John Seigenthaler Are We Writing About?,' " *ASNE Bulletin* (February 1989): 15–21.

John Sengstacke

(25 November 1912 –)

John De Mott
Memphis State University

MAJOR POSITIONS HELD: Vice-president and general manager, Robert S. Abbott Publishing Company (1934–1940); president and chairman of the board, Sengstacke Enterprises (1940–   ).

John Herman Henry Sengstacke, who founded the Negro Newspaper Publishers Association in 1940, heads the largest group of black-owned newspapers in the United States and is publisher of the only black-owned daily newspaper in the United States. In 1992 the Biographical Center of Cambridge, England, named Sengstacke its "International Man of the Year 1991–92," honoring his many achievements as an internationally known leader in the field of social justice.

Descended from a long line of Christian ministers, Sengstacke was born on 25 November 1912 in Savannah, Georgia, to the Reverend Herman Alexander Sengstacke and Rose Mae (Davis) Sengstacke, a missionary worker. The couple lived in nearby Woodville, Georgia. One of six children — three boys and three girls — the future editor and publisher was introduced to journalism at an early age. His father edited and published a small weekly newspaper, and an uncle, Robert Sengstacke Abbott, was publisher of the *Chicago Defender,* a weekly newspaper that he had launched in 1905. "From the time I was a small boy," Sengstacke recalls, "my uncle devoted considerable time to me. My interest in the printing trade developed naturally."

The newspaper edited by Alexander Sengstacke had been established by Abbott's father as the *Woodville Times.* Alexander changed its name to the *Woodville West End Post.* Young Sengstacke worked for his father, engaging in the newspaper's printing, advertising, and editorial activities. Sengstacke says that he "began at the bottom, as a printer's devil, eventually working up to an assistant to my father."

"My uncle took charge of my education," Sengstacke recalls, "giving it the direction that led to my association with the Chicago Defender." Fol-

John Sengstacke

lowing the completion of his elementary schooling in Savannah, he attended the Knox Institute in Athens, Georgia, and then a junior college in Brick, North Carolina. After graduation from junior college in 1929, Sengstacke enrolled at Hampton Institute in Virginia, from which his uncle Robert had been graduated before going to Chicago to study at the Kent School of Law. Prohibited from practicing law as a result of racial discrimination, Abbott put the education in printing that he had acquired at Hampton to work and achieved fame as a newspaper publisher.

While at Hampton, Sengstacke informed his uncle, "I am reading books in journalism, newspaper work, and taking a course in advertising. I am going to do some research work on the topic, 'Problems Confronting the Advertising Managers of Negro Newspapers.' " Although a business administration major at Hampton, Sengstacke was active in campus journalism, writing and editing for the campus paper, the *Hampton Script*. He participated in the musical activities of the Hampton Quartette and became a member of the Omicron Society. He was also active in athletics, capturing medals in the mile and two-mile runs.

However, most of Sengstacke's time went into his study of journalism. In recalling his uncle's interest in preparing him for that, Sengstacke stated that the *Defender* publisher sent him to school so that "I could learn the ins and outs of the newspaper business." Under his uncle's tutelage Sengstacke spent his summer breaks from Hampton working on the *Defender*. While working in Chicago during the summers, Sengstacke studied at the Mergenthaler Linotype School, the Chicago School of Printing, and Northwestern University, where he took courses in journalism and business administration.

After receiving a bachelor of science degree from Hampton in 1933, Sengstacke did postgraduate work at Ohio State University. In 1934 he joined the *Defender* staff as a full-time special assistant to the publisher. Under the credo "American race prejudice must be destroyed" – which continues to appear on the newspaper's editorial page in the 1990s – the *Defender* devoted its enterprise to opening up trades and trade unions to blacks, promoting African-American representation in the presidential cabinet, and urging federal legislation to prohibit lynching and to create "full enfranchisement of all" U.S. citizens.

First published by Abbott in a basement room in Chicago's "Bronzeville" community – with original assets consisting of twenty-five cents, a typewriter, and a kitchen table – the *Defender* by 1934 had acquired a national reputation and great influence. During the era called the "Great Migration," beginning shortly after World War I and continuing for many years thereafter, Abbott and the *Defender* played a major role in persuading tens of thousands of blacks to leave the South and go to Chicago, where their chances of enjoying good jobs, education, and freedom generally were much better.

The mission and philosophy of the *Defender* were articulated by Abbott in a statement issued on the paper's twenty-fifth anniversary:

Before I started on my life's work – journalism – I was counseled by my beloved father that a good newspaper was one of the best instruments of service and one of the strongest weapons ever to be used in defense of its citizenship rights. For 25 years I have hearkened to the sacred advice of my father, and have endeavored to give expression to my love for him, my race and humanity through the columns of THE CHICAGO DEFENDER.... I have endeavored to bring to the attention of the reading public all the inhuman treatment, discrimination, segregation, disfranchisement, peonage and all other injustices directed at my people.

In 1933 Abbott started the *Louisville* (Kentucky) *Defender,* and in 1936 he launched the *Michigan Chronicle,* a weekly newspaper for Detroit's rapidly growing black community. As his uncle's assistant, with the title of vice-president and general manager of the Abbott Publishing Company, Sengstacke wrote editorials for both the Detroit and Louisville papers, as well as the company's flagship publication in Chicago. Sengstacke married Myrtle Elizabeth Picou on 9 July 1939. The couple had three sons: John Herman Henry III, Robert Abbott, and Lewis Willis. In 1992 only Robert survived, serving as president of Sengstacke Enterprises.

John Sengstacke's increasing role in the growth and development of the *Defender* coincided with a decline in its aging publisher's health. Abbott decided that his nephew would succeed him, and in 1939 he willed two-thirds of his estate to Sengstacke, leaving the remaining one-third to his wife. Near the end of his life Abbott spent most of his time in bed, dictating an autobiography. It remained unfinished when he died in February 1940.

A few months before his uncle's death, Sengstacke played an important part in the creation of the Negro Newspaper Publishers Association (NNPA), a national organization of which he later served three terms as president. Abbott had prepared him well for command of the *Defender* enterprises. Sengstacke moved smoothly into the company's chief executive position.

At the time Sengstacke became its president, the *Chicago Defender* had achieved a reputation for leadership in the coverage of black news throughout the country, as well as in its home state of Illinois and neighboring states. In 1940 the paper's net worth was estimated at three hundred thousand dollars. Under Sengstacke's management the *Defender* and its associated newspapers were destined to reach even greater heights. First, however, the new executive had to manage his company's survival through World War II.

As a newspaper editor, Sengstacke was exempted from military service. However, he voluntarily served as chairman of the U.S. Office of War Information advisory committee on the Negro press. In Chicago he chaired Rationing Board No. 2, believed to have been the nation's largest such local board. In an effort to assist black servicemen, he became a supporter of the United Service Organization, a civilian group providing hospitality and assistance to servicemen in the United States and overseas.

Throughout World War II the *Defender* devoted its columns to patriotic concerns, such as the sale of U.S. government defense bonds. It chronicled the exploits of black American soldiers and sailors, as did other Negro newspapers, and the contributions of black workers in defense industries. Nevertheless, the *Defender* did not cringe from exposing and deploring discrimination against blacks in the military, regardless of whether such discrimination occurred in the services themselves, in Red Cross canteens, or in commercial establishments.

President Harry Truman shared the concern over frequent incidents reflecting friction between black and white servicemen. He called Sengstacke to suggest that a national conference be called to discuss the situation. Such a conference was unnecessary, the editor advised Truman, because he could provide a solution to the entire problem at that instant, over the telephone: "Integrate the armed forces." Truman responded to that suggestion, issuing his historic order the next day.

Despite the war and its difficulties, Sengstacke's efforts to build an ever-stronger association of black newspaper publishers continued. By 1944, when Sengstacke began the first of his terms as its president, the NNPA's accomplishments included the official accreditation of Negro correspondents to the White House conferences and in war coverage, and the establishment of a Washington news bureau serving black newspapers around the country. A year later, when Sengstacke was succeeded by Frank Stanley, editor of the *Louisville Defender,* a national Negro news agency was planning to open bureaus in New York, Washington, and Chicago. These were to serve fifty-three newspapers represented by the NNPA.

While serving as president of the NNPA, Sengstacke published a trade periodical, *Publisher, Editor and Printer,* dedicated to fostering greater cooperation among black newspapers. With such assistance from Sengstacke and other leaders of their national association, black newspapers were able during World War II to manage a transition from predominantly individual-subscription financing to support by advertising. The Negro press had been supported almost wholly through circulation revenues before the war. Afterward advertising provided about 75 percent of its revenues. Much of the gain in black-newspaper advertising resulted from the creation of Amalgamated Publishers, under Sengstacke's leadership. In 1992 he was still serving as president of the firm, which sold advertising for about seventy-five black newspapers around the country.

With national newsmagazines such as *Time, Life, Look,* and *Newsweek* receiving increasing interest as a result of U.S. involvement in World War II, Sengstacke created a news-and-picture magazine in 1944. Originally called *Headlines,* it was edited by Louis E. Martin, former editor of the *Michigan Chronicle.* John's brother Frederick D. Sengstacke served as its business manager. At first a small-format publication, the periodical was later converted to standard newsmagazine size and renamed *Headlines and Pictures.* The magazine was edited in New York and achieved a circulation of approximately thirty thousand. It still failed to command the desired readership, however, and died in 1946.

During the postwar period Sengstacke became increasingly active in public affairs on national, state, and local levels. In continuing his efforts to end discrimination in the military, he served as secretary of the Committee on Equality of Opportunity and Treatment in the Armed Services. For his role in the integration of the U.S. military – as well as for other extraordinary services to the newspaper industry and democratic society worldwide – Sengstacke was honored in 1950 by the National Urban League, which presented him with its Two Friends Award.

In addition to promoting military-service integration, Sengstacke played an important part in paving the way for Jackie Robinson to break professional baseball's color barrier and join the Brooklyn Dodgers. Earlier he had persuaded President Franklin D. Roosevelt to create jobs for blacks in the U.S. Postal Service. Aside from playing a major role in national affairs, Sengstacke continued to emphasize his newspaper's effort to improve Chicago. In 1948 the *Defender* received an award for outstanding community service from the Illinois Press Association.

Although Sengstacke identifies himself as an independent in politics, friendship prompted him to serve as cofounder and treasurer of the National Citizens Committee for the Re-election of President Harry Truman. Sengstacke's regard for Truman has been reflected in many ways. In 1947 the Rob-

Front page of the Chicago Daily Defender, *6–12 August 1966*

ert S. Abbott Memorial Award – presented by the *Defender* to the individual who has contributed most to the advancement of American democracy – went to Truman. The following year Truman's name led those of seventeen persons on the newspaper's "Honor Role of Democracy." Among the others were Eleanor Roosevelt, Congressman William L. Dawson of Illinois, Judge J. Waties Waring, Senator-elect Hubert Humphrey of Minnesota, Dr. Ralph Bunche, and columnist Drew Pearson.

In 1952 Sengstacke established the *Tri-State Defender,* a weekly newspaper serving Tennessee, Arkansas, and Mississippi, produced in Memphis. In 1956 Sengstacke converted the *Chicago Defender* into a daily newspaper. A morning tabloid, it is published Monday through Thursday and on Saturday. In 1992 it had an audited circulation of twenty-eight thousand daily and thirty thousand Saturday. Frederick Sengstacke serves as publisher, while William M. Majors is general manager. John Sengstacke retains the editorship.

In 1966 Sengstacke acquired the Pittsburgh Courier Company and its chain of eight newspapers. Founded in 1908 by Robert Vann – who saw, as did Abbott, the need for newspaper leadership in the struggle of black Americans to obtain equality with other U.S. citizens – the Courier newspaper enterprise has exerted great influence over the large black communities of the Eastern Seaboard. Reorganized by Sengstacke as the New Pittsburgh Courier Company, the enterprise is directed by Roderick Doss.

The parent corporation of the Sengstacke newspapers, Sengstacke Enterprises, is controlled by a board chaired by Sengstacke himself. Robert Sengstacke is its secretary; Frederick Sengstacke is the publisher of the *Chicago Daily Defender.* Corporate headquarters are at 2400 South Michigan Avenue in Chicago's "Near South Side." The building, which formerly served as headquarters for the Chicago Automobile Association, also houses the *Defender* publishing operation.

During its long history the *Chicago Defender* has achieved many "firsts" for the African-American press. It was the first weekly to print pictures in three-color process; the first to inaugurate a children's page; the first to reach a circulation of one hundred thousand; the first to produce two papers – national and local editions – in the same week. It was the first to offer a column on health; to print as many as forty-eight pages in a single edi-

tion; to publish a full page of comics; and to employ a regular cartoonist on its staff.

Sengstacke's journalistic achievements have been recognized in many ways. He was the first black newspaper publisher elected to the board of directors of the American Society of Newspaper Editors. He is also a member of the American Newspaper Publishers Association and the Chicago Press Club.

Loyal to his and his uncle's alma mater, Sengstacke has served as a member of the board of trustees of Hampton Institute and as president of the Chicago chapter of the national Hampton alumni association. In addition to supporting Hampton, Sengstacke has served as a trustee of Bethune-Cookman College in Daytona Beach, Florida, and has established a journalism scholarship in his uncle's name at Lincoln University in Jefferson City, Missouri.

Active in business affairs other than publishing, Sengstacke has served as a director of the Illinois Federal Savings and Loan Association of Chicago, which he founded, and is a director emeritus of the Golden State Mutual Insurance Company, also of Chicago. Sengstacke's many contributions to Chicago and its people include service as vice-chairman of the South Side Planning Board, as a director of the Urban League, and as a director of the Wabash Avenue YMCA, as well as membership on the Committee to Build a Greater Chicago, the Committee to Bring Olympics to Chicago, the Mayor's Committee on Human Relations, and the Freedom Train Committee. He has actively supported the USO and the Boy Scouts of America.

Sengstacke led the drive to build Provident Hospital in Chicago, and in 1992 he served as chairman of the Provident Hospital and Training School Association, working to renovate the hospital. His many honors include citations from the National Urban League, National Council of Negro Women, American Legion, Veterans of Foreign Wars, and Chicago Civil Liberties Committee.

References:

"Celebrating 86 Years of History," *Chicago Defender,* 20 October 1989, p. 1;

Armistead Pride, "Negro Newspapers: Yesterday, Today and Tomorrow," *Journalism Quarterly,* 28 (Spring 1951): 179–188;

"TSD Publisher 'Man of the Year,' " *Tri-State Defender,* 21 March 1992, p. 3;

Roland Wolseley, *The Black Press, U.S.A.* (Ames: Iowa State University Press, 1990).

Hazel Brannon Smith

(5 February 1914 –)

A. J. Kaul
University of Southern Mississippi

NEWSPAPERS OWNED: *Durant* (Mississippi) *News* (1936–1985); *Lexington* (Mississippi) *Advertiser* (1943–1985); *Banner County Outlook* (Flora, Mississippi) (1955–circa 1977); *Northside Reporter* (Jackson, Mississippi) (1956–1973).

For half a century Hazel Brannon Smith published weekly newspapers in Holmes County, Mississippi, a bastion of massive resistance to integration during the civil rights movement of the 1950s and 1960s. Her unflinching commitment to law and order, equal justice, and freedom of expression made her the target of segregationist reprisals – advertising boycotts, smear campaigns, bombings, cross burnings, and a rival newspaper established to drive her out of business. The plainspoken eloquence of her opposition to racial violence earned her the first Pulitzer Prize for editorial writing awarded to a woman.

She gloried in being a newspaperwoman, rejecting other labels. "I flinch every time I am called a crusading editor," she wrote. "But an honest editor who would truly serve the highest and best interest of the people will not compromise convictions to support a popular cause known to be morally wrong just to incur popular favor or support."

Hazel Freeman Brannon was born on 5 February 1914 in Alabama City, Alabama – near Gadsden, the county seat of Etowah County – a daughter of Dock Boad Brannon, an electrical contractor, and Georgia Freeman Brannon. Her middle-class southern childhood included a Negro nurse who was treated as a member of the family. "As a child I was taught to love everybody and not to hate anyone," she recalled decades later. "Respect and consideration for the rights of others were engrained in me for as long as I can remember."

She was graduated from Gadsden High School in 1930 at the age of sixteen, too young to enter college. For two years Brannon worked for the weekly *Etowah Observer*, contributing personal items at five cents per column inch before moving to page-1 reporting and selling advertisements on a 10 percent commission. Her successful advertising salesmanship and high commission earnings prompted the newspaper to put her on a weekly salary. By her own account she was making about fifty dollars a week when she resigned to enter the University of Alabama to study journalism in 1932.

She breezed through the university, was managing editor of the student newspaper, and was her Delta Zeta sorority's beauty queen. She dated, partied, and was graduated with a B.A. in 1935. Her *Observer* experience and journalism education fired an ambition to edit and publish her own newspaper, and she scoured the South to buy one.

On 4 August 1936 Brannon used a three-thousand-dollar loan to acquire the *Durant News,* a country weekly in Holmes County, Mississippi, on the eastern edge of the Delta cotton country. Many of the weekly's six hundred subscribers referred to it as the "Durant Excuse." Three editors had passed through the *Durant News* in the thirteen months before Brannon arrived. The "boys in the pool room" started a betting pool on how long she would last, she wrote thirty years later, and "the most any of them gave me was six months."

Mississippi lieutenant governor Billy Snider, himself a newspaper publisher, solemnly told her: "Young lady, Durant has long been known as the graveyard of Mississippi journalism. If you can make a go of this newspaper, you can have anything you want in Mississippi journalism, or anywhere else for that matter." Despite a decrepit Linotype and press that often broke down on publication nights, Brannon boasted that "we never missed an issue and were always at the post office in time."

She filled the *Durant News* with articles on arrests, births, deaths, club activities, family reunions, graduations, homecomings, and marriages. Her chatty front-page column, "Through Hazel Eyes," served as a stage from which she played the role of village scold, issuing blunt editorial commentary.

When local physicians opposed a public-health clinic to treat venereal diseases, she published the venereal-disease rates. Soon after, on a date with a local beau, she was told, "Ladies just don't talk about venereal disease." "Well, I ain't no lady," she quipped, "I'm a newspaper woman." The local-news formula doubled subscriptions to almost fourteen hundred, increased advertising revenues, and enabled her to pay off the newspaper's mortgage in four years to become sole owner.

"Welcome to Lexington Miss Hazel Brannon," read a front-page headline in the *Lexington Advertiser* on 8 April 1943, when she became the editor and publisher of the eighteen-hundred-subscriber independent weekly in the Holmes County seat. Two weeks later she pledged to readers: "We shall stand for upholding the traditions of the past and improving them." The twenty-nine-year-old publisher held traditional white southern attitudes and beliefs about segregation in a county whose population was two-thirds black. In a "Through Hazel Eyes" column republished "in response to many requests from our readers" as an editorial, "The South's Racial Problem," in July 1943, she expressed benign Jim Crow beliefs widely shared by her audience:

> The white man and the black man have dwelt together in peace and harmony in the south for many, many years, because each has known his place and kept it. Each has had his own ideals, customs, and habits and they have not conflicted ... as some of our meddling friends would have us believe.
>
> The good negro is just as proud of his race and its integrity as the white man, the Indian, or the Chinese. He realizes that God must have intended for there to be a great colored race or he would not have created it. He is not fooled by loose talk concerning "social equality." He knows there is no such thing as "equality," even among white men. . . .
>
> The wise man realizes, whether he be white or black, that as long as tastes and habits and appetites of people differ there can be no absolute "equality" among races. . . .
>
> The vast majority of the colored race in the south know that the white man is his friend; when he is in trouble the first person he goes to is a white friend. And the white friend doesn't let him down. He values highly the friendship of his negro friends. . . .
>
> But the south and America are a white man's country and both races know it. . . .
>
> That is why the so-called "negro problem" must be solved by southern white and negro people. It cannot be solved for us by our northern friends nor in Washington. . . .

Hazel Brannon Smith, 1965

> The good negro respects and likes the southern white man more than any other white man. He also knows that the person who would make trouble between him and his white friends is either his worst enemy or motivated by ignorance, or is just plain a trouble maker. . . .
>
> Southern white people are at last beginning to recognize the existence of trouble incited by people from the outside who have made a second car-

petbagging expedition into the south under the guise of the New Deal. . . .

We in our own way and in our own time as best we can will work out a better world for both ourselves and the negro in the south. But we will not be hamstrung nor dictated to by the group in this nation who would tell us how to run our elections and our state.

Brannon argued that the "half-baked ideas" of the New Deal had abandoned the Democratic party's "white supremacy principles," making President Franklin D. Roosevelt and his administration "as repugnant to Southerners as the worst carpetbaggers of reconstruction days." "A lot of things have been fostered by the New Deal administration which has violated every tradition held by southern people," she wrote in September 1944, citing "communists, coddled by the New Deal," who distributed a leaflet among government employees in Washington, D.C., urging them to outlaw the separation of white and Negro blood at blood banks. "Good negro citizens . . . no more want white blood in their veins than does the white man want negro blood. The communistic influences that would mix the two do not have the interest of either at heart."

Brannon's first extensive editorial campaign in the *Advertiser* sought to rid the "widespread lawlessness" of bootlegging and gambling in Holmes County. The six-month campaign began in November 1945 when she challenged local law-enforcement officials to enforce antiliquor and antigambling laws. Her "Through Hazel Eyes" column complained:

> Liquor joints line the highways going in and out of most towns in the county. They don't just sell liquor quietly. They are the loudest places in town. They display prominently in their doors slot machines and other gambling devices. . . . They flaunt it in the face of the people . . . as well as the officers. . . . Liquor selling has now reached the stage where it is the most profitable business in Holmes County.

A few days before Christmas 1945, the *Advertiser* editor reported the "astonishing information" that a Holmes County bootlegger had sold $221,000 worth of liquor in the first ten months of the year: "That this one man can do this much business in Holmes county without being raided over once in a two-year period is almost unbelievable." By late February 1946 the newspaper bluntly told its readers: "The only way our officials can prove they are not being paid off, in our opinion, is to start enforcing the law now and continue to enforce it until this country is rid of the bootlegging joints that line our public highways through-

out the county." And Brannon directly challenged Holmes County sheriff Walter L. Murtagh "to do something about it."

The sheriff's continued lackadaisical enforcement of liquor and gambling laws prompted a stronger editorial offensive. On 28 March 1946, three days before the Holmes County Circuit Court convened, Brannon published a signed, front-page "open letter" to District Attorney Howard Dyer, Holmes County attorney Pat M. Barrett, and members of the grand jury: "We think it your duty to do something about the lawlessness in Holmes County . . . whatever measures you deem necessary to cope with the situation." Failure to act, she wrote, would compel "a group of citizens . . . to take these matters up with the Governor or other officials." The grand jury's six-hour meeting on 1 April produced no indictments for liquor and gambling violations.

Holmes County circuit judge S. F. Davis reconvened the grand jury on 16 April after receiving a petition signed by many county residents, including Brannon. The petition implored the judge to recall the grand jury and charge it with investigating "the open sale of whiskey and display of gambling devices." Davis told the grand jury that the petition was "an indictment against . . . every officer in this county." If untrue, the petition was "a libelous article against every officer."

The three-day investigation returned fifty-two indictments for prohibition and gambling violations on 19 April 1946, the day after the *Advertiser* suggested that the sheriff resign or enforce the law. During questioning Murtagh told the grand jury that "in the future the policy of his office would be to rigidly enforce the prohibition and gambling laws of Holmes County," the *Advertiser* reported. Brannon was exuberant. The Holmes County law enforcement establishment – judge, jury, prosecutor, county attorney, and sheriff – was unaccustomed to a thirty-two-year-old newspaperwoman's stinging editorial criticism. They retaliated.

Six months later, at the October 1946 session of the Holmes County Circuit Court, Davis – who was pressured into reconvening the grand jury to investigate bootlegging and gambling – found Brannon guilty of contempt of court. The contempt citation was ostensibly unrelated to her editorial campaign. He had ordered witnesses in a murder trial not to talk to anyone except their lawyers. After the widow of the slain man had testified, Brannon interviewed the witness in a courthouse hallway in order to check a point in her notes.

A deputy sheriff reported the incident, and Dyer filed a sworn Information of Criminal Contempt, charging the editor with attempting to "embarrass," "hinder," and "impair" the trial. Davis issued a reprimand to the editor from the bench:

> I sympathize with you and am sorry you got in this mess, but you brought it on yourself. I realize you are putting on a great campaign for law and order but if you read history you will see that the only perfect being didn't make much of a hit with his reform. He reformed a few and left this advice, "Before you clean up someone else clean up yourself" . . . I have been around a long time and know the job. . . . I don't believe you can do it. I am of the opinion that when Gabriel blows his horn and rolls back the scroll of Heaven he will find the world like it is today. . . . I wish you had stayed out of this mess. It reminds me of what the Irishman said when he saw the bull run head-on into the train. "I admire your spunk but doubt your judgment." You have run head-on to this court. When called up you proceeded to give the Court a curt lecture as to his duties.

The judge sentenced the editor to pay a fifty-dollar fine and spend fifteen days in the Holmes County jail, suspended on condition that she violate no municipal, state, or federal laws for two years. Brannon appealed the contempt conviction to the Mississippi Supreme Court. " 'The freedom of the press' is no idle and meaningless term," Justice L. A. Smith, Sr., wrote in his 7 April 1947 opinion, which found "wholly insufficient proof" for contempt and overturned the conviction.

An ultraconservative states' rights Dixiecrat, Brannon served as secretary of the Holmes County Democratic Executive Committee between 1940 and 1948 and was a delegate to the Democratic National Conventions in 1940 and 1944. She held staunchly anti-Communist views. She wrote that the election of President Dwight D. Eisenhower in 1952 would bring about "thorough housecleaning that will rid our national government of all the pinks and reds and the pro-Soviet sympathizers that have been feeding at the expense of the American taxpayers for so long." She defended Senator Joseph McCarthy of Wisconsin against censure by the Senate: "Every pink and left-winger in the country will share in the victory scored by the Communist party which has inspired and directed the campaign against McCarthy in a well-planned and officially endorsed policy."

Profits from the *Durant News* and the *Lexington Advertiser* allowed her to indulge a penchant for expensive designer clothes and white Cadillac convertibles. "Honey, I had the most eligible bachelor in Durant and the most eligible bachelor in Lexington," she recalled in her early seventies, "and my only trouble was that I couldn't have them both.

That's true. I was something." In 1949 she took an ocean cruise and met the ship's purser, Walter Dyer "Smitty" Smith; they were married on 21 March 1950 in Holmes County. He became administrator of the Holmes County Community Hospital, and they settled into the comfortable routine of small-town social life in Lexington.

On 17 May 1954 a unanimous U.S. Supreme Court decision in *Brown* v. *Board of Education* declared segregated public schools unconstitutional. "Separate educational facilities are inherently unequal," Chief Justice Earl Warren wrote, sending shock waves through the segregated South and prompting massive resistance strategies to court-ordered integration. Three days later Smith's front-page column in the *Advertiser* told readers: "Perhaps if we had done as much as we should to improve our Negro schools throughout the South in the past decade we would never have had these cases in the courts." She continued:

> The Supreme Court may be morally right when it says that "separate educational facilities are inherently unequal."
>
> But we know, for practical purposes, that separate educational facilities are highly desirable in the South and other places where the two races live and work side by side. We know that it is to the best interest of both races that segregation be maintained in theory and in fact — and that where it isn't maintained trouble results. . . .
>
> The present situation has all of the ingredients necessary for a bloody revolution — if people don't keep their heads.

Less than a month after the Supreme Court decision was announced, Smith declared her racial credo on the front page of the *Advertiser:* "We believe that all men of all races and colors and creeds are the same before God . . . and should be equal before the law — should have the same protection of the law and courts." However, she guarded the color line in Holmes County: "We feel that our efforts should be toward self-advancement within the boundaries of our race." Her only concession was to equality before the law.

Massive resistance to integration took the form of citizen's councils, grassroots pressure groups comprised of prominent businessmen and public officials that rapidly spread from Mississippi throughout the South. The first citizen's council sprang up not far from Holmes County, in Indianola, home of arch-segregationist James O. Eastland, a U.S. senator. The councils advocated legal, nonviolent resistance tactics to assure total community compliance and conformity to segregation.

In July 1954 a leading resident of Lexington sought the cooperation of Smith and her newspapers in the formation of a citizen's council. "If a Nigra won't go along with our thinking on what's best for the community as a whole, he'll simply have his credit cut off," the editor was told. "What do you think the Negroes are going to think when they hear that the white men are organizing?" she asked. "Well, it might be a good thing for them to be a little scared," she was told. The editor responded:

No, it's not a good thing for anyone to be a little scared. People can't live under fear, and it will end up with all of us scared, and it will be a big scare. What you're proposing to do is to take away the freedom of all of the people in this community.

Citizen's council organizer Edwin White, a Holmes County representative in the state legislature, told *Advertiser* readers in August 1954 that implementation of the *Brown* decision would "violate God's Creation and Law, and when any court decision violates His law it is sinful, unholy and unworthy of obedience." A month later the editor's "Through Hazel Eyes" column contained a veiled reference to citizen's council tactics: "There are some who seek to stir up strife for purposes of their own. They appeal to prejudice and to ignorance – and their religion is the doctrine of hatred and greed implemented by the weapons of fear and distrust." Her objection to citizen's council tactics of fear and economic reprisal put the editor in a precarious position in a county whose traditionally rigid color line was rapidly becoming a segregationist wall.

Smith crossed over the color line in Holmes County on 15 July 1954 when she published a signed editorial, "The Law Should Be For All": "The laws in America are for everyone – rich and poor, strong and weak, white and black and all the other races that dwell within our land." A week earlier the *Advertiser* had reported on its front page: "Negro Man Shot in Leg Saturday in Tchula; Witness Reports He was Told To 'Get Goin' by Holmes County Sheriff." County sheriff Richard F. Byrd had encountered twenty-seven-year-old Henry Randle "in a Negro section of Cox Town for the purpose of getting the people home." The sheriff asked Randle "what he meant by 'whooping.'" Byrd reportedly "struck the Negro on the head" with a blackjack and told him to " 'get going.' " Randle fled. Byrd fired his gun "several times, one

of the bullets entering the left thigh and passing through the leg to the front. . . . No charges have yet been filed against Sheriff Byrd in the shooting."

"The Law Should Be For All" blasted the sheriff:

This kind of thing cannot go on any longer.
It must be stopped.
The vast majority of Holmes county people are not red necks who look with favor on the abuse of people because their skins are black. . . .
In our opinion, Mr. Byrd as Sheriff has violated every concept of justice, decency and right in his treatment of some of the people in Holmes county. He has shown us without question that he is not fit to occupy that high office.
He should, in fact, resign.

Byrd sued Smith for libel, claiming $57,500 in damages from the news story and editorial. "We don't know whether to be flattered at being sued for so much – or surprised that the Sheriff places the value of his reputation at so little," she commented in "Through Hazel Eyes." On 12 October 1954 a Holmes County Circuit Court jury awarded Byrd a ten-thousand-dollar judgment for libel. The editor immediately appealed to the Mississippi Supreme Court, and she continued to criticize Byrd: "There are some sheriffs in office in Mississippi now who have lied to every man, woman and child in their counties, but they have no more remorse than an egg-sucking dog."

The Mississippi Supreme Court took more than passing notice of the libel case, given the religious veneration of freedom of expression codified in the state constitution in 1890: "The freedom of speech and of the press shall be held sacred." Although acknowledging uncertainty concerning who actually shot Randle, the high court concluded in November 1955 that Smith and her newspapers had "substantially recited the circumstances" of the shooting, and the libel judgment was overturned. However, the court went far beyond a narrow adjudication of libel.

Viewing the facts "most favorably for the sheriff," the court found "no justification for hitting the Negro with the blackjack or shooting him. . . . And since the blow and the shot were both unjustified, it follows that the Negro was unlawfully assaulted in both instances." The Mississippi Supreme Court had vindicated Smith and chastised Byrd. "I am a firm believer in our Southern traditions and racial segregation," Smith wrote when she published the libel opinion, "but not at the expense of justice and truth."

Hazelwood, Smith's mansion on the outskirts of Lexington, Mississippi (photograph by Kevin Cooper)

Smith's husband became a target of his wife's enemies two months after the libel decision was overturned. At a special meeting of the newly elected Holmes County Community Hospital trustees on 4 January 1956, he was fired as the hospital's administrator. His successor, C. B. Read, "the successful operator of a modern poultry farm," became administrator on 10 January 1956. The firing came despite a 30 December 1955 resolution of the hospital's medical staff that called Smith "a man of absolute integrity and sound judgment" and commended him for "his splendid unselfish service."

The physicians' resolution deplored "the effort to inject politics" into the hospital's management and asked the trustees "to make no change whatever in the office of administrator." The editor's husband echoed the resolution in a signed "Open Letter" on the front page of the *Advertiser* on 5 January 1956. It opposed "any move to permit personalities or politics . . . to become involved in the management of the hospital," citing "a small group" that was "exerting pressure" on the trustees to fire him.

The official reasons for firing Smith were a cover for deeper antagonisms generated by his wife's editorial stands, including her opposition to the citizen's councils and the sheriff. One hospital trustee told a *Jackson* (Mississippi) *Daily News* reporter that his firing "stems from the fact his wife has become a controversial figure." Smitty became a full-time partner in his wife's newspapers. "He became a newspaperman the next morning, and a damn good one," she quipped years later.

Meanwhile, massive resistance to public-school desegregation mounted, reaching into the U.S. Congress and the Mississippi legislature. In early March 1956 nineteen U.S. senators and seventy-eight congressmen signed "A Declaration of Constitutional Principles." The declaration, commonly called the "Southern Manifesto," was drafted by Senator John C. Stennis of Mississippi and four other southern senators; the entire Mississippi congressional delegation signed.

The Southern Manifesto criticized the *Brown* v. *Board of Education* decision for substituting "naked power for established law." Condemning "outside agitators" and "meddlers," the manifesto commended "the motives of those states which have declared the intention to resist forced integration by any lawful means." In Mississippi a bill introduced in the state senate proposed stripping the property-tax exemption from churches that used their premises for nonsegregated purposes – allowing Negroes to attend services. The *Advertiser* editor objected, supporting the traditional separation of church and state: "We do not favor integration in any form, in the churches, schools or socially. But neither do we favor any legislative body seeking to use pressure to compel churches to do their bidding."

In November 1958 citizen's council members organized the *Holmes County Herald* to provide head-to-head competition to drive the *Advertiser* out of business. The newly formed publishing company was capitalized for thirty thousand dollars at twenty-five dollars a share. The largest shareholder, Chester Marshall, became the rival newspaper's first editor. The former general manager of the *Lexington Advertiser* and the *Durant News* – hired fifteen months earlier with the expectation that he would become editor of the two newspapers – resigned on 24 November 1958 to join the opposition against Smith. "The price of betrayal comes high these days," she commented. "A long time ago it was only 30 pieces of silver."

The first edition of the *Holmes County Herald* appeared in January 1959. For months its editorial columns were filled with inflammatory segregationist rhetoric. Even the statehood of Hawaii invited ridicule: "Hawaii was noted for pineapple and communists. But we guess this country had to add a few more reds to keep the ones in Washington company." When the *Advertiser* called for "mutual tolerance, equal justice, understanding and good will" in a 4 June 1959 editorial, "Race Hatred is Not the Answer," the *Herald* condemned the publication for "agitating" about race only to attract readers.

After six months of competition, the *Advertiser* claimed circulation superiority with twenty-eight hundred subscribers; the *Herald* boasted more advertising than the other county weeklies combined. Lexington businessmen began boycotting the *Advertiser,* diverting their advertising dollars to the *Herald.* The revenue base of the *Advertiser* began to deteriorate. "Economic pressure and its usual accompanying gangster tactics . . . can ruin a community or paralyze a nation," the *Advertiser* editor warned.

The *Herald* undercut the financial base of the *Advertiser* in February 1960, when the rival weeklies bid for county contracts to publish legal advertisements and public notices. The *Advertiser* submitted a bid of thirty dollars a month for a two-year contract, half the state-set maximum rate. The *Herald* bid only one cent and thus won the contract from

the Holmes County Board of Supervisors, whose head was *Herald* shareholder W. Leslie Smith. Hazel Brannon Smith wrote that the lowball bid convinced many Holmes County residents of the "conspiracy" to drive her out of business.

Smith won the Elijah Parish Lovejoy Award for Courage in Journalism on 17 July 1960. Sponsored by the Southern Illinois University School of Journalism, the Lovejoy Award was named after an abolitionist editor killed by a mob in Alton, Illinois, in 1837. The Lovejoy citation recognized Smith for "daring to resist the merciless attack of an organized pressure group . . . which sought to silence her by means of reprisals . . . personal vilification . . . economic boycott . . . and by means of the launching of an opposing newspaper." The *Holmes County Herald* reported that she had been "the target of a group which opposes her news and editorial policies supporting integration," with "supporting integration" in boldface type.

Below the story announcing the Lovejoy Award in the *Lexington Advertiser,* Smith published her letter to Marshall, demanding "a proper correction": "Since you know of your own knowledge, Chester, having been in my employ for some 15 months, that I have never advocated integration of the races either in my newspapers, or in any other way, you must have known that you were printing a lie."

Marshall was fired in mid October 1960. "Judgment Day has come for a former Holmes County editor – and sooner or later it is going to catch up with those who were and are responsible for him," Smith commented. The new editor of the *Herald* was twenty-two-year-old Jack A. Shearer, Jr., who was graduated in August from Millsaps College in Jackson, Mississippi, with a degree in political science.

Reprisals against Smith continued. On 31 October 1960 several teenage boys put a burning cross on the editor's lawn and set off firecrackers to attract attention. The culprits fled, leaving their car behind. Smith shot a photograph of the burning cross, took the license plate off the parked vehicle, and later found the car parked behind the home of county attorney Pat Barrett, a *Herald* shareholder whose fifteen-year-old son had participated in the Halloween prank. In an editorial, "A Cross Burns – Symptom of a Community Illness," that accompanied her photograph, she dismissed the idea that the incident was "an innocent Halloween prank of high school boys."

Smith celebrated her twenty-fifth anniversary as a newspaper editor in August 1961, publishing a full-page "personal letter" to readers. "I do not take myself too seriously or fancy myself as a Saviour of the people of Holmes County," she wrote. "I flinch every time I am called a 'crusading editor.'" A few weeks earlier she had been vilified in several thousand "little white tracts" anonymously mailed to Holmes County residents. The tracts called the editor a "moderate" – "a dirty word" in "race-conscious Holmes County." Her letter asked readers to "let the world know" her newspaper had their "loyalty and support."

Pulitzer Prize winner Hodding Carter II, publisher of the *Delta Democrat-Times* in Greenville, Mississippi, formed the Tri-Anniversary Committee in July 1961 to raise money to offset her newspapers' sagging advertising revenues. "Tri-Anniversary" referred to three historic benchmarks: Smith's twenty-five years as editor, the centennial of the *Durant News,* and the 125th anniversary of the *Lexington Advertiser.* Committee members included prominent southern journalists Ralph McGill of the *Atlanta Constitution,* Mark Ethridge of the *Louisville Courier-Journal,* and J. N. Heiskell of the *Arkansas Gazette.*

The *Herald* responded to the Tri-Anniversary Committee with front-page name-calling in November 1961, two weeks after the *Advertiser* carried a full-page advertisement placed by Nelson Poynter, Jr., publisher of the *St. Petersburg* (Florida) *Times.* Poynter's advertisement saluted "with admiration" Smith's twenty-five-year editorship. The *Herald* called the Tri-Anniversary Committee "a group of out-of-state agitators, masquerading as do-gooders and moderates," who "continually espouse the NAACP line." Two weeks later the *Herald* ran a seven-column headline across its front page: "Lexington Advertiser, Durant News Receiving Assistance From Member of Top Communist Front Organization." The *Herald* accused Poynter of onetime membership in a citizens' group that a 1944 U.S. House of Representatives Special Committee on Un-American Activities called "the major Communist front organization of the moment." A month before he resigned – effective 1 December 1962, when Paul Tardy became the third editor of the *Herald* in four years – Shearer lambasted Smith, calling her a "witchy ole heifer," and her husband, a "lopeared hound dog mascot."

The court-ordered integration of the University of Mississippi in September 1962 prompted Governor Ross Barnett to defy the order admitting James Meredith. His televised defiance speech led President John F. Kennedy to order federal troops to occupy the Oxford campus to enforce the order and to quell rioting that claimed two lives. The governor's "ridiculous grandstand play" had fomented "rebellion and open insurrection," Smith complained. She wrote that he was primarily responsible for the bloodshed and calumny brought upon the state: "No infant now living will ever see the day when the stain is completely removed. We must face the unpleasant fact that now we are largely regarded throughout the civilized world as an ignorant, narrow, bigoted, intolerant people with little or no regard for human rights and Christian values."

Racial tension in Holmes County exploded on 8 May 1963 when the five-room home of Tchula farmer Hartman Turnbow was firebombed. Three white men shot at the fifty-eight-year-old Turnbow – who had tried to register to vote a month earlier – his wife, and sixteen-year-old daughter when they fled their home. The sheriff and constable arrived five hours later to investigate, the constable reportedly telling Turnbow that he had been keeping "the wrong kind of company with them outside agitators" who were trying to register Negro voters. Turnbow was arrested for firebombing his own home and charged with arson; four voter-registration workers also were arrested in connection with the firebombing, detained for five days, and released.

Smith wrote that the firebombing was "a vicious act" against "all of the people of Holmes County, both white and black." Turnbow's arrest was "a grave disservice" that never would have happened "if we had demanded that all citizens be accorded equal treatment and protection under the law." She applauded an investigation of the incident spearheaded by the U.S. Justice Department.

The FBI investigation of the Turnbow affair led the Justice Department to file a civil suit in U.S. District Court in Jackson. The department sought court orders to stop Turnbow's prosecution and to require Holmes County officials to accept Negro voter-registration applications without harassment or interference. Smith testified during the trial that she had heard then-sheriff Andrew Smith tell the Holmes County Board of Supervisors in 1956: "I don't intend that any Negroes will vote while I'm sheriff." The *Holmes County Herald* disputed Smith's testimony, quoting the deputy sheriff's emphatic denial. Her front-page editorial rejoinder, "A Lying Newspaper is No Good," accused *Herald* editor Tardy of dishonestly slanting and mismanaging news to please "certain individuals, officers and groups."

The shooting death of decorated World War II navy veteran Alfred Brown in early June 1963 exacerbated racial tension in Holmes County. Two Lexington policemen attempted to arrest the thirty-eight-year-old Negro – who had recently been released from a veteran's hospital where he was a mental patient – on suspicion of being publicly intoxicated. Brown pulled out a pocketknife after being hit with a blackjack; he was shot twice. A crowd gathered at the scene where the stricken Brown lay bleeding for fifteen minutes before an ambulance was summoned.

Smith called the shooting "senseless" in a front-page editorial that insisted the death could have been avoided if the policemen "either knew or cared what they were doing." The victim's "natural resentment of an unprovoked arrest on a false and baseless charge" was understandable. "Officers guilty of lawless or unbecoming conduct should be made to give an accounting of their actions. . . . An honest and complete investigation should be made by competent authorities – and no 'whitewash' attempted," she wrote. "And officers should be ordered to treat with respect and dignity all people with whom they come in contact. If they can't or won't do this they should resign or be fired."

In May 1964 Smith became the first woman to win the Pulitzer Prize for editorial writing. The Pulitzer committee cited "the whole volume of her work" and "steadfast adherence to her editorial duties in the face of great pressure and opposition." The associate publisher of the *Delta Democrat-Times,* Hodding Carter III – son of the Pulitzer Prize winner who had formed the Tri-Anniversary Committee – nominated her. The *Delta Democrat-Times* commented:

> Her independence, courage and integrity have not been late-blooming roses. . . . Hazel Smith has stuck to her convictions for almost three decades of Mississippi newspapering. . . . These have not been easy years . . . but she has not endured them because of some distorted martyr complex, but because she fiercely believes in what the bill of rights of the U.S. Constitution proclaims about individual freedom and press responsibility.

While she was in Atlantic City, New Jersey, working as a delegation reporter for NBC at the Democratic National Convention in August 1964, a homemade bomb was tossed through a window of her suburban Jackson, Mississippi, weekly, the *Northside Reporter,* causing an estimated fifteen hundred dollars in damage. She published a front-page signed letter "To The Person or Persons Responsible For The Bombing Of The Northside Reporter":

> If, by your cowardly deed, you hope to kill this newspaper, I tell you now – you are doomed to failure. It takes more than the sneak act of a criminal to destroy a free and independent press. A hundred bombs will not stop our publication.
>
> If, by chance, it was your purpose to frighten, harass, or intimidate, you'd better think again. Others, more expert than you, have tried it and failed. They have merely strengthened our resolve to maintain an honest press so that the people of Mississippi, who want it, may know the truth.
>
> We shall continue to print the truth and state editorially our opinion – in spite of bombing or other pressures and threats made by those who do not want the people to know, those who would arrogantly force all of us to live in a valley of fear, afraid to express an opinion if it does not conform to their selfish dictates.

The ten-year advertising boycott took its toll on Smith and her newspapers. She was eighty-thousand dollars in debt, she told the *New York Herald Tribune* in May 1964, and she had mortgaged personal property, cut the newspaper staff, and borrowed money to continue publishing. She discontinued the *Banner County Outlook* and sold the *Northside Reporter* during the 1970s; she had acquired the *Outlook* in 1955 and the *Reporter* in 1956. Smith's many journalism awards won her national recognition: National Federation of Press Women editorial awards in 1948, 1955, and 1961; the National Editorial Association's Herrick Award in 1956; Theta Sigma Phi's Headliner Award in 1962; the Golden Quill Award of the International Conference of Weekly Newspaper Editors in 1963; and a "Woman of Conscience" citation from the Council of Women of the United States in 1964. Her reputation for being Mississippi's "lady editor" and "a maverick in the magnolia patch" became a springboard for speaking tours that raised money to keep her newspapers afloat, but her debts continued to mount.

Passage of the Civil Rights Act of 1964 brought profound changes to the South, Mississippi, and Holmes County. The failure of the state's lobbying effort to water down the bill demonstrated, she wrote, "how far the South has gone out of the mainstream of American thought and policy and how little sympathy the rest of the country has for us." Lexington's public schools were integrated in September 1966 when an estimated 130 Negro students enrolled. "I Am So Proud of Lexington," her front-page editorial proclaimed: "This facing up to reality, this courageous stand for the preservation of the public schools, deserves the highest commendation." More than 5,000 Negroes had

Ruins of the Lexington Advertiser *office in November 1992, seven years after Smith went bankrupt (photograph by Kevin Cooper)*

registered to vote in Holmes County. An early supporter of the editor was elected in 1967 to represent Holmes County in the state legislature, the first black legislator elected since Reconstruction.

With the dismantling of segregation and enfranchisement of Negroes during the 1960s and 1970s, blacks gained political power and won public offices in Holmes County. Blacks no longer needed whites, including Smith, to defend their civil rights and speak for them. Eventually the black leadership broke with her. "It was almost like a child coming of age who no longer needs his mother," commented Bruce Hill, who became publisher of the *Holmes County Herald* in the early 1970s. "Hazel was a great help to blacks for a long time, but as they came into their own in Holmes County, they developed their own leadership. It was another era, and they didn't need her."

Ostracized by the white community and abandoned by blacks, Smith struggled with ever-mounting debts to publish the *Advertiser*. She had borrowed thousands of dollars, pouring much of it into Hazelwood, the fourteen-room Greek Revival mansion – modeled after Tara in *Gone With the Wind* – that she and Smitty had built on the western edge

of town. Smitty died in November 1983 when he fell from the roof while cleaning gutters. After her husband's death Smith's health began to deteriorate noticeably, her failing memory and erratic behavior later recognized to be the onset of Alzheimer's disease.

The last edition of the *Lexington Advertiser* appeared on 19 September 1985. Two weeks earlier the *Holmes County Herald* had published a legal notice that she had filed for bankruptcy. She owed more that $250,000, including $34,000 in printing bills for her newspaper. She got lost en route from Lexington to a mandatory bankruptcy-court hearing in Jackson in November, and her bankruptcy case was dismissed for her failure to appear. The bank foreclosed, taking her newspaper and repossessing Hazelwood; her furniture was auctioned. In February 1986 Smith's sister quietly took her back to an obscure and penniless retirement in Gadsden, Alabama.

Smith began her fifty-year weekly newspaper career with ultraconservative Dixiecrat beliefs in segregation. Her views moderated when her law-and-order brand of Christian morality confronted the racial bigotry and violence that erupted during the mid 1950s. "You finally come to a point when you must decide whether you're for law and order or against it," she told the *Christian Science Monitor* in July 1966, "and it's also been a matter of people being able to pressure the free press with its rights and responsibilities." Even though she voiced admiration and praise for slain civil-rights leaders Martin Luther King, Jr., and Medgar Evers, Smith was never a staunch integrationist: "We had never advocated school integration at the time of the 1954 high court decision (nor since for that matter)," she wrote eight months after winning the Pulitzer Prize.

Nevertheless, her southern detractors and northern admirers called her a "liberal." *New York Herald Tribune* writer Ann Geracimos's assessment was overdrawn: "She is probably the only liberal editor in Mississippi, one of the few liberal women at all in the state and one of only a handful in the whole South." Hodding Carter, Jr., offered a more temperate view in *First Person Rural* (1963), noting that a northerner with similar views would hardly be called a liberal. "The supreme irony is that nowhere outside the Deep South would Hazel Brannon Smith be labeled even a liberal in her racial views," he wrote. "If she must be categorized, then call her a moderate."

Her moderate editorial pleas for equal justice for all races *were* "liberal" within the inflammatory context of the Deep South's closed society. "If she would have been a man, they would have lynched her," observed William F. Minor, dean of Missis-

sippi journalists and a longtime friend. "She wrote some beautiful things that needed to be said."

Hazel Brannon Smith saw herself merely as "a little editor in a little spot" who refused to let her newspaper be intimidated into silence. "Honey," she said, "I'm not on any crusade. I'm simply committed to speaking out about whatever I think is right."

References:

Hodding Carter, Jr., "Woman Editor's War on Bigots," in his *First Person Rural* (Garden City, N.Y.: Doubleday, 1963), pp. 217–225;

Dudley Clendinen, "Delta Blacks Rally for 'Woman of Principle,' " *New York Times,* 31 March 1986, pp. A1, A17;

Lee Freeland, "Time Closes Lexington Newspaper that Battled Racism," *Jackson* (Mississippi) *Clarion Ledger,* 5 January 1986, pp. A1, A17;

Fred Grimm, "Hazel Smith, Champion of Civil Rights, Fights Final Battle Alone and Forgotten," *Chicago Tribune,* 27 March 1986, pp. 1, 3;

T. George Harris, "The 11-year Siege of Mississippi's Lady Editor," *Look,* 29 (16 November 1965): 121–128;

"Mississippi, Determined Lady," *Columbia Journalism Review,* 2 (Fall 1963): 37–38;

Mark Newman, "Hazel Brannon Smith and Holmes County, Mississippi, 1936–1964: The Making of a Pulitzer Prize Winner," *Journal of Mississippi History,* 54 (February 1992): 59–87.

Arthur Hays Sulzberger

(12 September 1891 – 11 December 1968)

and

Arthur Ochs Sulzberger

(5 February 1926 –)

Ronald S. Marmarelli
Central Michigan University

MAJOR POSITIONS HELD: **Arthur Hays Sulzberger:** Publisher, *New York Times* (1935–1961); president (1935–1957), chairman of the board (1957–1968), New York Times Company.

Arthur Ochs Sulzberger: Publisher, *New York Times* (1963–1992); president (1963–1979), chairman of the board (1973–), New York Times Company.

Throughout the twentieth century members of the Ochs-Sulzberger family led the *New York Times* to its position as the standard-bearer in daily print journalism in the United States. The leadership task passed to the fourth generation of the family on 16 January 1992, when Arthur Ochs Sulzberger, Jr., took his father's place on the fourteenth floor of the Times Building on West Forty-third Street in New York City. In keeping with family tradition, the new publisher, like his father and grandfather before him, had prepared for the job by working in several departments at the *Times*.

Prior to his appointment, Sulzberger, Jr., served for almost four years as deputy publisher, with responsibility for the news and business departments of the newspaper. As his predecessors had, he pledged in a message on the editorial page his allegiance to the guiding precept set down for the *Times* by Adolph S. Ochs ninety-six years earlier: "To give the news impartially, without fear or favor, regardless of any party, sect or interest involved." The new publisher asserted that his title "stands for a history of excellence – one that is renewed daily by the finest newspaper staff ever assembled anywhere."

Arthur Hays Sulzberger, 1953

Each time power was transferred at the *Times* that "history of excellence" meant that new leadership received a newspaper that was stronger and more firmly established. Because of the accomplishments of his father in twenty-nine years as publisher, Sulzberger, Jr., took the helm of a newspaper that was in many ways different and much improved in comparison to the one his father had taken over. Similarly, Arthur Hays Sulzberger's leadership had made the *New York Times* of which Arthur Ochs Sulzberger took command in 1963 very different from the newspaper of 1935, when Adolph Ochs died and his son-in-law succeeded him as publisher.

Upon his appointment Sulzberger, Jr., said that he would consider himself a success if, when it came time for him to turn the newspaper over to a new generation, he had done as well as his father had. His father, noting that the *Times* was "stronger than ever" and looking forward to the transition into the twenty-first century, commented that the new publisher and "his team" would continue the position of the *Times* "as the nation's preeminent newspaper."

That status was achieved under Ochs, who took over the failing newspaper in August 1896, gained full control in June 1900, and made it into a prestigious national institution. Ochs insisted that his successors sustain the newspaper's integrity and independence. His will called upon them to "perpetuate *The New York Times* as an institution charged with a high public duty" and to maintain it "as an independent newspaper, entirely fearless, free of ulterior influence, and unselfishly devoted to the public welfare, without regard to individual advantage or ambition, the claims of party politics, or the voice of religious or personal prejudice or predilection."

Under the Sulzbergers, the *Times,* while always growing stronger, continued in substantive ways to be much the same newspaper it had been since 1896. While remaining faithful to Ochs's wishes, the Sulzbergers succeeded in perpetuating and enhancing the quality of their newspaper to an extent unprecedented in the history of family newspaper ownership.

Neither his own family background nor his early education and training had provided Arthur Hays Sulzberger with the opportunity to be a success in the newspaper business. He was born 12 September 1891 in New York City, the fourth child and third son of Cyrus Lindauer Sulzberger and Rachel Peixotto Hays Sulzberger. His father was a prosperous textile importer and cotton merchant; his mother, a former teacher in New York City public schools and at Hunter College.

After attending New York City public schools and the Horace Mann School, Sulzberger entered Columbia College in 1909 to study engineering, looking toward a career as a sanitary engineer. He received a B.S. degree in 1913, then worked at N. Erlanger,

Blumgart and Company, the textile firm where his father was president and later chairman of the board. In 1917 he was commissioned a second lieutenant in the U. S. Army Reserve and trained as an artillery officer.

While a student, Sulzberger met Iphigene Ochs, daughter of the *New York Times* publisher and a student at Barnard College, where she earned a B.A. degree in 1914. They became reacquainted in 1915. When they announced their intention to marry, her father was not pleased. He had hoped his only child would marry a newspaperman. In his history of the *New York Times,* Meyer Berger writes: "The officer suitor was clean-cut and alert, but the publisher could not overlook the fact that Sulzberger was not of the inky tradition and that his father, for all his excellent business and civic reputation, was a cotton merchant and not of the Fourth Estate."

Despite Adolph Ochs's misgivings, Sulzberger and Iphigene were married on 17 November 1917 in the Ochs's home at 308 West Seventy-fifth Street. After their wedding, military service took the Sulzbergers first to Camp Wadsworth in Spartanburg, South Carolina. Although he was expecting overseas duty, Sulzberger was transferred first to Chillicothe, Ohio, then to other units in the United States before being discharged from active service in 1918.

Shortly after Sulzberger's discharge, his father-in-law put him to work at the *Times,* starting on 7 December 1918. Years later, Sulzberger described his "system" for getting to be publisher of a great newspaper: "You work very hard, you never watch the clock, you polish up the handle of the big front door. And you marry the boss's daughter. That is how I did it." This assessment irked his wife. "The success Arthur made of himself," she wrote, "was wholly his own."

Sulzberger's title at the *Times* was assistant to the executive manager, but his duties were not specified. Ochs was determined that Sulzberger would have to work his way into a responsible job at the newspaper. The only guidance offered to him was that he try his hand at whatever came his way.

He first involved himself in the newspaper's annual Hundred Neediest Cases appeal. After that, Berger comments, Sulzberger found new tasks but "wandered, rather lonely, in the plant, affable and pleasant, but with no fixed duties, a minister without portfolio." Nevertheless, he took advantage of the opportunity his situation offered him to become familiar with many elements of the operation and earned promotion within a decade to a vice-presidency.

The first important responsibility that Sulzberger was assigned required him to become an expert on newsprint production and supply. He was to make sure that the *Times* would have a sufficient supply of the vital paper, and he did. Ochs suggested he begin his familiarization firsthand at the company's Tidewater Paper Mill in South Brooklyn. In 1926 he represented the *Times* in the development of a $30 million cooperative venture with the Kimberly-Clark Company to build the Spruce Falls Power and Paper Company paper mill in Kapuskasing, Ontario. The mill opened in 1928.

During those early years of his work at the *Times,* Sulzberger and Iphigene had four children – Marian Effie, Ruth Rachel, Judith Peixotto, and Arthur Ochs, the future publisher – all born in New York City. Arthur, born 5 February 1926, soon acquired the nickname "Punch." His father wrote and illustrated a book to celebrate his birth, declaring that the new addition to the family had "come to play the Punch to Judy's endless show."

The nickname seemed for a time to be more of a certainty than his given name. His sister Ruth explained:

> Grandfather Ochs, who was already well pleased with his crop of girls, took one look at the heir and announced that he would be spoiled rotten. This so riled the new mother than she erased Ochs from his name and dubbed him Arthur Hays Sulzberger, Jr. Six months later ... Mrs. Sulzberger felt more kindly disposed to perpetuating her father's name. The Ochs was reinstated, which was fitting, because along with the name the child inherited the ears.

In the 1930s Ochs's declining health and bouts of depression brought Sulzberger increasing responsibilities for representing and managing the newspaper. At public events and ceremonies he often spoke for freedom of the press and the important role of journalism in a democracy, as well as the principles that Ochs had enunciated as representing the character and purpose of the *Times.* He pledged that the *Times* would continue to adhere to those principles.

In addition to the day-to-day activities in which his new responsibilities involved him, he suggested and supervised development of the newspaper's own system for transmitting photographs over telephone lines as an alternative to leasing costly Wirephoto lines from the Associated Press. As a result, the newspaper was able to start its Wide World Wirephoto service in February 1935.

Arthur Ochs Sulzberger, 1963

Less than two months later, Ochs died on 8 April 1935, leaving controlling interest in the *Times* in trust to the Sulzbergers' children, with Iphigene and Arthur Hays and Julius Ochs Adler, Ochs's nephew, as trustees and executors of the estate. Ownership was to pass to the children after Iphigene's death. (Ochs's will also left to his heirs the *Chattanooga Times,* his first newspaper, as a separate corporation.) Sulzberger was chosen by the trustees to succeed Ochs, and on 7 May 1935 the company's board of directors elected him president of the company and publisher of the newspaper. Circulation of the *Times* stood at 465,000 daily and 713,000 on Sunday. Gross income was about $17 million.

Besides naming Sulzberger publisher, the trustees also took steps to preserve the trust's controlling interest, foreshadowing similar actions in later years to keep the *Times* firmly in family hands. By selling the trust's preferred stock in the New York Times Company to the company, the trustees raised the $6 million needed to pay inheritance taxes, attorneys' fees, and other costs incurred because of Ochs's death. The action meant the trust gave up some $480,000 in annual income from the stock. Sulzberger said later that the trustees did not wish "any bank, or group of banks" to control the *Times,* "and we were prepared to make any sacrifice to avoid that."

Upon taking over as publisher, Sulzberger decided that any major changes he might wish to make would be put off for a time. He did not want anyone to think the newspaper would be altered in fundamental ways. He also did not wish it to appear that he had been waiting for Ochs to die before making changes. "Let's just go along on existing lines for a year," he said at the time. "We'll take up changes then." The willingness to change the *Times,* but to do so carefully and cautiously, reflected the character trait that enabled him, as longtime *Times* writer James Reston noted later, to combine "reverence to the symbol and tradition of the *Times*" with a remarkable "fearlessness of revision."

In addition to noting the depth and quality of his character, judgment, and integrity, contemporaries and colleagues also described Sulzberger as a handsome and urbane man, relaxed and easygoing, with a broad sense of humor that included a fondness for puns. In its account of his having been named publisher, *Literary Digest* said of him: "Tall and good-looking, his hair parted in the middle, he dresses smartly but quietly. His taste runs to fine and expensive objects, such as ornately-bound books. . . . He combines a gift for writing light verse with an aptitude for poker."

Years later, in its obituary of its late publisher, the *Times* noted that "the square set of his shoulders and his trim physique" conveyed the impression that he was "a tall and dominating man, although he was of average height — 5 feet, 9 inches." It continued, "Because he was handsome and carried the newspaper aura with him and because he liked to do things with style, he was characterized often as having glamor."

Sulzberger's management style consisted of delegating authority but paying close attention to details. In a 1945 speech he stated that the publisher's control of the newspaper's policies depended upon working in harmony with carefully chosen associates, "talking things out and, on many occasions, being willing to give *way* rather than to give *orders.*"

Turner Catledge, who rose from reporter to managing editor under Sulzberger, wrote that the publisher's inclination was not to be aggressive or dominating, not to be a boss who hurled "thunderbolts at an awed staff." Rather, he was "more reserved, more subtle, and I think more effective." Sulzberger often used humor to ease the tension of contentious meetings. Catledge also said Sulzberger

could be "irritable on small issues" but "had unerring good judgment on the big issues."

The years of Sulzberger's leadership were, the *Times* wrote later, "marked by striking changes gradually introduced." Besides continued financial strength and technical progress, he oversaw steady change and improvement in news coverage and content that included increases in specialization, interpretation, background, and analysis; more concise, brighter writing; and greater use of photographs. The comprehensive and authoritative coverage of national and international affairs that had become a trademark of the *Times* under Ochs continued and expanded under Sulzberger and his editors.

The editorial page also received Sulzberger's attention. In November 1938 he named Charles Merz editor of the page. That move reflected a shift in emphasis from the Ochs years, during which *Times* editorials were noted for their ability to see both sides of an issue. As Berger explains, "Merz and Sulzberger did not share Ochs's inhibitions about the strong editorial stand on vital issues. They felt certain that *The Times* was so thoroughly established as a *news* paper, first and above all else, that there was no longer reason to fear that editorial crusading would spill over into its news columns."

Sulzberger's experience in developing the Wirephoto service had increased his interest in news photography, and he championed expanded use of photographs in the *Times,* both on the front page and on inside pages. In this and other ways his modernizing of the newspaper was, Berger notes, "taking place so subtly that many readers did not notice it." Sulzberger, however, recalled that he was, at times, worried that he might be making changes too quickly:

> I was anxious to perfect *The Times*'s readability. I wanted the paper to move editorially out of the ivory tower. I saw the effect that radio commentators were having; it called for more news interpretation on our part because news was growing almost alarmingly complex. It was clear to me that it was time for change, but I feared that I might be ruining *The Times*. The changes had to be made without affecting the basic Ochs formula.

In reflecting that basic formula Sulzberger often emphasized the newspaper's responsibility to present news honestly, fully, and intelligently. In 1945, for example, he stated that the main responsibility of the newspaper "lies in reporting accurately that which happens." He added, "Whichever way the cat should jump, we should record it, and we should not allow our excitement about the direction which it takes, or plans to take, to interfere with our primary mission."

In order for the *Times* to focus more concertedly on its mission, Sulzberger took several steps to tighten the newspaper and reduce operating costs. In his first several years as publisher, he sold its subsidiary publications, the *Annalist*, *Current History*, and *Mid-Week Pictorial*; sold Wide World Photos to the Associated Press; and merged the newspaper's rotogravure section with the Sunday magazine.

Restrictions on the supply of newsprint during World War II presented Sulzberger and other publishers with a dilemma – how to find space for the kind of reporting the war merited. He opted for the kind of comprehensive coverage that the *Times* had made a key ingredient of its formula. On occasion this policy called for restricting advertising in order to make sufficient space available for news. Any temporary loss of advertising revenue that occurred during the war was offset by a surging circulation afterward, which resulted in increased advertising revenue. Figures from the war years show that circulation dipped slightly, while total advertising lineage remained steady.

For Punch the war also brought challenge and opportunity. He was an indifferent student, attending several private schools. "They were all delighted to have him, but wanted him as something other than a spectator," his sister Ruth wrote. His teachers "found him charming," she said, but they admitted "they were not 'getting through' to him." In 1943 Punch, then seventeen, left the Loomis School to enlist in the Marines. His parents reluctantly consented. He worked briefly for the *Times* in the Wirephoto department, then entered the Marines in January 1944, training as a radio operator. World War II, he said later, "gave me the excuse to finally quit school, otherwise I might still be up there in Loomis, trying to graduate."

He reacted well to the tight discipline of the Marines and was able to achieve success to a degree he had not experienced in school. He served in the Philippines as a naval intercept radio operator and was a driver at the headquarters of Gen. Douglas MacArthur. In April 1946 he was discharged as a corporal and soon passed a high-school equivalency examination to qualify for college.

He was accepted provisionally as a special-studies student at Columbia University but soon qualified for regular-student status. He majored in English and history, did well, and received his B.A. in 1951. "I settled down in a hurry," he recalled.

During the war the elder Sulzberger, who had become a leading figure in the American Red Cross,

journeyed on two trips of some twenty-seven thousand total miles each to inspect Red Cross installations and, as a publisher, to see the war zones firsthand. One development that, in part, grew out of his first trip was the *Overseas Weekly,* a tabloid newspaper for the armed forces that first appeared in August 1943.

A condensed version of the "News of the Week in Review" from the Sunday *Times,* it was distributed on sixteen fronts by the Army Exchange Service. In 1949 it developed into the *Times International Edition,* published in Europe. Sulzberger expanded that edition in October 1960 so that it could be published at the same time and on the same day as the domestic edition.

Sulzberger also expanded the *Times* domestically on at least two fronts. The newspaper's production facilities were increased with the building of an extension to its Forty-fourth Street plant in 1944; a new plant was built on West End Avenue in 1959. The company moved into a new communications field in 1944 with the purchase of radio station WQXR in New York.

The rise of labor unions brought new challenges to Sulzberger and the *Times*. He had first signed union contracts in the 1940s and was not resistant to organized labor. Although he opposed a closed union shop for news and editorial employees, he generally agreed to union economic demands, being reluctant to force a strike. But, Catledge wrote, Sulzberger was saddened because "the growth of unionism lessened his ability to guide the paper in the fatherly manner he preferred."

In 1953 a photoengravers' strike supported by most of the news staff shut down the newspaper for almost two weeks, and the *Times* failed to publish for the first time in its history. Sulzberger's thirty-fifth anniversary with the *Times* occurred during the strike, prompting him in his despair to write a poem that ended with the lines:

He worked very hard and he never watched the clock
And he polished up the handle on the big front door.
By dint of hard labor he rose to the top
And in thirty-five years the *Times* was no more.

His opposition to a closed union shop for news and editorial personnel was based on his commitment to the ideal of impartiality in the presentation of the news. That commitment also caused him to bar Communist-party members from working in some departments of the newspaper that he thought to be sensitive. In 1955 he fired a reporter who refused to answer questions before a Senate commit-

Arthur Ochs Sulzberger, his wife, Carol, Abby Catledge, and Turner Catledge on board a ship bound for Europe, 1964

tee, believing that neither the newspaper nor the reporter could retain readers' confidence in their impartiality. He later decided against a blanket rule in such cases.

Sulzberger thought the appearance of impartiality so important that he used the pseudonym "A. Aitchess" (A.H.S.) in letters to the editor to disguise his own opinions. His son continued the tradition, signing his letters "A. Sock." Iphigene Sulzberger signed hers with the names of deceased relatives.

Punch worked briefly as a reporter at the *Times* in 1951 after receiving his degree from Columbia and before being recalled for service in the Marines during the Korean War. Commissioned a second lieutenant, he served in Korea as an information officer, then was transferred to Washington, D.C., where he worked in the office of the legislative assistant to the commandant of the Marines. He was released from active duty in 1953 as a first lieutenant and went back to work as a reporter at the *Times*.

In February 1953 he went to the *Milwaukee Journal* to work in the newsroom. He returned to the *Times* in February 1954, worked three months on the foreign-news copy desk, and in June 1954 went to Europe for service as a correspondent in the Paris, London, and Rome bureaus. He was recalled to New York and named assistant to the publisher in January 1956.

That same year he was divorced and remarried. He had married Barbara Grant on 2 July 1948, while a student at Columbia. They had two children, Arthur Ochs, Jr., and Karen Alden. He married Carol Fox Fuhrman on 19 December 1956. They had a daughter, Cynthia, and Punch adopted Carol's daughter, Cathy Jean.

In April 1957 Orvil E. Dryfoos, the husband of Marian Sulzberger, was named president of the company, and Punch was named assistant treasurer. Dryfoos, who had worked at the *Times* since 1942, was in line to move up to publisher. When the elder Sulzberger's health declined after a series of strokes, he retired on 25 April 1957 and was succeeded by his son-in-law. Sulzberger retained his position as chairman of the board.

The *Times* had grown considerably during Sulzberger's twenty-five years as publisher. Daily circulation had increased by 40 percent to 744, 763, and Sunday circulation had nearly doubled to 1.4 million. Advertising lineage had increased more than three times, and gross income had increased by about $100 million, to more than $117 million. The number of *Times* employees had grown to 5,189 in 1961, more than double the number in 1935.

Punch was one of those employees in 1961, and his duties were as unspecified as his father's had been years earlier. "I was 'assistant' of everything," he said later. Former *Times* writer Gay Talese reported that Sulzberger "was often seen around the third floor, a clean-cut, dark-eyed young man puffing a pipe, smiling, then looking up at the walls in the newsroom inspecting the paint, or scrutinizing the air-conditioning ducts, appearing to be endlessly fascinated by the mechanical system and machinery around the building. . . . His opinions on news coverage, however, were rarely solicited or expressed, and he was often ignored by some top *Times* men."

Dryfoos was not inclined to give him much responsibility. Sulzberger recalled, "My career didn't look very promising. I'd go up to Orv occasionally and ask him to give me something to do." Dryfoos, then forty-eight, was expected to serve as publisher until his retirement, perhaps two decades later. Punch would be in line to succeed him. But when Dryfoos died of a heart ailment on 25 May 1963 – fifty-five days after the end of a printers union strike that lasted from December 1962 through March 1963 – the Sulzbergers faced the decision on succession years ahead of schedule.

For a time they seemed uncertain that Punch was ready to take on the job. His father had noted his maturation during the long strike in a letter dated 31 March 1963: "You went into it something of a boy and came out of it a man whose judgment was generally respected." But, as Iphigene said later, "We had all hoped that Punch would have many years more training before having to take over."

Perhaps for that reason they considered having him serve as publisher, but with shared authority. However, he insisted that if he were to be publisher, it had to be without conditions. So, on 20 June 1963 Arthur Ochs Sulzberger was named publisher and president at age thirty-seven, one year younger than his grandfather had been when he took over the *Times* in 1896. "We had to take a chance on

Punch," his mother recalled. "Maybe because he was the youngest he hadn't been considered so much. But he turned out so well. He was better than anyone could have expected."

In a statement announcing the appointment, the elder Sulzberger said: "It is our intention to maintain this family operation and insure continuance of the newspaper that the *Times* has come to be under those who by sentiment and training are particularly tied to its principles and traditions." Punch said later that he felt "shell-shocked" when he took over. After his first day on the job, he told one of his sisters, "I've made my first executive decision. I've decided not to throw up."

That anecdote, which was repeated in various forms over the years, reflects the informality, affability, and humor (often self-deprecating and much like his father's) everyone knew Punch brought to his job. However, many did not know of the decisiveness with which he would act in doing that job. Catledge said the new publisher "was energetic and impatient, filled with ideas and criticisms, filled also with wit and high spirits."

Catledge said that Punch proved to be a more aggressive publisher than either his father or brother-in-law had been; he asked questions and challenged assumptions like Adolph Ochs, who often said, "I always question the obvious." Referring to Punch as "the Harry Truman of the *Times*," in that he "was undertrained and underestimated," James Reston said he "proved that common sense and a little humanity go a long way." Rather than "worry about problems," Reston wrote, "he decided them."

Decisions he made in leading the Times Company through a series of challenges over three decades produced stunning changes that transformed the company and the newspaper, ensured their financial stability, and enhanced the quality of the *Times*. He realized those changes were absolutely necessary in order for the *Times* to continue to be the newspaper that it had come to be, as his father had said the family intended.

Punch knew that financial strength was vital to the journalistic mission of the newspaper but felt that profitability and quality could be maintained simultaneously. The newspaper's primary mission, he said later, was to make a profit, because "if we're not profitable, we can't have any other mission." Beyond that, he said, the mission is "to cover the news – to call the shots as we see them," echoing his father's earlier statements.

While making a profit was primary, maximum profit was not the goal. "The important thing is not how much money the *New York Times* makes, but how good the *New York Times* is," Punch remarked. His greatest pride was in the quality of the newspaper: "We don't run it to maximize the profits of the paper." If that were the goal, he said, profits could be doubled by closing bureaus, using the wire services and stringers, and cutting the news content. That would not take genius, he said, "and we'd just be like everybody else."

Of immediate concern to the new publisher were problems made obvious during and after the long 1962–1963 strike. The 114-day shutdown had a major immediate impact on the company's finances at the same time it was losing $5 million a year on its West Coast and international editions. For the first quarter of 1963 the company posted a net loss of more than $4 million. For the year – for the first time in its history – it lost money on its newspaper operations, more than five hundred thousand dollars. Total newspaper revenues for the year were below the level of 1962, when the paper earned only about six hundred thousand dollars.

Sulzberger was especially concerned about the company's reliance on what the *Times* brought in for most of its revenue and its consequent vulnerability to a strike, especially a long one. The unions could use strikes or threats of strikes to prevent the company from pressing for agreements that would permit automation to reduce production costs. The company clearly had to broaden its sources of revenue in order to confront the unions and to strengthen its ability to withstand strikes.

The lack of a plan for doing that was symptomatic of broader problems at the Times Company. By modern standards the company was deficient in such basic business practices as budgeting, planning, and developing a growth strategy. Sulzberger noted that while the quality of the newspaper "was reasonably good," the real problem "was on the business side." Consequently, he had to give priority attention to the business problems.

As his father had, Punch took steps to reduce costs and tighten the company's operations. A major step was shutting down the *Times* West Coast edition in January 1964. Dryfoos had started the "Westward Ho" project in October 1962, but it had failed to establish sufficient circulation and advertising and was losing $3 million a year. Sulzberger announced in the spring of 1967 that he was folding the international edition, which had lost money for most of its eighteen years.

In its place the Times Company joined as a one-third partner with Whitney Communications and the Washington Post Company in the operation of the *International Herald Tribune*. The Times and Post companies later took over operation of the newspaper as equal partners. Following the closing of the morning *New York Herald Tribune* and the afternoon *New York World Journal Tribune,* Sulzberger started – then stopped in October 1967 – work on an afternoon newspaper to be published by the Times Company. A prototype, using a six-column format, was prepared in the summer of 1967, but Sulzberger suspended the project because the new newspaper might have drained the resources of the *Times.*

One of the organizational problems that Sulzberger tackled was the existence within the newspaper and the company of various "internal fiefdoms," in which editors and executives operated as if they were independent entities. The split between the daily news and Sunday departments represented the most notorious example. "We were running two separate newspapers here," Sulzberger recalled. "They did not talk to one another."

Catledge, noting Sulzberger's fondness for "neat organization," which matched the publisher's personal neatness, said the split "seemed untidy to Punch, and he proposed to remedy it." The publisher announced that on 1 September 1964 the departments would be unified under Catledge as executive editor. For various reasons, however, completion of the merger did not occur until twelve years later, when Sulzberger insisted to his new executive editor, A. M. Rosenthal, "Now look, that's it. No more."

Soon after taking over as publisher, Sulzberger began steps toward diversification, mainly through the acquisition of other companies, which added to company earnings and strengthened its position in dealing with unions. In doing so he had to work against the company's traditional aversion to investing in other enterprises, which was based on a concern that the *Times* would be accused of editorial bias in favor of the company's other interests. "It took a while to convince my father that we should change," Punch said.

In 1963 the company increased its involvement in paper manufacturing by acquiring a minority interest in the Gaspesia Pulp and Paper Company in Quebec and established the Times Book Division. Over the following five years the company bought the Microfilming Corporation of America, Teaching Systems Corporation, Arno Press, and Quadrangle Books. In 1967 the *Times* began the *Large Type Weekly,* printed in eighteen-point type for readers with vision problems.

Front page of the New York Times, *1 July 1971*

In Sulzberger's first five years as publisher, daily circulation of the *Times* rose from 740,000 to 1 million; Sunday circulation, from about 1.4 million to 1.54 million. Advertising lineage rose steadily, from an all-time high of more than 67 million in 1964 to another all-time high of more than 86 million in 1968.

As chairman of the board of the Times Company, Arthur Hays Sulzberger shared in his son's early success. Four days after having marked his fiftieth anniversary at the *Times,* however, he died on 11 December 1968 in New York City at age seventy-seven. At a memorial service James Reston said the elder Sulzberger "presided over the *Times* with rare good judgment, unfailing human consideration, and a remarkable combination of seriousness and merriness." Despite his initial lack of training and expertise in the newspaper business, he was "a remarkable success," Reston said.

After 1968 Punch Sulzberger's expansion and diversification program continued over the next twenty-three years, transforming the family business from a basically one-product, privately held company that was dependent upon the *Times* for most of its revenue into a $1.7 billion, publicly held communications conglomerate. The biggest step in that direction was taken in March 1971, with the acquisition of fourteen properties of Cowles Communications for $52 million in *Times* stock and the assumption of $15 million of debt. The purchases included *Family Circle* magazine, a Memphis television station, a textbook company, three Florida newspapers, and a group of medical magazines. "We started to grow from there," Sulzberger said.

The company bought other daily and weekly newspapers, consumer and trade magazines, book-publishing companies, educational media companies, television stations, and cable television systems. In 1985 alone the company spent $400 million on acquisitions. Several of the properties were subsequently sold — the cable systems for $420 million in January 1989. In 1991 the company sold its interest in the Spruce Falls Power and Paper Company, which had been jointly owned with Kimberly-Clark since Arthur Hays Sulzberger arranged the deal in 1926.

In January 1992 – besides the *New York Times,* its news service, and feature syndicate, and WQXR radio – the company's properties included thirty-two regional newspapers (twenty-four daily, eight weekly) in Florida and ten other states; seventeen consumer and trade magazines, including *McCall's, Family Circle, Child, Golf Digest, Tennis,* and *Cruising*

World; and five TV stations. It also had interests in three paper mills.

In June 1971, the year of the Cowles deal, the *Times* was selling almost 850,000 copies daily and almost 1.5 million on Sunday. The Sunday edition of 13 June that year marked another dramatic milestone in Sulzberger's tenure as publisher, one that led to a confrontation with the U.S. government, a landmark Supreme Court decision, and a Pulitzer Prize for the newspaper. The *Times* published a series of stories that Sunday and the following Monday and Tuesday based on a secret Pentagon study of the making of policy on Vietnam. It also published pages of documentary material from the study, which the *Times* referred to as "Vietnam Archive." A temporary court injunction halted publication, and fifteen days of litigation in the federal courts, ending in the Supreme Court, followed. After the Supreme Court decision on 30 June, publication resumed on 1 July and continued through 5 July.

Despite his initial misgivings about the project, and advice from the newspaper's attorneys against publication, Sulzberger, without consulting members of his family and the company's board of directors, approved running the stories, specifying how much space should be devoted to them. He also decided to continue the series on Tuesday, refusing a government request to cease publication. Sulzberger said later that he thought the *Times* had handled the stories appropriately and that the decision to publish them and to contest the government's efforts to suppress publication was correct. "If we hadn't done it," he said, "people would have said the spunk and fight have gone out of the *New York Times.*"

The Pentagon Papers episode marked one of several notable journalistic achievements for Sulzberger's *Times* in the 1960s and 1970s, beginning with the *Times* v. *Sullivan* decision of the Supreme Court in 1964, which protected journalists against libel suits by public officials. With its coverage of civil-rights efforts in the South, the Vietnam War (and its vigorous editorial opposition to U.S. policy on Vietnam from 1965 on), and Watergate, the *Times* played a key role in expanding and asserting the press's role as public watchdog.

According to *Times* historian Harrison E. Salisbury, publication of the Pentagon Papers marked the newspaper's "transition from 'good gray *Times,*' repository of moral enlightenment, historical record and beyond-the-need-of-duty loyalty to the Establishment, to its new but still unacknowledged role of guardian of public interest, of living embodiment of the First Amendment principles bestowed upon the press by the founding fathers." Salisbury also wrote that the episode symbolized a change in the *Times* "from a newspaper which recorded the action to one which has become, like it or not, a very considerable part of the action."

That new status of the *Times* did not translate into prosperity for the newspaper, for reasons not directly related to its publication of the Pentagon Papers or its coverage of social and political issues. In the early and mid 1970s the newspaper faced serious economic problems in a period of national economic recession, which included the bankruptcy of New York City. Rising production and distribution costs, changes in reading habits and readers' interests, and increased competition for advertising from television and suburban newspapers took their toll on the newspaper's financial health. Revenues increased, but net income dropped for both the company and the newspaper. Advertising in the *Times* fell 25 percent from 1969 to 1974.

Sulzberger – who, in addition to his publisher and president titles, was named chairman of the board in November 1973, filling the post vacant since his father's death – looked on the editorial page of the *Times* as one place where change was needed to improve the newspaper's situation. (A decision that he had made earlier brought about the start, on 21 September 1970, of the "Op-Ed" page, an idea that had been talked about for four years but had been stalled because of internal disputes between editors.)

Sulzberger felt that the *Times* was perceived as being antibusiness, primarily because of its editorials. Although he believed that the newspaper's editorial policy was misunderstood by the business community, he knew that the perception could harm the newspaper. "If we're going to outrage the businessman, we're not going to get his advertising or his readership, both of which are important to us," he said.

The major change that he made was to ask his cousin John Oakes, editor of the editorial page since 1961, to retire early. He was succeeded by Max Frankel on 1 January 1977. A few years later Sulzberger said the newspaper had not "violently changed" its editorial position: "I think we just became a little more thoughtful, a little less preachy, a little more considerate of the fact that there is usually more than one side to an issue and that everybody on the other side isn't a liar or a thief or something like that." He said he preferred that the editorial page "be perceived as being, first of all, thought-

ful, fair, somewhat liberal, international, not overly regional."

Other, more far-reaching changes in the newspaper contributed significantly to its achieving a turnaround in its fortunes during the late 1970s. Sulzberger directed a fundamental redesign of the "good gray *Times*" that attracted advertisers and readers in large numbers. The daily *Times* went from being a two-section paper, using the same formula and format it had used for years, to being a four-section paper that carried a feature section designed to appeal to affluent readers and to advertisers. One observer termed the change the "sectional revolution of the seventies."

Sulzberger worked closely with editors, production people, and business-office executives in developing and adding the sections from 1976 through 1978, starting with the Friday "Weekend" section in April 1976, which quickly attracted thirty-five thousand new readers. The other sections were "SportsMonday," "Science Times" (Tuesday), "Living" (Wednesday), and "Home" (Thursday). The new fourth section, "Business Day," debuted in May 1978. A new advertising slogan, "More Than Just the News," emphasized the paper's expanded coverage of family life, food, culture, religion, science, sports, women's news, and other spheres.

Along with the content changes came revisions in layout and page design, use of graphics, and conversion from the traditional eight-column format to six columns. "It's not only a newspaper of good hard news every day," Sulzberger said later, "but it's basically a magazine also, with those C sections, which have been very good for us."

The redesign, Sulzberger recalled, "was a response to a business need," primarily a circulation problem. "We had to do something that would excite our readers, something new, something fresh, something they really wanted," and something that "would be interesting to advertisers." With the new sections, the *Times* reversed weekday circulation losses and brought in more advertising revenue, which went from $195 million in 1975 to $254 million in 1980. Total revenues also increased, from $283 million in 1970 to $731 million in 1980.

The changes in content and design were related to changes the *Times* was making in its production facilities and its use of new printing and communications technology. The *Times* moved into photocomposition of classified and display advertising and toward computerization of editing and typesetting of news copy, and on 1 July 1978 it completed the conversion to cold-type photocomposition. In October 1976 a $35 million automated satellite printing plant in Carlstadt, New Jersey, began operation as one of the largest and most advanced offset plants in the nation. In 1977 renovation started transforming the newspaper's block-long newsroom, with its sea of gray desks and manual typewriters, into a modern, bright newsroom with reporters and editors working at video display terminals.

Conversion to new, automated production technology required Sulzberger to work out new arrangements with unions representing *Times* employees, a task that began soon after he took over as publisher. It took several years to complete because of the newspaper's vulnerability to strikes and its previous dealings with the unions. Sulzberger recalled: "We were perceived as the giveaway boys in terms of industrial relations for years and years and years. I am reminded on occasion that my father was supposed to have said, and probably did say, that never would *The New York Times* take a strike over an economic issue."

The 1962–1963 strike had been settled with the *Times* agreeing to a 47 percent wage settlement and getting no right to automate its production. Gradually, however, as Sulzberger strengthened the company through diversification, the unions agreed to automation in return for lifetime job guarantees for production workers. One setback was an eighty-eight-day strike in 1978, but in the settlement the *Times* obtained the power to reduce personnel through attrition and retirement incentives.

New technology also enabled Sulzberger to create, in March 1980, a two-section national edition of the *Times,* made possible by the availability of satellite communications. By 1991 the national edition was being printed in several cities around the country; circulation was 250,000 daily. The *Times* also started a new California–West Coast edition in April 1988.

Further expansion came in July 1987 when the company's board of directors approved spending $400 million for a new plant in Edison, New Jersey. In addition to expanding the press operations of the *Times,* the new plant, a one-million-square-foot automated printing and distribution facility, was intended to enable the introduction of color into some sections of the Sunday paper. After agreements were negotiated with the unions representing workers there, the new plant was put into operation in September 1992.

Sulzberger acted to diversify and strengthen the Times Company, expand and modernize its production facilities, work out new arrangements with unions, and redesign the *Times* in order to ensure

Arthur Ochs Sulzberger, Jr., publisher of the New York Times *since 1992 (photograph © Gene Maggio,* New York Times)

the survival of the newspaper in an era that saw the number of daily newspapers in New York City drop from seven in the 1960s to three in 1992. He also sought to maintain the *Times* as an independent newspaper, in keeping with Adolph Ochs's wishes, and to continue family ownership.

When Iphigene Ochs Sulzberger died on 26 February 1990 at the age of ninety-seven, the trust that her father had created was terminated, and control of the company was passed to new trusts for her children, thirteen grandchildren, and twenty-four great-grandchildren. Those trusts are to last well into the twenty-first century.

The new arrangement included an agreement restricting the sale of Times Class B stock outside the family. The company had first offered its stock publicly in 1968 in two classes, A and B, with A having limited voting rights. In 1992 the Sulzbergers' trusts controlled about 84 percent of the Class B stock.

Under Arthur Ochs Sulzberger, the Times Company grew into a large, prosperous communications conglomerate. Despite the effects of economic recession, which cut into advertising revenues, company revenues were reported to be almost $1.8 billion in 1991, compared to $100 million in 1963. Daily circulation of the *Times* was 1.1 million in January 1992, and Sunday circulation, 1.7 million.

Sulzberger's accomplishments earned him lavish praise from a wide range of public figures. "Above all, he took the quality of the product up to an entirely new level," Katharine Graham, chairman of the Washington Post Company, said. He is, she observed, "an outstanding publisher and a modest and wonderful man — and he's really funny."

During Sulzberger's tenure as publisher the *Times* and its staff received thirty-three Pulitzer Prizes, adding to the twenty-three received when his father was publisher and continuing the dedication of the *Times* under Ochs and the Sulzbergers to, as a *Times* writer put it, "serious journalism, to good taste and to progressive values."

References:
"Arthur Hays Sulzberger, Times Chairman, 77, Dies," *New York Times,* 12 December 1968, pp. 1, 41;

"Arthur Ochs Sulzberger Named Times Publisher," *New York Times,* 21 June 1963, pp. 1, 17;

Brooks Atkinson, "Arthur Hays Sulzberger," *New York Times,* 15 December 1968, sec. 4, p. 13;

Meyer Berger, *The Story of the New York Times, 1851–1951* (New York: Simon & Schuster, 1951);

Turner Catledge, *My Life and the Times* (New York: Harper & Row, 1971);

Ellis Cose, "The Cathedral: *The New York Times,*" in his *The Press* (New York: William Morrow, 1989), pp. 187–279;

Edwin Diamond, "Old Times, New Times," *New York,* 24 (30 September 1991): 28–35;

Debra Gersh, "Turning Over the Reins," *Editor & Publisher,* 125 (25 January 1992): 9, 35;

Ruth Sulzberger Golden, "My Brother the Publisher," *Times Talk* (July–August 1963): 1;

Joseph C. Goulden, *Fit to Print: A. M. Rosenthal and His Times* (Secaucus, N.J.: Lyle Stuart, 1988);

"Iphigene Ochs Sulzberger Is Dead; Central Figure in Times's History," *New York Times,* 27 February 1990, pp. A1, B6;

Alex S. Jones, "Arthur Ochs Sulzberger Passes Times Publisher's Post to Son," *New York Times,* 17 January 1992, pp. A1, A19;

Roger Kahn, "The House of Adolph Ochs," *Saturday Evening Post,* 238 (9 October 1965): 32–60;

Harry Levinson and Stuart Rosenthal, "Arthur O. Sulzberger, New York Times Company," in their *CEO: Corporate Leadership in Action* (New York: Basic Books, 1984), pp. 219–258;

Charles Merz, "An Appreciation: Arthur Hays Sulzberger," *New York Times,* 13 December 1968, p. 46;

The Pentagon Papers as Published by the New York Times (New York: Quadrangle, 1971);

James Reston, *Deadline: A Memoir* (New York: Random House, 1991);

Nan Robertson, *The Girls in the Balcony: Women, Men, and the New York Times* (New York: Random House, 1992);

Harrison E. Salisbury, *Without Fear or Favor: An Uncompromising Look at the New York Times* (New York: Times Books, 1980);

Leonard Silk and Mark Silk, "Church, State, and Counting House: *The New York Times,*" in their *The American Establishment* (New York: Basic Books, 1980), pp. 66–103;

Arthur Ochs Sulzberger, Jr., "From the Publisher," *New York Times,* 17 January 1992, p. A28;

Iphigene Ochs Sulzberger, *Iphigene: Memoirs of Iphigene Ochs Sulzberger of the New York Times Family, as Told to Her Granddaughter, Susan W. Dryfoos* (New York: Dodd, Mead, 1981);

"Sulzberger Heads the Times," *Literary Digest,* 119 (18 May 1935): 36;

"Sulzberger Stressed News Coverage, Financial Strength, and Technical Progress," *New York Times,* 12 December 1968, pp. 40–41;

Gay Talese, *The Kingdom and the Power* (New York: World, 1969);

Sheldon Zalaznick, "The Evolution of a Pleasant Young Man," *New York,* 6 (6 May 1974): 29–33.

Papers:

The Sulzbergers' papers are in the *New York Times* Archives.

John Hay Whitney

(17 August 1904 – 8 February 1982)

Charles L. Robertson
Smith College

MAJOR POSITIONS HELD: Publisher (1957–1966), editor in chief (1961–1966), *New York Herald Tribune*; director and editorial committee member, *World-Journal-Tribune* (1966–1967); chairman, *International Herald Tribune* (1967–1982).

John Hay ("Jock") Whitney was master of one of America's great fortunes, a sportsman, a philanthropist, an art collector, and a diplomat. He also, over the course of a decade, poured nearly $40 million and all of his enormous energy into a gallant, ultimately futile attempt to save the once great *New York Herald Tribune* in the late 1950s and early 1960s.

Whitney took control of the *Herald Tribune* in 1959, when the *Times* and the *Tribune* were the last two serious, competing morning newspapers in the city, and the only two with national and international reputations. The *Times* had a distinctly Democratic tinge. The *Herald Tribune* – which traced its ancestry to the *New York Herald,* founded in 1835 by James Gordon Bennett, and the *New York Tribune,* established by Horace Greeley in 1841 – was long a mainstay of the Republican party.

The *Herald Tribune* had a special place in the hearts and minds of a whole class of New Yorkers. Newspapermen regarded it as the best-edited, best-written newspaper in the United States, one with which some of the greatest names in American journalism had been associated. The challenge that Whitney accepted when approached to save the newspaper in 1958 was therefore to maintain some measure of competition in New York; to keep alive a national voice for moderate, independent Republicanism; and to preserve a journalistic institution. Saving the *Tribune* was one of the most important enterprises he undertook in his lifetime and one of the few at which he failed.

There remains one influential legacy of that attempt: the *International Herald Tribune* – formerly the European edition of the *New York Herald Tribune* – edited in Paris but printed and distributed all over the world, and jointly owned by the *New York Times* and the *Washington Post.* Without Whitney, there seems little question that the European edition would have failed too, and the *International Herald Tribune* would never have come into existence in its present guise in 1967.

Whitney was born on 17 August 1904 in Ellsworth, Maine, the son of Payne and Helen Hay Whitney. When Payne died in 1927, he left the largest estate ever to be settled in the United States. John, then attending Oxford University, became an extremely wealthy man in his own right. Although he led the life of an affluent socialite all through the following decade, becoming a prominent member of what in the late 1930s was known as "café society," he also inherited a sense that a fortune must be preserved and put to good use.

Payne and Helen Hay Whitney both came from a rarefied stratum of enormously rich Americans, many of whom combined their wealth with a sense of public service. Helen's father, John Hay, had been ambassador to the Court of Saint James and secretary of state, as well as editor of the *New York Tribune* for a short time; Payne's father, William Whitney, had been secretary of the navy. The Whitney Museum of American Art was founded by sculptor Gertrude Vanderbilt Whitney, John's cousin. The Metropolitan Museum of Art, the Museum of Modern Art, and many other institutions, including Yale University, owe immensely to the Whitneys – and especially to John – as benefactors.

Whitney was highly conscious of this family tradition. A friend once said that for him "money has three purposes: to be invested wisely, to do good with, and to live well off." He attended Groton and then Yale University, following in family footsteps. A big man, a bon vivant, and a sportsman with a lifelong interest in horse breeding and racing, he numbered Fred Astaire and Robert Benchley among his closest friends, and he escorted such actresses as Tallulah Bankhead, Paulette Goddard, and Joan Crawford to social

315

John Hay Whitney

events. Whitney's marriage to Mary Elizabeth Altenus in 1930 – the high point of the Philadelphia social season – ended in divorce. In 1942 he married Betsy Cushing Roosevelt – former wife of James Roosevelt, the eldest son of President Franklin D. Roosevelt – and subsequently adopted her two daughters.

He first displayed an interest in publishing while at Yale, where as assistant editor of the *Yale Review* he was able to secure articles from such friends as Dorothy Parker, Donald Ogden Stewart, and Benchley. When he returned from Oxford after his father's death, he began to manage the vast family fortune. He invested in a variety of enterprises, most notably in theatrical productions and films. He backed the introduction of Technicolor in motion pictures; he became a partner in the Selznick International movie studio, playing an important role in bringing *Gone With the Wind* to the screen in 1939. He persuaded a reluctant David Selznick to buy the film rights to the novel in 1936. In these years he also became the Museum of Modern Art's trustee in charge of its new film archive and library, and then a vice-president of the museum.

In 1940 Whitney took his first flier into newspaper journalism, investing in Ralph Ingersoll's new, advertisement-free New York tabloid, *PM*. His doubts about the enterprise grew almost as quickly as its heavy leftist slant became evident. The social responsibility of wealth did not have to countenance the kind of bias the publication exhibited, and he sold out his share – for one-fifth of what he had contributed – to Marshall Field III. In a United States divided between isolationists and interventionists, he became active in pro-Allied activities. In 1940 he went to work running the Motion Picture Division of Nelson Rockefeller's Office of Coordinator of Inter-American Affairs, an organization meant to keep Latin America out of the Axis orbit.

The work for Rockefeller was not enough for Whitney once the United States was drawn into the war, and in 1942 he secured a commission in the air force, serving in intelligence operations in London and then North Africa. Anxious to get a little closer to action than his office-bound activities allowed, he managed to get himself sent to the south of France to investigate how well resistance networks there were operating. The Germans took him prisoner,

Whitney and David O. Selznick in Hollywood, circa 1939

putting him in a cattle car headed for Germany. A daring escape after some eighteen days of Allied bombardments and shunting about brought him back into Allied-held territory.

The war and his brief period of captivity worked a change in Whitney that ultimately brought him to the *Herald Tribune*. He later told how shocked he was that the American soldiers he met in captivity had no idea of why they were fighting Nazi Germany: the only thought they had was, "We were dragged in; the only doubt by whom." Only a handful of the forty-five men in the cattle car chose to attempt escape with him, and of those, two-thirds were officers. The rest preferred prison camp to the possibility of having to go back into battle. For the first time he discovered the gulf that separated him and his class from most ordinary Americans, and his subsequent career reflected how much this had perturbed him.

He continued to enjoy his wealth and to manage investments that continually increased his fortune. But upon his return to New York he insisted

on the removal of his name from the New York Social Register. He created J. H. Whitney and Company to provide venture capital to new and risky enterprises with limited appeal to conventional sources of financing. Most important, Whitney began to turn to more socially involved activities.

As a new member of the United States National Commission for UNESCO, he managed to get youth representation on the commission when he discovered there was none. As a vice-president of New York Hospital, which his father had so richly endowed, he saw to it that the board of trustees elect its first Jewish member. In the winter of 1946 he created the remarkable John Hay Whitney Foundation, dedicated to the promotion of the humanities. Under its aegis he developed the Opportunity Fellowship program for individuals from minority and disadvantaged groups who had shown some promise in their chosen fields. The program also gave distinguished professors at large American universities the opportunity to continue teaching after retirement at smaller colleges that could not have

Whitney, Irene Mayer Selznick, Olivia de Havilland, David O. Selznick, Vivien Leigh, and Laurence Olivier at the 28 December 1939 opening of Gone With the Wind in Los Angeles, which followed the world premiere in Atlanta

otherwise afforded their services. The John Hay Fellowships gave more than two thousand high school teachers the opportunity to take time off to study at universities such as Columbia, Yale, Harvard, and Northwestern. During the 1970s the foundation shifted from individual-based philanthropy to community improvement. In the 1980 annual report Whitney reiterated his views:

> Central to the philosophy of the Foundation is its desire to help people achieve social and economic justice, with particular focus on the problems of minority persons and poor people and with a special concern for equality of opportunity for women.

Whitney, for all his comfort with Democrats and even Socialists of varying stripes, remained vaguely a Republican, but one dissatisfied with conventional and conservative party members. The advent of Dwight D. Eisenhower's candidacy changed his mind. He threw himself into fund-raising outside of the regular party organization, garnering in the process the services of lawyer Walter Thayer, who would remain a close ally, and developing a deep friendship with Eisenhower. Writing to the

new president in the summer of 1953, Whitney declared, "You are reshaping the Party into what John Hay, my grandfather, often called it: 'the party fit to rule'; and I am at last proud to be 'a Republican.' "

In the course of this campaign, he came to know an early Eisenhower booster, Bill Robinson, business manager of the *Herald Tribune*. In 1953 Robinson approached him about investing in the ailing newspaper, whose chief hope at the time was that an Eisenhower presidency would somehow redound to its benefit. Whitney gave the possibility only passing consideration, though he gave more to a second approach a year later by young Whitelaw Reid, president of the paper. This time Whitney consulted with partners of J. H. Whitney and Company but decided that, in light of the company's commitments, he could not participate. Nevertheless, his interest in the paper had been aroused.

His services to the second Eisenhower campaign in 1956 earned him the ambassadorship to the Court of Saint James, for which a private fortune was necessary for maintenance of the embassy, but for which Whitney was also unusually well suited. During the course of his four years in London, he managed to do much to mend the rift that had developed when Eisenhower forced the British and French to withdraw from their invasion of Egypt over the Suez Canal in 1956. It was also during his ambassadorship that his involvement with the *Herald Tribune* began.

The *Herald Tribune* was in parlous shape by the mid 1950s. Created in 1924 when Ogden and Helen Reid bought the *New York Herald* to merge with their *Tribune,* the *Herald Tribune* was then one of sixteen English-language newspapers in New York. When Ogden took it over from his absentee father in 1912, the *Tribune* had a daily circulation of 25,000. In 1925 the *Herald Tribune* had a circulation of 275,000. Twenty years later, at the end of World War II, only the *Times* and the *Trib* – as it was usually called – remained in the morning field, apart from two tabloids. The *Trib* was livelier, better edited, carried more features, and had columnists in the fields of sports, politics, music, and other areas that the *Times* could not match. It was a much better looking paper than the *Times,* and many of its features and writers were syndicated throughout the United States. Its advertising revenues were 80 percent of those of the *Times,* but it was only sixth in circulation among the remaining nine New York newspapers, with a daily circulation only 63 percent of that of the *Times.*

The seemingly flourishing *Trib* had several fundamental weaknesses. Ogden Reid had been an able owner-publisher, but in later years he absented himself more and more from the activities of the newspaper. Helen Reid was an able advertising executive, but when she took over the paper after Ogden's death in 1946, some of her choices of subordinates were questionable. Whitelaw, who became editor after his father's death, was an intelligent, unassuming, and likable man who could not provide the tough editorial leadership the paper needed at the time. His younger brother, Ogden, Jr., who took over from Whitelaw in a palace coup engineered by their mother in 1955, was far more energetic, but that energy tended to be misguided. In the crucial postwar decade, the paper lacked the leadership it needed.

At the time of the 1937 recession Ogden and Helen Reid decided to economize, and to leave the "virtue" of completeness to the *Times.* The *Trib* cut back severely in foreign coverage, leaving much of it to the wire services. In light of radio competition, its managers argued, people wanted shorter, brisker papers. But in the long run this meant that people seeking completeness shifted to the *Times.* In the following years the precariousness of the financial sit-

uation at the *Trib* was reflected in its failure to do what the *Times* was doing: plowing profits back into the paper, modernizing equipment and distribution. The *Trib* owed money to the Reid family; debt had not been transformed into equity when it could have been, with the result that the *Trib* could not seek outside funding when it badly needed it during the early 1950s.

The healthier financial situation of the *Times* also allowed it to follow policies that proved ruinous for its financially weaker rival in the years following World War II. The *Times* made costly concessions to labor and maintained a low newsstand price at a time when increased labor expenses forced the weaker *Trib* into raising prices, which cost it circulation. Demographics gradually caught up with the *Trib:* its readership was largely aging, upper class, white, Anglo-Saxon, and Protestant. These readers were moving to the suburbs and doing less of their shopping in town. With advertisers relying more and more on market research rather than responding to the pleas of old friends, they found the higher-cost advertising in the *Trib* – always justified in the past by the supposed higher income of its readership – simply not worth it and shifted to the *Times* and suburban papers. The *Times* continued to plow income back into its expanding Sunday edition, distribution in and coverage of the suburbs, foreign coverage, and its reputation for being "the newspaper of record."

In the 1950s *Trib* management sought desperate expedients out of the economic predicament. But it failed to deal with fundamentals and tried to find the solutions to its problem in its ties to the Eisenhower administration, which would presumably gain it recognition as a political force; in puzzles and gimmicks; and in a costly and failed attempt at an early edition that would catch suburbanites on their way home at night. Over the course of the first postwar decade, the paper's circulation dropped from seven hundred thousand to slightly more than half a million, while that of the *Times* rose to a million. In the two years Ogden Reid, Jr., was at the helm, circulation rose temporarily but then dropped further. This was the newspaper in which Whitney was asked to invest – in 1953, in 1954, and in 1957, while he was ambassador to the Court of Saint James.

He turned over investigation of the paper's finances to his associates. Thayer estimated that Whitney might be able to turn the paper around in three years at an estimated cost of $3 million a year. Others were more pessimistic: it would take ten years at $5 million a year. Newspaper owner Sam-

Managing editor Eric Hawkins, production manager Andre Bing, Whitney, an unidentified compositor, and composing room foreman Richard Beecher at the Herald Tribune, *1957*

uel Newhouse told Thayer it could not be done at all, because the paper had been badly run for too long. Nevertheless, Ogden Reid, Jr., was able to get reluctant family members to transform $11 million worth of notes into stock, making the paper a credible investment vehicle. In September 1957 Whitney agreed to lend the *Trib* $1.2 million; in the New York and Paris offices there was jubilation. With Whitney's backing, most people believed all would be well.

For Whitney, saving the paper offered something important to do following his ambassadorship: a genuine public service that he could perform, an exciting challenge, a way, once again, to put his large fortune to good use. In the next few months, however, losses mounted much faster than anticipated, and Whitney's associates decided there was no use pouring money in without some measure of control over its use. As a result, Whitney resolved to buy the newspaper from the Reids, who had wanted to maintain control. But there was no longer any way for them to do this; the continued losses deprived them of any bargaining power.

Nevertheless, a last-minute attempt by the Reids to retain a foothold lost Whitney the man his people wanted as editor – Lee Hills, of the *Detroit*

Free Press – and led Whitney to withdraw from the whole deal. Only the direct intervention of Eisenhower, assuring him that the Reids would accept his terms, persuaded him to carry through. The turnover was achieved through a reorganization agreement completed in August 1958. Stanley Walker, legendary former city editor of the *Trib,* wrote in the *Saturday Review:*

> The coming of Mr. Whitney was a specific in itself. His name and personality alone brought a certain confidence. The people at the paper felt better, the readers were reassured somewhat, and even the advertisers felt a new, healthy glow, a sort of pride to have a part in a Whitney venture . . . the old-timers, who never quite give up hope, are in his corner.

However, there was no way to wipe the slate clean; the new owner had to take over debts and an ongoing losing proposition. The paper – Thayer wrote to Whitney before he returned from London – was losing $5,479.45 a day every day of the year. Another associate told Whitney that the drain the paper would be on his resources meant he would have to hold back on major contributions to other causes. In Paris, where the advent of Whitney ownership was celebrated with grandiose plans for expansion of the European edition, a painful realization set in that penny-pinching would still be in order. In order to make the ailing, costly New York newspaper operate without excessive drain on Whitney's resources, Thayer devised a complicated strategy. Whitney created a company ultimately to be known as Whitney Communications, designed to acquire profitable publications as well as a television chain, all of which would be required to supply enough profit to support the expenditures on the *Trib.*

There was no reason for optimism unless Whitney could resolve the problem of who was to run the paper. With the loss of Hills and with Whitney still in London, the Whitney people plucked a young unknown, Robert M. White II of the *Mexico* (Missouri) *Evening Ledger,* for the editorial side while continuing to use veterans on the business side. The first two years proved to be mostly a holding operation. White lasted for only those two years, although he later declared that he had just come for a transitional period. As a small-town newspaperman in a very big town he moved cautiously and found that his actions were circumscribed by supervision from the business side. In part he could not respond to the need to settle the direction the paper should take.

The fundamental dilemma was that Whitney had undertaken to save the *Trib* because of its national and international standing and its literate style, and White and the people he hired tried to restore these. But Whitney was advised that he could not match the *Times* in the first two domains, that he should attempt to make the *Trib* a more popular paper, city-centered, stressing local crusades – almost an upgraded tabloid. A Roper Associates poll concluded that *Trib* readership was "too old, too Republican, too upper class, too suburban, too highly college educated, too Protestant and too heavily male" for it to compete with the *Times.* For too long it had bet on the rich and refined; it was failing as an advertising medium.

No one really wanted or dared to take the expensive, risky, and not always palatable suggestions for overcoming these failings. Thayer, as Whitney's watchdog in New York, was convinced that White had failed in even trying to maintain the paper, much less taking the initiatives necessary for success. Following the election of John F. Kennedy to the presidency in 1960, Whitney told White that he was returning to New York and would assume an active role, taking the titles of editor in chief and publisher and establishing Thayer as president.

Whitney secured the services of John Denson, former managing editor of *Newsweek,* as editor.

Denson brought excitement to the newspaper, and circulation – which had dropped to less than four hundred thousand – began to increase. But there were conflicts with the business side and complaints that he paid too much attention to the front page and not enough to the rest of the paper. In the meantime the antiquated plant imposed high costs, and expensive labor practices continued at a time when automated printing technology began to sweep the industry. The situation was exacerbated by a strike in 1963, shortly after Denson left and the new editor, James Bellows, was promoted from within. When the strike ended and publication resumed, daily circulation was down by ninety-two thousand and yearly labor costs had increased by more than a million dollars.

Whitney became more and more involved, trying to define the newspaper in a way that would differentiate it from the *Times* and find a new audience. He was still optimistic; he could write in July 1963 that he detected among acquaintances a special enthusiasm for the paper that existed for no other, a sense that it was the only interesting newspaper in New York. He would not jeopardize its integrity. When the paper editorially lambasted the Kennedy administration over its handling of the Billie Sol Estes scandal and the White House canceled its subscriptions to the *Trib,* he refused to bow to pressure. On the other hand, once the conservative Barry Goldwater was nominated for the presidency in 1964, a front-page editorial headlined "We Choose Johnson" declared: "Travail and torment go into these simple words, breaching as they do the political traditions of a long newspaper lifetime. But we find ourselves, as Americans, even as Republicans, with no other acceptable course." Many longtime readers canceled their subscriptions.

In 1963 and 1964 the paper lost $4 million each year. In 1965 another strike occurred, over the issue of automation. Whitney considered moving the paper to an afternoon slot, but this would have required printing at the *Times* plant, and the *Times* was not about to help out the *Trib.* Finally, in a last desperate move, lengthy negotiations ensued over a merger with the afternoon Scripps *World-Telegram* and the Hearst *Journal-American.* The proposed merger would have led to a morning *Herald-Tribune,* an afternoon *World-Journal,* and a Sunday *World-Journal and Tribune.* Savings lay in the area of jobs; sixteen hundred positions would be eliminated. The *Trib* would abandon its midtown plant.

Whitney in the Herald Tribune *pressroom after the 1963 strike that halted production of the newspaper*

Again, a strike intervened. It lasted 113 days, and on 15 August 1966 Whitney gave up. The morning *Trib* would never again appear. An attenuated *World-Journal-Tribune* appeared for 233 days and then disappeared. The disappearance of the *Trib* led to an outpouring of genuine lamentation. Whitney was right: people were deeply attached to the *Trib*. But their attachment did not translate into increases in circulation or advertising. Whitney Communications had put $39,475,929 into trying to keep the paper alive.

Whitney was still not out of the newspaper business. He had the European edition, published in Paris since James Gordon Bennett, Jr., had founded it in 1887 as a Paris edition of his *New York Herald*. It was, in its earliest years, the paper for a wealthy, mobile, cosmopolitan class, who could find it in reading rooms all over Europe. It remained in Paris during World War I, supporting the Allied effort and campaigning for America to enter the war. During the interwar period it catered to a different class – primarily businessmen and somewhat less affluent tourists – and passed through a dark period when it supported appeasement, partly because

its editor-publisher was pro-fascist, partly because he did not want to lose advertising from Nazi Germany and Fascist Italy.

Ogden Reid finally took control of the situation in 1938 and then closed the paper when the Nazis marched into Paris. Revived in December 1944, it waxed and waned while remaining the primary American newspaper for Americans in Europe. It wound up engaging in a struggle with the *New York Times* when the latter decided to publish its own Paris edition in 1960.

In Paris it was called the "Battle of the Boulevards," and the struggle paralleled the one in New York. But in Paris it was the *Times* that had to try to catch up with the *Trib*. While the latter held down expenses at the insistence of Whitney's men, the New York office of the *Times* poured money into its European edition. In 1962 the European edition of the *Trib* celebrated its seventy-fifth anniversary with much self-congratulation, and Whitney became a Chevalier de la Legion d'Honneur. By 1965, however, with the *Times* creeping up in both circulation and advertising, it looked as though the outcome in Paris would parallel that in New York, although

Front page of the New York Herald Tribune, *25 November 1963*

Whitney was determined to keep the Paris edition out of any New York merger deal and expressed his continued commitment to it.

Thayer sought out possible partners for the European edition, pressing the *Wall Street Journal* to come aboard. In 1966 *Washington Post* publisher Katharine Graham agreed to buy in, seeking to give the *Post* wider exposure. With this, the *Times* people knew they had lost. The infusion of *Post* money meant they would have to fight a much longer battle, so they negotiated a slightly less than one-third interest in what was renamed the *International Herald Tribune*. Whitney retained slightly more than a one-third share.

The merged paper – with Whitney people as publisher and editor, and with the format of the *Trib* – began to take off in a manner neither its new nor old owners had imagined. In short order new technology allowed it to do what previous Paris publishers had wanted to do – increase sales in areas the Paris edition previously could not reach in time. In 1974 the first international facsimile link allowed it to be printed in a London suburb and in Paris simultaneously. Soon new facsimile-printing sites sprang up throughout the world – in Zurich, Marseilles, and Frankfurt, and then Hong Kong, Singapore, and Tokyo – so that the *International Herald Tribune* could truly claim to be a global newspaper.

Its readership included political leaders as well as the business and financial elite. Journalists all over the world relied on it for more balanced views and coverage than their local press could provide. The vast news-gathering resources of the *Times* and the *Post* were at the disposal of the *International Herald Tribune,* which moved out of Paris proper into highly automated, computerized facilities in the suburb of Neuilly. In the era of global communications the *IHT,* as many people called it, was no longer the parochial old Paris paper of the interwar and postwar periods. It had become an indispensable news source for people the world over. Its success was heralded by a *New Yorker* cartoon that showed a new arrival in Heaven facing a newsstand displaying the *IHT.*

Whitney, who took little active part in the running of Whitney Communications after the demise of the New York paper, maintained his active interest in the Paris-based paper. He was one of the founders of a sort of Republican think tank in 1962, the Ripon Society. One of its members, Lee Huebner, acted as Whitney's troubleshooter when the paper faced modernization problems in 1977, and then became its publisher. By the time Whitney's activities were curtailed by a heart attack in 1976, the *IHT* had already become an international institution. He lived on for six more years, a quiet witness to his beloved newspaper's growing success, and died of heart failure on 8 February 1982 in Manhasset, Long Island, New York, leaving his wife Betsy, his two adopted daughters, and eight grandchildren.

Whitney, in the words of his biographer E. J. Kahn, Jr., was one of an outmoded breed – the "vanishing patrician . . . with a genuine social conscience." He brought both excitement and something unusual to the normally cynical New York newspaper scene: high purpose. The excitement was short-lived, but the purpose lives on in what many readers consider one of the best newspapers in the world.

References:

E. J. Kahn, Jr., *Jock: The Life and Times of John Hay Whitney* (Garden City, N.Y.: Doubleday, 1981);

Richard Kluger and Phyllis Kluger, *The Paper: The Life and Death of the New York Herald Tribune* (New York: Knopf, 1986);

Charles L. Robertson, *The International Herald Tribune: The First Hundred Years* (New York: Columbia University Press, 1987);

David Thomson, *Showman: The Life of David O. Selznick* (New York: Knopf, 1992).

Papers:

Whitney's papers are at the Sterling Library, Yale University.

Checklist of Further Readings

Altschull, Herbert J. *Agents of Power: The Role of News Media in Human Affairs*. New York: Longman, 1984.

Aronson, James. *The Press and the Cold War*. Indianapolis: Bobbs-Merrill, 1970.

Bagdikian, Ben H. *The Information Machines: Their Impact on Men and the Media*. New York: Harper & Row, 1971.

Bagdikian. *The Media Monopoly*. Boston: Beacon, 1983.

Bayley, Edwin R. *Joe McCarthy and the Press*. Madison: University of Wisconsin Press, 1981.

Beasley, Maurine H., and Richard R. Harlow. *Voices of Change: Southern Pulitzer Winners*. Lanham, Md.: University Press of America, 1979.

Biagi, Shirley. *Media/Impact: An Introduction to Mass Media*. Belmont, Cal.: Wadsworth, 1992.

Blum, Eleanor. *Basic Books in the Mass Media*. Urbana: University of Illinois Press, 1972.

Bogart, Leo. *Press and Public: Who Reads What, When, Where, and Why in American Newspapers*. Hillsdale, N.J.: Erlbaum, 1981.

Broder, David S. *Behind the Front Page: A Candid Look at How the News Is Made*. New York: Simon & Schuster, 1987.

Brogan, Patrick. *Spiked: The Short Life and Death of the National News Council*. New York: Priority Press, 1985.

Brown, Lee. *The Reluctant Reformation: On Criticizing the Press in America*. New York: McKay, 1974.

Brucker, Herbert. *Freedom of Information*. New York: Macmillan, 1949.

Casey, Ralph D., ed. *The Press in Perspective*. Baton Rouge: Louisiana State University Press, 1963.

Cater, Douglass. *The Fourth Branch of Government*. Boston: Houghton Mifflin, 1959.

Clark, Peter, and Susan H. Evans. *Covering Campaigns: Journalism in Congressional Elections*. Stanford, Cal.: Stanford University Press, 1983.

Commission on Freedom of the Press. *A Free and Responsible Press*. Chicago: University of Chicago Press, 1947.

Cose, Ellis. *The Press*. New York: Morrow, 1989.

Cross, Harold L. *The People's Right to Know: Legal Access to Public Records and Proceedings*. New York: Columbia University Press, 1953.

Crouse, Timothy. *The Boys on the Bus*. New York: Random House, 1973.

Czitrom, Daniel J. *Media and the American Mind: From Morse to McLuhan.* Chapel Hill: University of North Carolina Press, 1982.

Daniel, Walter C. *Black Journals of the United States.* Westport, Conn.: Greenwood, 1982.

Devol, Kenneth S., ed. *Mass Media and the Supreme Court: The Legacy of the Warren Years.* Mamaroneck, N.Y.: Hasting House, 1990.

Douglas, Sara U. *Labor's New Voice: Unions and Mass Media.* Norwood, N.J.: Ablex, 1986.

Emery, Michael. *America's Leading Daily Newspapers.* Indianapolis: Berg, 1983.

Emery. *The Press and America: An Interpretive History of the Mass Media.* Englewood Cliffs, N.J.: Prentice Hall, 1992.

Ernst, Morris Leopold. *The First Freedom.* New York: Macmillan, 1946.

Evans, Harold. *Front Page History: Events of Our Century That Shook the World.* London: Quiller Press/Photo Source, 1984.

Fenby, Jonathan. *The International News Services.* New York: Schocken, 1986.

The Front Page, 1887–1980. New York: Arno, 1981.

Ghiglione, Loren, ed. *The Buying and Selling of America's Newspapers.* Indianapolis: Berg, 1984.

Ghiglione, ed. *Gentlemen of the Press: Profiles of American Newspaper Editors.* Indianapolis: Berg, 1984.

Gillmor, Donald M. *Free Press and Fair Trial.* Washington, D.C.: Public Affairs Press, 1966.

Goldstein, Tom. *The News at Any Cost: How Journalists Compromise Their Ethics to Shape the News.* New York: Simon & Schuster, 1985.

Goldstein, ed. *Killing the Messenger: 100 Years of Media Criticism.* New York: Columbia University Press, 1989.

Grauer, Neil A. *Wits and Sages.* Baltimore: Johns Hopkins University Press, 1984.

Hachten, William A. *The World News Prism: Changing Media, Clashing Ideologies.* Ames: Iowa State University Press, 1981.

Halberstam, David. *The Next Century.* New York: Morrow, 1991.

Halberstam. *The Powers That Be.* New York: Knopf, 1979.

Hess, Stephen. *The Washington Reporters: Newswork.* Washington, D.C.: Brookings Institution, 1981.

Hill, George H. *Black Media in America: A Resource Guide.* Boston: G. K. Hall, 1984.

Hohenberg, John. *Free Press/Free People – The Best Cause.* New York: Columbia University Press, 1971.

Hohenberg. *The Pulitzer Prizes: A History of the Awards.* New York: Columbia University Press, 1974.

Hynds, Ernest C. *American Newspapers in the 1980s.* New York: Hasting House, 1980.

Isaacs, Norman E. *Untended Gates: The Mismanaged Press*. New York: Columbia University Press, 1986.

Kern, Montague, and Patricia W. Levering. *The Kennedy Crisis: The Press, the Presidency and Foreign Policy*. Chapel Hill: University of North Carolina Press, 1983.

Kessler, Lauren. *The Dissident Press: Alternative Journalism in American History*. Beverly Hills, Cal.: Sage, 1984.

Kobre, Sidney. *Development of American Journalism*. Dubuque, Iowa: Wm. C. Brown, 1969.

Kozol, Jonathan. *Illiterate America*. Garden City, N.Y.: Doubleday, 1985.

Leonard, Thomas C. *The Power of the Press: The Birth of American Political Reporting*. New York: Oxford University Press, 1986.

Lindstrom, Carl E. *The Fading American Newspaper*. Garden City, N.Y.: Doubleday, 1960.

Lippy, Charles H., ed. *Religious Periodicals in the United States*. Westport, Conn.: Greenwood, 1986.

MacBride, Sean, et al. *Many Voices: One World*. New York: Unipub, 1980.

MacDougall, Allan Kent, ed. *The Press: A Critical Look from the Inside*. Princeton, N.J.: Dow Jones, 1972.

Marbut, Frederick B. *News from the Capital: The Story of Washington Reporting*. Carbondale: Southern Illinois University Press, 1971.

Marzolf, Marion. *Up from the Footnote: A History of Women Journalists*. New York: Hasting House, 1977.

Merrill, John C., et al. *Global Journalism: A Survey of the World's Mass Media*. New York: Longman, 1983.

Miller, Sally M., ed. *The Ethnic Press in the United States: A Historical Analysis and Handbook*. Westport, Conn.: Greenwood, 1987.

Mills, Kay. *A Place in the News: From the Women's Pages to the Front Page*. New York: Dodd, Mead, 1988.

Mollenhoff, Clark R. *Washington Cover-Up*. Garden City, N.Y.: Doubleday, 1962.

Mott, Frank Luther. *American Journalism: A History, 1690–1960*. New York: Macmillan, 1962.

Nelson, Harold L. *Libel in News of Congressional Investigating Committees*. Minneapolis: University of Minnesota Press, 1961.

The New Media Barons. New York: Gannett Center for Media Studies, 1989.

Osmer, Harold H. *U.S. Religious Journalism and the Korean War*. Lanham, Md.: University Press of America, 1980.

Peck, Abe. *Uncovering the Sixties: The Life and Times of the Underground Press*. New York: Pantheon, 1985.

Pember, Don R. *Mass Media in America*. New York: Macmillan, 1992.

Pickett, Calder M. *Voices of the Past: Key Documents in the History of American Journalism*. Columbus, Ohio: Grid, 1977.

Pollard, James E. *The Presidents and the Press: Truman to Johnson*. Washington, D.C.: Public Affairs Press, 1964.

Porter, William E. *Assault on the Media: The Nixon Years*. Ann Arbor: University of Michigan Press, 1967.

Powell, Jody. *The Other Side of the Story*. New York: Morrow, 1984.

Press, Charles. *The Political Cartoon*. Rutherford, N.J.: Fairleigh Dickinson University Press, 1981.

Price, Warren C., and Pickett. *An Annotated Journalism Bibliography, 1958–1968*. Minneapolis: University of Minnesota Press, 1970.

Read, William H. *America's Mass Media Merchants*. Baltimore: Johns Hopkins University Press, 1976.

Reston, James B. *The Artillery of the Press: Its Influence on American Foreign Policy*. New York: Harper & Row, 1967.

Rivers, William L. *The Opinionmakers*. Boston: Beacon, 1965.

Rivers. *The Other Government: Power and the Washington Media*. New York: Universe, 1982.

Rivers, et al. *Backtalk: Press Councils in America*. San Francisco: Canfield, 1972.

Rivers, and Wilbur Schramm. *Responsibility in Mass Communication*. New York: Harper & Row, 1969.

Rosenberg, Norman L. *Protecting the Best Man: An Interpretive History of the Law of Libel*. Chapel Hill: University of North Carolina Press, 1986.

Rucker, Bryce W. *The First Freedom*. Carbondale: Southern Illinois University Press, 1968.

Rucker, ed. *Twentieth Century Reporting at Its Best*. Ames: Iowa State University Press, 1964.

Rutland, Robert. *The Newsmongers: Journalism in the Life of the Nation, 1690–1972*. New York: Dial, 1973.

Schilpp, Madelon G., and Sharon Murphy. *Great Women of the Press*. Carbondale: Southern Illinois University Press, 1983.

Schudson, Michael. *Discovering the News: A Social History of American Newspapers*. New York: Basic Books, 1978.

Sim, John Cameron. *The Grass Roots Press: America's Community Newspapers*. Ames: Iowa State University Press, 1969.

Sloan, William D. *The Media in America*. Worthington, Ohio: Publishing Horizons, 1989.

Sloan, ed. *Pulitzer Prize Editorials: America's Best Editorial Writing, 1917–1979*. Ames: Iowa State University Press, 1980.

Smith, Anthony. *Goodbye Gutenberg: The Newspaper Revolution in the 1980s*. New York: Oxford University Press, 1980.

Snyder, Louis L., and Richard B. Morris. *Treasury of Great Reporting*. New York: Simon & Schuster, 1962.

Spear, Joseph C. *Presidents and the Press: The Nixon Legacy*. Cambridge, Mass.: MIT Press, 1984.

Sterling, Christopher H., and Timothy R. Haight. *The Mass Media: Aspen Institute Guide to Communication Industry Trends*. New York: Praeger, 1978.

Stoler, Peter. *The War Against the Press: Politics, Pressure and Intimidation in the 1980s.* New York: Dodd, Mead, 1986.

Talese, Gay. *The Kingdom and the Power.* New York: World, 1969.

Tebbel, John. *The Compact History of the American Newspaper.* New York: Hawthorn Books, 1963.

Thomas, Dana L. *The Media Moguls.* New York: Putnam's, 1981.

Thomas, Helen. *Dateline: White House.* New York: Macmillan, 1975.

Turner, Kathleen J. *Lyndon Johnson's Dual War: Vietnam and the Press.* Chicago: University of Chicago Press, 1985.

Udell, Jon G. *Economic Trends in the Daily Newspaper Business, 1946 to 1970.* Madison, Wis.: American Newspaper Publishers Association, 1970.

UNESCO. *News Agencies: Their Structure and Operation.* Paris: UNESCO, 1953.

UNESCO. *World Communication Report.* Paris: UNESCO, 1989.

Weisberger, Bernard A. *The American Newspaperman.* Chicago: University of Chicago Press, 1961.

Wiggins, James Russell. *Freedom or Secrecy.* New York: Oxford University Press, 1964.

Williams, Herbert Lee. *The Newspaperman's President: Harry S Truman.* Chicago: Nelson-Hall, 1984.

Wittke, Carl. *The German-Language Press in America.* Lexington: University of Kentucky Press, 1957.

Wolseley, Roland E. *The Black Press, U.S.A.* Ames: Iowa State University Press, 1971.

Wolseley. *The Journalist's Bookshelf: An Annotated and Selected Bibliography of United States Print Journalism.* Indianapolis: Berg, 1986.

Contributors

Edward E. Adams ....*Ohio University*

June N. Adamson ....*University of Tennessee*

Morgan David Arant ....*Memphis State University*

Maurine H. Beasley ....*University of Maryland – College Park*

Margaret A. Blanchard.......................*University of North Carolina at Chapel Hill*

James Bow...*Mt. Pleasant, Michigan*

Michael Buchholz ....*Indiana State University*

Ginger Rudeseal Carter ....*Northeast Louisiana University*

Edward Caudill...*University of Tennessee*

David A. Copeland ....*University of North Carolina*

David C. Coulson ....*University of Nevada at Reno*

John M. Coward...*University of Tulsa*

Patrick J. Daley ....*University of New Hampshire*

Douglass K. Daniel ....*Ohio University*

John De Mott ....*Memphis State University*

Michael J. Dillon...*Pennsylvania State University*

Betty Farmer...*University of Tennessee*

Jean Folkerts ....*George Washington University*

Cecilia Friend...*Utica College of Syracuse University*

Marie Myers Hardin..*Georgia State University*

William Herbert ....*Mt. Pleasant, Michigan*

Carol Sue Humphrey...*Oklahoma Baptist University*

William E. Huntzicker..*University of Minnesota*

Terry Hynes ....*California State University, Fullerton*

Joel Kaplan ....*Syracuse University*

A. J. Kaul ....*University of Southern Mississippi*

Robert F. Keeler ....*Newsday*

Louis W. Liebovich ....*University of Illinois*

Gregory C. Lisby ....*Georgia State University*

Alfred Lawrence Lorenz ....*Loyola University in New Orleans*

Charles H. Marler ....*Abilene Christian University*

Ronald S. Marmarelli...*Central Michigan University*

Aralynn Abare McMane ....*University of South Carolina*

Michael D. Murray ....*University of Missouri – St. Louis*

Dan O'Neill ....*University of Alaska at Fairbanks*

Mary Elizabeth Padgett...*Greenville Piedmont*

Daniel W. Pfaff...*Pennsylvania State University*

Alf Pratte ....*Brigham Young University*

Charles L. Robertson ....*Smith College*

Jeffrey B. Rutenbeck ....*University of Denver*

Rodger Streitmatter..*American University*

Herb Strentz ....*Drake University*

Mary Ann Weston ....*Northwestern University*

Wendy Swallow Williams ....*American University*

Cumulative Index

Dictionary of Literary Biography, Volumes 1-127
Dictionary of Literary Biography Yearbook, 1980-1991
Dictionary of Literary Biography Documentary Series, Volumes 1-10

Cumulative Index

DLB before number: *Dictionary of Literary Biography,* Volumes 1-127
Y before number: *Dictionary of Literary Biography Yearbook,* 1980-1991
DS before number: *Dictionary of Literary Biography Documentary Series,* Volumes 1-10

A

E

K

M

N

O

P

W

Y

Z

ISBN 0-8103-5386-5

90000

1860, edited by Catharine Savage Brosman (1992)

120 American Poets Since World War II, Third Series, edited by R. S. Gwynn (1992)

121 Seventeenth-Century British Nondramatic Poets, First Series, edited by M. Thomas Hester (1992)

122 Chicano Writers, Second Series, edited by Francisco A. Lomelí and Carl R. Shirley (1992)

123 Nineteenth-Century French Fiction Writers: Naturalism and Beyond, 1860-1900, edited by Catharine Savage Brosman (1992)

124 Twentieth-Century German Dramatists, 1919-1992, edited by Wolfgang D. Elfe and James Hardin (1992)

125 Twentieth-Century Caribbean and Black African Writers, Second Series, edited by Bernth Lindfors and Reinhard Sander (1993)

126 Seventeenth-Century British Nondramatic Poets, Second Series, edited by M. Thomas Hester (1993)

127 American Newspaper Publishers, 1950-1990, edited by Perry J. Ashley (1993)

Documentary Series

1 Sherwood Anderson, Willa Cather, John Dos Passos, Theodore Dreiser, F. Scott Fitzgerald, Ernest Hemingway, Sinclair Lewis, edited by Margaret A. Van Antwerp (1982)

2 James Gould Cozzens, James T. Farrell, William Faulkner, John O'Hara, John Steinbeck, Thomas Wolfe, Richard Wright, edited by Margaret A. Van Antwerp (1982)

3 Saul Bellow, Jack Kerouac, Norman Mailer, Vladimir Nabokov, John

Updike, Kurt Vonnegut, edited by Mary Bruccoli (1983)

4 Tennessee Williams, edited by Margaret A. Van Antwerp and Sally Johns (1984)

5 American Transcendentalists, edited by Joel Myerson (1988)

6 Hardboiled Mystery Writers: Raymond Chandler, Dashiell Hammett, Ross Macdonald, edited by Matthew J. Bruccoli and Richard Layman (1989)

7 Modern American Poets: James Dickey, Robert Frost, Marianne Moore, edited by Karen L. Rood (1989)

8 The Black Aesthetic Movement, edited by Jeffrey Louis Decker (1991)

9 American Writers of the Vietnam War: W. D. Ehrhart, Larry Heinemann, Tim O'Brien, Walter McDonald, John M. Del Vecchio, edited by Ronald Baughman (1991)

10 The Bloomsbury Group, edited by Edward L. Bishop (1992)

Yearbooks

1980 edited by Karen L. Rood, Jean W. Ross, and Richard Ziegfeld (1981)

1981 edited by Karen L. Rood, Jean W. Ross, and Richard Ziegfeld (1982)

1982 edited by Richard Ziegfeld; associate editors: Jean W. Ross and Lynne C. Zeigler (1983)

1983 edited by Mary Bruccoli and Jean W. Ross; associate editor: Richard Ziegfeld (1984)

1984 edited by Jean W. Ross (1985)

1985 edited by Jean W. Ross (1986)

1986 edited by J. M. Brook (1987)

1987 edited by J. M. Brook (1988)

1988 edited by J. M. Brook (1989)

1989 edited by J. M. Brook (1990)

1990 edited by James W. Hipp (1991)

1991 edited by James W. Hipp (1992)